AMERICAN LAW YEARBOOK 2009

A GUIDE TO THE YEAR'S MAJOR LEGAL CASES AND DEVELOPMENTS

ISSN 1521-0901

AMERICAN LAW YEARBOOK 2009

A GUIDE TO THE YEAR'S
MAJOR LEGAL CASES AND
DEVELOPMENTS

GALE
CENGAGE Learning

Detroit • New York • San Francisco • New Haven, Conn • Waterville, Maine • London

American Law Yearbook 2009

Project Editor: Jeffrey Wilson

Editorial: Brigham Narins

Product Manager: Kate Hanley

Editorial Support Services:
Andrea Lopeman

Indexing Services: Dave Hendree

Rights Acquisition and Management:
Dean Dauphinais

Composition: Evi Abou-El-Seoud

Manufacturing: Rita Wimberley

Imaging: John Watkins

Product Design: Pam Galbreath

ISBN 978-1-4144-3389-9
ISBN 1-4144-3389-1
ISSN 1521-0901

Gale
27500 Drake Rd.
Farmington Hills, MI, 48331-3535

This title is also available as an e-book.
ISBN-13: 978-1-4144-5755-0   ISBN-10: 1-4144-5755-3
Contact your Gale, a part of Cengage Learning sales representative for ordering information.

Printed in the United States of America
1 2 3 4 5 6 7 13 12 11 10 09

CONTENTS

Preface . . . . *vii*

Abortion 1
Admiralty and Maritime Law 3
Age Discrimination 5
Alien 6
Americans With Disabilities Act 8
Antitrust Law 9
Appellate Advocacy 11
Arbitration 12
Armed Robbery 16
Attorney 17
Attorney General 20
Automobiles 21
Bankruptcy 25
Banks and Banking 26
In Focus
    The Debate Over Nationalization
       of Banks 28
Biden, Joseph 29
Birth Control 30
Capital Punishment 33
Clean Water Act 37
Clemency 38
Commerce Clause 40
Computer Crime 42
Confrontation 43
Copyright 44
Corruption 49
Covenant 53
Craig, Gregory 54
Crime 55
Criminal Law 56
Criminal Procedure 57
Department of Justice 63

Discrimination 64
DNA 70
Double Jeopardy 72
Drugs and Narcotics 73
Duty of Tonnage 76
Economy 79
Education Law 80
Elections 84
Employment Law 86
Environmental Law 89
Espionage 93
Evidence 94
Federal Communications Commission . 97
Federal Deposit Insurance Corporation 98
First Amendment 100
Food and Drug Administration 106
In Focus
    FDA Comes Under Fire 107
Foreign Intelligence Surveillance Court 109
Fourth Amendment 110
Fraud 114
Freedom of Information 116
Freedom of Speech 117
Gay and Lesbian Rights 119
In Focus
    Constitutional Amendments to
       Same-Sex Marriages 124
Geithner, Timothy 126
Habeas Corpus 129
Holder, Eric 132
Identity Theft 135
Immigration 136
Immunity 140

Internet 142
Judges 145
Jurisdiction 148
Jury 149
Labor Law 153
Libel 154
Manslaughter 159
Military Law 160
Military Tribunal 162
Mortgage 164
Murder 165
Napolitano, Janet 169
National Security 170
Native American Rights 171
Obstruction of Justice 175
Palin, Sarah 179
Pensions 180
Peremptory Challenge 181
Perjury 182
Preemption 184
Product Liability 185
Punitive Damages 187
Religion 189
RICO 190
Riparian Rights 192
Safe Haven 195
Search and Seizure 196
Securities 197
Sentencing 198
Sex Discrimination 202
Sex Offenses 204
Sixth Amendment 205
Sotomayor, Sonia 210

Sovereign Immunity 211
Sovereignty 213
Sports Law 214
Suicide 216
Supremacy Clause 217
Terrorism 219
Tobacco 222
Tort Law 224
Torture 226
In Focus
    Dilemma Over Prosecutions for the
       'Torture Memos' 228
Trade 230
Veterans' Rights 233
Voting 234
In Focus
    The Internet is the New Face of
       Political Campaigning 236
War Crimes 241
Whistleblowing 242
Wiretapping 244

Appendix 247
   Discrimination 247
   Drugs and Narcotics 248
   Terrorism 249

Bibliography 253

Glossary 271

Abbreviations 287

Table of Cases Cited 305

Index by Name and Subject 309

The need for a layperson's comprehensive, understandable guide to terms, concepts, and historical developments in U.S. law has been well met by *West's Encyclopedia of American Law* (*WEAL*). Published in a second edition in 2004 by The Gale Group, *WEAL* has proved itself a valuable successor to West's 1983 publication, *The Guide to American Law: Everyone's Legal Encyclopedia.* and the 1997 first edition of WEAL.

Since 1998, Gale, a part of Cengage Learning, a premier reference publisher, has extended the value of *WEAL* with the publication of *American Law Yearbook* (*ALY*). This supplement adds entries on emerging topics not covered in the main set. A legal reference must be current to be authoritative, so *ALY* is a vital companion to a key reference source. Uniform organization by *WEAL* term and cross-referencing make it easy to use the titles together, while inclusion of key definitions and summaries of earlier rulings in supplement entries—whether new or continuations—make it unnecessary to refer to the main set constantly.

UNDERSTANDING THE AMERICAN LEGAL SYSTEM

The U.S. legal system is admired around the world for the freedoms it allows the individual and the fairness with which it attempts to treat all persons. On the surface, it may seem simple, yet those who have delved into it know that this system of federal and state constitutions, statutes, regulations, and common-law decisions is elaborate and complex. It derives from the English common law, but includes principles older than England, along with some principles from other lands. The U.S. legal system, like many others, has a language all its own, but too often it is an unfamiliar language: many concepts are still phrased in Latin. *WEAL* explains legal terms and concepts in everyday language, however. It covers a wide variety of persons, entities, and events that have shaped the U.S. legal system and influenced public perceptions of it.

FEATURES OF THIS SUPPLEMENT

Entries

ALY 2009 contains 164 entries covering individuals, cases, laws, and concepts significant to U.S. law. Entries are arranged alphabetically and use the same entry title as in *WEAL* or *ALY*—when introduced in an earlier *Yearbook* (e.g., September 11th Attacks). There may be several cases discussed under a given topic.

Profiles of individuals cover interesting and influential people from the world of law, government, and public life, both historic and contemporary. All have contributed to U.S. law as a whole. Each short biography includes a timeline highlighting important moments in the subject's life. Persons whose lives were detailed in *WEAL*, but who have died since publication of that work, receive obituary entries in *ALY*.

DEFINITIONS

Each entry on a legal term is preceded by a definition, which is easily distinguished by its sans serif typeface. The back of the book includes a Glossary of Legal Terms containing the definitions for a selection of the most important terms **bolded** in the text of the essays and biographies. Terms bolded but not included in the Glossary of Legal Terms in ALY can be found in the Dictionary volume of WEAL.

CROSS REFERENCES

To facilitate research, *ALY 2009* provides two types of cross-references: within and following entries. Within the entries, terms are set in small capital letters (e.g., FIRST AMENDMENT) to indicate that they have their own entry in *WEAL*. At the end of each entry, additional relevant topics in *ALY 2009* are listed alphabetically by title.

APPENDIX

This section follows the Glossary of Legal Terms and includes ten organization biographies, covering groups not previously included in prior editions of WEAL or ALY.

TABLE OF CASES CITED AND INDEX BY NAME AND SUBJECT

These features make it quick and easy for users to locate references to cases, people, statutes, events, and other subjects. The Table of Cases Cited traces the influences of legal precedents by identifying cases mentioned throughout the text. In a departure from *WEAL,* references to individuals have been folded into the general index to simplify searches. Litigants, justices, historical and contemporary figures, as well as topical references are included in the Index by Name and Subject.

CITATIONS

Wherever possible, *ALY* includes citations to cases and statutes for readers wishing to do further research. They refer to one or more series, called "reporters," which publish court opinions and related information. Each citation includes a volume number, an abbreviation for the reporter, and the starting page reference. Underscores in a citation indicate that a court opinion has not been officially reported as of *ALY*'s publication. Two sample citations, with explanations, are presented below.

Miranda v. Arizona, 384 U.S. 436, 86 S.Ct. 1602, 16 L.Ed. 2d 694 (1966)

1. *Case title.* The title of the case is set in i and indicates the names of the parties. The suit in this sample citation was between Ernesto A. Miranda and the state of Arizona.

2. *Reporter volume number.* The number preceding the reporter abbreviation indicates the reporter volume containing the case. The volume number appears on the spine of the reporter, along with the reporter abbreviation.

3. *Reporter abbreviation.* The suit in the sample citation is from the reporter, or series of books, called *U.S. Reports,* which contains cases from the U.S. Supreme Court. Numerous reporters publish cases from the federal and state courts; consult the Abbreviations list at the back of this volume for full titles.

4. *Reporter page.* The number following the reporter abbreviation indicates the reporter page on which the case begins.

5. *Additional reporter citation.* Many cases may be found in more than one reporter. The suit in the sample citation also appears in volume 86 of the *Supreme Court Reporter,* beginning on page 1602.

6. *Additional reporter citation.* The suit in the sample citation is also reported in volume 16 of the *Lawyer's Edition,* second series, beginning on page 694.

7. *Year of decision.* The year the court issued its decision in the case appears in parentheses at the end of the cite.

Brady Handgun Violence Prevention Act, Pub. L. No. 103-159, 107 Stat. 1536 (18 U.S.C.A. § § 921-925A)

        1   2   3 4 5 6   7   8

1. *Statute title.*

2. *Public law number.* In the sample citation, the number 103 indicates this law was passed by the 103d Congress, and the number 159 indicates it was the 159th law passed by that Congress.

3. *Reporter volume number.* The number preceding the reporter abbreviation indicates the reporter volume containing the statute.

4. *Reporter abbreviation.* The name of the reporter is abbreviated. The statute in the sample citation is from *Statutes at Large.*

5. *Reporter page.* The number following the reporter abbreviation indicates the reporter page on which the statute begins.

6. *Title number.* Federal laws are divided into major sections with specific titles. The number preceding a reference to the U.S. Code stands for the section called Crimes and Criminal Procedure.

7. *Additional reporter.* The statute in the sample citation may also be found in the *U.S. Code Annotated.*

8. *Section numbers.* The section numbers following a reference to the *U.S. Code Annotated* indicate where the statute appears in that reporter.

COMMENTS WELCOME

Considerable efforts were expended at the time of publication to ensure the accuracy of the information presented in *American Law Yearbook 2009.* The editor welcomes your comments and suggestions for enhancing and improving future editions of this supplement to *West's Encyclopedia of American Law.* Send comments and suggestions to:

    American Law Yearbook

    Gale

    27500 Drake Rd.

    Farmington Hills, MI 48331-3535

ABORTION

The spontaneous or artificially induced expulsion of an embryo or fetus. As used in legal context, usually refers to induced abortion.

Fourth Circuit Strikes Down Ban on Partial Birth Abortions

In May 2008, the Fourth **Circuit Court** of Appeals held that a Virginia law banning partial birth abortions was unconstitutional. The court's decision came just a year after the U.S. SUPREME COURT had ruled that a similar federal ban is constitutionally permissible. The Fourth Circuit based its decision on distinctions between the Virginia law and the federal law. However, critics of the Fourth Circuit's ruling opined that the ruling was based more on the political beliefs of the two judges who voted to strike down the Virginia **statute**.

In 2003, the Virginia General Assembly passed the statute that prohibited doctors from performing "partial birth infanticide." The statute defined this procedure as

> any deliberate act that (i) is intended to kill a human infant who has been born alive, but who has not been completely extracted or expelled from its mother, and that (ii) does kill such infant, regardless of whether death occurs before or after extraction or expulsion from its mother has been completed.

The statute excluded several abortion procedures from the statute's definition of partial birth infanticide.

The act further defined the phrase "human infant who has been born alive" as:

> [A] product of human conception that has been completely or substantially expelled or extracted from its mother, regardless of the duration of pregnancy, which after such expulsion or extraction breathes or shows any other evidence of life such as beating of the heart, pulsation of the umbilical cord, or definite movement of voluntary muscles, whether or not the umbilical cord has been cut or the placenta is attached.

The statute provided a limited exception that allowed a physician to use a procedure necessary to save the life of a mother. However, the statute contained no additional provision that allowed a doctor to perform an abortion when the mother's health was at risk.

The Richmond Medical Center was a facility that provides a variety of reproductive health services, including those necessary for women who have had miscarriages. Dr. William G. Fitzhugh performed abortions and treated women who have had incomplete miscarriages. In 2003, the Richmond Medical Center and Fitzhugh brought suit in the U.S. **District Court** for the Eastern District of Virginia to challenge the statute's enforcement. Senior Judge Richard L. Williams agreed with the plaintiffs and issued an injunction that prohibited the statute's enforcement. According to Williams' order, the statute placed an undue burden on a woman's right to choose to have an abortion.

Moreover, Williams concluded that the statute's exception that applied to a physician saving the life of the mother was constitutionally inadequate. Because the statute was unconstitutional, Williams issued the injunction barring the statute's enforcement. *Richmond Medical Center v. Hicks*, 301 F. Supp. 2d 499 (E.D. Va. 2004).

The Commonwealth of Virginia appealed the ruling to the Fourth Circuit. A three-judge panel reviewed the case in 2005. Writing for a 2-1 majority, Judge M. Blane Michael concluded that the Virginia statute indeed violated the Constitution. *Richmond Medical Center for Women v. Hicks*, 409 F.3d 619 (4th Cir. 2005). Michael reviewed the Supreme Court's precedent and concluded that the lack of a health exception in the statute was fatal by itself. Judge Diana Gribbon-Motz joined Michael in the decision. Both Michael and Motz were originally appointed by President BILL CLINTON. One of President George H.W. Bush's appointees, Paul V. Niemeyer, dissented. According to Niemeyer, "The majority's opinion is a bold, new law that, in essence, constitutionalizes infanticide of a most gruesome nature."

In 2007, the Supreme Court reviewed the constitutionality of the federal Partial Birth Abortion Ban Act of 2003, which is similar in many respects to the Virginia statute. In *Gonzales v. Carhart*, 550 U.S. 124, 127 S. Ct. 1610, 167 L. Ed. 2d 480 (2007). In a 5-4 decision, with the lead opinion written by Justice ANTHONY KENNEDY, the Court upheld the federal law. Significantly, Kennedy concluded that the absence of a provision protecting the health of the mother did not render the law unconstitutional on its face.

Less than a week after the Court decided *Carhart*, the Court vacated the decision in *Hicks* and remanded the case to the Fourth Circuit for review in light of *Carhart*.

Commentators followed the Fourth Circuit's reevaluation of *Hicks*. Abortion-rights activists feared that the Supreme Court's decision in *Carhart* would lead many state legislatures to adopt the partial-birth bans approved by the Supreme Court. On the other hand, commentators believed that there was a good chance that the Fourth Circuit would again strike down the Virginia statute due to the makeup of the court. Though the Fourth Circuit itself is generally conservative, the same judges who heard the case in 2005 again

reviewed the case when it returned to the court in 2007.

The panel again decided that the Virginia statute was unconstitutional. Writing again for the 2-1 majority, Judge Michael focused heavily on the Supreme Court's decision in *Carhart*. The majority found a key distinction between the federal statute and the Virginia statute. The federal law provided protection from prosecution for a doctor who set out to perform a standard dilation and evacuation procedure (which was not covered by the statute) but who accidentally performs an intact procedure (which was banned under the statute). This distinction was enough for the majority to conclude that the statute was unconstitutional "because it imposes an undue burden on a woman's right to obtain an abortion." *Richmond Medical Center for Women v. Herring*, 527 F.3d 128 (4th Cir. 2008).

Abortion opponents decried the decision. According to Victoria Cobb, president of the Family Foundation of Virginia, "It is disappointing that yet again just two people can thwart the will of the people, the action of a legislature, and simple justice for nearly born children." Other supported the decision. Stephanie Toti, who represented the Center for Reproductive Rights, said, "The court recognized Virginia's law is extreme—that it effectively banned the most common method of second-trimester abortion, and that is unconstitutional."

Anti-Choice Measures Fail in Three States

Prior to the November 2008 election cycle, political pundits expressed concern that the landmark 1973 U.S. SUPREME COURT case of *Roe v. Wade* (granting certain legal protections to women seeking abortions) was in **jeopardy**. That concern appeared groundless as voters in South Dakota, Colorado, and California resoundingly defeated anti-choice initiatives in those states. That was not to say that voters were overwhelmingly pro-abortion, but rather, that they believed the proposed restrictions on abortions were too narrowly-drawn.

South Dakota's "Measure 11" was the most publicized. Voters in that state had previously rejected (by a 10-point margin) an all-out ban on abortions in 2006. Proponents of the new and revised Measure 11 had hoped that, by creating exceptions for such things as rape and incest, the initiative would pass in 2008.

Measure 11 was handily defeated, even with the provided exceptions. Most voters found the exceptions still too narrow. "South Dakotans have affirmed by their votes tonight that no vague law can account for every individual circumstance," Sarah Stoesz, regional president and CEO of Planned Parenthood, was quoted as saying in a post-election *Los Angeles Times* article. But Leslie Unruh, local activist and proponent of the ban (also quoted in the article) countered, "We'll be back. Third time's the charm."

Measure 11, like other similar measures, began by declaring, "as a matter of scientific and biological fact," that "all induced abortions, whether surgically or chemically induced, terminate the life of an entire, unique, living human being, a human being separate from his or her mother." The state went on to declare its duty to protect the life of all human beings, including the life of an unborn child.

Section 2 of the measure provided that,

"except as permitted by section 3,4,5,6 of this Act, any person who knowingly performs any procedure upon a pregnant woman, or uses any instrument upon a pregnant woman, or administers any medicine or drug or substance or device to a pregnant woman, or prescribes or procures or sells any medicine or drug or substance or device for use by a pregnant woman, or employs any other means, with the intent of causing the termination of the life of an unborn human being, is guilty of performing an illegal abortion, which is a Class 4 felony."

Sections 3,4,5, and 6 excepted, respectively, the life or health of a pregnant woman, rape, or incest. Prior to performing an abortion pursuant to any of these sections, the physician was required to meet several reporting requirements or risk felony charges and up to 10 years in prison.

Other requirements bothered South Dakota voters as well. For example, rape or incest-excepted abortions required identification of the assailant and proven paternity through DNA testing.

But it was the Section 4 exception (the woman's health) that seemed to provoke most controversy and objection, begging the question of how ill must a woman be to qualify under this exception? Voters, legal experts, and physicians alike found the language dangerously vague (although explanatory language was included in the Section). Critics argued that those disputes would be settled in a courtroom, after the fact, rather than left to the sound judgment of physicians consulting with their patients.

Colorado's Measure 48 would have defined a fertilized egg as a legal human being, invoking all the protections afforded thereto, including due process and inalienable rights. The measure was not classified as an anti-abortion or anti-choice one, but rather, entitled the 'person-hood' measure. It received more than 130,000 signatures in the petition stage (to request that it be placed on the ballot for general vote). But legal experts concluded that when Colorado voters read through its entirety and understood its potential far-reaching consequences, support would dwindle. Opponents (and even some proponents) opined that if Measure 48 were passed, it could ban nearly all abortions as well as other procedures or activities, including in vitro fertilization and certain forms of birth control (e.g., the "morning after" pill). On November 5, 2008, Colorado's Measure 48 was defeated by a 3-1 ratio. As in South Dakota, Colorado voters, many united in general sentiment against abortions, nonetheless believed this measure went "too far."

California's measure was to require physicians to notify the parents of any minor requesting abortion services. It also would have required a 48-hour waiting period before a minor could undergo the procedure. This was the third time that voters failed to pass the measure.

It is common in nearly all states to periodically place issues on the ballot for voters to decide by majority vote. Twenty-four states have a process that allows citizen-sponsored measures to be placed on a ballot for general election vote if enough citizens sign a petition requesting the issue to be placed on the ballot.

ADMIRALTY AND MARITIME LAW

A field of law relating to, and arising from, the practice of the admiralty courts (tribunals that exercise jurisdiction over all contracts, torts, offenses, or injuries within maritime law) that regulates and settles special problems associated with sea navigation and commerce.

Atlantic Sounding Co. v. Townsend

Maritime law, among other things, provides for specific types of remedies for injuries incurred on sea vessels. One such remedy is the right of a seaman to receive what is known as maintenance and cure. When a vessel owner refuses to provide maintenance and cure, courts in the past have concluded that **punitive damages** may be available for the injured seaman. In 2009, the U.S. SUPREME COURT reviewed these standards in light of recent cases and concluded that punitive damages were indeed available in a case involving a vessel owner's refusal to provide maintenance and cure. *Atlantic Sounding Co. v. Townsend*, No. 08-214, 2009 WL 1789469 (2009).

Edgar Townsend was a seaman and crew member aboard the Motor Tug Thomas. On July 5, 2005, Townsend slipped and landed on his shoulder on the steel deck of the boat. Townsend injured his shoulder and clavicle as a result of the fall. The owners of the Motor Tug Thomas were Atlantic Sounding Co., Inc. and Weeks Marine, Inc. After Townsend's injury, the owners informed him that they would not pay "maintenance and cure," which applies specifically when a seaman becomes ill or is injured while serving aboard a vessel. Maintenance and cure covers medical care, a living allowance, and wages.

After informing Townsend that they would not pay maintenance and cure, the owners filed suit in the U.S. **District Court** for the Middle District of Florida. The owners sought a **declaratory judgment** that they were not required to pay maintenance and cure to Townsend. Two days later, Townsend filed suit against the owners. Townsend's suit included claims for negligence, unseaworthiness, arbitrary and willful failure to pay maintenance and cure, and wrongful termination. Townsend filed his claims under both general maritime law and under the Jones Act, 46 U.S.C. § 688. Townsend thereafter filed the same claims as counterclaims to the owners' declaratory action. Townsend sought punitive damages on the claim for maintenance and cure.

The owners moved to dismiss Townsend's claim for punitive damages. The district court denied the claim, relying on the holding in *Hines v. J.A. LaPorte, Inc.*, 820 F.2d 1187 (11th Cir. 1987). The court agreed to certify this question to the Eleventh Circuit for review through **interlocutory** appeal. In *Hines*, the Eleventh Circuit held that when a shipowner willfully and arbitrarily refuses to pay maintenance and cure, the injured seaman may recover both reasonable attorney's fees and punitive damages.

On appeal, the owners argued that the Eleventh Circuit's decision in *Hines* had been superseded by the Supreme Court's decision in *Miles v. Apex Marine Corp.*, 498 U.S. 19, 111 S. Ct. 317, 112 L. Ed. 2d 275 (1990). The Court in *Miles* ruled that under the Jones Act, the family of a seaman who died at sea could not recover for loss of society. The Court observed:

> We no longer live in an ERA when seamen and their loved ones must look primarily to the courts as a source of substantive legal protection from injury and death; Congress and the States have legislated extensively in these areas. In this era, an admiralty court should look primarily to these legislative enactments for policy guidance. We may supplement these **statutory** remedies where doing so would achieve the uniform vindication of such policies consistent with our constitutional mandate, but we must also keep strictly within the limits imposed by Congress.

The owners argued that the Court's reasoning in *Miles* suggested that courts should apply damage standards uniformly, whether a seaman brings a claim under the Jones Act, general maritime law, or any other law. Since the Jones Act does not permit recovery of punitive damages, the owners argued that Townsend could not recover such damages under general maritime law.

The Eleventh Circuit rejected the owners' argument. The court noted that *Miles* itself did not involve punitive damages or any issue involving maintenance and cure. Instead, the court stressed that the owners' argument relied only on the reasoning of *Miles* rather than its holding. Other circuits considered the effect that *Miles* may have on maintenance and cure, and each concluded that *Miles* did not control the outcomes of those cases. The Eleventh Circuit therefore relied on its own decision in *Hines* and ruled that punitive damages were available to Townsend. *Atlantic Sounding Co. v. Townsend*, 496 F.3d 1282 (11th Cir. 2007).

The owners appealed the decision to the U.S. Supreme Court. On June 25, 2009, the Court reached a 5-4 decision in favor of Townsend.

Justice Clarence Thomas wrote the opinion for the majority. Thomas noted that punitive damages have long been a remedy available in maritime actions, dating back to the English **common law** and the colonial years in America. A number of nineteenth century cases concluded that punitive damages were indeed available in maritime actions. Other cases also established the right of a seaman to receive maintenance and cure. In numerous instances, courts held that punitive damages were available when a vessel owner failed to provide maintenance and cure.

Thomas then turned his attention to the Jones Act. Congress enacted the Jones Act in response to the Court's decision in *The Osceola*, 189 U.S. 158, 23 S. Ct. 483, 47 L. Ed. 760 (1903), in which the Court prohibited a seaman or his family from recovering for injury or death based on the negligence of the vessel owner. The Jones Act effectively overruled this decision by providing a statutory **cause of action** for negligence. However, Thomas stressed that the Jones Act did not eliminate any of the preexisting remedies available under general maritime law. An injured seaman may elect to bring an action under the Jones Act or under general maritime law, but the remedies available under the Jones Act are not exclusive remedies.

Thomas also addressed the owners' argument focusing on the application of the *Miles* decision. Like the Eleventh Circuit, Thomas concluded that *Miles* did not apply to the question of whether punitive damages were available in cases involving maintenance and cure. The Court therefore affirmed the decision of the Eleventh Circuit. *Atlantic Sounding Co. v. Townsend*, No. 08-214, 2009 WL 1789469 (2009).

Justice Samuel Alito dissented and was joined by three other justices. Alito argued that the Court should have applied the analytical framework established in *Miles*. According to Alito, few courts have addressed the issue of punitive damage awards in the context of maintenance and cure, and Alito argued that the Court should not have departed from the rationale of *Miles* in reaching its decision.

AGE DISCRIMINATION

Gross v. FBL Financial Services

Employees are protected from age discrimination in the workplace through the provisions of the Age Discrimination in Employment Act (ADEA).

Though this act contains some similar components as other civil rights statutes, including Title VII of the Civil Rights Act, the courts have not always treated the ADEA in the same manner as other civil rights laws. In 2009, the Supreme Court determined that a jury instruction standard that applies to Title VII cases is inapplicable to ADEA cases. The result of the ruling was that the Court determined that the **burden of persuasion** in an ADEA case never shifts to the employer. *Gross v. FBL Financial Services, Inc.*, No. 08-441, 2009 WL 1685684 (2009).

The Supreme Court's case focused on Jack Gross, who was born in 1948. He began working at FBL Financial Services in 1987 and was promoted during the years 1990, 1993, 1997, and 1999. His highest position achieved was Claims Administration Vice President. The company reorganized in 2001, and the company assigned Gross to the position of Claims Administration Director. Although his job responsibilities did not change at that time, Gross viewed the reassignment as a demotion because the position change reduced his points under the company's point system for salary grades.

FBL reassigned Gross yet again in 2003, when Gross was 54 years old. At that time, the company gave him the position of Claims Project Coordinator. The company created a new position with the title of Claims Administration Manager, and many of Gross's old duties were transferred to the new position. The company hired a woman in her forties to serve in the newly created position. Gross believed that his position change was another demotion because though he received the same salary and pay grade, the new position lacked a job description or specifically assigned duties.

Gross brought suit against FBL in 2004 in the U.S. **District Court** for the Southern District of Iowa. Gross argued that the company had demoted him due to his age in violation of the Age Discrimination in Employment Act (ADEA), 29 U.S.C. § 623(a). This **statute** makes it unlawful for an employer to take adverse action against an employee "because of such individual's age." At trial, Gross introduced evidence suggesting that that age was a motivating factor in his reassignment. The company presented evidence, though, that the reassignment was due to corporate restructuring and that Gross' new position was better suited for his skills.

At the close of trial, the district court instructed the jury that it must return a verdict in favor of Gross if the jury found that FBL had demoted Gross to claims project coordinator and that age was a motivating factor in the company's decision. Under these instructions, the jury could find that age was a motivating factor if age played a role in the company's decision to demote Gross. Conversely, the court instructed the jury that it must render a verdict in favor of FBL if the jury determined that the company would have demoted Gross regardless of his age. The trial concluded with the jury awarding Gross $46,945 in lost compensation.

FBL appealed the decision to the Eighth **Circuit Court** of Appeals. The Eighth Circuit reviewed the District Court's application of the Supreme Court's decision in *Price Waterhouse v. Hopkins*, 490 U.S. 228, 109 S. Ct. 1775, 104 L. Ed. 2d 268 (1989). The *Price Waterhouse* case focused on the proper **allocation** of the burden of persuasion under Title VII of the Civil Rights Act of 1964, 42 U.S.C. § 2000e *et seq*. More specifically, the decision focused on so-called mixed motives cases, where an employee alleges that an employer has taken an employment action because of both permissible and impermissible considerations. The *Price Waterhouse* decision was a highly fractured one that resulted in a **plurality** opinion and several concurrences and dissents.

The Eighth Circuit applied the opinion of Justice Sandra Day O'Connor to the FBL case. Using Justice O'Connor's opinion, the court determined that Gross had to present "[d]irect evidence ... sufficient to support a finding by a reasonable fact finder that an illegitimate criterion actually motivated the adverse employment action." Once an employee presented this **direct evidence**, the court concluded that the burden shifted then to the employer to "convince the trier of fact that it is more likely than not that the decision would have been the same absent consideration of the illegitimate factor." Applying these standards to Gross' case, the Eighth Circuit determined that the district court's jury instructions were flawed. These instructions allowed the employee to shift by the burden to the employer by producing any category of evidence showing that age was a motivating factor. Since the district court did

not require the employee to produce direct evidence to shift this burden, the Eighth Circuit reversed the district court. *Gross v. FBL Financial Servs. Inc.*, 526 F.3d 356 (8th Cir. 2008).

Gross appealed the decision to the U.S. SUPREME COURT. The parties asked the Court to determine whether a plaintiff is required to present direct evidence of discrimination in an ADEA case before the burden of persuasion shifts to the employer. In a 5-4 decision, the Court determined that the burden of persuasion in an ADEA case never shifts to the party defending a mixed-motives discrimination claim brought under the ADEA.

The majority opinion written by Justice Clarence Thomas noted that *Price Waterhouse* and several other cases relied upon by Gross and the lower courts only apply in the context of a Title VII action. The burden-shifting framework under Title VII never applies to an ADEA case, according to Thomas. In fact, Congress had addressed the mixed-motives cases by amending Title VII, but Congress did not amend the ADEA at that time to address similar issues in the context of age discrimination cases. According to the majority, the employee in an ADEA case retains the burden of persuasion to show that but for the age discrimination, the employer would not have taken the adverse employment action. Accordingly, the Court vacated the Eighth Circuit's decision. *Gross v. FBL Financial Services, Inc.*, No. 08-441, 2009 WL 1685684 (2009).

Justice JOHN PAUL STEVENS, joined by three other justices, dissented. According to Stevens, the Court engaged in "unnecessary lawmaking" by adopting a causation requirement in the ADEA that is inconsistent with the requirements under Title VII.

ALIEN

An individual who is not a citizen or a national of the United States.

Report Finds U.S. Homeland Security Failed to Protect Undocumented Minors

The term "repatriation" refers to the official removal and return of persons who have entered the country illegally to their own countries of birth or origin. In November 2008, the Center for **Public Policy** Priorities (CPPP), a nonprofit, nonpartisan policy institute focused on improving conditions for low and moderate-income residents of Texas, released its report on the removal/repatriation from the United States of undocumented, unaccompanied children. Entitled *A Child Alone and Without Papers,* the report was critical of the U.S. Department of Homeland Security's handling of these minors. Specifically, it reported that the U.S. government often compromised the rights, safety, and well-being of such children, in contravention of international law and U.S. child welfare standards.

CPPP's report focused on what it estimated as approximately 43,000 undocumented, unaccompanied children entering the United States annually, the vast majority of children coming from Mexico and Honduras. Its findings were premised on both policy analyses and interviews with adults and children within the system.

As background, the Homeland Security Act of 2002, P.L. 107-296, 116 Stat. 2153, created the Department of Homeland Security (DHS). It also consolidated or abolished several prior agencies and absorbed or reassigned their duties. One such non-surviving **entity** was the former Immigration and Naturalization Service (INS). Under the Act, the functions of border security and immigration services became the Bureau of Customs and Border Protection and the Bureau of Immigration and Customs Enforcement (ICE), respectively. While ICE was given the task of prosecuting undocumented children, the Office of Refugee Resettlement (ORR), under the Department of Health and Human Services, was now given the task of protecting such children. This relieved the legal tension of conflicting duties to both prosecute and protect undocumented children being vested in the same entity. Under the prior INS, such children were apprehended, detained, tried, and deported all by the same agency. The Act further established that the ORR and DHS were expected to collaborate on decisions affecting placements of undocumented, unaccompanied minors.

In addition to the reorganization under DHS that established it as an enforcer (and the ICE as caretaker), only one section of the federal Code of Regulations (CFR) was promulgated specifically for unaccompanied children entering the country at one of the borders or airports, for example, and taken into ICE custody. Under such circumstances, there were

two legal options. They could apply to remain in the United States or seek an order of voluntary departure (which would not bar future legal entry).

CFR Section 236.3 provided specific instructions that required written notice to the child of his or her legal rights, and if unable to read or understand, or under the age of 14, the notice should be read and explained in a language he or she understood. The Section also provided for a child's right to communicate with a parent, laying out criteria for release to a family member. While awaiting a hearing before an immigration judge, unaccompanied children were housed in federally-funded facilities as established by ORR, such as foster care, group homes, detention facilities, or transitional housing.

According to CPPP's report, these provisions might have sounded sufficient to address the problem, but in reality lacked coordination and/or detail. Report author Amy Thompson, in a CPPP press release, summarized,

> "The U.S. treats undocumented, unaccompanied children with a shocking lack of concern. Our domestic child welfare system has shaped international standards on child treatment, but we have not extended our standards to this vulnerable population. Policymakers should act swiftly and forcefully to prioritize the welfare of all children in U.S. custody."

With respect to findings on the U.S. side, the CPPP was critical of the fact that U.S. immigration law did not address child treatment during federal custodianship, resulting in a lack of clear policy and procedure. Even where bi-national agreements existed, the CPPP found underutilization or non-recognition, and with respect to Honduras, none existed.

There were also reported incidents of inattention to repeated requests for medical attention, lack of adequate food and water, and general mistreatment. Fifty to 70 percent of children lacked legal counsel or an assessment of their rights, and CPPP interviews indicated that Vienna Convention provisions regarding notification of consulates from the country of origin were not regularly being followed. Children were being returned to Mexico in covered trucks and Honduras by commercial flight. Many were unsafe, and the United States regularly failed to give **advance** notice of arrivals, often made in the middle of the night. This resulted in many children arriving without escort and often returned to unsafe conditions. In turn, said the report, such lack of policy and procedure resulted in increased incidence of repeat migration, child trafficking, and forced conscription into illegal activities.

On the Mexican and Honduran sides, CPPP reported a prevalent lack of policies and procedures resulting in regional variations in the collection of critical data, such as whether a repatriated child had been previously returned and from where. Moreover, CPPP found a lack of family reunification efforts in Honduras, as well as some instances of patent discrimination against disabled children, and other degrading detention conditions.

The CPPP recommended that the United States, among other things, guarantee the right to legal counsel and representation to any unaccompanied and undocumented children facing removal; the establishment of transparent and consistent standards and protocols for removal and repatriation; collection of statistics for interagency information-sharing; discontinuance of transportation methods placing children at unnecessary risk; provision of reintegration assistance; and establishment of bi-national standards for data collection and sharing.

AMERICANS WITH DISABILITIES ACT

Congress Overturns Supreme Court ADA Rulings

The Supreme Court is charged with interpreting federal statutes and determining congressional intent. Sometimes Congress objects to these interpretations by enacting legislation explicitly overruling Court decisions. Such was the case with provisions of the Americans with Disabilities Act dealing with the definition of "disability." On September 25, 2008, President Bush signed the Americans with Disabilities Act Amendments Act of 2008 Pub. L. No. 110-325, 122 Stat. 3553. The Act makes important changes to the definition of the term "disability" by rejecting the holdings in two Supreme Court decisions and portions of EEOC's ADA regulations. Congress specifically overruled the decisions in *Sutton v. United Airlines*, 527 U.S. 471, 119 S.Ct. 2139, 144 L.Ed.2d 450 (1999) and *Toyota Motor Manufacturing, Kentucky, Inc. v.*

Williams, 534 U.S. 184, 122 S.Ct 681, 151 L.Ed.2d 615 (2001).

In *Toyota* the Court held that a person's impairment could not be considered a disability under the ADA unless the impairment prevented the worker from performing "any major life activity." The Court stated forcefully that a person who could not perform certain jobs because of an impairment did not meet the definition of disabled by that fact alone. The person must also show impairment that affects day-to-day life activities outside of work. Ella Williams worked at the Toyota automobile manufacturing plant in Georgetown, Kentucky from 1990 to 1996. After operating pneumatic tools on the assembly line, she developed carpal tunnel syndrome, which can cause pain and a loss of feeling in the hands, wrists and arms. Based on this diagnosis, Toyota reassigned Williams to a series of jobs that produced little physical strain on her hands and arms. Her physical condition deteriorated in the fall of 1996, when Toyota assigned her a job that required her to hold her hands and arms around shoulder height for a significant amount of time. The plant physician diagnosed inflammation in her shoulder blade area and nerve compression. Williams eventually stopped coming to work in late 1996 after Toyota declined to reassign her to another, less physically stressful, job. Toyota fired her in January 1997 for her absenteeism.

The Supreme Court, in a unanimous decision, rejected the Sixth Circuit's standard for assessing disability. The Court noted that "Merely having an impairment does not make one disabled for purposes of the ADA." A person must also prove that the impairment limits a major life activity. Third, the person must show that the limitation on a major life activity is "substantial." Applying this three-step requirement to Williams, the Court agreed that Williams suffered from physical impairments. The key questions were whether what major life activities had been affected and whether these limitations had been substantial.

The Court stated that the definition of "major life activities" needed to be strictly defined. In the Court's view the phrase meant "those activities that are of central importance to daily life," which included walking, seeing and hearing. In addition, the "impairment's impact must also be permanent or long-term."

Therefore, it was not enough for a person such as Williams to cite a medical diagnosis as evidence of an impairment. All employment ADA cases needed to be examined on their own unique facts. These "individualized assessments" needed to be made because the impairment caused by symptoms "varied widely from person to person." The Court made clear that placing a person in a broad class of disability did not settle the matter of ADA liability. Finally, the Court directed the lower courts to look at all aspects of a person's life, not just their work life, to determine disability.

Congress rejected this interpretation of the **statute**. In its findings for the 2008 amendments, Congress stated that the *Toyota* decision narrowed the broad scope of protection intended to be afforded by the ADA and interpreted the term "substantially limits" to require a greater degree of limitation than was intended by Congress. The act was intended in part to reject standards enunciated by the Supreme Court in Toyota that the terms "substantially" and "major" in the definition of disability under the ADA "need to be interpreted strictly to create a demanding standard for qualifying as disabled," and that to be substantially limited in performing a major life activity under the ADA "an individual must have an impairment that prevents or severely restricts the individual from doing activities that are of central importance to most people's daily lives." Congress concluded that the ruling created an inappropriately high level of limitation necessary to obtain coverage under the ADA, and that it was intent of Congress that the primary object of attention in cases brought under the ADA should be whether entities covered under the ADA have complied with their obligations. Congress also intended to convey that the question of whether an individual's impairment is a disability under the ADA should not demand extensive analysis.

In *Sutton v. United Airlines* the Supreme Court ruled individual who claimed a disability but had the ability to control or correct the impairment were not disabled within the meaning of the ADA. Congress specifically overruled this decision. In that case two severely myopic twin sisters sought to become commercial pilots for United Airline. Although their uncorrected visual acuity was 20/200 or worse, both women, when wearing eyeglasses, functioned identically to individuals without similar impairments. The airline rejected their applications because they did not meet the airline's minimum requirement of uncorrected visual acuity of 20/100 or better. The Supreme Court, in affirming the lower courts, held that the sisters did not have a physical impairment that substantially limited them in one or more major life activities. The Court concluded that the phrase "substantially limits" should be read to require that a person be presently, not potentially, substantially limited to demonstrate a disability. The use of corrective eyeglasses and contact lenses mitigates the individual's impairment, thus showing that there is no impairment that can be addressed by the ADA. The Court reasoned that a holding to the contrary would add 160 million individuals to the list of disabled persons.

In its findings for the 2008 amendments, Congress rejected the requirement enunciated by the Court in *Sutton* that whether an impairment substantially limits a major life activity is to be determined with reference to the ameliorative effects of mitigating measures. It also rejected the Court's reasoning with regard to coverage under the third prong of the definition of disability. Congress stated that it was reinstating the reasoning of a prior Supreme Court case, which set forth a broad view of the third prong of the definition of handicap under the Rehabilitation Act of 1973.

ANTITRUST LAW

Legislation enacted by the federal and various state governments to regulate trade and commerce by preventing unlawful restraints, price-fixing, and monopolies, to promote competition, and to encourage the production of quality goods and services at the lowest prices, with the primary goal of safeguarding public welfare by ensuring that consumer demands will be met by the manufacture and sale of goods at reasonable prices.

Pacific Bell Telephone Company, dba AT&T California, v. Linkline Communications, Inc.

The Telecommunications Act of 1996 was enacted to increase competition within the industry and to end state-sanctioned monopolies. The act came in the aftermath of the breakup in the early 1980s of American Telephone and Telegraph's (AT&T) **monopoly** over virtually all aspects of the telephone business. AT&T settled an antitrust lawsuit in 1982 by divesting itself of its local operating companies, while retaining control of its long distance activities. Seven regional telephone companies, known as Baby Bells, were given responsibility for local telephone service. With the growing demand for high-speed Internet access in the 2000s, the Baby Bells developed a retail market for digital subscriber line (DSL) service using its telephone lines. Competing DSL providers have entered the market, but they must obtain access to the Baby Bells' networks. In *Pacific Bell Telephone Company, dba AT&T California, v. Linkline Communications, Inc.*, __U.S.__,129 S.Ct. 1109, L.Ed.2d (2009), the Supreme Court reviewed an antitrust case based on an allegation that a Baby Bell subjected several DSL providers to a "price squeeze" that violated the Sherman Antitrust Act. The Court rejected the use of the price squeeze theory where the facts indicated the Baby Bell had no duty at the wholesale level to sell at the retail level to the DSL providers.

Linkline Communications is a digital subscriber line (DSL) service provider, competing against AT&T, which owns much of the infrastructure and facilities needed to provide DSL service in California. AT&T controlled most of what is known as the "last mile"—the lines that connect homes and businesses to the telephone network. Competing DSL providers must generally obtain access to AT&T's facilities in order to serve their customers. The FEDERAL COMMUNICATIONS COMMISSION abandoned a requirement in 2005 that had required companies such as AT&T to sell transmission service to independent DSL providers. However, AT&T was bound by a merger requirement to provide wholesale DSL access to independent firms at a price no greater than the retail price of AT&T's DSL service. Linkline and three other DSL providers sued AT&T under § 2 of the Sherman Act, claiming that AT&T engaged in a "price squeeze," reducing their profit margins by setting a high wholesale price for DSL transport and a low retail price for DSL Internet service. By doing so, the plaintiffs alleged AT&T preserved and maintained its monopoly control of DSL access to the Internet.

AT&T moved to dismiss the action, contending that price-squeeze claims could only proceed if they met the two established requirements for predatory pricing: below-cost retail pricing and a "dangerous probability" that the defendant will recoup any lost profits. These requirements are from *Brooke Group Ltd. v. Brown and Williamson Tobacco Corp.*, 509 U.S. 209, 113 S.Ct. 2578, 125 L.Ed.2d 168 (1993). The **district court** and the Ninth **Circuit Court** of Appeals disagreed with this argument, leading the Supreme Court to hear the case to resolve a conflict in the federal circuit courts of appeal.

The Supreme Court, in a unanimous decision, reversed the Ninth Circuit ruling. Chief Justice JOHN ROBERTS, writing for the Court, held that a price-squeeze claim may not be brought under §2 when the defendant has no antitrust duty to deal with the plaintiff at wholesale. Businesses are generally free to choose the parties with whom they will deal, as well as the prices, terms, and conditions of that dealing. In this case Linkline did not allege predatory pricing nor was there an antitrust duty for AT&T to deal with Linkline. Linkline had argued that under a price squeeze theory AT&T had operated in both the wholesale ("upstream") and retail ("downstream") markets. By raising the wholesale price of inputs while cutting its own retail prices, the AT&T had raised competitors' costs while putting downward pressure on their revenues. Linkline and the other plaintiffs had asserted that AT&T must leave them a "fair" or "adequate" margin between wholesale and retail prices.

The Court rejected this theory. Roberts concluded that where there is no duty to deal at the wholesale level and no predatory pricing at the retail level, a firm is not required to price both of these services in a manner that preserves its rivals' profit margins. Moreover, the Court found no merit in Linkline's claim that AT&T had set its retail prices too low, thereby supporting the price-squeeze claim. In this case AT&T's retail price remained above cost. To approve a price-squeeze claim would invite a decline in competition, as firms might raise retail prices or refrain from aggressive price competition to avoid potential antitrust liability.

Finally, Roberts expressed "institutional concerns" that counseled against recognizing such price-squeeze claims. Noting the importance of clear rules in **antitrust law**, allowing price-squeeze claims to go forward "would require courts simultaneously to police both the wholesale and retail prices to ensure that rival firms are not being squeezed. Courts would be aiming at a moving target, since it is the interaction between these two prices that may result in a squeeze. Moreover, firms seeking to avoid price-squeeze liability will have no safe harbor for their pricing practices. The most commonly articulated standard for price squeezes is that the defendant must leave its rivals a "fair" or "adequate" margin between wholesale and retail prices; this test is nearly impossible for courts to apply without conducting complex proceedings like rate-setting agencies.

APPELLATE ADVOCACY

The act of pleading or arguing a case or a position in a court of appeals.

Bell v. Kelly

Just a few days after hearing oral arguments in the case of *Bell v. Kelly*, No. 07-1223, 555 U.S. ___(2008), the U.S. SUPREME COURT, without comment, dismissed the case as improvidently granted (after having had, earlier in 2008, granted **certiorari** review of the matter.) The appealed case involved convicted murderer Bell's claim of ineffective counsel during the sentencing phase of his trial, and the admissibility of evidence relating thereto.

Generally, when the Supreme Court either declines review or dismisses without opinion, it essentially and effectively "lets stand" the decision from a lower court that was being appealed. In this case, the decision being appealed was from the U.S. Court of Appeals for the Fourth Circuit. But because the Fourth Circuit's opinion was "unpublished," it is not considered binding precedent in that circuit.

A jury had convicted Edward Bell for the murder of a Winchester, Virginia police officer in 1999. At the sentencing phase of the trial, the state presented evidence alluding to Bell's violent past, including handgun possessions and previous violent acts. The state prosecutor also presented evidence about the impact of the police officer's death upon his surviving family.

Bell's defense counsel, on the other hand, only presented evidence (in the form of testimony from Bell's father and sister) about the impact of the case upon their own (Bell's) family. Defense counsel did not present any witnesses to testify about mitigating factors such

as Bell's family relationships, background, or character.

The jury sentenced Bell to death, based on "the probability that he would commit criminal acts of violence in the future that would constitute a continuing serious threat to society" (Va. Code Ann. §19.2-264.2). Bell appealed both his conviction and his death sentence to the Supreme Court of Virginia, which affirmed on both.

Next, Bell filed for **habeas corpus** relief (challenging the lawfulness of his detainment) with the Virginia Supreme Court. In this petition, Bell brought 21 claims, including one for ineffective counsel (an alleged violation of his SIXTH AMENDMENT right to assistance **of counsel**). Bell's claim was based on his attorney's failure to present mitigating evidence during the sentencing phase of the trial. Specifically, Bell argued that he wanted to introduce five witnesses (his ex-wife and her sister, an ex-girlfriend and her mother, and a co-worker) to show his non-violent, hard-working, and loving side.

The Virginia Supreme Court denied his habeas petition, without holding an evidentiary hearing for Bell's proposed witnesses or considering what they would have potentially said. Instead, the Virginia high court concluded that Bell had failed to meet the requirements needed to prove "ineffective counsel" as outlined in a previous U.S. Supreme Court case, *Strickland v. Washington*, 466 U.S. 668 (1984). In *Strickland*, the Supreme Court laid out two prongs that needed to be satisfied before such a claim would be considered. A claimant must show not only that his trial counsel departed from a reasonable professional standard, but also, that such departure resulted in prejudice because "there is a reasonable probability that, but for counsel's unprofessional errors, the result of the proceeding would have been different." (466 U.S. at 688, 694). The Virginia Supreme Court found that Bell's claims satisfied neither of these prongs.

Not to be deterred after exhausting all available state remedies, Bell next brought his case to the U.S. **District Court** for the Western District of Virginia. (A federal **writ** of habeas corpus permits prisoners to challenge the lawfulness of their state-court convictions.) However, the Antiterrorism and Effective Death Penalty Act of 1996 (AEDPA), 28 USC §2254(d) limits federal court relief only to cases where a challenged state court's **adjudication** of a prisoner's claim either "resulted in a decision that was contrary to, or involved an unreasonable application of, clearly established Federal law, as determined by the SUPREME COURT OF THE UNITED STATES; or resulted in a decision that was based on an unreasonable determination of the facts in light of the evidence presented in the state court proceeding."

The district court, for the first time, heard testimony evidence from Bell's five witnesses, then affirmed the state court decision and denied habeas relief (in the form of a stay of execution). It found, in particular, that although the performance of Bell's counsel was deficient, The Virginia Supreme Court was reasonable in concluding that Bell's five witnesses likely would not have altered the jury's decision.

Next, Bell appealed the federal district court's decision to the U.S. **Circuit Court** of Appeals for the Fourth Circuit. (The Fourth Circuit's unpublished decision was the one ultimately appealed to the U.S. Supreme Court.) Notwithstanding, the Fourth Circuit upheld and affirmed the federal district court. In so doing, the **appellate court** stated, in part,

> After review, we conclude that the district court correctly concluded that the finding of the Supreme Court of Virginia on prejudice was reasonable. Evidence from each of these witnesses was cross-purpose because it would have allowed the prosecution to emphasize multiple instances of Bell's infidelity; **abandonment** of his children, wife, and girlfriend; domestic abuse; and failure to provide child support. When weighed against the aggravating factors of Bell's criminal record and propensity for violence, we find it reasonable for the Supreme Court of Virginia to conclude that the factors in **aggravation** outweighed the mitigation evidence. Accordingly, we affirm the district court's decision denying Bell's petition for writ of habeas corpus.

The original certiorari granted (in May 2008) for Supreme Court review was limited to the following question: Did the Fourth Circuit err when, in conflict with decisions of the Ninth and Tenth Circuits, it applied a deferential standard of 28 USC 2254(d), which is reserved for claims "adjudicated on the merits" in state court, to evaluate a claim predicated on evidence of prejudice *not considered* by the state court, and that was properly received for the first time in a federal evidentiary hearing (Bell's five

witnesses' testimony)? Because of the Court's later dismissal without comment, it appeared that perceived conflict among circuits would need to wait until another ripe case presented itself on this question.

ARBITRATION

The submission of a dispute to an unbiased third person designated by the parties to the controversy, who agree in advance to comply with the award–a decision to be issued after a hearing at which both parties have an opportunity to be heard.

Arthur Andersen LLP v. Carlisle

Arbitration is designed to avoid the need to go to court to resolve disputes. The Federal Arbitration Act (FAA) contains a provision that deals with situations where a party files a lawsuit in federal court despite an arbitration clause. In such cases a litigant can ask the court to stay the court action until the arbitration occurs. If the court denies the stay request, the litigant is allowed to file an **interlocutory** appeal that challenges this denial. Interlocutory appeals occur before the case has been tried and, for that reason, are generally denied. The Supreme Court dealt with these FAA provisions in *Arthur Andersen LLP v. Carlisle*, __U.S.__, 129 S.Ct. 1896, __L.Ed.2d__ (2009), ruling that an appeals court had jurisdiction to hear the interlocutory appeal and that a third-party to the arbitration agreement could seek a stay.

Wayne Carlisle and two other business colleagues sought to minimize their taxes after they sold their construction-equipment company in 1999. They consulted with Arthur Andersen LLP, which had served as the company's accountant, auditor, and tax adviser. Arthur Andersen introduced them to Bricolage Capital, LLC, which in turn introduced them to another firm for legal advice. The advisers from these companies recommended a tax shelter designed to create fictional losses through foreign-currency-exchange options. The men entered into an agreement with Bricolage to handle the tax shelter, which required any disputes about the contract to be arbitrated in New York City. The tax shelter proved to be a financial disaster for Carlisle and his colleagues. The tax shelter they invested in proved almost entirely worthless, and the IRS determined in 2000 that the scheme was illegal. The IRS offered conditional amnesty to them, but the financial advising firms failed to inform them. They eventually settled the matter by paying the IRS all taxes, penalties,and interest owed.

Carlisle and his colleagues filed a federal lawsuit in Kentucky against Bricolage, Arthur Andersen, and others, alleging **fraud**, civil conspiracy, malpractice, breach of **fiduciary** duty, and negligence. Arthur Andersen filed a motion with the court, asking it to stay the lawsuit and force the plaintiffs and Bricolage to arbitrate their claims. The court denied the motion, and Andersen filed an interlocutory appeal with the Sixth **Circuit Court** of Appeals. The appeals court dismissed the case for lack of jurisdiction and Andersen appealed to the Supreme Court.

The Court, in a 6-3 decision, reversed the Sixth Circuit ruling. Justice ANTONIN SCALIA, writing for the majority, concluded that a provision of the FAA "in clear and unambiguous terms" entitled a litigant to an immediate appeal of a denial of the stay "regardless of whether the litigant is in fact eligible for a stay." The Sixth Circuit clearly had jurisdiction to consider the matter, but it had mistakenly conflated "the jurisdictional question with the merits of the appeal. The FAA provision made the underlying merits irrelevant, "for even utter frivolousness of the underlying request" for a stay could not turn a denial into something other than an order refusing a stay described in the FAA.

The Court also addressed whether Arthur Andersen, as a third-party, could ask for the stay. The Sixth Circuit had determined it could not, but Justice Scalia ruled otherwise. He stated that the FAA did not alter "background principles of state contract law regarding the scope of agreements (including the question of who is bound by them.)" If state contract law allows third parties to seek enforcement of a contract, then the FAA will not stand in the way.

Justice DAVID SOUTER, in a dissenting opinion joined by Chief Justice JOHN ROBERTS and Justice JOHN PAUL STEVENS, argued that the FAA did not open the door to interlocutory appeals by someone who had not signed the arbitration agreement. He concluded that the longstanding congressional policy of limiting interlocutory appeals disallowed such appeals by third parties. He found it strange to think

Congress meant to grant the right to appeal a stay denial "to anyone as peripheral to the core agreement as a nonsignatory."

Vaden v. Discover Bank

In 2009, the U.S. SUPREME COURT reviewed a case involving the question of whether a federal **district court** had the power to compel arbitration under the Federal Arbitration Act. Though both a district court and the Fourth **Circuit Court** of Appeals ruled that the federal court could order arbitration, the Supreme Court reversed. The Court determined that the lower courts had erred in reaching their conclusions because they determined that the **federal courts** had jurisdiction based on counterclaims rather than the plaintiff's claims.

Congress enacted the Federal Arbitration Act (FAA), 9 U.S.C. §§ 1 *et seq.* to establish a national policy favoring arbitration and also to overcome judicial prejudice against arbitration clauses. Section 4 of the FAA establishes that a federal district court may issue an order that compels arbitration if the court would have jurisdiction over the suit. A dispute over an arbitration clause alone is not enough to establish federal jurisdiction. Instead, a party seeking to compel arbitration in federal court must establish that the court's jurisdiction lies in the underlying dispute that is subject to arbitration.

In June 2003, Discover Financial Services, Inc. (DFS) sued a credit card customer named Betty Vaden in the U.S. District Court for the District of Maryland. DFS was an service affiliate of Discover Bank, which is a federally insured bank incorporated in Delaware. DFS's suit, filed in state court in Maryland, was based on state law claims stemming from Vaden's nonpayment of credit card charges amounting to more than $10,000. Vaden filed counterclaims also based on Maryland state law. These counterclaims alleged that DFS had breached the contract with Vaden and had illegally assessed finance charges, late fees, and interest rates.

Vaden's original agreement with Discover did not include an arbitration provision. However, Discover changed the agreement in 1999, adding a mandatory arbitration agreement. Pursuant to this arbitration provision, Discover filed a petition with the district court. The district court granted the motion, and Vaden appealed. On appeal, the Fourth Circuit Court of Appeals determined that whether the district court had authority to compel arbitration depended on whether the district court had **subject matter jurisdiction** over the underlying dispute between the parties. *Discover Bank v. Vaden*, 396 F.3d 366 (4th Cir. 2005).

The Fourth Circuit thus remanded the case so that the district court could determine whether it indeed had subject matter jurisdiction in the case.

On remand, the court focused principally on Vaden's counterclaims to determine whether the court had jurisdiction. Vaden's counterclaims were based on state commercial law statutes in Maryland. The statutes in question regulate the assessment of finance charges and late fees on a **consumer credit** card account. These provisions of Maryland law differ significantly from similar provisions of Delaware law, which is much more favorable to the credit card companies.

The court reviewed the nature of Vaden's counterclaims in light of the Federal Deposit Insurance Act (FDIA), 12 U.S.C. § 1831d(a). This **statute** expressly preempts any state law that applies to interest rates charged by banks. Under the FDIA, the law that applies to interest rates is the law of the state where the bank is located. The Supreme Court had never determined that this provision of the FDIA completely preempts state laws related to interest rates. The Court, though, previously held that similar provisions of the National Bank Act, 12 U.S.C. §§ 85, 86 (2006) completely preempts state **usury** laws in claims brought against national banks. *Beneficial Nat'l Bank v. Anderson*, 539 U.S. 1, 123 S. Ct. 2058, 156 L. Ed. 2d 1 (2003). The district court concluded that the FDIA preempted Vaden's counterclaims and that the court had jurisdiction over the case based on the federal statute's **preemption** of the state law claim. *Discover Bank v. Vaden*, 409 F. Supp. 2d 632 (D. Md. 2006).

Vaden appealed the decision to the Fourth Circuit for a second time. In a 2-1 panel decision, the Fourth Circuit affirmed the district court's decision. The lead opinion written by Judge James H. Wilkinson III recognized that a case ordinarily cannot be removed to federal court based solely on a defense or counterclaim based on state law. However, Wilkinson noted that the complete preemption doctrine is an exception to the rule that applies to a defense or counterclaim. Under the doctrine of complete preemption, "any claim purportedly based on [a] preempted state law is considered, from its inception, a federal claim, and therefore arises under federal law." *Caterpillar Inc. v. Williams*, 482 U.S. 386, 107 S. Ct. 2425, 96 L. Ed. 2d 318 (1987). Since Wilkinson concluded that Vaden's counterclaims were completely preempted, Wilkinson's opinion concluded that that district court had jurisdiction over the underlying claims in the case. *Discover Bank v. Vaden*, 489 F.3d 594 (4th Cir. 2007).

The Supreme Court granted **certiorari** to review the case. In a 5-4 decision, the Court reversed the Fourth Circuit. Justice Ruth Bader Ginsberg wrote the opinion for the majority, concluding that the Fourth Circuit had erred by applying the complete preemption doctrine to a counterclaim. Ginsburg noted that it is true that a complaint that purports to rest on state law could be recharacterized as one that has arisen under federal law "if the law governing the complaint is exclusively federal." On the other hand, this rationale does not apply to counterclaims. Because the majority determined that the federal court did not have jurisdiction, the Court held that the district court could not compel arbitration. *Vaden v. Discover Bank*, ___ U.S. ___, 129 S. Ct. 1262, ___ L. Ed. 2d ___ (2009).

Chief Justice JOHN ROBERTS, joined by three other justices, concurred in part and dissented in part. Roberts agreed with the majority that courts should "look through" the dispute to determine whether the federal court has jurisdiction over the underlying dispute. However, Roberts argued that the Court's analysis of counterclaims ran counter to the language and policy of the FAA.

14 Penn Plaza LLC v. Pyett

U.S. businesses have increasingly sought to resolve disputes with their employees by using arbitration. Though the courts have generally upheld arbitration clauses in employment contracts, there have been conflicts over the use of them in contracts negotiated with labor unions through a collective bargaining process. In cases where the employee alleges discrimination that is barred by federal civil rights laws, the Supreme Court had ruled that a **collective bargaining agreement** could not waive workers' rights to a judicial forum. However, in *14 Penn Plaza LLC v. Pyett*, __U.S.__, 129 S. Ct. 1456, __L. Ed. 2d__ (2009), the Court rejected its prior ruling and allowed arbitration of civil rights claims.

Steven Pyett and other members of the Service Employees International Union, worked within the building-services industry in New York City as building cleaners, porters, and doorpersons. The union had exclusive rights to bargain on behalf of its members with the Realty Advisory Board on Labor Relations (RAB), a multiemployer bargaining association for the New York City real-estate industry. The collective bargaining agreement between the union and RAB contained a clause that required union members to submit all claims of employment discrimination to binding arbitration under the agreement's grievance and dispute resolution procedures.

In August 2003, 14 Penn Plaza LLC, a member of RAB, changed security companies at the office building it owned and operated. Pyett and other union members worked as night lobby watchmen in the building and were directly employed by the prior security company. The union consented to the change in companies, as the new security company agreed to keep the watchmen. However, the new company hired licensed security guards to monitor the lobby and entrances to the building. It reassigned Pyett and the other watchmen to jobs as night porters and light duty cleaners in other locations in the building. The watchmen filed a grievance, arguing that the reassignments had led to a loss in income, caused them emotional distress, and were less desirable. The dispute was not resolved through the grievance process, so the union requested arbitration. The union alleged, among other grievances, that the workers had been reassigned on account of their age. While the arbitration process was underway the union withdrew the age discrimination claims and filed a federal civil rights lawsuit against Penn Plaza. In the federal suit the age discrimination claim was reasserted. Penn Plaza sought to have the lawsuit dismissed, citing the binding arbitration clause in the CBA. The **district court** rejected the dismissal motion, finding that the arbitration clause was unenforceable when dealing with civil rights claims. The Second **Circuit Court** of Appeals upheld this ruling, finding that a Supreme Court precedent prohibited the enforcement of arbitration clauses in collective bargaining agreements when federal civil rights laws were at issue. However, the court also noted that this precedent was in tension with a more recent Supreme Court case that held that an individual employee could waive his rights to a federal court and be compelled to arbitrate a claim under the Age Discrimination in Employment Act (ADEA).

The Supreme Court, in a 5-4 decision, overturned the Second Circuit ruling. Justice Clarence Thomas, writing for the majority, agreed that the two Supreme Court decisions on arbitration were in tension. He concluded that the more recent decision dealing with individual employment agreements should be extended to the collective-bargaining context. A waiver is enforceable as long as the agreement to arbitrate **statutory** antidiscrimination claims is "explicitly stated" in the collective bargaining agreement. In this case the agreement did explicitly state the waiver, yet the union contended that an individual employee must personally waive a right to proceed in court for the waiver to be "knowing and voluntary" under the ADEA. Justice Thomas found no merit in this argument, as federal labor law gave the union and RAB the authority to collectively bargain for arbitration and Congress had no explicitly terminate that authority with respect to ADEA discrimination claims.

The Court noted the difference between waiving a substantive right to be free from workplace discrimination and waiving the right to seek relief from a court in the **first instance**. The prior ruling barring waiver of filing claims in court in a collective bargaining agreement confused the two types of waiver. That decision wrongly concluded that waiving the right to go to federal court "was tantamount to a substantive waiver of those rights." Justice Thomas noted that the prior ruling had been made at a time when arbitration was viewed with suspicion by the courts and courts held unwarranted fears about the fairness of the arbitration process. Arbitration had now become an accepted means of dispute resolution and courts should not stand in the way of allowing unions and employers to negotiate arbitration provisions.

Justice JOHN PAUL STEVENS, in a dissenting opinion, argued that the majority's 'subversion

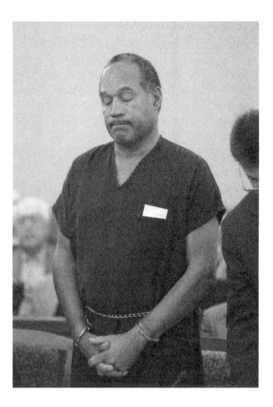

O.J. Simpson in court, December 5, 2008.

AP IMAGES

of precedent' was not based on legal reasoning. Instead, the Court was 'espousing a policy favoring arbitration.'

ARMED ROBBERY

O.J. Simpson Sentenced to 33 Years in Hotel Holdup Case

More than 14 years after being charged with the murder of his wife and another man, former football star O.J. Simpson was convicted on a variety of charges stemming from his role in breaking into a hotel room in an effort to retrieve memorabilia. The Nevada judge who presided over the case showed no mercy for Simpson, sentencing the celebrity to 33 years in prison. Simpson would not be eligible for parole for nine years.

Simpson first became a national celebrity during his days as a college football star at the University of Southern California. In 1968, he won the Heisman Trophy award at the nation's best football player. He was drafted by the Buffalo Bills, and he played professional football for 11 seasons in Buffalo and San Francisco. He became even more well-known when he appeared in several commercials for Hertz rental cars. After his football career ended,

Simpson remained in the spotlight as a television commentator and pitch man. He also appeared in the "Naked Gun" movies during the 1980s and 1990s.

In June 1994, Simpson's former wife, Nicole Brown Simpson, was found slain along with a companion, Ronald Goldman. Less than a week later, Simpson was charged with the murder. The case quickly evolved into one of the most publicized trials of the 20th century. A "dream team" of high-profile lawyers represented Simpson, and millions of people followed the pre-trial and trial proceedings in 1994 and 1995. To the shock of many, Simpson was acquitted of the murder on October 5, 1995.

Immediately after the acquittal, the families of Goldman and Nicole Brown Simpson sued Simpson for **wrongful death**. In February 1997, a civil jury in Santa Monica, California found Simpson liable for the deaths and awarded the families $33.5 million in damages. After the civil trial, Ronald Goldman's father, Fred Goldman, pursued Simpson aggressively, making every effort to collect anything that Simpson owned. Simpson was able to maintain his lifestyle thanks to a substantial **pension** he received from the National Football League. Simpson also allegedly received money for giving autographs, but Goldman had difficulty proving that Simpson was receiving this money.

Many of Simpson's items of value, including his Heisman Trophy, were sold at auction to satisfy the Goldman judgment. A market existed for Simpson items, due in large part to the novelty of having items that once belonged to the disgraced star. During the 2000s, Simpson attempted to write a book, entitled "If I Did It," which Simpson said was a hypothetical account of how he might have committed the murders. In June 2007, a federal bankruptcy judge in Miami awarded the rights to the book to the Goldman family. The Goldman family retitled the book as "If I Did It: Confessions of the Killer" and published the book on September 13, 2007.

As the Goldmans aggressively pursued the items, Simpson continued his efforts to hide personal possessions. At one point, Simpson's former manager, Mike Gilbert, allegedly removed several valuables from Simpson's home so that the Goldmans could not recover the items. Simpson and Gilbert later fought over money, and in response, Gilbert sold some of the items. Simpson was furious about the sale and decided to try to recover these items. Gilbert later wrote a book entitled "How I Helped O.J. Get Away With Murder: The Shocking Inside Story of Violence, Loyalty, Regret and Remorse," in which Gilbert explained his role in hiding items of value from the Goldman family.

On the same day that the Goldmans published "If I Did It: Confessions of the Killer," Simpson and five others convened at the Palace Station hotel-casino in Las Vegas. Simpson forcibly entered the room of two memorabilia dealers named Alfred Beardsley and Bruce Fromong, who allegedly purchased the items from Gilbert. Another memorability dealer named Thomas Riccio secretly recorded the break-in, during at least one of the men brandished a gun. Fromong later said that Simpson never brandished a gun. However, Riccio maintained that Simpson was the one who organized the break-in, which lasted about five or six minutes.

Simpson had organized the break in to retrieve several items that Simpson said belonged to him. The others who accompanied Simpson were Clarence "C.J." Stewart, Walter "Goldie" Alexander, Michael "Spencer" McClinton, Charles Ehrlich and Charles Cashmore. Fromong had purchased the collectibles, which included signed footballs and photographs, along with other items. However, it was unclear whether Fromong had acquired the items legally. On the tape that Riccio produced, Simpson clearly accused the men of stealing his items. Fromong and Beardsley reported the incident as an armed **robbery**.

Within days, Simpson and his accomplices were arrested and charged with several crimes, including kidnapping and armed robbery. On September 19, Simpson was freed on $125,000 bail, after which he returned to his home in Florida. Within a month, three of Simpson's accomplices agreed to plea deals that would require them to testify against Simpson. On November 14, 2007, Simpson, Stewart, and Ehrlich were charged with 12 crimes, to which the defendants pleaded not guilty. Ehrlich eventually agreed to testify against Simpson in a plea bargain.

Simpson had been ordered not to contact his co-defendants, but he violated this order by leaving a message for Stewart with a bail bondsman. On January 16, 2008, Judge Jackie Glass reprimanded Simpson and doubled Simpson's bail. Up to this time, it appeared to be questionable whether the prosecution would move forward. The witnesses had given conflicting accounts of the incident, and most involved were perceived to be shady characters.

Nevertheless, on September 8, 2008, jury selection for the trial began. The jury consisted of a total of nine women and three men. The trial lasted from September 15 through October 2. Simpson's lawyers attempted to discredit the witnesses and tried to convince the jury that Simpson's motive was simply to retrieve items that belonged to him. Simpson did not testify during the trial, which some experts said was a mistake. At the conclusion of the trial, the jury deliberated for 13 hours before rendering its verdict. Simpson and Stewart were both found guilty on all 12 counts, including kidnapping, armed robbery, conspiracy, coercion, **burglary**, and assault with a deadly weapon.

At his sentencing hearing, Simpson gave a rambling speech during which he said, "I didn't want to steal anything from anyone.... I'm sorry, sorry." Despite Simpson's plea, Judge Glass showed no leniency. On December 5, Glass sentenced Simpson to a maximum of 33 years in prison. He is currently serving time at Lovelock Correctional Center in Lovelock, Nevada. In a twist of fate, the items that Simpson sought to retrieve from the memorabilia dealers ended up in the hands of Goldman. When Simpson was sentenced, Goldman told reporters, "We are thrilled, and it's a bittersweet moment. It was satisfying seeing him in shackles like he belongs."

ATTORNEY

A person admitted to practice law in at least one jurisdiction and authorized to perform criminal and civil legal functions on behalf of clients. These functions include providing legal counsel, drafting legal documents, and representing clients before courts, administrative agencies, and other tribunals.

Attorneys Convicted in Fen-Phen Settlement Proceeds Case

In April 2009, two Kentucky attorneys were each convicted of eight counts of wire **fraud** and one count of conspiracy for their self-serving misappropriation of millions of dollars in class-action settlement proceeds involving the diet-drug Fen-Phen. The criminal charges stemmed from their wire transfer of escrowed funds from the $200 million settlement into their own personal and business accounts. Both men had been previously disbarred from the practice of law following a state investigation stemming from the same case. Moreover, a civil lawsuit filed by clients they had represented in the class-action suit resulted in a $42 million verdict against them.

Ironically, a Covington, Kentucky federal jury could not agree on a verdict in 2008 and a mistrial had been declared. It was later learned that the previous hung jury were split 10-2 in favor of acquittal. This time around, prosecutors issued a superseding indictment raising the charges against the attorneys from one count to nine counts. Jurors deliberated for ten hours over two days before issuing their guilty verdict. Following the verdict, U.S. **District Court** Judge Danny Reeves refused bail, determining them as flight risks, and bound them over to federal prison awaiting sentencing.

Fen-phen was a drug "cocktail" popular in the early 1990s for the treatment of obesity. Each of its two main pharmaceutical components had been used separately to aid in weight loss for years. Fenfluramine released the hormone serotonin into the body, while phentermine acted as a stimulant to counteract the drowsiness and altered moods often associated with high levels of serotonin. The two drugs were combined and manufactured as Fen-phen by American Home Products (now known as Wyeth) as a popular weight loss drug.

Concurrent with its market success, Fen-phen began to cause concern among scientists and researchers. In 1997, the Mayo Clinic reported that 24 patients developed heart valve disease after taking Fen-phen. A public health advisory was announced, and the U.S. FOOD AND DRUG ADMINISTRATION (FDA) recommended that patients stop taking the drug. Several health problems attributed to the drug were publicized, including heart murmurs, lung damage, and potentially fatal heart disease.

In July 1998, William Gallion and Shirley Cunningham, Jr., along with another attorney (Melbourne Mills) filed a **civil action** in Kentucky on behalf of what eventually would become a class-action suit involving 440 plaintiffs.

In 2001, the suit was settled for $200 million. Evidence and testimony at trial established that Gallion and Cunningham deliberately withheld facts from their clients about the total amount of the settlement, but instead fraudulently convinced each plaintiff to accept a low value for his or her claim. Further, the attorneys suggested the possibility of imprisonment if plaintiffs revealed their individual settlement amounts to others.

Meanwhile, as established at trial, the two attorneys were wiring millions of dollars from the **escrow** account holding the settlement money to their own individual accounts. The third attorney, Mills (who was acquitted in the first trial) said in a deposition that the other two attorneys advised him that the case had been settled for $150 million, not $200 million. He further said that the three men privately decided how to divvy up an extra $10 million among themselves and keep the distribution secret.

By 2002, the Kentucky Bar Association had launched an investigation into the way the settlement had been handled. It requested a subpoena for the escrow account and financial records of Gallion and Cunningham. Evidence at trial established that after Gallion and Cunningham were made aware of the subpoena request, they used money already diverted to their personal accounts to pay a second distribution to the class-action plaintiffs. During this second distribution, the plaintiffs were advised that if there were any additional money left over, they could have those amounts donated to a trust for charity. Those class-action plaintiffs who testified at the trial against the attorneys all stated that they believed the amount going to charity would be negligible/miniscule.

But, in fact, the two attorneys had gotten sealed orders from the Fen-phen trial court authorizing the establishment of the Kentucky Trust for Healthy Living, and appointing themselves as trustees for which they would each be compensated at $5,300 per month during the life of the trust. They placed $20 million of the escrowed settlement money into the trust. All of this was done without the knowledge or consent of their class-action clients.

Kentucky Judge Joseph Bamberger, who approved the $200 million settlement, said in his deposition that the lawyers never told him how much they had paid themselves, and that he approved the settlement without reading it.

He was forced to resign from the bench and was publicly admonished for his handling of the case, his conduct referred to by the Judicial Commission as "shock[ing] the conscience."

Cincinnati, Ohio **class action** expert Stanley Chesley, who negotiated the 2001 settlement, testified for the prosecution that each of the 440 plaintiffs should have been told the total settlement amount and received an accounting of all funds before agreeing to settle his or her individual claim for a specified sum. He further testified that the attorneys had no authority, without their clients' approval, to place $20 million in the trust and collect more than $10,000 monthly as fees, instead of distributing this amount to their clients.

The successful prosecution of Gallion and Cunningham followed a $42 million civil verdict against them by former plaintiffs in the class action.

Democratic Fund Raiser Convicted for Unauthorized Practice of Law

A well-known fund raiser from Corpus Christi, Texas was convicted in 2009 on charges that he practiced law without a license. Mauricio Celis ran a well-known law firm in Corpus Christi despite the fact that he was not a licensed attorney in Texas. Celis received a sentence of 10 years' probation.

Celis was born in Texas and educated in Mexico. He owned CGT Law Group International in Corpus Christi. CGT regularly referred large cases to litigation firms in South Texas. Celis earned a reputation as a major donor by giving large donations to Democratic candidates and hosting fund raising events. He also served on the boards of such organizations as the Catholic Charities of Corpus Christi.

Questions circled for some period of time about whether Celis was even a lawyer. During the spring of 2007, one lawyer in a deposition regarding a disputed legal fee questioned whether CGT Law Group could even operate as a law firm. According to the lawyer, CGT Law Group was a "sham law firm operating illegally" and that the firm was "nothing more than a runner ambulance-chasing referral organization that has a history of referring cases that they have solicited improperly, and sent off to other lawyers."

Under Texas law, a person who practices law without a license is guilty of a **felony**. A lawyer cannot share fees with non-lawyers, and a non-lawyer generally cannot own an interest in a law firm. Celis was not licensed to practice law in Texas, but he was regularly identified as a lawyer in such publications as the *Chicago Tribune* and *Texas Monthly*. His website and stationary referred to him as an attorney, with licenses to practice law in California and Washington, D.C., as well as Mexico.

Thomas J. Henry, a personal injury lawyer based in Corpus Christi, filed a complaint in May 2007 with the Unauthorized Practice of Law Committee of the State Bar of Texas. Henry also submitted written complaints to the Texas attorney general and to the Nueces County district attorney. Celis responded by asserting that he earned a law license in Mexico and that he could own a law firm in Texas based on the firm's affiliation with one in Texas. According to legal experts, though, Celis should not have operated his Texas law firm, and other firms should not accept referrals from Celis.

Notwithstanding the laws forbidding unauthorized practice, authorities did not respond to Henry's complaint. After months of waiting, Henry decided to go public with his accusations by running a series of advertisements. On September 28, 2007, Henry appeared in the ad, holding up his law license. During the commercial, Henry said:

> I'm Thomas J. Henry. I proudly display my law license. However, Mauricio Celis with the law firm of CGT International Law Group does not have a law license in the state of Texas, nor does he have a license to practice law anywhere in the world. If you have hired this law firm, you may be entitled to a refund of attorney's fees paid. Contact me immediately.

The ad ran for 30 seconds.

Celis immediately obtained a temporary restraining order to remove the ad from the air. Attorneys in Corpus Christi and elsewhere debated about whether Henry's charges had merit. Firms that had accepted clients based on Celis' referrals started questioning whether they could continue representation. Celis continued to claim that he was merely the general manager and chief administrator at the firm and that he did not actively practice law.

In November 2007, Celis was charged with a variety of crimes, including practicing law without a license, impersonating a police officer, theft, and perjury. Celis was accused of flashing a badge at one time so that he could accompany a client being questioned. He was also accused of illegally keeping money belonging to a client and of lying under oath about his educational background. Two judges initially recused themselves due to their prior dealings with Celis. A third judge, J. Manuel Bañales, agreed to preside over the case. Bañales instructed Celis to place a sign at the CGT firm indicating that Celis is not a lawyer.

Celis and his firm faced more legal problems. The Texas attorney general brought a **civil action** against Celis based on the unauthorized practice charge. A committee of the Supreme Court of Texas also brought an action against five attorneys in Celis' firm. The committee alleged that even though the attorneys in the firm were authorized to practice law, they had aided and **abetted** Celis in practicing law without a license and had shared fees with him unlawfully. The committee sought a court order that would require the lawyers to return legal fees to clients. In December 2007, Evanston Insurance Company sued Celis, claiming that the company should not have to pay Celis' legal bills because he had lied on an application for professional liability insurance.

In April 2008, a **grand jury** in Nueces County heard testimony about the charges. During a three-week period, the grand jury heard testimony from lawyers that knew Celis as well as from investigators from the office of the Texas attorney general. On April 25, the grand jury returned two indictments against Celis, charging him with **money laundering** and impersonating a lawyer. Celis maintained his innocence, saying that the charges were politically motivated.

Celis chose to face different charges in separate trials. He was faced 22 counts on charges related to unauthorized practice of law. Prosecutors brought in thousands of pages of documents, including thirteen boxes of seized evidence. In February 2009, a jury found Celis guilty on 14 of the 22 charges. Celis' attorney attempted to argue that the prosecutors had failed to prove that Celis was not licensed to practice in Mexico, but the defense did not persuade the jury. Based on the charges, a visiting judge who presided over the case initially sentenced Celis to one year in prison and 10 years probation. However, in May 2009, Bañales ruled that the prison term was not warranted and sentenced Celis to 10 years' probation.

Celis must still stand trial on other charges, including money laundering.

ATTORNEY GENERAL

Report Finds Alberto Gonzales Mishandled Classified Documents

The Office of the Inspector General (OIG) within the U.S. Department of Justice (DOJ) released an investigation report in September 2008 clearly critical of former U.S. Attorney General Alberto Gonzales. Although the DOJ was precisely the department that Gonzales oversaw, he was not subject to internal department discipline: he had already resigned a year prior (September 2007) amid a stormy controversy in Congress over his role in the firing of nine U.S. Attorneys.

The "Report of Investigation Regarding Allegations of Mishandling of Classified Documents by Attorney General Alberto Gonzales" was the result of a matter referred to the DOJ by Kenneth Wainstein, former Assistant Attorney General for the National Security Division, on August 10, 2007. The White House Office **of Counsel** had already notified the DOJ that the referral was coming, after Wainstein had consulted with other senior Department officials.

Initially, the allegations concerned Gonzales's handling of documents containing classified information about the National Security Agency's (NSA) sensitive surveillance program relating to national intelligence. That information was classified as Top Secret/Sensitive Compartmented Information (TS/SCI). However, during the course of the investigation, the OIG learned of other instances of potential mishandling of classified documents by Gonzales.

The OIG conducted the investigation by interviewing Gonzales on three separate occasions, as well as attorneys in the White House Counsel's Office and other staff members of the OAG. The OAG also reviewed all of the classified documents at issue and consulted with other officials knowledgeable in the handling of classified documents.

Gonzales served as White House Counsel for then-President GEORGE W. BUSH from 2001 to 2005, at which time he was sworn in as Attorney General. The first of the incidents covered in the investigative report occurred shortly thereafter. It involved very critical and high-classified (TS/SCI) information about the NSA's wiretapping initiative (the government's most sensitive national security program). The report found that Gonzales carried around notes about the NSA's program in his unlocked briefcase, then took them home. His private residence contained a special locked safe (still less secure than the required SCIF-level, see below) in conjunction with his official duties, but Gonzales apparently did not even put the documents in the safe because he "could not remember the combination." When questioned later by investigators, Gonzales stated that he could not recall whether he took home the highly-classified documents, and that he did not know if they contained classified information, despite his own markings of "top secret-eyes only" written on them.

An NSA official who reviewed the documents indicated that they contained specific references to operational aspects of the wiretapping initiatives, including a top-secret code word for the program,—unequivocal information that should have been "zealously protected." The classified papers included personal notes that Gonzales had drafted to memorialize a classified briefing of congressional leaders regarding the wiretap program, draft and final legal opinions about both the NSA surveillance program and a detainee interrogation program, correspondence from congressional leaders to the Director of Central Intelligence (CIA), and other memoranda relating to the two classified programs. By regulation, such documents must be stored in a Sensitive Compartmented Storage Facility (SCIF).

Investigators concluded that Gonzales stored these documents in his briefcase for an "indeterminate" amount of time. Thereafter, he stored them in a safe outside his JUSTICE DEPARTMENT office. However, several employees had access to the safe who lacked not only the security clearances needed, but also the "need to know" what those documents contained. Regulation required that the documents be stored in a safe that was contained in a SCIF.

The investigation report indicated the Gonzales never inquired whether the safe he used satisfied security requirements, nor did he ask whether the OAG had a SCIF. The report further indicated that Gonzales made the classified documents accessible to individuals not "cleared" into the two compartmented programs.

At least five staff members had access to the safe; none of them had been cleared into the NSA surveillance program, and four of the five were not cleared into the detainee interrogation program. All had access to the safe.

Gonzales told investigators that he never gave "conscious consideration" to the fact that such persons would have access to those documents, and referred to those individuals as "trusted people." He said he doubted that his assistants would open and read the contents of an envelope marked "AG-EYES ONLY." The investigators additionally learned that two of those assistants had likely gone through all those documents in response to a Freedom of Information (FOIA) request. However, since neither had an appropriate clearance, investigators could not show them the documents or query them with descriptive terms to ascertain whether they recalled seeing any of the documents during the FOIA review.

The security compromise unequivocally violated Justice Department policies. The Federal Criminal Code also contains statutes relating to the improper handling of classified documents, e.g., 18 USC 1924. In light of the breaches of security that the investigation uncovered, the report was forwarded to the National Security Division for review. After reviewing the report, the National Security Division declined prosecution.

AUTOMOBILES

Automaker Bailout Talks Lead to Greater Oversight of the Automotive Industry

One of the industries hit hardest by the economic downturn in 2008 was the automotive industry. Nearly every automaker lost money in 2008, though the so-called "Big Three" of General Motors, Ford, and Chrysler were hit hardest. When executives with these companies approached Congress for bailout money, the business strategies of the Big Three came into question. Though the government eventually agreed to provide the loans these companies requested, the loans came with a steep price: unprecedented government oversight of the automotive industry.

The major American automakers for years focused their attention on manufacturing larger vehicles, such as trucks and SUVs. There were several reasons for this. First, demand for these types of vehicles remained fairly constant among U.S. consumers. Second, the cost of producing these types of vehicles was less than the cost of producing more fuel efficient passenger cars. And third, because of the lower manufacturing costs, the profit margin of these larger vehicles was greater than the profit margin of a typical passenger car.

U.S. automakers saw a sharp decline in its domestic market share during the past decade. Between 1998 and 2008, the market share of the Big Three fell from 70% to 53%. During this period, the number of car sales in the U.S. fell significantly from the all-time high of 17.4 million in 2000. The growth in the number of cars during the current decade outgained the growth in the total number of drivers during the same time period. Jobs in the automotive industry also suffered a steady decline. Part of the difficulty that U.S. automakers have had related to labor costs, which were higher due to collective bargaining agreements reached with the United Auto Workers.

Rising oil prices in 2008 turned the decline of the automakers into a crisis. With gas prices rising well above $4 per gallon, consumers seeking more fuel-efficient models turned away from the vehicles offered by the Big Three and instead opted for models offered by overseas competitors. Compounding the problems for U.S. automakers was the credit crisis that deeply affected the economy in 2008. As consumers lost their ability to borrow money to make auto purchases, sales continued to drop significantly.

With each of the Big Three on the verge of bankruptcy, executives during the fall of 2008 began to lobby Congress for bailout loans that would help the companies survive the crisis. In September 2008, Congress and President GEORGE W. BUSH approved $25 billion in loans to the automakers. The plan for these loans had been in the works for some time, but the need became more pressing with the dire economic news. The companies received a very low interest rate (estimated at about 4%) and did not need to begin paying off the loans for five years.

Even with these loans, the Big Three said that the corporations needed more assistance to survive. Executives with Chrysler, Ford, and General Motors appeared before Congress in November to request more money, but they were met with scrutiny from members of the Senate Banking Committee. Committee Chairman Christopher Dodd (D.-Conn.) said that the automotive business had been "devoid of vision." Republicans also chimed in, with Senator Michael Enzi (R.-Wyoming) expressing doubt that the proposed bailout "will do anything to promote long-term success." On the flip side, the companies, along with the head of the United Auto Workers, said that if one of the companies collapsed, the other two would probably follow soon thereafter. A collapse of these companies could result in the loss of some two million jobs, which would further drive the economy downward.

As the debate raged on, one proposal that emerged focused on the appointment of an individual who would oversee that the conditions attached to the bailout money were being followed through. This so-called "car czar" would ensure that the automakers turned in a direction that would make them "viable and competitive," according to White House spokeswoman Dana Perino. As of December 2008, proposals called for the automakers to receive loans up to about $17 million. Executives had initially requested $34 billion. Under the proposal at that time, then-president George W. Bush would select the car czar by working with the team of president-elect Barack Obama. Despite Bush's willingness to consider the bailout proposal, though, Republican members of Congress continued to express concern about whether the bailout proposal would make any difference in the long term. Even some Democrats expressed reservations about the viability of the bailout proposal.

Congress in December agreed to $17.4 billion in loans to the automakers that came out of a $700 billion bailout package authorized two months earlier. Despite the availability of money from these loans, Chrysler and General Motors continued to suffer. The credit crisis in the United States had not ended by early 2009, and the automotive industry accordingly felt the heat caused by this crisis. In the first two months of 2009, Chrysler had to make several requests for billion-dollar loans from the bailout package just so that the company could stay afloat. By the spring of 2009, however, Ford executives said that the company had enough credit that it may not need to take its part of the loans.

As the automakers continued to struggle, Obama announced an alternative strategy to the car czar proposal. In February 2009, Obama announced the formation of a task force that would oversee the bailout of Chrysler and General Motors. Two key members of the task force included Treasury Secretary Timothy Geithner and White House economic advisor Lawrence Summers. The administration added another key member, Steven Rattner, in March. Rattner brought a wealth of experience to the task force. He is a former investment banker, a well-known fundraiser for the DEMOCRATIC PARTY, and a foreign correspondent with the *New York Times*. In April 2009, the *Times* referred to Rattner as "Obama's top auto industry troubleshooter."

Obama's active role in the crisis led to criticism. On March 30, 2009, Obama requested that General Motors CEO Rick Wagoner resign, leading at least one commentator to refer to Obama as "CEObama." The news worsened later in April when allegations arose that Rattner may have been involved in a **pension** scandal. The administration expressed support for Rattner, but the commentators said the controversy hurt the task force's credibility. Meanwhile, General Motors in April was probably headed for bankruptcy. Whether GM filed for bankruptcy would be based on a joint decision made by GM's board and the auto task force.

BANKRUPTCY

A federally authorized procedure by which a debtor—an individual, corporation, or municipality—is relieved of total liability for its debts by making court-approved arrangements for their partial repayment.

Travelers Indemnity v. Bailey

In the consolidated cases of *Travelers Indemnity v. Bailey* and *Common Law Settlement Counsel v. Bailey,* No. 08-307, 556 U.S. ___ (2009), the U.S. Supreme Court faced the question of whether a bankruptcy court had the authority to block private lawsuits seeking damages for injuries against one of the settling insurance carriers of a company in bankruptcy. By a 7-2 decision, the Court held that the lawsuits were barred by the 1986 settlement agreement in bankruptcy court. Because the case before the Court concerned a settlement agreement involving bankrupt Johns-Manville Corporation and its insurer Travelers Indemnity Company, the decision had limited application. In any event, its decision reversed the holding of the U.S. Court of Appeals for the Second Circuit. That court ruled that the bankruptcy court lacked authority to block private common law suits alleging wrongdoing by Travelers even though they were separate from that of its insured, Johns-Manville.

Johns-Manville (Manville) was an asbestos supplier and manufacturer of asbestos-containing products. Travelers Indemnity and related companies (Travelers) was the company's main

liability insurer from 1947 to 1976. When the dangers of asbestos became apparent, Manville became the target of products liability lawsuits alleging exposure-related personal injuries. It sought protection in bankruptcy court, petitioning for reorganization. During the period leading up to the reorganization, Manville was caught up in litigation with its own insurers (including Travelers) over the scope and limits of liability coverage. Travelers also faced lawsuits from third parties, including Manville factory workers and vendors of Manville products seeking asbestos exposure-related damages. Manville's liability insurers were also fighting with each other, filing cross-claims, indemnity claims, and claims for contribution.

Because asbestos-related injuries may not manifest for several years, Manville's insurance policies were its most valuable asset it the bankruptcy estate. In a settlement that became the cornerstone of the Manville reorganization, Manville ultimately settled with its insurance carriers for $770 million, most of which was placed in the Manville Personal Injury Settlement Trust. Travelers had settled with Manville for $80 million in exchange for "a full and final release of all Manville-related claims." Another insurer, Common Law Settlement Counsel (party in the companion case), obtained a similar settlement.

In December 1986, the bankruptcy court issued its Insurance Settlement Order. Its relevant provisions stated that, upon the insurers' payment of the settlement funds to the Trust, all claims that were "based upon, arose out of, or related to" Manville's liability insurance policies would be directed against the Trust fund.

Importantly, and at issue in the present case, the Insurance Settlement Order provided that, (upon the insurers' payment of the settlement funds to the Trust), "all Persons are permanently restrained and enjoined from commencing and/or continuing any suit, arbitration or other proceeding of any type or nature for Policy Claims against any or all members of the Settling Insurer Group," Thereafter, the insurers were "released from any and all Policy Claims," which were to be directed to the Trust Fund. The Order expressly defined "Policy Claims" as

> "any and all claims, demands, allegations, duties, liabilities and obligations (whether or not presently known) which have been, or could have been, or might be, asserted by any Person against … any or all members of the Settling Insurer Group based upon, arising out of or relating to any or all of the Policies."

Years after the 1986 Settlement Order, Congress amended the Bankruptcy Code in 1994 to expressly authorize bankruptcy court "injunctions barring derivative claims against third party insurers." 11 USC §524(g).

This did not prevent the filing of several subsequent lawsuits directly against Travelers in 2001. Although these direct actions were asbestos related, they were not related to Manville's wrongdoing, but instead, alleged wrongdoing by Travelers. Specifically, they claimed violations of state consumer protection laws or common law violations of failure to warn or disclose dangers, conspiracy to conceal pertinent facts, etc. Lawyers filing the actions argued that they fell outside the purview of the bankruptcy court's Settlement Order because these claims directly involved Travelers' wrongdoing and not the bankrupt Manville estate.

In response, Travelers invoked the 1986 Settlement Order and asked the bankruptcy court to enjoin 26 of these direct actions against it. Ultimately, a settlement was reached in 2004 with several of these plaintiffs, (for an aggregate $500 million) in exchange for an order from the bankruptcy court reiterating its earlier 1986 decision barring such suits (the Clarifying Order). In conjunction with the Clarifying Order, the bankruptcy court made extensive factual findings essentially concluding that Travelers' knowledge of asbestos was derived from its relationship with Manville, and that Travelers' alleged wrongdoing was based on acts or omissions arising from or related to the insurance policies. The Clarifying Order expressly reiterated that the 1986 Order therefore barred these and other pending new claims.

Those who did not settle appealed. The federal district court affirmed the bankruptcy court's Order, but the U.S. Court of Appeals for the Second Circuit reversed. It held that the bankruptcy court lacked jurisdiction to enjoin these actions because they sought to recover on the basis of Travelers' independent conduct, not Manville's conduct.

The U.S. Supreme Court reversed the Second Circuit, agreeing instead with the district court and the bankruptcy court. Justice Souter delivered the opinion of the Court and cautioned that its decision was a narrow one ("Whether the bankruptcy court had jurisdiction [to bar such lawsuits] in 1986 [prior to Congress' 1994 amendments to the Bankruptcy Code] was not properly before the [Second Circuit] Court of Appeals in 2008 and is not properly before us [now]," said the 7-2 majority opinion). "Almost a quarter-century after the 1986 orders were entered, the time to prune them is over." The 1986 orders became final on direct review more than two decades previously, Justice Souter said.

Justice Stevens, joined by Justice Ginsburg, dissented. "Because I am persuaded that the 1986 Insurance Settlement Order did not encompass independent actions and that the Bankruptcy Court improperly enjoined such actions in 2004, I respectfully dissent," wrote Stevens.

BANKS AND BANKING

Authorized financial institutions and the business in which they engage, which encompasses the receipt of money for deposit, to be payable according to the terms of the account; collection of checks presented for payment; issuance of loans to individuals who meet certain requirements; discount of commercial paper; and other money-related functions.

Cuomo v. Clearing House Association

The National Bank Act (NBA) establishes limitations on the ability of the states to exercise certain types of supervisory powers over national banks. The Office of the **Comptroller** of Currency (OCC) approved a regulation that strictly limited the types of powers that states could exercise over the national banks. When the former attorney general of New York sought to obtain records from national banks in conjunction with an investigation of possible instances of racial discrimination in lending, the OCC blocked the action, arguing that the investigation violated both the NBA and the OCC regulation. On June 29, 2009, the Supreme Court concluded that the NBA only prohibits the exercise of certain powers over national banks and that the OCC regulation was an unreasonable interpretation of the NBA.

The NBA applies to the creation of national banks. Under 12 U.S.C. § 484(a):

> No national bank shall be subject to any visitorial powers except as authorized by Federal law, vested in the courts of justice or such as shall be, or have been exercised or directed by Congress or by either House thereof or by any committee of Congress or of either House duly authorized.

The statute establishes the OCC to serve as the federal agency responsible for overseeing "the business of banking" under the NBA. According to 12 U.S.C. § 93a, the OCC has authority "to prescribe rules and regulations to carry out the responsibilities of the office." The OCC may also define "incidental powers" of national banks beyond the powers that are listed in the statute.

In *Guthrie v. Harkness*, 199 U.S. 148, 26 S. Ct. 4, 50 L. Ed. 130 (1905), the Supreme Court defined "visitation" as "the act of a superior to superintending officer, who visits a corporation to examine into its manner to conducting business, and enforce an observance of its laws and regulations." The Second **Circuit Court** of Appeals also observed that the purpose of the restriction on visitorial powers is to "prevent inconsistent or intrusive state regulation from impairing the national system." *Wachovia Bank, N.A. v. Burke*, 414 F.3d 305 (2d Cir. 2005).

The OCC in 1996 adopted a regulation providing that "the exercise of visitorial powers over national banks is vested solely in the OCC." 12 C.F.R. § 7.4000. The OCC subsequently revisited this regulation and made modifications. The rule establishes that state officials have no right to inspect or require the production of books of a national bank except as provided by the NBA. The rule also forbid states from bringing "prosecuting enforcement actions" against national banks because these actions are prohibited state visitorial powers. Section 7.4000 provides several examples of the types of visitations prohibited by the regulation, including:

> (i) Examination of a bank; (ii) Inspection of a bank's books and records; (iii) Regulation and supervision of activities authorized or permitted pursuant to federal banking law; and (iv) Enforcing compliance with any applicable federal or state laws concerning those activities.

Beginning in 2005, New York State Attorney General Eliot Spitzer began to investigate whether several national banks and their subsidiaries had engaged in racial discrimination. The investigation began when data showed that a significantly higher percentage of high-interest home mortgage loans had been issued to African- and Hispanic-American borrowers compared with those issues to white borrowers. The data was available to the public through the federal Home Mortgage Disclosure Act (HMDA), 12 U.S.C. §§ 2801-10.

The attorney general's office responded to these concerns by sending letters of inquiry to those mortgage lenders, which included the national banks and their subsidiaries. The attorney general's office selected these lenders based on implications determined from the HMDA data. The letters stated that the disparities in loans based on race were "troubling on their face, and unless legally justified may violate federal and state anti-discrimination laws...." The letter requested, "in lieu of issuing a formal subpoena," that that lenders voluntarily produce certain non-public data about their mortgage policies and practices. The letter also requested information about loans related to real property in New York.

The OCC concluded that the attorney general's efforts violated the NBA and OCC's regulations. The OCC concluded that the attorney general could not investigate the banks or enforce provisions of the anti-discrimination laws, because these investigative and enforcement actions constituted exercises of visitorial powers that the regulations prohibit. A consortium of national banks—The Clearing House Association—also filed a complaint against the attorney general, seeking to enjoin the attorney general from continuing the investigation. The attorney general filed a counterclaim against the OCC, arguing that the OCC regulation should be set aside under the Administrative Procedure

THE DEBATE OVER NATIONALIZATION OF BANKS

The banking industry in 2008 and 2009 experienced one of the biggest crises in generations. Many banks became insolvent, and more would have become insolvent had the federal government not stepped in to provide bailout funds. While the federal bailout may have saved some banks, the price tag was enormous. In exchange for billions of dollars in aid, the government received equity interests in these banks.

The idea that the federal government would become so actively involved in saving these banks might appear at first blush to draw the ire of those concerned with big government. As Barack Obama prepared to take over as president in January 2009, the health of several of the largest banks in the United States—Bank of America, Citigroup, and Wells Fargo—looked shaky. Stock in those banks fell by as much as 20 percent just before Obama's inauguration.

Though the stock prices did not remain low, many expressed concerns

the federal government may need to step in to take over one of the nation's largest banks. At the time of Obama's inauguration, the government had already used a significant part of the $700 billion of the Troubled Asset Relief Program (TARP), which was designed to allow the government to purchase toxic financial assets from banks so that the banks could remain afloat. Congress at the time was already debating how to allocate more money to kick start the ailing economy, and the Obama administration had to determine how to spend the second half of the $700 billion TARP package.

The numbers involved in the banking crisis were staggering. By early 2009, banks had already written off more than $1 trillion in losses. Other potential losses also numbered in the trillions when economists took into account losses in real estate loans, consumer credit-card debt, bonds, loans, and so forth. In January, the government provided $120 billion in aid to Bank of America in the

form of capital and absorbed losses. The government had previously given $300 billion in aid to Citigroup. The amount of aid would have been enough for a private company to have acquired those banks.

Early in 2009, economists publicly suggested that the federal government should consider nationalizing banks. Two professors from New York University, Matthew Richardson and Nouriel Roubini, wrote an op-ed piece that was published in the *Washington Post* on February 15. According to Richardson and Roubini, the federal government should determine which banks were insolvent and which banks were solvent. The authors said that the government should take over (nationalize) the insolvent banks. This strategy would not involve a permanent takeover, but would instead allow the government to clean up the banks and then reprivatize those banks. Richardson and Roubini wrote:

> The eventual outcome would be a healthy financial system with

Act, 5 U.S.C. § 706, because the OCC regulation was not in accordance with law.

The U.S. **District Court** for the Southern District of New York reviewed the case and ruled in favor of the OCC. The district court concluded that the OCC regulation was entitled to deference under the Supreme Court's standard set forth in *Chevron U.S.A., Inc. v. Natural Res. Def. Council*, 467 U.S. 837, 104 S. Ct. 2778, 8 L. Ed. 2d 694 (1984). By deferring to the agency regulation, the court concluded that the attorney general did not have the authority to investigate the claims or enforce the anti-discrimination laws. *Office of the Comptroller of the Currency v. Spitzer*, 396 F. Supp. 2d 383 (S.D.N.Y. 2005). The attorney general appealed the decision to the Second Circuit Court of Appeals, which affirmed the district court's opinion as the opinion applied to the application

of the OCC regulation. *Clearing House Ass'n v. Cuomo*, 510 F.3d 105 (2d Cir. 2007).

The U.S. SUPREME COURT reviewed the case and issued an opinion on June 29, 2009. In a 5-4 decision, the Court reversed part of the Second Circuit's judgment but affirmed other parts of the lower court's opinion. The majority opinion written by Justice ANTONIN SCALIA reviewed the history of the NBA and the meaning of the term "visitation" as it is used in the NBA. According to Scalia's review of the cases, the Court has treated a state's power to enforce the law as something separate from visitorial powers. A state exercises its visitorial powers when it establishes a form of administrative oversight over corporations. By comparison, when a state brings a lawsuit to enforce a state law against a national bank, the state is acting as a law enforcer rather than as a supervisor.

many new banks capitalized by good assets. Insolvent, too-big-to-fail banks would be broken up into smaller pieces less likely to threaten the whole financial system. Regulatory reforms would also be instituted to reduce the chances of costly future crises.

Support for these nationalization proposals had not necessarily depended on party alliances or political beliefs. Some Republicans spoke in support of nationalizing some of the banks—surprising some who would think that conservatives would oppose such a move. In one television exchange, Senator Lindsey Graham (R.-S.C.) said that nationalization may be necessary. He said:

This idea of nationalizing banks is not comfortable. But I think we've got so many toxic assets spread throughout the banking and financial community, throughout the world, that we're going to have to do something that no one ever envisioned a year ago, no one likes. To me, banking and housing are the root cause of this problem. I'm very much afraid any program to salvage the banks is going to

require the government... I would not take off the idea of nationalizing the banks."

One of the other Democratic panel members, Senator Chuck Schumer (D.-N.Y.), opposed nationalization, noting that he did not "think government is good at making these decisions."

Talk of nationalization during 2009 sent investors into panic. News of a possible government takeover of any bank typically sent that bank's stock spiraling downward—at least during the short term. Part of the reason for this reaction was been that a government takeover of a bank would mean that public shares in these banks would become worthless. Although depositors are insurance by the FEDERAL DEPOSIT INSURANCE CORPORATION, those that stood to lose included bondholders, creditors, and those with deposits above the amount insured by the FDIC.

A second concern about nationalization of banks is that such a takeover would not address the underlying problems that caused the banking crisis. Losses caused by bad subprime loans and other financial assets could continue to lose the value, and a government

takeover would not end these losses. In the event of a takeover, the government would need to continue to pump more money into the banks to help to cover these losses, but a takeover of any of these banks would not itself prevent these losses.

Throughout the spring of 2009, the Obama administration continued to oppose taking over the banks. Treasury Secretary Tim Geithner noted that "for basic practical reasons that our system will be stronger if it remains in private hands, with support from the government to make sure those institutions can play their critical role going forward." At the same time, a report submitted by Inspector General Neil Barofsky concluded that TARP had exposed the government (and hence, taxpayers) to large losses.

In May 2009, Geithner and Federal Reserve Chairman Ben Bernanke announced the results of a stress test that evaluated the health of 19 of the nation's largest banks. The report was optimistic, concluding that the banks needed about $75 billion in capital to continue to withstand the recession. Talk of nationalizing banks began to die down after the release of the report.

Based on this reasoning, the majority concluded that the attorney general's threat to issue executive subpoenas fell under the category of the state acting as a supervisor. Thus, the Court upheld the injunction prohibiting the attorney general from issuing these subpoenas. However, the Court concluded that the OCC regulation was not a reasonable interpretation with regard to an action by the attorney general to enforce the anti-discrimination laws. *Cuomo v. Clearing House Ass'n*, No. 08-453, 2009 WL 1835148 (2009).

New York Attorney General Andrew M. Cuomo applauded the ruling, noting that it was "a huge win for consumers across the nation." Cuomo noted that the decision reaffirmed the role of state attorneys general "in protecting consumers from illegal and improper practices by our country's biggest and most powerful banks."

❖ BIDEN, JOSEPH

Joseph Biden served as a United States Senator before joining Barack Obama as his vice presidential choice in the 2009 presidential election. Biden was born in 1942 to a working-class family in Scranton, Pennsylvania, and grew up in suburban Wilmington, Delaware. Biden enrolled at the University of Delaware, where he played safety on the football team. In the classroom he depended less on hard study than on his native intelligence and glib wit. "He had a talent for getting it done when it had to get done," college roommate and future law partner David Walsh told the *Wilmington News Journal*. During spring break of his junior year, Biden met Syracuse University student Neilia Hunter. He quit football before his senior year to spend more time with her and, after graduating, enrolled in

Joseph Biden.
AP IMAGES

Syracuse University Law School. They married in 1966 and two years later moved to Delaware, where Biden opened a law practice. He quickly became prominent in Wilmington by defending the accused in the toughest criminal cases.

Biden, who registered as a political independent in 1970, was asked to run for the New Castle County Council by Delaware Republicans impressed with his legal oratory skills. Biden decided to run, but as a Democrat. Although the district was 65 percent Republican, Biden—at 27—won by a large margin. The next day he began planning his Senate U.S. campaign. Just two years later, at 29, Biden challenged J. Caleb Boggs, 63, a two-term senator who had held office in Delaware for 26 years. No other Democrat wanted to challenge the popular Boggs, who was said to have known every state resident on a first-name basis and sent cards to every Delaware family at Christmas. So when the unknown Biden entered the race, people saw him as a sacrificial lamb.

But Biden gained recognition by meeting voters in six coffee klatches a day throughout the state and by deploying battalions of high school students to pass out leaflets. He argued that Boggs was a do-nothing senator who would prefer to retire. His tenacity impressed donors, and money began to pour in. In the end, the campaign spent $300,000, the most for a statewide campaign in Delaware at that time. On election night, Biden won took Boggs' seemingly safe seat by 3,162 votes.

In December 1972, Neilia Biden and daughter Naomi were killed in an automobile accident. Biden planned to resign in order to raise his surviving sons, but he was persuaded to stay on as senator, being named to several important committees.

In 1978, Biden was re-elected with 58 percent of the vote. Much of his support came from his position as the Senate's leader in opposing busing for school integration. In the mid-70s, Biden successfully proposed an amendment to prevent the Department of Health, Education and Welfare from ordering school districts to institute busing. Two years later he proposed a bill that failed by two votes on the Senate floor to restrict court-ordered busing. "Is it racist because people don't want to send their kid instead of across the street to a school six miles away?" he asked on the Senate floor. Such stands created a confusing image of Biden. For every liberal

1942	Born, Scranton, Pennsylvania
1968	Graduated Syracuse Law School
1972	Elected U.S. Senator for Delaware
1988	First failed presidential run
2008	Became U.S. Vice President

act—opposition to U.S. involvement in Vietnam in the 1970s and El Salvador in the 1980s, grilling of the CIA over covert espionage—there was an equal and opposite conservative act—opposing busing, aiming to cut off federal funds for abortion, beefing up the defense budget.

Yet by 1984, Biden ranked fifth in how often he had voted in opposition to President Ronald Reagan, according to Congressional Quarterly. Two years later, the Democratic Party recaptured control of the Senate, elevating Biden to the post of chairman of the powerful Judiciary Committee. He came to be regarded as an expert on criminal justice and foreign policy. In 1983 he co-sponsored a comprehensive anti-crime bill criticized by some as anti-liberal. He was a Senate leader on such issues as the MX missile, arms control, Lebanon, U.S. Soviet relations and civil rights. A run for the Democratic presidential nomination in 1988 was derailed when Biden was shown to have used parts of speeches by British politican Neil Kinnock without credit.

Biden's attempt to run for the Democratic nomination in 2008 fell short again, but on August 23, 2008, Obama announced he had chosen Biden as his vice-presidential running mate. Biden was viewed as a shrewd choice, given his years of political experience, including deep knowledge of foreign policy and in national security issues, helped offset the Illinois senator's youth.

BIRTH CONTROL

A measure or measures undertaken to prevent conception.

Illinois Courts Wrestle with Emergency Contraception Laws

By 2009, a significant minority of states had enacted laws related to emergency contraception. When taken within 72 hours of sexual intercourse, these pills can prevent pregnancy. Several states became concerned about whether hospitals, individual doctors, or pharmacists would prescribe or dispense emergency contraceptive pills, especially in situations involving sexual assault. Many of the statutes related to emergency contraception address these concerns. However, issues have arisen in a number of states about how these laws apply.

In 2006, the FOOD AND DRUG ADMINISTRATION approved a pill known as Plan B as an emergency contraceptive. The pill consists of a concentrated dose of progestin, which is a hormone commonly found in birth control pills. Estimates about how effective Plan B pills are at preventing pregnancy vary, but generally range from 80 to 90 percent in terms of effectiveness. Plan B differs significantly from the abortion pill known as RU-486, which can end a pregnancy up to seven weeks after conception. Women ages 18 and older can obtain Plan B over-the-counter, but girls 17 and under can only obtain the drug through a prescription.

According to the National Conference of State Legislatures, a total of 20 states had enacted emergency contraception statutes as of February 2009. Fifteen of these states have enacted legislation that either requires hospitals to provide information about emergency contraception or mandates that the hospital initiate emergency contraception to women who have been sexually assaulted. Nine other states have enacted statutes that permit pharmacists to initiate emergency contraception drug therapy so long as the pharmacist is working in conjunction with a physician or has completed a training program in emergency contraception.

The Illinois Legislature in 2002 and 2008 amended the state's Sexual Assault Survivors Emergency Treatment Act. The statutes define emergency contraception and require dissemination of information about emergency contraception to women who are sexual assault victims. The state's Department of Public Health must approve hospital plans for emergency services to women who are the survivors of sexual assault. The hospitals must provide accurate verbal and written information about emergency contraception, including how to obtain the drug and the drug's possible side-effects.

In 2005, two pharmacists determined that their religious beliefs prevented them from dispensing the Plan B pill. Women who sought to obtain the Plan B pill from these pharmacies filed complaints when the pharmacies refused to dispense the Plan B pills. Several national and local women's organizations condemned the pharmacies' actions and advocated for a change in state rules that would require pharmacies to fill Plan B prescriptions. In April 2005, former Illinois governor Rod Blagojevich announced that a new rule would take effect mandating that pharmacies must fill valid Plan B prescriptions "without delay, consistent with the normal time frame for filling any other prescription." At the time he announced the rule change, Blagojevich said, "I have a sneaking suspicion that in all likelihood, [the refusal to dispense the Plan B pills] is part of a concerted effort to deny women access to birth control. Those may be getting away with this in other states, but here in Illinois, we are not going to let that happen."

In September 2005, the state initiated proceedings against the pharmacies that refused to dispense the pills. State officials said they would engage in an effort to "vigorously" enforce the new rule. The pharmacies responded by filing a motion for a restraining order, asking the trial court to enjoin enforcement of the new rule. The state responded by arguing that the pharmacies could not challenge the rule because the pharmacies had not yet been sued and disciplined by the state. According to the state's argument, the pharmacies' case was not ripe because the pharmacies first had to exhaust their administrative remedies before seeking a **declaratory judgment**. On November 18, 2005, Illinois Circuit Judge John Belz dismissed the plaintiff's case.

The pharmacies appealed the circuit court's decision to the Fourth District **Appellate Court** in Illinois. The **district court** reviewed the case to determine whether the issues were ripe for consideration and relied on factors previously articulated by the U.S. SUPREME COURT. According to the **appellate** court, the pharmacies' chances for suffering future hardship as a result of the state's actions were too slim to outweigh the courts' "traditional reluctance to get involved in administrative determinations." Accordingly, the court held that the issues in the case were not ripe, and because of this conclusion, the court did not have to address whether the pharmacies had to exhaust their administrative remedies before filing suit. *Morr-Fitz, Inc. v. Blagojevich*, 867 N.E.2d 1164 (Ill. App. Ct. 2007).

The pharmacies appealed the decision to the Illinois Supreme Court. The pharmacies argued that the rule violated their rights under both the Illinois Health Care Right of Conscience Act, 745 Ill. Comp. Stat. 70/1 *et seq.* and the Illinois Religious Freedom Restoration Act, 775 Ill. Comp. Stat. 35/1 *et seq.* The court first analyzed whether the pharmacies' claims were ripe. The court disagreed with the lower court's conclusion that the pharmacies would not suffer hardship if the courts were not involved. Prior to the case being appealed to the Illinois Supreme Court, the state had amended the rule by adding additional requirements with which pharmacies had to comply. Provisions of the previous version of the rule along with the new requirements affected the pharmacies' day-to-day operations. Therefore, the Illinois Supreme Court determined that the issue was ripe for review.

The court then turned its attention to whether the pharmacies had to exhaust their administrative remedies before seeking judicial intervention. The court determined that the pharmacies did not have to exhaust these remedies, but the court refused to consider the pharmacies' substantive arguments about why the emergency contraceptive rule was invalid under Illinois law or constitutional theories. The Illinois Supreme Court remanded the case for further proceedings. *Morr-Fitz, Inc. v. Blagojevich*, 901 N.E.2d 373 (Ill. 2008). In April 2009, Belz ruled that the state could not force the pharmacies to dispense the pills over the religious objections of the pharmacies or pharmacists.

Other courts have had to wrestle with similar issues. For instance, the U.S. District Court for the Western District of Washington enjoined a Washington state agency from enforcing a rule that prohibited a pharmacy from refusing to dispense Plan B pills and instead referring a customer to another pharmacy. The Ninth **Circuit Court** of Appeals reviewed the case, and in May 2008, declined to invalidate the injunction. *Stormans Inc. v. Selecky*, 526 F.3d 406 (9th Cir. 2008).

CAPITAL PUNISHMENT

The lawful infliction of death as a punishment; the death penalty.

Kentucky Conducts Its First Criminal Execution in Nine Years

In the wake of the U.S. Supreme Court's 2008 ruling in *Baze v. Rees*, 553 U.S. ___ (in which the Court held that execution by three-drug lethal injection did not constitute "cruel and unusual punishment"), several states declared their intentions to resume criminal executions that had been stayed pending the high court's decision. The State of Kentucky went forward with its first execution in nine years when it executed, by lethal injection, convicted killer Marco Allen Chapman on November 21, 2008. Chapman had murdered two children in 2002 and attempted to murder their mother and another child (who both survived the attack).

What made Chapman's execution more noteworthy than cases in other states was that Chapman had created a string of appeals, not to challenge his execution, but rather, to ask the court to proceed with his execution and dismiss his court-appointed counsel. This followed his own admission and confession of guilt and his voluntary request for the death penalty.

After a series of competency hearings and appeals, the Supreme Court of Kentucky granted Chapman's motion to dismiss all pending motions for stay of execution filed on his behalf, as "against [his] wishes and beliefs,"

and allowed the execution to go forward. The state's highest court also ruled on an issue of **first impression**, holding that a competent criminal defendant was entitled to plead guilty to a capital offense and seek to receive the death penalty (as Chapman did in this case).

Chapman's crime was a particularly heinous one, and he knew his victims. In the early morning hours of August 23, 2002, after coming down from an apparent two-day crack and cocaine binge, he began banging on the door of Carolyn and Charles Marksberry, neighbors and friends of his ex-girlfriend. Charles was out of town on business, but Carolyn, recognizing Chapman, answered the door and let him in. He immediately placed a knife to Carolyn's neck, bound her hands to a bed frame with duct tape, raped her, then stabbed her. The knife broke off in her chest. In her presence, he then got a larger knife, stabbed and slit the throats of two of her children, stabbed a third (who played dead), and continued to stab Carolyn. The stabbed ten-year-old child (who had played dead) escaped and ran to a neighbor's house. Chapman, upon seeing her escape, burglarized the home then fled in his truck. In the aftermath, Carolyn underwent emergency surgery for a collapsed lung, blood-filled other lung, and stab wounds to her esophagus and larynx. She and her 10-year-old daughter survived to identify their attacker. Dead were her two other children, 6-year-old Cody and 7-year-old Chelbi, of multiple stab wounds and slit throats.

Confessed child killer Marco Chapman.
AP IMAGES

The murders occurred in northwestern Kentucky. Chapman was captured several hours later in Shrewsbury, West Virginia. In December 2004, Chapman, without full explaining his actions, pleaded guilty to the murders and attacks before a Boone County, Kentucky judge, then voluntarily asked for the death penalty.

In the ensuing months and years, Chapman appeared in court on numerous occasions, not to challenge his sentence but rather to fight for its enforcement against the wishes and arguments of his public defenders. He underwent four competency hearings and was found competent in all. He motioned repeatedly to fire his court-appointed counsel and have all pending motions for stay of execution dismissed.

In August 2007, the Supreme Court of Kentucky, in *Chapman v. Commonwealth,* No. WL 2404429, 265 S.W.3d 156, held, among other things, that (1) Chapman's right to proceed *pro se* (without counsel) was not violated when the trial court appointed the attorneys he fired as stand-by counsel; (2) Chapman was mentally competent to plead guilty, seek the death penalty, waive jury sentencing, and forgo the presentation of mitigating evidence; and (3) the trial court's failure to require Chapman to recite at length his involvement in the crimes to which he pleaded guilty, in order to establish a factual basis for the plea, did not constitute reversible error. Further, and as an issue of first impression in Kentucky, the court held that a defendant is entitled to plead guilty to

a capital offense and to seek to receive the death penalty.

But even this did not end the appeals. On October 27, 2008, the Department of Public Advocacy filed two more motions for stay of execution with the Franklin **Circuit Court** in Kentucky. Chapman filed a separate verified and certified *pro se* response, stating that these motions were filed against his will and knowledge. He asked the court to dismiss them as "filed against my wishes and beliefs. So I ask this court one last time to dismiss all motions and allow my execution [sic] go forward as planned without any further delays or proceedings." On November 17, 2008, the Franklin Circuit Court, after hearing testimony from both Chapman and yet another court-appointed medical expert, found that Chapman was competent for purposes of "making decisions concerning his own defense and legal representation." Two days later, the Supreme Court of Kentucky upheld the competency findings and the dismissal of motions for stay of execution that were filed against Chapman's wishes.

Meanwhile, Kentucky Governor Steve Beshear denied a **clemency** petition for Chapman filed by area church leaders and Catholic bishops. He noted that Chapman had freely admitted guilt and had been found competent in four separate proceedings. Further, he noted the particularly heinous nature of the murders, stating his belief "that capital punishment is appropriate" in such cases.

Chapman was executed without incident on November 21, 2008. Surviving victim Carolyn Marksberry and her husband were witnesses in an adjoining room.

Lethal Injections Resume in States After *Baze*

In September 2007, the U.S. SUPREME COURT granted **certiorari** (review) of a Kentucky case challenging the use of a three-stage lethal injection protocol for criminal executions. From September 2007 until April 2008, when the Court rendered its decision, no death-row criminals were executed in the United States, as all states and the federal government exercised a self-imposed moratorium while awaiting the high court's decision.

Finally, on April 23, 2008, the Court issued its ruling in *Baze v. Rees,* 553 U.S. ___, in which the Court held that Kentucky's lethal injection procedures did not violate the EIGHTH AMENDMENT to the U.S. Constitution's ban on **cruel and unusual punishment**. Just a few days later, the Court, without comment, rejected appeals of 11 other death row inmates in Texas, Mississippi, Alabama, Arizona, Ohio, Georgia, and Missouri.

The Court's ruling effectively ended the issuance of last-minute stays of execution on the basis of lethal-injection challenges. At the time of the decision, nearly all of the 35 other death-penalty states and the federal government employed similar lethal injection protocols as that used in Kentucky. This involved the administration of three drugs in succession: first, an anesthetic barbiturate; second, pancuronium bromide, a paralytic to stop respirations; and third, potassium chloride to stop the heart. Approximately 40 inmates around the country had secured stays of execution from courts or state officials while awaiting the challenge to the lethal injection protocol.

Following the Supreme Court's ruling, several states immediately announced their intentions to resume executions that had been placed on hold pending the decision. Texas, which had executed 26 persons the year prior to the moratorium (more than the rest of all states combined) announced it would resume executions as soon as May 2008. Oklahoma, Florida, Georgia, Virginia, Mississippi, and Arizona soon announced similar intentions.

However, not all states resumed their executions immediately, instead scheduling reviews of their respective procedures and protocols, and revising them as deemed appropriate.

In May 2008, a federal judge in Delaware extended a stay on all executions pending an evidentiary hearing on the state's protocol procedure. Delaware changed its execution procedure to one based on Kentucky's protocol, following the *Baze* decision. A class-action lawsuit on behalf of all death row inmates remained pending in early 2009.

In June 2008, a federal judge ordered the State of Ohio to eliminate two of the three drugs used in lethal injection protocol and instead use only a single anesthetic (barbiturate)(*Ohio v. Ruben Rivera*). The state then filed an appeal in July. An evidentiary hearing was scheduled for December 2008 after the judge ordered the state

to turn over all information regarding the state's protocol, including that involving the training and qualifications of executioners. As of early May 2009, no decision had been issued by the **appellate court**.

In August 2008, a Pulaski County, Arkansas Superior Court Judge ruled that Arkansas' lethal injection protocol was invalid because it had not been subjected to public review as required by the state's Administrative Procedures Act. However, the state argued that during the 2008-2009 legislative session, lawmakers had approved Act 1296 of 2009, which declared all procedures used in the lethal injection process exempt from the state's Administrative Procedures Act. The case, originally filed by death-row inmate Frank William Jr., was still pending before the Arkansas Supreme Court as of May 2009. The question before the court was whether William's argument was rendered moot by the enactment of Act 1296.

Similarly, the California Court of Appeals, in November 2008, affirmed a lower court's decision declaring California's lethal injection protocol to be invalid because it also was not adopted in compliance with the state's Administrative Procedures Act.

The North Carolina Supreme Court, in November 2008, heard oral arguments over whether physicians could be present and/or participate in lethal injection executions in that state, as required by state law. The STATE DEPARTMENT of Corrections had been unable to find doctors willing to monitor executions for fear of discipline from the state medical board. It sued the state medical board, which had taken the position that such participation violated a doctor's code of ethics to preserve life. On May 1, 2009, the state high court issued its opinion, ruling that the state medical board lacked authority to interfere with or stop doctors participating in executions. It also could not discipline or threaten to discipline doctors for their participation. *North Carolina Department of Corrections v. North Carolina Medical Board*, No. 51PA08 (2009). At the time of the state court's ruling, 163 inmates were on death row in North Carolina.

In one of the more convoluted series of legal sequelae following *Baze*, the U.S. Supreme Court, in *Stenson v. Vail*, No. 08A471, 555 U.S. ___ (December 2008), voided a stay of execution in the state of Washington that had been granted by local U.S. **District Court** Judge Lonny Suko. The federal court had ordered the stay after the state revised its lethal injection protocol without announcement or going through a rule-making process, as allegedly required by the state's administrative procedure regulations.

But a state-ordered stay of execution remained in effect, after the Washington Supreme Court denied a Clallam County request to vacate the county judge's stay. (The federal stay was in response to a challenge to lethal injections, whereas the state stay involved a last-minute former inmate who came forward as a potential defense witness. The stay of execution was to allow DNA testing related to the new witness's testimony.) Eventually, the state Department of Corrections cancelled the execution and announced a new date would not be scheduled for at least 90 days. As of early May 2009, hearings were still being scheduled in Stenson's case.

Meanwhile, in the midst of the legal wrangling, four persons designated to administer lethal injections at the Washington State Penitentiary resigned, fearing their identities would become public as a result of the court battles. Following their April 2009 resignations, officials from other states offered to send lethal injection teams to Washington if needed, as the state prepared to assemble a new team. The last execution in Washington was in 1991.

Supreme Court Denies Review of Victim Impact Evidence Cases

In November 2008, the U.S. SUPREME COURT denied **certiorari** (review), with noted objections from Justices Stevens, Souter, and Breyer, in two California cases that argued against "victim impact evidence" being used in death penalty cases. *Kelly v. California*, No. 07-11073, and *Zamudio v. California*, No. 07-11425, 555 U.S. ___ (2008). The Court's action served to leave intact existing California rules permitting its use (with some restrictions) during the penalty phase of capital trials.

Victim impact evidence refers to that evidence intended to show the trier of fact (generally a jury) the "impact" (emotional and personal) a crime has had upon the victim or the victim's family. The proffered evidence does not speak to or address the guilt or innocence of the defendant, or the circumstances of the crime. Its purpose is to cause the jury to appreciate and understand the crime's impact as though they (the jurors) were in the shoes of the victim or victim's family.

Opponents to the admission of victim impact evidence generally argue that it is powerfully prejudicial and inflammatory, in that its emotional impact on a jury may cause the jurors to react more strongly or severely than the outer limits of **probative** evidence (evidence tending to prove or disprove a fact) would permit. This may cause them to deliberate on emotional grounds, not on reasoned judgment.

For that reason, the Supreme Court had previously announced, in *Booth v. Maryland*, 482 U.S. 496 (1987), that juries in capital cases were categorically prohibited from considering victim impact evidence that "described the personal characteristics of the victims and the emotional impact of the crimes on the family." The Court's justification for the *per se* prohibition of such evidence in capital cases was in noting the unique character of the death penalty as a "punishment different from all other sanctions."

But the Court overruled itself just four years later, in 1991, with the capital case of *Payne v. Tennessee*, 501 U.S. 808. In *Payne*, testimony by the mother of the deceased victim in a particularly heinous crime powerfully conveyed her grandson's agony at having witnessed the murder of his mother and sister. Even though this was a capital case, the Supreme Court declared that the mother's testimony, offered at the penalty phase, was "simply another form or method of informing the sentencing authority about the specific harm caused by the crime in question." The Court then further acknowledged that prosecutors should have the right to present such evidence, including evidence about the life "which [the] defendant chose to extinguish."

Importantly, the *Payne* case did not present or articulate the parameters of, or any standards defining, the permissible victim impact evidence. It did, however, offer guidance in the form of noting that,

> "[i}n the event that evidence is introduced that is so unduly prejudicial that it renders the trial fundamentally unfair, the Due Process Clause of the FOURTEENTH AMENDMENT provides a mechanism for relief."

(Said Justice Stevens in the present case, "That statement represents the beginning and end of the guidance we have given to lower courts considering the admissibility of victim impact evidence in the first instance.") Accordingly, states have developed their own standards and rules for admissibility, using the Court's term of "unduly prejudicial" as a parameter for gauging admissibility.

The convicted capital defendants in the two California cases argued that the victim impact statements used at their respective trials had crossed *Payne's* "unduly prejudicial" line. In the first case, Kelly had been convicted of murdering 19-year-old Sara Weir. The prosecutors played a 20-minute composite video of photographs and video clips of Weir's life, e.g., surrounded by friends and family members, swimming, horseback riding, attending school and social functions, etc., from her infancy up to a few days before her death. The victim's mother narrated the video, with soft music playing in the background. The end of the video contained views of her grave marker.

In the second case, Zamudio was convicted of robbing and murdering an elderly couple. The victims' daughters and two grandchildren testified about the effects the murders had on their lives and their families. During some of this testimony, prosecutors played a video containing photographs of the victims at various times during their lives, e.g., raising their children, serving in the military, celebrating holidays, vacationing together, fishing, attending family events, etc. As in the other case, the video ended with views of their graves, each accompanied by a vase of flowers.

In both cases, the California Supreme Court upheld the admission of the videos as victims' impact statements. The state high court found the videos lacking in outrage or calls for vengeance, but instead, simply "implied sadness." One dissenting judge expressed concern that the video shown during Zamudio's penalty phase had the potential to "imbue the proceedings with 'a legally impermissible level of emotion,'" but the majority found that the video was "not unduly emotional."

Justice Steven's objection spoke only to his opinion that the Court should revisit the issue and provide more guidance. He wanted to ensure that jurors focused on the crime and the criminal, not the impact on the victim's family. Justices Souter and Breyer agreed that the Court should take up the issue. However, it takes a minimum of four votes to grant certiorari for an appealed case.

CLEAN WATER ACT

Entergy Corporation v. Riverkeeper, Inc.

The federal Clean Water Act (CWA), 33 U.S.C. § 1251 et seq, sets standards and review processes for industries that discharge material into navigable waters. The act governs the use and discharge of water by electric powerplants, which need it to cool their facilities. The extraction of water poses different threats to the environment and includes the destruction of aquatic organisms that live in the water sources. The ENVIRONMENTAL PROTECTION AGENCY (EPA), which administers the CWA and adopts regulations to carry out the law's mandates, did not promulgate regulations concerning powerplants until 2001, nearly 30 days after the enactment of the CWA. Up until 2001 the EPA determined on a case-by-case basis what the **statute** called the "best technology available" for minimizing adverse environmental impact from cooling water intake structures. The 2001 regulations dealt with the construction of new powerplant cooling water intake structures and in 2004 the EPA adopted regulations governing existing facilities. Over 500 facilities, which account for 53 percent of the electric-power generating capacity in the U.S., were subject to the 2004 regulations. The EPA used a cost-benefit analysis in determining the content of the 2004 regulations, which triggered a lawsuit from an environmental group that contended the CWA did not allow such an analysis. The Supreme Court, in *Entergy Corporation v. Riverkeeper, Inc.*, __U.S.__, 129 S.Ct. 1498, __L.Ed.2d__ (2009), sided with the EPA and ruled that the law did not specifically bar cost-benefit analysis for that part of the law dealing with powerplant cooling water structures.

The 2004 regulations permitted the issuance of site-specific variances from national performance standards governing cooling water if a facility could demonstrate either that costs of compliance were "significantly greater than" the costs considered by the EPA in setting the standards, or that the costs of compliance "would be significantly greater than the benefits of complying with the applicable performance standards." Riverkeeper, Inc., an environmental advocacy group that sought to protect U.S.

rivers from damage, filed a lawsuit challenging the new regulations with the Second **Circuit Court** of Appeals. The appeals court remanded the regulations to the EPA, concluding that the agency could not use cost-benefit analysis, which "compares the costs and benefits of various ends, and chooses the end with the best net benefits." The Supreme Court accepted the EPA's appeal to decide whether the CWA authorized the EPA to compare costs with benefits in determining the best technology available for minimizing environmental damage at cooling water intake structures.

The Court, in a 6-3 decision, overruled the Second Circuit decision. Justice ANTONIN SCALIA, writing for the majority, noted that if the CWA allows the EPA to take into account the cost of "best technology available", then the Court must permit that view as long as it is a reasonable interpretation of the statute. It might not be the only possible interpretation or the most reasonable interpretation, but administrative agencies are shown deference by the courts if the interpretation is reasonable. The Second Circuit had read "the best technology available minimizing adverse environmental impact" to mean the technology that provided the greatest reduction at a cost that can reasonably be borne by the industry. Scalia agreed it was a "plausible" interpretation of the CWA provision, but "best technology" could also describe technology that produces "a good at the lowest per-unit cost, even if it produces a lesser quantity of that good than other available technologies."

Riverkeeper argued that the statute used the word "minimize" to mean the reducing of the adverse impact to the smallest amount possible. Scalia disagreed, finding that the "minimize" is a "term that admits degrees and is not necessarily used to refer exclusively to the 'greatest possible reduction.'" He pointed to other CWA provisions where Congress used "plain language" to "mandate the greatest feasible reduction in water pollution." The cooling water provision "did not unambiguously preclude cost-benefit analysis." The language did not require the power industry to "spend billions to save one more fish or plankton."

Justice JOHN PAUL STEVENS, in a dissenting opinion joined by Justices DAVID SOUTER and RUTH BADER GINSBURG, argued that cost-benefit analysis "often, if not always, yields a result that does not maximize environmental protection." He contended that Congress did not explicitly authorize the use of cost-benefit analysis for cooling water intake structures as it did elsewhere in the CWA.

CLEMENCY

Leniency or mercy. A power given to a public official, such as a governor or the president, to in some way lower or moderate the harshness of punishment imposed upon a prisoner.

Bush Grants Clemency to Convicted Border Patrol Agents

On his last full day in office, President GEORGE W. BUSH granted **clemency** to two former border patrol agents. In 2006, Ignacio Ramos and Jose Alonso Compean were convicted of shooting a Mexican drug runner who was trying to run across the border and back to Mexico. The convictions of Ramos and Compean were met with heavy criticism from a variety of circles, and both Republicans and Democrats alike expressed approval of Bush's decision.

In February 2005, Osvaldo Aldrete-Davila entered the United States illegally by driving a van across the border. The van contained 743 pounds of marijuana. When agents Ramos and Compean spotted Aldrete-Davila near Fabens, Texas, they began to pursue him. Aldrete-Davila immediately attempted to return to Mexico, first in the van and then on foot. At some point during the pursuit, Compean tried to hit the suspect with the butt of a shotgun. As Aldrete-Davila continued to flee, Compean and Ramos drew their weapons and shot at the suspect. Ramos hit Aldrete-Davila in the buttocks with a shot.

Border patrol regulations require agents to report a shooting. However, Compean and Ramos failed to do so. Instead, the agents attempted to cover up the scene by removing spent shell casings that were ejected from their guns. After the shooting, the Homeland Security Department's Office of Inspector General (OIG) began an investigation. After a review, the OIG determined that Ramos and Compean knew about the shooting but had failed to report it. Moreover, the OIG concluded that the agents had destroyed evidence and made false statements.

Ramos and Compean were arrested pursuant to a warrant. After their arrest, they were

Former US Border Patrol agent Ignacio Ramos hugs two sons upon returning to Texas, February 17, 2009.

AP IMAGES

placed on indefinite suspension without pay. A federal **grand jury** indicted both agents. Compean faced nine charges, while Ramos faced seven. According to Ramos, he responded to a request for backup from Campean, who had seen the suspicious fan on a levee road along the Rio Grande River. Ramos argued that when he shot at Aldrete-Davila, Compean was already injured. Ramos said he believed that the suspect was armed. Ramos was an eight-year veteran of the Naval Reserve and had previously received an award as an outstanding border patrol agent.

Investigators with the OIG also sought to interview Aldrete-Davila, who temporarily went missing after the incident with the agents. Aldrete-Davila finally contacted U.S. authorities

on March 11, claiming that the bullet was still lodged in his body. He agreed to cooperate in the investigation of the border patrol agents so long as U.S. officials agreed not to prosecute him. Aldrete-Davila admitted to fleeing from the agents, but he denied that he shot at the agents or even that he had a weapon on his possession at the time. A doctor removed the bullet from Aldrete-Davila's body, and U.S. officials took possession of the bullet. During an investigation of the location where the incident took place, however, investigators were unable to locate any evidence that a shooting had taken place. In 2008, Aldrete-Davila pleaded guilty to drug-smuggling charges after a long delay in his prosecution. His sentence of 114 months

(9.5 years) sparked outrage because it was less than the sentences given to the agents.

After a two-week trial in the U.S. **District Court** for the Western District of Texas, a jury found the agents guilty. The convictions included charges for assault with a deadly weapon, assault with serious bodily injury, discharge of a firearm in the commission of a crime of violence, tampering with official proceedings, and deprivation of rights under the **color of law**. The jury found the agents not guilty of assault with intent to commit murder or aiding and **abetting**. On October 19, 2006, U.S. District Judge Kathleen Cardone sentenced Ramos to 11 years in prison and Cardone to 12 years in prison. One week later, Ramos and Compean were officially terminated as border patrol agents.

Many critics openly decried the convictions, arguing that the agents were merely doing their job. One of the most vocal critics was Congressman Dana Rohrabacher (R.-Cal.). He referred to Ramos and Compean as "unjustly convicted men who should have never been prosecuted in the first place." The convictions were the subject of extensive media attention. Critics of the convictions argued that the men should not have been charged under a law that boosts sentences for using a gun during the commission of a crime. According to the critics, the law should not have applied because law enforcement officers are required to carry a weapon.

Ramos and Compean appealed their convictions to the Fifth **Circuit Court** of Appeals. The agents argued that the district court had erred by refusing to admit evidence related to the amount of marijuana present in the van at the time of the incident. The agents also argued that they should have been able to introduce evidence related to later drug-smuggling charges filed against Aldrete-Davila. Moreover, the agents attacked the statutes under which they had been prosecuted. Writing for a three-judge panel, Circuit Judge E. Grady Jolly affirmed the convictions on all but one point. The agents convinced the **appellate court** to reverse the obstruction of justice charges, and the panel remanded the case to the trial court for resentencing. *United States v. Ramos*, 537 F.3d 439 (5th Cir. 2008). In November 2008, Cardone resentenced both agents to their original terms.

While the agents were incarcerated, several groups put pressure on Bush either to pardon the agents or to grant the agents clemency. Several members of Congress appealed to Bush to act on the case. In fact, nearly the entire congressional delegation from the State of Texas visited Bush to ask the president to take action. However, as a general matter, Bush was reluctant to issue pardons or to grant clemency. During his eight years in office, he only granted 189 pardons and ten commutations. These total numbers were far below the totals of previous two-term presidents BILL CLINTON (396 pardons, 61 commutations) and RONALD REAGAN (393 pardons, 13 commutations).

Notwithstanding Bush's reluctance, he granted the agents clemency on January 19, 2009. The agents were released from prison in February and remained in house confinement for about a month after their release. On March 23, the U.S. SUPREME COURT denied **certiorari** to review their case.

COMMERCE CLAUSE

The provision of the U.S. Constitution that gives Congress exclusive power over trade activities between the states and with foreign countries and Indian tribes.

Sixth Circuit Strikes Down Kentucky Wine Law

The Sixth **Circuit Court** of Appeals in December 2008 decided that several **statutory** sections in Kentucky related to the sale of wine violated the **Commerce Clause** of the U.S. Constitution. Relying on Supreme Court precedent, the Sixth Circuit determined that the statutes discriminated against interstate commerce, mostly because the laws favored in-state interests over out-of-state interests.

The Commerce Clause of the Constitution grants power to Congress to regulate interstate commerce. The U.S. SUPREME COURT has determined that the Commerce Clause has a socalled "dormant" component, meaning that the clause prohibits a state from discriminating against interstate commerce. Under the cases construing the dormant Commerce Clause, a court must make several conclusions to determine whether a **statute** is unconstitutional. The court must first determine whether the statute indeed discriminates against interstate commerce. This discrimination may be present "on the face" of the statute, meaning that it is clear from the statute's language. Alternatively, the statute may have a discriminatory purpose or may discriminate in practical effect. When a statute is not discriminatory, the statute is valid "unless the burdens on interstate commerce are 'clearly excessive in relation to the **putative** local benefits.' " On the other hand, a statute that is discriminatory is invalid unless the state shows that the statute "advances a legitimate local purpose that cannot be adequately served by reasonable nondiscriminatory alternatives."

The 21st Amendment to the U.S. Constitution is seldom the subject of legal analysis, but occasionally courts will analyze its provisions. This amendment repealed the 18th Amendment, which prohibited the manufacture, sale, or transportation of intoxicating liquors in the United States. Under section 2 of the 21st Amendment, "[t]he transportation or importation into any State, Territory, or possession of the United States for delivery or use therein of intoxicating liquors, in violation of the laws thereof, is hereby prohibited." U.S. Const. amend. XXI. § 2. The courts that have reviewed this amendment have concluded that the amendment gives broad authority to the individual states over the importation and distribution of alcohol within the states.

In *Granholm v. Heald*, 544 U.S. 460, 125 S. Ct. 1885, 161 L. Ed. 2d 796 (2005), the U.S. Supreme Court reviewed the 21st Amendment's application in light of dormant Commerce Clause **jurisprudence**. The Court reviewed New York and Michigan statutes that prohibited out-of-state wineries from shipping wine to customers within those states. The Court determined that both statutes were unconstitutional because they violated the dormant Commerce Clause. In reaching this conclusion, the Court noted that "the TWENTY-FIRST AMENDMENT ... does not displace the rule that States may not given discriminatory preference to their own producers."

Shortly after the *Granholm* decision, several parties challenged statutory provisions in Kentucky that were similar to the New York and Michigan wine statutes. One plaintiff was Huber Winery, based in Indiana. Other plaintiffs in the case were Kentucky residents who had been prohibited from having wine shipped directly to them from wineries in states other than Kentucky. An Oregon-based winery also joined in the case. The defendants in the case were Lajuana S. Wilcher, the Secretary of the Kentucky Environmental and Public Protection Cabinet, and Lavoyed Hudgins, the Executive Director of the Kentucky Department of Alcoholic Beverage Control. After the case was filed, Wine and Spirits Wholesalers of Kentucky Inc. intervened.

The plaintiffs claimed that four specific provisions of Kentucky law were unconstitutional:

1. Section 244.165 of the Kentucky **Revised Statutes** (K.R.S.) prohibits the shipment of alcohol by out-of-state sellers to a Kentucky resident other than a wholesaler or distributor.

2. Section 243.032 of the K.R.S. requires restaurants to purchase wine from wholesalers (rather than directly from out-of-state sellers).

3. Section 243.155(1)(f) of the K.R.S. allows small and farm wineries to ship up to two cases of wine directly to a consumer who purchased the wine in-person at the winery.

4. Section 243.156(1)(d) also applied to small and farm wineries, but it was repealed in 2007.

According to the plaintiffs' arguments, these statutes had the effect of discriminating against out-of-state wineries in favor of the interests of in-state wineries. The Kentucky legislature amended several of these statutes, effective in 2007, but the U.S. **District Court** for the Western District of Kentucky nevertheless reviewed these provisions because the legislature established a prospective effective date. The court concluded that the pre-revision statutes violated the Commerce Clause. However, the court determined that the revisions to the statutes rendered the statutes constitutional. Conversely, the court held that the statutory requirement of having a consumer visit a winery in person before the consumer could have wine delivered to him was constitutionally impermissible. The court therefore enjoined the state from enforcing the in-person requirement. *Cherry Hill Vineyards, L.L.C. v. Hudgins*, 488 F. Supp. 2d 601, 625 (W.D. Ky. 2006).

Although the state defendants chose not to challenge the case any further, the wholesalers who intervened appealed the district court's decision to the Sixth Circuit. The **appellate** court reviewed the constitutionality of the requirement that consumers purchase the wine in-person prior to shipment. This provision was not discriminatory on its face because it allowed consumers to order wine in person from an out-of-state winery and then have the wine shipped to the consumer in Kentucky. The plaintiffs argued, though, that this requirement had a discriminatory effect because it required consumers to travel as far as 4,800 miles to purchase the wine in person prior to the shipment.

A panel of the Sixth Circuit agreed with the plaintiffs and held that the statute was unconstitutional. According to the court, the statute failed to "advance a legitimate local purpose that cannot be adequately served by reasonable nondiscriminatory means." The court also agreed with the district court's remedy of nullifying the in-person requirement. Therefore, the court affirmed the district court's decision. *Cherry Hill Vinyards L.L.C. v. Lilly*, 553 F.3d 423 (6th Cir. 2008).

COMPUTER CRIME

The use of a computer to take or alter data, or to gain unlawful use of computers or services.

VA Agrees to $20 Million Settlement Over Stolen Laptop

As the collection and retention of personal data on computers has grown, so have concerns about the security of this data. The focus has been on computer hackers who seek to break into computer networks and secure financial and personal data that can be used for **fraudulent** purposes. However, with the advent of powerful portable laptop computers, databases can be easily transferred from an office desktop computer to a laptop or, in some cases, an external hard drive or flash memory drive. Computer security consultants discourage this practice, especially when the data has not been encrypted. The perils of unsecured data on laptops was brought to national attention when in 2006 thieves stole a Department of Veterans Affairs (VA) laptop computer and external hard drive that contained the birthdates and Social Security numbers for millions of veterans and military personnel. Concerns about identity theft led to the filing of five **class action** suits by veterans groups that charged the VA with negligence for allowing an employee to bring

home sensitive information. Although the laptop and hard drive were recovered within two months and the FBI concluded that no one had accessed the data, the VA agreed to a settlement of the consolidate class actions cases in January 2009. The VA agreed to pay $20 million to compensate veterans for any costs associated with protecting their credit. Whatever money remained after paying these claims will go to charity.

A VA employee brought home the laptop and external hard drive to his Aspen Hill, Maryland home. He was authorized to bring home the equipment and use agency software to access data. The equipment was stolen on May 3, 2006, and local police were notified. However, the FBI was not told for two weeks. The database on the computer contained Social Security numbers and other personal information for almost 17.5 million veterans, active military personnel, 430,000 NATIONAL GUARD members, and 645,000 reserve members. The VA did not alert the public until May 22 As time went on, public anger grew. The VA responded by setting up a call center to handle questions and sending letters to veterans about the theft. By the end of June the Bush administration asked Congress for $165 million to pay for one year of free credit monitoring for veterans and military personnel. Before this request, veterans were advised to purchase credit monitoring services. Several veterans groups responded by filing class action lawsuits.

The laptop and hard drive were recovered on June 28 from a person who had seen news accounts and the $50,000 award announcement from local police. The FBI **forensic** computer specialists analyzed the laptop and hard drive and concluded that the sensitive data had not been accessed. Despite this good news, the VA came under withering criticism by members of Congress for poor data security and slow response to the theft. It came to light that the VA secretary was not told about the **burglary** for 13 days. The theft resulted in the forced retirement or dismissal of several VA employees, yet Congress concluded that changes needed to be made to the system. A later report from the inspector general faulted both the employee who took the laptop home and his supervisors for putting veterans at unreasonable risk.

The class action lawsuits were consolidated and heard in the U.S. DISTRICT COURT for the

DISTRICT OF COLUMBIA. The plaintiffs alleged that the VA violated federal the Federal Privacy Act by not properly securing sensitive personal information. The class was composed of all veterans, spouses of veterans, and military personnel who had actual damages during the period between the computer equipment was stolen and the time it was recovered. In January 2009 the VA and the plaintiffs agreed to a settlement. Members of the class can recover actual damages, which include out-of-pocket expenses incurred as a direct result of the theft. Examples include money spent to protect or monitor personal or financial information from identity theft and money spent to treat physical symptoms of emotional distress linked to the theft. To recover money, class members must complete a claim form, with public notices published in military and civilian publications to alert potential claimants. A toll-free number was to be established as well for answering questions. Veterans who can show harm from the data theft will be eligible to receive payments ranging from $75 to $1,500. If any of the $20 million is left over after making these payments, the remainder will be donated to veterans' charities agreed to by the parties.

As for the VA itself, it made sweeping changes in how computer technology and data are handled by the agency, reorganizing and centralizing information technology. It strengthened policies and procedures, bolstered training for employees on privacy and security of sensitive data, and worked with government and commercial entities that have veteran information for business reasons to ensure there were proper safeguards. The VA also contracted with private firms to analyze the strengths and weaknesses of its data security, and to supply services that can immediately analyze whether data has been improperly accessed. The 2006 theft also spurred agencies throughout the federal government to pay more attention to encrypting data on laptops and other mobile devices and to improving security for telecommuters who access government data from home.

CONFRONTATION

A fundamental right of a defendant in a criminal action to come face to face with an adverse witness in the court's presence so the defendant has a fair chance to object to the testimony of the witness and the opportunity to cross-examine the witness.

Melendez-Diaz v. Massachusetts

The Sixth Amendment's Confrontation Clause gives criminal defendants the right to examine witnesses who are against them. The Supreme Court, in *Crawford v. Washington*, 541 U.S. 36, 124 S.Ct. 1354, 158 L.Ed.2d 177 (2004), issued a landmark decision that held that "statements of witnesses absent from trial" were admissible "only where the declarant is unavailable, and only where the defendant has had a prior opportunity to cross-examine [the witness]." An unanswered question was whether **forensic** analysts who prepare reports for the prosecution would be required to testify about their reports, so as to give defendants the right to cross-examine their findings and methods. The Court, in *Melendez-Diaz v. Massachusetts*, __U.S.__, S.Ct. , __L.Ed.2d__ 2009 WL 1789468 (2009), answered in the affirmative, introducing a requirement that could change the way criminal trials are conducted in the U.S.

Luis Melendez-Diaz was arrested by Massachusetts police and charged with distributing cocaine. At trial the prosecution placed into evidence bags that had been seized and introduced three "certificates of analysis" that contained the results of forensic analysis of the contents of the bags. The certificates reported the weight of each bag and stated, "The substance was found to contain: Cocaine." The certificates were sworn before a **notary public** at the state laboratory. The defendant objected to the admission of the certificates, contending that under *Crawford* the analysts were required to testify in person. The trial court overruled the objection, and Melendez-Diaz was found guilty. He appealed, arguing that the certificates violated the Confrontation Clause. The state appeals court rejected this argument, and the Supreme Judicial Court denied review. He then petitioned the U.S. SUPREME COURT.

In a 5-4 decision, the Court overturned the state court decision and agreed with Melendez-Diaz that the Confrontation Clause required the analysts to testify. Justice ANTONIN SCALIA, who authored the *Crawford* opinion, wrote the majority opinion. He characterized the case as a "little more" than the application of the *Crawford* holding. The SIXTH AMENDMENT did not permit the prosecution to submit out-of-court affidavits unless the persons who submitted the affidavits appeared in court. A defendant has the right to confront those who "bear testimony" against him. The certificates in question were clearly "testimonial statements," as they were "functionally identical to live, in-court testimony." In this case the certificates had the sole purpose under state law to provide evidence of the composition, quality, and the net weight of the analyzed substance. The analysts had to be aware of the evidentiary purpose of the certificates.

Justice Scalia devoted the remainder of his opinion responding to the arguments from the state and the dissenting justices that such certificates should not be brought under the Confrontation Clause requirements. The state argued that the analysts were not subject to confrontation because they were not "accusatory" witnesses." They did not directly accuse a defendant of wrongdoing but offered testimony that was only inculpatory when taken together with other evidence that linked the defendant to the illegal substances. Justice Scalia rejected this distinction, noting that the Sixth Amendment guaranteed the defendant the right to confront witnesses against him. Clearly the testimony was against Melendez-Diaz, proving one fact necessary for his conviction. The state and the dissent also contended that the analysts were not "conventional witnesses" because they did not observe the crime. Justice Scalia found no merit in this argument because it would exempt all expert witnesses from confrontation by a defendant.

The state claimed that there was a difference between recounting historical events, which are prone to distortion and manipulation, and "neutral, scientific testing." Moreover, having the analyst look at the defendant while repeating the results of a scientific test would have little value. Justice Scalia noted that testing is not as neutral or as reliable as the state suggested. He cited a recent study by the National Academy of Sciences that found the majority of laboratories producing forensic evidence are administered by law enforcement agencies. An analyst may feel pressure or have an incentive to alter the evidence to favor the prosecution. In addition, other studies reported that invalid forensic testimony contributed to the convictions in 60% of the cases later overturned with exonerating evidence. The Melendez-Diaz case illustrated the potential perils of allowing forensic reports to be submitted without confrontation, as the reports did not state what tests were performed, whether the tests were routine, and whether interpreting the results required the exercise of judgment or skill that the analysts might not possess.

Justice Scalia acknowledged that this new requirement was burdensome on the prosecution, but "that is equally true of the right to trial by jury and the privilege against self-incrimination." The Confrontation Clause "is binding, and we many not disregard it our convenience." Responding to the dissenting opinion's claim that guilty defendants will go free on technical grounds, Scalia noted that such rules are in place in many states and that "[p]erhaps the best indication that the sky will not fall after today's decision is that it has not done so already."

Justice ANTHONY KENNEDY, in his dissenting opinion, argued that the confrontation clause did not encompass forensic reports and that the majority's decision "disregards a century of jurisprudence." He focused on the practical effects that the new requirement will impose on prosecutors. The FBI's forensic laboratory has 500 employees who conduct over a million tests each year. The new requirement meant that "before any of those million tests reach a jury, at least one of the laboratory's analysts must board a plane, find his or her way to an unfamiliar courthouse and sit there waiting to read aloud notes made months ago."

Defense lawyers were understandably happy with the decision, while prosecutors expressed concerns about an extra burden to be shouldered at a time when states are cutting back budgets. Others pointed out that 95% of drug cases are resolved with a guilty plea and that defense attorneys may stipulate to the admission of the reports to avoid antagonizing the jury.

COPYRIGHT

An intangible right granted by statute to the author or originator of certain literary or artistic productions, whereby, for a limited period, the exclusive privilege is given to the person to make copies of the same for publication and sale.

Congress Enacts Law that Authorizes Appointment of Copyright Czar

The U.S. economy relies on the fruits of intellectual property. The U.S. CHAMBER OF

COMMERCE has estimated that U.S. intellectual property is worth more than $5 trillion and that it accounts for more than half of all U.S. exports. Businesses that produce such property, including film, recording, and software companies, have complained for many years about the damage done to their businesses by pirating of their goods. After years of lobbying, Congress passed the PPrioritizing Resources and Organization for Intellectual Property ACT (Pro-IP), Pub. L. No. 110-403, 122 Stat. 4256, and President GEORGE W. BUSH signed it into law on October 13, 2008. Among its provisions, which aim at enhanced enforcement efforts, is the creation of a cabinet-level "copyright czar" in the office of the President. One controversial provision was deleted before passage that would have authorized the Attorney General to sue on behalf of copyright holders.

Senators Patrick Leahy (D-Vt) and Arlen Spector (R-Penn) introduced the Pro-IP Act in July 2008. The measure encountered little opposition in the SENATE JUDICIARY COMMITTEE. However, before passage, Title 1 of the bill, "Authorization of Civil Copyright Enforcement by Attorney General," was removed at the request of Senator Ron Wyden (D-Ore). The Department of Justice (DOJ) strongly opposed this section, which not only authorized the attorney general to pursue civil remedies for copyright infringement, but required attorney general to secure "restitution" damages and remit them to the private owners of infringed copyrights." The department lodged three objections. First, civil copyright enforcement has always been the responsibility and prerogative of private copyright holders, and U.S. law already provided them with effective legal tools to protect their rights. Second, if enacted the provision could result in DOJ prosecutors serving as **pro bono** lawyers for private copyright holders regardless of their resources. In effect, taxpayer-supported lawyers would pursue lawsuits for copyright holders, with monetary recovery going to industry. Third, DOJ had limited resources to dedicate to particular issues, and civil enforcement actions would occur at the expense of criminal actions.

Stripped of this provision, the law encountered little opposition from legislators. Public advocacy groups such as the ELECTRONIC FRONTIER FOUNDATION and the American Library Association opposed the bill, concluding that it gave too much protection to large media companies and little benefit to the public and artists. Congress gave final approval to the legislation in late September, just as the U.S. financial crisis began. President Bush signed the bill despite his objection to the creation of a copyright czar that would be part of the Executive Office.

Pro-IP became effective upon the President's signature. It contained several major changes to copyright and trademark law. First, the act raised the minimum and maximum **statutory** damages award a successful copyright or trademark owner can receive. The level of statutory damages in counterfeiting cases had not been raised since 1996. Congress doubled the possible statutory damages awards, raising it to $1000 to $200,000 per piece of intellectual property counterfeited and offered for sale or distributed. If the violation was willful, a court may now award up to $2 million per piece of intellectual property offered for sale. Second, the law imposed substantial penalties on some parties that intentionally assist copyright or trademark violators. Where a party provided goods or services necessary to an intentional violation and knew they would be used for counterfeiting by the recipient, the party it must pay treble damages and attorneys' fees. Prior to Pro-IP, Previously, the only the party that sold or distributed the goods was liable for these damages and fees. A new criminal provision increases the maximum penalties for trafficking in counterfeit goods where the defendant knowingly or recklessly causes or attempts to cause serious bodily injury or death.

Most of the attention to Pro-IP centered on the creation of the position of a "Copyright Czar." The actual title is the Intellectual Property Enforcement Representative (IPEC), who will be appointed by the President with the advice and consent of the Senate. The IPEC will work with in the Executive Office of the President and will be charged with coordinating the development of a Joint Strategic Plan at the federal level to reduce copyright and trademark infringement in various ways. The IPEC will be the President's principal advisor on domestic and international intellectual property enforcement policy. In this role the IPEC will also advise federal departments and agencies on intellectual property policy issues, but will not have any enforcement powers. An advisory committee made up of representatives from various agencies, including the FBI, the STATE DEPARTMENT, the Copyright Office, and the PATENT AND TRADEMARK OFFICE, will assist the IPEC in developing policies.

The Pro-IP also provided for improved investigative and **forensic** resources for those enforcing intellectual property criminal laws and it allocated funds for investigating and prosecuting intellectual property crimes and other criminal activity involving computers. As of May 2009, President Barack Obama had not appointed the IPEC.

Orphan Works Act of 2008

For years, legislators had struggled to find amicable middle ground between copyright holders and those wishing to "copy" or use likely copyrighted works, but unable to identify and/or locate the copyright holder for permissions. The term "orphan works" refers to such works.

Despite several years in the making and an unanimous passage by the Senate, The Orphan Works Act of 2008 (S. 2913 and H.R. 5889) failed to make it into law by the close of the 110th Congress in January 2009. Lost in the House of Representatives' efforts to pass the massive $700 billion economic "bailout" legislation following the November 2008 elections, the "Shawn Bentley Orphan Works Act of 2008" expired at the end of the Congressional term (as all bills do that are not acted upon) without final action in the House. Notwithstanding, Senator Orin Hatch (R-UT), in a speech before the World Copyright Summit held in Washington DC in June 2009, vowed to continue efforts to pass orphan works legislation in the 111th Congress. In his speech, Senator Hatch told the audience,

> Last year, the Senate unanimously passed bipartisan legislation to encourage the use of orphan works-works that may be protected by copyright but whose owners cannot be identified or located. Countless artistic creations-books, photos, paintings and music-around the country are effectively locked away and unavailable for the general public to enjoy because the owner of the copyright for the work is unknown.
>
> Unfortunately, it isn't easy to identify or find these owners of copyrighted work. To make matters worse, many are discouraged or reluctant to use these works out of fear of being sued should the owner eventually step forward.

For years, I have been working with industry stakeholders and copyright experts, including Marybeth Peters, Register of Copyrights, to pass orphan works legislation. The bill seeks to unite users and copyright owners, and to ensure that copyright owners are compensated for the use of their works. I couldn't agree more with Register Peters when she said, "A solution to the orphan works problem is overdue and the pending legislation is both fair and responsible."

The orphan works problem was the unintended fallout of the 1976 revision to the Copyright Act. The 1976 Act removed the requirement that prospective owners of protect-eligible works affirmatively register those works with the U.S. Copyright Office (a requirement of the original 1909 Act). Works are now protected from the moment they are fixed in a tangible medium of expression, such as ink, print, paint, film, audio recording, etc. By virtue of removing the requirement to register a works for copyright protection, the new Act essentially eliminated the requirement for a copyright owner to file a renewal registration to extend the term of protection.

Whereas the old law created a retrievable record (for the Register of Copyrights) to ascertain whether a work was copyrighted, whether the copyright had expired without extension and was now in the **public domain**, and who the registered owner of the copyright was, the new law created excessive caution on the part of potential users. Literally thousands of copyrighted works went expired, yet, because of unknown status, were never used by the public at large as "fair use" exceptions or as works now in the public domain. Some examples of problems that orphan works legislation was intended to cure included, e.g., the inability to restore an old wedding photograph of grandparents because one could not locate the original photographer; a public library's inability to display letters of American soldiers written during WORLD WAR II because it could not locate the soldiers or their descendents; or a museum's inability to display or exhibit old photographs, letters, cards, etc. from the Great Depression because the creators/authors were not found.

Orphan works legislation was intended to bridge the gap between releasing all orphan works to the public domain or holding users fully accountable should the owner eventually come forward. It would do this by limiting

statutory liability for uses of orphan works. It would encourage prospective users to proceed with their use, knowing in **advance** the maximum remedy they would face if, after such use, a copyright owner came forward.

The pending legislation would enable users to display, exhibit, or incorporate into other creative works a particular orphan work only after a thoroughly documented search that showed an inability to locate the owner (if any). Language in the proposed legislation provided for not only the criteria for conducting such a search, but also court review to determine whether such a search was adequate and done in **good faith**. If the copyright owner should later come forward, the user would need to pay reasonable compensation to the owner, but could avoid the full statutory damages (as much as $150,000) in the existing copyright statutes. No protection was afforded for failures to conduct diligent searches or searches done in **bad faith**.

A contentious area of the proposed legislation related to just how much of a "diligent effort" (to find the copyright owner) a prospective user would have to make (and prove) prior to proceeding with an infringing use.

In sum, the proposed act would have created a new section 514 of Title 17 to provide a limitation on remedies in such circumstances of copyright infringement in which a user was unable to locate the owner of the work despite a diligent search. The proposed act also provided no award of damages if the user was a nonprofit educational institution, museum, library, archive, or public broadcasting **entity** that met additional criteria as to the infringing use.

Technically, the original bill was introduced as the Orphan Works Act of 2008 (H.R. 5439) by Representative Lamar Smith (R-TX) in May 2006, and was then folded into the Copyright Modernization Act of 2006 but never passed. The September 2008 version introduced by Senator Patrick Leahy (D-VT) was amended and passed to the House Committee on the Judiciary. The amendment was "to modify provisions relating to diligent efforts, guide searches, recommend practices, limitations on injunctive relief, and for other purposes."

RIAA Changes Position on Suing Individuals Who Illegally Download Music

Protecting intellectual property in the age of the Internet remains a difficult task. In the music industry, record companies, recording artists, and songwriters have seen the sale of CDs plummet while illegal downloads of their music has increased. Online music sales of digital downloads through sites such as iTunes and Amazon.com has gained popularity, but the industry's trade group, the Recording Industry Association of America (RIAA), has pursued a legal strategy that sought to discourage illegal behavior. The RIAA filed lawsuits against thousands of individuals, demanding thousands of dollars for uploading and downloading music files. Many individuals agreed to out-of-court settlements, but the RIAA's strategy hit a roadblock with the first suit went to trial in Minnesota. At the end of 2008, the RIAA announced it would abandon the use of lawsuits and concentrate on working with Internet Service Providers (ISPs) to discourage users from illegally uploading music. However, in 2009 the RIAA made clear that it had only agreed to file new cases; those still pending would either be settled or taken to trial.

The Minnesota court case demonstrated the difficulty of successfully suing a music uploader. Jammie Thomas, a 30-year-old single Brainerd mother of two who works for the Mille Lacs Band of Objibwe, allegedly copied or distributed 24 songs by placing them on the Kazaa file-sharing network. The RIAA believed she had actually uploaded over 1,700 songs but concentrated on just 24. It warned her about her behavior and then asked Thomas for $4,740 to settle the matter. After she refused the RIAA filed a lawsuit in Minnesota federal **district court**. The case went to trial in October 2007. The jury heard a computer **forensic** expert testify that he had identified and linked Thomas' Internet Protocol (IP) address and cable modem to pirated music on Kazaa in 2005. However, he conceded on cross-examination that he could not determine if Thomas was the person who had done the sharing. Her lawyer argued that an Internet hacker had used her computer without her knowledge. The RIAA also argued that she had replaced her hard drive soon after she was notified that she was under investigation, suggesting that Thomas was trying to destroy evidence. A Best Buy Geek Squad employee weakened this argument by testifying that the hard drive was replaced under warranty and that Best Buy would not replace a hard drive unless it was not working properly.

The jury found Thomas liable and awarded the RIAA $222,000, but soon after the trial Judge Michael Davis notified the parties that he had second thoughts about a jury instruction he issued. The instruction went to the heart of the case: what level of proof was needed for the RIAA to prevail. The jury instruction stated that the RIAA did not have to prove that anybody downloaded the songs that Thomas placed in her Kazaa folder. As long as she had made the files available the jury could find that she had committed copyright infringement. In September 2008, Davis declared a mistrial because of his "erroneous" instruction. For the RIAA to prevail it had to prove that the songs had actually been transferred to another computer. The RIAA complained that this burden of proof was impossible to meet. In addition, Judge Davis held that the amount of damages were "wholly disproportionate to the damages suffered." *Capitol Records Inc. v. Thomas*, 579 F.Supp.2d 1210 (D.Minn.2008)

Faced with the fact that it had never prevailed at trial on Internet copyright infringement, the RIAA rethought its strategy. New York State Attorney General Andrew Cuomo worked with the recording industry and ISPs to negotiate an agreement that would end litigation. In late December 2008, RIAA announced that it had stopped filing mass lawsuits and was now working with major ISPs on a new approach. In the past the RIAA had filed lawsuits against ISPs, demanding that ISPs disclose the identities of file sharers. The new graduated response plan, which is modeled on European programs, involved negotiating agreements with ISPs to perform certain actions when notified that customers are file sharing. Once the ISP receives an email notification from the RIAA, it will either forward the message to the customer or notify the customer that she appears to be uploading music illegally and asks the customer to stop. If the customer persists in uploading the ISP will send one or two more emails and may slow down the person's connection. As a last resort the ISP will cancel the customer's service. However, the RIAA reserved the right to sue heavy file sharers or individuals who ignore repeated warnings. It believed the new approach would be effective because it will let people know they are not anonymous.

It is unclear if this voluntary, non-government approach will work. ISPs may benefit by reducing network congestion tied to peer-to-peer file sharing. Comcast notified its customers that it had capped the monthly amount of bandwidth available to accounts. The RIAA made clear that it would continue to litigate that had already been identified before the change in strategy. In April 2009 it filed more such lawsuits, signaling that there will be more court fights over the burden of proof needed for finding liability.

Studios Clash Over Rights to "Watchman" Movie

Two of the major film studios—Twentieth Century Fox and Warner Brothers—became involved in a dispute in 2008 and 2009 regarding distribution rights to the film *Watchmen*. Several studios were involved in different production efforts for the film, which was based on a popular comic book published in the 1980s. Fox and Warner Brothers settled the case early in 2009, and the film was released in March.

A writer named Alan Moore and an artist named Dave Gibbons developed *Watchmen* as a book-length comic book. The book appeared in 12 issues that were published between September 1986 and October 1987. The book establishes an alternate history of the United States where a group of superheroes help to save the United States. The series focused on tensions between the United States and the Soviet Union during the 1980s. The main characters (the superheroes) were an unusual collection—very different than superheroes in typical comic books. Critics praised the series, with *Time* referring to *Watchmen* as "a heart-pounding, heartbreaking read and a watershed in the evolution of a young medium."

Plans to develop *Watchmen* as a movie project began as early as 1986. Twentieth-Century Fox (Fox) was the first studio to become involved with the project, but several efforts stalled. In 1991, Fox transferred some of its rights to *Watchmen* to Lawrence Gordon, a former studio chief. Fox maintained that the agreement with Gordon gave the studio distribution rights to the film version of *Watchmen*. Development of the film stalled, and Fox in 1994 entered into another agreement with Gordon. Under the 1994 contract, Gordon could try to sell the project to another studio.

However, the actual terms of the 1994 contract were subject to dispute. Fox claimed that Gordon could not have full control of the movie's production rights until Gordon repaid the studio for development costs that the studio had incurred. The agreement also included other limitations on Gordon's rights to the film. For instance, the studio retained the right to join the production once again if Gordon made certain creative changes to the film, such as changing the director or screenwriter. The so-called "changed element" clause is common in deals for film rights because studios insist on protecting their rights in the event that a project becomes more appealing.

In 2001, Gordon presented the film to Universal Studios. Universal was hesitant to accept the project, and in 2004, Paramount Studios became involved. Paramount paid Universal a custom fee of 10% of Universal's development costs. Had Paramount eventually produced the film, the company would have to pay Universal the remaining 90% of those costs. It appeared for a time that Paramount would indeed produce the film, but the studio became concerned about the film's script and large budget of more than $100 million. In June 2005, Paramount shut the film down.

Warner Brothers became involved in the film project in December 2005. During 2006, Warner Brothers named Zach Snyder as director. Disagreements between the different studios began at that point. Warner Brothers was not required to pay any of Paramount's production fees, but because Paramount had not reimbursed Universal, Paramount did not have any transfer rights. Paramount and Warner Brothers eventually agreed that Paramount would own 25% of the film, and Warner Brothers allowed Paramount to distribute the film outside the United States.

Fox stepped in and began to argue that Warner had infringed on Fox's rights to the movie. Fox claimed that Warner's deal for *Watchmen* violated Fox's rights under the 1991 and 1994 contracts between Fox and Gordon. Warner claimed that it did not know about either of those contracts. Warner later claimed that the 1994 contract between Gordon and Fox did not confer any distribution rights to Fox. In February 2008, Fox sued Warner in U.S. **District Court** of the Central District of California, claiming that Warner Brothers had

infringed on Fox's copyright. According to Fox, since Gordon did not pay Fox's production costs, Gordon never acquired Fox's distribution rights. Therefore, Gordon could not have transferred those rights to Warner Brothers or any other studio.

In August 2008, U.S. District Judge Gary Feess denied Warner Brothers' motion to dismiss. Fox subsequently filed a motion for **summary judgment** on its copyright claims, arguing that Fox at least owned distribution rights. In December, Feess agreed and granted summary judgment in favor of Fox.

> In the Court's view, Gordon's agreement to and execution of the [1994 agreement] indicates a clear understanding that Fox owned important rights in "Watchmen," including, at the very least, a distribution right, and that Gordon was required to comply with the terms and conditions of the buy-out if he wanted to acquire those rights. Because Gordon never paid the buy-out price, he never acquired Fox's rights in "Watchmen," and those rights therefore remain with Fox. Moreover, nothing in any later agreement altered or terminated Fox's ownership interest. In particular, Warner Brothers exercised its option to acquire Gordon's rights after being placed on notice of Fox's claim and having received the documentation upon which this Court bases its ruling. Thus, Warner Brothers cannot argue that its interest in "Watchmen" takes priority over Fox's interest.

Twentieth Century Fox Film Corp. v. Warner Brothers Entertainment Corp., No. CV 08-00889 GAF, 2008 WL 5429687 (C.D. Cal. Dec. 24, 2008).

In January 2009, Fox and Warner Brothers announced that they had agreed to settle the case. Fox did not receive distribution rights under the settlement, but the studio received cash along with a percentage of the film's revenues. The film opened on March 6 and earned more than $180 million at the box office.

CORRUPTION

Illinois Governor Rod Blagojevich Impeached

In one of the most closely-watched political stories of 2008 and 2009, Illinois governor Rod Blagojevich was impeached by the Illinois House of Representatives and removed from office by the state's Senate. Blagojevich was

Rod Blagojevich, April 21, 2009, leaving court in Illinois.

AP IMAGES

charged with a number of crimes, including a plot to sell Barack Obama's seat on the U.S. Senate once Obama was elected as president. Blagojevich became the first governor in the history of Illinois to be impeached.

Blagojevich was at one time a prosecutor, and he served in the Illinois Legislature during the 1990s. In 1996, he won a seat in the U.S. House of Representatives. While he was a member of Congress, the sitting governor in Illinois, George Ryan, was embroiled in controversy stemming from corruption allegations. When Ryan decided to step down in 2002, Blagojevich became a candidate for the governor's office. Blagojevich became the first Democrat to serve as governor of Illinois in 25 years when he defeated former Illinois Attorney General Jim Ryan (who is not related to George Ryan). Blagojevich won a reelection bid in 2006. Meanwhile, George Ryan was convicted on federal corruption charges in 2006, and he was sentenced to more than six years in prison.

Even before he was charged in 2008, Blagojevich had been the subject of allegations related to corruption. In 2006, Blagojevich's top fundraiser, Antoin Rezko, was indicted on federal charges that he sought millions of dollars in illegal kickbacks and campaign contributions from firms that sought to be involved in the state's **pension** business. Rezko had recommended several friends to serve in high-level positions in Blagojevich's administration. Moreover, Blagojevich had made thousands in 2004 on real estate deals with Rezko. Blagojevich maintained that he was innocent of any wrongdoing, but his approval rating fell due

to these controversies. In 2007, the *Chicago Tribune* openly questioned whether Blagojevich should be removed from office.

The investigation and trial of Rezko focused more attention on Blagojevich. Court documents in the Rezko trial referred to someone as "Public Official A," and in 2008, U.S. District Judge Amy St. Even revealed that the official was Blagojevich. Allegations in the Rezko case raised suspicions that Blagojevich had exchanged influence in government contracts and legal work for campaign contributions. For instance, prosecutors alleged that Rezko had offered the brother of one of his business partners a seat on the Illinois Banking Board in exchange for a $50,000 contribution to Blagojevich's campaign. This example was one of several so-called "pay-to-play" schemes associated with Blagojevich.

One of these pay to play schemes was especially heinous. When the chief executive officer of the Children's Memorial Hospital in Chicago refused to donate $50,000 to Blagojevich's campaign, Blagojevich allegedly responded by threatening to revoke $8 million in funding commitments to the hospital. Prosecutors also alleged that Blagojevich threatened to hold back funds related to the sale of Wrigley Field in Chicago unless the Tribune Company, owner of the *Chicago Tribune*, fired certain members of the newspaper's editorial board.

The allegation that attracted the most public attention focused on Blagojevich's efforts to benefit from the selection of Obama's seat on the U.S. Senate. When Obama was elected president in November, he had to vacate his seat on the Senate. Blagojevich had the responsibility to appoint Obama's successor. Blagojevich used this power as a bargaining tool, seeking a number of possible benefits in exchange for the selection to the Senate. He allegedly wanted to be selected for a position on Obama's cabinet. Blagojevich also considered moves that might help to lead to a presidential run in 2016.

Blagojevich was unaware that federal authorities had placed wiretaps at the governor's home and campaign offices. In several recordings, Blagojevich was brash, noting that the power to select Obama's replacement was something of value that he could shop around. In the recording, Blagojevich said, "I've got this thing, and it's [expletive] golden. And I'm just not giving it up for [expletive] nothing. I'm not going to do it. And I can always use it. I can parachute me there." Blagojevich commonly used **profanity** when he spoke to staff members.

By December, federal prosecutors had enough evidence to bring charges against the governor. On December 9, 2008, federal authorities arrested Blagojevich at his home in Chicago. At the time of Blagojevich's arrest, U.S. attorney Patrick Fitzgerald said that Blagojevich had "taken us to a truly new low" and had gone on "a political corruption crime spree." Fitzgerald filed a 78-page criminal complaint that specified a number of allegations in addition to the attempt to sell Obama's Senate seat.

Members of the Illinois Legislature, as well as Lieutenant Governor Pat Quinn, called for Blagojevich to step down as governor, either permanently or temporarily while the investigation was ongoing. Obama also called for Blagojevich to resign, expressing concern that the governor could lead effectively given the charges. In addition to concerns about Blagojevich's future as governor, lawmakers also demanded that Blagojevich not appoint Obama's Senate replacement. Blagojevich brashly claimed his innocence and refused to step down. On December 30, Blagojevich appointed former Illinois Attorney General Roland Burris to succeed Obama.

By the time Blagojevich appointed Burris, the governor was already facing an impeachment inquiry, which began in mid-December. On January 8, 2009, a House committee recommended Blagojevich's impeachment, and on January 9, the House voted 114-1 in favor of impeachment. Blagojevich claimed that the move in the House was "politically motivated" and that he would fight the legislature's actions "every step of the way." The case proceeded to the Senate by the end of January. Blagojevich appeared before the Senate on January 29, making an impassioned speech about why the Senate should not remove him from office. Nevertheless, the Senate approved his removal by a unanimous vote of 59-0. With the vote, Blagojevich became the eighth governor in U.S. history to be removed from office following an impeachment. The Senate also voted to bar Blagojevich from holding public office in Illinois ever again.

Blagojevich was indicted by a federal **grand jury** on April 2, 2009. Also indicted were John

Ted Stevens, April 7, 2009.

AP IMAGES

Harris, the former governor's former chief of staff; Robert Blagojevich, Rod's brother; Alonzo Monk, a lobbyist; Christopher Kelly, Blagojevich's former campaign fund chair; and William F. Cellini, Sr., an Illinois businessman.

Senate Ted Stevens Loses Senate Election Following Conviction

Long-time Alaska senator Ted Stevens was convicted in 2008 on charges that he failed to disclose gifts he had received from an oil company in exchange for certain political influence. The conviction came just days before Stevens was defeated in the 2008 election. The loss marked an end to Stevens' 40-year career in the Senate. In April 2009, though, Stevens' conviction was set aside because prosecutors had failed to share interview notes with the defense.

Stevens was born in Indianapolis and raised in Chicago. He graduated from Harvard Law School in 1950 and worked for a firm in Washington, D.C. to begin his legal career. He moved to Alaska in 1952 and worked behind the scenes when the United States considered adding Alaska as a state. During the 1960s, Stevens served in the Alaska Legislature. He failed in his first campaign for a seat on the U.S.

Senate, but due to the death of one of the incumbents, he was appointed to serve on the Senate by Alaska Governor Walter Hickel. Stevens was elected to the Senate in 1970, and he was reelected in 1972, 1978, 1984, 1990, 1996, and 2002. With his election in 2002, he became the longest-serving Republican senator in U.S. history (Senator Strom Thurmond, who served longer than Stevens, was originally a Democrat).

During his career, Stevens was influential in federal legislation that benefited Alaska. He served as the chair of the Senate Appropriations Committee from 1997 to 2001 and again from 2003 to 2005. His position of influence helped him to direct more than $3 billion in federal money to Alaska. He was well-respected in the state he represented. He received an award as "Alaskan of the Year," and the largest airport in the state was named after him. He was not without his critics, however. One group criticized him heavily for wasteful government spending.

More damaging allegations came from a 2003 story in the *Los Angeles Times*, which accused him of using his political power for personal financial gain. According to the story, Stevens had not benefited financially for most of his career in the Senate. However, beginning in 1997, he used his influence in exchange for private deals that earned Stevens millions of dollars. For instance, the newspaper alleged that Stevens helped an Alaskan company to obtain millions in defense contracts. In exchange, the company reportedly paid $6 million to lease a building owned by Stevens.

VECO Corporation, an Alaskan oil pipeline company, became the focus of an investigation. Between 2002 and 2007, Ted Steven's son, Ben, was paid more than $243,000 for consulting work by VECO founder and chief executive officer Bill Allen. VECO lobbied aggressively on certain proposals before the Alaska Legislature. One piece of legislation focuses on the rate that the state would tax for profits on oil. VECO lobbyist Rick Smith urged legislators to limit the tax to 20%. Although the state's senate originally agreed to 22.5% rate, the debate ended in a stalemate when the House and Senate could not agree on a rate.

Federal authorities began to investigate allegations that VECO had made illegal gifts to lawmakers. On August 31, 2006, agents with the FEDERAL BUREAU OF INVESTIGATION raided the offices of six members of the legislature, including Ben Stevens' office. The investigation led to charges brought against three former members of the legislature in 2007. On May 7, 2007, Allen and Smith of VECO pleaded guilty to bribing members of the legislature in exchange for votes. Both resigned from VECO, and the company was later purchased by another firm.

Just weeks after the raids, the *Anchorage Daily News* revealed that federal agents had begun to investigate a major remodeling project at Ted Stevens' personal residence in Girdwood, Alaska. A federal **grand jury** called Stevens' neighbor to submit documents related to the work on Stevens' home. According to reports, investigators found evidence that contractors on the project were either hired or supervised by VECO. In July, Stevens filed a financial disclosure form, asserting that he and his wife had paid for the renovations "with their own money." FBI agents raided Stevens' home on July 30, 2007.

Despite the allegations, Stevens filed for reelection to the U.S. Senate in February 2008. The investigation continued, however, and on July 29, 2008, the grand jury indicted Stevens on seven counts related to concealment of his alleged receipt of things of value from VECO. According to the indictment, Stevens received more than $250,000 in goods and services from VECO, including the home improvements, automobile exchanges, and household goods. The indictment alleged that Stevens had violated the Ethics in Government Act, 5 U.S.C. § 101 **et seq.**, which requires members of Congress to file financial disclosure forms. Under the **statute**, Stevens was required to detail specific transactions that he engaged in during the previous year, including receipt of gifts over a certain amount.

Stevens' trial began on September 22, 2008. The trial lasted more than the month, which included testimony from Allen about gifts given to Stevens and free labor provided for the home renovations. Both Stevens and his wife also testified. Both claimed that they did not want the gifts that Allen had given to them. Ted Stevens also accused Allen of lying about the transactions. Stevens' denials did not sway the jury, which convicted Stevens on all seven counts on October 27. Stevens' conviction came just days before the November election for Stevens' seat on the Senate. Although Stevens led Anchorage mayor Mark Begich according to early returns, Begich pulled out the win thanks to thousands of votes submitted through absentee ballots. Stevens bid farewell to the Senate on November 20.

In December, an FBI whistleblower revealed that prosecutors had withheld evidence from the defense in Stevens' trial. According to the informant, prosecutors had taken notes during an interview with Allen in April 2008. During the interview, Allen made statements that were inconsistent with statements that Allen later made at trial. This disclosure led Attorney General Eric Holder to dismiss the indictment against Stevens. On April 2, U.S. district judge Emmet Sullivan set aside Stevens' conviction.

COVENANT

An agreement, contract, or written promise between two individuals that frequently constitutes a pledge to do or refrain from doing something.

Right to Dry Laws

Legal controversies often arise when one group advocates for a legitimate social goal and is blocked by another group with a competing worthy social goal. In the United States the goal of reducing dependence on energy in hopes of reducing climate change has run into long-held legal principles concerning real property. Advocates of using clotheslines to dry clothes rather than dryers have discovered that most condominium and homeowners associations and many communities ban the use of clotheslines. Out of this conflict has come a movement that seeks the enactment of "Right to Dry" laws that would override covenants in real estate agreement and local ordinances and allow the installation of clotheslines. Opponents object out of fear that clotheslines will reduce property values and project an unsuitable image about their communities. Though only a few states have enacted right to dry laws, advocates continue to press state legislatures for action.

The use of clothes dryers is a relatively recent development in modern society. In the 1950s dryers started to attract consumers, but since then they have grown ever more popular. By 2005 there were 88 million dryers in the U.S., consuming over 1 thousand kilowatt hours of energy per household and creating over 2,200 pounds of carbon dioxide emissions. In 1995 Alexander Lee founded Project Laundry List to promote the use of clotheslines, reasoning that the drying of clothes by sunshine and air would reduce energy and carbon emissions to zero for each household and save the household hundreds of dollars a year in utility costs. However, it soon became apparent that higher-income communities and condominium associations would not permit clotheslines from being erected because of local ordinances and, more importantly, legal covenants tied to the purchase of real estate. When an individual buys a house with a covenant in the contract or deed that forbids the use of clotheslines or basketball hoops, the purchaser agrees to follow the terms of the contract or face legal sanctions.

Lee and other advocates have lobbied a number of state legislatures, seeking laws that will override covenants and ordinances. It is estimated that 60 million Americans live in areas governed by over 300,000 homeowner's associations and many ban clotheslines, making this a national issue. By 2009 only Florida, Utah, and Colorado had enacted laws that give residents the right to use a clothesline. At least 10 other state legislatures have seen right to dry laws introduced, but it has proved difficult to enact them. Homeowners associations have lobbied against the bills, believing it important to maintain curb appeal by maintaining good aesthetics and to preserve residents' expectations. Concerns about a loss in property value also motivate opponents. They have noted a 2007 Zogby International poll of people living in community associations that found 75 percent opposed government rules about clotheslines, while 18 percent favored them. Environmental concerns must be balanced against the desires of those who find the sight of clothes hanging in a yard unsightly and out of place. Opponents also point out that associations have elected board members. Right to dry advocates should embrace the democratic process and seek election to these boards.

Advocates of clotheslines consider these objections trivial when compared to the environmental benefits to be gained. Moreover, hanging out clothes requires exercise and time outside, which are social goods. Some believe that the objections to clothesline are class-based as well, suggesting that only lower-income people would not use a dryer in today's world.

The Florida right to dry law expressly states that no governing body may adopt ordinances that prohibit the installation of clotheslines. In addition, no deed restrictions, covenants, or other binding agreements running with the real estate may prohibit clotheslines. The Utah **statute** does not explicitly create a right to dry but it permits municipalities to decide whether to override covenants and permit solar collectors, clotheslines, or other renewable energy devices. The 2008 Colorado law overrides homeowners association prohibitions on clotheslines but only if the clotheslines are retractable. The statute permits restrictions on clotheslines only if the restrictions do not unreasonably impede their use or drive up the cost.

Clothesline advocates have tried to mitigate aesthetic objections by not objecting to reasonable time and use rules. Some advocates have negotiated with associations to allow air drying during certain hours, such as weekdays between 10 a.m. and 4 p.m., and have agreed that only retractable or removable clotheslines are permitted.

❖ CRAIG, GREGORY

Following the election of Barack Obama as President of the United States, his choice for White House counsel was Gregory Craig. This was not Craig's first affiliation with a Democratic White House; in September of 1998, Craig was chosen to lead, along with Charles Ruff, U.S. President BILL CLINTON'S legal defense in impeachment proceedings. Craig has made a career of representing high-profile defendants in distasteful cases, counting John Hinckley, Jr. and William Kennedy Smith, among his clients. Craig has had an equally strong career in politics, serving as Senator Ted Kennedy's foreign policy advisor, and as the State Department's director of policy planning.

Craig was born in Norfolk, Virginia, in 1945, the son of a World War II officer, but grew up in Palo Alto, California. He graduated magna cum laude from Harvard University. It was at Harvard that he first displayed the style of debate for which he would become famous: forceful yet disarmingly cordial. He led anti-Vietnam War protests at Harvard, participating in a reasoned, carefully-articulated debate with United Nations Ambassador Arthur Goldberg, and criticizing fellow protestors for shouting

Gregory Craig.
AP IMAGES

down United States defense secretary Robert McNamara. Although against the war, Craig nevertheless presented his objections to the draft board rather than become a conscientious objector. "I thought it was the only honorable thing to do," he later told the Washington Post. Craig was rejected for service because of a bad shoulder.

Craig received his law degree from Yale University, where he met future president Bill Clinton and Clinton's then-girlfriend, Hillary Rodham. The three were close enough that Craig gave up his New Haven apartment for the couple. Craig and the Clintons remained friends, and Craig has said that no political event excited him more than when Clinton won the Arkansas governorship.

After law school, Craig went to work for the Washington, D.C. law firm of Williams & Connolly. It was here in 1982 that Craig, along with Vincent Fuller, represented John Hinckley, Jr. in his trial for an assassination attempt on President Ronald Reagan. Craig and Fuller successfully argued that Hinckley was not guilty because he was insane. Craig, on CNBC in 1996, quoted in the New York Times, said the insanity plea had a "very, very good pedigree" and "represents the belief, I think, that society will not hold someone responsible for his acts or her acts if he doesn't have the capacity to make a decision" or "cannot distinguish between right and wrong."

Craig left Connolly & Williams in the mid-1980s to join Senator Edward Kennedy's staff as his foreign policy advisor. Craig advised Kennedy on policy on Latin America and South America, and arranged a trip by the senator to South Africa—a trip that helped win a congressional vote in 1986 for economic sanctions against South Africa in opposition to apartheid. After his return to Connolly & Williams, Craig was again called upon to help his former employer. Kennedy asked Craig to advise him during the investigation surrounding the trial of William Kennedy Smith, the senator's nephew. Kennedy had been called on to testify, and Craig successfully guided him through the proceedings. Smith was eventually acquitted.

Craig left Connolly & Williams again to work for the State Department as Director of Policy Planning. It was from this post, considered by many to be a plum job, that Craig was called to head President Clinton's defense team

1945	Born, Norfolk, Virginia
1972	Graduated from Yale University
1982	Represented John Hinckley, Jr
1986	Joined Senator Edward Kennedy's staff
2009	Named White House Counsel

preparing the case for the president's impeachment trial. Impeachment proceedings revolved around allegations by Independent Council Kenneth Starr that President Clinton lied under oath when questioned about his sexual affair with former White House intern Monica Lewinsky, and thus committed perjury.

Craig participated in the Obama campaign leading up to the 2008 presidential election, and accepted the position of White Counsel in January 2009.

CRIME

Acts or omissions that are in violation of law.

FBI Reports Two-Year Decline in Violent Crime

For the second year in a row, the Federal Bureau of Investigation's (FBI) Preliminary Semiannual Uniform Crime Report, released in January 2009, showed measurable declines in violent crimes, property crimes, and arsons. The report covered January through June of 2008, and compared statistics with the same time period in 2007. (Annual reports, incorporating the semiannual findings, are not released until late in the year following the reported year.)

The FBI report is based on data received from more than 11,500 law enforcement agencies reporting through the Uniform Crime Reporting Program (UCR). By standardizing and defining specific crimes, the UCR focuses on those more useful in predicting trends and patterns. The crimes specifically measured for this report were: murder and non-negligent **manslaughter**, forcible rape, **robbery**, **aggravated assault**, **burglary**, larceny-theft, motor vehicle theft, and arson. According to the FBI, the UCR Program focuses on the above crimes because they are serious ones that occur most frequently and most often come to the attention of state and local law enforcement personnel.

The full report summarized crime levels in both city groupings (broken down further by city populations), metropolitan counties, and non-metropolitan counties. The entire country was also divided into four national regions (Northeast, Midwest, West, and South) for the purpose of other statistics.

Significantly and across the board in all populations nationwide, violent crime fell a full 3.5 percent and property crime 2.5 percent during the first half of 2008. Breaking down violent crime, murders were down by 4.4 percent, aggravated assaults by 4.1 percent, forcible rape by 3.3 percent, and robbery by 2.2 percent. Non-violent crimes also dropped by palpable percentages. National statistics showed a 0.8 percent decline in burglary, 1.2 percent decline in larceny-theft, motor vehicle theft by 12.6 percent, and arson by 5.6 percent.

On a regional basis, law enforcement agencies reported a 6.0 percent drop in violent crime in the Midwest, 5.0 percent in the West, 2.9 percent in the Northeast, and 1.5 percent in the South. Property crimes fell in the Midwest by 4.7 percent, 6.1 percent in the West, and 0.4 percent in the South. Forcible rapes were down in the South (4.7 percent), the Midwest (4.2 percent) and the West (2.9 percent).

Arsons also dropped in all geographic regions and among all population groups, with the exception of cities with populations of 250,000–500,000, where it increased by 2.0 percent. However, that precise population group (250,000–500,000) saw the greatest decline in violent crime (5.2 percent) for the same reported period.

With respect to populations, cities with populations of 250,000–500,000 saw the most significant decrease in overall violent crime, down 5.2 percent. In metropolitan counties, violent crimes fell by 4.1 percent; in non-metropolitan counties, violent crimes fell 7.5 percent. Isolating just the crime of murder, cities with higher populations of 500,000–1,000,000 reported the largest decrease in reported murders (down 11.3 percent). Yet, cities with populations less than 10,000 posted the largest increase in murders (up 9.8 percent).

Most city population groups reported declines in forcible rapes, with the exception of large cities with populations greater than 1,000,000 (a 3.4 percent increase). Forcible rapes increased by 1.0 percent in metropolitan counties, but there was a major decline (12.7) in non-metropolitan counties.

Property crimes decreased in all population groupings. The largest decline was recorded in cities with 250,000–500,000 inhabitants.

Notwithstanding, some increases in crimes were also noted. Murder and non-negligent manslaughter were up 3.3 percent in mid-sized cities (populations of 50,000–100,000) and 9.8 percent in smaller cities (populations under 10,000). Arson increased only in cities with populations between 250,000–500,000 (by 2.0 percent).

On a regional basis, the Northeast showed a slight increase in forcible rapes (0.6 percent), burglaries (2.7 percent) and larceny-theft (2.9 percent). Property crimes also rose in the Northeast by 1.7 percent. Also, on a regional basis, the South reported an increase in burglaries (0.6 percent) and larceny-thefts (0.5 percent), but a decline in forcible rapes (4.7 percent).

The UCR Program and FBI reports are valuable, not only to law enforcement personnel and legislators, but also to the public at large. Insurance companies also utilize the information for risk-assessment and claim trends.

CRIMINAL LAW

A body of rules and statutes that defines conduct prohibited by the government because it threatens and harms public safety and welfare and that establishes punishment to be imposed for the commission of such acts.

Craig v. State

The legal saga surrounding Senator Larry Craig's (R.-Idaho) Minnesota airport restroom incident came to end in December 2008, just weeks before his U.S. Senate term expired. The Minnesota Court of Appeals, in *Craig v. State*, 2008 WL 5136170 (Minn.App.2008), ruled that Craig could not withdraw his guilty plea to the **misdemeanor** offense of **disorderly conduct** and that the disorderly conduct **statute** was not unconstitutionally overbroad. The events that took place on June 11, 2007 in a public restroom led to national ridicule and the end of Craig's political career.

Craig, a three-term senator, sought to undue his guilty plea at both the trial and **appellate** level once the events of June 11 became national news. On that day Craig was at the Minneapolis-St. Paul airport, waiting for a connecting flight. He entered a public restroom, which according to airport police, was a site for homosexual sex. Sergeant David Karsnia, dressed in plain clothes, had entered the bathroom 15 minutes earlier, and was sitting in a toilet stall with its door close. According to Karsnia, Craig appeared outside of the stall where he was sitting and looked into it several times through the crack in the doorway. When a stall next to Karsnia's came open, Craig entered and placed his roller bag in front of the stall. This tactic is apparently used to block the view from the front of the stall in order to conceal sexual activity. Craig allegedly began to tap his right foot, which is another sign that he wanted to solicit sex. At one point, Craig moved his right foot so that it touched Karsnia's left foot. Craig then made gestures by running his hand underneath the divider between the stalls. This activity continued for about four minutes until Karsnia displayed his badge underneath the stall door and motioned for the exit to the restroom. Craig responded by shouting "No!" and left the stall without flushing the toilet. Craig was taken to the police operations center and after initially denying he had done anything illegal, agreed to enter a guilty plea to charges of interference with privacy and disorderly conduct, which were lesser offenses to the more serious public **lewdness** charges that could have been brought. Craig, who did not appear in person when his plea was filed, paid a $500 fine.

After the incident and plea became public in late August of 2007, Craig expressed regret that he had pleaded guilty. That fall he sought to withdraw his guilty plea, but Minneapolis **district court** judge Charles Porter denied Craig's request. The judge noted that Craig had signed the plea agreement and had been advised of his rights. Craig then filed an appeal with the Minnesota Court of Appeals.

The three-judge panel unanimously upheld the trial court decision. Chief Judge Edward Toussaint, writing for the court, rejected a series of arguments made by Craig. Toussaint ruled that the plea petition was not flawed because it did not describe the alleged conduct in detail. Because Craig did not appear, the plea petition was the only account given to the trial court of Craig's version of the offense. However, the complaint made by airport police that contained the details was available to the trial court when it accepted the plea. Craig contended the judge had not read the complaint, but his argument was severely weakened because he had not ordered a transcript of the plea hearing for his appeal. In addition, Craig had failed to seek a postconviction evidentiary hearing to establish what had taken place at the proceeding. The appeals court had no factual record of what happened at the hearing, and therefore Craig failed to carry his burden of evidence on this point.

Craig had also alleged that the factual basis for the disorderly conduct plea was lacking because the police had failed to show that "others," in addition to the undercover officer, would have been alarmed or disturbed by his conduct, as required by the disorderly conduct statute. The appeals court found no merit in this argument, noting that a **statutory** reference to "others" did not "necessarily mandate the presence of more than one other person." Finally, the court rejected Craig's claim that Karsnia had entrapped him by at least partially inviting Craig's conduct. **Entrapment** exists only where the criminal intent originates in the police officer rather than in the mind of the accused. The complaint clearly indicated that the criminal intent originated in the mind of Craig.

The Minnesota chapter of the AMERICAN CIVIL LIBERTIES UNION (ACLU) filed a brief arguing that the disorderly conduct statute was unconstitutionally overbroad on its face, while Craig contended it was overbroad as applied to him. The court found that the law was not facially overbroad because it required the perpetrator to know or have reasonable grounds that the alleged conduct would tend to arouse "alarm, anger or resentment" in others. Given the "wide variety of circumstances" in which the type of conduct that the law seeks to proscribe can occur, "no more specific standard could reasonably be provided." As to Craig's claim the law was unconstitutional as applied to him, the court concluded that the "right to be left alone" in a public restroom was "very strong." The place the conduct occurred in this case "as much as or more than the *nature* of the conduct" determined its offensive nature.

CRIMINAL PROCEDURE

The framework of laws and rules that govern the administration of justice in cases involving an individual who has been accused of a crime, beginning with the initial investigation of the crime and concluding either with the unconditional release of the accused by virtue of acquittal (a judgment of not guilty) or by the imposition of a term of punishment pursuant to a conviction for the crime.

Cone v. Bell

The Due Process Clause of the FOURTEENTH AMENDMENT bars prosecutors from suppressing evidence favorable to an accused that is material to guilt or to innocence. The Supreme Court announced this holding in *Brady v. Maryland*, 373 U.S. 83, 83 S.Ct. 1194, 10 L. Ed.2d 215 (1963). Though the holding in *Brady* is straightforward, one inmate on death row worked for almost 27 years to put before a jury suppressed evidence that might mitigate his sentence. His efforts brought this case before the Supreme Court three times. The latest, and perhaps last, *Cone v. Bell*, __U.S.__, __S.Ct.__, __L.Ed.2d__ 2009 WL 1118709 (2009), led the Court to remand his case to the **district court** for a full consideration of his *Brady* argument.

Gary Cone, a Vietnam veteran, went on a crime spree in Tennessee and Florida in August 1980. Over the course of several days Cone committed assault, **burglary**, **robbery**, and two murders. At his Tennessee jury trial in 1982, Cone did not challenge the charges against him but claimed that he was not guilty by reason of insanity. His lawyer argued that Cone's severe drug addiction attributable to his military experience in Vietnam was the root cause for his criminal behavior. Expert witnesses testified that he committed the crimes while suffering from chronic amphetamine psychosis, a disorder linked to Cone's drug abuse. The prosecution rebutted this line of defense by portraying Cone as a calculating, intelligent criminal who was in control of his decisions and actions. The prosecution presented expert and lay testimony to show that Cone was not addicted to drugs. One witness, Ilene Blankman, proved damaging to Cone's case. She testified that she was a former heroin addict, who had spent time with Cone several months before the murders. She claimed that she had never seen Cone use drugs and had never seen him show signs of paranoia. The jury convicted Cone on all counts and then had to consider in a penalty hearing whether he should be sentenced to death. Cone's lawyer did not present any new evidence but argued that his client's drug addiction was a mitigating factor. The jury thought otherwise and returned a sentence of death.

Cone lost his direct appeals in the Tennessee courts and then pursued postconviction proceedings. He argued that the prosecutor had suppressed evidence favorable to him and that under *Brady* he should be retried. However, he had no proof that this evidence existed and the state appeals court rejected his claims. The situation changed dramatically in 1992 when the Tennessee Court of Appeals held for the first time that the state's public records law allowed a criminal defendant to review the prosecutor's file in his case. Cone exercised his right and found a number of statements that indicated the state knew he had been using drugs in the days before the murders. In addition, there was evidence in the file that Blankman had been an untruthful and biased witness. Despite the new evidence Cone could not get the state courts to look at it. The prosecutors convinced the courts on separate occasions that he had either waived this argument years before or that he had never raised it before. These contradictory arguments confused the **federal courts** when Cone filed for a petition of **habeas corpus** in 1997. His case went to the U.S. SUPREME COURT twice on other issues before returning in 2008.

The Court, in a 6-3 decision, ruled that there were no procedural bars under habeas corpus law to prevent the federal district court from hearing Cone's claims and reviewing the suppressed evidence. Cone did not argue that the evidence would change the finding of guilt but instead contended that some jurors would not have voted for the death penalty if they had seen the suppressed evidence of drug use and wild behavior in the days leading to the crimes. Justice JOHN PAUL STEVENS, writing for the majority, took to task the state prosecutors and the state and federal appeals courts for confusing the procedural and *Brady* issues for decades.

Justice Stevens examined the suppressed evidence and found that "both the quantity and quality" of it lent support to Cone's claim at trial that he was addicted to drugs and that his drug use affected his behavior during his crime spree. Therefore, the Court ordered a full review

of the suppressed evidence and its effects by the federal district court.

In a dissenting opinion, Justice ANTONIN SCALIA argued that Cone had failed to establish a reasonable probability that had the suppressed evidence been disclosed the sentencing proceeding result would have been different.

Hedgpeth v. Pulido

On December 8, 2008, the U.S. SUPREME COURT vacated a ruling of the Ninth **Circuit Court** of Appeals regarding jury instructions given in a murder case from California. In the case, the jury had been instructed on alternative theories of guilt, and after California state courts had affirmed the conviction, the defendant sought **habeas corpus** relief in federal court. A federal **district court** granted relief, and the Ninth Circuit affirmed. However, the Supreme Court vacated the Ninth Circuit's decision, holding that the lower federal court had applied the wrong standard in determining whether the state court's error in reviewing the defendant's conviction was harmless.

During the early morning hours on May 24, 1992, someone shot a cashier at a Shell gas station in San Mateo, California. The weapon used was a .45-caliber pistol, which killed the cashier within seconds. A witness heard the shooting and also heard a voice yelling after the shooting. According to the witness, it sounded to the witness as if the person was yelling at someone else. The gas stations' cash register went missing, but authorities found it the next day in some bushes elsewhere in San Mateo.

Michael Pulido, then age 16, was arrested on an unrelated charge of auto theft, and while he was in custody for that charge, he told officers that he had information about the **robbery** of the Shell station. Based on the information he provided, officers found discarded and unused .45-caliber cartridges with marking similar to those used in the shooting at the gas station. Pulido made a number of inconsistent statements, implicating more than one person as the actual shooter. At the time of the shooting, Pulido was staying with an uncle named Michael Aragon. Aragon had previously been convicted of **burglary**, possession of cocaine, and contributing to the delinquency of a minor. Because he had these prior convictions, Aragon told Pulido to discard the weapon. Aragon and his cohabitant, Laura Moore, testified that

Pulido was home at about midnight prior to the shooting but that he was gone by 3 a.m. The next morning, they said he was back in the house asleep with his clothes on. According to Aragon, Pulido displayed money to Aragon, and Moore later discovered that Pulido was carrying the handgun. Moore said she made Pulido disassemble the weapon, and that Pulido and Aragon threw the pieces of the gun away near Candlestick Park in San Francisco. Aragon said he later confronted Pulido about the crime, and Pulido at that time confessed to the shooting.

Pulido testified that Aragon was the actual shooter. According to Pulido's testimony, Aragon had found Pulido's pistol and had it on his possession when Aragon and Pulido went driving. On two occasions on the night of the shooting, Aragon stopped to purchase and smoke cocaine. After smoking the cocaine, Aragon went to the Shell station. Without telling Pulido what his intention was, Aragon went inside the store. Pulido said he heard a shot, and then ran inside the store to see what had happened. When he entered, the clerk was laying on the floor bleeding. Pulido ran from the store, followed by Aragon, who was carrying the cash register. According to Pulido, Aragon got into the car and threw the cash register onto Pulido's lap. Pulido pried open the cash register, and the two discarded it in some bushes along the road. At trial, Pulido's attorneys attacked Aragon's credibility, showing evidence that Aragon was using cocaine despite his statements that he was clean.

Under California law, Pulido could be convicted of both robbery and murder even if he was not the actual shooter. The jury could not reach a verdict on charges that Pulido was the actual shooter. Thus, at least some members of the jury apparently believed that Aragon was the actual shooter and that Pulido was an accomplice. Pulido was sentenced to life in prison without the possibility of parole. The verdict was based on the application of the **felony-murder rule**, under which a person may be convicted of murder if a killing occurs during the commission of another **felony**, such as a robbery. The felony-murder rule applies not only to the actual shooter, but also to those who conspire with the shooter or aid and **abet** the shooter in the commission of the other felony. In Pulido's case, he aided and **abetted** Aragon during the commission of a robbery,

and since Aragon shot the clerk during the robbery, Pulido could be convicted of murder under the felony-murder rule.

He appealed his conviction, arguing that he had not intended to aid and abet the robbery until after Aragon had committed the murder. The California Supreme Court agreed with Pulido's legal argument about whether a person aids and abets a felony *after* the killing has occurred should be criminally liable under the felony-murder rule. According to the California Supreme Court, a "late joiner" in a felony should not be liable for a killing that occurred prior to the time that the person joins the **felonious** enterprise. The jury in the case had not been instructed that Pulido would not be liable for the murder if he formed the intent to participate in the robbery after the murder had taken place. However, when the California Supreme Court reviewed the jury instruction given in the case, the court held that error in the jury instruction did not prejudice the defendant. Therefore, the California Supreme Court affirmed the verdict. *People v. Pulido*, 936 P.2d 1235 (Cal. 1997).

Pulido sought habeas corpus relief, first through the California state courts and then through the **federal courts**. In 2005, the U.S. District Court for the Northern District of California reviewed Pulido's habeas corpus petition and decided to grant the petition. According to the district court, the error in the jury instruction prejudiced Pulido, and so the court granted habeas relief. Under the district court's order, the state was required to vacate the murder conviction and retry Pulido on robbery and auto theft convictions. *Pulido v. Lamarque*, No. C 99-4933 CW (PR), 2005 WL 6142229 (N.D. Cal. Mar. 24, 2005). The state appealed the district court's decision to the Ninth Circuit Court of Appeals. In a **per curiam** opinion, a three-judge panel affirmed the Ninth Circuit's ruling. According to the panel, the state trial court had made a "structural" error, meaning that the form of the instruction allowed the jury to convict a defendant on a constitutionally invalid ground. When an error is considered to be a structural error, the court will set aside a conviction irrespective of whether the error prejudiced the defendant. Because the Ninth Circuit determined that error in the jury instruction regarding the application of felony-murder in Pulido's case was a structural error, the Ninth Circuit agreed with the district court that the conviction should be set aside. *Pulido v. Chrones*, 487 F.3d 669 (9th Cir. 2007).

The case reached the Supreme Court in 2008. Before the Court, both parties agreed that the error in this case was not a structural error, thus contradicting the Ninth Circuit's analysis. In a per curiam opinion, the Court vacated the Ninth Circuit's decision and remanded the case. According to the Court's opinion, the lower federal courts should have determined whether the error in the jury instruction prejudiced Pulido. *Hedgpeth v. Pulido*, ___ U.S. ___, 129 S. Ct. 530, ___ L. Ed. 2d ___ (2008). Justice JOHN PAUL STEVENS, joined by Justices DAVID SOUTER and RUTH BADER GINSBURG, dissented. According to the dissent, the Court merely corrected a misnomer in the Ninth Circuit's opinion. The dissent argued that the district court had analyzed the case under the correct standard and the Supreme Court had made a mistake in remanding the case to the Ninth Circuit to repeat the analysis.

Puckett v. United States

Thousands of criminal cases in the United States never make it to trial because the parties (prosecutors and defendant) have agreed to a "plea" arrangement. For example, in return for not having to prove its case and go through the expense of trial, prosecution instead may agree to accept a guilty plea from the defendant for a lesser charge, or a guilty plea as charged for one or more crimes in return for other charges being dropped. It is important to note that only the judge in the case can accept or reject the plea arrangement; prosecution can only recommend to the judge that the parties have agreed to one. Further, in placing an accepted plea arrangement on record, evidence is taken in **open court** (in the form of testimony from the defendant) that he or she fully acknowledges and understands that by pleading guilty, he or she is waiving the right to a trial on the matter.

In *Puckett v. United States*, No. 07-9712, 556 U.S. ___ (2009), prosecution agreed to recommend a reduced sentence in return for a guilty plea as charged. The guilty plea was entered on the record (as above). However, prior to the sentencing hearing (set for a subsequent date), defendant committed another crime. Therefore, at sentencing, prosecutors for the Government

reneged on the plea deal and did not recommend a reduced sentence. Defense counsel did not object on the record (that the Government had broken its plea deal promise), and defendant was sentenced to 262 months in prison.

Generally, if an error is "not preserved on the record," i.e., counsel has not objected to it at the time that it happens, it is considered waived. Notwithstanding, Federal Rule of **Civil Procedure** (FRCP) 52(b) nonetheless provides for **appellate** review of a "plain error that affects substantial rights," even if it was not raised at the trial court. The question before the U.S. SUPREME COURT in *Puckett* was whether FRCP 52(b)'s "plain-error standard of review" applies when defense fails to preserve a claim that the government breached a plea agreement?

In a 7-2 majority opinion, the Supreme Court said yes. However, Puckett did not benefit from the decision, for the Court also found that he failed to meet all prongs of the standard (see below), in that Puckett's "substantial rights" had not been affected. (A party's substantial rights are affected if the alleged "error" affects the outcome of the court proceedings or adjudication.)

In 2002, James Benjamin Puckett was charged in the U.S. **District Court** for the Northern District of Texas with bank **robbery** and the use of a firearm in the commission of a crime of violence (which invokes a higher minimum sentence). In return for pleading guilty to both counts, the government agreed to support a three-level reduction in his offense level (for "accepting responsibility" for his crimes), which would make him eligible for a shorter prison term.

Puckett's sentencing was delayed more than two years, after he had a seizure and was treated for a benign brain tumor. Due to the long delay in sentencing, the district court ordered Puckett's probation officer to interview him and update the original pre-sentence investigation report. Unfortunately, Puckett admitted to the probation officer his role in helping another inmate defraud the U.S. POSTAL SERVICE during the time between plea deal and sentencing. The probation officer noted this in his report and recommended that Puckett not receive an offense-level reduction, and he did not.

Puckett appealed to the U.S. Court of Appeals for the Fifth Circuit. Among other things, he argued that the district court abused its discretion in not allowing him to withdraw his guilty plea because the government's breach of the plea agreement made the agreement unenforceable and his waiver of trial invalid.

The Fifth Circuit reviewed the matter under the "plain-error standard." This required Puckett, on appeal, to show that (1) the error had not been affirmatively "waived;" (2) the error was clear and obvious; (3) and this affected Puckett's substantial rights. While the Court found the first two prongs of the standard were met, it concluded that Puckett's substantial rights had not been affected. This was because, at the sentencing hearing, the district court judge had stated on the record that "acceptance-of-responsibility" reductions in offense level were so rare as "to be unknown" where a defendant has continued to engage in criminal activity while awaiting sentencing for a previous crime. In other words, even if the government had

recommended a reduced offense level, the district court would likely have rejected it because of Puckett's recent criminal activity. Therefore, he had suffered no adverse consequence to any substantial right as a result of the government's breach of the plea deal.

The U.S. Supreme Court affirmed. Justice Scalia wrote the majority opinion, in which he was joined by all except Justices Souter and Stevens, who dissented. The dissenting opinion agreed with the majority that the plain error standard was the proper test, but disagreed as to what interest (of Puckett's) was at stake. The majority opinion held that the substantial right affected was the length of incarceration for the offense charged. The dissent opined that the "relevant effect is conviction in the absence of a trial or compliance with the terms of the plea agreement dispensing with the Government's obligation to prove its case."

DEPARTMENT OF JUSTICE

The Department of Justice (DOJ) is the executive-branch department responsible for handling the legal work of the federal government.

Justice Department Probe Finds Misconduct in Politically-Motivated Hirings

On July 28, 2008, two watchdog offices within the U.S. Department of Justice (DOJ) jointly released a scathing investigation report that found politicized and discriminatory hiring practices within that Department. Specifically, the U.S. Office of the Inspector General and the Office of Professional Responsibility determined that Monica Goodling, former White House Liaison (and Senior Counsel to then-Attorney General Alberto Gonzales), as well as D. Kyle Sampson, former Chief of Staff, had been evaluating and assessing prospective career job candidates according to their political affiliations. The 140-page report concluded that Goodling's and Sampson's actions constituted illegal misconduct in violation of JUSTICE DEPARTMENT policy. Gonzales consistently advised investigators that he had no knowledge of the wrongdoing. Gonzales was cleared of any wrongdoing.

The investigation was triggered in March 2007 following allegations that several U.S. Attorneys were forced to resign for improper reasons, including political purposes. The investigation then expanded to include an allegation that Goodling had discriminated on the basis of political affiliation or political ideology in the hiring process for career Department employees. The allegation named a specific example involving a candidate for an Assistant U.S. Attorney position.

The scope and methodology of the investigation involved interviewing more than 85 individuals and sending written surveys to every person identified as having been interviewed by Goodling or others in the OAG, reviewing thousands of documents, and searching e-mail accounts and computer hard drives. The Office of the Attorney General had 25 employees in **fiscal** year 2006. Gonzales, who succeeded JOHN ASHCROFT, served as Attorney General from February 2005 to September 2007.

The report, entitled "An Investigation of Allegations of Politicized Hiring by Monica Goodling and Other Staff in the Office of the Attorney General [OAG]," culminated the one-year probe into the matter. The report's "Introduction" cites Goodling's May 2007 testimony before the U.S. House of Representatives Committee on the Judiciary. In return for a grant of immunity, Goodling gave both a written statement and verbal testimony, acknowledging that she indeed took political considerations into account in assessing candidates for career Department positions.

Goodling's testimony included statements that "[I]n a very small number of cases, I believe that my decisions may have been influenced in part based on political considerations." To wit, Goodling expounded that "[I]n some cases, I learned and considered political information" when assessing candidates who applied for temporary detail positions in the Office of the Deputy Attorney General, the Office of Legal Policy, the Office of the Associate Attorney General, the National Security Division, and the Executive Office for United States Attorneys." She also admitted taking political considerations into account when reviewing resumes and/or soliciting applications for immigration judges and members for the Board of Immigration Appeals.

It is important to note that not all attorney positions within the Department are nonpolitical. The DOJ has several political attorney positions, including presidential appointees requiring Senate approval (e.g., U.S. Attorneys and Assistant Attorneys General), and Schedule C positions commonly referred to as political appointments. However, most positions are designated by the Office of Personnel Management (OPM) as Schedule A positions "which are not of a confidential or policy-determining character," 5 C.F.R. §213.3101 and §213.3102(d). These are considered career positions, and include trial attorneys, Assistant U.S. Attorneys, and immigration judges.

The investigative report expressly stated,

> "It is not improper to consider political or ideological affiliations in making hiring decisions for political positions. However, both Department policy and federal law prohibit discrimination in hiring for career positions on the basis of political affiliations. Our investigation found that Goodling improperly subjected candidates for certain career positions to the same politically based evaluation she used on candidates for political positions, in violation of federal law and Department policy."

Further, the report concluded that Goodling often used political or ideological affiliations to select, reject, or extend career attorney candidates for temporary details to Department offices.

But the most systematic use of political or ideological affiliation as an improper factor in considering career candidates involved the selection of immigration judges, which implicated Kyle Sampson. In 2004, Sampson had implemented a new process for the selection of immigration judges, ensuring that all were selected by OAG staff, using the AG's direct

appointment authority, which Goodling and her predecessor, Jan Williams, utilized. Sampson told investigators he implemented the new policy because he believed that immigration judges were political appointees not subject to civil service rules. He also stated that his belief was premised on advice he had been given by the Deputy Director in the Executive Office for Immigration Review, but this was not supported or collaborated by other evidence/findings.

In summary, the investigation concluded that Goodling, Sampson, and Williams "committed misconduct" by considering political and ideological affiliations in soliciting and selecting various candidates for civil service and career positions outside of the parameters of political appointments. It further concluded that Goodling had committed misconduct in providing inaccurate information (in the form of a denial) when responding to requests by a Civil Division attorney who was defending a lawsuit brought by one of the unsuccessful candidates for immigration judge.

Before leaving office, AG Gonzales approved several new processes restoring prior (and implementing new) hiring and selection practices intended to restore confidence and prevent recurrence of improper conduct. The investigation report made several additional recommendations which the successive Attorney General, Michael Mukasey, announced his Department would implement.

Goodling had taken an indefinite leave of absence in March 2007 and formally resigned on April 6, 2007. In September 2008, members of the Virginia Bar Association drafted a complaint asking the Bar to conduct an ethics investigation of Goodling. However, AG Mukasey indicated that he would not prosecute Goodling or the others, when he spoke before the AMERICAN BAR ASSOCIATION (ABA) House of Delegates in August 2008.

DISCRIMINATION

In constitutional law, the grant by statute of particular privileges to a class arbitrarily designated from a sizable number of persons, where no reasonable distinction exists between the favored and disfavored classes. Federal laws, supplemented by court decisions, prohibit discrimination in such areas as employment, housing, voting rights, education, and access to public facilities. They also proscribe discrimination on the basis of race, age, sex, nationality, disability, or religion. In addition, state and local laws can prohibit discrimination in these areas and in others not covered by federal laws.

Ashcroft v. Iqbal

The Supreme Court in 2009 reviewed a case involving a Pakistani Muslim who brought a civil suit against federal officials and agents based on their treatment of him in prison. Following the SEPTEMBER 11TH ATTACKS in 2001, Javaid Iqbal was detained on criminal charges and was soon moved into a high security facility. Iqbal claimed that he was entitled to damages based on deprivation of his constitutional rights, but the Supreme Court ruled that his case should have been dismissed because he failed to plead his case properly.

In the months following the September 11th attacks, the FEDERAL BUREAU OF INVESTIGA-TION (FBI) and other agencies engaged in a massive investigation to find those responsible for the attacks and to prevent future attacks. In the first week after the attack, the FBI had received 96,000 tips and other leads regarding potential suspects. The FBI assigned more than 4,000 special agents and about 3,000 other personnel to the investigation. The FBI questioned more than a thousand potential suspects, and the FBI held 762 of these suspects on immigration charges. Agents designated 184 of these suspects to be of "high interest" to the investigation.

The details of the investigation were subject to dispute. According to Iqbal's complaint, the FBI classified many of the men considered "of high interest" based on the suspect's race, religion, and national origin. On November 2, 2001, agents with the FBI and the Immigration and Naturalization Service arrested Iqbal, a Pakistani Muslim, and charged him with conspiracy to defraud the United States and **fraud** with identification.

Authorities initially held Iqbal in the general prison population at the Metropolitan Detention Center (MDC) in Brooklyn, New York. Two months after his initial arrest, he was moved to a special section of the facility known as the Administrative Maximum Special Housing Unit ("ADMAX SHU"). Those inmates who were placed ADMAX SHU were subject to the most restrictive security conditions allowable

under regulations of the Federal Bureau of Prisons regulations. Detainees in this facility were confined to their cells for 23 hours per day, and during the one hour that they were allowed outside their cell, they were handcuffed and placed in leg irons. All interactions were strictly non-contact, and the detainees were escorted by four officers and otherwise monitored by video cameras. The detainees were cut off from outside communications for several weeks at a time.

According to Iqbal's complaint, prison officials did not review the files of those assigned to ADMAX SHU. Instead, the detainees were left in the facility until FBI officials approved their release to the general population. Several suspects were left in ADMAX SHU for months even without evidence linking the suspect to terrorism. Iqbal claimed that he was subject to numerous injustices while assigned to ADMAX SHU. He claimed he was kept in solitary confinement and that the staff deliberately left the lights on 24 hour a day. The staff also made the climate conditions uncomfortable but turning on the air conditioning during the winter and by turning on the heat during the summer. While in custody, Iqbal claimed he lost 40 pounds due to inadequate food. He also said he was beaten on two occasions and that he was denied medical care after the second beating in March 2002. Moreover, he said he was subject to several strip and body-cavity searches. Iqbal pleaded guilty to the charges. After his pleading, he was released to the general prison population. He was released from prison on January 15, 2003 and was subsequently removed to Pakistan.

In May 2004, Iqbal filed a *Bivens* action pursuant to the U.S. Supreme Court's decision in *Bivens v. Six Unknown Federal Narcotics Agents*, 403 U.S. 388, 91 S. Ct. 1999, 29 L. Ed. 2d 619 (1971). This type of action allows a plaintiff to recover damages when federal agents have violated the plaintiff's constitutional rights. Iqbal asserted 21 causes of action against 34 federal officials along with 19 "John Doe" corrections officers at MDC.

Iqbal's complaint focuses on his treatment while he was assigned to the ADMAX SHU. Many of the defendants were employees of the prison, including correctional officers who had day-to-day contact with Iqbal as well as wardens at the prison. Also named where high-ranking officials within the federal government. These officials included former U.S. Attorney General JOHN ASHCROFT and former FBI director Robert Mueller. Other defendants included agents and officials with the FBI. According to Iqbal, Ashcroft and Mueller, along with the other members of the FBI, had given directives and developed policies that led to the arrest of Iqbal and many others based on race, religion, or national origin. These types of classifications, Iqbal asserted, violated his rights under the First and Fifth Amendments.

Ashcroft, Mueller, and the other defendants filed motions to dismiss the suit on several grounds, including qualified immunity. According to the defendants, the events that followed the September 11th attacks created special circumstances that justified their actions, including the actions taken towards Iqbal. Moreover, the defendants argued that Iqbal had failed to state specific allegations that showed the defendants' involvement in clearly established unconstitutional conduct.

After the U.S. **District Court** for the Eastern District of New York denied the defendant's motion to dismiss (with a few exceptions), the defendants appealed the case to the Second **Circuit Court** of Appeals. The Second Circuit reviewed the case in light of the Supreme Court's decision in *Bell Atlantic Corp. v. Twombly*, 550 U.S. 544, 127 S. Ct. 1955, 167 L. Ed. 2d 929 (2007), which focused on the standard under which a complaint is sufficiently detailed to survive a motion to dismiss. The Second Circuit rejected the defendants' claims that Iqbal's pleadings were inadequate, and thus the **appellate court** affirmed most of the district court's decision. *Iqbal v. Hasty*, 490 F.3d 143 (2d Cir. 2007).

The Supreme Court agreed to review the case. In a 5-4 opinion, the Court reversed the Second Circuit. The majority opinion written by Justice Anthony Kennedy reviewed the pleading standard in *Twombly*. Following *Twombly*, the Court engaged in a two-pronged approach to reviewing whether the plaintiff's pleadings should survive a motion to dismiss. The first prong focuses on whether the Court should determine whether legal conclusions stated in the complaint are grounded on well-pleaded factual allegations. The second prong focuses on whether the pleading states a plausible **claim for relief**. Regarding the first prong, the general principle that a court reviewing a motion to dismiss must accept all allegations as true does not apply to legal conclusions. Thus, "[t]hreadbare recitals of the elements of a **cause of action**, supported by mere conclusory statements, do not suffice."

According to Kennedy, Iqbal's complaint could not satisfy the first prong under *Twombly*. Kennedy concluded that many of Iqbal's allegations were merely conclusory and that the Court should not assume that the facts were true. Because of inadequate pleadings, the Court concluded that Iqbal had failed to state a claim for purposeful and unlawful discrimination. *Ashcroft v. Iqbal*, ___ U.S. ___, 129 S. Ct. 1937, ___ L. Ed. 2d ___ (2009).

Voting for the Supreme Court's decision was based largely on the division between the conservative and liberal views of the justices. Joining Kennedy on the majority was Chief Justice JOHN ROBERTS and justices Clarence Thomas, Samuel Alito, and ANTONIN SCALIA. Among the others on the Court, justices DAVID SOUTER and STEPHEN BREYER both filed dissenting opinions, and justice RUTH BADER GINSBURG and JOHN PAUL STEVENS joined Justice Souter's dissent. Souter argued that the Court misapplied *Twombly* and that the Court should have taken into account concessions made by Ashcroft and Mueller regarding their potential liability.

Congress Enacts Genetic Information Nondiscrimination Act

The Genetic Information Nondiscrimination Act of 2008 (GINA), Pub. L. No. 110-343, 122 Stat. 3765, was signed into law on May 21, 2008. The sections on health insurance take effect May 2009, and those relating to employers will take effect by November 2009. The law deals with concerns about discrimination that might keep some people from getting useful genetic tests that could benefit their health. The law also enables people to take part in research studies without worrying that their DNA information might be used against them when applying for health insurance or for a job. However, the law does not cover life insurance, disability insurance and long-term care insurance. The federal law sets a minimum standard of protection that must be met in all states, but it does not weaken the protections provided by any state law dealing with these issues.

The term "genetic information" is broadly defined under GINA. The term is defined to mean with respect to any individual, information about the individual's genetic tests; the genetic tests of family members of the individual; and the manifestation of a disease or disorder in family members of the individual. GINA states that any reference to genetic information concerning an individual or family member includes genetic information of a fetus carried by a pregnant woman and an embryo legally held by an individual or family member utilizing an assisted reproductive technology.

Title I of GINA deals with genetic nondiscrimination in health insurance. The law amends the EMPLOYEE RETIREMENT INCOME SECURITY ACT of 1974 (ERISA), the PUBLIC HEALTH SERVICE Act (PHSA), and the INTERNAL REVENUE CODE to prohibit a group health plan from adjusting premium or contribution amounts for a group on the basis of genetic information. GINA prohibits a group health plan from requesting or requiring an individual or family member of an individual from undergoing a genetic test. However, if a test is conducted this section mandates that the plan request only the minimum amount of information necessary to accomplish the intended purpose. This title also prohibits a group health plan from requesting, requiring, or purchasing genetic information for underwriting purposes.

Companies that violate these provisions of GINA face great liabilities. Under amendments to ERISA made by GINA, group health plan noncompliance can attach liability to both the plan and its sponsor. Participants or beneficiaries will be able to sue group health plans for damages and equitable relief. If the participant or beneficiary can show an alleged violation would result in irreparable harm to the individual's health, the participant or beneficiary may not have to exhaust administrative remedies before bringing suit.

Individuals may file private lawsuits, and the government may impose penalties against employers and other sponsors of group health plans that violate applicable requirements of GINA of up to $500,000.

GINA also amended the Health Insurance Portability and Accountability Act (HIPAA). Among its provisions, HIPAA imposes privacy rules on patient information collected and maintained by group health plans, health insurers, health care providers, and health care clearinghouses. Under GINA, information that falls within its definition of "genetic information" is now protected health information for purposes of HIPAA. HIPPA privacy violations can trigger the imposition of civil penalties of $100 per violation, up to $250,000 by the Department of Health & Human Services Office of Civil Rights, criminal prosecution leading to imprisonment for up to 10 years, or both.

GINA also applies to employers, employment agencies, labor organizations or joint labor-management committees. Title II prohibits employment discrimination on the basis of genetic information against an employee, individual, or member including: (1) for an employer, by failing to hire or discharging an employee or otherwise discriminating against an employee with respect to the compensation, terms, conditions, or privileges of employment; (2) for an employment agency, by failing or refusing to refer an individual for employment; (3) for a labor organization, by excluding or expelling a member from the organization; (4) for an employment agency, labor organization, or joint labor-management committee, by causing or attempting to cause an employer to discriminate against a member in violation of this Act; or (5) for an employer, labor organization, or joint labor-management committee, by discriminating against an individual in admission to, or employment in, any program established to provide apprenticeships or other training or retraining. Under GINA, employees and individuals can sue to obtain damages and other relief as is currently recoverable for other prohibited employment practices under Title VII of the Civil Rights Act of 1964 and other nondiscrimination laws.

Section 206 of GINA requires an employer, employment agency, labor organization, or joint labor-management committee that possesses any genetic information about an employee or member to maintain such information in separate files and treat such information as a confidential medical record. Section 208 provides that disparate impact on the basis of genetic information does not establish a **cause of action** under GINA.

The law also establishes the Genetic Nondiscrimination Study Commission to review the developing science of genetics. Six years after enactment of the Act, this Commission will make recommendations to Congress regarding

President Barack Obama, seated, presents pen used to sign Lilly Ledbetter Bill, to Lilly Ledbetter, January 29, 2009.

AP IMAGES

whether to provide a disparate impact cause of action under this Act. It also authorizes appropriations to the EQUAL EMPLOYMENT OPPORTUNITY COMMISSION (EEOC) to carry out this section.

Congress Enacts the Lilly Ledbetter Fair Pay Act

In January 2009, Congress enacted the Lilly Ledbetter Fair Pay Act of 2009, Pub. L 111-2, 123 Stat. 5. The law overturned the Supreme Court decision in *Ledbetter v. Goodyear Tire & Rubber Company, Inc.*, __U.S.__, 127 S.Ct.

2162, 167 L.Ed.2d 982 (2007) that required employees to file within 180 days of a specific allegedly discriminatory event, such as receiving a smaller raise because of her gender. Under this ruling, employees could no longer recover by establishing a pattern of discrimination that reached back many years. Though the case involved sex discrimination, the ruling applied to Title VII's other protected classes.

Lilly Ledbetter worked as a supervisor at Goodyear Tire and Rubber's plant in Gadsden, Alabama from 1979 to her retirement in 1998. During her tenure she worked as an area manager, a position dominated by men. When she started in 1979 her salary was equal to men who did substantially similar work, but over time she earned less than other managers. By 1997 Ledbetter was the only female area manager, with a monthly salary of approximately $3,700. The lowest-paid male area manager earned $4,300 while the highest paid manager earned $5,200. In July 1998 Ledbetter filed a charge of discrimination with the EEOC, alleging she was underpaid because of her sex. After she took an early retirement in November 1998, Ledbetter filed a federal civil rights lawsuit under Title VII and the Equal Pay Act (EPA), 29 U.S.C.A. § 206(d). The federal **district court** dismissed her EPA claim but allowed the Title VII claim to proceed to trial. At trial she introduced evidence that suggested she had been given poor job evaluations because she was a woman. These evaluations result in lower raises than her male counterparts. The jury found in Ledbetter's favor and awarded her backpay and damages. The company appealed to the Eleventh **Circuit Court** of Appeals, which reversed the verdict. The appeals court held that the company had not discriminated against Ledbetter in 1997 and 1998 during the EEOC charging period. The remainder of her claims was barred by the 180-day **statute of limitations**, thereby eliminating almost 20 years of alleged discrimination. Ledbetter appealed to the Supreme Court.

The Supreme Court, in a 5-4 decision, upheld the Eleventh Circuit ruling. The Court concluded that a line of Title VII cases supported the conclusion that unequal pay claims must be filed within 180 days of the allegedly discriminatory act. Though the Court admitted that the 180-day deadline is "short by any measure," it believed that Congress had made its intent clear that prompt resolution of these types of claims was important. In Ledbetter's case, it would be unfair for Goodyear to try to defend itself for actions that allegedly occurred many years before. The better course was to acknowledge that "strict adherence to the procedural requirements specified by the legislature is the best guarantee of evenhanded administration of the law." Because she had failed to show that Goodyear had intentionally discriminated against her in the 180-day period before she complained to the EEOC, she could not recover under Title VII. The Court noted, however, that alleged

sex discrimination in pay could be pursued under the Equal Pay Act, which does allow plaintiffs to show a long pattern of unfair pay disparity.

Justice RUTH BADER GINSBURG, in a dissenting opinion joined by three other justices argued that the Court had ignored the realities of the workplace. Employees rarely know the pay of the co-workers and may only find out many years later. She contended that the Court "does not comprehend, or is indifferent to, the insidious way in which women can be victims of pay discrimination." Pay disparities often grew in small increments that, over time, lead a person to suspect that discrimination is the cause. Justice Ginsberg, noting that the majority believed it was upholding the intent of Congress, suggested that this "cramped interpretation of Title VII" should be corrected by Congress. The 1991 Civil Rights Act overruled several Supreme Court decisions and Justice Ginsburg suggested that "Once again, the ball is in Congress' court.

Congress enacted the Lilly Ledbetter Fair Pay Act in early 2009, making it the second piece of legislation signed by President Barack Obama. Ledbetter, who had campaigned for the president, was invited to the White House for the signing. The act was effective retroactively to the date of the Supreme Court decision: May 27, 2007. Congress, in its findings, stated that the Supreme Court ruling "significantly impairs **statutory** protections against discrimination in compensation that Congress established and that have been bedrock principles of American law for decades. The Ledbetter decision undermines those statutory protections by unduly restricting the time period in which victims of discrimination can challenge and recover for discriminatory compensation decisions or other practices, contrary to the intent of Congress."

The act states that an unlawful employment practice occurs, with respect to discrimination in compensation," when a discriminatory compensation decision or other practice is adopted, when an individual becomes subject to a discriminatory compensation decision or other practice, or when an individual is affected by application of a discriminatory compensation decision or other practice, including each time wages, benefits, or other compensation is paid, resulting in whole or in part from such a decision or other practice." Congress also made this provision applicable to the Age Discrimination in Employment Act, the Americans with Disabilities Act, and the Rehabilitation Act.

DNA

Osborne v. District Attorney's Office for the Third Judicial District

Use of DNA testing to evaluate biological evidence has become widespread throughout the U.S. judicial system. However, a criminal defendant's right to have the evidence tested is not without limitations. In 2009, the U.S. SUPREME COURT determined that the State of Alaska was not required to release evidence so that a convicted felon could conduct DNA testing of the evidence. In so ruling, the Court distinguished between a defendant's rights to testing before trial and the defendant's post-conviction rights.

The case arose from an incident in March 1993 in Alaska. A female prostitute with the initials K.G. was taken by two men to a secluded area of Anchorage. She was forced at gunpoint to perform sexual acts on the two men. One of the men did not wear a condom, but the other did. After the incident, K.G. refused to leave the car. One of the men hit her in the head with a gun, and the other man choked her. K.G. managed to leave the car, but the men beat her and shot at her. She pretended to be dead, and the men left her in the snow. A passing car later picked up K.G. and took her home, and though K.G. did not wish to cooperate initially, she eventually told her story to the police.

During a physical examination, examiners collected hair and blood samples. The examiners did not perform a vaginal examination, though, because one of the attackers wore a condom and because K.G. had bathed several times since the attack. Investigators discovered a used blue condom, part of a condom wrapper, a spent shell casing, and K.G.'s pants that were stained with blood. The condom and shell casings were found very close to one another and near bloody patches of snow. The investigators could also identify tire tracks made not only by K.G.'s rescuers, but also by the assailants.

One week after the incident, military police stopped Dexter Jackson for a traffic infraction. During the stop, police saw a gun case that

William Osborne, January 26, 2009.
AP IMAGES

could hold a .380-caliber pistol. Police conducted a search of the car and found a box of ammunition as well as a pocketknife. The military police believed that Jackson and his passenger at the time of the stop (who turned out to be an innocent **third party**) matched the descriptions of K.G.'s attackers, and so the police contacted Anchorage Police. Jackson thereafter told Anchorage Police that the other assailant was William Osborne.

Police brought K.G. in to assist in the investigation. She identified Jackson and Osborne from photographic arrays. She also identified Osborne as the one who was most likely the passenger in the car on the night of the attack. K.G. was also able to identify Jackson's car as well as the pocketknife found in Jackson's car. Police matched tire tracks to Jackson's car, and ballistics tests showed that the shell casings found at the crime scene came from Jackson's pistol.

The state's crime lab tested the sperm found on the used condom. The type of DNA testing that the lab used was able to eliminate K.G., Jackson, and another man as possible donors. The results showed that the sperm could have been Osborne's but the results could have been consistent with one out of every six or seven

African-American males. A more discriminating type of DNA testing was available during pretrial, but the crime lab decided not to run the second test. At that time, the crime lab needed a better quality sample to perform a competent test. Osborne's defense counsel met with the state crime lab's DNA expert. The counsel also researched articles about DNA testing. Because he believed that Osborne stood a better chance at trial without the more discriminating DNA testing, defense counsel did not pursue the matter further.

Several other items of evidence also pointed to Osborne as the accomplice. Hair samples found on K.G. sweatshirt were consistent with those of Osborne (though the crime lab did not test these samples). Police also found at the crime scene paper tickets from an arcade, and Osborne had been at that arcade on the night of the attack.

Osborne raised several defenses, arguing that this was a case of mistaken identity and that he had a credible alibi for his whereabouts on the night of the attack. Osborne also tried to attack K.G.'s testimony, noting that she was not wearing her glasses on the night of the attack and that her stories before and during trial had inconsistencies. The jury, however, rejected Osborne's defenses and convicted him of kidnapping, first-degree assault, first-degree sexual assault. Osborne appealed his conviction to the Alaska Court of Appeals, which affirmed. Osborne did not seek review from the Alaska Supreme Court.

Osborne later sought post-conviction relief in an Alaska Superior Court, arguing that his counsel had been ineffective for failing to pursue DNA testing. The superior court denied relief. Osborne later appealed this decision, leading to two cases before the Alaska Court of Appeals. In 2007, the Alaska Court of Appeals ruled against Osborne, and the Alaska Supreme Court denied Osborne's petition for the high court to hear the case.

At the same time that he sought relief in the Alaska state courts, Osborne filed an action in federal court against several officials in Anchorage. Osborne's principal argument was that these officials had violated his constitutional rights by depriving him of post-conviction access to evidence so that the evidence could be subjected to DNA testing. In his complaint, which was brought under 42 U.S.C. § 1983,

Osborne wanted to subject the DNA evidence from the condom and a hair sample found on K.G.'s shirt.

The case continued in the U.S. **District Court** for the District of Alaska, as well as the Ninth **Circuit Court** of Appeals. In 2006, the district court concluded that Osborne had a "very limited constitutional right to the testing sought." Several of the officials appealed the decision to the Ninth Circuit, which affirmed the district court's decision. According to the Ninth Circuit, Osborne had a due process right to access to the biological evidence used against him at trial. The Ninth Circuit relied on the case of *Brady v. Maryland*, 373 U.S. 83, 83 S. Ct. 1194, 10 L. Ed. 2d 215, which held that a prosecutor had the duty to disclose exculpatory evidence. *Osborne v. District Attorney's Office for the Third Judicial District*, 521 F.3d 1118 (9th Cir. 2008).

The Supreme Court agreed to review the case. In a 5-4 decision, the Court reversed the Ninth Circuit. Writing for the majority, Chief Justice JOHN ROBERTS noted that DNA testing "has an unparalleled ability both to exonerate the wrongly convicted and to identify the guilty." On the other hand, Roberts noted that the availablity of this testing does not mean that every criminal conviction based on biological evidence should be cast in doubt. Alaska is one of only a few states that has not enacted a **statute** directed specifically at DNA testing, though the Alaska courts have undertaken to develop standards regarding this testing.

The Court noted that though Osborne had a liberty interest in obtaining the DNA evidence, this interest is limited in the post-conviction context. After concluding that Alaska's post-conviction procedures were adequate, the Court determined that the Anchorage officials had not violated Osborne's due process rights for failing to provide access to the evidence. The Court also concluded that the Ninth Circuit's reliance on *Brady v. Maryland* was misplaced because that case only applies in the preconviction context. The Court therefore reversed the Ninth Circuit's decision. *District Attorney's Office for the Third Judicial District v. Osborne*, No. 08-6, 2009 WL 1685601 (2009).

Justice JOHN PAUL STEVENS dissented, arguing that the Court had "blessed" Alaska's "arbitrary denial of the evidence Osborne" sought on "highly suspect grounds." Stevens noted that Osborne had merely requested the opportunity to test the DNA evidence at his own expense.

DOUBLE JEOPARDY

A second prosecution for the same offense after acquittal or conviction or multiple punishments for same offense. The evil sought to be avoided by prohibiting double jeopardy is double trial and double conviction, not necessarily double punishment.

Yeager v. United States

The Double Jeopardy Clause of the Fifth Amendment to the U.S. Constitution protects an individual from being prosecuted or tried by the government more than once for the same offense. A parallel doctrine, "collateral estoppel," prohibits parties from re-litigating issues of fact that have already been determined in a previous court proceeding. In *Yeager v. United States*, No. 08-67, 557 U.S. ___ (2009), The U.S. Supreme Court showed how these two doctrines could work together to prevent a re-trial on criminal counts that were the subject of a mistrial because of a hung jury.

A federal district court jury acquitted Yeager and other defendants of conspiracy, wire fraud, and securities fraud. However (as to Yeager), the jury was hung on 20 counts of insider trading and 99 counts of money laundering, and the district court declared a mistrial on these counts. Four months later, government prosecutors recharged defendant Yeager on several of the insider trading and money laundering counts. Yeager moved to dismiss the charges against him on the basis that, if the jury had already acquitted him on fraud counts, they had already necessarily decided that he did not have the requisite "insider information" required to prove fraud. In other words, argued Yeager, the government was precluded from retrying him on this issue. Was this Double Jeopardy?

Both the district court and U.S. Court of Appeals for the Fifth Circuit said no. Collateral estoppel on the underlying factual scenario relating to both charges did not bar retrial in Yeager's case. But the U.S. Supreme Court, by a 6-3 majority, found otherwise and reversed.

As background, Yeager served as senior vice president of strategic development for Enron Broadband Services, an acquired telecommunications business of the Enron Corporation. In the summer of 1999, Enron circulated press releases touting the superiority of its new fiber-optic telecommunications system. At the company's annual equity analysts' conference on January 20, 2000, Yeager and some of the other defendants allegedly made false and misleading statements about the value and performance of the telecommunications project. One day later, Enron's stock price rose from $54 to $67. The following day, it soared to $72. At that point, Yeager sold more than 100,000 shares of his own personal stock and within six months had sold an additional 600,000 shares. Ultimately, his stock sales generated more than $54 million in proceeds and $19 million in personal profit.

In the end, the value of the telecommunications project proved illusory. The telecommunications system touted to the public was riddled with technological problems and was never fully developed. In 2004, a grand jury indicted Yeager on 126 counts of five different federal offenses (as above). The government's theory was that Yeager and others intentionally deceived the public about the telecommunications system in order to inflate the value of Enron stock and ultimately enrich themselves for their own personal benefit, resulting in the fraud charges.

Yeager additionally was charged with insider trading was also for selling his own Enron stock while in possession of non-public information about the telecommunication system's true performance and its true value to Enron. The money laundering charge stemmed from various transactions Yeager conducted with the proceeds of his stock sales.

After the government re-charged Yeager on the insider trading and money-laundering counts, the district court denied Yeager's motion and the Fifth Circuit affirmed in March 2008. The appellate court noted that Yeager had the burden of proving that the jury necessarily found him not guilty of insider trading (which it had not; it was hung on this issue). Since the jury had found him not guilty on other related charges, it certainly had been acting rationally and could just as easily have found him not guilty of insider trading. But instead, there was a hung jury on that count. Therefore, it was unclear what the jury's rationale was as to these counts and Yeager could be retried for them.

On appeal to the U.S. Supreme Court, Yeager argued that the impossible burden placed on him by the Fifth Circuit Court of Appeals was inconsistent with the Fifth Amendment's protection against Double Jeopardy. The Supreme Court's majority agreed. The majority opinion characterized the question before it as "whether an apparent inconsistency between a jury's verdict of acquittal on some counts and its failure to return a verdict on other counts affects the preclusive force of the acquittals under the Double Jeopardy Clause of the Fifth Amendment."

Justice Stevens, writing for the 6-3 majority said, "The fact that petitioner has already survived one trial should be a factor in favor of, rather than against, applying a Double Jeopardy bar."

Both the Fifth Circuit and the Supreme Court acknowledged that there was an apparent inconsistency between the jury's verdict of acquittal on the fraud counts and its failure to return a verdict on the other counts. However, the Supreme Court, in reversing the Fifth Circuit, said that the inconsistency did not affect the acquittals' "preclusive force under the Double Jeopardy Clause."

Importantly, the Supreme Court said that this case was controlled by *Ashe v. Swenson*, 397 U.S. 436. Clearly in that case, the Court had expressly held that the Double Jeopardy Clause prevented the government from re-litigating any issue that was necessarily decided by a jury's acquittal in a prior trial.

A jury's verdict of acquittal represents its collective judgment regarding all the evidence and arguments presented to it, said the Court. Thus, if the possession of insider information was a critical issue of ultimate fact in all of the charges against Yeager, a jury verdict that necessarily decided that issue in his favor on some of the counts protected him from prosecution for any other counts for which that was an essential element. Accordingly, in the present case, the Supreme Court characterized Yeager's insider trading and money-laundering counts (undecided upon by a previous jury) as "non events" that should be given no weight in the issue preclusion analysis.

Justice Stevens was joined by Chief Justice Roberts and Justices Souter, Ginsburg and Breyer. Justice Kennedy filed a separate opinion concurring in part and concurring in the judgment. Justice Scalia filed a dissenting opinion, joined by Justice Thomas and Alito,

in which he found that the majority's result "neither accords with the original meaning of the Double Jeopardy Clause nor is required by the Court's precedents." (Justice Alito filed his own dissenting opinion, in which Justices Scalia and Thomas also joined, saying that he did not think the Double Jeopardy Clause "precludes retrial on the 'hung' counts.")

DRUGS AND NARCOTICS

Drugs are articles intended for use in the diagnosis, cure, mitigation, treatment, or prevention of disease in humans or animals, and any articles other than food intended to affect the mental or body function of humans or animals. Narcotics are any drugs that dull the senses and commonly become addictive after prolonged use.

Abuelhawa v. United States

In the matter of *Abuelhawa v. United States*, No. 08-192, 556 U.S. ___ (2009), the U.S. SUPREME COURT was asked to interpret the meaning of the term "facilitates" as found in a section of the federal Controlled Substances Act (CSA), 21 USC §843(b). Congress had enacted the CSA as part of the Comprehensive Drug Abuse Prevention and Control Act of 1970, 21 USC §801, *et seq.*. The factual scenario in this case involved the use of a cell phone for the purchase of illegal drugs for personal use. The high court's interpretation meant the difference between a **misdemeanor** vs. **felony** crime for the defendant, Salman Khade Abuelhawa.

FBI agents had been watching Mohammed Said, a suspected drug dealer in the Washington, D.C. area, for some time. After agents obtained a warrant in early 2003 to wiretap Said's cellular phone lines, they listened to all incoming and outgoing calls on his cell phone. They were then able to obtain a warrant to determine the identify of Said's callers involved in any drug transactions.

Said had at least six conversations on his cell phone with defendant Abuelhawa in July 2003. The conversations were spoken in Arabic, but translated by a government language specialist (to the satisfaction of all parties involved). In them, Abuelhawa requested, and arranged to purchase, small amounts of cocaine (one half to one gram) in two separate transactions, with a street value of about $80 to $120. The conversations also involved plans to meet at certain times and places for the purpose of completing the drug sales.

Armed with the wiretapped and recorded conversations as evidence, FBI agents arrested Abuelhawa in October 2003 for purchasing the drugs from Said. Abuelhawa confessed to the purchases from Said and others, and admitted that he had used his cell phone to call Said to set up the drug transactions.

The two purchases (for personal use) were misdemeanors under §844 of the CSA, while Said's two sales were felonies under §841(a)(1) and (b). Notwithstanding, the U.S. government charged, and a federal **grand jury** indicted Abuelahawa on felony charges under §843(b) for "unlawfully, knowingly, and intentionally using a communications facility-a telephone-in committing, causing, and facilitating" the distribution of cocaine. (The actual language of 21 USC §843(b) makes it a felony "to knowingly or intentionally use any communication facility in committing or in causing or facilitating the commission of any [drug crime under the CSA.]")

After a federal jury in the Eastern District of Virginia convicted Abuelhawa on six felony counts, he appealed to the U.S. Court of Appeals for the Fourth Circuit, arguing that his misdemeanor-level drug purchase for personal use could not be construed as "facilitating" Said's felony sales. But the **appellate court** affirmed his conviction, specifically finding that "facilitat[e]" should be given its ordinary meaning, and therefore, Abuelhawa's use of a phone to buy cocaine "facilitated" the commission of a drug "felony," i.e., it made Said's distribution of drugs easier.

In November 2008, the U.S. Supreme Court granted **certiorari** (review) of the case (based on conflict among the circuit courts of appeal over interpretation of 21 USC §843(b)), and in May 2009, reversed the Fourth Circuit.

In essence, the Court held that using a telephone to make a misdemeanor drug purchase did not rise to the level of "facilitating" felony drug distribution in violation of 21 USC §843(b). "We are skeptical," said the Court. Looking at the plain meaning of the word "facilitate," the Court noted that "[a] word in a **statute** may or may not extend to the outer limits of its definitional possibilities" (quoting from *Dolan v. Postal Service*, 546 U.S. 481, 486).

Here, it did not, said the Court. Sweeping the definition of "facilitate" to include one

party as "facilitating" the conduct of another would have the effect of treating both parties to the drug transaction equally (as both having committed felonies). But this did not comport with Congress's intent, since Congress had expressly made the "sale" of drugs a felony under §841(a), and the purchase of drugs for personal use a misdemeanor under §844. Therefore, using the language of §843(b)("to use any communication facility in.facilitat[ing] felony distribution [of drugs]," in order to support the enhancement of a §844 misdemeanor offense to the level of a felony, made the Government's argument "just too unlikely," said the Court. It then reversed the judgment of the Court of Appeals for the Fourth Circuit and remanded the case for further action consistent with its reversal.

Justice Souter delivered the opinion for an unanimous Court.

Voters Approve Marijuana Initiatives

In 2008, voters in Michigan and Massachusetts approved ballot measures focused on marijuana. Voters in Michigan passed a proposal that permitted the cultivation of marijuana for medical purposes. Opponents attempted to defeat the measure with a series of advertisements that appeared just before the November elections. However, more than 60% of the voters approved the measure. A total of 13 states have approved the use of medical marijuana. However, in most of the states, the sale of marijuana remains illegal. Authorities in Michigan struggled with the new law in 2009 as the state tried to work through issues about how the law should be implemented.

For those suffering through chemotherapy, marijuana can offer some relief from pain and nausea. In the 1990s, supporters of the use of marijuana for this purpose pushed legislatures to consider proposals that would allow marijuana for medical use. The first state to approve such a measure was California in 1996. Voters in that state approved a ballot initiative that removed criminal penalties on those who grow, use, or possess marijuana, so long as the use is prescribed by a physician. The U.S. SUPREME COURT later determined that the Controlled Substances Act, 21 U.S.C.A. § 841(a), did not recognize a medical use for marijuana. *United States v. Oakland Cannibis Buyers' Co-op.*, 532 U.S. 483, 121 S. Ct. 1711, 149 L. Ed. 2d 722 (2001). Nevertheless, several other states on the west coast approved similar measures. These states included Alaska (1998), Oregon (1998), and Washington (1998). In the years that followed, more states throughout the nation approved medical marijuana. These states have included: Colorado (2000), Hawaii (2000), Nevada (2000) Maryland (2003), Montana (2004), Vermont (2004), Rhode Island (2006), and New Mexico (2007).

Of the 13 states, nine approved the medical marijuana laws through ballot initiatives. The other states have approved the laws through legislative enactments. As of 2009, the only effort to legalize marijuana for medical uses that has failed occurred in South Dakota.

Several groups supported the ballot measure introduced in Michigan. According to campaign finance reports, proponents raised $1.5 million for the initiative, much of which came from the Washington, D.C.-based Marijuana Policy Project. The major support group in Michigan was the Michigan Coalition for Compassionate Care. This organization had supported a number of citywide medical marijuana initiatives, which ended local prosecution of marijuana possession when used for medical purposes. These cities included Detroit (2004), Ann Arbor (2004), Ferndale (2005), Traverse City (2005), and Flint (2007). A number of the major newspapers in the state also supported the marijuana proposal.

The statewide proposal in Michigan met with resistance. A group known as the Citizens Protecting Michigan's Kids consisted of a number of leaders from medical, law enforcement, and anti-drug organizations, as well as a group of prosecuting attorneys. The chairman of the committee was Judge Bill Schuette of the Michigan Court of Appeals. In the weeks leading up to the November election, opponents ran advertisements showing so-called "pot shops" that became prevalent in California when the medical marijuana law passed there. The opponents of the Michigan measure said they were concerned that the law would lead to the proliferation of the use of marijuana for illicit purposes.

Notwithstanding the opposition, about 63% of the voters approved the Michigan proposal. The law features several provisions that are common among medical marijuana laws. Those who use marijuana for medical purposes must receive approval from their doctors. Those who ware seriously ill with cancer, HIV, AIDS, and glaucoma. Patients are allowed to cultivate their own marijuana, though the law limits how much a person can possess. The law also prohibits the public use of marijuana and driving while under the influence of marijuana.

In April 2009, the Michigan Department of Community Health implemented new rules pursuant to the new law. However, the law's application had already caused problems. Individuals who had been charged with marijuana possession after the law's enactment raised defenses based on the act. The courts were initially uncertain about how to rule on these defenses. Under the rules approved in April, medical marijuana users can receive cards indicating that these users are growing and possessing marijuana for appropriate purposes. However, what effect these cards have when police investigate marijuana possession remains unclear. According to a spokesperson with the Michigan Department of Community Health, "There are so many gray areas in this law I truly believe it's going to create a lot of litigation and instances where they are going to end up in court for a judge to decide what is intended."

Massachusetts voters in 2008 also approved a marijuana-related law, but this law focused on what supporters called a "more sensible" approach to possession of marijuana in the state. Under the proposal, the state would decriminalize possession of one ounce or less of marijuana. Someone caught with less than an ounce of marijuana would receive a citation and no more than a $100 fine. Moreover, the charge would not appear on the person's criminal history. On November 4, voters approved the ballot initiative with 65% support. The principal supporter of this initiative was the Committee for Sensible Marijuana Policy. According to Whitney Taylor, the chairwoman of this committee, "The people were ahead of the politicians on this issue; they recognize and want a more sensible approach to our marijuana policy. They want to focus our limited law enforcement resources on serious and violent crimes. They recognize under the new law that the punishment will fit the offense."

The new law in Massachusetts took effect in January 2009. According to guidelines released by the state's Executive Office of Public Safety and Security, the law applies to any substance that contains tetrahydrocannabinol, or THC, which is what gives users a high.

DUTY OF TONNAGE

A fee that encompasses all taxes and customs duties, regardless of their name or form, imposed upon a vessel as an instrument of commerce for entering, remaining in, or exiting from a port.

Polar Tankers, Inc. v. City of Valdez

Article I of the U.S. Constitution contains a clause preventing states from imposing a duty on tonnage without the consent of Congress. In 2009, the Supreme Court reviewed an **ad valorem** property tax imposed by the City of Valdez, Alaska. In a splintered opinion, the Court determined that the tax was unconstitutional because it violated the Constitution's Tonnage Clause.

The City of Valdez during the 1990s had suffered an erosion of its tax base, which is based heavily on property related to oil and gas. In 1990, the city adopted an **ordinance**, providing for an ad valorem property tax on vessels of at least 95 feet in length. The ordinance applied to such vessels that docked at private facilities in the city. The ordinance also applied to vessels that had "acquired a taxable situs" by principally docking at other ports. The city imposed a tax scheme under which vessels were taxed in an amount that reflected the total **market value** of the property that fairly reflected the property's use in the City of Valdez.

The City applied a formula to calculate this tax. Under the formula, the city determined how many days the vessel spent in Valdez as well as the total number of days that the vessel spent in any port, including Valdez. The owner was required to pay a tax based on 100 percent of the vessel's value times the ratio of the number of days spent in Valdez divided by the total number of days spent in all ports. The ordinance provided for certain exceptions, and the ordinance allowed a taxpayer to request the use of an alternative **apportionment** formula.

Polar Tankers, Inc. ran tanker vessels that transported crude oil. The company would load crude oil from a private terminal in Valdez and then transported the oil to the ports in Washington, California, and Hawaii. After Valdez enacted its ordinance, Polar paid the ad valorem property taxes under protest for the years 2000, 2001, 2002, 2003, and 2004. In 2000, Polar sued the City of Valdez, arguing that the tax was unconstitutional under the Due Process Clause, the **Commerce Clause**, and the Tonnage Clause of the U.S. Constitution.

The Due Process Clause of the FOURTEENTH AMENDMENT provides, "No state … shall … deprive any person of life, liberty, or property, without due process of law." In the context of taxation, the Supreme Court has established that due process requires: (1) that taxed property should have a physical presence and minimal connections with the taxing sovereign, thus giving the sovereign a "tax situs;" and (2) that the tax should be fairly apportioned to "opportunities, benefits, or protection conferred or afforded by the taxing [authority]." *Ott v. Miss. Valley Barge Line Co.*, 336 U.S. 169, 69 S. Ct. 432, 93 L. Ed. 585 (1949). The Supreme Court has established a similar test that applies to whether a tax on mobile property satisfies the Commerce Clause. This test requires: (1) that the property taxed have a "substantial nexus" with the taxing jurisdiction; (2) that the tax is fairly apportioned; (3) that the tax does not discriminate against interstate commerce; and (4) that the tax be fairly related to the services provided by the jurisdiction. *Complete Auto Transit, Inc. v. Brady*, 430 U.S. 274, 97 S. Ct. 1076, 51 L. Ed. 2d 326 (1977).

Article I of the Constitution also contains what is known as the Tonnage Clause. This clause prohibits states from laying "any Duty of Tonnage" without the consent of Congress. The Supreme Court has defined a duty on tonnage as any tax or duty that "operate[s] to impose a charge for the privilege of entering, trading in, or lying in a port." *Clyde Mallory Lines v. Alabama ex rel. State Docks Commission*, 296 U.S. 261, 56 S. Ct. 194, 80 L. Ed. 215 (1935).

In Polar Tankers' case, a superior court in Alaska determined that the ad valorem tax did not violate the Tonnage Clause but that the tax did violate the Due Process and Commerce Clauses. The Superior Court concluded that a constitutional apportionment formula should take into account a ratio of the number of days each vessel spent in Valdez divided by 365 days. Thus, according to the superior court, the city could impose the tax, but the city would have to adjust its formula.

Both the city and Polar appealed parts of the superior court's ruling. The city challenged the court's decision about the application of the Due Process and Commerce Clauses, while Polar challenged the conclusion about the Tonnage Clause. The Alaska Supreme Court reviewed the case in 2008. The Alaska Supreme

Court noted that the *Complete Auto* test regarding the Commerce Clause applied to both the Commerce Clause and Due Process arguments, so the court only applied the *Complete Auto* test to the case. The court disagreed with the superior court that the tax was not fairly apportioned because the city's apportionment formula created a risk of duplicative taxation. The Alaska Supreme Court determined that the Valdez tax was fair even if it produced a risk of duplicative taxation. The court likewise concluded that Polar had attained a **taxable situs** in Valdez. Therefore, the court ruled that the tax did not violate the Commerce Clause or Due Process Clause.

The Alaska Supreme Court then turned its attention to the Tonnage Clause issue. The court noted that a "fairly apportioned property tax is not a tonnage duty." Since the Valdez tax was an ad valorem tax on personal property, the Court ruled that this tax was not a tonnage duty and did not violate the Tonnage Clause. *City of Valdez v. Polar Tankers, Inc.*, 182 P.3d 614 (Alaska 2008).

The U.S. SUPREME COURT reviewed the decision in 2009. In a splintered decisions in which several justices only joined parts of the majority opinion, the Court reversed. Stephen Breyer's majority opinion focused exclusively on the Tonnage Clause issue. Breyer noted that the purpose behind the Tonnage Clause was to restrain the states from exercising taxing power in a manner that injured the interests of the other states. The Valdez tax was closely related to cargo capacity and almost exclusively related to oil tankers. It applied to no other form of personal property. Thus, the Court rejected the city's argument that the tax was truly a property tax, because vessels under the Valdez tax were not taxed in the same manner as other forms of property in the city. *Polar Tankers, Inc. v. City of Valdez, Alaska*, No. 08-310, 2009 WL 165086 (2009).

Chief Justice JOHN ROBERTS and Justice Samuel Alito both concurred. They agreed that the tax violated the Tonnage Clause, but they both argued that the clause's application was broader than what Breyer's opinion suggested. Justice JOHN PAUL STEVENS dissented, arguing that the Valdez tax was not the type of charge that implicates the Tonnage Clause.

ECONOMY

Congress Enacts $789 Billion Stimulus Package

Facing a recession caused in large part to the mortgage meltdown in 2007 and 2008, Congress in February 2009 enacted the American Recovery and Reinvestment Act of 2009, Pub. L. No. 111-5. Passage of the bill occurred just weeks after President Barack Obama took office. Supporters of the bill stressed that it would help the economy and preserve or create millions of jobs. However, critics have charged that the bill's spending provisions are wasteful and will not accomplish the bill's goals.

The economic situation in the United States began to decline in 2006 and 2007 due to a variety of factors. One of the most significant of these factors was the mortgage meltdown caused by subprime lending practices. Major lenders in the U.S. had marketed loans given to those with poor or no credit. These loans had terms that were less favorable to borrowers than conventional, fixed-rate loans. The adjustable-rate mortgage became one of the most popular types of subprime loans. These loans were offered at a certain interest rate, but lenders were able to adjust the interest rate (usually upward) during the life of the loan. Values of homes began a continuous fall in 2006 and 2007, while lenders continued to raise the rates of the adjustable rate mortgages. As a result, the percentage of homeowners who became delinquent in their mortgage payments increased. Mortgage-backed securities eventually lost value, and most of the major Wall Street firms lost millions or billions. Several economists have blamed overall reliance on consumer debt as the principal contributor, with the mortgage crisis making the recession of 2008 more severe.

In response to the recession, President GEORGE W. BUSH signed several bills designed to aid the economy. In February 2008, he signed the Recovery Rebates and Stimulus for the American People Act of 2008, Pub. L. No. 110-85, 121 Stat. 823, which provided tax breaks to individuals and businesses. Congress in July 2008 passed the Housing and Economic Recovery Act of 2008, Pub. L. No. 110-289, 122 Stat. 2654, which was designed to help troubled subprime mortgage companies. Several firms nevertheless either collapsed or nearly collapsed during September 2008, leading Congress to pass the Emergency Economic Stabilization Act of 2008, 110 Pub. L. No. 343, 122 Stat. 3765, which authorized the TREASURY DEPARTMENT to purchase mortgage-backed assets from banks and bank holding companies.

The economy was a major focus of the debates leading to the presidential election in 2008. As a candidate, Obama made several promises about how he would steer the country through the economic turmoil, and his team began working on an economic stimulus proposal even before he took office. Although Obama suggested that 2009 would mark "clean break" from practices in the past, early ideas for economic stimulation focused in part on tax breaks for individuals and businesses. The debate over the stimulus proposals continued after Obama took office on January 20, with experts disagreeing about what parts of the expensive proposal were necessary. Most reports suggested that an economic stimulus bill would cost in the range of $800 billion.

Some commentators suggested that the president needed to "go for something big" with regard to the amount sought from Congress. Many of these commentators suggested that Congress needed to eliminate the "toxic" mortgage debt securities that plagued the economy as a whole. A more moderate effort by Congress may slow down the economy's decline, these commentators said, but such an effort would not provide a long-term cure. Critics of the proposals stressed that the country would effectively mortgage its future by going further in debt. Conversely, lack of action could have the most dire effects, with some experts predicting that unemployment could reach double-digits by 2010 without any congressional action.

After a month of intense debating over the contents of the bill, Congress on February 16, 2009 passed H.R. 1. The vote was largely based on party lines. The House of Representatives approved the bill by a vote of 246-183, while the Senate passed the bill by a vote of 60-38. President Obama signed the bill on February 17. At the time he signed the bill, which provides for $789 billion in spending, Obama commented:

> I don't want to pretend that today marks the end of our economic problems. Nor does it constitute all of what we're going to have to do to turn our economy around. But today does mark the beginning of the end—the beginning of what we need to do to create jobs for Americans scrambling in the wake of layoffs; the beginning of what we need to do to provide relief for families worried they won't be able to pay next month's bills; the beginning of the first steps to set our economy on a firmer foundation, paving the way to long-term growth and prosperity.

A major part of the act was an effort to create or to save jobs. According to several analysts, the act could save three to four million jobs during the two years following act's passage. Supporters also promised that the act would focus on spending, with at least 75% of the stimulus package paid out within 18 months of passage. Among the other major goals of the act include the following:

- Establishment of a plan to double the capacity of generating renewable energy over a three-year period. If the plan meets its goals, renewable energy production in three years would double the level achieved over the last thirty years.

- Modernization of 75% of federal buildings along with two million homes.

- Computerization of every American's health care records within five years.

- Upgrading of approximately 10,000 schools, with improved learning environments for about five million children.

- Increase in the investment in the nation's roads, bridges, and mass transit systems.

In an effort to make spending under the act transparent, the government established a website, Recovery.gov, which provides data and news releases related to spending under the bill.

EDUCATION LAW

The body of state and federal constitutional provisions; local, state, and federal statutes; court opinions; and government regulations that provide the legal framework for educational institutions.

Minnesota School District Violates Equal Access Act

The associational rights of public secondary school students are protected by the Equal Access Act (EAA). The EAA prohibits public secondary schools with a "limited open forum" from discriminating against students desiring to hold meetings on the basis of political, religious, philosophical, or other content of the speech. 20 U.S.C.A §§ 4071 (a), (b). A schools creates a "limited open forum" whenever it "grants an offering to or opportunity for one or more noncurriculum related student groups to meet on school premises during noninstructional time." Therefore, a school's obligations under the EAA are "triggered" even if the school only permits one noncurriculum group to meet. Once triggered, the EAA forbids a school from prohibiting other groups, based on the content of their speech, from having "equal access" to meet on school premises.

In *Straights and Gays for Equality v. Osseo Area Schools-District 279*, 540 F.3d 911 (8th Cir. 2008), the Eighth **Circuit Court** of Appeals ruled that a Minnesota school district violated the EAA by providing greater access to other noncurriculum-related student groups than they did for a group known as Straights and Gays for Equality (SAGE). An association of students enrolled at Maple Grove Senior High School, SAGE was formed to "promote tolerance and respect for [MGSH] students and faculty through education and activities relevant to gay, lesbian, bisexual, and transgender ("GLBT") individuals and their allies."

In 2005, SAGE sued the Osseo, Minnesota school district in federal **district court** after officials at Maple Grove Senior High denied the group status as a "curricular" student organization. Though the group could meet, having curricular status allowed a school organization to make announcements over the school public address system, put up signs in the school, and meet during school hours. The district challenged the status of SAGE, contending that it was not a curricular organization because its activities were not connected to the high school's curriculum.

The group asked the district court for a **preliminary injunction** based on the EAA that would require the school district to grant SAGE the same access as other non-curriculum groups. The senior high school recognized 60 student groups, including SAGE and classified them as either "curricular" or "noncurricular" under the Student Group Framework (SGF). This framework defined "curricular" groups as those related to the school's curriculum. These groups were sponsored by the school and entitled to use the public address system, the yearbook, and other tools for communication. The groups were permitted to participating in fundraising and field trips. Curricular groups included cheerleading and synchronized swimming. Noncurricular groups like SAGE were not sponsored by the school. They could only announce meetings by placing posters on a community bulletin board. There were nine noncurricular groups at the school, including SAGE.

The district court issued a preliminary injunction, finding that cheerleading and synchronized swimming, like SAGE, were noncurriculum-related groups yet they were granted greater rights than SAGE. The school district appealed the preliminary injunction to the Eighth Circuit Court of Appeals, which issued its first decision in the case in 2006. The appeals court rejected the school district's claim that the district court abused its discretion in issuing the preliminary injunction. The district claimed that its physical education curriculum justified classifying the cheerleader and swimming groups as curricular. The U.S. SUPREME COURT had defined "noncurriculum related student group" as a group that does not directly relate to the body of courses offered by the school." The court noted that a scuba-diving group would not directly relate to the school curriculum even if swimming is taught as a physical education, when scuba diving is not taught as a regular class and does not result in academic credit. In this case, there were no classes offered at the high school for cheerleading and synchronized swimming. Therefore, SAGE was entitled to the same avenues of communication offered to those two groups.

The parties returned to the district court to have the court determine whether a permanent injunction should be issued against the district. The court found that two other noncurricular groups, Spirit Council and Black Achievers, had greater access than SAGE. The court imposed a permanent injunction that accorded SAGE the same access for meetings, avenues of communication, and other miscellaneous rights as those afforded to curricular groups. The district appealed this order as well.

The Eighth Circuit upheld the permanent injunction. It found no merit in the district's claim that the Spirit Council was a subdivision of the high school's student government group. The group's activities centered on planning homecoming, winter and spring dances, the student prom, and other events fostering school pride. The court pointed out that these activities were not related to any courses offered at the school. Therefore, the appeals court concluded that the permanent injunction was proper.

The Louisiana Science Education Act of 2008

On June 23, 2008, Louisiana Governor Bobby Jindal signed into law the Louisiana Science Education Act, S.B. 733, dubbed by opponents as "an anti-evolution law" but overwhelmingly supported by the state's legislature as an act to, among other things, "promote students' critical thinking skills and open discussion of scientific theories." The new law did not mention the words "creationism" or "intelligent design."

Prior to passage, the proposed bill was introduced as a measure to encourage robust debate in science classrooms. In a two-hour public forum before the state Senate Education Committee in April 2008, detractors characterized the proposed bill as a back-door attempt to inject creationism into the classroom. But proponents argued that students wanted and needed to be challenged in the classroom by debating and questioning subject matter presented to them.

The state legislature also considered outside commentary and criticism. The American Institute of Biological Sciences, in correspondence to Louisiana state representatives, warned of consequences if the bill were passed:

> By promoting the discussion of patently non-scientific ideas in the science classroom, SB 733 threatens the quality of science education and risks setting the students of Louisiana well behind their national and international counterparts. At a time when national political and business leaders are calling for a reinvestment in our scientific research and education enterprise, passage of SB 733 would set Louisiana on a path counter to that of the rest of the nation."

The bill (known as Senate Bill 561 prior to amendment) passed through the Senate Education Committee without opposition. On June 11, 2008, the bill passed the full Louisiana House by a vote of 94 to 3. The Senate requested, and was given, two amendments: language specifying the scientific theories covered by the bill, and language specifying that teachers present material from the standard textbook prior to introducing any supplemental material. The bill, now identified as SB 733, passed the Senate on June 16 by a vote of 36 to 0.

Section 285(B)(1) of the Act states,

> The State Board of Elementary and Secondary Education, upon request of a city, parish, or other local public school board, shall allow and assist teachers, principals, and other school administrators to create and foster an environment within public elementary and secondary schools that promotes critical thinking skills, logical analysis, and open and objective discussion of scientific theories being studied including, but not limited to, evolution, the origins of life, global warming, and human cloning.

Section 285(C) provides that after teaching the material contained in a standard textbook supplied by the school system, a teacher may use supplemental textbooks and other instructional materials "to help students understand, analyze, critique, and review scientific theories in an objective manner."

Section 285(D) expressly states, "This Section shall not be construed to promote any religious doctrine, promote discrimination for or against a particular set of religious beliefs, or promote discrimination for or against religion or non-religion."

In September 2008, the Society of Vertebrate Paleontology urged Louisiana legislators and citizens to **repeal** the new law. It characterized the Act as one intended to garner support and legal protection for the introduction of religious and/or creationist concepts, including intelligent design, into the science classroom. It further expressed concern that local school boards could henceforth choose to define science and science education to suit their own agendas.

Despite critics' backlashing, an early 2009 poll by the Louisiana State University's (LSU) **Public Policy** Research Lab showed that a resounding majority (nearly 58 percent) of polled Louisiana residents favored the teaching of creationism along with evolution in public schools. A different Louisiana survey, sponsored by the Manship School of Mass Communication's Reilly Center for Media & Public Affairs at LSU, reported in April 2009 that at least 40 percent of polled Louisiana residents believed evolution was not "well-supported by evidence or widely accepted within the scientific community." Nearly as many, 38.8 percent, said that it was. Another 11.4 percent responded that they did not know.

The Louisiana Science Education Act was one of several similar bills introduced in state legislatures in 2008, including those in Alabama, Florida, Michigan, Missouri, and South Carolina. Only Louisiana's was enacted in 2008. Michigan's remained pending in both houses (without hearing or action) until the end of the legislative session(s).

As of early 2009, new "Academic Freedom" legislation was introduced in Oklahoma (SB 320); Alabama (HB 300); Iowa (HF 183); Missouri (HB 656); New Mexico (SB 433); and Texas (HB 224). Oklahoma's bill, entitled

"The Scientific Education and **Academic Freedom** Act," was considered the first "anti-evolution" bill of 2009. Its language clearly paralleled that of Louisiana's bill, providing for teachers to "help students understand, analyze, critique, and review in an objective manner the scientific strengths and scientific weaknesses of existing scientific theories pertinent to the course being taught." It would require state and local authorities to assist teachers "to find more effective ways to present the science curriculum where it addresses scientific controversies." Specific topics mentioned included "biological evolution, the chemical origins of life, global warming, and human cloning."

No Private Cause of Action under No Child Left Behind Act

The Third **Circuit Court** of Appeals in November 2008 ruled that the No Child Left Behind Act did not provide a private **cause of action** for aggrieved parents. The case arose when a group of parents in Newark, New Jersey sought to enforce the provisions of the act against the public schools in Newark. The issues before the Third Circuit was a matter of **first impression** in the **federal courts** of appeal.

Education was a major focal point in many of the elections of the 2000s. As a presidential candidate, GEORGE W. BUSH promised immediate action in the area of education, and one of his first proposals focused on improving educational standards. The proposal evolved into the No Child Left Behind Act (NCLB), Pub. L. No. 107-110, 115 Stat. 1495 (codified at 20 U.S.C. §§ 6301 *et seq.*). This act received bipartisan support and was signed into law on January 8, 2002. The focus of the act was on standards-based educational reform, which relies heavily on standardized testing as a gauge of a school's quality. The NCLB Act is one in a long line of federal education statutes, but its provisions have come under fire by educators and politicians alike. In the final year of his term, Bush continued to press for the renewal of the act, despite the criticism.

Congress enacted the NCLB Act pursuant to Congress' spending power under Article I, § 8 of the Constitution. The act's provisions are not technically mandatory. Instead, a state must agree to the statute's terms to receive federal funds attached to the provisions. When a state complies with the act, then Congress provides funding to state educational agencies, which in turn provide funding to local educational agencies. To become eligible for the federal funds, the state must submit a plan demonstrating that the state has "adopted challenging student academic content standards and challenging student academic achievement standards that will be used by the State, its local educational agencies, and its school." The state plan must ensure that all schools in the state are held accountable with regard to educational quality. Each local educational agency is charged when making sure that schools are making adequate yearly progress. If a school fails to make progress, the local educational agency must identify the school for corrective action. If the corrective action fails, then the local agency must identify the school for "restructuring."

When a school is identified for improvement, corrective action, or restructuring, the **statute** requires a local educational agency to notify parents about the deficiency and to inform parents about what steps the local or state educational agency will take to correct the deficiency. The statute also requires the local educational agency to explain to parents in writing that they have the option of transferring their student to another school. The agency must also explain that parents may obtain supplemental educational services (SES) for their children. With regard to SES, the NCLB Act puts a priority on children from low-income families and then on children with the lowest achievement levels on standardized tests.

The statute also includes an enforcement provision. Under this provision, the Secretary of Education may impose a penalty on the school by withholding federal funds from the state educational agency that fails to meet the NCLB Act's requirements. Nothing in this section, however, establishes civil liability. Moreover, the statute does not provide any specific remedy for parents should a state fail to comply with the statute's requirements.

A substantial number of schools in Newark were identified as failing each year from 2003 through 2007. In fact, the number of failing schools increased each year during that time period—from 37 during the 2003-04 **academic year** to 51 in 2006-07. There are 81 schools in the Newark public school system, which is managed by Newark Public Schools, a corporate body. Newark Public Schools also serves as the local educational agency responsible for these schools. In 2005, the Office of the Inspector General of the U.S. DEPARTMENT OF EDUCATION investigated five New Jersey school districts, including those in Newark. According to the Inspector General's report, the Newark Public Schools "failed to meet even the minimum NCLB [Act's] Notice Provisions pertaining to parents' rights to transfer their children to a non-failing school and to obtain SES for their children."

A group of parents and guardians, represented by the Newark Parents Association, sued the Newark Public Schools and individual administrators. According to the plaintiffs, Newark Public Schools contravened the NCLB Act by wholly failing to notify parents that: (1) their children were enrolled in deficient schools; (2) the parents had the right to transfer their children from failing schools to non-failing schools; (3) the parents had the right to request SES for their children; and (4) the parents had the right to request professional obligations about the teachers in the Newark schools. Other plaintiffs claimed that they sought SES for their children but were denied. The plaintiffs based most of their causes of action specifically on provisions of the NCLB Act.

The **district court** determined that the NCLB Act did not provide causes of action for the parents. The lower court relied heavily on *Gonzaga University v. Doe*, 536 U.S. 273, 122 S. Ct. 2268, 153 L. Ed. 2d 309 (2002). In *Gonzaga*, the U.S. SUPREME COURT reviewed a case brought by a student at Gonzaga University under the Family Educational Rights and PRIVACY ACT OF 1974 (FERPA), 20 U.S.C. § 1232g. The student argued that the school had violated a nondisclosure provision under the FERPA by revealing to a prospective employer that the student had been accused of committing an act of sexual misconduct. However, the Court determined that the FERPA did not provide a private cause of action and dismissed the case. According to the district court in the case of the Newark parents, the NCLB Act's provisions were similar to those of FERPA. Therefore, the district court concluded that the NCLB Act did not establish a private cause of action for the children.

The parents appealed the decision to the Third Circuit Court of Appeals. In an opinion written by Judge Maryanne Trump Barry, the panel that reviewed the case agreed with the district court. The court acknowledged that the statute creates obligations on the part of the state, and thus the provisions create law. However, the court concluded that the same provisions do not confer rights that are enforceable by private individuals. Therefore, the court affirmed the district court's dismissal of the parents' case. *Newark Parents Association v. Newark Public Schools*, 547 F.3d 199 (3d Cir. 2008).

ELECTIONS

The processes of voting to decide a public question or to select one person from a designated group to perform certain obligations in a government, corporation, or society.

Contest of General Election Held on November 4, 2008, for the Purpose of Electing a United States Senator from the State of Minnesota

Close elections are not uncommon in local contests but the 2008 U.S. Senate race in Minnesota pitting Republican Senator Norm Coleman, Democratic challenger Al Franken, and Independent Party challenger Dean Barkley resulted in Coleman and Franken ending in almost a dead heat. Out of 2.9 million votes cast, the election night results gave Coleman a lead of 286 votes over Franken. The closeness triggered an automatic recount that gave Franken the lead, which resulted in Coleman filing an election contest with the Minnesota Supreme Court. The ensuing litigation, which deprived the Democrats in the Senate from attaining a 60-vote, filibuster-proof majority, came to an end on June 30, 2009, when the supreme court ruled 5-0 against Coleman. *Contest of General Election Held on November 4, 2008, for the Purpose of Electing a United States Senator from the State of Minnesota*, __N.W.2d__ 2009 WL 1856379 (Minn. 2009) That same day Coleman conceded and Governor Tim Pawlenty (Rep.) signed the election certificate that Franken could present to the Senate the following week for his admission to the body. Though the concession of Coleman drew most of the attention, legal commentators gave high marks to the state court for its 32-page decision that analyzed Coleman's legal claims.

Though Barkley ran a spirited campaign, the senate race was a dual between Franken and

Coleman. State and local fundraising by the two candidates led to the spending of over $50 million, most of which went to television advertising. Coleman carried baggage from his close association with President W. Bush and his policies, while Franken's career as a professional comedy writer, comedian, author, and radio talk-show host produced embarrassing examples of his raw humor. The day after the election, Coleman asked Franken to concede, saying he would have done it if he had lost. Franken refused, noting that under Minnesota law when the margin between candidates is less than one-half of one percent of the total votes cast, an automatic recount must be conducted by election officials.

The statewide recount began on November 19, 2008 and concluded on January 5, 2009. During this time election officials corrected clerical errors, and reviewed individual ballots. The two campaigns lodged about 6,000 challenges to these ballots and the State Canvassing Board convened in late December to review the challenges. The board, which consisted of Secretary of State Mark Ritchie (Dem.), Chief Justice Eric Magnuson, Associate Supreme Court Justice G. Barry Anderson, and District Court Judges Edward Cleary and Kathleen Gearin, conducted its business in public. The board grew exasperated at the number of frivolous challenges and the campaigns quickly began withdrawing most of them. In the end the board reviewed just over 1,000 ballots, which resulted in Franken taking the lead by 49 votes. The board also opened 933 absentee ballots that election officials agreed had been improperly rejected. After these ballots were counted, Franken's lead grew to 225 votes. On January 5, the board certified Franken the victor.

Coleman filed a notice of election contest the next day, challenging the canvassing board's certification. A week later the Minnesota Supreme Court appointed a three-member panel of trial judges to hear the evidence and determine the contest. Testimony began in late January and concluded on March 12, 2009. The contest court determined that 351 additional absentee ballots should be opened and counted. Franken's margin grew to 312 votes after the counting was completed. On April 13, the panel issued its ruling, rejecting all of Coleman's legal arguments and factual claims, and concluding that Franken was entitled to receive the certificate of election.

Al Franken, with wife Franni, speaking on April 13, 2009.

AP IMAGES

Though public opinion polls revealed that Minnesotans had grown weary over the long process and wished it over, Coleman appeal the contest court decision to the supreme court. Briefing took place in May and oral argument occurred on June 1. Because Magnuson and Anderson had served on the canvassing board, they recused themselves from the case. The remaining five justices, lead by senior Justice Alan Page, expressed great skepticism over the arguments that Coleman had lodged. Though some commentators expected a quick decision, the court took the entire month to decide the case and prepare the opinion. On June 30, the court issued a unanimous *per curiam* opinion. Such an opinion is not signed by one judge but rather is a collective decision.

The court upheld the contest court's legal and factual conclusions. It held that Coleman had failed to establish that contest court had violated his due process rights by requiring that absentee voting standards were satisfied before counting a rejected absentee ballot. Moreover, Coleman had not proved that either the contest court or local election officials violated the Equal Protection Clause where counties had different standards for rejecting absentee ballots. The Court rejected the application of the U.S. Supreme Court's ruling in the 2000 presidential Florida recount, *Bush v. Gore*, 531 U.S. 98, 121 S.Ct. 525, 148 L.Ed.2d 388 (2000). The court noted that unlike Florida, Minnesota had strict standards for counting absentee ballots. Moreover, Coleman needed to prove that officials acted with illegal intent to deny the counting of these ballots. Just because election officials in some counties applied the law differently did not make this a violation of equal protection. If that were the case, then there would be few elections where similar claims would not be made. Another difference between the Florida and Minnesota elections involved what officials reviewed. In Florida, individual ballots were examined for voter intent. The possibility of political shenanigans was real. In Minnesota the issue involved uncounted absentee ballots, which were inside unopened envelopes. No one knew who the each voter selected for the Senate seat, so the chance of political corruption was very low.

Legal commentators who specialize in election law uniformly lauded the court decision as well-reasoned, well-written, and a model of judicial impartiality in a politically-charged case. Within two hours of the opinion's release, Coleman conceded, abandoning his previous statements that he might take the matter to the U.S. Supreme Court. Twenty-four hours later, Franken held a long-delayed victory rally in front of the State Capitol, just a few hundred feet from the Minnesota Judicial Center and the justices who decided his political future.

EMPLOYMENT LAW

The body of law that governs the employer-employee relationship, including individual employment contracts, the application of tort and contract doctrines, and a large group of statutory regulation on issues such as the right to organize and negotiate collective bargaining agreements, protection from discrimination, wages and hours, and health and safety.

A Tightening Job Market and Its Legal Implications

According to the World Economic Forum's "Global Competitiveness Report," which ranks the world's most competitive economies, the United States had fallen from first to sixth place by 2008. The economic fallout invited legal and political sequelae as well. Fewer jobs meant that it was an employers' market, and hiring practices became more closely scrutinized as employers focused on getting the best return for their investment. The hiring of illegal immigrants was a prominent issue, as was the rising number of claims for unemployment benefits and general aid that put state budgets "in the red." Health care insurance became a key platform issue for the November 2008 presidential election. The negative effects of the collapsing auto industry rippled through the job market in all major sectors.

U.S. Citizenship and Immigration Services (CIS) had been issuing approximately 65,000

An empty Fisher plant employee parking lot, March 2009.

AP IMAGES

H-1B employment visas yearly. H-1B visas are non-immigrant temporary visas for U.S. employment in critical or specialized fields, or where employers can demonstrate insufficient numbers of domestic applicants. Generally the quota was exhausted on the first day petitions were received by CIS (April 1) each year. But in 2009, there were still several thousand H-1B visas available by mid-year.

Worker verification remained at the heart of all immigration debates, with more than 22,000 companies participating in E-Verify (an Internet-based system for verification of U.S. status for employment.) The program was operated by the U.S. Department of Homeland Security and Social Security Administration.

Other legal consequences centered on healthcare. In the first half of 2008, more than half of company CEOs polled in the Business Roundtable's latest "Economic Outlook Survey" listed healthcare as the greatest source of cost pressure on companies. In 2005, less than 50 percent of employers believed that employees exhibiting unhealthy habits and behaviors (smoking, obesity, etc.) should pay a larger portion of their health benefit costs. By 2008, that number had jumped to more than 62 percent, and there was an increased trend in employers instituting penalties for such behaviors/habits.

According to the National Association of Colleges and Employers' (NACE) student survey of more than 35,000 students from more than 840 colleges and universities nationwide, less than 20 percent of 2009 graduates who had applied for a job, had one in hand by the time of graduation. However, the survey results also showed that there were fewer 2009 graduates who actually sought out jobs (59 percent). Several reasons were cited, including the considerable attention paid to the nation's high unemployment, the global financial crisis, and the impact of such developments on the recruitment and hiring of new graduates by specific industries. Twenty-six percent of 2009 graduates indicated they would move on to graduate school, as compared to 24 percent in 2008 and 20 percent in 2007.

The Wall Street scandals and stock market declines also caused baby-boomers to work longer than expected or to return to the employment sector because of shrinking retirement investments. The tight market adversely affected teen employment as well, particularly in those sectors traditionally dominated by young employees (fast-food servers, music clerks, camp counselors and lifeguards, etc.). But now employers were opting for experience, as the job market flooded with workers willing to take positions below their skill levels. Ultimately, unemployment rates for teens threatened to reach 20 percent at times, the highest rate since 2003.

According to the 2008 Job Market Report published by Lee Hecht Harrison, the ten fastest growing occupations were (1) network systems and data communications analysts; (2) physicians assistants; (3) computer software engineers, applications; (4) dental hygienists; (5) physical therapist assistants;(6) computer software engineers, systems software; (7) network and computer systems administrators; (8) database administrators; (9)physical therapists; and (10) forensic science technicians. With respect to legal careers, the stock market fiasco, immigration reform, intellectual property rights, healthcare regulation, and privacy concerns all contributed to the growth of the profession.

Demographically, baby-boomers worked predominantly in educational services, transportation, health services, and public administration. Occupations most affected by the Boomer generation were: administrative assistants, elementary and secondary school teachers, registered nurses, bookkeeping and accounting clerks, college and university professors, education administrators, and farmers.

Regionally, the West remained the best place for jobs in information technology (IT) and construction. The Northeast remained the best place for jobs in healthcare and science, biomedical, education, and technology in general. The Southeast was best for jobs in engineering, finance, construction and healthcare. The Southwest was best for technology, engineering, and healthcare, while the Midwest was best for technology, finance, and construction. However, the Midwest was home to the states with the highest unemployment rates.

Over the next decade, demand for temporary labor was expected to exceed the growth of overall employment. The top five occupations experiencing the largest annual growth in temporary employment were all in the IT sector. The most commonly-placed skilled temporary workers were registered nurses, as a continuing shortage of healthcare workers was expected to extend into the next decade.

Crawford v. Metropolitan Government of Nashville and Davidson County, Tennessee

When employees report employment discrimination they may be subject to retaliation by their supervisors and employers. Congress sought to prevent retaliation by including in Title VII of the Civil Rights Act of 1964 an antiretaliation provision. This provision forbids retaliation by employers against employees who report race or gender discrimination. However, the law has been unclear whether this provision protects an employee who does not speak out against discrimination on her own initiative but merely answers questions during an employer's investigation. The Supreme Court, in *Crawford v. Metropolitan Government of Nashville and Davidson County, Tennessee,* __U.S.__, 129 S.Ct. 846, __L.Ed.2d__ (2009), ruled that employees are protected when they give information during an investigation.

Vicky Crawford, a 30-year employee of the Metropolitan Government of Nashville and Davidson County, Tennessee (Metro), worked for the Metro school district. A Metro human resources officer began investigating rumors that Gene Hughes, the school district's employee relations director, had sexually harassed female employees. When the officer asked Crawford whether she had witnessed inappropriate behavior by Hughes, she described incidents of sexual harassment. Two other employees also reported sexually harassing behavior by Hughes. The district took no action against Hughes but fired Crawford and the two other accusers shortly after the conclusion of the investigation. The district claimed Crawford was discharged for **embezzlement**, but she claimed retaliation. She filed suit under Title VII, seeking protection from the antiretaliation provision.

The federal **district court** dismissed Crawford's complaint. The antiretaliation provision contains two clauses: the "opposition clause" and the "participation clause." The opposition clause bar retaliation against an employee who "has opposed any practice made an unlawful employment practice" by Title VII. The participation clause prohibits retaliation against an employee who "has made a charge, testified, assisted, or participated in any manner in an investigation, proceeding, or hearing" under Title VII. In this case the district court concluded that Crawford could not satisfy the opposition clause because she had not "instigated or filed any complaint." She had merely answered questions in an "already-pending investigation initiated by someone else. The court also ruled that her claim failed under the participation clause because the Sixth **Circuit Court** of Appeals had held that this clause was confined to participating in an investigation required by a pending EQUAL EMPLOYMENT OPPORTUNITY COMMISSION (EEOC) charge. No EEOC complaint had been filed at the time the school district started its investigation.

Crawford's appeal to the Sixth Circuit failed because of this precedent. The appeals court held that the opposition clause demanded "active, consistent" opposing activities, whereas Crawford had not initiated any complaint prior to the investigation, Moreover, it found that the participation clause did not cover the government agency's internal investigation because it was not conducted pursuant to a Title VII charge pending with the Equal Employment Opportunity Commission. The Supreme Court agreed to hear her appeal because other circuit courts of appeal decisions conflicted with the Sixth Circuit's decision.

The Supreme Court, in a unanimous decision, overturned the Sixth Circuit decision. Justice DAVID SOUTER, writing for the Court, held that the antiretaliation provision's protection extended to an employee who speaks out about discrimination not on her own initiative, but in answering questions during an employer's internal investigation. Because "oppose" is undefined by **statute**, Souter took a close look at the definition of the word. He concluded that it carried its ordinary dictionary meaning of "resisting or contending against." Therefore, Crawford's statement was covered by the opposition clause, as an ostensibly disapproving account of Hughes's sexually harassing behavior toward her. Justice Souter made clear that "oppose" goes beyond "active, consistent" behavior in ordinary discourse, and may be used to speak of someone who has taken no action at all to **advance** a position beyond disclosing it. Thus, a person can "oppose" by responding to someone else's questions just as surely as by provoking the discussion.

The Court also found the Sixth Circuit's precedent inconsistent with the goals of Title VII.

Souter stated that nothing in the statute required a "freakish" rule protecting an employee who reports discrimination on her own initiative but not one who reports the same discrimination in the same words when asked a question. The school district had claimed that employers would be less likely to raise questions about possible discrimination if a retaliation charge was easy to raise when things go badly for an employee who responded to enquiries. The Court rejected this argument, noting that employers have a strong inducement to seek out and put a stop to discriminatory activity in their operations because prior court decisions on sexual harassment in the workplace hold that "[a]n employer [is]... subject to **vicarious liability** to a victimized employee for an actionable hostile environment created by a supervisor with ... authority over the employee." The Sixth Circuit's ruling could undermine this scheme, along with the statute's "primary objective" of "avoid[ing] harm" to employees. The Court expressed concern that if an employee reporting discrimination in answer to an employer's questions could be penalized with no remedy, prudent employees would have a good reason to keep quiet about Title VII offenses.

ENVIRONMENTAL LAW

An amalgam of state and federal statutes, regulations, and common-law principles covering air pollution, water pollution, hazardous waste, the wilderness, and endangered wildlife.

Coeur Alaska, Inc. v. Southeast Alaska Conservation Council

The U.S. SUPREME COURT in June 2009 considered a case focused on the authorities of certain agencies to issue permits that would allow a company to begin a mining project in Alaska. The operation would require the company to deposit rock materials into a lake near a mine. In a 6-3 decision, the Court concluded that the U.S. Army Corps of Engineers was the proper agency to issue a permit for such an operation.

The Kensington Gold Mine operated a mine in southeast Alaska from 1897 to 1928. Coeur Alaska, Inc. decided to use the site to mine gold. The mining operation would mostly be subterranean, although the site would have some above-ground facilities. Coeur Alaska would

have to construct a froth-flotation mill facility to process the gold ore that was retrieved from the mine. In this froth-flotation process, rock containing the gold ore is moved through a series of mechanical crushing and grinding procedures until it is finely ground. The ground rock is then fed into a tank containing water and chemicals. The tank is then pumped with air, which produces bubbles that attach to the gold. The gold rises to the top because of these bubbles, and the gold can be skimmed off the top.

As a result of this process, tons of the ground rock (without gold ore) remains as waste product. The residual ground rock is known as tailings. Of 2,000 tons of ore that Coeur could process daily, only about 100 tons, or five percent, would yield valuable gold minerals. Coeur could use about 40 percent of the tailings as backfill in the mine, but a significant portion would remain. Coeur maintained that the volume of remaining tailings was too large to transport off the site.

Coeur ininitially developed a plan for disposing of the tailings by depositing these tailings on higher ground. After 10 to 15 years, the company would cover the disposal area with native material to allow new vegetation to grow. However, after the the U.S. Forest Service, the U.S. Army Corps of Engineers, and the ENVIRONMENTAL PROTECTION AGENCY (EPA) approved this plan, the price of gold dropped dramatically. Coeur would have to find a less expensive way to deposit the tailings.

The Kensington facility is located near Lower Slate Lake, which is a 23-acre lake in the Tongass National Forest. The lake is a

The entrance tunnel and water treatment facility for Kensington Gold Mine near Juneau, Alaska.

AP IMAGES

habitat to fish and other wildlife. Coeur proposed that it would deposit about 210,000 gallons of process wastewater, including 1,440 tons of tailings, into the lake each day. Over the course of about 10 to 15 years, Coeur would deposit about 4.5 million tons of tailings into the lake. During the course of the period, the discharge would raise the bottom of the lake by 50 feet and triple the lake's surface area. The operation would raise the pH factor in the water considerable, and the process would kill all of the aquatic life in the lake. Because of the concentrations of potentially hazardous minerals, including aluminum, copper, lead, and mercury. It was unclear whether the lake would ever be able to support aquatic life even after the mining operations ended.

Coeur also made other proposals. Because the operation would expand the size of the lake, the company would build a large dam as well as a diversion ditch. Construction of the ditch would require the company to cut trees on 7.6 acres of property. Moreover, the company would divert a creek that ran through Lower Slate Lake through the use of a pipeline.

The case involved several sections of the Clean Water Act of 1972, 33 U.S.C. §§ 1251 et seq. Congress enacted the Clean Water Act "to restore and maintain the chemical, physical, and biological integrity" of the waters in the United States. The act establishes strict standards that apply to the discharge of pollutants. Section 402 of the act establishes the EPA at the principal body responsible for reviewing proposals regarding discharge of the pollutants. Section 404 of the act, conversely, applies to the discharge of "dredge or fill material," and the agency responsible for issuing permits under section 404 is the Corps of Engineers.

In 2004, the Forest Service approved Coeur's plan. The Corps of Engineers determined that the discharge of tailings involved fill material, so the agency concluded that section 404 applied. On July 17, 2005, the Corps issued a permit to allow Coeur to discharge the tailings into the Lower Slate Lake. Two environmental groups, including the Southeast Alaska Conservation Council, the SIERRA CLUB, and the Lynn Canal Conservation, filed suit in the U.S. **District Court** for the District of Alaska. The plaintiffs argued that the proposal violated several sections of the Clean

Water Act and that the Corps should not have issued the permits.

In 2006, the district court granted **summary judgment** in favor of Coeur and other defendants. The district court reasoned that since the case was governed by section 404 of the act, other provisions of the Clean Water Act prohibiting discharge of pollutants were inapplicable. The plaintiffs appealed the decision to the Ninth **Circuit Court** of Appeals. In 2006, the Ninth Circuit enjoined further construction activities by Coeur.

The Ninth Circuit issued an opinion on the merits on May 22, 2007. The court reviewed the language and intent behind several sections of the Clean Water Act. The court disagreed with Coeur's argument that section 404 of the act does not require compliance with other provisions of the Clean Water Act, whereas section 402 does require such compliance. The court concluded that the mine needed to comply with the EPA's standard that applies to froth-flotation operations, rather than the more relaxed regulatory standard that applies to fill material. Accordingly, the Ninth Circuit reversed the district court's decision. *Southeast Alaska Conservation Council v. United States Army Corps of Engineers*, 486 F.3d 638 (9th Cir. 2007).

Coeur and the other defendants appealed the decision to the U.S. Supreme Court. In a 6-3 decision, the Supreme Court reversed the Ninth Circuit. The majority opinion written by Justice ANTHONY KENNEDY focused on both the Clean Air Act as well as EPA regulations. The EPA itself adopted a regulation providing that discharge of fill material is regulated by section 404 and that permits issued pursuant to section 402 are not required.

The Court read the provisions of the Clean Air Act but determined that the **statute** was ambiguous. As a result, the Court turned its attention to the agencies' interpretation of the statute. An internal EPA memorandum concluded that section 402 only applies to the discharge of water from a lake into a downstream creek and that the section does not apply to the discharge of a mixture of solids and liquids (slurry) into a lake. The Court deferred to this opinion and concluded that section 404 governed in the case rather than section 402. The Court therefore reversed the Ninth Circuit. *Coeur Alaska, Inc. v. Southeast*

Alaska Conservation Council, No. 07-984, 2009 WL 1738643 (2009).

Justice RUTH BADER GINSBURG, joined by two other justices, dissented. Ginsburg argued that the Clean Air Act's text, structure, and purpose mandate adherence to pollution-control requirements established by the EPA. Ginsburg therefore agreed with the Ninth Circuit's conclusion and would have affirmed the lower court's opinion.

Obama Administration Shifts Policy on Auto Emissions Regulation

When the Obama Administration took office in January 2009, it quickly signaled that it would make major changes in how the federal government will address climate change. Within six days of being sworn in, President Barack Obama directed the Department of Transportation and the ENVIRONMENTAL PROTECTION AGENCY (EPA) to move quickly to review an application by California and 13 other states to impose strict auto emission and fuel efficiency standards. Under the Bush Administration the applications were rejected by the EPA, leading the states to file federal lawsuits challenging the denials. Though the review would take time and lawsuits by automakers were possible if the applications were granted, the states were encouraged by this development.

California had received more than 40 waivers from the federal government under the Clean Air Act to toughen environmental regulations when it applied to the EPA in 2005 to impose standards on automakers tougher than those established by the federal government. Under the proposed standards, automakers would have been forced to cut emissions by 30 percent from cars and light trucks, and 18 percent for SUVs, beginning with the 2009 model year. However, the EPA did not act on the proposal until December 2007, when it finally denied the application. If adopted, the state regulations would raise the fuel efficiency in U.S. car and light trucks from 27 miles per gallon to 35.

EPA director Peter L. Johnson concluded that a single, unified national standard was better than a state-by-state scheme of regulations. (Observers noted that because of California's large automobile market, its emission and fuel economy standards would force automakers to make these the defacto national standard.)

Johnson noted that the Energy Independence and Security Act of 2007 required automakers to reach industry-wide fuel efficiency for cars, SUVs, and small tracks of 35 miles per gallon by 2020. In contrast, California's plan would raise fuel efficiency to 42 miles per gallon by 2020.

California's efforts had encouraged 13 other states to follow suit. With the denial of the application, California filed an appeal in federal court in January 2008. Meanwhile, Rep. Henry Waxman (D-Cal.), Chair of the House Oversight and Government Reform Committee, demanded that EPA turn over all its internal documents to his committee. Waxman alleged that the decision by the Bush Administration was driven by politics rather than science. EPA documents were soon disclosed that showed EPA employees had recommended approval of the waiver. One memo stated that there was no "legal or technical justification" for denying the waiver application. At a congressional hearing, Johnson refused to say whether the White House had pressured him to deny the application. He justified his decision by noting that the "impacts of global climate change in California" were not sufficiently different from the rest of states to allow it to go its own way. Democrats in both houses introduced bills that sought to overturn the denial but they were not enacted. Waxman issued a report that concluded the White House had played a "significant role" in the EPA decision, despite unanimous support from EPA career employees that the waiver should be approved.

On January 26, 2009, President Obama issued a memorandum that ordered the EPA to reconsider California's application, as well as the those from the other 13 states. Because of the long delay, California had moved its deadline to 2016 for compliance with its standards. The administration also instructed the Department of Transportation to draft new interim mileage standards starting in 2012 that will ensure new vehicles reach the 35-mile-a-gallon target set by Congress for 2020. The Bush administration guidelines for 2011 models were allowed to go forward due to the short timetable.

In March 2009, the EPA conducted a hearing to solicit comments on California's waiver application. Automakers and dealers testified and expressed concern over several points in the plan, noting the perilous financial condition of GM, Ford, and Chrysler. In addition, dealers pointed out that the rules would limit choices at dealerships in California and the other states, leading consumers to cross borders to other states to buy less fuel efficient vehicles. The public comment ended in April and a decision by the EPA was expected by July 2009.

With pressure building for state regulations, automakers and members of Congress expressed more interest than in the past for stronger national efficiency standards. The Obama Administration began efforts on this front, but the financial problems of GM and Chrysler have pushed environmental issues to a lower priority. California officials stated that they do not object to national standards, but they must be as tough as their state regulations, which force all types of new vehicles conform to the one standard. In contrast, automakers have continued to push for separate standards for light cars, trucks, and SUVs.

Summers v. Earth Island Institute

Environmental organizations have become watchdogs over state and federal lands, often taking the federal government to court in an attempt to stop the government from selling natural resources to private business. Such was the case when the U.S. Forest Service approved a salvage sale of timber on 238 acres of fire-damaged land in the Sequoia National Forest without going through the normal notice, comment, and appeal process. Five environmental groups and the Forest Service eventually resolved their legal dispute over the timber sale but the federal **district court** allowed the groups to continue its lawsuit over certain regulations. The federal government objected, arguing that with the timber sale issue settled, the groups did not have standing to challenge the regulations. The Supreme Court, in *Summers v. Earth Island Institute*, __U.S.__, __S.Ct.__, __ L.Ed.2d__ 2009 WL509325 (2009), agreed with the government, ruling that the groups lacked standing to challenge the regulations still at issue absent a live dispute over a concrete application of those regulations.

In the summer of 2002 fire burned a substantial area of the Sequoia National Forest. In September 2003 the Forest Service approved the Burnt Ridge Project, which authorized a salvage sale of timber on 238 acres damaged by the 2002 fire. Under Forest Service regulations, salvage sales of less than 250 acres did not have to provide the notice, comment, and appeal process mandated by the Appeals Reform Act, Pub. L. No. 102-381, 106 Stat. 1419 (1992). The Earth Island Institute and other environmental organizations filed a complaint in California federal district court in December 2003, challenging the Forest Service's failure to follow the Appeal Reform Act and the regulations that exempted notice and comment. The district court issued a **preliminary injunction** that halted the timber sale, and soon after the parties settled their dispute over the Burnt Ridge Project. At this point the government asked the court to dismiss the lawsuit because there we no other projects before the court in which the groups were threatened with actual injury. Therefore, the groups did not have standing to challenge the underlying regulations. The court rejected this argument and proceeded to invalidate five regulations and impose a nationwide injunction against their application. The Ninth **Circuit Court** of Appeals agreed with the government that three of the regulations were not at issue in the Burnt Ridge Project and therefore there was no **case or controversy** before the court. However, the appeals court found that the two other regulations were applicable to the Burnt Ridge Project. The court upheld the district court on these regulations and upheld the nationwide injunction.

The Supreme Court, in a 5-4 decision, overturned the Ninth District's ruling on the two regulations and the injunction, finding that Earth Institute lacked standing to challenge them. Justice ANTONIN SCALIA, writing for the majority, noted that Article III of the Constitution restricts the judicial power to cases and controversies. The Supreme Court has developed the doctrine of standing to determine whether a plaintiff has a sufficient personal stake in the outcome of the controversy to warrant federal-court jurisdiction. A plaintiff seeking an injunction must show that he is under threat of suffering "injury in fact" that is concrete and particularized. The threat must be actual and imminent and not hypothetical. Moreover, the threat must be traceable to the challenged action of the defendant.

Justice Scalia then applied these principles of the standing doctrine to Earth Island Institute's claims. The organization said that its members had a recreational interest in the National Forest and submitted an affidavit from a member who had repeatedly visit the Burnt Ridge site and intended to do so in the future. This was sufficient to grant standing at the beginning of the litigation but when the parties settled the member had his injury in fact remedied. Scalia stated that there was no precedent for the "proposition that when a plaintiff has sued to challenge the lawfulness of certain action or threatened action but has settled that suit, he retains standing to challenge the basis for that action (here, the regulation in the abstract),apart from any concrete application that threatens imminent harm to his interests." The environmental groups could not identify any other application of the invalidated regulations that threatened imminent harm to its members. This too deprived the groups of the standing.

The groups also claimed standing because they had suffered procedural injury from the denial of their ability to file comments on the Forest Service actions. Moreover, they will continue to be deprived of this ability. Justice Scalia dismissed this argument because deprivation of a procedural right must be tied to some some concrete interest that is affected by the deprivation. In this case there were no concrete interests since the Burnt Ridge Project as "off the table." Therefore, the groups had no standing to contest the regulations.

Justice STEPHEN BREYER, in a dissenting opinion joined by three other justices, argued that the the organizations had raised a "realistic threat" of injury brought about by "reoccurrence of the challenged conduct that the Forest Service thinks is lawful and *admits* will reoccur."

ESPIONAGE

The act of securing information of a military or political nature that a competing nation holds secret. It can involve the analysis of diplomatic reports, publications, statistics, and broadcasts, as well as spying, a clandestine activity carried out by an individual or individuals working under a secret identity for the benefit of a nation's information gathering techniques. In the United States, the organization that heads most activities dedicated to espionage is the Central Intelligence Agency.

U.S. Naturalized Citizen Sentenced as Chinese Spy

In the early years of the new millennium, U.S. military officials warned that China and Russia were stepping up military spying activities focused on advanced weapons technology. Indeed, by 2008, more than a dozen cases were pending that either involved traditional spying or economic espionage related to China, and represented an increasingly serious counterintelligence challenge.

Earlier in 2008, two separate cases came up for trial. The California trial of a Chinese-American engineer who was charged with stealing military and aerospace trade secrets was postponed until mid-2009. Another Chinese-born engineer was sentenced by a federal court to 24 years in prison for attempting to pass on "sensitive data" to China.

But the case that got the most attention was that of Taiwan-born but since-naturalized American citizen Tai Shen Kuo, a New Orleans furniture salesman who persuaded a Pentagon official to give him classified military information. Posing as a Taiwanese agent, he actually passed the information on to the People's Republic of China (China). In August 2008, a federal district court sentenced him to 16 years in prison. The former Pentagon official, Gregg W. Bergersen, a weapons system policy analyst, had been sentenced in July 2008 to 57 months, and Kuo's girlfriend, Yu Xin Kang, who helped transmit the documents, was sentenced to 18 months.

Initial assessment by the U.S. Department of Defense determined that the actual damage inflicted upon U.S. national security by the compromise of this classified information was minimal. The Associated Press reported that Taiwanese officials said the information was damaging but had not compromised Taiwan's key defense technology. The Chinese government, for its part, called the espionage allegations groundless and accused the United States of "Cold War thinking."

Court documents revealed a professional friendship between Kuo and Bergersen and Bergersen's interest in eventually leaving the Department of Defense to start a defense contracting business with Kuo. Kuo allegedly bestowed gifts upon Bergersen, including gambling money, but the district court discounted a "quid pro quo" arrangement. Prosecutors had advised the court that Kuo had cultivated Bergersen as a source of information without explicitly agreeing to "buy" information from him.

For his part, Bergersen pleaded guilty in April 2008 to conspiring to pass national defense information to unauthorized persons. He testified that he thought Kuo was a Taiwanese agent and that he (Bergersen) was unaware that Kuo was passing the information on to China.

According to court documents, the actual classified information that Bergersen gave Kuo included all projected U.S. military sales to Taiwan for the next five years. There were also details about a Taiwanese communications system, Po Sheng, that collected and transmitted information for the armed forces.

Just a week before the Kuo-Bergersen espionage case came to trial, U.S. officials had contacted China after the Pentagon advised that it had mistakenly sent nuclear warhead fuses to Taiwan in 2006. Defense Secretary Robert Gates ordered an investigation into the matter, but stressed that the mishap did not signal any change in U.S.-Taiwan policy.

U.S. military support for Taiwan had been an ongoing sore point between the United States and China, which threatened to regain control of Taiwan (a nearby island nation that China considered a renegade province) by force if necessary. In justification for U.S. support, Taiwan had pointed to China's steady buildup of missiles capable of hitting Taiwan.

The U.S. government began tracking Bergersen and Kuo in March 2007 and continued surveillance until their arrests in February 2008. At one meeting, Kuo stuffed $3,000 in Bergersen's pocket and was given several documents which had jagged edges where Bergersen had snipped off the "classified" markings. Court documents indicated that Kuo, in turn, received approximately $50,000 for the data from an unidentified Chinese agent, who lured him into espionage with promises of lucrative business deals in China.

Kuo, 58, came to the United States in 1972 and attended Nicholls State University in Louisiana on a tennis scholarship. He was a member of a prominent Taiwanese family and the son-in-law of Xue Yue, a Chinese nationalist general and close associate of Chiang Kai-shek. Kuo was also a prominent Louisiana businessman.

District Court Judge Leonie Brinkema gave lower-range sentences to Bergersen and Kang, but refused a defense request to do the same for Kuo. The court held that he was the more culpable and that his actions had ensnared Kang in a criminal enterprise in which she would otherwise not have been involved.

Kuo was arrested in February 2008 at the home of another Pentagon official, James W. Fondren, Jr., 62. Fondren, with a top secret clearance, was the deputy director of the Washington liaison office for the U.S. Pacific Command. In May 2009, federal prosecutors announced that Fondren was being charged with giving classified information to Kuo through "opinion papers" which he sold to Kuo for between $350 and $800 apiece. The activity allegedly occurred between 2004 and Kuo's arrest at Fondren's residence in February 2008. Fondren also claimed that he thought Kuo was working for Taiwan.

In an unrelated matter, in December 2008, federal prosecutors indicted former Motorola software engineer Hanjuan Jin for stealing thousands of confidential and proprietary technical documents and highly-sensitive trade secrets. U.S. Customs officials arrested Jin at Chicago's O'Hare International Airport in February 2007, about to depart on a one-way ticket to China. According to an FBI affidavit filed in court, Jin's luggage contained over 1,000 electronic and paper documents from Motorola (she had just quit her job there), along with Chinese documents for military telecommunications technology. The court case involved several other Chinese engineers who also allegedly downloaded proprietary documents from both Motorola and Lemko, along with source code. No trial date had been set as of May 2009.

EVIDENCE

Any matter of fact that a party to a lawsuit offers to prove or disprove an issue in the case. A system of rules and standards used to determine which facts may be admitted, and to what extent a judge or jury may consider those facts, as proof of a particular issue in a lawsuit.

Corley v. United States

The April 2009 U.S. SUPREME COURT case of *Corley v. United States*, No. 07-10441, 556 U.S. ___, shed some light on resolving criminal evidence conflicts between federal law, federal rules of **criminal procedure**, and Supreme Court precedent. The narrow 5-4 decision (with Chief Justice JOHN ROBERTS, Jr. and Justices Alito, Scalia, and Thomas dissenting) held that its previous decisions were not supplanted (superceded or trumped) by a section of the United States Code (USC) enacted by Congress after those decisions. Rather, said the Court, Congress intended to limit and not eliminate the general rule articulated therein.

Specifically, two prior and longstanding U.S. Supreme Court cases (see below) made it clear that confessions given by suspects during periods of detention were not admissible as evidence at criminal trials, if they were made in violation of the "prompt presentment" requirement of Federal Rules of Criminal Procedure (FRCP)5(a). The term "presentment" refers to the requirement for an arresting officer to bring or "present" his suspect before a judge for authority to bind over the prisoner. FRCP 5(a) states that a "person making an arrest.must take the defendant without unnecessary delay before a **magistrate** judge."

Both *McNabb v. United States,* 318 U.S. 332 (1943) and *Mallory v. United States,* 354 U.S. 449 (1957) articulated that an arrested person's confession would be inadmissible if given after an unreasonable delay in bringing him before a judge. The cases, and what they represented, were collectively referred to (in legal jargon) as the *McNabb-Mallory* rule." In *McNabb,* federal agents had interrogated several murder suspects for days before "presenting" them before a magistrate (after they finally got confessions). The Court ruled the confessions were inadmissible.

Following yet another famous Supreme Court case, *Miranda v. Arizona,* 384 U.S. 436 (1966), Congress believed too many dangerous criminals were being released because their confessions had been made prior to having had their constitutional rights (to remain silent and request legal counsel) ("Miranda" rights) read to them. In response, it enacted 18 USC §3501 two years later, in 1968.

Section (a) of §3501 provides that "a confession shall be admissible in evidence if it is voluntarily given," and §3501(b) lists several considerations for a court to address when determining the "voluntariness" of a confession. But Subsection §3501(c) was intended to address the *McNabb-Mallory* rule. It provides that "a confession made by a defendant while under arrest shall not be inadmissible solely because of delay in bringing such person before a magistrate judge if such confession is found by the trial judge to have been made voluntarily and.within six hours [of arrest]." That subsection also extends the time limit when further delay is "reasonable considering the means of transportation and the distance to the nearest available [magistrate]."

The facts surrounding the present *Corley* case did not appear to fit conveniently within these existing rules. Johnny Corley was suspected of robbing a bank in Pennsylvania. After federal officers discovered he was already wanted by police for a local matter, they obtained a warrant, and subsequently found him pulling out of a driveway in his car. A scuffle and chase ensued, during which Corley pushed one officer down, but Corley was finally caught and arrested for assaulting a police officer. The arrest occurred at approximately 8:00 a.m.

FBI agents first kept Corley at a local police station while questioning nearby residents. Just before 12:00 noon, they took him to a local hospital to treat a minor cut on his hand acquired during the chase. At 3:30 p.m., they took him from the hospital to the Philadelphia FBI office, at this time informing him that he was a suspect in the bank **robbery**. Despite a magistrate judge's office being located within the same building, FBI agents did not present him before a magistrate, but instead continued to question him, hoping to get a confession. At about 5:30 p.m. he began to confess that he robbed the bank. It was now more than nine hours after his arrest.

At around 6:30 p.m. Corley asked for a break and was held overnight. The next morning, agents resumed their interrogation, ending with Corley's signed confession. He was presented before a magistrate judge at 1:30 p.m. and charged with armed bank robbery.

At his criminal trial, Corley tried to suppress his confession, but the **district court** denied his motion, citing FRCP 5(a) and *McNabb-Mallory*. The court also found that the six-hour window of §3501(c) had been met because the hours spent at the hospital should be excluded. Further, the court found no unreasonable delay in the continued interrogation the next morning because it was

Corley who requested a break, which was granted. But for that, the court reasoned, he would have been presented sooner to a magistrate.

Corley was convicted and the Third **Circuit Court** of Appeals affirmed. The Third Circuit went further to opine that §3501(c) actually replaced the *McNabb-Mallory* rule with a pure "voluntariness" test. It concluded that if the district court had found the confession voluntary under §3501(a) and (b), despite any alleged delay, it was admissible.

The narrow majority of the U.S. Supreme Court disagreed. Justice Souter, writing for the Court, opened with,

> The question here is whether Congress intended 18 USC §3501 to discard, or merely to narrow, the rule in *McNabb* and *Mallory*, under which an arrested person's confession is inadmissible if given after an unreasonable delay in bringing him before a judge. We hold that Congress meant to limit, not eliminate, *McNabb-Mallory.*

The Court explained that the government claimed that §3501(a) eliminated *McNabb-Mallory* by making all confessions admissible

as long as they were voluntary under §3501(b). Conversely, Corley argued that those sections (a) and (b) were meant to overrule *Miranda,* and not applicable to his case. Only §3501(c) was intended to address the *McNabb-Mallory* rule, and since the government did not meet its requirements, his confession should have been suppressed.

Corley had the better argument, said the Court. If the government's argument were adopted (that §3501(a) and (b) made all confessions admissible if they met the "voluntary" test), then there would be no need for §3501(c) (the six-hour test). The Court further noted that the legislative history of 18 USC §3501 favored Corley's argument. In summary, Corley's confession, even if voluntary, was inadmissible for failure of officials to bring him before a magistrate in a timely manner.

The dissent, written by Justice Alito, found the language in 18 USC §3501 unambiguous in stating, "[I]n any criminal prosecution brought by the United States.a confession.shall be admissible in evidence if it is given voluntarily."

FEDERAL COMMUNICATIONS COMMISSION

Federal Communications Commission v. Fox Television Stations, Inc.

In 2004, the FEDERAL COMMUNICATIONS COMMISSION (FCC) changed its 30-year policy on the broadcasting of indecent language. A broadcast television or radio station could be subjected to fines and revocation of its federal license if it broadcast someone speaking a the F- and S-Words, even if the word was used just once. Using this policy the FCC issued notices of apparent liability against a national broadcaster, Fox Television States, Inc. for two incidents. Though a federal appeals court held that the FCC's policy was defective, the Supreme Court in *Federal Communications Commission v. Fox Television Station*, __U.S.__, 129 S.Ct. 1800, 173 L.Ed.2d 738 (2009), found the policy legitimate. The Court left for another day whether the FCC policy was constitutional under the FIRST AMENDMENT.

The FCC had a long-standing policy against the use of indecent language, but it did not prosecute one-time occurrences. The commission rethought its position after presenters and award-winners at a series of television awards shows in 2002 and 2003. It made three significant findings in changing the policy: (1) bleeping/delay systems technology had advanced; (2) the F-Word and the S-Word always invoke a coarse excretory or sexual image,

making it irrelevant whether a word was used as an expletive or a literal description; and (3) the new policy's "contextual" approach to indecency was better than the previous "categorical" approach which offered broadcasters virtual immunity for the broadcast of fleeting expletives.

Armed with this new policy, the FCC in 2003 issued a notice of apparent liability against the Fox network for allowing Cher to use the F-Word music awards show and for allowing Nicole Richie to utter both the F- and S-Words. Under the Federal Communications Act the commission could impose large fines on stations and even revoke station licenses. After hearing evidence from Fox the commission entered an order finding the broadcasts in question indecent, but it did not impose sanctions. Nevertheless, Fox, along with ABC, CBS, and NBC, appealed the order to the Second **Circuit Court** of Appeals. The networks contended that the new policy was arbitrary and capricious and that it raised First Amendment censorship concerns.

The Second Circuit, in a 2-1 decision, agreed that the shift in policy was arbitrary and capricious. It declined to rule on constitutional issues. The application of the commission's new "fleeting expletive" policy had to be considered in light of its previous policy and the reasons justifying the new one. Though administrative agencies should be accorded great deference in managing their responsibilities, when they make policies there must be a "rational connection between the facts found and the choice made." The networks contended, and the court agreed, that the FCC had acted arbitrarily because it made a complete about-face on its treatment of "fleeting expletives" without providing a reasoned explanation that justified its action.

The appeals court found no compelling reasons to justify the change. The commission's primary reason for the crackdown was a so-called "first blow" theory. Because the airwaves entered the privacy of the home uninvited and without warning, allowing isolated or fleeting expletives "unfairly forces viewers (including children) to take "the first blow." The court rejected the claim that this served as a "reasoned basis" for overturning the prior policy for several reasons. The FCC had not provided a reasonable explanation for why it had changed its perception, after 30 years, that a fleeting expletive was not a harmful "first blow."

The Supreme Court, in a 5-4 decision, overturned the appeals court decision and upheld the FCC policy. Justice ANTONIN SCALIA, writing for the majority, found that there was no basis in the Administrative Procedure Act that all agency change must be subjected to more searching review. An agency must show that there are good reasons for the new policy but it "need not demonstrate to a court's satisfaction that the reasons for the new policy are *better* than the reasons for the old one." Based on this assumption, Justice Scalia noted that the FCC had announced it was breaking new ground. In addition, its reasons for expanding the scope of enforcement was "entirely rational." It was reasonable to conclude that "it made no sense to distinguish between literal and nonliteral uses of offensive words, requiring repetitive use to render only the latter indecent." Moreover, that fact that technological advances make it easier for broadcasters to bleep out offending words supported the commission's policy. The Court remanded the case to the Second Circuit, where the broadcasters can **advance** their constitutional arguments. In a revealing concurring opinion, Justice Clarence Thomas announced he was ready to overturn prior rulings on First Amendment grounds that have underpinned the regulation of indecency in broadcasting.

Justice STEPHEN BREYER, in a dissenting opinion joined by three other justices, argued that the FCC had utterly failed to provide reasonable grounds for the change in policy. Moreover, he believed the FCC approach was unconstitutional and that the Court should have ruled so without a remand to the appeals court.

FEDERAL DEPOSIT INSURANCE CORPORATION

FDIC Steps in to Try to Curb Foreclosure Crisis

With foreclosures in the U.S. continually rising, many looked to the government to take appropriate steps to end the crisis. One of the advocates for government intervention was the chair of the FEDERAL DEPOSIT INSURANCE CORPORATION (FDIC), who began offering warnings of the crisis throughout 2008. The new presidential administration under Barack Obama moved the **foreclosure** crisis to the forefront of the government's concern, but this crisis continued during the first several months of 2009.

The 1990s saw a rise in what is known as subprime lending. This type of lending applies to individuals who cannot qualify for traditional loans due to poor credit or lack of credit. These types of loans take into account the greater risk that a lender assumes, and so these loans benefit the lenders more so than with traditional loans. A common example of a subprime loan is an adjustable rate mortgage. When a borrower takes out a mortgage such as this, the interest rate will begin at one figure but will then change during the course of the loans (usually the interest rate will increase). When the interest rate increases, the borrower must pay a higher monthly rate. A traditional loan, by comparison, usually involves a fixed interest rate.

After the recession of 2001, interest rates as a whole dropped significantly. In the wake of that recession, housing prices began to rise. Between 2002 and 2005, the combination of the lower interest rates and the increases in housing prices created a real estate boom. Due in large part to the increase in housing prices, lenders eased their credit standards, gambling that the housing prices would continue to increase. In 2006, though, the housing prices began to decline, which resulted in an increase in delinquency rates for mortgage payments. Many of those who fell behind on their mortgage payments had subprime loans.

The number of defaults on subprime loans continued in 2007. In May 2007, Federal Reserve Chairman Ben Bernanke said that the number of defaults would not cause serious harm to the U.S. economy. However, by July 2007, Bernanke told the Banking Committee of the Senate that there may be as much as $100 billion on losses resulting from subprime mortgages. Beginning in September 2007, the Federal Reserve began making cuts in the interest rates, citing concerns with the effect of the mortgage crisis on the economy as a whole.

The mortgage crisis did not improve in 2008. In January 2008, one of the biggest subprime mortgage lenders, Countrywide, was purchased by Bank of America for about $4 billion. The response of the Bush administration was to ask lenders to voluntarily modify loans so that borrowers could afford their mortgage payments. Critics of the administration said that this strategy was not going to be effective. Sheila Bair, chairwoman of the Federal Deposit Insurance Corporation, became vocal in 2008 about the need for government intervention in the housing crisis. With regard to the Bush administration's strategy, Bair said:

> [Treasury] Secretary [Henry] Paulson has been aggressively involved in calling senior management of servicers and telling them they need to modify loans. But because of the scale of the problem, the pace is just now what it really needs to be.

The situation became worse during the summer of 2008. On July 11, 2008, federal regulators had to take control of IndyMac Bancorp Inc. after depositors made a run on the bank, depleting the bank's cash supply. The overall economic situations continued to worsen, and on September 7, the government seized control of Fannie Mae and Freddie Mac, the two largest mortgage-finance companies in the United States. During the month of September, several prominent Wall Street companies failed or were on the verge of failing. This month was one of the worst periods since the Great Depression.

In October, Bair appeared before the Senate Banking Committee as members of Congress were pressing the administration to do more to slow down the rate of foreclosures. Bair said that the FDIC was working closely with the TREASURY DEPARTMENT on a program that would provide assistance to those struggling with mortgages. Bair testified, "Specifically, the

A foreclosure sign in Denver, August 29, 2007.

AP IMAGES

government could establish standards for loan modifications and provide guarantees for loans meeting those standards. By doing so, unaffordable loans could be converted into loans that are sustainable over the long term." Assistant Treasury Secretary Neel T. Kashkari also told the committee about the Treasury Department's plans. These plans included a strategy to purchase troubled assets from financial firms. Members of the committee were skeptical of the plans of both the FDIC and the Treasury Department, arguing that the banks receiving government assistance had not been asked to do enough to help struggling homeowners.

After Barack Obama won the 2008 presidential election, one of the first crises he addressed was the foreclosure crisis. In an interview that appeared on "60 Minutes," Obama said:

> We've got to set up a negotiation between banks and borrowers so that people can stay in their homes. That is going to have an impact on the economy as a whole. And, you know, one thing I'm determined is that if we don't have a clear focused program for homeowners by the time I take office, we will after I take office.

Shortly after Obama made those comments, the FDIC announced a proposal that called for the government to spend $24 billion to allow 1.5 million households to avoid foreclosure.

Although much of the focus of the foreclosure crisis had been on bad subprime loans, the crisis also affected more affluent borrowers who had taken out traditional, fixed-rate loans. This was especially true in California, which had seen an explosion in the housing market throughout most of the decade come to a halt beginning in 2007. Housing prices dropped severely, leaving many homeowners with houses worth less than the balance of the large mortgages. In several reported cases, homeowners owed hundreds of thousands more on their mortgages than their homes were worth, leaving these owners with few choices.

Some fear that the crisis is not over, given how many adjustable rate mortgages are scheduled to reset (likely meaning increase) over the next two years. The Obama administration has taken steps to prevent further problems. In February 2009, Obama announced a $75 billion plan called Making Home Affordable, which would offer assistance to as many as nine million homeowners. On April 23, 2009, Bair expressed some optimism, noting that the crisis among banks and the housing market were over and that regulators were in the "clean-up stage."

FIRST AMENDMENT

Eleventh Circuit Partially Rejects Challenge to Florida Pledge of Allegiance Law

In a decision handed down in 2008, the Eleventh **Circuit Court** of Appeals partially rejected an argument regarding the constitutionality of a Florida law requiring students to recite the pledge of allegiance. In *Frazier ex rel. Frazier v. Winn*, 535 F.3d 1279 (11th Cir. 2008), the court determined that requiring a student to obtain parental consent to be excused from reciting the pledge did not violate the student's constitutional rights. However, the court concluded that requiring the student to stand during the recitation of the pledge violated the student's FIRST AMENDMENT rights.

The courts have considered numerous challenges related to shows of respect to the American flag. For instance, in *West Virginia State Board of Education v. Barnette*, 319 U.S. 624, 63 S. Ct. 1178 (1943), the U.S. SUPREME COURT held that a state could not constitutionally require students to salute the flag. Later cases have upheld the right of schools to require students to recite the pledge of allegiance. However, most courts have concurred that students should be allowed to refuse to participate in reciting the pledge. Thus, in *Goetz v. Ansell*, 477 F.2d 636 (2d Cir. 1973), the Second

Circuit Court of Appeals ruled that a school could not require a student to stand in silence when others are reciting the pledge. Instead, the court in *Goetz* concluded that the student must be allowed to remain seated.

Section 1003.44(1) of the Florida Statutes requires students at elementary, middle, and high schools to recite the pledge of allegiance each day before class. The **statute** specifies, "When the pledge is given, civilians must show full respect to the flag by standing at attention . . . ." The statute requires schools to inform students that the students have a right to refuse to participate. However, the statute requires the student to obtain written permission from the student's parent before refusing to participate.

The district board of education at Boynton Beach Community High School in Palm Beach County, Florida adopted a policy requiring students to recite the Pledge of Allegiance each day, consistent with the state statute. The school's administration maintained a form containing the school's policy with a line for the parent's signature showing parental consent for refusal to recite the pledge. However, even when the student's parent signed the consent form, the school's policy required every student to stand while others recite the pledge.

Cameron Frazier was an eleventh grade student at Boynton in December 2005. Ordinarily, students recited the pledge early in the day, and Frazier had always remained seated and refused to recite the pledge. He had not previously received parental permission to refuse to recite the pledge, and other teachers had not punished him for refusing to participate. On December 8, 2005, the school recited the pledge later in the day than normal. Frazier was present in Cynthia Alexandre's math class at that time. When the students stood to recite the pledge, Frazier remained seated. Alexandre ordered Frazier to stand several times, but Frazier continued to refuse.

The altercation between Alexandre and Frazier became more heated. Alexandre showed Frazier a copy of the school policy that recited the provisions of section 1003.44 of the Florida Statutes. When Frazier continued to refuse, Alexandre called the principal's office to have Frazier dismissed from class. Salvatore Camp, the school's assistant principal, escorted Frazier from the class to the principal's office and handed Frazier a copy of the school policy.

Camp informed Frazier that Frazier's mother would have to sign the policy. However, Camp said that Frazier would still have to stand during the reciting of the pledge.

Acting through his mother, Frazier brought suit against the school district, Alexandre, and Camp. Frazier argued that the school and the school employees had violated his First Amendment rights. He sought injunctive relief as well as damages under 42 U.S.C. § 1983. Judge Kenneth L. Ryskamp of the U.S. **District Court** for the Southern District of Florida agreed with Frazier, holding that the school violated Frazier's constitutional rights both by requiring Frazier to obtain parental consent and by requiring him to stand during the recitation of the pledge. The judge granted Frazier's motion for **summary judgment** and required the school district to end its practice of enforcing the policy regarding the pledge.

The school district appealed the decision to the Eleventh Circuit Court of Appeals. In a **per curiam** decision, a three-judge panel reviewed the constitutionality of different aspects of the school's policy. *Frazier ex rel. Frazier v. Winn*, 535 F.3d 1279 (11th Cir. 2008). The first aspect related to the school's requirement than any "civilian" stand at attention during the recitation of the pledge. The second aspect related to the provision requiring a student to obtain parental consent before refusing to recite the pledge.

The court resolved the first issue relatively easily because the Eleventh Circuit had previously concluded that students have a clearly established right to remain seated during the pledge of allegiance. In *Holloman ex rel. Holloman v. Harland*, 370 F.3d 1252 (11th Cir. 2004), the court concluded that a student not only had the right to remain silent during the pledge, but he also had the right to raise his fist during the recitation of the pledge.

Boynton argued that the court should construe the statute to allow the school to require students to stand, but the court rejected this argument. However, the court concluded that the requirement that civilians stand during the pledge was severable from the rest of the statute. Therefore, the court struck the standing requirement and considered the rest of the statute separately.

The court characterized the parental consent provision of the statute is more focused on parental rights. Since the statute's concern focuses on the rights of parents to interfere with the wishes of their children, the court concluded that the state's interest in protecting the parent's rights is great enough to restrict the student's speech. Therefore, the court concluded that the parental consent requirement was constitutional under the First Amendment.

Frazier requested an **en banc** review of the panel's decision. However, the court denied the petition. Circuit Judge Rosemary Barkett wrote a dissent from the denial of rehearing, arguing that the court did not properly consider precedents when reaching the decision. Florida Attorney General Bill McCollum was pleased with the result, however, noting, "[We] see it as a significant issue for parents and families."

Third Circuit Again Strikes Down Child Online Protection Act

In a case that parties litigated for more than a decade, the Third **Circuit Court** of Appeals in 2008 struck down the Child Online Protection Act. This **statute** provided civil and criminal penalties for anyone who posted on the Internet material that would have been harmful to minors. However, the statute never went into effect because immediately after its enactment, parties successfully enjoined the statute's application. The Supreme Court declined to review the Third Circuit's decision, meaning that the litigation surrounding the case has probably come to an end.

Concerned with protecting children from harmful content found on the Internet, Congress enacted the Communications Decency Act as part of the Telecommunications Act of 1996, Pub. L. No. 104-104, 108 Stat. 56. The AMERICAN CIVIL LIBERTIES UNION (ACLU) and other parties immediately challenged the statute, arguing that the statute violated FIRST AMENDMENT rights of Internet users. The case reached the Supreme Court, which struck down the CDA. *Reno v. ACLU*, 521 U.S. 844, 117 S. Ct. 2329, 138 L. Ed. 2d 874 (1997).

Immediately after the Court's decision in *Reno*, Congress enacted the Child Online Protection Act (COPA), Pub. L. No. 105-277, 112 Stat. 2681-736 as part of an **omnibus** appropriations statute. The text of COPA provided that:

> Whoever knowingly and with knowledge of the character of the material, in interstate or foreign commerce by means of the World

Wide Web, makes any communication for commercial purposes that is available to any minor and that includes material that is harmful to minors shall be fined not more than $50,000, imprisoned not more than 6 months, or both.

In defining what is "harmful to minors," Congress borrowed language from the Supreme Court's definition of obscenity as set forth in *Miller v. California*, 413 U.S. 15, 93 S. Ct. 2607, 37 L. Ed. 2d 419 (1973).

Opponents of the statute immediately challenged it in federal court. The U.S. **District Court** for the Eastern District of Pennsylvania enjoined the enforcement of the statute in 1999, and the case was appealed to the Third Circuit. The Third Circuit in 2000 determined that the "community standards" provision of the statute was overly broad, rendering the statute unconstitutional. *ACLU v. Reno*, 217 F.3d 163 (3d Cir. 2000). The government appealed the case to the Supreme Court, which disagreed with the Third Circuit and held that the community standards provision was not unconstitutional on its own. *Ashcroft v. ACLU*, 535 U.S. 564, 122 S. Ct. 1700, 152 L. Ed. 2d 771 (2002).

The appeals continued. The Third Circuit in 2003 again determined that the statute violated the First Amendment, in part because the statute was not the least restrictive means to prevent minors from being exposed to harmful material on the Internet. *ACLU v. Ashcroft*, 322 F.3d 240 (3d Cir. 2003). The Supreme Court affirmed the Third Circuit's decision but also remanded the case to the district court so that the district court could make a factual finding about whether Internet filters were a more effective means of restricting minors from accessing harmful information. In 2007, the district court concluded in a lengthy opinion that COPA violated the First Amendment. Accordingly, the lower court enjoined the government from enforcing the statute. *ACLU v. Gonzales*, 478 F. Supp. 2d 773 (E.D. Pa. 2007).

In issuing the injunction, U.S. District Judge Lowell A. Reed Jr. noted that he was personally unhappy with the decision he had to reach. He wrote, "Despite my personal regret at having to set aside yet another attempt to protect our children from harmful material." On the other hand, Reed determined that the provisions in COPA would have more long-term damaging effects on children because the statute would infringe on their free speech rights. "Perhaps we

do the minors of this country harm if First Amendment protections, which they will with age inherit fully, are chipped away in the name of their protection," Reed wrote.

Sitting for the Third Circuit was a three-judge panel consisting of Judges Morton I. Greenberg, Thomas L. Ambro, and Michael A. Chagares. Before the court, the government argued that the district court had erred in concluding COPA did not satisfy the **strict scrutiny** standard. This standard required the government to prove that COPA: (1) served a compelling governmental interest, (2) was narrowly tailored to achieve that interest, and (3) was the least restrictive means of advancing that interest. Previous Supreme Court cases had established that protecting the physical and psychological well-being of minors was a compelling governmental interest. *Sable Communications of Cal., Inc. v. FCC*, 492 U.S. 115, 109 S. Ct. 2829, 106 L. Ed. 2d 93 (1989). The Third Circuit panel agreed and turned its attention to the other elements of the strict scrutiny standard.

The government argued that the statute was narrowly tailored because the statute allowed web developers to avoid prosecution by using age verification tools. The government also argued that the district court had erred by focusing too much attention on website owners who provided adult content for free, rather than focusing on commercial pornographers. The Third Circuit panel disagreed, noting that the statute placed an undue burden on all of the website owners, whether they were the principal focus of the statute's provisions or not. The court also disagreed that COPA's provisions were no different than so-called "blinder racks," which hide the covers of adult-themed publications.

The court also concluded that COPA's provisions were not the least restrictive means of advancing the government's interest in protecting minors. The court reviewed the district court's findings of fact, which focused heavily on whether COPA was necessary given the availability of Internet filters. The district court noted that "unlike COPA there are no fines or prison sentences associated with filters which would chill speech. Also unlike COPA, . . . filters are fully customizable and may be set for different ages and for different categories of speech or may be disabled altogether for adult use. As a result, filters are less restrictive than COPA." *Gonzales* 478 F. Supp. 2d at 813. The government argued that the filters are not less restrictive than COPA because the filters are part of the "status quo." The court disagreed, however.

The Third Circuit additionally determined that the statute was overly broad and vague. For these reasons, the court affirmed the district court's 2007 order. *ACLU v. Mukasey*, 534 F.3d 181 (3d Cir. 2008). The Supreme Court denied **certiorari** on January 21, 2009, meaning that enforcement of COPA will be enjoined permanently.

Pleasant Grove City, Utah v. Summum

The FIRST AMENDMENT includes both the Free Speech Clause and the Establishment Clause. The first guarantees the right of persons to free expression, while the second prohibits government from supporting religious organizations. The two clauses came into conflict in *Pleasant Grove City, Utah v. Summum*, __U.S.__, 129 S.Ct.1125, ___ L.Ed.2d ___ (2009), when a small religious organization was denied the right to place a religious monument in a public park that contained a Ten Commandments monument. The Court held that First Amendment free speech protections did not prevent the city from denying the request.

Pioneer Park, a public park in Pleasant Grove City, Utah has 15 permanent displays on its grounds. Eleven of these displays have been privately donated, including a Ten Commandments monument. They include an historic granary, a wishing well, and a September 11 monument. Summum is a religious organization founded in 1975 and based on Gnostic Christianity. Summum's headquarters are located in Salt Lake City, Utah. In 2003, Summum twice wrote the the mayor of Pleasant Grove City requesting that it be permitted to erect a stone monument which would contain the "Seven Aphorisms of Summum." The proposed monument was to be similar in size and nature to the Ten Commandments monument, which had been donated by the Fraternal Order of Eagles in 1971.

The city denied both of Summum's requests. The city informed the organization that its practice was to limit monuments in the park to those that were either directly related to the history of the city or were donated by

groups with longstanding ties to the Pleasant Grove community. In 2004 the city passed resolution that put this policy into writing. Summum renewed its request in 2005 but did not describe the monument's historical significance or the organization's connection to the Pleasant Grove community. The city council rejected this request.

Summum then filed suit in federal **district court**, claiming that the city had violated the Free Speech Clause of the First Amendment by accepting the Ten Commandments monument but rejecting the Seven Aphorisms monument. It asked the federal court to issue an injunction that would permit Summum to erect its monument in the park. The district court denied this request. Summum then appealed to the Tenth **Circuit Court** of Appeals on its free speech claim. The appeals court reversed the lower court decision, noting a previous ruling of the circuit that found the Ten Commandments monument in Pioneer Park to be private rather than government speech. Finding that public parks have traditionally been treated as public forums, the appeals court held that the city could not reject the Summum monument unless it had a compelling justification that could not be served by more narrowly tailored means. Concluding that the city was unlikely to meet these requirements, the court ruled that Pleasant Grove City was required to erect the Seven Aphorisms monument. The city then appealed to the U.S. SUPREME COURT.

The U.S. Supreme Court has examined many First Amendment issues involving free speech, yet this was the first time it was called upon to examine whether the Free Speech Clause governed the acceptance of privately donated, permanent monuments for erection in a public park. A long line of cases have dealt with free speech and the use of government property to exercise First Amendment rights. The public forum doctrine recognizes that members of the public may exercise free speech rights on public streets and in public parks. However, the government make impose reasonable **time, place, and manner restrictions** on the public's use of these public areas. Such restrictions will be subjected to **strict scrutiny**, a constitutional standard of review that requires the government to show that the restrictions are narrowly tailored to serve a compelling government interest.

In this case the Tenth Circuit had found that the city's reasons for rejecting the monument did not survive strict scrutiny under the Free Speech Clause. The Supreme Court, in a unanimous decision, overturned the appeals court, finding that issue was not the private speech rights of Summum but the free speech rights of government. In a recent line of cases the Court has established a government speech doctrine in which the First Amendment does not apply to government-made expression. Though the decision was unanimous, four justices wrote separately to express their concerns about this new doctrine and the possibility it could be misused. Justice Samuel Alito wrote the lead opinion, joined by seven other justices.

The Court extended a government entity's right to free expression to situations where private sources assist in delivering the government-controlled message. However, it acknowledged that government speech is not totally unregulated. The First Amendment's Establishment Clause places limits on how far the government may go in its support of religion. In addition, government officials may be limited in their public advocacy by law, regulation, practice, and the electorate. Citizens are free to choose different officials who espouse different views.

In this case the city officials were using government speech when they chose which monuments could be installed in the public park. The Court noted that since ancient times, governments have used monuments to speak to the public. Monuments are a means of government expression even if they are privately financed and donated and accepted by the government for erection on public lands. Examples of privately financed federal monuments include the Statue of Liberty, the Marine Corps War Memorial, and the Vietnam Veterans Memorial. States and cities have also received thousands of donated monuments since the beginning of the Republic. Privately donated monuments save tax dollars and provide means of public expression that the government could not have afforded. However, government entities exercise their discretion in accepting privately funded monuments, as to the the design and content. Monuments that are accepted are meant to convey a government message; this constitutes government speech.

Summum had argued that the government speech doctrine could be used as a subterfuge for favoring certain private speakers over others based on viewpoint. It suggested that a government **entity** that accepted a privately donated monument use a formal process that would require the adoption of a resolution embracing the "message" that the monument conveys. If the government did not adopt the message, then the monument would be considered private speech and subject to a violation of the Establishment Clause. The Court rejected this requirement as unworkable. Government entities would have to retroactively adopt the message of thousands of monuments. Moreover, the "message" of a monument can shift over time and, in fact, each person who views a monument may see a different viewpoint expressed.

Finally, the Court rejected the public forum argument advanced by Summum and adopted by the Tenth Circuit. A park can accommodate a large number of public speakers without defeating the basic function of a park. In contrast, a park can contain only a limited number of permanent monuments. Adopting the Summum position would force government entities to either allow a park to be overwhelmed by monuments or to remove long-standing monuments filled with historical and cultural significance. Therefore, Pleasant Grove City was not subject to the Free Speech Clause.

In a set of concurring opinions, four justices expressed their concerns about the government speech doctrine. Justice DAVID SOUTER, in particular, counseled against moving too quickly in defining the doctrine. In his view the interplay between the government speech doctrine and Establishment Clause principles have not been addressed at all.

Ysursa v. Pocatello Education Association

The FIRST AMENDMENT guarantees **freedom of association** and freedom of expression. The Supreme Court places heavy burdens on government when it attempts to restrict First Amendment rights. However, the Court has ruled that state government may impose restrictions on the First Amendment rights of state and local government employees if it can demonstrate a rational basis for the regulation. This is in contrast to private citizens, where the Court employs a **strict scrutiny** test to determine if the government has a compelling interest in imposing the regulation and carries out the regulation in the least restrictive manner. Government usually prevails when the **rational basis test** is applied, while it has more difficulty when the strict scrutiny test is used. The difference in outcome is illustrated in *Ysursa v. Pocatello Education Association*, __U.S.__, 129 S.Ct. 1093, __L.Ed.2d__ (2009), where the Supreme Court upheld a state law that prohibited state and local governments from allowing public employees to have union dues dedicated to political activities deducted from their paychecks. The Court rejected the application of strict scrutiny that the lower **federal courts** had used and instead applied rational basis.

The state of Idaho has enacted a Right to Work Act, which states that the right to work will not be infringed or restricted based on union membership or a refusal to join a union. Until 2003, employees, both private and public, could authorize both a payroll deduction for general union dues and a payroll deduction for union political activities. In that year the legislature amended the Right to Work Act, prohibiting payroll deductions for political activities. These activities included "electoral activities, independent expenditures, or expenditures made to any candidate, political party, political action committee or in support or against any ballot measure." Unions in Idaho objected to this change, as it would make the collection of these types of dues very difficult and costly. A group of labor organizations sued state and local government officials, contending that the amendment violated the First Amendment.

The federal **district court** rejected this argument as to state public employees because the First Amendment does not compel the state to subsidize speech by providing at its own expense payroll deductions. However, the court ruled that the amendment did violate the First Amendment rights of local governments and private employees because the state had failed to identify any subsidy it provided to these employers to administer payroll deductions. Idaho filed an appeal in which neither party challenged the rulings as to private and state-level employees. The only issue on appeal to the Ninth **Circuit Court** of Appeals was the application of the ban to local government employees. The Ninth Circuit sided with the district court, holding that the relationship between the state and its local government

subdivisions was analogous to that between the state and a regulated private utility. This analogy allowed the Ninth Circuit to apply strict scrutiny, which led to the ruling that the law was unconstitutional.

The Supreme Court, in a 6-3 decision, overturned the Ninth Circuit ruling. Chief Justice JOHN ROBERTS, writing for the majority, noted that while government may in some situations accommodate expression, "it is not required to assist others in funding the expression of particular ideas, including political ones." Idaho was under no obligation to aid the unions in their political activities and the state's decision not to do so was not "an abridgment of the union's speech." Because the state had not infringed the unions' First Amendment rights the Court did not need to apply strict scrutiny. The state only had to show it had a rational basis to justify the prohibition on political payroll deductions of its employees. In this case Idaho justified the ban to avoid the reality or the appearance of government favoritism or entanglement with partisan politics.

As to the ban on local governments to make payroll deductions, the unions contended strict strict scrutiny did apply because the state was no longer declining to facilitate speech through its payroll system was was obstructing speech in the local governments' payroll systems. The Court found no merit in this argument. Chief Justice Roberts held that rational basis was the appropriate way to review this part of the law. Municipal and county governments are not sovereign entities but subordinate units of government created by the state. Therefore, Idaho could withhold from all public employers "the power to provide payroll deductions for political activities." The same state interests that justified the ban on state employee deductions applied as well to employees "at whatever level of government."

Three justices dissented and filed individual opinions. Justice JOHN PAUL STEVENS argued that the was unconstitutional as applied because "it is clear to me that the restriction was intended to make it more difficult for unions to finance political speech." The avowed purpose in avoiding employer political involvement was inconsistent with the state's failure to restrict deductions for charitable activities. Charitable deductions "will often present a similar risk of creating an appearance of political involvement as deductions for covered political activities." The law as meant to target union political activity. Viewed in this way, strict scrutiny would render the **statute** unconstitutional under the First Amendment.

FOOD AND DRUG ADMINISTRATION

Salmonella Outbreak Leads to Hundreds of Illnesses

In 2008 and 2009, several hundred people became ill as a result of an outbreak of Salmonella Typhimurium. In early 2009, U.S. health officials determined that the outbreak was caused by certain products containing peanut butter. Authorities traced the outbreak to one Georgia-based plant owned by the Peanut Corporation of America (PCA). By April 2009, a total of 714 people had been infected in 46 states. Half of those infected were younger than 16 years of age.

Salmonella is a form of bacteria that most typically infects cattle and poultry. Salmonella appears in a number of different strains, including Salmonella Typhimurium, which can lead to salmonellosis. Symptoms of salmonellosis include high fever, vomiting, diarrhea, and stomach cramps. The majority of those infected with salmonellosis can recover without treatment. However, the infection can become severe, leading to death, especially when the victims are elderly or very young.

Prior to the peanut butter outbreak, the PCA had been the subject of investigations by the FOOD AND DRUG ADMINISTRATION (FDA). On two different occasions, the FDA had found in PCA plants the presence of afltoxins, which are toxins created by mold. Until recent years, however, the PCA did not make peanut butter. The PCA first started producing peanut butter in 2006 at its plant in Blakely, Georgia. The FDA inspected the plant in 2007 and required the PCA to make corrections.

PCA was under inspection again in 2008. In April, a distributor in Canada discovered that PCA peanuts contained metal fragments, leading the distributor to refuse PCA shipments. About two months later, the Georgia DEPARTMENT OF AGRICULTURE conducted a seven-day inspection of the PCA's plant at Blakely. The inspection revealed a number of problems related to cleanliness. The Georgia Department of Agriculture conducted further inspections later in 2008. In October, the inspection revealed that mildew was growing on the ceiling of one of the plant's storage rooms.

At Gleaners Food Bank, Indianapolis, students open packages of peanut butter crackers, February 7, 2009, during the salmonella scare.

AP IMAGES

FDA Comes Under Fire

Throughout the twentieth century, the United States attempted to protect consumers with the enactment of several statutes related to food and drug safety, proper labeling of food and drug items, and so forth. The first of these statutes was the Pure Food and Drug Act, ch. 384, 34 Stat. 768 in 1906. The predecessor to the U.S. FOOD AND DRUG ADMINISTRATION (FDA) was responsible for implementing the 1906 act, and the FDA celebrated its 100th anniversary in 2006 based on the passage of the 1906 act.

Notwithstanding passage of these statutes, the FDA has increasingly come under fire for its failure to detect problems that have led to food and drug scares in recent years. Advocacy groups have called for a comprehensive reform of the agency as part of an effort to ensure safety of not only food products but also other areas that fall under the FDA's **purview**, including drugs and medical devices.

Food companies have fallen under a great deal of pressure to reduce food prices, especially during the recession in 2008 and 2009. The global market for food ingredients may reach more than $34 billion in 2010. To reduce prices, companies often subcontract parts of the processing work to smaller companies, and so the food companies ultimately responsible for preparation of the food items and for distributing the food items may not know the source of food that may be contaminated.

In 2007, an estimated 15,000 people became ill due to frozen pot pies containing salmonella. FDA officials could not determine what ingredients carried the bacteria, despite comprehensive testing. ConAgra Foods, which prepared the pot pies, also could not determine which individual ingredients were the cause, and efforts by the company to prepare the food differently by cooking the foods at higher temperatures failed. ConAgra eventually conceded that it could not guarantee the safety of its foods and relied instead on cooking instructions that were supposed to make the food safer. These instructions required the consumer to measure the internal temperature of the pot pie with a cooking thermometer.

ConAgra's concession about the safety of its frozen pot pies was not a remote event. Other food companies such as Nestle, Blackstone Group (which makes the Swanson and Hungry-Man brands), and General Mills have also acknowledged that they could not guarantee the safety of the food. General Mills was forced to recall five million frozen pizzas in 2007 because of an outbreak of the E. coli bacteria. The company has since advised consumers to cook food in conventional ovens rather than microwaves.

Several hundred people in 2008 and 2009 became sick when salmonella appeared in certain peanut products. Prior to the outbreak, FDA officials had inspected peanut plants owned by the Peanut Corporation of America. Despite the inspection, the FDA failed to identify that the salmonella had come from the same plant. The peanut salmonella scare was just another of several food poisoning scares that had shaken consumer confidence in the safety of its food products.

Concerns about the FDA's competency in ensuring safety of products has certainly not been limited to food products. Legislation during the early 1990s was designed to shorten the time it would take for the FDA to approve

---

The first incident involving Salmonella occurred around September 1, 2008, according to the Centers for the Disease Control and Prevention (CDC). The CDC began to monitor the salmonella problem in November, after the outbreak had spread to 12 states. On November 24, a 78-year-old woman in Kingsport, Tennessee died after suffering from high fever and diarrhea for a week. By the time of the woman's death, salmonella incidents had spread to a total of 16 states.

Early in December 2008, the FDA and the CDC stepped up their investigations of the salmonella illnesses. The agencies conducted a number of interviews and attempted to identify the food item that was the likely cause of these illnesses. Peanut butter emerged as the likely source of the outbreak. Between December 21, 2008 and January 4, 2009, three elderly women who had been infected with salmonella died, and at least two of these women consumed peanut butter frequently.

In early January, the FDA looked more closely at institutional food service sources of peanut butter. The FDA determined that the PCA's plant in Blakely was the likely source for the salmonella outbreak. The facility made a brand of peanut butter that was distributed to nursing homes. The company also made a peanut paste that was used by manufacturers in products such as cereal, cookies, crackers, and ice cream. On January 15, FDA officials asked food companies that had purchased peanut butter and peanut paste from PCA's

FDA COMES UNDER FIRE

(CONTINUED)

drugs, but an effect of this legislation was that it increased the workload of FDA officials responsible for reviewing the drugs. Critics have said that the FDA's failures in the context of drug approval have been due in part to the agency's close relationship with drug manufacturers. A series of drugs were introduced to the marketplace with great fanfare, only to be recalled later when tests revealed side effects or other problems. Examples include Vioxx, Bextra, Zelnorm, Tysabri, NeutroSpec, Cylert, Permax, Baycol, and Palladone.

Although concerns regarding the FDA existed before the 2000s, some Democrats placed blame for the agency's shortcomings on policies under the administration of former President GEORGE W. BUSH. According to Representative Henry Waxman (D.-Cal.):

> FDA was our country's first **consumer protection** agency and Americans have relied on FDA to ensure the safety of their food and drugs for 100 years. Under the Bush Administration, FDA has undermined enforcement and betrayed its consumer-first legacy. FDA must start enforcing the law and

return to a culture that places public health concerns ahead of industry profits.

Critics were not limited to politicians. In 2004, an FDA researcher named David Graham appeared before the Senate Finance Committee. According to Graham, the FDA had wholly failed to act on evidence that the painkiller Vioxx was causing heart problems and that the drug had caused some users to suffer heart attacks. Moreover, Graham asserted that the FDA was incapable of protecting the public from future problems with the side effects of drugs. About a year later, Graham said in interviews that the FDA had become worse since the time of his testimony, asserting that steps the FDA had taken in response to the Vioxx fiasco was little more than window dressing.

Congress addressed some of the concerns regarding the FDA by passing the Food and Drug Administration Amendments Act of 2007, Pub. L. No. 110-85, 121 Stat. 823. Although the legislation was designed to increase the resources that the agency had available, critics said that the legislation did not offer enough by way of reform. The act focused primarily on the agency's review

of drugs and medical devices, rather than food inspection. A review conducted by the Department of Health and Human Services in 2007 noted that the FDA suffered from ineffective oversight.

As Barack Obama worked on his transition to the presidency, it became clear that reforming the FDA needed to be one of his tasks. Prior to his inauguration, a group of FDA scientists sent a letter to Obama asking the president-elect to restructure the agency. According to these scientists, managers with the FDA had coerced and intimidated the scientists to manipulate data illegally. The scientists concluded that the agency was "fundamentally broken."

Obama appointed Margaret Hamburg as the new FDA commissioner in May 2009. As she took office, she said that the public could expect a "modern food-safety system focused on prevention of contamination." Hamburg's statements demonstrated that the FDA was not only concerned with dangerous pharmaceuticals, but also with food contamination. Hamburg's first task may be her most difficult: restoring the integrity of the agency responsible for ensuring food and drug safety.

Blakely facility to test products for salmonella contamination. Although about 85 companies purchased products from PCA, the outbreak had not affected the major brands of peanut butter.

On January 27, the FDA completed its investigation of the Blakely plant. According to an FDA statement, the PCA's records showed that the company had discovered salmonella in its products on 12 occasions. These test took place in 2007 and 2008. When a test was positive for salmonella, the company had its products retested by an outside lab. If the outside lab's results were negative, then the company shipped the products, notwithstanding the company's positive test. FDA spokespersons stressed that the company had violated

standard practices related to food quality. The company had not previously revealed these test results to the FDA or the Georgia Department of Agriculture.

Shortly after the FDA released its statement, the PCA announced that it would recall every peanut product produced at the Blakely plant over a two-year period. The recall was one of the largest in U.S. history, affecting nearly 4,000 products distributed by an estimated 361 companies. The PCA decided to close the Blakely facility during the investigation. On January 30, the FDA announced that it would further intensify its probe by involving the agency's criminal division. The FEDERAL BUREAU OF INVESTIGATION (FBI) raided the Blakely plant as part of the probe.

The investigation expanded to Texas. The PCA on February 10 announced that it would close its plant in Plainview, Texas, pending the results of the FDA's investigation. Days later, officials with the Texas DEPARTMENT OF STATE Health Services ordered the PCA to recall all products produced by the Plainview plant. The plant had opened in 2005 and operated for four years without being inspected. Texas officials tested the facility and discovered the presence of the salmonella bacteria.

On February 13, the PCA announced that it had filed for Chapter 7 bankruptcy with a U.S. Bankruptcy Court in Virginia. Following the announcement, company officials said they would no longer respond to customer complaints and inquiries about PCA products. One week after the PCA's announcement, Texas officials announced that the Texas Department of State Health Services would take over the recall of PCA's products from the Plainview plant.

The result of the peanut butter recall had a devastating effect on the peanut industry. Although major brands were not directly affected by the salmonella outbreak, customers shied away from purchasing peanut products out of fear of infection. Members of the peanut industry estimate that the outbreak cost the industry about $1 billion.

FOREIGN INTELLIGENCE SURVEILLANCE COURT

Justice Department Reports Increase in Surveillance Warrants

The perceived tension between protecting civil liberties and accommodating domestic national security requirements creates many opportunities for challenge. Never was this more palpable than with the outrage expressed by many Americans when they learned that the U.S. government had authority, without a warrant, to intercept private telephone and internet communications for the purpose of gathering intelligence against foreign terrorists acting within the United States. But that authority was more limited than most Americans understood.

The Foreign Intelligence Surveillance Act of 1978 (FISA), 50 USC 1801 *et seq.,* was enacted to create judicial and Congressional oversight of foreign intelligence surveillance activities conducted in the name of national security. To that end, FISA, as amended over the years,

establishes procedures for the authorization of electronic surveillance, use of pen registers and trap and trace devices, physical searches, and business records for the purpose of gathering foreign intelligence. FISA requires an annual report to Congress from the U.S. Department of Justice regarding activities covered by the Act.

Importantly, and at issue here, Section §1803 of FISA created the U.S. Foreign Intelligence Surveillance Court (FISC). The FISC, in turn, holds non-public sessions to oversee requests for surveillance warrants (primarily from federal agencies, including the FBI) against suspected foreign intelligence agents operating inside the United States. Section §1802 contains an exception to allow the President to authorize electronic surveillance without a court order for a warrant. Under this exception, the Attorney General must certify that there is "no substantial likelihood that the surveillance will acquire the contents of any communication to which a U.S. person is a party," provided the surveillance is directed solely at communications between foreign powers or "the acquisition of technical intelligence.from property or premises under the open and exclusive control of a foreign power."

The annual report released by the JUSTICE DEPARTMENT in April 2008 showed that the number of secret surveillance warrants granted had more than doubled since the terrorist attacks against the United States on September 11, 2001. According to the report, the FISC approved 2370 requests in 2007, compared to 1102 in 2000. It further showed that in 2007, the FISC made substantive changes to 86 of the government's requests before granting them, denied one in part, and denied three surveillance requests in their entirety.

The FISA Amendment Act of 2008, enacted by Congress in July 2008, expanded some wiretapping powers for the Bush Administration by, among other things, transferring the National Security Agency's (NSA) Terrorist Surveillance Program under the authority of FISC, thereby making its wiretap requests "secret" and non-public. The amendments contained protections for Americans, e.g., the NSA could not intentionally target Americans or snag purely domestic communications. It could, however, engage in surveillance of any particular American who engaged in overseas communications, but a FISC warrant order would be required, specifically naming the target. Moreover, the amendments allowed surveillance monitoring of any/all Americans outside of the country.

The amendments further provided that telecommunications companies (e.g., AT&T or Google) could be ordered to assist the government surveillance of domestic telephone and internet facilities in an attempt to capture communications suspected to involve at least one foreign agent. Previously, FISA had limited such surveillance to those approved on an individual basis if conducted within the United States.

In July 2008, the AMERICAN CIVIL LIBERTIES UNION (ACLU) challenged the enactment of the new FISA provisions by filing a petition with the FISC to be included in FISC's secret review of wiretapping warrant requests. This was its third such request, and the FISC court denied it three times. In dismissing the latest plea, FISC Judge Marya Mclaughlin found no right for the public to be included in the court's activities, stating,

> "The FISC has no tradition of openness, either with respect to its proceedings, its orders or to Government briefings filed with the FISC. Although it is possible to identify some benefits which might flow from public access to Government briefs and FISC orders, any such benefits would be outweighed by the risks to national security created by the potential exposure of the Government's targeting and minimization procedures."

The judge also rejected ACLU's request to file a brief challenging the constitutionality of the law and its targeting procedures, advising that it would not be helpful, since only the court and the Government understood the workings of the intelligence community.

ACLU, after three rejections, responded by filing suit in the U.S. **District Court** for the Southern District of New York. *Amnesty International v. McConnell*, No. 08-Civ.6259. (The 2008 FISA amendments also provided retroactive amnesty for telecommunication companies who had previously cooperated with the Government for warrantless surveillance prior to the effective date of the amendments.) As of April 2009, the case was still pending.

FOURTH AMENDMENT

Arizona v. Gant

Though the FOURTH AMENDMENT requires police to secure a warrant before searching and seizing property in a criminal investigation, the Supreme Court has carved out exceptions based on the need to protect police officers from harm. Police may stop and frisk a person for reasonable cause and may search an automobile after arresting the driver. However, there has been great debate within the law as to limitations on the search of the automobile. Though the Court, in *New York v. Belton*, 453 U.S. 454, 101 S.Ct. 2860, 69 L.Ed.2d 768 (1981), authorized such searches, confusion as to the scope of this ruling led law enforcement to conclude that a vehicle search is allowed incident to the arrest of a recent occupant even if there is no possibility the arrestee could gain access to the vehicle at the time of the search. In a major decision, the Court in *Arizona v. Gant*, __U.S.__, 129 S.Ct. 1710 , 173 L.Ed.2d 485 (2009), rejected this broad interpretation and placed stringent requirements on warrantless automobile searches.

Rodney Gant was arrested for driving with a suspended license by Tucson, Arizona police. The police responded to an anonymous tip that drugs were being sold at house by knocking on the door. Gant, a visitor, told the officers that the owner would be returning later. The officers left the residence and conducted a records check on Gant, discovering that there was an outstanding warrant for his arrest for driving with a suspended license. The officers returned to the house in the evening and arrested two people in a car parked in front of the residence. Gant soon arrived behind the wheel of his car and pulled into the driveway. He got out of the car and shut the door, meeting the officers about 12 feet from his vehicle. He was immediately arrested, handcuffed, and placed in the back of a patrol car. Two officers then searched his car and found a gun and a packet of cocaine in a pocket of a jacket on the backseat.

Gant was charged with possession of narcotics for sale and possession of drug paraphernalia (the plastic bag containing the cocaine). Gant challenged the admissibility of the evidence, arguing that the **search and seizure** violated the Fourth Amendment. He contended that *Belton* did not authorize the search of his car because he posed no threat to the officers after he was handcuffed in the patrol car and because he was arrested for a traffic offense for which no evidence could be found in his vehicle. The court rejected his claim, finding that the search was permissible as a search incident to an arrest. The Arizona Supreme Court reversed this decision, holding that police may not conduct a search incident to an arrest once the scene is secure. The Court came to this conclusion by relying on an earlier U.S. SUPREME COURT case, *Chimel v. California*, 395 U.S. 752, 89 S.Ct. 2034, 23 L.Ed.2d 685 (1969). In this case the Court held that a search-incident-to-an-arrest exception warrant requirement was justified by interests in officer safety and evidence preservation. The Arizona court held that absent the *Chimel* justifications, a warrantless search of a vehicle is not permitted. The U.S. Supreme Court agreed to hear the state's appeal so that it could clarify this area of the law.

The Court, in a 5-4 decision, upheld the Arizona Supreme Court's ruling and its reasoning. Justice JOHN PAUL STEVENS, writing for the majority, noted that federal circuit courts of appeal had given different answers as to the application of *Belton*. That decision had stated that the vehicle must be within an arrestee's reach to justify a vehicle search incident to arrest. Over time lower court decisions had led police to view this type of search as an "entitlement" rather than as an exception justified by the two factors in *Chimel*. This broad reading of *Belton* could not stand. Stevens held that a vehicle search "incident to a recent occupant's arrest only when the arrestee is unsecured and within reaching distance of the passenger compartment at the time of the search." Moreover, even if police meet these requirements, they must also have a reasonable belief "evidence relevant to the crime of arrest might be found in the vehicle. He noted that Gant had been arrested for a traffic offense, which meant police had no reason to search the vehicle. Absent a warrant, police did not have the right to search Gant's car.

Justice ANTONIN SCALIA, in a concurring opinion, stated that he did not agree with the way *Belton* had been applied but he also disagreed with the "within arrestee's reach" holding crafted by Justice Steven. The new standard did not provide clear guidance to arresting officers and "also much room for manipulation, inviting officers to leave the scene unsecured (at least where dangerous suspects are not involved) in order to conduct a vehicle search." He argued the best course was to abandon *Belton* and restrict vehicle searches

incident to an arrest to those where police have reasonable belief that there is evidence in the vehicle for which the arrest was made. With four justices siding with Justice Stevens and four justices in dissent who wanted the broad reading of *Belton*, Justice Scalia sided with the former as the lesser of two evils.

Herring v. United States

The U.S. SUPREME COURT has enforced the Fourth Amendment's prohibition against unreasonable searches and seizures by prohibiting the use of any illegally seized evidence at a criminal trial. The suppression of evidence through the **exclusionary rule** was meant to deter law enforcement officials from using unconstitutinal practices. However, since the application of the FOURTH AMENDMENT to the states in the 1960s the Court has developed polices that do allow evidence to be used even if it was seized improperly. Such was the case in *Herring v. United States*, __U.S.__, 129 S.Ct. 695, __L.Ed.2d__ (2009), where the Court held that evidence could be use that was seized as a consequence of negligence by the police records department.

In 2004 an Alabama sheriff's investigator found out that Bennie Herring was coming to the county sheriff's office to retrieve something from his impounded truck. Herring was well-known in the local law enforcement community, so the investigator asked the county's warrant clerk to check for any outstanding warrants. Though the clerk found none, the investigator told the clerk to call the adjoining county and check there. The clerk in that county checked the computer database and told the clerk that Herring had an active **arrest warrant** for Herring's failure to appear on a **felony** charge. Armed with information, the investigator and a deputy followed Herring as he left the impound lot, pulled him over, and arrested him. A search revealed methamphetamine in Herring's pocket and a pistol in his vehicle. Meanwhile, the clerk in the adjoining county went to her files and could not locate the arrest warrant. She called the local courthouse and discovered that the warrant had been recalled five months earlier. For whatever reason, the recall notice had not been entered into the computer database. The county clerk relayed this information to the investigator but Herring had already been arrested and searched. The elapsed time for this entire episode was no more than 10 to 15 minutes.

Herring was indicted in Alabama federal **district court** for illegally possessing the gun and drugs. He asked the court to employ the exclusionary rule and suppress the evidence on the grounds that his initial arrest had been illegal because the arrest warrant had been recalled. The district court rejected Herring's motion because the arresting officers had acted in **good faith** that the arrest warrant was still outstanding. Therefore, even if there was a Fourth Amendment violation the exclusionary rule should not be used because there was no reason to believe that employing it "would deter the occurrence of any future mistake." The Eleventh **Circuit Court** of Appeals agreed with the district court's ruling. The negligent act was much different from a deliberate or tactical choice to act. Therefore, the evidence was admissible under the good-faith rule created by the Supreme Court. However, other circuit courts of appeal had excluded evidence obtained through similar police errors, so the Supreme Court accepted Herring's appeal to resolve this conflict.

The Court, in a 5-4 decision, upheld the Eleventh Circuit's ruling. Chief Justice JOHN ROBERTS, writing for the majority, noted the Eleventh Circuit's conclusion that the failure to update the arrest warrant information was negligent but not reckless or deliberate. This was crucial, as the point of the exclusionary rule is to deter future Fourth Amendment violations. It is meant to deter "deliberate, reckless, or grossly negligent conduct, or in some circumstances recurring or systemic negligence." In this case the error did not rise to the level. Herring had failed to prove that the police had been shown to be reckless in maintaining a warrant system or to have knowingly "made false entries to lay the groundwork for future false arrests." Therefore, the officers had acted in good faith when they arrested and searched Herring.

Justice RUTH BADER GINSBURG, in a dissenting opinion joined by three other justices, argued that law enforcement record-keeping errors have grave consequences for individuals. Because of this there was a need for a "forceful" exclusionary rule. In many cases the rule is the only effective way to **redress** a Fourth Amendment violation.

Ninth Circuit Rules that Employee Text Messages are Protected by the Fourth Amendment

The Ninth **Circuit Court** of Appeals in 2008 ruled that a public employer in Ontario, California

violated the constitutional and **statutory** rights of an employee by reviewing the employee's personal text messages. The case could have significant ramifications for employers who want to monitor their employees' electronic communications. On the other hand, the result in the case may have been different had the city's operational policy followed the city's written policy more closely.

In October 2001, the City of Ontario entered into an agreement with Arch Wireless Operating Company, Inc. Under the contract, the city became a subscriber to the company's two-way alphanumeric text-messaging pagers, which were used by city employees. The city paid a monthly subscription rate to Arch Wireless, and this rate allotted 25,000 characters per month for each pager. If any individual user exceeded 25,000 characters, the city would have to pay additional charges. The city issued the pagers to each member of the police department's SWAT team, including Sergeant Jeff Quon.

The city did not adopt a specific policy governing the use of the pagers. However, the city had previously adopted a statement entitled "Computer Usage, Internet and E-Mail Policy," which each employee had to review and sign. This policy contained several provisions, including the following:

- The policy specified that access to Internet sites would be recorded and periodically evaluated. Moreover, the policy specifically noted that "[u]sers should have no expectation of privacy or confidentiality when using these resources."

- Under the policy, electronic information produced on city computer systems was considered to be city property.

- The policy specified that use of inappropriate, derogatory, obscene, suggestive, defamatory or harassing language in the e-mail system would not be tolerated.

In 2002, the Ontario police department notified personnel that messages sent via the two-way pagers were considered email messages and that the department would apply the email policy to these pager messages. Although supervisors told employees that the pager messages would be subject to audit, the department was unable to review the contents of the messages directly. Instead, the department had to contact an Arch Wireless representative to request a transcript of the message. Notwithstanding the police department's policy or any other statements made by supervisors to employees, the written policy conflicted with the departments actual operational practices. The department generally did not audit use of the pagers, even when an employee used more than 25,000 characters in a certain month. In such situations, the employee had the option of paying the overage charges. Only if the employee disputed the overage charges would the department decide to audit the contents of the pager messages.

Shortly after the pagers were issued in 2002, Lieutenant Steven Duke notified Quon that Quon had exceeded the maximum number of characters allowed on the pager. Duke gave Quon the option of paying the overage charges so that Quon's messages would not be audited. Quon and several other employees frequently exceeded the 25,000-character limit. Duke later testified that he became tired of "being a bill collector" when it came to these overages. Department supervisors were also concerned that the employees were using the pagers for personal use rather than for department-related business. The police chief ordered Duke to audit the messages sent by Quon and another officer to determine how many messages were private in nature. Transcripts of Quon's messages revealed that many of the messages were very private in nature, including sexually-explicit messages from a woman with whom Quon was having an extra-marital affair. This discovery led to a full investigation by the department's internal affairs department.

In February 2003, Quon and his wife brought suit against the City of Ontario, the Ontario Police Department, Arch Wireless, and several other individuals related to the case. The Quons alleged that the defendants violated the federal Stored Communications Act, 18 U.S.C. § 2701 *et seq.*. The Quons also argued that the defendants had violated the Quons' FOURTH AMENDMENT rights.

The U.S. **District Court** for the Central District of California first considered the issues after both parties filed motions for **summary judgment**. In an effort to frame the question before the court, Judge Stephen Larson wrote:

What are the legal boundaries of an employee's privacy in this interconnected, electronic-communication age, one in which

thoughts and ideas that would have been spoken personally and privately in ages past are now instantly text-messaged to friends and family via hand-held, computer-assisted electronic devices?

In his decision, Larson first concluded that none of the defendants were liable under the Stored Communications Act. The judge then decided that Quon and other employees had a reasonable privacy expectation in the content of the pager messages. Larson concluded that a genuine issue of material fact existed as to whether the audit of the messages was constitutionally permissible. *Quon v. Arch Wireless Operating Co.*, 445 F. Supp. 2d 1116 (C.D. Cal. 2006).

The plaintiffs appealed the decision to the Ninth Circuit Court of Appeals. Writing for a three-judge panel, Judge Kim McLane Wardlaw disagreed with the lower court on several points. The court determined that Arch Wireless had violated the Stored Communication Act because Arch Wireless had provided an "electronic communication service" to the city. When Arch wireless knowingly turned over the transcripts to the city instead of to the intended recipient of the communication, Arch Wireless violated the **statute**.

The court then turned its attention to the Fourth Amendment issue. The Ninth Circuit panel agreed with the district court that the employees had a reasonable expectation of privacy in the content of the pager messages. *Quon v. Arch Wireless Operating Co.*, 529 F.3d 892 (9th Cir. 2008). Had the police department simply followed its written policy, the court's opinion suggests that Quon and the other plaintiffs would have had no reasonable privacy expectation. However, the fact that the department's "operational reality" differed from the written policy led to a different result. When Page informed the employees that the department would not review overage charges, this statement gave the employees a reasonable expectation of privacy in those messages.

The Ninth Circuit judges further concluded that the search of the messages was also unreasonable. The court noted, "There were a host of simple ways to verify the efficacy of the 25,000 character limit . . . without intruding on [the] Appellants' Fourth Amendment rights." The court offered several examples of these less intrusive means, such as having Quon refrain

from using the pager for personal communications and informing him that the contents would be reviewed from that point forward to ensure that the pager was being used for work-related purposes. Instead, the city chose an "excessively intrusive" means of searching the messages, which violated Quon's Fourth Amendment rights.

The Ninth Circuit declined to review the decision *en banc*, allowing the panel's decision to stand. One civil liberties advocacy group called the panel's decision a "tremendous victory" for online privacy. On the other hand, the attorney representing Arch Wireless countered, "I think right now service providers are going to be a little leery of providing anything to the subscriber because of this case."

FRAUD

A false representation of a matter of fact—whether by words or by conduct, by false or misleading allegations, or by concealment of what should have been disclosed—that deceives and is intended to deceive another so that the individual will act upon it to her or his legal injury.

Investors Lose Billions in Bernard Madoff's Ponzi Scheme

In one of the biggest **fraud** cases in history, investors lost as much as $65 billion in a massive **Ponzi scheme** run by respected Wall Street investor Bernard Madoff. The victims ranged from international banks to large charitable organizations to ordinary individuals who depended on those investments for income. Madoff pleaded guilty to several charges related to the scheme and was sentenced to 150 years in prison.

Madoff opened his firm, Bernard L. Madoff Investment Securities LLC., in 1960. He was a pioneer in the business known as market making. A market maker is a firm that buys and sells a particular stock at a publicly stated price. A market maker is an essential function of a market such as Nasdaq, which does not have an actual trading floor where buyers and sellers can trade face-to-face. A firm such as Madoff's would act as a middle man between buyers and sellers of stock. Madoff was instrumental in the development of Nasdaq and served as its chairman.

A Ponzi scheme is an illegal pyramid scheme named after Charles Ponzi, who fraudulently received millions of dollars from investors in a postage stamp speculation scheme in the 1920s. These schemes have been used on both small and large scales. The basic plan for such a scheme is that the perpetrator will lure investors with promises of huge returns. When the perpetrator receives money from new investors, the perpetrator will use the money to pay the earlier investors, making the system appear to be legitimate. In these schemes, the money invested is not secured by anything. When too many investors attempt to receive their returns, these schemes generally collapse.

The exact time when Madoff began running his Ponzi scheme is in question. Investigators have said they thought the scheme began in the 1970s, but Madoff claims the scheme did not begin until the 1990s. Regardless, Madoff's reputation helped him to attract some huge investors. He was a philanthropist who served on the boards of several nonprofit corporations. Madoff's principal clients were charitable foundations, which do not withdraw a significant percentage of their investments annually. Madoff also limited his business to a rather exclusive clientele, advertising his investment strategies as being too complicated for average investors to understand.

The returns that Madoff investors received were about 10% annually, which is modest compared with most Ponzi schemes. Even when the markets fluctuated, Madoff consistently provided returns that outperformed other investments. The reasons for Madoff's success were subject to some speculation in financial publications, but none of these publications raised the question of whether Madoff's methods were **fraudulent**. Madoff's firm had become one of the biggest securities dealers in the world.

Some outside analysts began to question Madoff's methods. A Massachusetts financial analyst named Harry Markopolos in 2000 asked the SECURITIES AND EXCHANGE COMMISSION to investigate Madoff's firm. The SEC largely ignored Markopolos' claims despite his repeated efforts. Others were also allegedly informed that Madoff was running a scheme. For instance, papers filed by New York University in a civil suit filed against J. Ezra Merkin of Gabriel Capital Group suggested that Merkin has been told several times in the 1990s that Madoff's claimed returns were not possible. Merkin revealed in 2008 that he had lost $2.4 billion to Madoff in the Ponzi scheme.

As the stock market plunged in 2008, Madoff continued to claim that his funds were earning money. By November 2008, investors were beginning to panic and sought redemptions from Madoff. During November and December, Madoff allegedly mailed about a million dollars worth of jewelry and other heirlooms to relatives and friends. His wife, Ruth, withdrew more than $15 million from a brokerage firm linked to Madoff.

The scheme finally came to an end when Madoff, on December 10, 2008, attempted to give his two sons a bonus. Both sons worked for their father, but neither worked with his asset management business. Madoff's sons questioned him about how he could pay them their bonus when he was unable to pay his investors. At that point, Madoff admitted to his sons that his firm had been running a giant Ponzi scheme. One day later, his sons alerted authorities about Madoff's business. Agents with the FEDERAL BUREAU OF INVESTIGATION visited Madoff and asked whether there was an "innocent explanation" for what Madoff had told his sons. Madoff responded, "There is no innocent explanation." He told agents that he "paid investors with money that wasn't there" and expected to go to prison.

Authorities immediately arrested Madoff and then began a massive effort to track down assets of both Madoff and Madoff's firm. According to records maintained by the National Association of Securities Dealers, Madoff was managing about $17 billion in client assets as of November 2008. Some entities had invested billions with Madoff's firm. The biggest investor was the Fairfield Greenwich Group run by investment guru Walter Noel. Noel and his firm had worked with Madoff for a number of years. Fairfield Greenwich had invested roughly half of its assets under management with Madoff, and it appeared that the firm would lose between $7.3 and $7.5 billion because of the scheme.

The *New York Times* called the scheme the first worldwide Ponzi scheme. Madoff attracted investors from Europe, Asia, and Middle East. Several prominent Jewish executives and organizations were Madoff's clients, including Yeshiva University and charities set up by the likes of director Steven Spielberg. Other investors included Hall of Fame pitcher Sandy Koufax as well as actors John Malkovich, Kyra Sedgwick, and Kevin Bacon. Madoff admitted to prosecutors that he lost more than $50 billion to investors, though by some estimates, the amount reached closer to $65 billion.

In March 2009, Madoff pleaded guilty to 11 counts related to the fraud. The charges included: investment advisor fraud, **mail fraud**, wire fraud, international **money laundering**, domestic money laundering, false statements, perjury, false filing, and theft from an employee benefit plan. Madoff faced up to 150 years in prison on these charges. In addition, the Securites and Exchange Commission filed a civil complaint against Madoff, seeking to have Madoff pay a fine and return money to investors. By April, about $1 billion had been recovered. A series of lawsuits have been filed to retrieve more of the money lost.

The fallout over the Madoff scheme had wide-reaching effects. For instance, the head of the SEC's enforcement division, Linda Chatman Thomsen, resigned after being grilled by members of Congress over the SEC's refusal to investigate Madoff's firm. Thomsen had been the head of the enforcement division since 2005 and had been with the SEC for fourteen years.

Madoff's wife was also part of the focus as authorities attempted to retrieve assets. In

March, she submitted a special filing in connection with the SEC's suit against Madoff. She insisted that the $70 million in assets she owned were not part of the criminal enterprise. Some sources noted that she acquired some of the assets as early as 1984 and that these assets were not connected at all with the Ponzi scheme. However, prosecutors have aggressively pursued Ruth Madoff's assets, including a $7 million New York penthouse.

FREEDOM OF INFORMATION

President Obama Signs Executive Order Amending Presidential Records Act

In one of his first official acts, President Barack Obama signed Executive Order 13489 on January 21, 2009, which revoked previous Executive Order 13233 from the Bush administration that had severely restricted release to the public of presidential records. President Bush's E.O. was a controversial order that gave ex-presidents *and their heirs,* in perpetuity, unprecedented control over the release of White House records. "Let me say it as simply as I can," Obama stated at the signing, "[T]ransparency and the rule of law will be the touchstones of this presidency."

The Presidential Records Act of 1978 (PRA, 44 USC 2201 *et seq.,*) governed the official records of Presidents and Vice Presidents that were created after January 20, 1981. Its main purpose (particularly after the Watergate scandal of the Nixon administration) was to change the legal ownership of such official records from private to public. It also established a new statutory scheme for Presidents to manage their records. The Act further provided for an incumbent President to dispose of records that no longer had historical, administrative, informational, or evidentiary value, contingent upon having obtained the views of the Archivist of the United States on the proposed disposal.

Importantly, the Act established procedures for restriction and/or public access to these records. Specifically, it allowed for public access to records through the Freedom of Information Act (FOIA) commencing five years after the end of the President's administration. Exceptions provided for longer restrictions in the interests of national security or privacy. The Act also established procedures for Congress and the courts (as well as subsequent administrations)

to obtain special access to records that remained closed to the public, following a 30-day notice period to the former and current Presidents.

Over the years the Act remained intact, through the administrations of Presidents Ronald Reagan, George H.W. Bush, and Bill Clinton. One exception, Executive Order 12667 from President Reagan in 1989, established procedures for the National Records and Archive Administration (NARA) and former and incumbent presidents to implement provisions under the PRA.

Then in 2001, President George W. Bush signed Executive Order 13233, which expressly superceded Reagan's E.O. 12667 and essentially nullified the PRA itself. Bush's E.O. contained sweeping changes regarding the use of "executive privilege" and who could invoke it. The Order gave Presidents and Vice Presidents, and for the first time, their heirs and/or designees, in perpetuity, unprecedented authority to block access to or refuse release of White House records for any reason. This privilege also extended retroactively to include former Presidents and their heirs. Moreover, Bush's E.O. removed the FOIA standard for release of records to the public, and replaced it with a requirement that requests for White House records show a 'demonstrated, specific need" to see them. That standard was not required by FOIA for the release of other government records.

For eight years, historians, archivists, political scientists, and other stakeholders on Capitol Hill and in the federal courts tried in vain to have Bush's E.O. revoked on legal grounds or by Congressional act. Then-Senator Obama campaigned on a promise of more transparency and openness in government. Executive Order 13489 was clearly in furtherance of that objective.

Obama's Executive Order restored the presumption that an incumbent President, and not former Presidents or their heirs and designees, was the proper person to assert claims of executive privilege. Section 4 of the E.O. expressly states that only "living former President[s]" could exercise the privilege, eliminating the most contentious portion of Bush's E.O. Moreover, Obama removed Bush's provision allowing former Vice Presidents to assert the privilege, by including Vice Presidential records under the definition of "Presidential

Records." Section 1(e) of E.O. 13489 expressly defined "Presidential Records" as "those documentary materials maintained by NARA pursuant to the Presidential Records Act, including Vice Presidential records." Finally, the E.O. restored the function of the Archivist of the United States as an independent arbiter of initial claims of privilege.

A concurrent White House Press Release stated the following:

> "The Executive Order on Presidential Records brings those principles to presidential records by giving the American people greater access to these historical documents. This order ends the practice of having others besides the President assert executive privilege for records after an administration ends. Now, only the President will have that power, limiting its potential for abuse. And the order also requires the Attorney General and the White House Counsel to review claims of executive privilege about covered records to make sure those claims are fully warranted by the Constitution."

President Obama also signed two other memoranda focusing on transparency and openness. One directed the Attorney General to issue new guidelines to agencies for complying with the letter and spirit of the FOIA. In the other, Obama tasked three senior officials with producing an "open government" directive within the first 120 days of the administration. Said Obama, "[T]he old rules said that if there was a defensible argument for not disclosing something to the American people, then it should not be disclosed. That era is now over. Starting today, every agency and department should know that this administration stands on the side not of those who seek to withhold information but those who seek to make it known."

FREEDOM OF SPEECH

The right, guaranteed by the First Amendment to the U.S. Constitution, to express beliefs and ideas without unwarranted government restriction.

Third Circuit Strikes Down Temple University Sexual Harassment Policy

The Third **Circuit Court** of Appeals in 2008 struck down the sexual harassment policy of Temple University in Philadelphia. A former graduate student challenged the policy on FIRST AMENDMENT grounds, arguing that the policy effectively "chilled" his speech. In *DeJohn v. Temple University*, 537 F.3d 301 (3d Cir. 2008), a three-judge panel with the Third Circuit agreed and ruled that the policy was unconstitutional.

Christian DeJohn served as a member of the Pennsylvania NATIONAL GUARD. In January 2002, he enrolled as a graduate student at Temple, seeking to obtain a master's degree in military and American history. The program required DeJohn to complete a series of courses. Once he finished these courses, he would have the option of taking a comprehensive exam or completing work on a master's thesis. The school required DeJohn to finish these requirements within three years of his enrollment.

During his first semester at Temple, DeJohn took four classes. After one semester, the military called him into active duty. He was deployed to Bosnia. During his time in active duty, he took a correspondence course and earned credit at Temple. He returned to Temple and completed his courses by the end of the fall 2003 semester. In January 2004, he began work on a master's thesis. He worked on the thesis between 2004 and 2006, submitting a final draft in March 2006. He did not enroll in as a student at Temple after the spring semester in 2006.

Temple University established a sexual harassment policy that was in force while DeJohn was a student. The policy read in relevant part:

> For all individuals who are part of the Temple community, all forms of sexual harassment are prohibited, including the following: an unwelcome sexual **advance**, request for sexual favors, or other expressive, visual or physical conduct of a sexual or gender-motivated nature when . . . (c) such conduct has the purpose or effect of unreasonably interfering with an individual's work, educational performance, or status; or (d) such conduct has the purpose or effect of creating an intimidating, hostile, or offensive environment.

In February 2006, DeJohn filed an action with the U.S. **District Court** for the Eastern District of Pennsylvania. DeJohn argued that Temple's sexual harassment policies violated his First Amendment rights. He claimed that as a graduate student in military and history, he felt inhibited to express his beliefs about the role of women in armed combat in general. He moreover felt concerned that if he expressed his political, social, cultural, or religious views that he could be sanctioned by the university. Accordingly, many of his claims focused on his assertion that the sexual harassment policy had the effect of chilling his speech. His principal argument was that the policy was overly broad on it face.

Temple filed a motion to dismiss DeJohn's complaint in May 2006. The district court granted the motion with regard to several of the counts, but the court required the university to submit an answer with respect to other counts related to the sexual harassment policy. In January 2007, Temple decided to modify its sexual harassment policy. Afterward, the university submitted several motions designed to prevent DeJohn from continuing with discovery in the case. However, the district court denied the university's motions, finding that the university could easily reinstate its old policies once the case was dismissed.

Once the parties completed discovery, DeJohn filed a motion for **summary judgment** on his claims. The district court on March 21, 2007 granted DeJohn's motion on two counts and declared that Temple's sexual harassment policy that existed prior to January 15, 2007 was unconstitutional on its face. The court issued an order prohibiting the university from implementing or enforcing the old policy. The court later issued a final judgment, permanently enjoining the university from applying the old policy. The court awarded **nominal damages** in the case to DeJohn in the amount of $1.

Temple appealed the decision to the Third Circuit Court of Appeals. One of the more difficult issues the court had to address was whether the issues before the court were moot because the university had voluntarily modified its policy. The court analyzed whether the case was indeed moot under the Supreme Court's decision in *Los Angeles County v. Davis*, 440 U.S. 625, 99 S. Ct. 1379, 59 L. Ed. 2d 642

(1979). In *Davis*, the Court noted that even when a party voluntarily ceases its illegal conduct, a case focused on that conduct is not moot unless there is virtually no chance that the party will repeat its illegal conduct. The Third Circuit concluded that there was no assurance that Temple would not revert to its old policy once the case was completed. The court also rejected the argument that the case was moot because DeJohn was no longer a student at Temple.

The court then turned its attention to the First Amendment issues. In a long line of cases, the Supreme Court has established that free expression is vitally important at the university setting. The Court has concerned itself with a "chilling effect" that an action may have on protected speech. Although the Court has recognized the significance of sexual harassment policies, those policies cannot interfere with protected speech under the Supreme Court's doctrine. Thus, a sexual harassment policy that suppresses or chills protected speech by imposing content-based restrictions on the speech violates the First Amendment.

The Third Circuit evaluated the Temple policy in light of these First Amendment concerns. The court evaluated whether the policy could be "susceptible to a reasonable limiting construction." In the language of the policy, a person could be disciplined for expressive conduct of a gender-motivated nature, which the court concluded was highly subjective, and whether an expression was gender-motivated would depend heavily on the viewpoint of both the speaker and the listener. For these reasons, the policy was overly broad on its face because it could effectively suppress protected speech.

Temple expressed disappointment in the decision, noting that the policy's language was very similar to language used by the EQUAL EMPLOYMENT OPPORTUNITY COMMISSION.

GAY AND LESBIAN RIGHTS

The goal of full legal and social equality for gay men and lesbians sought by the gay movement in the United States and other Western countries.

Arkansas Voters Ban Adoption and Foster Parenting by Unmarried Couples

Though much attention has been focused on the issue of same-sex marriage, gay and lesbian advocacy groups have sought to overturn laws that ban same-sex couples from adopting or foster parenting. The November 2008 elections saw Arkansas voters approve an initiative that bars all unmarried couples from being adoptive or foster parents, regardless if the couples are heterosexual or homosexual. Arkansas joined Florida, Nebraska, Utah, and Mississippi as states that either directly or indirectly prohibit adoptions by gays. A lawsuit was filed after election, challenging the constitutionality of the initiative, but no decision had been made as of May 2009.

The Arkansas ballot initiative came after a lengthy dispute over the state's Child Welfare Agency Board administrative policy that banned gays from serving as foster parents. The AMER-ICAN CIVIL LIBERTIES UNION (ACLU) challenged this policy and after seven years of litigation the Arkansas Supreme Court ruled it unconstitutional. A bill sponsored by the conservative Arkansas Family Council Action Committee failed to gain legislative approval in 2007 after concerns were raised about its constitutionality. The council then drafted an initiative that is sought to have on the November 2008 ballot. The state attorney general, who must approve the language of proposed initiatives, rejected the first application because it referred to marriage as the ideal child-rearing environment and it asserted that cohabiting households were more susceptible to instability, poverty, and other social problems. The council stripped the offending language from the initiative and the attorney general approved and certified it. The next task of the council, which gained assistance from Focus on the Family and other Christian religious groups, was to gather the required 62,000 signatures need to have the initiative placed on the ballot. The signature drive came up 4,000 names short after verification by the secretary of state. The group was given 30 days to make up the shortfall and it delivered an additional 31,000 signatures by the August 2008 deadline.

Opponents of the initiative first threatened to file a lawsuit challenging the validity of signatures, the constitutionality of the initiative, and whether the ballot title was accurate and sufficient. Many opponents argued that the initiative would restrict the number of foster and adoptive homes. Other opponents contended that the proposal was really aimed at homosexual adoption. However, they rethought their position and decided to devote financial resources to defeating the initiative. Arkansas voters decisively approved the initiative on

November 8, 2008, gaining 57 percent of the vote to the opponents 43 percent.

On December 30, 2008, the ACLU and 29 adults and children filed a lawsuit in state court challenging the initiative. The plaintiffs argued that the law violated state and federal constitutional rights to **equal protection** and due process. The total exclusion of an entire class of potentially qualified foster and adoptive parents, whether gay or heterosexual, was not constitutional nor was it in the best interest of children. The lawsuit named as defendants the state, the attorney general, and two state agencies that deal with child welfare. Moreover, the law was really targeted at homosexual couples.The case was initially assigned to Circuit Judge Timothy Fox. In 2004, Fox had ruled that the state regulation banning gays from the state foster program was illegal. The defendants asked that Fox not hear the case and it was soon transferred to Judge Chris Piazza.

In March 2009, Judge Piazza conducted a hearing on the case. The judge refused the state's motion to dismiss the entire case and set a trial date of December 7, 2009. At the hearing Piazza agreed with the state that a ballot title challenge (a condensed version of the proposal that appears on the ballot) must be dismissed. Ballot title challengers must be heard before an election. The judge stated that he had doubts about some of the constitutional arguments advanced by the ACLU but concluded that there was merit in the plaintiffs' argument that the state owed a duty to children in custody that is comparable to the duty the state owes prisoners and mental patients committed to state hospitals. In Piazza's view the key claim was likely to be the due process rights the state owed its children. The judge did dismiss the state from the lawsuit based on the doctrine of **sovereign immunity** but left the state agencies and their directors as defendants.

A lawyer for the Family Council Action Committee told the court that the ACLU was asserting a constitutional right that did not exist— the right of children to be adopted or placed in foster care. In his view adoption and foster care were not constitutional issues bur rather **statutory** issues that the citizens of Arkansas could control. The fact that 57 percent of state voters had approved the measure should control.

In April 2009 the group NowThyNeighbor. org posted on its website the names of more than 83,000 Arkansas residents who signed the petition to place the initiative on the ballot. The public data was provided by the secretary of state. The group, which advocates for same-sex marriage, sought to publicize the names of the signers in hopes that friends and neighbors would start a dialogue on gay and lesbian issues.

California Supreme Court Upholds Same-Sex Marriage

In May 2008, the California Supreme Court, to resolve several lawsuits going back as far as 2004, ruled that California legislative measures limiting marriage to opposite-sex couples (a man and a woman) violated the state's constitution and the rights of same-sex couples. *In re Marriage Cases*, No. S147999, 183 P.3d 384. When the 121-page, 4-3 majority opinion became final 30 days later, gay and lesbian couples crowded local courts and state offices to legalize their relationships. The victory appeared short lived. In November 2008, a clear majority of California voters approved "Proposition 8," a ballot initiative to amend the state constitution limiting marriage to unions between men and women.

The California Supreme Court case was significant because it squarely addressed many of the recurring and basic arguments about fundamental rights of same-sex couples. Those issues were not before the court in its earlier 2004 decision, *Lockyer v. City and County of San Francisco*, 33 Cal.4th 1055. In that more limited case, the state's high court held that San Francisco officials had no legal authority to issue marriage licenses to same-sex couples without a judicial determination that the state's statutes (e.g., Family Code section 3.8.5), which limited marriage to opposite-sex couples, were unconstitutional. In fact, the *Lockyer* opinion expressly noted that its decision did not reflect any view on the substantive constitutional issue, thereby leaving the door open for that challenge down the road.

The present consolidated cases, filed in 2004 by the City and County of San Francisco and several same-sex couples, followed the *Lockyer* decision and brought the substantive issue squarely before the court. The consolidated plaintiffs claimed California's **statutory** provisions were unconstitutional.

The California Supreme Court first examined the scope of California's statutory Family

Code section 308.5, the state's "marriage statute," interpretation of which was being challenged by the same-sex couples. But the court concluded that the statute's correct interpretation (and intent) was indeed to impose a limitation on marriages to those between a man and a woman.

Next, the state supreme court addressed the nature and scope of the constitutional right (not the above statutory right) to marry under the California Constitution. The opinion noted, "history alone is not invariably an appropriate guide for determining the meaning and scope of this fundamental constitutional guarantee." It then referred to one of its earlier landmark decisions (1948), *Perez v. Sharp*, 32 Cal.2d 711, in which it ruled as unconstitutional a then-existing California **statute** banning interracial marriages. The present court then concluded that "in view of the substance and significance of the fundamental right to form a family relationship, the California Constitution properly must be interpreted to guarantee this basic civil right to all Californians, whether gay or heterosexual, and to same-sex couples as well as to opposite-sex couples.

The court also took time to note that the state's recently-enacted comprehensive domestic partnership legislation afforded same-sex couples most of the substantive legal benefits and privileges embodied in the constitutional right to marry. (Denial of these substantive elements has often been the stated justification for challenging bans on same-sex marriages.) But the court opined that even if the basic rights were the same, assigning a different name for the family relationship of same-sex couples (i.e., "domestic partnership") threatened to deny same-sex couples the "dignity and respect" accorded to family relationships of opposite-sex couples.

Finally, the court addressed **equal protection** challenges, to wit, whether assignment of a different name for the official family relationship of same-sex couples violated the state equal protection clause. The court rejected arguments that treating the couples differently by name constituted discrimination on the basis of sex or gender, therefore requiring a "strict scrutiny" standard under which the case must be reviewed. Notwithstanding, the court concluded that a **strict scrutiny** standard of review was still required, but for a different reason. The court

found that discrimination based on sexual orientation was a constitutionally-suspect basis for differential treatment. The court concluded that California's statute was unconstitutional because the state had failed to articulate a necessary or "compelling interest" for the differential treatment.

Concurring opinions agreed with the narrow majority's conclusion, but urged that the future definition of marriage be decided by the democratic process, not the courts. These opinions also noted that there were ample grounds for upholding the assignment of a name other than marriage to same-sex couples. Most of the dissent focused on the opinion that the court's ruling exceeded its authority to overrule a vote of the people.

In fact, as earlier stated, subsequent to the court's May 2008 opinion, a majority of Californians adopted Proposition 8 in the November 2008 elections. Proposition 8 was to amend the constitution, thereby negating the court's opinion and defining marriage as between one man and one woman. After voters passed Proposition 8, it was legally challenged, and this matter also ended up for review by the California Supreme Court. After oral arguments in March 2009, the court strongly indicated it would rule that Proposition 8 validly abolished same-sex marriages in California, which it did, upholding Proposition 8 in their May 2009 ruling. However, the court further indicated it would allow same-sex couples married prior to the November election to remain legally married.

Meanwhile, as of April 2009, only three state high courts [Connecticut (2008), Iowa (2009), and Massachusetts (2004)] have ruled in favor of same-sex marriage.

Connecticut and Iowa Supreme Courts Find Same-Sex Marriage Bans Unconstitutional Under State Constitutions

On October 28, 2008, the Supreme Court of Connecticut ruled that denying same-sex couples the same rights, responsibilities, and designation of being "married" violated the **equal protection** clause of the state's constitution. *Kerrigan v. Commissioner of Public Health,* SC 17716. Just weeks later, on November 12, 2008, the state began to issue marriage licenses to same-sex couples.

Jody Mock and Beth Kerrigan obtain a marriage license, November 12, 2008.

AP IMAGES

At the time, Connecticut became the third state ever to issue marriage licenses to same-sex couples, following Massachusetts (2004) and California (2008). The California Supreme Court had ruled just five months earlier, in May 2008. (*In re Marriage Cases*, No. S147999, 183 P.3d 384.) However, subsequent to California's court decision, California voters reversed the ruling through Proposition 8, a ballot initiative in the November 2008 elections that would amend California's constitution. California's reversal left only two states permitting same-sex marriages until the Iowa Supreme Court, on April 3, 2009, legalized gay marriages by also ruling that Iowa restrictions violated the state's constitution. This ruling again brought the total to three states upholding such marriages.

Connecticut had no similar statewide initiative process (as California) that would allow its high court's ruling to be reversed. Although Connecticut voters could have supported a ballot measure calling for a convention to amend the state constitution, the measure failed. Under its state constitution, a question may appear on a ballot only once every 20 years. Therefore, Connecticut's high court ruling was not affected by the November 2008 elections. Notwithstanding, opponents of same-sex marriage vowed to change the new law in future elections.

The premise for the Connecticut's high court's ruling in *Kerrigan* was equal protection. That ground for constitutional challenge had increasingly failed in many courts around the country over the last several years, as states began creating new legislative measures to afford gay couples the same state benefits and amenities generally afforded to married couples. But that still was not enough for the Connecticut court.

The plaintiffs in *Kerrigan* comprised eight same-sex couples who had applied for, but were denied, marriage licenses by the town of Madison. They filed suit for **declaratory judgment**, claiming that Connecticut's law prohibiting same-sex marriage violated their rights to **substantive due process** and equal protection under the state constitution.

While their suit was pending, the state legislature enacted PA 05-10, creating civil unions for same-sex couples, affording them "all the same benefits, protections, and responsibilities under law.as are granted to spouses in marriage, which is defined as the union of one man and one woman."

The trial court rejected plaintiffs' argument, noting that the statutes did allow civil unions, which afforded the same legal rights as marriage. Because the plaintiffs in civil unions enjoyed the same legal rights as married couples, they suffered no harm. Therefore, the trial court concluded, the plaintiffs had not established a constitutionally-cognizable harm or **cause of action**.

But the state supreme court believed otherwise. It noted the history of discrimination against gays and lesbians, in combination with the fact that the institution of marriage carried with it a status and significance that (in the eyes of the court) the new classification of "civil union" did not. Therefore, the court concluded, segregating heterosexual and homosexual couples into separate institutions constituted a cognizable harm for which plaintiffs could sue.

The court further concluded that because the state scheme discriminated on the basis of sexual orientation (by limiting same-sex couples to "civil unions"), its reasons for so doing would be subject to a heightened or intermediate level of scrutiny upon **judicial review**. That level of scrutiny was rationalized on the basis that, for purposes of the equal protection provisions of the U.S. Constitution, classifications predicated on gender were considered quasi-suspect. Accordingly, reasoned the court, sexual orientation constitutes a quasi-suspect classification for purposes of the equal protection provisions of the state constitution.

The court found the state did not carry its burden of providing sufficient justification for the different treatment in excluding same-sex couples from the institution of marriage.

Just a few months later, in April 2009, the Iowa Supreme Court, in *Varnum v. Brien,* **Docket** No. 07-1499, similarly held that the prohibition of same-sex marriages under Iowa's statutes violated the equal protection clause of the state's constitution. That case, involving six gay and lesbian Iowa couples and their children as plaintiffs, had been working its way through the courts since 2005. The Iowa Supreme Court's decision upheld the August 2007 ruling by Polk County **District Court** Judge Robert Hanson, who found the state's restriction of marriage to only a man and a woman violated the state's constitutional rights of equal protection.

Michigan Supreme Court Prohibits Public Employers from Providing Healthcare Benefits to Same-Sex Partners

As in many states, a sound majority (nearly 60 percent) of Michigan voters approved a state constitutional amendment (in 2004) banning same-sex marriages. The amendment stated, "To secure and preserve the benefits of marriage for our society and for future generations of children, the union of one man and one woman in marriage shall be the only agreement recognized as a marriage or similar union for any purpose"(Article I §25).

But unlike other states, the quintessential legal challenge before the Michigan Supreme Court in 2008 was not the constitutionality of the amendment (e.g., whether such amendment violated any **equal protection** clause[s] found elsewhere in the state's constitution). Rather, the state high court was asked whether such amendment could be interpreted to prohibit public employers (state and local governments, institutions of higher learning, hospitals, etc.) from providing employment (healthcare) benefits to same-sex partners of employees ("domestic partnership benefits"). In *National Pride at Work v. Granholm,* 748 N.W. 2d 524 (Mich. 2008), the Michigan Supreme Court said yes.

Months after the marriage amendment was approved, Michigan's Attorney General (AG) issued an opinion in which he concluded that the amendment prohibited public employers from providing domestic partnership benefits. His reasoning was comparatively simple and direct: if voters have banned same-sex marriages in the state, then public employers may not use taxpayer money to provide domestic partnership benefits to their employees.

His opinion was immediately challenged. Filed in Ingham County Court against Michigan Governor Jennifer Granholm, the above-captioned lawsuit sought a declaration that the constitutional amendment did not impose such a ban. Plaintiffs included the non-profit organization National Pride at Work (an AFL-CIO affiliate) and several same-sex couples affected by the AG's opinion.

The **circuit court** sided with the plaintiffs. It concluded that just because the public employers at issue provided healthcare benefits to same-sex partners of their employees, this did not mean that the public employers were recognizing such unions as "similar" to marriage, in violation of language in the amendment, i.e., ".the union of one man and one woman in marriage shall be the only agreement recognized as a marriage or similar union for any purpose"(see above). Further, noted the court, health insurance was not a benefit of marriage, so providing it to same-sex partners did not violate the amendment's purpose, as articulated in its preamble clause, i.e., "To secure and preserve the benefits of marriage for our society."

The Court of Appeals of Michigan reversed, following appeal by the state's Attorney General. Instead of focusing on the amendment's pre-ambular clause (which indicated the purpose for the amendment), the **appellate court** focused on the amendment's operative clause, to wit, that voters recognized only the union of one man and one woman as a marriage "or similar union *for any purpose*" (emphasis added). The **appellate** court then noted that criteria used by public employers to determine who qualified for domestic partner healthcare benefits were "functionally the same" as the eligibility criteria for marriage under Michigan law. For example, the employee and his or her partner could not be blood relations and had to be of a certain gender in relation to one another. Accordingly, concluded the appellate court, the public employers' reliance on this criteria amounted to an impermissible recognition of

CONSTITUTIONAL AMENDMENTS TO SAME-SEX MARRIAGES

Supporters of gay marriage have celebrated some recent victories in both the courts and in state legislatures. In 2008, it appeared that a decision by the California Supreme Court may accelerate the gay marriage movement. Gay rights activists likened the decision in *In re Marriage Cases*, 183 P.3d 384 (Cal. 2008) to some of the major CIVIL RIGHTS CASES of the twentieth century. However, opponents of the decision relied on a strategy that has proven to be the most effective in defeating gay marriage movements within the states—ask voters to approve a constitutional amendment that defines marriage as a union between one man and one woman.

The strategy of approving such a constitutional amendment is based on the realization among gay marriage opponents that **equal protection** arguments in the courts were losing strength. Over time, a person's status as being gay or lesbian progressively became less of a stigma—a conclusion that conservatives

could not effectively deny. When gays and lesbians began to advocate for equal rights in all contexts, including marriage, opponents of the gay and lesbian rights movement became concerned that courts would apply equal protection **jurisprudence** to gay marriage in a manner similar to the approach in cases dealing with racial or gender discrimination.

By the 1990s, gay and lesbian rights supporters indeed began to challenge laws banning gay marriage on equal protection grounds. In 1994, two Alaskan men named Jay Brause and Gene Dugan filed for a marriage license. When the state's Office of Vital Statistics denied the application, Brause and Dugan challenged the decision, arguing that denying them a marriage license violated guarantees in the Alaska Constitution guaranteeing rights to privacy and equal protection. A Superior Court in Anchorage agreed with the men, holding that marriage is a fundamental right and that Alaska's ban on same-sex marriage (incorporated in a 1996 amendment to

the Alaska marriage **statute**) violated the men's fundamental right.

Rather than attempt to fight the decision in the **appellate** courts, opponents of the decision chose to pursue a constitutional amendment. The Alaska Family Coalition, the principal supporter of the constitutional amendment, received financial and other support from a number of groups outside Alaska. The amendment provided:

> This measure would amend the Declaration of Rights section of the Alaska Constitution to limit marriage. The amendment would say that to be valid, a marriage may exist only between one man and one woman. It would also say that no provision of the Alaska Constitution may be interpreted by a court to to require the state to recognize or permit marriage between individuals of the same sex.

Alaska voters approved the amendment by a vote of 68 percent to 32 percent.

domestic partnerships as unions that were "similar" to marriage.

The Michigan Supreme Court affirmed that decision in 2008. Its rationale and analysis closely paralleled that of the Court of Appeals, comparing the eligibility criteria for marriage under Michigan law with the eligibility criteria used for domestic partnership benefits offered by the public employers. The 5-2 majority opinion concluded that the domestic partnerships at issue were "similar" to marriage under Michigan law because both were defined in terms of individuals' gender and the absence of a close blood relationship. Therefore, the public employers' reliance and use of this criteria to provide healthcare benefits was in violation of the marriage amendment.

The dissenting opinion examined the amendment's history and found that, during the campaign period prior to voting day, the organization responsible for placing the amendment on the ballot (Citizens for the Protection of Marriage) advised the public that the amendment was unrelated to domestic partnership benefits. The dissent then focused on pointing out the differences between domestic partnerships and marriage, noting that the domestic partnerships at issue were not similar to marriage.

Immediately affected by the decision were the University of Michigan, Michigan State University, Wayne State University, and Eastern Michigan University, all of which had been using taxpayer dollars to fund benefits offered to employees and their partners.

Ten years after the decision by the Alaska voters, the strategy of attacking same-sex marriage by changing state constitutions remained effective.

The approval of the California proposition in 2008 demonstrates why the strategy of amending constitutions has been so potent. In a widely followed case, the California Supreme Court reviewed the state's marriage statute, which incorporated a ban on same-sex marriage. Advocates in the case asked the court to recognize not only that marriage is a fundamental right, but that gays and lesbians should be treated as a suspect class. If this argument prevailed, then the court would review the same-sex marriage ban under a heightened standard, known as **strict scrutiny**. In *In re Marriage Cases*, the court indeed recognized gays and lesbians as belonging to a suspect class, thus meaning that gay and lesbian advocates could challenge discriminatory laws more effectively.

Family, religious, and other groups rallied to place a ballot proposition on same-sex marriage during the 2008 election. After the proposal received more than 1.1 million signatures, Proposition 8 became an item for the election. Advocates on both sides of the debate raised a total of more than $80 million, far more than similar campaigns in other states. In fact, the total surpassed the amounts raised in other states for any election other than the presidential election. Several public officials, including California Governor Arnold Schwarzenegger, said that they would not support such an amendment. Several polls leading up to the election suggested that the proposition may not pass. Nevertheless, just over 52 percent of the voters approved the proposition. Voters in many of the counties along the Pacific coast voted against Proposition 8, but voters in many of the other (typically more conservative) counties voted in favor of the proposal.

Gay rights advocates protested across the nation following the vote. However, the California proposition was not the only ballot initiative on gay marriage to pass in 2008. In Arizona, 56 percent of the voters approved a ballot initiative that stated, "Only a union of one man and one woman shall be valid or recognized as a marriage in this state." Senator John McCain (R.-Ariz.) stated during the 2008 presidential election that he opposed same-sex marriage and that he supported the Arizona amendment. Voters in Florida approved a similar proposal, with more than 62 percent of the voters supporting the ban.

As of 2009, a total of 29 states had approved such constitutional amendments, including: Alabama (2006), Alaska (1998), Arizona (2008), Arkansas (2004), California (2008), Colorado (2006), Florida (2008), Georgia (2004), Kansas (2005), Idaho (2006), Kentucky (2004), Louisiana (2004), Michigan (2004), Mississippi (2004), Missouri (2004), Montana (2004), Nebraska (2000), Nevada (2002), North Dakota (2004), Ohio (2004), Oklahoma (2004), Oregon (2004), South Carolina (2006), South Dakota (2006), Tennessee (2006), Texas (2005), Utah (2004), Virginia (2006) and Wisconsin (2006).

Although these ballot initiatives may have stalled efforts among gay rights advocates, studies of the California vote have suggested that the age of a voter had a significant effect on whether the voter supported or opposed the proposal. One study showed that fewer than half of those under the age of 65 supported Proposition 8, while 67 percent of those age 65 and older voted in favor of the proposal. This data might suggest that that opposition to same-sex marriage may be on the decline and that after time has passed, a similar vote may fail.

North Coast Women's Care Medical Group, Inc. v. San Diego County Superior Court

The FIRST AMENDMENT guarantees freedom of religion but the Supreme Court has made clear that the state may regulate the behavior of believers when an important societal interests are at stake. Since the early part of this century some doctors, nurses and pharmacists have asserted that their religious beliefs prevent them from serving certain types of patients or dispensing birth control prescriptions. These religious objections have come into conflict with federal and state civil rights laws that mandate nondiscriminatory treatment. In *North Coast Women's Care Medical Group, Inc. v. San Diego County Superior Court*, 44 Cal.4th 1145, 189 P.3d 959, 81 Cal. Rptr.3d 708 (2008), the California Supreme Court ruled that physicians may not decline to perform fertility procedures because the patient is a lesbian. The court based its ruling on a state civil rights act and U.S. SUPREME COURT precedents.

Guadalupe Benitez and her lesbian partner, Joanne Clark, lived in San Diego County. They wanted Benitez to become pregnant and attempted intravaginal self-insemination, a nonmedical process in which a woman inserts sperm into her own vagina. Benitez and Clark used sperm from a sperm bank, but after these efforts failed Benitez was diagnosed with a medical disorder characterized by irregular ovulation. Her physician referred Benitez to the North Coast Women's Care Medical Group, Inc., which specialized in fertility treatments. The couple met with Dr. Christine Dr. Brody,

Tim Geithner.
AP IMAGES

an obstetrician and gynecologist employed by North Coast. Brody informed them at some point intrauterine insemination (IUI) might have to be employed. She said that if a IUI was needed, her religious beliefs would prevent her from performing the procedure on Benitez but other physicians in the clinic would be willing to handle it.

For almost a year Dr. Brody treated Benitez for infertility. In July 2000 Benitez sought an IUI using a friend's fresh sperm. Brody said that using her friend's sperm would pose a problem for the clinic, as there were more requirements for using donated fresh sperm than with using sperm from a sperm bank. Benitez then chose to use sperm from a sperm bank for the IUI. Dr. Brody noted this in Benitez's medical records and then went on an out-of-state vacation. Dr. Douglas Fenton took over treatment of Benitez but was unaware of her decision not to use her friend's fresh sperm. He later claimed the the updated record had been left in Dr. Brody's in box while she was on vacation. Fenton, the only doctor licensed to prepare fresh sperm, refused to prepare it because of his religious objections. Fenton referred Benitez to a physician outside North Coast's medical practice. Benitez conceived in June 2001 with the help of this doctor. In August 2001 she sued North Coast, Brody, and Fenton, seeking damages and an injunction. Benitez argued that the refusal to treat her violated California's Unruh Civil Rights Act.

The trial court ruled that the defendants could not use as an **affirmative defense** the rights of free speech and freedom of religion set forth in the U.S. and state constitutions. The defendants immediately contested this decision in the Court of Appeals, which allowed the Brody and Fenton to employ this affirmative defense. Benitez then filed an appeal with the California Supreme Court.

The court, in a unanimous ruling, over-turned the appeals court decision. Justice Joyce Kennard, writing for the court, noted that the U.S. Supreme Court's recent holdings stated that a person had no federal constitutional right to an exemption from a neutral and valid law of general applicability on the ground that com-plying with the law was contrary to the person's religious beliefs. On the defendant's assertion of federal constitutional rights, the court con-cluded that the Unruh Civil Rights Act was a

neutral and valid law of general applicability. The act required businesses to provide "full and equal accommodations, advantages, facilities, privileges, or services" to all persons regardless of their sexual orientation.

Justice Kennard found no merit in the defendants' state constitution claims. The consti-tution guaranteed the free exercise of religion but there was no religious exemption from a valid and neutral state law. Even if highest level of constitutional review, **strict scrutiny**, was applied, the claim failed. The state had a com-pelling interest in "ensuring full and equal access to medical treatment irrespective of sexual orientation, and there are no less restrictive means for the state to achieve that goal." The physicians could avoid liability be either per-forming the IUI procedure on all patients, regardless of sexual orientation, or North Coast could refuse to the procedure on any patient.

❖ GEITHNER, TIMOTHY

In November of 2008, Timothy Geithner was nominated by president-elect Barack Obama to be the Secretary of the Treasury in his Cabinet. Geithner had extensive experience in interna-tional economics, including serving as an assistant financial attaché at the American embassy in Japan. Before being nominated for Treasury secretary, he served as the chief executive officer (CEO) of the Federal Reserve Bank of New York. Geithner was born on August 18, 1961, in New York City. He earned his B.A. degree in government and Asian studies from Dartmouth College in 1983, then entered the Johns Hopkins School of Advanced Inter-national Studies. There, Geithner earned a master's degree in international economics and East Asian studies in 1985.

After completing his education, Geithner joined Kissinger Associates Inc., where he worked from 1985 to 1988. Beginning in 1988, he worked for the federal government, spending seven years as the assistant financial attaché at the U.S. embassy in Japan. After short stints as the deputy assistant secretary of international monetary and financial policy at the U.S. Department of the Treasury and the senior deputy assistant secretary of the Treasury for international affairs, Geithner became the assis-tant secretary of international affairs. From 1998 to 2001, Geithner served as the undersec-retary of the Treasury for International Affairs.

During his time with the government, he was the representative of the United States at international financial meetings with key countries and helped negotiate financial services trade agreements.

In 2001 Geithner spent six months as a senior fellow in international economics at the Council on Foreign Relations before joining the International Monetary Fund as the director of the Policy Development and Review Department. In this position, he helped design and implement the policies of the organization. In 2003 Geithner took on a role of even greater importance when he was named the CEO of the Federal Reserve Bank of New York, where he played a key role in developing the United States' interest rate policies. Geithner also helped manage crises in both the American and international financial systems. When the American economy hit the skids in 2008, he played a significant role in crafting the Fed's response by having cash infused into troubled investment and financial companies.

While serving as the head of the Federal Reserve, Geithner was nominated to be the Secretary of the Treasury by incoming president Obama in November of 2008. In this post,

1961	Born, New York City
1998	Began as undersecretary of the Treasury for International Affairs
2003	Named CEO of Federal Reserve Bank of New York
2008	Nominated to be Secretary of Treasury

Geithner was to be the leading economic official in the Obama administration, poised to face the most challenging American economic crisis in decades. Because his work with the Federal Reserve was so highly regarded by Wall Street, news of his appointment caused a sagging stock market to surge nearly 500 points on that day. Of Geithner's appointment, Kevin Hassett of the American Enterprise Institute told Jim Puzzanghera and Peter G. Gosselin of the Los Angles Times, "It's a terrific choice. He's been in the middle of this [economic crisis], he has been at Treasury and he's a very bright guy, highly respected by people in both parties."

HABEAS CORPUS

Latin, "You have the body." A writ (court order) that commands an individual or a government official who has restrained another to produce the prisoner at a designated time and place so that the court can determine the legality of custody and decide whether to order the prisoner's release.

Harbison v. Bell

If death-row inmates seek **clemency** from state governors or Pardon Boards, can they request federally-appointed (and funded) attorneys to represent them, if no other attorneys are available to prepare a clemency petition? In *Harbison v. Bell*, No. 07-8521, 556 U.S. ___ (2009), the U.S. SUPREME COURT, by a 7-2 decision, said yes.

Edward Jerome Harbison was convicted and sentenced to death by a Tennessee state court in 1983. In 1997, after finally exhausting all his state court appeals, the U.S. **District Court** in Tennessee appointed a federal public defender for the purpose of filing, on his behalf, a federal **writ** of **habeas corpus** under 28 USC §2254. Although counsel ultimately developed substantial evidence potentially mitigating for Harbison (according to the Supreme Court), the habeas petition was denied. Harbison then requested an attorney to represent him in a last-ditch effort for state clemency proceedings.

Tennessee law no longer authorized the appointment of state public defenders for clemency proceedings. Therefore, Harbison's federally-appointed attorney moved the district court to expand the scope of her representation to include the state clemency proceedings, relying on 18 USC §3599 (which provides for the appointment of federal counsel) for authority. Section 3599 (a)2 expressly refers to the federal habeas **statute** sections 2254 and 2255, providing for the appointment **of counsel** in "both state and federal post-conviction proceedings." Section 3599 (e) in relevant part, states that counsel is available to any defendant sentenced to death in "proceedings for executive or other clemency as may be available to the defendant." Despite the language, there had been a split in the federal circuit courts as to whether Section 3599 provided for federally-funded attorney only in executive clemency proceedings from the President, or also clemency from state governors or pardon boards.

The district court denied the motion, and the Sixth **Circuit Court** of Appeals affirmed. A question had also been raised on appeal about Harbison's failure to obtain a certificate of appealability under 28 USC 2253(c) and whether that deprived the Sixth Circuit of jurisdiction over the appeal? The U.S. Supreme Court granted **certiorari** on both questions. That is to say, (1) whether a certificate of appealability was required to appeal an order denying a request for counsel under Section 3599, and (2) whether Section 3599(e) provided for such federally funded counsel for representation in state clemency hearings.

The U.S. Supreme Court concluded that the certificate of appealability was not required; therefore, there was no problem with the Sixth Circuit's jurisdiction over the matter. The Court then overturned the Sixth Circuit's decision, holding instead that Section 3599 did indeed authorize federally appointed counsel to represent counsel in state clemency proceedings.

As to the issue of appealability, the Court found that §2253(c) governed only final orders that disposed of habeas corpus proceedings on the merits. In this case, Harbison never got that far. His case was only at the stage of requesting federal counsel to represent him in a habeas appeal.

Regarding the more substantive issue of whether Section 3599 would cover state clemency proceedings, the Court found that it not only authorized such federally-appointed counsel, but also entitled them to compensation for their representation. Again, the language of Section 3599(e) states that counsel is available to any defendant sentenced to death in "proceedings for executive or other clemency as may be available to the defendant," Clearly, state clemency proceedings are "available" to state petitioners. Therefore, those state petitioners such as Harbison, who had already obtained Section 3599 representation for federal habeas proceedings could also have counsel represent them in subsequent clemency proceedings, either state or federal.

Justice Stevens delivered the opinion of the Court, joined by Justices Kennedy, Souter, Ginsburg, and Breyer. Chief Justice Roberts wrote a separate opinion in which he concurred with the judgment, but would have resolved it by interpreting Section 3599(e) differently. He agreed that nothing in the text of §3599(e) excluded proceedings for state clemency proceedings, and there were good reasons to expect federal habeas counsel to continue their representation through such clemency hearings. Yet Justice Roberts noted that it was highly unlikely the Congress intended this effect. Therefore, he opined, the best reading of Section 3599(e) would interpret the phrase "subsequent stage[s] of available judicial proceedings" to not include state judicial proceedings after federal habeas proceedings because they were not "subsequent" but were actually "new" proceedings. Justice Thomas also separately concurred in the judgment.

Justice Scalia, with whom Justice Alito joined, concurred in the majority opinion about Harbison not needing a certificate of appealability, but dissented in agreeing that Section 3599(e) gave state prisoners the right to federally funded counsel to pursue state clemency. The dissent opined that Harbison's right to federally-funded counsel was limited to capital defendants appearing in a federal forum.

Jiminez v. Quarterman

The **federal courts** continue to grapple with the procedural rules governing petitions for writs of **habeas corpus** that Congress included in the Anti-Terrorism and Effective Death Penalty Act of 1996 (AEDPA), Pub. L. No. 104-132. AEDPA sought to reduce the number of habeas filings by imposing strict timelines on petitions, but the federal courts must rely on state court determinations on whether a petition is timely. Each state has different laws and rules of procedure that affect the calculation of time for filing a timely petition for habeas corpus. This has forced the U.S. SUPREME COURT to make a steady stream of rulings on habeas time limits. In *Jiminez v. Quarterman*, __U.S.__, 129 S.Ct. 681, __ L.Ed.2d __ (2009) , the Court had to determine whether a state court's grant of an out-of-time direct appeal reset the date when the conviction became final for AEDPA purposes, or whether the clock started running on the prisoner's original deadline for filing a direct appeal in state court. In this case the Court concluded that the clock started running from the issuance of the out-of-time appeal decision.

Carlos Jiminez was sentenced for **burglary** in 1995. His lawyer filed an appellate brief with the Texas Court of Appeals stating that he could not find any nonfrivolous grounds on which to base an appeal. The lawyer left a copy of brief at the county jail where he thought Jiminez was housed, along with a letter explaining that Jiminez had the right to file his own **appellate** brief. However, Jiminez had already been transferred to state prison and never received the brief and the letter. In 1996 the appeals court dismissed the appeal filed by the lawyer and served the notice of dismissal at the county jail address. Again, Jiminez never saw the document.

In time Jiminez discovered what had happened and filed for a **writ** of habeas corpus, arguing that his right to a meaningful appeal had been denied because of the mixup with the jail address. The Texas Criminal Court of Appeals ruled in his favor in September 2002 and granted him the right to file an out-of-time appeal. Jiminez's appeal was unsuccessful, with the appeals court ruling in October 2003. His time for filing an appeal with the U.S. Supreme Court expired in January 2004. He filed for a second habeas writ in December 2004 and it was denied on June 29, 2005. Jiminez then filed a federal petition for a writ of habeas corpus on July 19, 2005.

The federal **district court** looked to AEDPA provisions on timeliness. Under the **statute** a state prisoner has a one-year time limit for filing a federal habeas corpus petition. That year runs from the latest of four specified dates. In this case that was "the date on which the judgment became final by the conclusion of direct review or the expiration of time for seeking such review." Jiminez argued that the January 2004 was the trigger date–the date when time expired for him to seek review by the U.S. Supreme Court of his out-of-time appeal. In addition, he argued that the time his second habeas petition was pending in state court was excluded from the one-year limitations period. Therefore, he contended that 355 days had passed between the January 2004 expiration date and the filing of his federal habeas petition in July 2005. The district court disagreed. It concluded that the one-year limitations period started in October 1996, when Jiminez's time for seeking a direct appeal of his conviction expired. The court stated that it could not take into account the out-of-time appeal because it was bound by precedent of the Fifth **Circuit Court** of Appeals. The appeals court precedent stated that "AEDPA provides for only a linear limitations period, one that starts and ends on specific dates, with only the possibility that tolling will expand the period in between." Therefore, the district ruled his time for filing for a federal habeas writ expired in October 1997. The Fifth Circuit upheld this ruling and Jiminez appealed to the Supreme Court.

The Supreme Court, in a unanimous decision, reversed the Fifth Circuit ruling and its AEDPA precedent on time calculation. Justice Clarence Thomas, writing for the Court, rejected the state's claim resetting the one-year limitations based on the out-of-time appeal would undermine the policy of finality that Congress established. He pointed out that AEDPA sought to give state courts the first opportunity to review claims of constitutional violations. The statute requires a federal court to "make use of the date on which the entirety of the state direct appellate review process was completed." However, the Court made clear its decision was a narrow one, dealing only with out-of-time appeals.

Knowles v. Mirzayance

In *Knowles v. Mirzayance,* No. 07-1315, 556 U.S. ___ (2009), the U.S. SUPREME COURT reversed the decision of the Ninth **Circuit Court** of Appeals and unanimously rejected a federal habeas petition that claimed defendant Alexandre Mirzayance suffered ineffective assistance **of counsel** at his trial for first-degree murder. The claim was premised on defense counsel's decision to not pursue a "not guilty by reason of insanity" defense, which was the only defense available. On the substantive question, the Supreme Court held that deciding not to assert the defense, which was almost certain to fail, did not constitute ineffective assistance of counsel. Moreover, the Court held that Knowles did not meet the threshold criteria for federal habeas relief in the first place.

As background, California state law provides for a bifurcated, or two-phase criminal trial when dealing with a potential defense of insanity. During the first phase, a jury must find the defendant guilty as charged (the guilt phase). If a jury so finds, then a second trial phase allows the jury to consider level of culpability in light of any plea of "not guilty by reason of insanity" (NGI) (the NGI phase). Further, under California law, a first-degree murder conviction can be avoided by presenting medical testimony that the defendant was insane at the time of the murder and therefore, lacked the necessary premeditation or deliberation. This would reduce the culpability to that of second-degree murder.

Despite a confession that he stabbed and shot to death his cousin, defendant Mirzayance, through defense counsel, entered pleas of not guilty and not guilty by reason of insanity at his state court trial. Therefore, a full trial commenced. During the guilt phase of the trial, Mirzayance's counsel offered evidence, in the form of medical testimony, that he was insane at the time of the murder. The jury apparently gave little or no weight to the evidence and convicted Mirzayance of first-degree murder.

The trial moved on to the NGI phase, but when Mirzayance's parents refused to testify on their son's behalf, his counsel advised him to withdraw his NGI defense, which he did. (The state had carried the burden to prove his guilt, which it did, but since Mirzayance raised the defense of insanity, he, and not the government, would have to prove it.)

A series of state appeals followed, all rejecting post-conviction relief on Mirzayance's claim that this advice (to drop the NGI plea) constituted ineffective assistance of counsel under the SIXTH AMENDMENT to the U.S. Constitution. Mirzayance then petitioned for federal **habeas corpus** relief, denied by the federal **district court**. However, the Ninth Circuit Court of Appeals reversed and remanded the case for an evidentiary hearing into the reasons behind defense counsel's recommendation to drop the NGI defense.

During that hearing, a **magistrate** judge concluded that the medical evidence that would have been introduced at the NGI phase would have duplicated the same evidence already presented to and rejected by the jury during the guilt phase of the trial. The magistrate further found that after Mirzayance's parents refused to testify on his behalf, and after discussing the dilemma with other experienced defense attorneys, counsel made a careful and reasoned decision not to proceed with the NGI defense. Notwithstanding all this, the magistrate also concluded that counsel's performance was nonetheless deficient because he had "nothing to lose" by going forward with the NGI defense. The magistrate found prejudice in this, opining that a jury might reasonably find Mirzayance insane had counsel pursued the NGI defense (the only defense available). The magistrate recommended habeas relief for Mirzayance, and this time, the federal district court accepted the recommendation and granted the **writ**. On reviewing the case again after remand, the Ninth Circuit affirmed, finding that Mirzayance was entitled to federal habeas relief under 28 USC 2254(d)(1) because the California **Court of Appeal** had "unreasonabl[y] appli[ed] clearly established Federal law."

The above language comes from a provision found in the Antiterrorism and Effective Death Penalty Act (AEDPA), [28 USC 2254(d)(1)]. This section limits federal habeas relief for state-court adjudications only if the state court's decision "was contrary to, or involved an unreasonable application of, clearly established Federal law, as determined by the Supreme Court of the United States." The clearly-established federal law in the present case was the standard established in *Strickland v. Washington,* 466 U.S. 668 (1984), which required proof that (1) counsel's performance fell below an objective standard, and (2) that, but for the deficient performance, a jury would likely have reached a different result.

The U.S. Supreme Court reviewed the Ninth Circuit's reversal of the California Court of Appeals, which had denied Mirzayance post-conviction relief. Justice Clarence Thomas, writing for an unanimous Court, concluded that, whether the case was reviewed *de novo,* under the AEDPA provision, the Court still would have reversed the Ninth Circuit because Mirzayance failed to establish that his counsel's performance was deficient. The California **appellate** court's denial of Mirzayance's ineffective counsel claim violated no "clearly established federal law." No "clearly-established" Supreme Court precedent ever pronounced the notion that not pursuing a course of action or tactic, because "there was nothing to lose," would constitute ineffective counsel. All justices joined in this part.

Secondly, even under *Strickland's* more general standard, evidence was lacking to establish that either defense counsel was ineffective/deficient in performance at all, or that the outcome would have been different had the NGI defense been pursued. (Justices Scalia, Souter, and Ginsburg did not join in this part of the opinion.) Accordingly, the judgment of the Ninth Circuit was vacated and the case remanded for action pursuant to this holding.

❖ HOLDER, ERIC

Following the election of Barack Obama as U.S. President in 2008, Eric Holder was chosen as the incoming president's nominee for the post of U.S. attorney general, succeeding Michael Mukasey. Holder became the first African-American to hold the position as leader of the Justice Department.

Holder was born and raised in a working-class section of Queens, New York. His parents had both emigrated from Barbados. By virtue of his scholarship, he was accepted into the academically elite Stuyvesant High School in

Eric Holder.
AP IMAGES

Manhattan, and after graduation he enrolled at Columbia University. There he majored in American history, earning top grades, and he spent his spare time absorbing black culture at such notable Harlem landmarks as the Apollo Theater and the Abyssinian Baptist Church. Feeling a responsibility toward fellow black Americans who were less fortunate than himself, Holder began spending his Saturday mornings at a Harlem youth center and taking selected young people on trips around the city. He joined the Concerned Black Men, a national organization dedicated to helping minority youngsters.

Holder received his bachelor's degree in 1973, and immediately was accepted into Columbia's law school. When he graduated from that institution in 1976, he decided to join the Department of Justice. At the time he figured he would work there two or three years and then take a position in a private firm. Holder joined a relatively new division at Justice, the Public Integrity Unit. "It was formed ... with [the summer of 1972 incident, which eventually resulted in U.S. president Nixon's resignation, known as] Watergate still ringing in everyone's ears," he told the *Chicago Tribune*. The Public Integrity attorneys were charged with prosecuting high-level corruption cases, often involving respectable public figures. Among those Holder helped to prosecute were former South Carolina congressman John W. Jenrette—in the notorious "Abscam" case in the late 1970s—and a Philadelphia judge who accepted monetary gifts to "fix" cases. The list of people Holder prosecuted while with Public Integrity included Federal Bureau of Investigation (FBI) agents, politicians, organized crime figures, and even a fellow Justice Department lawyer. The job Holder thought he would stay in for two years consumed one dozen years of his life.

In 1988, President Ronald Reagan appointed Holder to the Superior Court of the District of Columbia. The rotating judgeship involved deciding every imaginable kind of case, from murders and armed robberies to

1951	Born, Queens, New York
1976	Graduated Columbia University School of Law
1988	Associate Justice for Superior Court of District of Columbia
1993	U.S. attorney
2009	U.S. attorney general

nonpayment of child support and school truancy. The job proved particularly difficult for a man committed to helping African-Americans in the city. Holder's sentiments as a judge—both sympathetic and pragmatic—helped endear him to the District of Columbia's political leaders. Many of these politicians felt that the district should have a black U.S. attorney, preferably a local citizen who had demonstrated an allegiance to the area. Holder was just that citizen, and he had even worked at the Department of Justice. After the presidential swearing-in of Bill Clinton in 1993, congressional delegate Norton commissioned a panel of Washington, DC lawyers and civic activists to make recommendations for the District's U.S. attorney slot. The panel chose Holder, and Norton passed his name along to the president. Holder was one of three candidates interviewed for the position, and the only qualm expressed about him was his lack of leadership experience.

Late in 1993, Clinton announced that he had chosen Holder to be Washington, DC's first black U.S. attorney. Holder provided direction for the prosecution of numerous local criminal suspects, including everyone from the local drug dealers to those who might wish to harm the president. In June 2008, Holder joined the Obama campaign, and eventually accepted the nomination to become attorney general. Holder was confirmed by a 75-21 vote in the U.S. Senate on February 2, 2009, and sworn in the following day.

IDENTITY THEFT

Flores-Figueroa v. United States

The use of forged Social Security and alien registration cards by illegal immigrants to secure employment is common in the United States. Sometimes fake IDs contain made up Social Security numbers and other data, while others are based on information taken from real persons. Congress enacted a criminal **statute** forbidding identity theft that imposes a mandatory consecutive two-year prison term upon individuals convicted of certain other crimes, if during the commission of these crimes the offender "knowingly" uses or possesses a "means of identification of another person." Some defendants convicted under this statute have appealed, arguing that the government is required to prove that they knew the fake ID was taken from another person. The appeals courts were divided on what the government had to prove, leading the Supreme Court, in *Flores-Figueroa v. United States*, __U.S.__, 129 S.Ct. 1886, 173 L.Ed.2d 853 (2009), to take up the question. The Court held that the government must prove the defendant knew that the identification document was stolen. Possessing false document was not sufficient.

Ignacio Flores-Figueroa, a Mexican citizen, entered the United States illegally. In 2000 he gave his new employer a false name, birth date, Social Security number and a counterfeit alien registration number. The Social Security number and the alien registration card number were not those of a real person. In 2006 Flores presented his employer with new counterfeit Social Security and alien registration cards. These cards used his real name, but the numbers on both cards were assigned to other people. His employer checked the numbers with the U.S. Customs and Immigration Enforcement agency, which reported that both numbers belonged to other people. The U.S. government charged Florida with three crimes: entering the United States illegally, misusing immigration documents, and aggravated identify theft. Flores sought acquittal on the identify theft charge because he claimed the government could not prove that he knew that the numbers on the counterfeit documents were assigned to other people. The government argued it did not have to prove that Flores knew he was committing identify theft. The **district court** sided with the government and after a **bench trial** convicted Flores on all three charges. The Eighth Circuit of Appeals upheld the district court's ruling. The Supreme Court agreed to hear Flores' appeal because two circuit courts of appeal agreed with the Eighth Circuit and three circuit courts of appeal disagreed, finding that the government needed to prove knowledge for the identity theft statute.

The Supreme Court unanimously overruled the Eighth Circuit ruling, concluding that the government had the burden of proving that the person using false identification knew that the numbers and information on the documents were assigned or belonged to another person. Justice STEPHEN BREYER, writing for the Court, based his analysis on a reading of the statute and on the legislative purpose behind the identity theft statute. Breyer found "strong textual reasons" for rejecting the government's position. The law stated that it was a crime if the offender "knowingly transfers, possesses, or uses without lawful authority, a means of identification of another." 18 U.S.C.A. §1028A(a)(1). The government conceded that the offender must know that he is transferring, possessing, or using something but contested the idea that the offender had to know he was using a real ID rather than a fake ID. It believed the word "knowingly" did not modify the law's last phrase concerning "a means of identification of another person." Breyer thought that it seemed "natural" to read "knowingly" as applying to all the subsequently listed elements of the crime. As an example of the absurdity of the governments' reasoning, Breyer queried whether a law that made it unlawful to knowingly possess drugs would apply to a person "who steals a passenger's bag without knowing that the bag has drugs inside?" Justice Breyer built on this textual argument by citing other decisions where the Court had read a phrase in a criminal statute that "introduces the elements of a crime with the word 'knowingly'" as applying that word to each element.

The Court also rejected the government's complaint that imposing the knowledge requirement would give potential offenders an incentive to avoid wrongly using IDs that belong to others. Justice Breyer concluded that legislative history was inconclusive as to whether Congress intended to allow convictions where the offender did not know or intend to use a fake ID that belonged to another person. The statute dealt with two issues: the unlawful use of false identification and identity theft. The legislative debates and the **fraud** statute from which this provision came from used the terms "identity fraud" and "identity theft." In the legislative history identity theft was attached to circumstances where the offender clearly knew that he was taking identifies another person. The Court admitted that its interpretation made enforcement more difficult but it was up to Congress to make any corrections to the language.

IMMIGRATION

The entrance into a country of foreigners for purposes of permanent residence. The correlative term emigration *denotes the act of such persons in leaving their former country.*

Lozano v. City of Hazelton, Pennsylvania

In a closely-watched case captioned *Lozano v. City of Hazelton, Pennsylvania,* (No.3:06cv1586, M.D. Pa., 2007) the U.S. District Court for the Middle District of Pennsylvania held that Hazelton City ordinances to regulate the rental housing and employment of illegal immigrants were preempted by federal law (dealing with immigration). Further, they violated both procedural due process and 42 USC §1981 (the civil rights statute enacted after the Civil War and the emancipation of slaves).

Hazelton, Pennsylvania, a town of less than 25,000 during the 2000 census, had its population balloon to more than 31,000, ostensibly from an influx of illegal immigrants. In response to perceived inaction by the federal government relating to issues posed by the presence of millions of undocumented aliens nationwide, some local governments, including Hazelton, sought to enact their own restrictions on illegal aliens' access to jobs, housing, and benefits. Cash-strapped Hazelton, through its City Council, adopted ordinances to deal with the crime, crowded schools, hospital costs, and demand for public services that it attributed to the rise in its illegal immigrant population. One ordinance precluded illegal immigrants from renting housing. Another prohibited the employment of "illegal aliens."

In 2006, the American Civil Liberties Union (ACLU) and others filed a lawsuit against the City of Hazelton. The lawsuit was held without prosecution after Hazelton agreed not to enforce its original ordinance. However, on September 12, 2006, Hazelton adopted two new separate ordinances, the "Illegal Immigration Relief Act," and the "Official English Ordinance." The first was passed by a vote of 4-1; the latter passed unanimously.

Hazelton's ordinance relating to housing provisions in the first ordinance barred persons from knowingly leasing or permitting occupancy by an "illegal alien." It additionally required apartment dwellers to obtain an occupancy permit by presenting proof of citizenship or lawful residency in the United States.

In October 2006, Pedro Lozano and several other individual Latinos joined with the Hazelton Hispanic Business Association and the Pennsylvania Statewide Latino Coalition as plaintiffs in a new lawsuit filed against the City of Hazelton. A bench trial was held in March 2007. On July 26, 2007, U.S. District Court Judge James M. Munley issued his decision, enjoining the City of aHaHazelton from enforcing the subject ordinances.

The City had first argued that the plaintiffs (who had originally sued anonymously for fear of disclosure of their immigration status to authorities) lacked standing. City lawyers argued that the plaintiffs did not have authorization to reside in the United States and had not suffered an injury for which they were entitled to relief. But the district court reasoned that even if denied residency permits in Hazelton, it did not follow that the plaintiffs lacked authorization to live anywhere in the United States. Under *Plyler v. Doe*, 457 U.S. 202 (1982), the U.S. Supreme Court held that even unlawfully present aliens were "persons" entitled to due process under the Fifth and 14th Amendments before being stripped of their rights.

Judge Munley held that the employment ban was both expressly and impliedly preempted by the federal 1986 Immigration Reform and Control Act (IRCA), 8 USC at §1324a(h)(2), which regulated the employment of aliens. Specifically, that provision preempted "any State or local law imposing civil or criminal sanctions (other than through licensing and similar laws) upon those who employ, or recruit or refer for a fee for employment, unauthorized aliens." City lawyers argued that its ordinance fell within the exception for "licensing and similar laws," because it sanctioned businesses for employing unauthorized aliens by suspending their business licenses and permits. But the district court found this nonsensical, because revoking the right to do business was "the ultimate sanction," and the exemption in the statute was for suspension of licenses for violating the IRCA, not a local ordinance. The district court further held that an implied preemption existed under IRCA because the Act was a "comprehensive scheme" covering the field of employment of unauthorized aliens, leaving no room for state or local regulation.

The district court also found that the housing ban in Hazelton's ordinance conflicted with federal immigration law by incorrectly assuming that the federal government sought removal of all aliens who lacked legal status. A conclusive determination of immigration status could only be made by a federal immigration judge, said Judge Munley. The district court further held that the housing ban violated 42 USC §1981, which guarantees all persons the same right to enter into contracts (in this case, leases). Moreover, said the district court, the plaintiffs were denied procedural due process, in that the right to work for a living and to enter into leases were both protected liberty interests. The employment ordinance failed to provide employers with adequate notice of the "identity information" they were required to provide and failed to outline procedures for verifying documents. The housing ordinance provided no notice to tenants subject to eviction, said the district court.

The City appealed the district court's ruling. A decision or other disposition of the case from the U.S. Court of Appeals for the Third Circuit was still pending as of June 2009.

Negusie v. Holder

The United States has strict rules on whether an alien may be admitted to the country as a refugee. The Immigration and Nationality Act (INA) bars an alien from obtaining refugee status in the United States if he "assisted, or otherwise participated in the persecution of any person on account of race, religion, nationality, membership in a particular social group, or political opinion." INA. §101(a)(42). This so-called "persecutor bar" applies to those seeking asylum or withholding of removal, but does not disqualify an alien from receiving a temporary deferral of removal under the Convention Against Torture and Other Cruel, Inhuman or Degrading Treatment or Punishment (CAT). The Supreme Court, in *Negusie v. Holder,* __U.S.__, 129 S.Ct. 1159, L.Ed.2d (2009), held that the Board of Immigrant Appeals (BIA) and the Fifth Circuit had misapplied a Supreme Court decision as mandating that whether an alien is compelled to assist in persecution is immaterial for persecutor-bar purposes.

Daniel Negusie was born and educated in Ethiopia but left, in 1994, at age 18 to visit his mother in Eritrea. Government officials took him into custody soon after he arrived. He was forced to perform hard labor and then was conscripted into the Eritrean military. When war broke out in 1998 between Ethiopia and Eritrea, Negusie was conscripted once more. He refused to fight against Ethiopia and was imprisoned. After two years he was released but was forced to serve as a prison guard for four years. The prisoners he guarded were persecuted under the terms of the INA **statutory** definition. Negusie claimed that although he was armed, he never shot at or directly punished any prisoner. Moreover, he claimed he had helped prisoners. In time Negusie escaped from the prison and hid in a container that was loaded on a ship bound for the United States. When he arrived in the states he applied for asylum as a refugee.

The immigration judge cited the persecutor bar in denying Negusie refugee status, despite the fact that he found Negusie's claims credible that he never directly punished a prisoner. Despite this ruling, the judge allowed Negusie to remain in the U.S. because he was likely to be tortured if he was returned to Eritrea. The BIA upheld both of these decisions. The fact that Negusie had been compelled to serve as guard and had not directly punished prisoners was "immaterial," as intent or motivation were irrelevant under the INA provision. The Fifth **Circuit Court** of Appeals affirmed the BIA ruling.

The Supreme Court, in an 8-1 decision, overturned the Fifth Circuit ruling. Justice Kennedy, writing for the majority, held that the appeals court had misapplied *Fedorenko v. United States*, 449 U.S. 490, 101 S.Ct. 737, 66 L. Ed.2d 686 (1981), as mandating that whether an alien is compelled to assist in persecution is immaterial for persecutor-bar purposes. The BIA must interpret the **statute**, free from this mistaken legal premise. Though the BIA is entitled to deference in interpreting ambiguous INA provisions, in this case the Court had not spoken on a matter that federal immigration laws place primarily in agency hands. Therefore, the Court's ordinary rule was to remand the case to allow the BIA to address the matter in the **first instance** in light of its own experience.

In denying Negusie's request for refugee status, the BIA had recited a rule it had developed in its cases: An alien's motivation and intent are irrelevant to the issue whether he

"assisted" in persecution; rather, his actions' objective effect controls. Justice Kennedy found that a reading of those decisions confirmed that the BIA had not exercised its interpretive authority but, instead, had deemed its interpretation to be mandated by *Fedorenko*. This error prevented the BIA from fully considering the statutory question presented. Its mistaken assumption stemmed from a failure to recognize the inapplicability of the statutory construction principle invoked in *Fedorenko*, as well as a failure to appreciate the differences in statutory purpose. The BIA was not bound to apply the *Fedorenko* to the persecutor bar here at issue. Therefore, the Court could not grant deference to the BIA's reasoning.

In its remand to the BIA the Court pointed out that there was substance to Negusie's contention that involuntary acts cannot implicate the persecutor bar because "persecution" presumes moral blameworthiness. Negusie also strongly rebutted the government's argument that the question at issue was answered by the statute's failure to provide an exception for coerced conduct. Because this provision of the INA was ambiguous, the Court directed the BIA to first address issue.

Nken v. Holder

In 1996, Congress passed the Illegal Immigration Reform and Immigrant Responsibility Act (IIRIRA), partly to tighten the opportunities used by aliens to remain in the United States after an agency has ordered their removal. The IIRIRA thus contained more strict standards of review for courts when overruling agency determinations for removal and allowing aliens to remain in the United States. Specifically, Section 1252(f)(2) of IIRIRA prohibits judges from stopping (enjoining) the removal of aliens unless the alien can show, by clear and convincing evidence, that the removal was prohibited by law.

In *Nken v. Holder*, No. 08-681, 556 U.S. ___ (2009), the U.S. SUPREME COURT was asked whether the stricter IIRIRA standards of review also applied to motions to stay deportation pending **judicial review** of the removal order. By a 7-2 decision, the majority held that the newer, stricter standard did not apply to "motions to stay," but only to motions for injunctive relief. It then explained the difference between the two, and why the stricter standard could not apply to both. In rendering its opinion, the Court vacated the decision of the U.S. **Circuit Court** of Appeals for the Fourth Circuit, which had applied the stricter standard. There had been a split between **appellate** circuits over the proper application of IIRIRA's Section 1252(f)(2), triggering the Supreme Court's grant of review.

Jean Marc Nken, a citizen of Cameroon, entered the United States in 2001 on a transit visa and remained after the visa expired. Later that year, he applied for asylum and other relief, claiming that he had participated in student protests against Cameroon's government in 1990 and would be subjected to persecution if returned there. An immigration judge (in an administrative hearing) denied relief, noting numerous discrepancies and finding Nken's story not credible. Nken appealed to the Board of Immigration Appeals (BIA), which upheld the immigration judge's decision and ordered his removal from the United States.

Administrative decisions of the BIA may be appealed in federal court. By the time Nken's case came before the U.S. Circuit Court of Appeals for the Fourth Circuit, he had married a U.S. citizen and fathered a child. His wife filed an I-130 Petition for Alien Relative application (for adjustment of status) in 2004, and Nken sought to have his case remanded in light of his new marital status. Both the BIA and Fourth Circuit denied relief, partly because his I-130 application was still pending.

In 2006, Nken's I-130 application was approved and he again filed a motion to reopen and have his case reconsidered based on his marital status. His was again denied relief by the BIA, and his petition for review of the BIA's removal order was again denied as well.

Meanwhile, in Nken's native country of Cameroon, President Paul Biya announced that he was altering the Cameroon Constitution and making himself dictator. This presented an opportunity to Nken to file a third motion to reopen his case, based on changed circumstances in Cameroon. The BIA found insufficient factual support (since Baya had actually been in control of Cameroon for the previous 25 years) and denied Nken's third motion. He again sought review in the Fourth Circuit Court of Appeals of the BIA's denial of his motion to reopen removal proceedings. Also, and importantly, Nken petitioned the Fourth Circuit to stay the order of removal while his appeal of the BIA's denial of his motion to reopen removal proceedings was pending.

In his motion to stay the removal order, Nken acknowledged that Fourth Circuit precedent required him to meet the stricter criteria of the IIRIRA's Section 1252(f)(2), under which he would need to prove, by clear and convincing evidence, that the removal was prohibited by law. However, Nken argued in his motion that this standard did not govern, noting the split among circuit courts of appeal over this issue. The Fourth Circuit denied his motion without comment.

In reversing the Fourth Circuit, Chief Justice Roberts, delivering the opinion of the Supreme Court, held that traditional factors used to review motions to stay, and not the stricter IIRIRA's standards, governed an appellate court's authority to stay an alien's removal pending judicial review.

Importantly, the Court noted that IIRIRA's Section 1252(f) did not refer to "stays," but rather to the authority to "enjoin [by injunction] the removal of any alien." The Court went on to explain the difference. A "stay" is a request to hold the matter in **abeyance** until a court could review the merits. A stay operates upon a judicial proceeding by halting or postponing some part of it. Conversely, an "injunction" is an order, directed toward a person or **entity** itself, to do something or refrain from doing something. An alien asking for a stay of removal pending **adjudication** of a petition for review, is not asking for a coercive order against the government, but only for a temporary reprieve against enforcing a removal order.

Accordingly, application of IIRIRA's Section 1252(f)'s stricter standards was not appropriate for a motion to stay a removal order. Rather, appellate courts should apply traditional standards for reviewing stays. The Court then enumerated the four-prong test that governs review of stays. First, there must be more than a mere possibility that relief (in the matter under review) will be granted. Second, there must be more than a mere possibility that **irreparable injury** will result if the stay is denied. The third and fourth factors assess whether the stay will injure the opposing party and what public interest is at stake.

Justice Kennedy, joined by Justice Scalia, wrote a separate concurring opinion, emphasizing that stays in such cases were extraordinary remedies not to be granted lightly. Justice Alito, joined by Justice Thomas, dissented. He argued that IIRIRA provided that immigration removal orders were "self-executing" and "not dependent upon judicial enforcement."

IMMUNITY

Exemption from performing duties that the law generally requires other citizens to perform, or from a penalty or burden that the law generally places on other citizens.

Pearson v. Callahan

The federal civil rights **tort law**, 42 U.S.C.A. § 1983, gives individuals the right to sue police officers for injuries caused by the officers' unconstitutional actions. Though individuals may have the right to file such a lawsuit, the Supreme Court has made it increasingly more difficult by constructing a qualified immunity doctrine. Unlike legislators and judges, who enjoy absolute immunity from civil damages lawsuits, enforcement officers only possess a qualified immunity. This means that a court must review their application for immunity and determine if they qualify. The qualifications for immunity have undergone a number of modifications since the 1960s, but the Supreme Court established a mandatory two-step process of analysis for the federal district courts to follow. This procedure proved to be very unpopular with the federal bench, leading the Court to make the process merely optional in *Pearson v. Callahan*, __U.S.__, 129 S.Ct. 808, __L.Ed.2d__ (2009).

Afton Callahan was convicted in Utah state court for possession and distribution of drugs, which he sold to an undercover informant. The Central Utah Narcotics Task Force had arranged for the informant to go to Callahan's trailer home and purchase a gram of methamphetamine for $100. Once the deal was consummated, the informant was to signal this fact to the officers with an electronic communications device. All went as planned. Callahan's daughter let the informant into the home, and the drug deal was made. Once the informant sent the signal the officers entered the trailer through a porch door and confronted Callahan, who dropped a bag of meth. The officers then searched the residence and found a large bag of meth, along with the $100 marked bill.

The trial court held that the warrantless search did not violate the FOURTH AMENDMENT because the police were working under exigent circumstances. This exception to the warrant requirement is justified if the officer believes evidence will be destroyed before a warrant can be obtained. The Utah Court of Appeals disagreed, finding that the search was illegal and the evidence of the search could not be used at trial. The prosecutor dropped criminal charges against Callahan, who then filed a § 1983 damages lawsuit against the police officers who had entered and search his house.

The **district court** granted the officers qualified immunity and dismissed the lawsuit, ruling that other courts had permitted warrantless entry once an informant was allowed into the house voluntarily and observes contraband in plain view. The Tenth **Circuit Court** of Appeals reversed, holding that the exception the district court used applied only to undercover police officers, not informants. It said that the constitutional right to be free in one's home from unreasonable searches and seizures was clearly established.

The Supreme Court, in a unanimous decision, overturned the Tenth Circuit ruling. Justice Samuel Alito, writing for the Court, noted that the appeals court had applied the mandatory procedure set out in *Saucier v. Katz*, 533 U.S. 194, 121 S.Ct. 2151, 150 L. Ed. 2d 272 (2001). The procedure required a court to first decide whether the facts that a plaintiff has alleged or shown make out a violation of a constitutional right. If the plaintiff has satisfied this first step, then the court must decide whether the right at issue was "clearly established" at the time of the defendant's alleged misconduct. Qualified immunity is granted unless the official's conduct violated a clearly established constitutional right. The Court concluded that this mandatory procedure did not work. Judge should be allowed to decide which of the two elements should be addressed first "in light of the circumstances in the particular case at hand."

Justice Alito found that the mandatory procedure resulted in substantial expenditure of judicial resources on "difficult questions that have no effect on the outcome of the case." In fact, there were "cases in which it is plain that a constitutional right is not clearly established but far from obvious whether there is such a right." These fruitless exercises also wasted parties' resources and defeated the very point of qualified immunity, which is to relieve defendants of the costs and time associated with civil litigation. Forcing defendants to go through the two-step process when the outcome clearly would result in immunity did not make sense.

Turning to the conduct of the officers in this case, the Court ruled that the officers were entitled to qualified immunity because the entry did not violate clearly established law. It did not matter if there was a violation of the Fourth Amendment because the informant warrant exception discussed by the district court and the Tenth Circuit had been accepted by a number of lower courts. Even though the exception had not been ruled on by the Tenth Circuit at the time of the search, the officers could have reasonably believed that their conduct was within the law.

Van de Kamp v. Goldstein

The Supreme Court has granted immunity from civil lawsuits to many types of public officials, preventing citizens from suing officials for damages over injuries allegedly caused by government officials. The Court has made clear that when criminal prosecutors perform the traditional functions of an advocate, they are absolutely immune from money damage lawsuits. Absolute prosecutorial immunity, however, does not extend to functions that are not associated with advocacy, such as administrative functions. In *Van de Kamp v. Goldstein*, __U.S.__, 129 S.Ct. 855, __L.Ed.2d__ (2009), a former prisoner alleged that the district attorney and chief deputy district attorney had failed to properly train and supervise other prosecutors who successfully convicted him of murder. The prosecution failed to give information to the defense that cast doubt on the credibility of a jailhouse informer who testified against the defendant. The former prisoner sued the two district attorneys for damages, alleging that their administrative failures were not protected by absolute immunity. The Supreme Court disagreed, ruling that they were entitled to absolute immunity because the alleged actions were intimately associated with the judicial phase of the criminal process.

In 1980 Thomas Goldstein was convicted of murder in Lost Angeles, California. At the trial a jailhouse informant's testimony played a critical part in convicting Goldstein. Goldstein claimed the testimony was false. It was not until many years later that Goldstein discovered that the informant had previously received reduced sentences for providing prosecutors with favorable testimony in other cases. Goldstein filed for a **writ** of **habeas corpus** in 1998, arguing that prosecutors should have disclosed this information to his attorney at trial. If the attorney had been given this information, he could have sought to impeach the credibility of the informant and prevent a wrongful conviction. After an evidentiary hearing the federal **district court** agreed that the informant had not been truthful and ordered the state to either retry Goldstein or release him. The state declined to retry Goldstein, who had already served 24 years in prison.

Goldstein, now a free man, filed a § 1983 federal civil rights lawsuit against John Van de Camp, who served as L.A. District Attorney in 1980, and Van de Kamp's chief deputy. He alleged that the two top prosecutors failed to properly train and supervise prosecutors, and failed to establish an information system containing potential impeachment material about informants. The defendants asked the court to dismiss the lawsuit by asking the court to grant them absolute immunity. The federal district declined to dismiss the case, concluding that the alleged misconduct was administrative and fell outside the scope of the prosecutor's absolute immunity. The defendants appealed this ruling and the Ninth **Circuit Court** of Appeals upheld the "no immunity" decision.

The Supreme Court, in a unanimous decision, overruled the appeals court. Justice STEPHEN BREYER, writing for the Court, restated the importance of shielding prosecutors from civil lawsuits filed by disgruntled criminal defendants. If prosecutors were not immune they would be deluged with lawsuits and their legal decisions might be influenced by the thought of future litigation. Breyer acknowledged that prosecutors lose absolute immunity when the actions taken in an investigative or administrative role and that Goldstein's claims were based on administrative procedures. However, these claims focused on administrative obligations that are "directly connected with the conduct of a trial." In this case an individual prosecutor's error in Goldstein's trial constituted an essential element of Goldstein's claim, unlike administrative duties such as hiring, payroll administration, and the maintenance of office space.

The management tasks at issue concerned how and when to make impeachment information available at trial. These tasks were "directly connected with the prosecutor's basic trial advocacy duties." More generally, Justice Breyer questioned whether a line could be drawn between general office supervision and specific supervision or training related to a particular case. In addition, he viewed Goldstein's strategy as a back-door way of avoiding immunity and attaching liability for courtroom actions. A plaintiff "could restyle a complaint charging a trial failure so that it becomes a complaint charging a failure of training or supervision." If his theory succeeded, prosecutors could make decisions out of fear of damages liability and defendants would bring a multitude of lawsuits. Another concern was the difficulty of defending prosecutorial decisions many years after they were made. A final concern was the creation of legal anomalies. Under Goldstein's theory, the trial prosecutor would retain immunity, even for intentional failings, but her supervisor might be liable for negligent training or supervision. Though immunity sometimes deprives a plaintiff compensation that "he undoubtedly merits," it was more important that the "fair, efficient functioning of a prosecutorial office" be maintained.

INTERNET

A worldwide telecommunications network of business, government, and personal computers.

Seattle "Spam King" Convicted

In Cyberspace, "SPAM" refers to unsolicited commercial e-mail. The CAN-SPAM Act of 2003 (Controlling the Assault of Non-Solicited Pornography and Marketing Act), 15 USC §7701-7713 and 18 USC §1037, endeavored to regulate commercial email by creating parameters for permissible use while providing penalties for violation. Five years after passage, there were just a few noteworthy prosecutions, and critics said the law should have banned rather than regulated such "commercial speech" for private e-mail addresses. According to *SpamLaws.com,* SPAM accounted for 14.5 billion global messages per day, or about 45 percent of all e-mail traffic.

CAN-SPAM became effective January 1, 2004, and covers e-mail whose primary purpose is advertising or promoting a commercial product or service. Among other things, it prohibits false or misleading header information (which must reveal the originating domain name and e-mail address); prohibits deceptive subject lines (to **entice** or mislead the recipient about the contents or subject matter of the body of the e-mail message); and requires that the e-mail give recipients an "opt-out" method for 30 days following the e-mail sent.

Enforcement of CAN-SPAM falls primarily with the FEDERAL TRADE COMMISSION, but the U.S. Department of Justice may enforce its criminal sanctions.

In July 2008, 28-year-old Robert Alan Soloway, dubbed the "Seattle Spam King" by several media sources, was sentenced in U.S. **District Court** for the Western District of Washington to nearly four years in prison. He also was ordered to pay $708,000 in **restitution**. Earlier in March 2008, he had pleaded guilty to **mail fraud**, **fraud** in connection with electronic mail, and willful failure to file a tax return. He had been indicted in May 2007.

Soloway allegedly operated the Newport International Marketing Corporation (NIM) between November 2003 and his indictment in May 2007. He and the corporation offered a "broadcast e-mail" software product and "broadcast e-mail" services. These product and service advertisements inherently constituted "spam" in that they were bulk high-volume commercial unsolicited junk e-mail messages. Moreover, the "broadcast" products and services Soloway and NIM sold allowed yet others (purchasers of their products/services) to harvest e-mail addresses from the Internet and create their own spam.

Criminally, Soloway's and NIM's e-mails contained false and forged "headers" (the "from" and "to" part of e-mail messages, as well as the routing information, including the originating domain name and e-mail address). Using networks of compromised proxy computers (botnets, also a violation of CAN-SPAM), Soloway relayed millions of e-mail messages containing not only false and forged headers, but also containing substantively false claims about the products and services offered. He then constantly "moved" the NIM website, which was hosted on at least 50 different domains.

According to records filed in the case, one claim broadcasted by Soloway and NIM stated that the e-mail addresses used for the products and services were "opt-in" e-mail addresses. (The CAN-SPAM requires that unsolicited commercial e-mail messages give recipients an "opt-out" method to request that no more e-mails or messages be sent to their e-mail address.) Moreover, Soloway's websites offered money-back guarantees with full refunds for customers who purchased the broadcast e-mail products. The investigation was triggered when customers complaining about the product and services they had purchased, and/or asking for refunds, were threatened with additional charges and referral to a collection agency. The case was investigated by the FBI, U.S. Postal Inspection Service, and the INTERNAL REVE-NUE SERVICE Criminal Investigations in conjunction with the Computer Hacking and Intellectual Property (CHIP) Task Force.

Just as news of Soloway's sentence became available to media, a U.S. Attorney's Office in Colorado announced the escape of 35-year-old Edward Davidson, Colorado's "spam king" who walked out of a minimum-security prison camp in Florence, Colorado, after his wife visited him. He had been sentenced two months earlier, in April 2008, to 21 months in prison after pleading guilty to tax evasion and criminal spam charges. Davidson had also been ordered to pay the IRS nearly $715,000. According to his plea agreement, he owned a business known as Power Promoters. Between July 2002 and April 2007, Davidson and Power Promoters sent out millions of unsolicited commercial "spam" promoting the visibility and sale of products for nearly 20 companies. The messages contained false header information.

In July 2008, Adam Vitale of Brooklyn, New York pleaded guilty to sending spam to approximately 1.2 million AOL subscribers. He was sentenced to more than two years in prison followed by three years of supervised release, and ordered to pay American Online (AOL) $183,000 in restitution. The stiffest spam penalty as of June 2009 was meted out to Jeremy Jaynes of Raleigh, North Carolina, sentenced in 2004 to nine years in a Virginia prison. He was found guilty under Virginia state law that prohibited e-mail marketers from sending more than a certain number of spams within a given time frame, and also prohibited the use of fake e-mail addresses.

JUDGES

A public officer chosen or elected to preside over and to administer the law in a court of justice; one who controls the proceedings in a courtroom and decides questions of law or discretion.

Caperton v. A.T. Massey Coal Co., Inc.

The question of when judges must recuse themselves from cases is usually resolved by a state **statute** or court rule. In most instances, the issue of judicial disqualification does not give rise to a constitutional concern. In some narrow circumstances, however, the courts have determined that due process requires recusal. In *Caperton v. A.T. Massey Coal Co., Inc.*, ___ U.S. ___, ___ S. Ct. ___, ___ L. Ed. ___, 2009 WL 1576573 (2009), the U.S. SUPREME COURT considered a case in which a judge refused to recuse himself even though one of the parties had contributed significantly to the judge's recent campaign. Based on the unique facts of that case, the Court determined that the judge's refusal to recuse himself violated the due process rights of one of the parties to the case.

The origins of the case began in 2002. In August of that year, a jury in West Virginia issued a verdict in favor of Hugh Caperton and other plaintiffs in a case brought against A.T. Massey Coal Co. The basis of liability was **fraudulent** misrepresentation, concealment, and **tortious** interference with existing contractual relations. The jury awarded the plaintiffs $50 million in compensatory and **punitive** **damages**. Massey filed post-trial motions to challenge the verdict and damages award. The trial court denied these motions, finding that Massey had "intentionally acted in utter disregard of [Caperton's] rights and ultimately destroyed [Caperton's] businesses because, after conducting cost-benefit analyses, [Massey] concluded it was in its financial interest to do so." The trial court's final action in the case occurred in March 2005, when the court denied Massey's motion for judgment.

Massey's chairman, chief executive officer, and president was Don Blankenship. He knew that the West Virginia Supreme Court of Appeals would review the trial court's judgment, and so he used the 2004 judicial elections to his advantage. One of the justices on that court, Warren McGraw, was up for reelection. Blankenship found an attorney, Brent Benjamin, to compete against McGraw in the election. Although judges are limited to receiving $1,000 in campaign contributions, Blakenship was able to contribute to Benjamin's campaign in other ways. Blankenship gave $2.5 million to a political organization, "And For The Sake Of The Kids," which supported Benjamin. Blankenship also spent more than $500,000 on advertising that supported Benjamin. The $3 million spent to support Benjamin's campaign was more than the total amount spent by all of Benjamin's other supporters combined and three times the amount spent by Benjamin's own campaign committee. Blankenship also spent $1 million more than the two candidates combined.

Benjamin won the 2004 election with 53.3 percent of the vote. Less than 50,000 votes among more than 700,000 total votes separated the two candidates.

Prior to Massey filing an appeal in the case, Caperton sought to remove Benjamin, arguing that the West Virginia CODE OF JUDICIAL CONDUCT required recusal based on the conflict of interest caused by Blankenship's campaign support for Benjamin. Benjamin, however, denied Caperton's motion. Benjamin wrote that he had found "no objective information . . . to show that this Justice has a bias for or against any litigant, that this Justice has prejudged the matters which comprise this litigation, or that this Justice will be anything but fair and partial." After Benjamin refused to recuse himself, Massey in December 2006 filed an appeal of the jury verdict.

The court in November 2007 reversed the $50 million verdict awarded to Caperton by a vote of three to two, which Benjamin voting with the majority. Although the majority agreed that Massey's conduct warranted the judgment, the court determined that a forum selection clause in the contract barred the West Virginia court from hearing the case. Moreover, the Supreme Court of Appeals determined that the doctrine of RES JUDICATA barred the suit based on a judgment rendered in an out-of-state judgment. Two justices in the case dissented, arguing that the decision was "legally and morally wrong" and that the majority misapplied the law.

Following the court's decision, Caperton asked for a rehearing and filed motions to disqualify three of the justices. One of the justices (not Benjamin) was seen vacationing with Blankenship in the French Riviera while the case was still pending. Another justice, who had filed one of the dissenting opinions, had criticized Blankenship during the 2004 elections. Both of these justices agreed to recuse themselves from the case. Benjamin, however, refused to step down.

The court rendered another decision and again ruled in Massey's favor by a vote of three to two. *Caperton v. A.T. Massey Coal Co.*, ___ S.E.2d ___, 2008 WL 918444 (W. Va. Apr. 3, 2008). One of the dissenting justices argued that Benjamin should have recused himself, noting that his participation in the case raised "genuine due process implications." Benjamin filed a concurring opinion in the case, supporting his decision not to step down by arguing that he had not "direct, personal, substantial, **pecuniary** interest" in the case. Benjamin cited articles showing that his opponent in the 2004 election, McGraw, was a controversial figure and that counsel in other cases did not request Benjamin's recusal.

The U.S. Supreme Court agreed to review the case, and in a 5-4 decision, ruled that Benjamin should have recused himself. The majority opinion, written by Justice ANTHONY KENNEDY, noted that the Constitution usually requires recusal in one of two instances. First, a judge who had a financial interest in the outcome of the case must recuse herself. And second, a judge who has been involved in a criminal contempt case (meaning that the judge has charged a party with criminal contempt) cannot later try and convict the party of the criminal contempt charge. Neither of these circumstances was present in the Caperton case, but the Court determined that the Due Process Clause of the FOURTEENTH AMENDMENT requires recusal depending on the degree in which a judge may be influenced to reach a decision.

In this case, Justice Kennedy and the majority concluded that Blakenship's role in Benjamin's election put Benjamin in a position where he was improperly influenced. The Court acknowledged that the case involved an extraordinary situation and that in most instances, state statutes or court rules will dictate whether a judge must recuse himself or herself. In this case, however, the majority concluded that due process required recusal.

Chief Justice JOHN ROBERTS, joined by three other justices, dissented. According to Roberts, the majority's decision "provides no guidance to judges and litigants about when recusal will be constitutionally required." Roberts also noted that the decision would lead to an increase in cases where parties will allege that judges are biased.

Two Pennsylvania Judges Plead Guilty to Kickback Scheme

Lawyers and judges are members of a profession that is governed by ethical rules of conduct. Judges play a central role in the U.S. justice system, ensuring that court rules are followed and that each case is treated impartially. Therefore, it was shocking news when two Pennsylvania trial judges pleaded guilty to tax evasion and wire **fraud** for a kickback scheme that resulted in 2,500 juveniles being sent to a private detention center for mostly minor offenses. The criminal enterprise also revealed a lack of oversight by the state courts and the failure of probation officers and other court employees to come forward and challenge the questionable activities they observed.

Mark Ciavarella Jr. and Michael Conahan were judges on the Pennsylvania Court of **Common Pleas** in Luzerne County. The men lived in the same neighborhood and socialized with their wives, often taking trips to Florida together. Ciavarella was the son of a brewery worker, while Conahan's father owned a funeral home and was the mayor of small town near Wilkes Barre. Ciavarella became the juvenile court judge for the county in 1996 and became known as a no-nonsense judge who meted out tough sentences. Things changed for both men when Robert Powell, a wealthy local lawyer and friend of Conahan, approached the two judges in 2000 an asked how he might secure a contract to build a private detention center. As the three men began to plot the building of a center they decided on a way for all of them to make money from it. In January 2002, Conahan became the presiding judge of the count. In this position he controlled the courthouse budget. He soon signed a secret deal with Powell in which the court would pay $1.3 million in annual rent for the facility. This was on top of the millions of dollars the county and state would pay to house juveniles adjudged delinquent. Conahan, in a final blow to competition, ended financing of the county detention center. He signed a "placement guarantee" agreement with the firm that required the courts to send the center enough juveniles to ensure that the firm was paid more than $1 million a year in public funds. In 2004 Powell's company signed a long-term deal with the county court worth $58 million. Ciavarella and Conahan demanded large kickbacks in return.

With all the elements now in place, Ciavarella in 2002 began a practice of sending most juveniles who appeared before him to the private detention center. The U.S. SUPREME COURT has mandated that juveniles are entitled to legal representation when brought before a juvenile court, but Ciavarella ignored this

requirement. From 1997 to 2003, juveniles appeared before him without a lawyer at more than five times the state average. From 2003 to 2007 the rate increased to 10 times the state average. The number of juveniles he sent to secure facilities more than doubled between 2001 and 2002. He continued this trend for the next six years, which was contrary to prevailing practice in other Pennsylvania courts. He more than doubled the state average for sending juveniles to detention centers.

There were numerous examples of juveniles being sent to the detention center for a first minor offense. A 13-year-old-boy was sent away for failing to appear as a witness at a hearing, even though his family had not been notified of the hearing. A girl who posted a humorous MySpace page about her vice-principal was adjudicated delinquent before she had a chance to present her side of the story. She was sent to the detention center for three months. Ciavarella's sentencing practices became so well known to local lawyers that they discouraged parents from retaining their services. It did not matter whether a juvenile was represented or not. Probation officers, who recommended light sanctions, were ignored by Ciavarella.

Local government officials became suspicious but Conahan saw to it that charges were either ignored or silenced. One judge who complained to county commissioners about detentions costs was transferred to another court. By 2004 the two judges accumulated so much money that it became difficult to handle. They purchased a $785,000 condominium together in Florida to conceal the payments and then disguised kickbacks as rent and other related fees. Parked in front of the condo was a $1.5 million, 56-foot yacht owned by Powell. The boat was named Reel Justice.

It is unclear how or when federal law enforcement authorities discovered the kickback scheme. However, one family challenged the decision of Ciavarella to send their daughter to the detention center, and in 2007 the Pennsylvania Juvenile Center, an organization that represents juveniles, filed a petition with the Pennsylvania Supreme Court that challenged Ciavarella's handling of 500 cases. By the summer of 2007 federal authorities had searched and seized files and records from the county courthouse. In February 2009 Ciavarella and Conahan appeared in federal **district court** and pleaded guilty to tax evasion and wire fraud. Powell was not charged, as he claimed he was forced to pay kickbacks. The two judges agreed to a plea agreement that will have them serve up to seven years in prison. They will also forfeit their judicial pensions

The Pennsylvania Supreme Court reconsidered the Juvenile Center petition and issued an order to review the adjudications of all juveniles charged with minor crimes in Luzerne County and heard by Ciavarella. The court intended to clear all of these juveniles of their charges. In addition, two **class action** civil lawsuits have been filed by juvenile victims against the former judges, their wives, Powell, and the detention center, seeking monetary damages.

JURISDICTION

The geographic area over which authority extends; legal authority; the authority to hear and determine causes of action.

Carlsbad Technology, Inc. v. HIF Bio, Inc.

Federal district courts generally have discretion to remand cases to state court. If a federal court remands a case because it lacks subject matter jurisdiction, then the decision is not reviewable on appeal. In *Carlsbad Technology, Inc. v. HIF Bio, Inc.,* ___ U.S. ___, 129 S. Ct. 1862, ___ L. Ed. 2d ___ (2009), the Supreme Court determined that a district court's decision to remand a case based on its refusal to exercise supplemental jurisdiction is not due to the district court's lack of subject-matter jurisdiction. Thus, the Supreme Court concluded that such a decision could be reviewed on appeal.

The case's origins began in 1999, when two researchers associated with a Korean university began to study the effect of a compound known as YC-1 on a protein complex that appears in human tumors. These researchers, Jong-Wan Park and Yang-Sook Chun, believed that YC-1 could be used to suppress the growth of blood vessels into animal tumors. The effect of this process would be that YC-1 would starve tumors of oxygen and nutrients. Thus, the research could lead to a treatment for cancerous tumors. Park and Chun conducted a series of experiments between 1999 and 2002, and the results confirmed their hypothesis about the effects of YC-1 on tumors. Two academic journals accepted and published papers that Park and Chen wrote about their findings.

In 2003, Park and Chen became embroiled in a dispute about who should received credit for the YC-1 discovery. Parties listed as defendants in the case filed U.S. patent applications that covered the "novel anti-angiogenic, anti-cancer properties of YC-1." These applications listed two other researchers as the inventors. Park and Chen subsequently assigned their rights to YC-1 to a party named BizBiotech, which later assigned its rights to HIF Bio, Inc.

In 2005, BizBiotech and HIF Bio filed a complaint in Los Angeles Superior Court. The plaintiffs argued that they owned the rights to the YC-1 invention and named as defendants several parties that had claimed ownership of the invention. Most of the plaintiffs' causes of action were based on state law, including: slander of title, conversion, **fraud**, intentional interference with contractual relations and prospective economic advantage, negligence interference with contractual relations; breach of contract, unfair competition, and unjust enrichment. The plaintiffs also alleged a federal **cause of action** based on violations of the Racketeer Influence and Corrupt Organizations Act (RICO), 18 U.S.C. §§ 1961-1968. The defendants removed the action to the U.S. **District Court** for the Central District of California.

Under 28 U.S.C. § 1367, when a federal district court has subject-matter jurisdiction over a claim, the court may exercise supplemental jurisdiction over state-law claims "that are so related to claims in the action within such original jurisdiction that they form part of the same case or controversy." Conversely, a federal district court may decline to exercise supplemental jurisdiction over a state law claim in one of four circumstances listed in 28 U.S.C. § 1367 (c): (1) the claim raises a novel or complex issue of state law; (2) the claim substantially predominates over the claim or claims over which the district court has original jurisdiction; (3) the district court has dismissed all claims over which it has original jurisdiction; or (4) in exceptional circumstances, there are other compelling reasons for declining jurisdiction.

The defendants filed motions to dismiss the case. The district court dismissed the RICO claims against the defendants because the plaintiffs had not proven a pattern of racketeering sufficient to prove a RICO violation.

Once the RICO claim was dismissed, the court was left only with state law claims. The court exercised its discretionary power under 28 U.S. C. § 1367(c) and remanded the case to state court. *HIF Bio, Inc. v. Yung Shin Pharmaceuticals Industrial Co.*, NO. CV-05-07976, 2006 WL 6086295 (C.D. Cal. June 9, 2006).

The issues became more complicated when the defendants appealed the case to the Federal Circuit Court of Appeals. Under 28 U.S.C. § 1447(c), a federal district court must remand a case to state court if the district court lacks subject-matter jurisdiction over the case. In an instance where a court remands based on lack of subject-matter jurisdiction, 28 U.S.C. § 1447 (c) establishes that the decision cannot be reviewed on appeal. However, the Supreme Court previously established that a decision to remand a case based on a reason other than lack of subject-matter jurisdiction can be reviewed by an appellate court. Most federal courts of appeal have relied on *Thermtron Products, Inc. v. Hermansdorfer*, 423 U.S. 336, 96 S. Ct. 584, 46 L. Ed. 2d 542 (1976) to support decisions to review a district court's remand of a case.

In *Powerex Corp. v. Reliant Energy Services, Inc.*, 551 U.S. 224, 127 S. Ct. 2411, 168 L. Ed. 2d 112 (2007), the Supreme Court ruled that appellate review was barred under 28 U.S.C. § 1447(d) if a remand decision was "colorably characterized as subject-matter jurisdiction." In the present case, the Federal Circuit believed that the Supreme Court had signaled a change in direction in *Powerex*. The appellate court concluded that every remand based on § 1367 (c) must involve a "predicate finding that the claims at issue lack an independent basis of subject matter jurisdiction ...." Thus, the Federal Circuit court concluded that a remand based on a district court's declining of supplemental jurisdiction was a remand based on lack of subject-matter jurisdiction. By applying § 1447(d), the appellate court concluded that it could not review the decision to remand the case. *HIF Bio, Inc. v. Yung Shin Pharmaceuticals Industrial Co.*, 508 F.3d 659 (Fed. Cir. 2007).

The Supreme Court agreed to review the Federal Circuit's decision. In a unanimous decision, the Supreme Court reversed the Federal Circuit. Writing for the majority, Justice Clarence Thomas reviewed the application of § 1367 and § 1447 in light of the Court's statement in *Powerex*. Thomas noted that a decision about whether to exercise supplemental jurisdiction is entirely discretionary. Even after dismissing the RICO claims, the district court could have retained jurisdiction over the remaining claims. The district court's decision to remand was not based a lack of jurisdiction over the subject matter, because § 1367 continued to establish a basis for the district court's jurisdiction.

Three different justices filed concurring opinions. Justices JOHN PAUL STEVENS and ANTONIN SCALIA suggested that the Court should have focused more heavily on its precedent in *Thermtron Products, Inc.* Justice STEPHEN BREYER in another concurrence suggested that "experts in this area of the law reexamine the matter with an eye toward determining whether **statutory** revision is appropriate."

JURY

In trials, a group of people selected and sworn to inquire into matters of fact and to reach a verdict on the basis of the evidence presented to it.

Kansas Supreme Court Rules that Juveniles Entitled to Jury Trial

The Kansas Supreme Court surprised many commentators in June 2008 when the court ruled that juveniles in the state have a constitutional right to a trial by jury. The court abrogated a 1984 decision that had rejected the argument that juveniles had a jury right. Court personnel throughout Kansas reacted immediately, noting that the decision could put a great deal of pressure on the state's justice system.

The United States Supreme Court in 1971 considered the question of whether the juveniles were entitled to a right to trial by jury. In *McKeiver v. Pennsylvania*, 403 U.S. 528, 91 S. Ct. 1976, 29 L. Ed. 2d 647 (1971), the Court reviewed the juvenile justice systems in New York and Pennsylvania, neither of which provided for a right to trial by jury for juveniles. A majority of the justices agreed that juveniles were not entitled to a jury under either the SIXTH AMENDMENT or the FOURTEENTH AMENDMENT. However, the justices could not agree on the reason for this conclusion. In a **plurality** opinion, the Court identified a number of attributes about the juvenile justice systems of the states in question. Historically, adjudications in cases involving juveniles have been more intimate and informal than criminal proceedings brought against adults. The plurality in *McKeiver* was concerned that requiring states to try juveniles before juries would destroy this system. Moreover, the plurality concluded that states needed to be able to experiment with different ways to handle juvenile problems. Recognizing a right to a jury would limit the ability of states to be able to conduct such experiments.

In 1984, the Kansas Supreme Court considered the question of whether juveniles in the State of Kansas were entitled to a jury. The court in *Findlay v. State*, 681 P.2d 20 (Kan. 1984) reviewed existing Kansas law in light of the decision in *McKeiver*. Under the version of the state's Juvenile Offenders Code that existed in 1984, a case brought against a juvenile was not considered to be a case that established a criminal act. Instead, the **statute** specifically mentioned that the state was exercising its parental power when it adjudicated a case brought against a juvenile.

In the years that followed *Findlay*, juvenile law changed significantly. The Kansas Juvenile Offenders Code (KJOC) was replaced with the Revised Kansas Juvenile Justice Code (KJJC). The KJJC specifies: "The primary goals of the juvenile justice code are to promote public safety, hold juvenile offenders accountable for their behavior and improve their ability to live more productively and responsibly in the community. Thus, the KJOC's focus on the rehabilitation of juveniles and the state's parental role were replaced in the KJJC with very different goals.

The issue of whether a juvenile has a right to a jury arose again when a juvenile was convicted of aggravated sexual **battery**. The juvenile, known by his initials L.M., had a midnight encounter with a female neighbor. After asking the neighbor for a cigarette, L.M. tried to kiss the neighbor. When she refused, L.M. kissed and licked her on the face while holding on to her. L.M. was later arrested and was taken to a hospital. He had been drinking prior to the incident. Officers questioned him at the hospital, and he was charged with aggravated sexual battery and being a minor in possession of alcohol. He was tried without a jury and convicted. Part of his sentence required L.M. to register as a sex offender.

L.M. appealed his conviction, arguing that he was entitled to a jury trial by the Due Process Clause of the U.S. Constitution as well as

provisions of the Kansas Constitution. The Court of Appeals of Kansas noted that *Findlay* had established three main points. First, whether a juvenile receives a jury trial is solely within the discretion of the trial judge. Second, the decision to grant or deny a jury trial to a juvenile does not involve the rights of the juvenile or the state. And third, the judge's decision is not subject to **appellate** review. The **appellate court** acknowledged that L.M. made "some rather good arguments" about why he was entitled to a jury trial. However, the court believed it was "duty bound to follow Kansas Supreme Court precedent, absent some indication that the court is departing from its previous position." Because the appellate court determined that the Kansas Supreme Court had not departed from *Findlay*, the court held that L.M. was not entitled to a jury trial. *In re L.M.*, 147 P.3d 1096 (Kan. Ct. App. 2006).

The Kansas Supreme Court granted L.M.'s petition for review. The sole issue before the court was whether L.M. had a right to a jury. The court reviewed both *McKeiver* and *Findlay* in light of the changes to Kansas juvenile law between 1984 and the current law. Under the KJJC, the Kansas legislature patterned many of the provisions applying to juveniles after analogous criminal provisions that apply to adults. Moreover, the legislature emulated the structure of the Kansas Sentencing Guidelines when it developed a sentencing matrix that applies to juveniles. According to the court, "These changes to the juvenile justice system have eroded the benevolent **parens patriae** [government acting on behalf of the child] character that distinguished it from the adult criminal system." Due to the "legislative overhaul" of the juvenile statutes, the court concluded that *Findlay* was no longer applicable. Therefore, the court concluded that L.M. was entitled to a jury trial. *In re L.M.*, 186 P.3d 164 (Kan. 2008).

Only a minority of states have granted juveniles the right to a jury trial. Several who commented on the decision said that the decision could tax the Kansas courts. According to Tom Stanton, the president of the state associations for local prosecutors, "It is going to be a shock to the system."

Waddington v. Sarausad

In a criminal trial conducted with a jury, jury instructions play an important role. Before the jury is sent to deliberate, the judge provides it with instructions on what law to apply to the facts that have been presented. Verdicts are sometimes overturned because the judge provided incorrect or ambiguous instructions. In addition, if jurors have questions about specific instructions the judge can only direct them to review the pertinent parts of the instructions; the judge cannot elaborate or change the instructions once given. There are also circumstances where the legal interpretation may change or be clarified, revealing the fact that the instruction given to the jury was unclear. Defendants often challenge instructions on this basis, arguing that the jury was confused as to what legal standards it was to apply. Such was the case in *Waddington v. Sarausad*, __U.S.__, 129 S.Ct. 823, __L.Ed.2d__ (2009), where a Washington state teenager was convicted for being the driver in a drive-by shooting. Confusion as to what he knew before the shooting and the jury instruction on being an accomplice led the lower **federal courts** to throw out his conviction. The U.S. SUPREME COURT disagreed, finding that any confusion was not substantial enough to void the conviction.

Cesar Sarausad was a member of the 23d Street Diablos gang in Seattle, Washington. The Diablos clashed with the Bad Side Posse, a rival gang headquartered at Ballard High School. A dispute between the gangs escalated to the point where Diablos member Brian Ronquillo retrieved a handgun and members of the gang set out for Ballard in a car driven by Sarausad. Ronquillo was in the front seat. As the car approached the high school, Ronquillo tied a bandana over the lower part of his face and readied the handgun. Just before reaching Ballard, another car of Diablos pulled next to the car and Sarausad asked them "Are you ready?" He then accelerated the car and sped toward the high school. Once he was in front of the school, Sarausad abruptly slowed down to about five miles per hour while Ronquillo fired 6 to 10 shots at a group of students standing in front of it. The gunfire killed one student and wounded another.

Sarausad, Ronquillo, and another gang member that was in the car were tried together for first-degree murder and second-degree assault. Sarausad and Reyes were tried as accomplices. They claimed that they could not have been accomplices to murder because they had no idea that Ronquillo had a gun when they returned to Ballard. They said that they expected to engage in a fistfight with the Bad Side Posse and were "totally and utterly dismayed when Ronquillo started shooting." Sarausad's lawyer told the jury that he could only be convicted of being an accomplice to murder if he had assisted Ronquillo with knowledge that their actions would promote or facilitate the commission of murder.The prosecutor argued that by slowing down the car in front of the students, Sarausad knew that a shooting was about to take place. She also made several statements that the escalation of violence was predictable between the gangs and that the key principle, "In for a dime, you're in for a dollar," applied in this instance. The judge gave the jury two instructions on accomplice liability, but the jury returned three times during deliberations to ask about the accomplice-liability standard. The jury ultimately convicted Ronquillo of first-degree murder and Sarausad of the lesser included crime of second-degree murder. The jury could not make a decision on the third defendant, so the judge declared a mistrial.

Sarausad appealed his conviction, arguing that the state had not proven that he had intent to kill. The Washington Court of Appeals affirmed his convictions and stated that the theory of accomplice liability could be reduced to the phrase "In for a dime, in for a dollar." The Washington Supreme Court denied discretionary review but soon after handed down a decision rejecting the "In for a dime, in for a dollar" theory. Instead, the court said an accomplice who knows of one crime—the dime—is not guilty of the greater crime—the dollar—if he has no knowledge of the greater crime. Sarausad sought postconviction relief because of this ruling but the state courts held that the judge had correctly told the jury that knowledge of the particular crime was required. Sarausad then filed for a **writ** of **habeas corpus** in federal court. The district granted his writ, concluding that the jury was confused about what elements were needed to establish guilt for second-degree murder. The Ninth **Circuit Court** of Appeals upheld this decision, finding that the state appeals court had unreasonably applied a U.S. Supreme Court precedent.

The Supreme Court, in a 6-3 decision, reversed the Ninth Circuit ruling. Justice Clarence Thomas, writing for the majority, noted that under the Anti-Terrorism and

Effective Death Penalty Act of 1996 (AEDPA), a federal court may grant habeas relief on a state court claim only if the decision "was contrary to, or involved an unreasonable application of, clearly established Federal law, as determined by the Supreme Court of the United States." To meet this standard, Sarausad had to show that the state's application of governing federal law was "not only erroneous, but objectively unreasonable." In this case the Washington courts "reasonably concluded" that the jury instructions were not ambiguous. Moreover, even if the instructions were ambiguous, the state courts were correct when they applied Supreme Court precedent that there was no "reasonable likelihood" that the prosecutor's **closing argument** citing the "In for a dime, in for a dollar" phrase caused the jury to apply the instructions incorrectly.

Justice DAVID SOUTER, in a dissenting opinion joined by two other justices, argued that the "discordant positions" on the accomplice-liability **statute** revealed the difficulty that judges, let alone jurors, had with the issue. In the face of this ambiguity, he concluded that the conviction should have been overturned.

LABOR LAW

An area of the law that deals with the rights of employers, employees, and labor organizations.

Locke v. Karass

An individual is not required to join a labor union that is the exclusive **bargaining agent** for a group of employees, but the U.S. SUPREME COURT has ruled that these individuals must pay a service fee to the union as a condition of their employment. Since 1956 the Court has issued rulings on what service fees may be charged to nonmembers without violating the FIRST AMENDMENT rights of nonmembers. The general approach to analyzing the components of a service fee has been to exempt from the fee political or ideological activities with which the nonmembers might disagree. The Court determined that the payment of the service fee furthered the government's interest in preventing free-riding by nonmembers who benefit from the union's collective bargaining actions and in preserving peaceful labor relations. Another component of the service was reviewed by the Court in *Locke v. Karass*, __U.S.__, 129 S.Ct. 798, __L.Ed.2d__ (2009). It ruled that a union could charge nonmembers for national litigation expenses as long as the litigation was of the type that would be chargeable if the litigation were local and the charge was reciprocal in nature.

The state of Maine required government employees to pay a service fee to the local union that acts as their exclusive bargaining agent, even if the employees disagree with the union and do not want to belong. The Maine State Employees Association was the local union for certain executive branch employees. In 2005 the full service fee the local charged nonmembers was about 49% of a member's union dues. Nonmembers paid about $9.70 a month. The service fee paid for ordinary representational activities (collective bargaining or contract administrative activities) , but did not pay for political, public relations, or lobbying activities. It did include an affiliation fee that the local paid its national union as well as a litigation fee that helped pay the national union's legal work.

A group of state employees challenged the legality of certain part of the service fee, including the litigation fee. They brought an action in federal **district court** and alleged that the First Amendment prohibited charging them for any part of the service fee that represented what the Supreme Court has called "national litigation." This term means any litigation that does not directly benefit the local union. The district court upheld the legality of the national litigation fee and the First **Circuit Court** of Appeals agreed with the court's decision. The Supreme Court agreed to hear the employees' appeal because other circuit courts of appeal had ruled that the fee was banned by the First Amendment.

The Court, in a unanimous decision, found that the litigation fee was valid under certain

153

circumstances. Justice STEPHEN BREYER, writing for the Court, noted that the Court had ruled on a number of the components of a labor union's service fee. Starting in 1956, the Court upheld the service fee arrangement as constitutional if the union did not charge for political or ideological activities. In 1961 and again in 1976 the Court reiterated that the First Amendment permits the payment of a service fee by nonmembers. In 1984 it ruled that the local union could charge nonmembers for the costs of a national convention, for the costs of social activities, and for the costs of those parts of publications that were not devoted to political causes. In that same decision the Court held that the local union could charge nonmembers for litigation expenses incidental to the local union's negotiation or administration of a **collective bargaining agreement**. In 1991 the Court decided that the local union could charge nonmembers for its payment of national union affiliation fees. It also examined payments for national litigation but a majority of the Court could not come to decision on this issue.

Justice Breyer concluded from this line of cases that an expense is chargeable when it bears an appropriate relation to collective-bargaining activity. Under the standards announced in the 1991 case the Court concluded that a local union may charge a nonmember an appropriate share of national litigation expenses if the subject-matter of the litigation is related to collective bargaining and the arrangement is reciprocal. In this context reciprocal would mean that the local's payment to the national organization was for services "that may ultimately **inure** to the benefit of the members of the local union." Breyer stated that there was no significant differences between litigation activities and other national activities that the Court had previously found chargeable.

Justice Samuel Alito, in a concurring opinion joined by Chief Justice JOHN ROBERTS, believed that the Court had not reached the question of what "reciprocity" means. The plaintiffs in the case had claimed that national litigation fees could never be assessed. Alito suggested that the Court will have to address in a future case what showing is required to establish that services benefited the members of the local union.

LIBEL

Libel is any defamation that can be seen, such as a writing, printing, effigy, movie, or statue.

Libel Suit Against Author John Grisham Dismissed

In September 2008, A federal judge in Oklahoma dismissed a libel case brought against author John Grisham. Two public officials who had been involved in a murder investigation during the 1980s claimed that Grisham's book, *The Innocent Man*, had made false statements and painted the officials in a false light.

On December 8, 1982, a 21-year-old waitress named Debra Sue Carter was found raped and murdered in her apartment in Ada, Oklahoma. The murder was especially gruesome, as the murderer and rapist strangled Carter and then wrote on her with ketchup. At the time of Carter's murder, Dennis Fritz was working as a high school teacher and raising a eight-year-old daughter. The mother of Fritz's daughter had been murdered several years earlier by a demented neighbor.

Fritz had befriended a man named Ron Williamson, who suffered from mental disorders. Fritz and Williamson played guitar together and would hang out at local bars. The two often visited the Coachlight Club, which is where Carter worked. Shortly after Carter's murder, a witness named Glen Core told authorities that Williamson was at the Coachlight Club on the night of the murder and had been bothering Carter. Authorities also suspected Fritz, and the police questioned both Williamson and Fritz. Williamson took a polygraph test, but the results did not produce any evidence. The police soon released both men.

Five years after Carter's murder, nobody had been charged with the crime. In 1987, a jailhouse snitch claimed that while Williamson was in jail on unrelated charges, Williamson had confessed to murdering Carter. Based on this information, police arrested both Williamson and Fritz. The police analyzed hair found at the crime scene and claimed that the hair matched both men. Other jailhouse snitches later claimed that Fritz had confessed to the crime. Prosecutors brought murder charges against Williamson and Fritz based principally on the hair evidence and snitches' testimony. Williamson and Fritz said they had little memory of where they were on the night of the murder.

The prosecutors' evidence was enough to convict both men of first degree murder in 1988.

Williamson's psychological health deteriorated in prison. He was first scheduled to be executed on September 22, 1994, but a public defender who represented Williamson filed a petition for a **writ** of **habeas corpus** in federal court in Oklahoma. The basis of Williamson's habeas corpus claim was that he received ineffective assistance **of counsel** at the time of his murder trial. Williamson received a stay of execution pending review of his petition. Fritz later sought assistance from The Innocence Project, a program that focuses on testing DNA evidence from old crimes. In 1999, DNA evidence revealed that neither Williamson nor Fritz had raped Carter, and the hairs did not belong to either man. Based on this evidence, both men were exonerated. Both men filed a civil suit against several parties, and the men settled their claims out of court.

Fritz later wrote a book entitled *Journey Toward Justice*, which detailed his ordeal. Two other authors also wrote books about the case as well as another murder in Ada during the 1980s. These authors include Robert Mayer, who wrote *The Dreams of Ada* in 1987, and Grisham, who wrote *The Innocent Man* in 2006. Each of these books criticized public officials involved in the investigation and prosecution. These officials included William Peterson, the Pontotoc County District Attorney; Gary Rogers, an agent with the Oklahoma Bureau of Investigation; and Melvin Hett, a criminalist with the Oklahoma Bureau of Investigation.

After the books were published, Peterson and Rogers filed a lawsuit in 2007 against the authors of the three books, along with Barry Scheck, who is co-director of the Innocence Project and who represented Fritz. The lawsuit asserted that the authors had conspired to commit libel against the officials and that the publications had placed the officials in a false light. Moreover, the suit alleged that the defendants had intentionally inflicted emotional distress on the officials. According to the complaint, "The defendants launched this attack through the use of speeches, interviews and simultaneously publishing three books that were all three strategically released in October of 2006."

The defendants filed a motion to dismiss the suit, which was filed in the U.S. **District Court** for the Eastern District of Oklahoma. Judge

A 2009 photo of author John Grisham.
AP IMAGES

Ronald White reviewed the case in light of the U.S. Supreme Court's decision in *New York Times Co. v. Sullivan* 376 U.S. 254, 84 S. Ct. 710, 11 L. Ed. 2d 686 (1964). *New York Times* established requirements that a public official must establish to bring a **defamation** action. White also analyzed the claims under the Oklahoma Constitution, which contains a free-speech-and-press clause that is worded more broadly than the analogous clause of the U.S. Constitution.

On September 17, 2008, White dismissed all claims against the defendants. According to White's opinion: "[T]he court is faced with this basic question: What two words best describe a claim for money damages by government officials against authors and publishers of books describing purported prosecutorial misconduct? Answer: Not plausible." White also wrote, "Where the justice system so manifestly failed and innocent people were imprisoned for 11 years (one almost put to death), it is necessary to analyze and criticize our judicial system (and the actors involved) so that past mistakes do not become future ones. The wrongful convictions of Ron Williamson and Dennis Fritz must be discussed openly and with great vigor." *Peterson v. Grisham*, No. CIV-07-317-RAW, 2008 WL 4363653 (E.D. Okla. Sept. 17, 2008).

Hatfill v. The New York Times

In *Hatfill v. The New York Times*, 532 F.3d 312, review denied without comment by the U.S. SUPREME COURT, 129 S.Ct. 756 (2008), scientist Steven J. Hatfill charged **defamation** and intentional infliction of emotional distress against *The New York Times* (*The Times*) and various media entities for linking him to the 2001 deadly anthrax mailings that killed five people. In July 2008, a three-member panel of the U.S. **Circuit Court** of Appeals for the Fourth Circuit unanimously found no liability for the defendants and confirmed **summary judgment** in the consolidated cases. The U.S. Supreme Court's denial of **certiorari** (review) let stand the Fourth Circuit decision and finally put an end to the protracted and costly litigation.

Essentially, the **appellate court** deemed Hatfill a "limited-purpose public figure" and "public official" who had "voluntarily thrust himself into the controversy." Therefore, said the court, the defamation standard articulated in the landmark case of *The New York Times v. Sullivan*, 376 U.S. 254 (1964) would apply. This meant that as a public official or figure, Hatfill needed to show "actual malice" to prove libel.

At issue was a series of editorial columns authored by Nicholas Kristof and appearing in *The Times* during the spring and summer of 2002. This followed the underlying anthrax attacks that triggered his remarks.

Just one week after the September 11, 2001 terrorist attacks on the World Trade Center and the Pentagon, and again a few weeks later, someone sent letters laced with deadly anthrax toxin to members of Congress and several news organizations. Five persons who touched the pieces of mail died, and seventeen more were injured. As the nation was made aware of the circumstances, media reporters and news organizations began to focus on the FBI's investigation.

One such journalist and columnist, Kristof, was a regular contributor to the editorial section of the *The Times*. In his columns, he was critical of what he saw as "lethargic" and "lackadaisical" investigations by the FBI in finding the perpetrator of the anthrax attacks. He intimated that the FBI's handling of information to either clear or conclusively identify the culprit was threatening national security and exposing everyone to future harm. Then, using information he had gleaned from experts and expert sources, Kristof began to focus (in his columns) on one person, whom Kristof referred to as "Mr. Z." Said Kristof in one of his editorials:

> Some in the biodefense community think they know a likely culprit, whom I'll call

Mr. Z. Although the bureau has polygraphed Mr. Z, searched his home twice and interviewed him four times, it has not placed him under surveillance or asked its outside handwriting expert to compare his writing to that on the anthrax letters.

Kristof also stated that certain scientific experts suspected "one middle-aged American who has worked for the United States military biodefense program and had access to the labs at Fort Detrick, Md.." With each successive column, Kristof continued to suggest that Mr. Z had knowledge of how to make anthrax toxin, was current with his vaccinations, and had a motive.

By August 2002, Kristof identified Mr. Z by name, saying the scientist, Steve Hatfill, had come forward and identified himself as the person of interest in the investigation, and telling his readers "there is reason to hope that the bureau may soon be able to end this unseemly limbo by either exculpating Dr. Hatfill or arresting him."

Hatfill was neither charged nor arrested. He sued *The Times* in federal **district court**, relying on Virginia defamation law and arguing that he was neither a public official nor a **public figure**. The district court granted summary judgment to *The Times* but was reversed on appeal in 2005. At that time, the Fourth Circuit held that Kristof's columns were capable of defamatory meaning under Virginia law. However, on remand, the district court again granted summary judgment to the *The Times* in January 2007. This time, the district court expressly held that (1) Hatfill was a "public official" as well as a "limited purpose public figure" and therefore needed to demonstrate *The Times* had published Kristof's columns with "actual malice." The court concluded that Hatfill had failed to prove **malice**, and for similar reasons, dismissed his claim for intentional infliction of emotional distress as well.

In the U.S. Supreme Court's landmark 1964 *Times v. Sullivan* case (also relied on by the **appellate** court in the present case), the Court held that "public officials" and "public figures" (by virtue of holding public offices or having assumed roles of special prominence) had thrust themselves to the forefront of particular public controversies and/or had voluntarily placed themselves in highly visible or "limelight" positions before the media, inviting comment and attention. Therefore, in order to prove libel (defamation in written form, as in a newspaper article), a public figure or official had to prove "actual malice." This meant either proving that the defamatory statements were published with the knowledge that they were false, or were published with reckless disregard of whether they were true or false. The Court assumed this different standard between a private citizen and a "public" figure or official "to encourage robust and uninhibited commentary on public issues."

Because the Fourth Circuit agreed that Dr. Hatfill, a research scientist at the U.S. Army's infectious disease laboratory, was both a public official and public figure, it affirmed the district's court's ruling that he had to prove "actual malice." It was uncontroverted that Hatfill, from 1997 to 1999, had voluntarily placed himself before the media, holding himself out as an expert in bioterrorism, advising the federal government, giving public speeches, participating in panels on the subject, and giving interviews to the press. Using the media, Dr. Hatfill had voluntarily thrust himself into the limelight and the debate, said the Fourth Circuit opinion. "He cannot remove himself now to assume a more favorable litigation posture," wrote Justice Paul Neimeyer. The appellate court also affirmed the district court's dismissal of the other claim for intentional infliction of emotional distress.

Notwithstanding (*The Times*) prevailing on appeal, Hatfill did receive at least $4.6 million from the U.S. Department of Justice to settle a separate lawsuit in which Hatfill claimed that JUSTICE DEPARTMENT officials had violated his privacy by speaking about him to the media.

Former Baseball Star Roger Clemens Sues Trainer for Libel

Former Cy Young award winner Roger Clemens in 2008 filed a **defamation** suit against his former trainer, who had alleged that Clemens had used steroids in the late 1990s and early 2000s. The case was just one of many steroid-related stories related to professional sports during the 2000s, and the defamation case was just part of Clemens' story regarding alleged steroid use. The U.S. **District Court** for the Southern District of Texas in February 2009 dismissed most of the claims brought against the trainer.

Clemens played high school baseball in Houston before being drafted by the Boston Red Sox in 1983. He quickly became a star in Boston, leading the Red Sox to the World Series in 1986. He won five Cy Young Awards in Boston as the best pitcher in the American League. However, during the last three or four years of his career in Boston, Clemens appeared to be slowing down as he barely won more games than he lost. In 1997, he signed with the Toronto Blue Jays, which whom he spent two seasons. His career had a resurgence in Toronto as he won two more Cy Young Awards.

While Clemens played in Toronto, he met a trainer named Brian McNamee. McNamee was a former police officer in New York City who later became a personal trainer. Following the 1998 season, Clemens joined the New York Yankees, and McNamee joined the Yankees one season later. At one point in 2001, McNamee faced rape charges in Florida, leading Clemens to sever ties with the trainer. However, Clemens rehired McNamee at some point after the 2001 season. McNamee followed Clemens to Houston when Clemens joined the Astros in 2004. Throughout his career, Clemens' principal residence has been in Texas.

Clemens retired after playing a final season with the Yankees. He was a productive player for a remarkably long time, especially considering that many baseball commentators thought that his career had started to decline in the mid-1990s. During the 2000s, the public became aware of the rampant use of steroids in baseball. Stars such as Gary Sheffield, Jason Giambi, and Barry Bonds were identified as possible steroid users (Sheffield and Giambi admitted to using steroids, while Bonds has denied it).

At some point in 1999 or 2000, McNamee spoke with Andy Pettitte, a pitcher with the Yankees and a friend of Clemens. During this conversation, McNamee told Pettitte that Clemens has used human growth hormone (HGH). In either 2003 or 2004, McNamee had another conversation with Pettitte during which McNamee said that Clemens used steroids. Both conversations took place in Texas. In 2006, the *Los Angeles Times* reported on a raid by FBI agents of former relief pitcher Jason Grimsley. According to the newspaper account, Grimsely named both Pettitte and Clemens as steroid users. However, a U.S. attorney later said the newspaper account contained inaccuracies.

Federal authorities contacted McNamee in 2007. When he met with these agents, the agents told him they had significant evidence that he was delivering packages of controlled substances, which could lead to a prison term. Although McNamee first denied that Clemens used HGH or steroids, he later told the agents that he had injected Clemens with steroids in 1998, 2000, and 2001 and with HGH in 2000. According to McNamee, these injections took place in New York. At some point after the agents interviewed McNamee, federal agents asked McNamee to repeat his story to Senator George Mitchell, who was conducting an investigation into steroid use in professional baseball. McNamee agreed and later told Mitchell about how he injected Clemens with steroids and HGH about 16 to 21 times overall. The Mitchell inquiry was not part of a government investigation.

On December 13, 2007, Mitchell released the report entitled *Report to the Commissioner of Baseball of an Independent Investigation Into the Illegal Use of Steroids and Other Performance Enhancing Substances by Players in Major League Baseball*. The contents of the so-called Mitchell Report were covered extensively by national media and by the local media in Texas. After the Mitchell Report was released, McNamee conducted an interview with a reporter with *Sports Illustrated*. In the interview, conducted in New York, McNamee repeated the same accusations.

Clemens fiercely denied the accusations and filed suit against McNamee for defamation in state court in Texas. McNamee later removed the case to federal court and filed a motion to dismiss. About a month after Clemens filed suit, both men appeared before the House Committee on Oversight and Government Reform, which was meeting about the steroid problem in baseball and elsewhere. Members of the committee said that Clemens did not sound believable, but the committee members also said that McNamee sounded like a drug dealer. Clemens never admitted to taking steroids, but in his first public statements about the controversy, made at a press conference in May 2008, Clemens apologized for his "mistakes." However, he refused to drop the case against McNamee.

In February 2009, U.S. District Judge Keith P. Ellison granted McNamee's motion to dismiss on several of Clemens' theories for recovery. According to Ellison, the district court in Texas did not have jurisdiction over statements that were made to investigators in New York. Therefore, Clemens would have to file the case again in a New York court. Ellison allowed the case to proceed with respect to the statements that McNamee made to Pettitte. *Clemens v. McNamee*, No. 4:08-cv-00471, 2009 WL 365740 (S.D. Tex. Feb. 12, 2009).

Clemens still denies the steroid allegations, which may very well ruin his chances to enter the Baseball Hall of Fame. In April 2008, four statistics professors issued a report questioning how Clemens could have improved late in his career when all of Clemens' contemporaries were slowing down. The report said that there must have been some "unusual factors" that helped Clemens to improve.

MANSLAUGHTER

The unjustifiable, inexcusable, and intentional killing of a human being without deliberation, premeditation, and malice. The unlawful killing of a human being without any deliberation, which may be involuntary, in the commission of a lawful act without due caution and circumspection.

Blackwater Security Indicted for Killing Iraqi Civilians

In December 2008, officials from the U.S. Department of Justice announced a 35-count criminal indictment against five Blackwater Security guards for their alleged roles in killing 14 unarmed Iraqi citizens and attempting to kill 20 more (who ultimately survived their injuries) on a crowded street in Baghdad. A sixth Blackwater operative had already entered a guilty plea to two charges as part of an agreement that required him to testify against his fellow guards. Blackwater Worldwide (which changed its name in early 2009 to, simply, "Xe") had been under contract with the U.S. government to provide personal security services in support of the U.S. mission in Iraq. Significantly, the company itself as well as its owner, Erik Prince, faced no charges.

The indictment represented the first time in more than five years of U.S. Iraqi occupation that the JUSTICE DEPARTMENT had brought charges against armed private contractors working to protect U.S. diplomats and personnel. It also represented the first prosecution under the Military Extraterritorial Jurisdiction Act (MEJA) against non-Defense Department private contractors. Blackwater was under contract with the DEPARTMENT OF STATE, formerly beyond the reach of MEJA prior to its 2004 amendments. All events/incidents alleged in the indictment occurred outside of the jurisdiction of any particular state or district but within the **venue** of the U.S. **District Court** of Columbia under 18 USC 3238.

The killings placed the company at the forefront of international infamy following the single incident that occurred on September 16, 2007 at Nisur Square in Baghdad. A formal investigation was conducted by the Federal Bureau of Investigations (FBI), assisted by the Iraqi Ministry of the Interior and the Iraqi National Police. According to them, events that day unfurled shortly after noon, when Blackwater forces fired upon a civilian vehicle in a crowded intersection. Inside the vehicle were a young Iraqi medical student and his mother; both were killed. This set off approximately fifteen minutes of sustained gunfire and chaos as civilians tried to flee the area.

Witnesses said the shooting was unprovoked, but Erik Prince testified before Congress in October 2007 that his guards were the victims of an armed ambush. He testified that Blackwater forces faced men with AK-47s firing on the convoy as well as other approaching vehicles that appeared to be suicide bombers. Based on everything known by Blackwater, Prince

Former Blackwater guard Donald Ball, January 6, 2009.

AP IMAGES

claimed, the guards had responded in an appropriate manner while operating in a very complex war zone.

But the FBI and military investigations, finding no evidence to support a claim that enemy activity was involved, determined that all the killings were unjustified, and termed the shootings "criminal." The investigation also found that many of the civilians were shot while attempting to flee the area.

Further, Jeremy Ridgeway, the sixth defendant who pleaded guilty, acknowledged in documents filed in support of the plea agreement that government evidence would prove he and the others "opened fire with automatic weapons and grenade launchers on unarmed civilians." Ridgeway also admitted that one man was shot in the chest while standing in the street with his hands up. Women and children were also shot and killed. Ridgeway admitted in his plea statement that there was no attempt to provide a "reasonable warning to the driver of the vehicle first targeted."

Counts 1-14 of the indictment charged the remaining five defendants with voluntary **manslaughter** for each of the 14 deceased Iraqi citizens; Counts 15-34 charged "attempt to commit manslaughter" for the 20 individuals who were shot but survived. Count 35 charged all defendants with knowingly using and discharging firearms, to wit, an SR-25 sniper rifle, M-4 assault rifles, M-240 machine guns, and M-203 grenades and grenade launchers,

during and in relation to a crime of violence. If convicted, each defendant faced a maximum sentence of ten years imprisonment for each count of manslaughter, seven years of imprisonment for each count of attempt to commit manslaughter, and a mandatory 30 year imprisonment for the firearms count.

The Iraqi Interior Ministry, from which private security companies working for the U.S. government were required to obtain a license, revoked Blackwater's license in September 2007 following the Nisur shootings. Notwithstanding, U.S. officials renewed the company's contract in April 2008. The Iraqi government could do little under the existing U.N. Security Council resolution, which granted immunity to private security contractors under Iraqi law. The resolution expired on December 31, 2008. The U.S. government was unable to persuade the Iraqi government to extend immunity under the new security agreement, effective January 1, 2009, which sharply curtailed American power in Iraq.

On January 28, 2009, the Iraqi government informed the U.S. Embassy in Baghdad that it would not issue a new license to Blackwater, and that the company and its personnel must leave the country as soon as a joint U.S.-Iraqi committee finalized new guidelines for private contractors under the new security agreement. Iraqi officials cited the Nisur shootings as a major factor. However, Blackwater employees not accused of improper conduct would be allowed to continue working as private security contractors if they switched employers. Two other security companies were operating in the area to protect American diplomats: DynaCorp International and Triple Canopy, both based in Northern Virginia. Blackwater's non-bid contract had provided that its security personnel would live inside a compound in the Green Zone and report to the embassy's security officer. An October 2007 congressional report indicated that Blackwater guards were paid more than $1,200 per day.

MILITARY LAW

The body of laws, rules, and regulations developed to meet the needs of the military. It encompasses service in the military, the constitutional rights of service members, the military criminal justice system, and the international law of armed conflict.

United States v. Denedo

In certain circumstances, a federal court may issue a **writ** of *coram nobis*, which is designed to allow a court to correct certain errors. In 2009, the U.S. SUPREME COURT ruled that military courts have authority to issue such a writ. The Court's decision in *United States v. Denedo*, ___ U.S. ___, ___ S. Ct. ___, ___ L. Ed. 2d ___, 2009 WL 1576568 (2009) allowed a former member of the Navy to seek to withdraw a guilty plea in a case that became final in 1998.

The case focused on Jacob Denedo, who immigrated from Nigeria to the United States in 1984. He enlisted in the U.S. Navy in 1989 and became a legal resident in 1990. Military authorities in 1998 charged him with crimes of **larceny**, forgery, and conspiracy, all in violation of the Uniform Code of Criminal Justice. The charges were based on a scheme to defraud a community college. Denedo received assistance from both military and civilian counsel. With counsel's assistance, he reached a plea bargain under which he pleaded guilty in exchange for military authorities referring his case to a special court martial. The special court martial at that time could not impose a sentence of longer than six months.

At the time he agreed to the plea bargain, Denedo was concerned with being deported back to Nigeria. When he informed his civilian counsel of his concern, the lawyer told him that he is pleaded guilty, he would avoid any risk of deportation. Denedo later alleged that his civilian counsel was an alcoholic who was drunk during the time of the representation. The case proceeded, and the military judge conducted an inquiry into whether Denedo's plea as provident. After concluding that Denedo had given the plea knowingly and voluntarily, the judge accepted the guilty plea. The judge sentenced Denedo to three months' confinement, a discharged based on bad conduct, and a reduction in pay. Denedo appealed the sentencing, arguing that it was severe. The Navy-Marine Corps Court of Criminal Appeals (NMCCA) affirmed the sentence in 1998. Denedo was discharged from the Navy on May 30, 2000.

Six years after his discharge, the HOMELAND SECURITY DEPARTMENT decided to commence deportation proceedings based on Denedo's conviction. Although the conviction had been final for eight years, Denedo challenged his conviction once again. He filed a petition for a writ of *coram nobis* ("the error before us"), which is a remedy designed to correct errors of fact. In his petition, Denedo argued that his guilty plea should be considered void because he entered a guilty plea based on ineffective assistance **of counsel**.

The government filed a motion to dismiss Denedo's case for want of jurisdiction. According to the government, the NMCCA lacked authority to conduct postconviction proceedings. The NMCCA denied the government's motion but also denied Denedo's petition. According to the NMCCA, the military could review its earlier decision under the All Writs Act, 28 U.S.C. § 1651(a). Denedo then appealed the decision to the United States Court of Appeals for the Armed Forces (CAAF). The CAAF agreed with the NMCCA that the All Writs Act allowed the military court to issue the writ. The All Writs Act provides that a court "established by Act of Congress" may issue "all writs necessary or appropriate in aid of their respective jurisdictions."

A writ of *coram nobis* developed under English **common law** as a means to allow a court to correct a factual error. For instance, the writ could be used to correct a technical error by the trial court. Later Supreme Court cases established that the writ could be used to correct other errors, including deprivation of constitutional rights. In *United States v. Morgan*, 346 U.S. 502, 74 S. Ct. 247, 98 L. Ed. 248 (1954), the Supreme Court held that the writ could be used in a case involving ineffective assistance of counsel. Under the Federal Rules of **Civil Procedure**, the writ is unavailable in civil cases, but it may still be used in criminal cases.

Use of the writ of *coram nobis* has particular application in a case such as Denedo's. Since Denedo was not in custody, he could not seek a writ of **habeas corpus**. The CAAF determined that Denedo had no other **adequate remedy at law**. Even though he faced a deportation hearing, the court concluded that the proper proceeding for post-conviction review was a **collateral** review proceeding in an **appellate court**. If the administrative court presiding over the deportation hearing heard the case, the administrative body would be compelled to give effect to the prior conviction. The CAAF also determined that Denedo had valid reasons for not seeking a review of his case earlier. Those reasons were based on the advice he had received from the civilian counsel who had told Denedo that he would not face deportation. For these and other reasons, the CAAF ruled that it had jurisdiction to review the case.

The court then turned its attention to Denedo's claim that he had receive ineffective assistance of counsel. The court determined that the NMCCA needed to determine whether the merits of Denedo's claims required a factfinding hearing regarding the counsel he received. Two judges dissented, with one arguing that Denedo's claim lacked merit and the other claiming that the court lacked jurisdiction. *Denedo v. United States*, 66 M.J. 114 (2008).

The Supreme Court agreed to review the case. In a 5-4 decision, the Court affirmed the CAAF's decision. Justice ANTHONY KENNEDY wrote the majority opinion, which focused heavily on whether the military courts had jurisdiction to consider and review Denedo's *coram nobis* request. The majority opinion reviewed both the All Writs Act and the UNIFORM CODE OF MILITARY JUSTICE (UCMJ). The government argued that one section of the UCMJ prohibits military courts from reviewing cases such as Denedo's because the section provides that **appellate** reviews of sentences by courts-martial are final and conclusive. However, Kennedy rejected this argument, finding that this section does not prohibit military courts from issuing *coram nobis* writs in extraordinary cases. The Court remanded the case for further proceedings to focus on Denedo's ineffective assistance claim.

Chief Justice JOHN ROBERTS, joined by three other conservative justices, concurred in part and dissented in part. Roberts disagreed that the military courts have authority to issue a writ of *coram nobis*, noting that neither the All Writs Act or the UCMJ specifically allow these courts to issue such writs.

MILITARY TRIBUNAL

Military Tribunal Convicts Bin Laden's Driver

On August 6 2008, a U.S. military jury, in the first military **tribunal** to be held since WORLD WAR II, convicted Guantanamo Bay (Cuba) detainee Salid Ahmed Hamdan of "providing material support" to terrorism. He was acquitted of the more serious charge of conspiracy to kill and/or maim U.S. citizens. Hamdan had served as chauffeur and sometimes bodyguard to Osama bin Laden, the alleged leader of the terrorist group known as "al-Qaeda."

In the larger scheme of things, Hamdan was considered a small player. But his protracted detention as an "enemy combatant" (see below) and his subsequent conviction on related charges were caught between two more significant legal events. First, against a backdrop of a U.S. SUPREME COURT case challenging presidential power to detain enemy combatants indefinitely, Hamdan's trial was the first to be conducted under a newly-enacted law (see below) creating such tribunals. Then, within months of his trial and conviction, a newly elected U.S. President Barack Obama announced his plans to close Guantanamo Bay and drop the term "enemy combatant" as a means to justify such detentions.

Still, Hamdan's relatively light sentence for his conviction (5.5 years, with credit for time served in detention), coupled with an acquittal on related conspiracy charges, helped to assuage human rights critics still skeptical of a process they believed was rigged to convict. "The decision showed what the jury thought Hamdan was worth," said the former chief prosecutor for the Guantanamo trials, U.S. Air Force Col. Morris Davis, in an August 2008 Associated Press telephone interview reported by MSNBC. com. "There is a perception that trying people in front of the military was going to be a rubber stamp process. This shows they [the military jurors] are conscientious, following instructions and are making rational decisions."

Hamdan, a 38-year-old Yemeni with only a few years' formal education, was captured in November 2001 by U.S. troops at a road block in Afghanistan (just two months after the September 11, 2001 terrorist attacks upon the United States). In his Toyota hatchback vehicle, U.S. soldiers found two SA-7 surface-to-air missiles. Such missiles were the only known air power involved in attacks against U.S. warplanes in the ongoing Afghan conflict. Hamdan told the officers he borrowed the car to take his family from the al-Qaeda stronghold in Kandahar to safety in Pakistan. The soldiers placed him in captivity in Afghanistan and interrogated him. Two defense witnesses would later testify in secret before the tribunal (because of protective orders issued by the court) that Hamdan tried to cooperate with his captors and offered U.S. Special Services an "opportunity" that was (according to the witnesses) "squandered" by the United States. Although that testimony is/was not available to the public, speculation has focused on possible information related to bin Laden's whereabouts at the time.

In prior years, alleged non-U.S. citizen terrorists such as Hamdan (to whom basic constitutional rights do not apply) could be tried only in courts under the laws of the United States civilian or military systems, or the Geneva Conventions. But after September 11, 2001, then-President GEORGE W. BUSH, by his own executive order, sought swift response and retribution through specially-empowered military tribunals.

From the outset, the new tribunals were besieged with legal and procedural challenges. Starting in 2004 (following Hamdan's original indictment under the old, challenged law, and while he was being held in confinement at Guantanamo), lawyers acting on his behalf held up the case against him with a series of court battles. It finally reached the U.S. Supreme Court in a much-watched showdown about **presidential powers**.

In *Hamdan v. Rumsfeld*, 126 S.Ct. 2749 (2005), the U.S. Supreme Court held that neither the U.S. Constitution (including the inherent powers of the Executive) nor any act of Congress expressly authorized the type of "military commissions" created by the Bush Administration to try detained enemy combatants for war crimes.

In response to the Court's ruling, Congress enacted the U.S. Military Commissions Act, Pub. L. 109-366, 120 Stat. 2600, on September 29, 2006. Its stated purpose was to "facilitate bringing to justice terrorists and other unlawful enemy combatants through full and fair trials by military commissions, and for other purposes." The Act specifically defined an "unlawful enemy combatant" as a person who engaged in hostilities or purposefully and materially supported such acts against the United States or our allies, who was not an enemy combatant (including a member of the Taliban, al-Qaeda, or associated groups); or someone who, after the date of enactment of the Act, was

determined to be an unlawful enemy combatant by a Combatant Status Review Tribunal or another competent tribunal established pursuant to the authority of the President or of the Secretary of Defense.

The following year (2007), Hamdan was subsequently re-charged and finally prosecuted under the new authority. Specifically, he was charged with violation of 10 USC 950v(b)(28) conspiracy, and violation of 10 USC 950v(b)(25) providing material support to terrorism. In support of these charges, the United States asserted (among other facts) that Hamdan had served as bodyguard and personal driver to bin Laden; that he had trained at an al-Qaeda camp and had driven bin Laden to such camps as well as press conferences and lectures; and that he had transported weapons, ammunition and other supplies to al-Qaeda members and associates with knowledge that such weapons were to be used to carry out an act of terrorism.

But Hamdan's defense team portrayed him as a ragtag orphan from the deserts of Yemen, who found his way to jihad in Afghanistan and simply needed the $200/month wages being offered for the job. Conversely, government prosecutors asserted that he had risen through the ranks of al-Qaeda to become a vital member of that terrorist group.

In the end, the jury of six senior military officers (five men and one woman) delivered the split verdict (with a required two-thirds vote) after eight hours of deliberation over a three-day period. Meanwhile, the U.S. JUSTICE

A courtroom sketch of Salim Ahmed Hamdan, July 24, 2008.

AP IMAGES

DEPARTMENT under the new Obama administration declared that it would henceforth hold (in custody) only terrorist suspects who "substantially supported" terrorist groups, and not those who only "provide unwitting or insignificant support" to al-Qaeda or the Taliban.

MORTGAGE

A legal document by which the owner (buyer) transfers to the lender an interest in real estate to secure the repayment of a debt, evidenced by a mortgage note. When the debt is repaid, the mortgage is discharged, and a satisfaction of mortgage is recorded with the register or recorder of deeds in the county where the mortgage was recorded. Because most people cannot afford to buy real estate with cash, nearly every real estate transaction involves a mortgage.

Subprime Lending Crisis Turns Into a Financial Meltdown

A crisis stemming from certain lending practices by major mortgage lenders developed into a crisis affecting the U.S. and global economy. The U.S. government in 2008 and 2009 attempted to intervene to help the situation, but the government's actions have led to further problems. The mortgage crisis contributed heavily to the recession of 2008 and 2009.

The 1990s saw a boom in the issuance of what is known as subprime lending. Lenders initially targeted those with impaired credit or no credit for the types of loans offered within the category of subprime loans. The most common of these loans has been the adjustable rate loan, under which a mortgage begins at a certain rate but which the mortgage company can change depending on the market situations. Other types of subprime loans include, for example, interest-only loans and zero-down loans involving more than one mortgage company (also known as piggy-back loans).

Although these subprime loan packages can help some homeowners to purchase houses these homeowners would not be able to purchase otherwise, many who have taken out subprime loans have run into unforeseen problems. In most instances, mortgage companies will increase the rates of adjustable rate mortgages. Thus, a borrower may be able to afford the initial rate of, for example, 7% interest, but when the lender increases the rate

to 8%, the borrower has more difficulty paying because the monthly payment increases. As the percentage continues to increase, the borrower's situation becomes progressively worse. Similar problems arise with interest-only loans and zero-down loans with piggy-backs, the terms of which favor mortgage companies and not the borrowers. Many of the subprime lenders have not require borrowers to show proof of income.

Prime loans have remained the most prevalent, representing 80% of the total mortgages in the United States. However, subprime loans became increasingly popular even for those with a sufficient credit history to qualify for a conventional loan. In many cases, the rate of a subprime loan (especially an adjustable rate mortgage) initially may have been less than a conventional loan. However, when the mortgage companies increased those rates, the rate of the subprime loan surpassed the rate of the conventional loan. Between 2001 and 2006, the percentage of new loans characterized as subprime or near-prime rose substantially.

Between 2002 and 2005, housing prices had steadily increased, which helped the subprime loan market. Companies also continued to ease their credit standards. Moreover, interest rates during this time remained low because of the recession of 2001. During this period, when many borrowers had difficulty making their mortgage payments, borrowers often had a few options. In many cases, borrowers could borrow against their homes through home equity loans to make mortgage payments. Borrowers could also sell their homes to settle their mortgage debts. Lenders took these circumstances into account when the lenders continued to market these subprime loans aggressively.

A variety of factors caused subprime lenders to begin to experience heavy losses. First, home prices in 2006 began to decline, meaning that borrowers lost equity in their homes. In many cases, subprime borrowers owed more on their mortgages than their homes were worth, meaning that the borrowers had few options when they could not make their payments. Delinquency rates of subprime loans issued in 2006 greatly exceeded the rates of 2004.

In April 2007, one of the nation's largest subprime lenders, New Century Financial, filed for bankruptcy. By the summer of 2007, Bear Sterns announced that it had experienced huge losses because of its subprime mortgage holdings. Bear Sterns had been one of the world's largest investment banks and securities and brokerage firms, but by 2008, the firm was in ruins. In March 2008, the Federal Reserve orchestrated the acquisition of Bear Sterns by JPMorgan Chase & Co. The Federal Reserve agreed to finance up to $29 billion to help JPMorgan to cover Bear Sterns' substantial losses. The government's act represented the first bailout of a broker since the Great Depression. Several firms that had loaned money to Bear Sterns experienced problems because of Bear Sterns' collapse. These firms included JPMorgan Chase, Merrill Lynch, Citigroup, and Goldman Sachs.

The crisis continued in 2008. In February, with the U.S. economy as a whole struggling, President GEORGE W. BUSH signed the Economic Stimulus Act of 2008, Pub. L. No. 110-185, 112 Stat. 613. The act injected $168 billion into the economy over the course of two years. However, the economy continued to suffer due to the mortgage crisis. By 2008, agencies that rate the value of securities reduced the ratings on $1.9 trillion in mortgage-backed securities. The rating reductions had the effect of lowering the stock value of several financial firms.

The situation hit rock bottom in September 2008. Fannie Mae and Freddie Mac, which owned or backed more than $5 trillion in mortgages, had experienced billions in losses in 2007 and 2008. On September 6, 2008, Treasury Secretary Henry Paulson announced that the government would take over those firms. The TREASURY DEPARTMENT also agreed to provide up to $200 billion in loans to provide funding for banks and other home lenders. Edward J. Pinto, a former executive with Fannie Mae, testified in December 2008 that Fannie Mae and Freddie Mac had engaged in "an orgy of junk mortgage development," which helped lead to the mortgage meltdown.

Several Wall Street firms also reached the point of collapse in September 2008. Insurance company American International Group (AIG) suffered more than $18 billion in losses during a nine-month period. The company sought and received loans from the Federal Reserve to help the company avoid bankruptcy. In return, the government received a large equity stake in the company, meaning that the government effectively took control of one of the world's biggest

insurers. One day later, the Bank of America announced that it had agreed to acquire Merrill Lynch, one of the largest brokerage firms in the world. Another major Wall Street firm, investment bank Lehman Brothers, was unable to receive a government bailout and was forced to file for bankruptcy protection. By mid-September, Lehman's stocks were virtually worthless. Another major player in the mortgage market, Washington Mutual, also collapsed. On September 15, 2008, the credit rating firm Standard and Poor's reduced Washington Mutual's rating to **junk bond** status. Several other firms suffered severe losses, but they survived. Banks such as Citigroup, Morgan Stanley, and Goldman Sachs lost billions as a result of the credit crisis. The meltdown led to record-setting decline in the stock market, as the Dow Jones average dropped precipitously throughout the final quarter of 2008.

The government under President Bush made efforts to help families who had become delinquent with their subprime loans. Under such plans as FHA Secure and Hope for Homeowners, some families have been able to refinance their subprime loans and obtain conventional fixed-rate mortgages. The government set aside up to $200 billion for these programs. However, the programs were met with criticism from those who were unable to obtain assistance through these programs. The government was also criticized for its efforts in bailing out companies such as AIG. In March 2009, critics became outraged when the company revealed it used part of its bailout money to pay bonuses to executives, several of whom were responsible for part of the company's downfall. In April 2009, the former CEO of AIG, Maurice Greenberg, testified that the bailout of AIG was a failure.

MURDER

The unlawful killing of another human being without justification or excuse.

Casey Anthony Murder Case Draws National Attention

A rather bizarre case involving a missing two-year-old child in Florida became one of the biggest murder stories of the decade in 2008 and 2009. The child, Caylee Anthony, went missing at some point in June 2008, but the child's mother, Casey Anthony, failed to report the

child's disappearance. Casey Anthony told a series of lies to investigators, but eventually authorities charged her with murdering her daughter.

Casey Anthony resided with her daughter in Orlando. On July 12, 2008, Caylee's grandparents (Casey's parents) confronted Casey about the whereabouts of Caylee, whom the grandparents had not seen in nearly a month. Casey insisted that she had been going to work every day and that she had been leaving Caylee with a babysitter. Casey claimed that she had been conducting her own investigation of the child's location. On July 15, the child's grandmother, Cindy Anthony, took Casey to an Orlando police station and claimed that Casey had stolen from her parents. Later that evening, Cindy told officers that she suspected that Caylee was missing and possibly dead, noting that she smelled what appeared to be a dead body in Casey's car.

Officers immediately began their investigation. Casey told the investigating officers that she had last seen her daughter around June 9 when she dropped the girl off at the apartment of a babysitter named Zenaida Fernandez Gonzalez. Casey provided officers with the address of the apartment. She also told officers that she was employed at Universal Studios and had been going to work every day. When the officers visited the apartment where Gonzalez allegedly lived, though, the officers discovered that nobody had lived there for months. Gonzalez told officers that she did not know Casey Anthony. Moreover, when the officers took Casey to Universal Studios so that she could show her office to the officers, she admitted that she was no longer employed at Universal Studios.

Investigators discovered even more inconsistencies in Casey Anthony's story. On June 26, her car ran out of gas, and she had to contact a friend to pick her up. At the time, Caylee was not with Casey. No family member had seen Caylee since June 15, when Caylee accompanied Cindy Anthony to a nursing home to visit Cindy Anthony's father. Casey claimed that she had spoken to her daughter by phone on July 15, but officers later discredited this claim. Officers took possession of Casey's car and found possible evidence of human decomposition. Investigators also searched Casey's home and backyard. On July 17, authorities officially charged Casey with one count of child neglect and two counts of obstruction of justice. Authorities held Casey on a $500,000 bond.

Investigators continued to try to discovery Caylee's whereabouts during the next several months. Media outlets released photographs of Casey Anthony dancing and engaged in somewhat lewd behavior with friends at Orlando nightclubs. Authorities noted that these photos were taken after Caylee had gone missing, raising suspicions that Casey had murdered her daughter so that she could be free to pursue these social activities. Documents that were released to the press in late August indicated that Cindy Anthony called Casey Anthony a sociopath and a "mooch." Other documents indicated that Casey wanted to give up Caylee for adoption but that Cindy Anthony would not allow it.

In mid-August, a bounty hunter named Leonard Padilla agreed to post the bond for Casey Anthony's release. On August 21, authorities fitted Casey with an electronic monitoring device and released her. Investigators, however, discovered evidence of crimes that were allegedly committed by Casey but that were unrelated to Caylee's disappearance. These charges included allegations of using a fraudulent instrument, petting theft, and fraudulent use of personal information. The charges stemmed in part from surveillance footage of Casey using forged checks. On August 29, Casey's original bond was revoked, and she was taken back into custody. However, an anonymous person posted a bond for Casey's release on September 4, and she was released again on September 5. On September 15, though, Casey turned herself in yet again for new economic charges related to an alleged theft. This was her third arrest, but she was released shortly after turning herself in.

On October 14, an Orlando **grand jury** indicted Casey on seven counts, including first-degree murder, aggravated child abuse, aggravated **manslaughter**, and four counts of obstruction of justice. About one week later, authorities dropped child neglect charges, noting that the authorities brought these charges under the assumption that Caylee was still alive. Evidence continued to suggest that the child was dead. For instance, an air sample from Casey Anthony's car showed evidence of human decomposition. Moreover, the report confirmed that chloroform was present in the car, suggesting that Casey may have rendered her daughter unconscious through use of the chloroform.

During October and November, searches for Caylee's body continued but revealed very little. At one point, divers at a lake near Casey Anthony's home found a plastic bag filled with bones and toys, but the bag did not contain Caylee's remains. On December 11, a meter reader named Roy Kronk found a skull with duct tape wrapped around it. Investigators found several other bones in the same area, and analysts determined that the bones were those of Caylee. Kronk said that he had originally seen the remains in August but that the deputy who visited the site did not want to investigate further because the area was under water and was infested by snakes. A private investigators named Jim Hoover later said he visited the area before Caylee's remains were found, but he was unable to find any evidence during his search.

During the investigation, authorities periodically released photos, videos, and other documents related to the case. Most of this evidence suggests that Casey Anthony is a deeply disturbed person who often acted inappropriately while she was being accused of and then charged with murder. For instance, after she had been charged with murder in October, videos showed her laughing with detectives before being taken to jail. Similarly, she did not cry when investigators found her daughter's body. Instead, she collapsed in her jail chair and appeared to hyperventilate. She later asked for a sedative but did not talk about her case. She rather talked about football until her defense attorney arrived.

Media sources, especially cable talk shows, spent many hours covering developments in the case. These programs focused much of their attention on such items as photographs of Casey Anthony dancing at a nightclub while her daughter was missing, video clips of Casey in jail while talking to her parents, and the contents of text messages exchanged between Casey and then-boyfriend Tony Rusciano.

In April 2009, the Florida State Attorney's Office announced that prosecutors would seek the death penalty in the case. According to a case filing, "sufficient aggravating circumstances exist to justify the imposition of the Death Penalty . . . ."

❖ NAPOLITANO, JANET

Janet Napolitano was nominated to become Barack Obama's Secretary of Homeland Security on December 1, 2008, leaving her position as governor of Arizona to accept the position. She had first come to national attention as a member of the legal team created to represent Anita Hill during her testimony to the Senate Judiciary Committee in October 1991, in which Hill detailed allegations of sexual harassment by then-Supreme Court nominee Clarence Thomas.

Napolitano was born in 1957, and graduated from the University of California-Santa Clara, and earning her legal degree from the University of Virginia in 1983.

As part of the Hill team, Napolitano acted as the law professor's counsel during meetings, which were arranged prior to her testimony by Judiciary Committee staff members. That this small role continued to define Napolitano caused her considerable irritation. A small scandal erupted the next year when Dennis DeConcini, Arizona's senior senator, nominated her to be U.S. Attorney for Phoenix. Napolitano responded that her representation of Hill had been "a four day representation in a ten year career."

Despite hardline Republican opposition, Napolitano's nomination was ultimately approved. However, she was once again drawn into the national spotlight by Republican ideologues looking to make headlines. In 1996, as

1957	Born, in New York
1976	Graduated University of Virginia Law School
1991	Part of Anita Hill legal team
2003	Governor of Arizona
2009	Secretary for Homeland Security

Janet Napolitano.
AP IMAGES

Republican presidential nominee Bob Dole's campaign found itself struggling in the polls, the former Kansas senator began searching through the records of Clinton appointees. He found that in January of that year, Janet Napolitano, as acting U.S. Attorney in Phoenix, had refused a request by the U.S. Postal Inspection Service (USPIS) to grant a warrant to search the home of a suspected consumer of child pornography. The warrant was later issued by a state judge, and the man was arrested and admitted to having had sex with underage boys. In May of that year, ABC news ran a story suggesting that Napolitano had refused to issue the warrant because she was sympathetic to homosexuals, an accusation she characterized as "fundamentally offensive" at a press conference the day after ABC aired the story. Napolitano's office was scandalized by the report and issued a response indicating that in ten requests for search warrants involving child pornography, Napolitano had issued nine–eight of which involved homosexual pedophilia.

In 1998, Napolitano won election as Arizona's state Attorney General. She followed that office up by running for and winning election as Arizona governor in a tight contest. Napolitano became known for issuing vetoes while serving as governor, issuing nearly 200 during her two terms. In 2008, Barack Obama selected her as his nominee for the post of Homeland Security secretary, one she accepted. She was confirmed in January 2009.

NATIONAL SECURITY

Winter v. National Resources Defense Council, Inc.

Balancing national security interests with other important societal interests can lead to litigation. Such was the case when environmental organizations raised concerns about the U.S. Navy's use of sonar in training exercises in southern California waters. These waters are the home of various mammal species, who, it is alleged, can suffer serious harm from exposure to sonar. The Navy, which has the used the waters for 40 years for training, that there had never been a documented sonar-related injury to any marine mammal. The dispute eventually moved to federal court, where the lower courts were sympathetic to the arguments from environmental groups. However, the Supreme Court in *Winter v. National Resources Defense Council, Inc.*, __U.S.__, 129 S.Ct. 365, 172 L.Ed.2d 249 (2008), ruled in favor of the Navy, concluding that national security interests were paramount.

The Navy places great emphasis on antisubmarine warfare, as modern submarines can operate almost silently, making them very difficult to detect and track. Potential adversaries of the United States have at least 300 of this type of submarine. The most effective way to identify submerged submarines within torpedo range is active sonar. Sonar technology involves emitting pulses of sound underwater and then receiving the acoustic waves that echo off the target. The Navy's use of "mid-frequency active" (MFA) sonar, which transmits sound waves at frequencies between 1 kHz and 10 kHz, led to concerns from environmental groups.

They contended that MFA sonar can cause serious injuries to marine mammals, including permanent hearing loss, decompression sickness, and and major behavioral disruptions. The groups pointed to several mass strandings outside of southern California waters of marine mammals that have been linked to the use of MFA sonar.

The federal Marine Mammal Protection Act of 1972 (MMPA) seeks to safeguard these mammals, but the Secretary of Defense has authority under the act to exempt any action or category of actions from the MMPA for national defense. In 2007 the DEFENSE DEPARTMENT granted the Navy a two-year exemption from the MMPA for the training exercises in southern California waters. The exemption was conditioned on the Navy taking steps to mitigate harm to mammals, including the reduction of sonar transmission levels if a marine mammal is detected within 1,000 yards of the bow of a vessel. The Navy also issues an environmental assessment that concluded the 14 training exercises schedule through January 2009 would not have a significant impact on the environment. The Navy's computer models predicted that only 8 dolphins would be seriously injured and 274 beaked whales would be suffer temporary injury or disruption.

Following the release of the environmental assessment, the National Resources Defense Council and several other environmental organizations sued the Navy, seeking an injunction that barred the use of MFA Sonar. They based claimed that the use of sonar violated the ENDANGERED SPECIES ACT of 1973 and the Coastal Zone Management Act of 1972. The **district court** granted the plaintiffs a **preliminary injunction** that prohibited the Navy from using MFA sonar during its remaining training exercises. The court concluded that the plaintiffs had demonstrated the probability of gaining a permanent injunction based on harm prohibited harm by the two federal statutes. The Navy appealed to the Ninth **Circuit Court** of Appeals, which ultimately upheld the district court. The Navy then appealed to the Supreme Court.

The Court, in a 7-2 decision, reversed the Ninth Circuit ruling. Chief Justice JOHN ROBERTS, writing for the majority, emphasized the importance of antisubmarine warfare training exercises for preserving national security. The Court agreed with the Navy that the the lower courts applied a lenient standard for granting the preliminary injunction. The courts had found that the plaintiffs had shown the "possibility" of irreparable harm, while the proper standard is the "likelihood" of irreparable harm. Roberts concluded that the courts had failed to show such a likelihood of harm; the plaintiffs had failed to provide sufficient evidence to counter the Navy's claim that harm to marine mammals from MFA sonar was not documented. In addition, the courts had failed to take into account the restrictions that the Navy placed on itself when marine mammals came too close.

Despite the Court's skepticism about irreparable harm, in the end the justices focused on balancing the equities between harm to marine mammals and harm to the overall public interest. The harm to an unknown number of marine mammals could not compare to "an inadequately trained antisubmarine force" that "jeopardizes the safety of the fleet." The Navy had no alternative for conducting realistic training exercises. Viewed this way, Roberts concluded that "the proper determination of where the public interest lies does not strike us as a close question." Therefore, the Court overturned the preliminary injunction and made clear to the lower courts that it would be an **abuse of discretion** to enter a permanent injunction. The analysis used by the Court in examining preliminary relief would be "applicable to any permanent injunction as well."

NATIVE AMERICAN RIGHTS

Carcieri v. Salazar

The federal government's policies concerning the treatment of Native Americans have shifted over the years. At several points the government sought to assimilate the Indian population but overall it has acted as a **trustee** for Native American tribes. The Indian Reorganization Act (IRA) authorizes the Secretary of the Interior to acquire land and hold it in trust for the purpose of providing land to Indians. Under the IRA, tribes may acquire land and then have the secretary accept it. In this way the property becomes tribal property that is exempt from state property taxes and local regulations. A dispute arose over the use of this authority when an Indian Tribe that was not recognized as a tribe at the time the IRA was enacted in

1934 sought to have the secretary take lands it had acquired. The Supreme Court, in *Carcieri v. Salazar*, __U.S.__, 129 S.Ct.1058, 172 L.Ed.2d 791 (2009), held that the **statute** clearly restricted the application of the IRA to tribes that were recognized as such at the time the IRA was passed.

The case involved the Narragansett Indian Tribe. At the time of colonial settlement the Narragansett occupied much of what is now Rhode Island. Hostilities between colonists and tribe in the 1670s led to the decimation of the tribe and in 1709 the colony of Rhode Island placed the tribe under formal guardianship. In 1880 the state of Rhode Island persuaded the Narragansett to relinquish its tribal authority as a way to assimilate tribal members into the local population. The tribe also sold all but two acres of its remaining reservation land but soon realized this had been a mistake. In the early 20th century the tribe sought economic support from the federal government and asked for a return of its tribal status. From the late 1920s to the late 1930s federal officials declined these requests, concluding that the Narragansett was, and had always been, under the jurisdiction of the New England states, not the federal government. In the 1970s the tribe sued to recover its ancestral land and in 1978 the claims were resolved in a federal law that gave the tribe 1,800 acres of land in Charlestown, Rhode Island in return for its relinquishing of all other land claims. In 1983 the federal government formally recognized the Narragansett as a tribe under federal jurisdiction. The tribe then asked the Secretary of the Interior to accept a **deed of trust** to the 1,800 acres and in 1988 the secretary agreed.

In 1991, the tribe's housing authority purchased 31 acres of land in Charlestown that was adjacent to the 1,800 acres. A dispute arose over whether the tribe needed to comply with local construction regulations for new housing. The Narragansett persuaded the secretary in 1998 to accept the 31-acre parcel into trust, thereby preventing local authorities from having jurisdiction over the land and the construction. The town and the state challenged the transfer in an administrative process but lost. They then filed a federal lawsuit but again the secretary's action was upheld. The federal **district court** concluded that the IRA defined "Indian" to include members of all tribes in existence in

1934 but did not require a tribe to have been federally recognized on that date. The First **Circuit Court** of Appeals upheld the lower court. Though it found that the language was ambiguous as it to what the word "now" meant, it deferred to the secretary's construction of the provision. The plaintiffs had failed to show that the secretary's interpretation was inconsistent with earlier practices of the DEPARTMENT OF THE INTERIOR.

The Supreme Court, in a 6-3 decision, rejected the reasoning of the court of appeals and found that the Narragansett Tribe did not qualify as a federally-recognized tribe. At the time of the enactment of the IRA the tribe was not recognized by the federal government. Justice Clarence Thomas, writing for the majority, used "settled principles of **statutory** construction" to guide the Court's decision. A provision of the IRA defined "Indian" to include "all persons of Indian descent who are members of any recognized Indian tribe now under Federal jurisdiction." The key issue was the meaning of the word "now." Using contemporary dictionaries, Justice Thomas noted that the ordinary meaning of the word as understood in 1934 was "at the present time" or "at this moment." This definition was consistent with other interpretations given to the word "now" by the Court in cases before and after the enactment of the IRA. In addition this interpretation "aligns with the natural reading of the word within the context of the IRA." Some parts of the law used the word "now" to indicate at the present time, while others used the phrase "now or hereafter." The Narragansett could only have qualified under the IRA if the definition of Indian had included the "or hereafter" language.

Justice Thomas concluded that the secretary's current interpretation was "at odds with the Executive Branch's construction of the provision at the time of enactment." The plain meaning of the provision barred the secretary from using the IRA to accept land in trust from the Narragansetts.

Justice JOHN PAUL STEVENS, in a dissenting opinion, argued that other provisions of the IRA made clear that the secretary had broad authority to carry out the purposes of the act, which were to revitalize tribal development and cultural **self-determination**. Focusing on the word "now" meant that the Narragansett were

not a tribe under the IRA despite the fact that the federal government recognized it as a tribe in 1983.

Native Americans Awarded $455 Million in Land Trust Case

In August 2008, a federal district judge in the U.S. **District Court** for the DISTRICT OF COLUMBIA ruled that the U.S. Government owed $455 million to Native American plaintiffs in a 12-year-old class-action lawsuit originally filed in 1996. The U.S. DEPARTMENT OF THE INTERIOR had been sued for mismanaging and withholding mineral royalties, grazing fees, and other revenues drawn from Indian lands over which it served as **Trustee**. The plaintiffs (nearly 500,000 certified in the class) had sought $47 billion in the case, and had rejected a $7 billion settlement offer from the government in 2007. *Cobell v. Salazar,* No. 1-96CV01285 (D. D.C. 2008). The case was originally captioned as *Cobell v. Babbitt,* and at the time of the above decision, was known as *Cobell v. Kempthorne,* these changes reflecting successive names of U.S. Secretaries of the Interior as defendants.

This did not settle the protracted matter. Both parties immediately filed appeals with the U.S. **Circuit Court** of Appeals for the D.C. Circuit. After oral arguments in May 2009, the matter was still pending in June, and the Obama administration expressed interest in settling the matter only after the **appellate** court's decision.

The case stems from an 1887 law known as the Dawes Act, under which the federal government divided millions of acres of land reserved for Native Americans into individually-parceled reservations. Since the Native Americans were not citizens of the United States, the government put the reservation lands into trusts and set itself up as trustee. According to the Act, proceeds from oil and mineral leasing rights were to be paid into the trusts.

According to the lawsuit, over the next 120+ years, the government's accounting system was faulty at best, suspect at worst. The case had been originally assigned to Judge Royce Lamberth. Lamberth's caustic treatment of government officials and JUSTICE DEPARTMENT lawyers prompted them to petition the D.C. Court of Appeals for his removal from the case. In July 2006, a three-member panel of the **appellate court** "reluctantly" agreed and reassigned the case to Judge James Robertson, who, in 2007, ordered a full trial. The June 2008 **bench trial** focused on the actual and realistic amount of royalty money that may have been mismanaged or withheld from trust accounts.

Elouise Cobell, a Blackfoot Indian and the class-representative (captioned) plaintiff in the case, became treasurer of the Blackfoot Nation at the age of 30. It was in performing her duties as treasurer that she became concerned about the government's accounting system. According to her complaint, when she sought answers from the Department of the Interior's Bureau of Indian Affairs (BIA), she allegedly was ignored and sought legal advice.

Meanwhile, prior to the eventual filing of her lawsuit but following her queries to the BIA, Congress passed the American Indian Trust Fund Management Reform Act of 1994. The Act created the Office of the Special Trustee for American Indians, tasked with overseeing the reform of Indian trust management and the implementation of new **fiduciary** and accounting systems. Its role was expanded two years later to include accounting, investment, and disbursement of beneficiary funds (funds owed to Native Americans). It also was tasked with maintaining trust records, conducting land appraisals, and providing beneficiary services including a call center.

Later, in 2001, the district court ordered historical accounting of trust funds, and pursuant to that order, the Office of Historical Trust Accounting (OHTA) was established to conduct the historical accounting of Individual Indian Money (IIM) accounts.

Attorneys for the plaintiffs alleged that the government improperly benefited from its mismanagement of trust funds. Judge Robertson agreed. But he did not accept plaintiffs' methods for calculating damages. For its part, the government, acknowledging the overwhelming task of managing the trusts, argued that the dollar amount in dispute was in the hundred-millions, not billions. Judge Robertson, in his ruling, noted that the Native American plaintiffs' calculations were prone to "numerous methodological flaws that were illuminated by the government's presentation and, in many instances, are obvious to anyone having basic familiarity with the case." His award of $455 million was more reflective of government estimates than plaintiffs'.

United States v. Navajo Nation

After years of litigation, the U.S. SUPREME COURT may have finally resolved a dispute between the Indian tribe of Navajo Nation and the federal government. The case has a long history, and the Supreme Court had already rendered a decision in the case prior to its decision on April 6, 2009. The dispute involved a claim brought against the Secretary of the Interior for damages allegedly caused by a breach of **fiduciary** duty. The Court determined that the Secretary owed no duty to the tribe and therefore concluded that the tribe's claims must fail.

The Navajo Nation covers more than 27,000 square miles of land in parts of Arizona, Utah, and New Mexico. Several statutes and regulations govern the development and sale of mineral resources on Indian reservation lands. These laws include the Indian Mineral Leasing Act of 1938, 25 U.S.C. §§ 396 *et seq.*, the Indian Mineral Development Act of 1982, 25 U.S.C. §§ 2101-2108, as well as regulations that implement these statutes. The government agencies responsible for supervising and regulating the development and sale of the mineral resources on these lands is the Secretary of the Interior and the Interior Department's Board of Indian Affairs (BIA).

The dispute between the Secretary of the Interior and the Navajo Nation began as a result of an agreement between the Navajo Nation and Sentry Royalty Company. In 1964, these two entities entered into an agreement regarding the mining of coal deposits on Navajo lands. Under the agreement, Sentry was required to pay a royalty of 37.5 cents per ton. The agreement provided that on the twentieth anniversary of the lease, the Secretary of the Interior could readjust the royalty rate to a reasonable level. Peabody Coal Company became the successor in interest to Sentry. By 1984, the rate of 37.5 cents per ton was well below the prevailing market rate. Peabody and Navajo began negotiations regarding this rate, but the two parties were unable to reach an agreement. Navajo Nation asked the Secretary of the Interior to resolve the dispute by setting the royalty at the **fair market value**.

An officer with the Bureau of Indian Affairs issued a decision to increase the royalty rate to 20% of the gross proceeds of the sale of the coal. Peabody appealed the decision, first to an official named John Fritz, who was Deputy

Assistant Secretary for Indian Affairs. Fritz affirmed the rate of 20%. However, the Secretary of the Interior, Donald Hodel, sent Fritz a memorandum instructing Fritz to withdraw the decision. In a memo to Fritz, Hodel wrote, "I suggest that you inform the involved parties that a decision on this appeal is not imminent and urge them to continue with efforts to resolve this matter in a mutually agreeable fashion." Hodel's actions thus clearly favored Peabody's interests and not Navajo Nation's interests. Navajo Nation eventually agreed to a rate of 12.5%, and the amendments to the lease were approved in 1987.

In 1993, Navajo Nation sued the United States government, arguing that the Secretary of the Interior had breached a fiduciary duty with the Indian tribe. As a general matter, the federal government cannot be sued without its consent. Under one federal **statute**, known as the Indian Tucker Act, the United States can be subject to liability to an Indian tribe if a contract or another federal statute mandates compensation by the federal government. 28 U.S.C. § 1505. Thus, for Navajo Nation to recover from the United States, the tribe had to argue successfully that a federal statute created a right or a duty that the Secretary of the Interior breached.

The Court of Federal Claims first ruled on the merits of the case in 2000. According to the court, the Navajo Nation's claims failed because the tribe could not cite to **statutory** authority that could be construed to mandate compensation by the government. *Navajo Nation v. United States*, 46 Fed. Cl. 217 (2000). The Federal **Circuit Court** of Appeals reversed, holding that the Indian Mineral Leasing Act of 1938 (IMLA), 25 U.S.C. §§ 396a *et seq.* effectively establishing that the United States owed a fiduciary duty to the Indian tribes because the statute gives the federal government such broad control over mineral leasing on

Indian lands. The Federal Circuit thus held that the government had breached its duty. *Navajo Nation v. United States*, 263 F.3d 1325 (Fed. Cir. 2001). The U.S. Supreme Court, though, disagreed, holding that the IMLA created no such duty. *United States v. Navajo Nation*, 537 U.S. 488, 123 S. Ct. 1079, 155 L. Ed. 2d 60 (2003).

On remand, the lower courts once again disagreed. In its briefs before the Court of Federal Claims, Navajo Nation cited a "network" of statutes and regulations, arguing that this network established that the federal government owed a fiduciary duty to the tribe. The Court of Federal Claims, though, could not find any support in these statutes for the assertion that statutory and regulatory network created a right which mandated that the government pay a money claim. *Navajo Nation v. United States*, 68 Fed. Cl. 805 (2005). The Federal Circuit once again disagreed with the Court of Federal Claims. According to the Federal Circuit, three statutory provisions established a duty on the part of the government. These statutes included two sections of the Navajo-Hopi Rehabilitation Act of 1950, 25 U.S.C. § 635(a), 638, as well as a section of the Surface Mining Control and Reclamation Act of 1977, 30 U.S.C. § 1300(e). *Navajo Nation v. United States*, 501 F.3d 1327 (Fed. Cir. 2007).

A unanimous Supreme Court once again reversed the Federal Circuit. Writing for the Court, Justice ANTONIN SCALIA reviewed each of the statutes relied upon by the Federal Circuit, but Scalia determined that none of these statutes provided a basis for the tribe's breach-of-trust claim. "This case is at an end," Scalia wrote. The opinion instructed the Federal Circuit to affirm the Court of Federal Claims' dismissal of the complaint. *United States v. Navajo Nation*, No. 07-1410, 2009 WL 901510 (U.S. April 6, 2009).

OBSTRUCTION OF JUSTICE

Detroit Mayor Pleads Guilty to Obstruction of Justice

Detroit Mayor Kwame Kilpatrick's personal, political, and legal travails came to a stunning conclusion when he pleaded guilty in September 2008 to two charges of obstruction of justice. As part of the plea agreement, Kilpatrick resigned from office and surrendered his law license. He served 99 days in jail and was placed on probation. Kilpatrick sought to regain his law license and he initiated a civil lawsuit against the telecommunications company that provided law enforcement with over 600 pages of text messages from Kilpatrick and others. The messages played a central role in Kilpatrick's criminal case.

The rise of Kilpatrick's political career was meteoric. The son of U.S. Congresswoman Carolyn Cheeks Kilpatrick (D.-Mich.), Kilpatrick earned a law degree from the Detroit College of Law and then entered politics in his mid-20s. Elected to his mother's former seat in the Michigan House of Representatives in 1996, Kilpatrick served five years before being elected mayor of Detroit at the age of 31 in 2001. He was dubbed the "hip hop" mayor because of his age, flashy suits, and a diamond stud in his ear, and soon was embroiled in controversy. Kilpatrick entertained strippers at the mayor's mansion,

leased an SUV for his family with city money, used city credit cards for personal expenses, and hired many of his friends. As his reelection campaign began in 2005, most observers believed that he had no chance to retain his position. However, he was reelected with 53 percent of the vote.

Political success gave way to personal and legal turmoil. Kilpatrick had conducted an extramarital affair in 2002 and 2003 with Christine Beatty, a former political advisor who served as his chief of staff. When rumors surfaced, Kilpatrick denied the affair. The affair issue reappeared when a former Kilpatrick bodyguard police officer and a deputy police chief filed a whistleblower lawsuit, alleging that they were fired because of an investigation into the mayor's **personal actions**. A jury awarded the two men $6.5 million dollars and the city quickly settled the lawsuit for $8.4 million after the police officers' attorney filed a motion containing evidence that Kilpatrick and Beatty had perjured themselves in their trial testimony; the new evidence would have led to further damages being levied against the city if another trial had taken place. Several Detroit newspapers successfully sued the city, requesting a copy of the settlement. The agreement revealed that the parties agreed to keep confidential all intimate text messages between Kilpatrick and Beatty.

The text messages served as the "smoking gun" in a criminal investigation into the testimony of Kilpatrick and Beatty. Ironically, Kilpatrick had issued a directive in his first term that that electronic communications transmitted on city-owned devices were not considered private or personal. These messages were thus stored electronically and could be retrieved. The whistleblowers' lawyer had obtained the messages through discovery from the communications provider SkyTel. In January 2008 the *Detroit Free Press* obtained 14,000 text messages exchanged between the pair, leading to calls for a criminal investigation. The messages clearly revealed that Kilpatrick and Beatty had conducted an affair and that other testimony at the whistleblowers' trial was false. The Detroit City Council voted 7-1 on a resolution asking the mayor to resign but Kilpatrick remained defiant. In March 2008 he and Beatty were charged with twelve criminal counts, including perjury, conspiracy to obstruct justice, obstruction of justice, and misconduct in office, but the mayor again refused to resign.

By September 2008, Gov. Jennifer Granholm had begun holding hearings on whether to remove Kilpatrick from office. However, on September 4 Kilpatrick agreed to resign and plead guilty to obstruction of justice charges. He also pleaded no contest to a **felony** count of

assault on a police officer who had tried to serve a subpoena on the mayor in August. Kilpatrick agreed to pay **restitution** to the city of $1 million, surrender his law license, forfeit his state **pension** to the city, and be barred from holding elective office for five years. He agreed to serve 120 days in the county jail and to be placed on probation for five years. Kilpatrick was formally sentenced in late October and began his jail sentence. Released in February 2009 after 99 days in jail, the former mayor began working for a local computer company soon after.

Kilpatrick's legal troubles did not end with his plea agreement. Accusations arose that he had used nearly $1 million in campaign funds to finance his legal defense. Michigan Secretary of State Terri Lynn was expected to issue a ruling by July 2009. If Kilpatrick violated the law he would be subject to fines and taxes. The trial judge also ordered him in March to pay the city $6 thousand a month in restitution. Though the former mayor agreed to surrender his law license, he later asked the state attorney discipline board to change the revocation to a suspension. If granted, it would have allowed him to petition for reinstatement before he had completed his five years of probation. However, in a January 2009 decision the board refused his request, stating that the criminal plea agreement set the terms of revocation. The board did not have the authority to modify the terms.

In March 2009, Kilpatrick filed a civil lawsuit against SkyTel, seeking $100 million in damages for violating his privacy by releasing the text messages to civil lawyers and prosecutors without his permission. His lawyer cited the federal Stored Communication Act that prohibits the release of any messages unless the sender and receivers are given prior notice. The **civil action** came soon after a judge approved the release of over 600 pages of text messages from Kilpatrick and others.

❖ PALIN, SARAH

Sarah Palin rose to national prominence quickly, having won election as governor of Alaska in 2006, and followed that by accepting John McCain's invitation to be his running mate in the 2008 presidential election. Palin, born in Idaho as Sarah Heath, the daughter of Chuck and Sally Heath, was raised in Skagway and Southcentral, Alaska. She graduated from Wasilla High School in 1982 and earned her undergraduate degree in journalism in 1987 from the University of Idaho. Her husband, Todd, raised in rural Alaska, is an oil field worker and commercial fisherman.

1964	Born, Idaho
1996	Mayor of Wasilla, Alaska
2006	Elected Alaskan governor
2008	Republican vice presidential nominee
2009	Resigned as governor

Sarah Palin.
AP IMAGES

Palin served two terms on the Wasilla city council, then two more as its mayor, beginning in 1996. She won the mayoral election, in part, by taking positions against abortion and gun control and receiving support from the state Republican party, an escalation of what used to be the town's friendly, low-key politics. She also criticized the incumbent mayor, John Stein, for wanting to use the growing town's tax revenues to expand services. As mayor, Palin oversaw the town's rapid development. She also took conservative social positions, such as a widely reported incident in which she questioned the procedure for banning books from the local library.

In 2002, Palin entered statewide politics, running for lieutenant governor of Alaska. She finished second in the Republican primary. Alaska's governor then appointed her as chair of the Alaska Oil and Gas Conservation Commission. However, she resigned from the post in January of 2004 after accusing a fellow commissioner, state Republican Party chairman Randy Ruedrich, of ethics violations. Eventually, Ruedrich paid a $12,000 fine, the largest civil fine in Alaska regarding an ethics matter. In 2005, Palin took on another fellow Republican over an ethics matter, filing an ethics complaint against attorney general and longtime Murkowski aide Gregg Renkes pertaining to an international coal deal he and Murkowski were drafting. Renkes resigned under pressure. Palin's actions infuriated Republican leaders, but they impressed the Alaskan public and press.

Palin then ran for governor in 2006, winning election with 49 percent of the vote. She took a more aggressive stance toward regulating two of the most powerful industries affecting Alaska, the oil industry and the cruise lines that bring many tourists there. Early in her term, Palin convinced the legislature to overwhelmingly pass a new law that created new rules for developing oil pipelines in Alaska. The law offered a half-billion dollars in incentives for developers, but spelled out strict rules for them. Palin also recalculated a tax on oil producers and turned the revenue over directly to Alaskans in 2008, sending every resident an energy refund check for $1,200.

Conservatives nationwide began paying attention to Palin's career, with many naming her as one of the Republican parties rising stars and a potential vice presidential candidate in 2008. In August 2008, McCain announced that Palin would be his vice-presidential running mate in the November 2008 elections. Controversy immediately followed, as Palin's 17-year-old-daughter was announced as expecting a child, leading to some criticism. However, Palin's initial impact on the McCain campaign was positive, with crowds caught up in her unusual personality. That swell of momentum slowed as coverage of her focused on her perceived lack of experience in foreign affairs, as well as incidents from her time as governor, including ethics charges.

In July 2009, Palin shocked many by unexpectedly resigning from her post as Alaskan governor, citing the pressures of the job and attacks on her ethics. Her failure to finish her term left many questioning her suitability for higher national offices.

PENSIONS

A benefit, usually money, paid regularly to retired employees or their survivors by private business and federal, state, and local governments. Employers are not required to establish pension benefits but do so to attract qualified employees.

Kennedy v. Plan Administrator for DuPont Savings and Investment Plan

The federal EMPLOYEE RETIREMENT INCOME SECURITY ACT of 1974 (ERISA)governs U.S. employee **pension** and benefits plans. This detailed **statute** requires employers to administer their plans very carefully, so as to avoid legal liability. A common occurrence for an employee is changing the designated beneficiary on the pension plan in the event the employee dies. This may occur when the employee divorces

and removes the former spouse as beneficiary. Failure to meet ERISA standards for doing this may result in the former spouse receiving the proceeds of the pension. Such was the case in *Kennedy v. Plan Administrator for DuPont Savings and Investment Plan*, __U.S.__, 129 S.Ct. 865, __L.Ed.2d__ (2009), where the Supreme Court ruled that language in a divorce decree was not sufficient to remove the former spouse as beneficiary.

William Kennedy worked for the E.I. DuPont de Nemours & Company and participated in the company's savings and investment plan (SIP). Under the plan Kennedy had the authority to designate a beneficiary or beneficiaries to receive all or part of his funds upon his death. The plan required Kennedy to complete an approved form for designating or changing a beneficiary. Moreover, under ERISA's anti-alienation provision the benefits cannot be assigned or alienated to a third-party. A beneficiary did have the right to submit a "qualified disclaimer" of benefits that had the effect of removing the beneficiary from any interest in the plan.

In 1971 he married Liv Kennedy and in 1974 signed a form designating her to be the beneficiary of his benefits under the SIP plan. He did not name an alternate or contingent beneficiary if Liv disclaimed her interest. The couple divorced in 1994, and in the divorce decree Liv agreed that she was divested of all claims to the SIP benefits. William, however, failed to complete the form that would have removed Liv as SIP beneficiary. He did execute a new beneficiary-designation form naming his daughter, Kari Kennedy, as the beneficiary of his DuPont Pension and Retirement Plan. When her father died in 2001, Kari was named the executrix of his estate. In this capacity she requested DuPont to give the SIP funds to William's estate. DuPont did not comply with this request and proceeded to pay $400,000 to Liv. DuPont relied on the original beneficiary-designation form that had never been rescinded by William.

The estate then sued DuPont and the SIP plan administrator, arguing that the terms of the divorce decree amounted to a waiver by Liv of the SIP benefits and that DuPont had violated ERIS by paying the benefits to Liv. The federal **district court** agreed with the estate and ordered DuPont to pay the value of the SIP benefits to it. The court relied on a precedent by the Fifth **Circuit Court** of Appeals that held a beneficiary can waive her rights to the proceeds of an ERISA plan if her waiver "is explicit, voluntary, and made in good faith." On appeal the Fifth Circuit reversed this decision and distinguished its prior decisions on **common law** waivers of ERISA benefits. The appeals court concluded that the divorce decree waiver constituted an assignment or alienation of her interest that was contrary to ERISA and therefore could not be honored. The Supreme Court agreed to hear the estate's appeal to resolved a split among **federal courts** of appeal and state supreme courts over a divorced spouse's ability to waive pension plan benefits through a divorce decree.

The Court, in a unanimous decision, upheld the Fifth Circuit's ruling but on different legal grounds. Justice D A V I D S O U T E R, writing for the Court, stated that Liv had not assigned or alienated anything to William or the estate. Instead, he looked at the law of trust that served as a backdrop for ERISA. Using this body of law, the Court concluded that Liv had not attempted to direct her interest in the SIP benefits to the estate or any other potential beneficiary.

The Court found that DuPont had met its duty under ERISA to distribute the SIP balance to Liv because it relied on the plan documents. ERISA was designed to promote uniform administrative schemes that contained a set of standard procedures to govern the processing of claims and disbursement of benefits. By requiring employees like William to complete a change of beneficiary form, ERISA foreclosed "any justification for enquiries into nice expressions of intent. " Otherwise plan administrators would be required to examine "a multitude of external documents that might purport to affect the dispensation of benefits." The present case indicated what would happen, as litigants fought over the meaning and enforceability of "purported waivers." Plan administrators would be forced to go into court to ensure they were making the proper distribution.

Justice Souter acknowledged that this "guaranty of simplicity" was not absolute. However, ERISA provided that administrators with objective criteria for determining whether a domestic relations order qualified as a valid waiver. This "relatively discrete" inquiry was a "far cry from asking a plan administrator to figure out whether a claimed federal common law waiver was knowing and voluntary." It made no sense for the administrator to venture into "factually complex and subjective determinations." The plan had provided William with an easy way for him to change the beneficiary designation yet for whatever reason he did not. The DuPont plan administrator did exactly what ERISA required by paying the person named as beneficiary.

PEREMPTORY CHALLENGE

The right to challenge a juror without assigning, or being required to assign, a reason for the challenge.

Rivera v. Illinois

In *Rivera v. Illinois,* No. 07-9995, 556 U.S. ___ (2009), an unanimous U.S. SUPREME COURT ruled that the Due Process clause of the U.S. Constitution did not require reversal of a criminal conviction because of the trial court's good-faith error in denying defense counsel's **peremptory challenge** to dismiss a juror. In so holding, the Supreme Court upheld the Illinois Supreme Court's conclusion that the wrongful denial did not require reversal of the jury's conviction for murder.

An Illinois jury had convicted Michael Rivera on two counts of first-degree murder and sentenced him to 85 years in prison. However, the jury foreperson had been the subject of a peremptory challenge by defense counsel prior to the trial. His motion was denied by the trial court.

In both federal and state courts, peremptory challenges allow each party to dismiss potential or prospective jurors without stating a cause or reason. Each party is allowed the same number of peremptory challenges, generally two. After this, a potential or prospective juror can only be dismissed from the jury pool "for cause."

In closed chambers with counsel prior to trial, the judge questioned Rivera's attorney about his reasons for wanting to strike Delores Gomez from the jury. A discussion ensued, after which the judge advised that the motion to strike Gomez would be denied. Defense counsel objected that no reason need be offered for peremptory challenges, but the motion was nonetheless denied, because, according to the trial judge, the request appeared to be discriminatory and defense counsel's stated reason was insufficient. The prosecuting attorney had expressed a similar opinion. The trial court did, however, allow defense counsel the opportunity to continue questioning Gomez in chambers, who continued to express her view that she could be impartial in evaluating the evidence. Gomez then served as jury foreperson, knowing that defense counsel had wanted to strike her from the jury. The jury found Rivera guilty and convicted him.

On appeal to the Illinois **Appellate Court**, Rivera's argument that the trial judge erred in denying the peremptory challenge was rejected, and both Rivera's conviction and sentence were affirmed. However, the Illinois Supreme Court remanded the case back to the trial court to better describe its reasons for denying the peremptory challenge. On remand, the trial judge articulated some facts and stated that he thought defense counsel's true reason for the peremptory challenge was based on gender.

Back before the Illinois Supreme Court, Rivera's conviction and sentence were affirmed, but the court did not affirm the trial court's denial of peremptory challenge, instead ruling that it should have been allowed. Notwithstanding, the state high court also ruled that this error did not warrant reversal of the conviction or sentence. Finding the error subject to "harmless error review," the court concluded that it was, indeed, harmless, i.e., did not affect the outcome of the case (the jury verdict).

The U.S. Supreme Court, generally reluctant to review decisions of states' highest courts, nonetheless granted **certiorari** (review) based on a substantial conflict among state high courts on whether convictions should be automatically overturned under such factual scenarios (wrongly seating a challenged juror) or whether the error was indeed "harmless."

The U.S. Supreme Court opinion was unanimous. In affirming the decision of the Illinois Supreme Court, Justice Ruth Ginsburg, writing for the Court, held that the SIXTH AMENDMENT right to due process and a fair trial did not require the automatic reversal of a conviction because of a trial court's good-faith error in denying a peremptory challenge. Since there is no constitutional right to a peremptory challenge, she reasoned, the mistaken denial of a peremptory challenge does not per se violate the Constitution. Rather, the decision whether such

an error was reversible error as a matter of law is vested with state courts. The Illinois Supreme Court acted within its powers in determining that the mistake denial of Rivera's peremptory challenge was **harmless error**.

Justice Ginsburg expressly noted that the Illinois Supreme Court, in reviewing the trial record before it, concluded that the presence of Gomez on the jury did not prejudice Rivera because "any rational trier of fact would have found [Rivera] guilty of murder on the evidence adduced at trial." Indeed, said Justice Ginsburg, Rivera received precisely what due process required: "a fair trial before an impartial and properly instructed jury."

PERJURY

A crime that occurs when an individual willfully makes a false statement during a judicial proceeding, after he or she has taken an oath to speak the truth.

Disgraced Track Star Marion Jones Spends Six Months in Prison for Perjury

Former Olympian track star Marion Jones was sentenced to six months in prison for lying to federal investigators about her use of steroids, as well as an unrelated check **fraud** case. Jones had spent years denying that she had used performance-enhancing drugs, but she finally admitted to using these drugs in 2007. She tried to rebuild her reputation during the fall of 2008 by appearing on well-known television shows, but several documents showed that statements she made after her release from prison were false or inaccurate.

Marion Jones first made national news in the months leading up to the 2000 Olympic games in Sydney, Australia when she announced that her goal was to win five gold medals. Prior to her Olympic run, she attended and graduated from the University of North Carolina at Chapel Hill, where she met her future husband, C.J. Hunter. Hunter was a shot putter who then served as a coach at North Carolina. Jones and Hunter were married in 1998. Both Jones and Hunter qualified for the Sydney Games, and Jones quickly became the darling of the games. Though she did not win five gold medals, she captured three gold and two bronze, which was an unprecedented feat for a female athlete.

Hunter made news of a different kind. Officials with the International Olympic

Committee (IOG) and the International Association of Athletics Federations (IAAF) announced that Hunter had tested positive four times for the prohibited steroid nandrolone. Hunter held a news conference, where he was joined briefly by Jones. Also joining Hunter was Victor Conte, who was then identified as Hunter's nutritionist. Hunter and Conte denied that Hunter had used steroids, with Conte asserting that the tests must have been inaccurate.

Conte was the founder of Bay Area Laboratory Co-Operative (BALCO), which turned out to be a company that developed steroids. A federal **grand jury** interviewed several athletes during the fall of 2003 about BALCO, and this investigation led to the revelation that many major athletes were using steroids. These athletes included baseball players Barry Bonds, Gary Sheffield, and Jason Giambi; football player Bill Romanowski; and a significant number of track and field stars. Jones was the most prominent name in track and field to be implicated during the grand jury investigation.

As Jones prepared for the 2004 Olympic Games in Athens, she steadfastly denied that she had used steroids. She and her attorneys stress that nothing during the grand jury investigation proved that she had used steroids, and she threatened to sue Olympic officials if they banned her from competing in Athens. Jones was allowed to participate in the 2004 Games, but she failed to win a medal. Less than four months after the Athens Games ended, the IOC opened an investigation into Jones' use of steroids after Conte said that he had supplied her with the steroids. Jones came under more scrutiny in 2005 when former Olympic champion Tim Montgomery was given a two-year ban for doping based on evidence that emerged from the BALCO investigation. Montgomery was Jones' boyfriend for two years, and the two had a child together.

Jones tried to prove her innocence by going on the attack. In December 2004, she filed a $25 million libel suit against Conte, and the two settled the case out of court in 2006. Nevertheless, the IOC said it would continue to investigate the steroid allegations against Jones. During the summer of 2006, she won the 100 meters at the U.S. track and field championships, but she had to withdraw from other events due to fatigue. Two months later, one of

Marion Jones leaves court after sentencing, January 11, 2008.

AP IMAGES

her steroid samples came up positive for an endurance-boosting hormone known as EPO. A second sample came up negative, though, so Jones was able to continue denying that she had taken the steroids.

By 2007, the major executives with BALCO pleaded guilty to a variety of charges, and those with knowledge of Jones' use testified that she had used the drug. Moreover, when Hunter appeared before the grand jury in the BALCO case in 2004, he admitted that he had helped Jones inject herself with performance-enhancing drugs, including human growth hormones. Similar to the excuse given by baseball star Barry Bonds, Jones claims she did not know what she was being given by her handlers, saying that she thought she was taking flaxseed oil. Experts said it was highly unlikely that a world-class athlete would not have noticed and questioned the effect of what she was taking.

Jones also became caught up in a completely unrelated investigation. Montgomery had allegedly engaged in a scheme to cash several million dollars worth of stolen or forged checks. Jones denied any knowledge of the scheme, but evidence later revealed that she indeed was aware of the scheme, even though she was not involved with it.

In October 2007, Jones finally admitted to using steroids. She was charged on two counts of perjury—one for the making false statements about using steroids, and another for lying about her knowledge of Montgomery's check scheme. Reading from a prepared statement outside a federal courthouse in New York,

Jones said, "It's with a great amount of shame that I stand before you and tell you that I have betrayed your trust. I have been dishonest and you have the right to be angry with me. I have let (my family) down. I have let my country down, and I have let myself down." She returned her Olympics medals to the IOC, and the IOC officially erased her results from the record books.

In January 2008, Jones was sentenced to six months in prison. She asked the judge for leniency, but U.S. District Judge Kenneth Karas refused to limit Jones' sentence to probation. Karas said, "Athletes in society . . . serve as role models to children around the world. When there is a widespread level of cheating, it sends all the wrong messages." Jones served her sentence in a Fort Worth prison from March through September 2008. While she was serving her time, Jones' former teammates received their own penalty. Members of both the 1,600-meter gold medal team and 400-meter bronze medal team at the Sydney Olympics lost their medals because Jones was a member of both teams.

Jones was broke when she emerged from prison. She tried to repair her reputation by appearing on such shows as the "Oprah Winfrey Show" and "Good Morning America." She repeatedly said that she did not know what she was taking when her coaches and others were giving her the performance-enhancing drugs. However, investigative reports published since her release from prison strongly indicate that she not only knew what she was taking but had also injected herself with the banned substances.

PREEMPTION

A doctrine based on the Supremacy Clause of the U.S. Constitution that holds that certain matters are of such a national, as opposed to local, character that federal laws preempt or take precedence over state laws. As such, a state may not pass a law inconsistent with the federal law. Or, a doctrine of state law that holds that a state law displaces a local law or regulation that is in the same field and is in conflict or inconsistent with the state law.

Wyeth v. Levine

The FOOD AND DRUG ADMINISTRATION (FDA) is charged with regulating, among other things, the marketing of prescription drugs. The Federal Food, Drug, and Cosmetic Act (FDCA) has long required FDA approval of new drugs, which includes labeling. Labels are crucial to doctors and nurses who dispense medication, as they contain recommended dosages, the best way to introduce the drug into a patient's body, and the potential side effects and injuries that can occur. When patients are injured by prescription drugs, litigation is often the next step. Drug manufacturers have fought efforts by plaintiffs to sue them in state courts based on a claim that drug labels failed to provide adequate warnings about the dangers of using the drug. The manufacturers have asserted that the FDA's drug approval system preempts any state-law tort claims. The Supreme Court, in *Wyeth v. Levine,__U.S.__,* 129 S.Ct. 1187, 173 L. Ed.2d 51 (2009), rendered an important decision, holding that plaintiffs could sue in state court on claims that drugs have been mislabeled.

Phenergan, made by Wyeth, was approved for use as an anti-nausea drug by the FDA in 1995. The warnings on Phenergan's label had not changed since its approval. The label advised medical personnel that the drug could be administered in either of two ways. The IV-drip method allowed the drug to be introduced into a saline solution in a hanging intravenous bag, from which it slowly descended through a catheter inserted in a patient's vein. The IV-push method introduced the drug by a direct injection into a patient's vein. Phenergan is a corrosive drug—it causes irreversible gangrene if it enters a patient's artery.

Diane Levine, a professional musician living in Vermont, suffered from frequent migraine headaches. In April 2000 she returned to her clinic to receive injections of Demerol for her migraine headache and Phenergan for her nausea. The combination failed to provide relief, so Levine returned later that day for a second round of injections. The physician's assistant again administered the Phenergan using the IV-push method. This time the drug entered Levine's artery. This could have been caused by the needle directly penetrating the artery or by the drug escaping the vein into the surrounding tissue. The results were devastating but predictable: Levine developed gangrene and doctors amputated her entire forearm. Apart from her pain and suffering, Levine lost her livelihood as a musician.

Levine accepted settlements from the health center and the doctors, and then sued Wyeth in Vermont state court on the tort theories of negligence and **strict liability**. A jury awarded Levine $7.4 million. Wyeth argued from the beginning of the lawsuit that federal law preempted the state lawsuit. The trial judge rejected this argument as did the Vermont Supreme Court. The court held that the lawsuit did not conflict with FDA labeling requirements because Wyeth could have warned against the IV-push method of administration without prior FDA approval. Moreover, federal labeling requirements create a floor, not a ceiling, for state regulation.

The Supreme Court, in a 6-3 decision, upheld the state supreme court's rulings. Justice JOHN PAUL STEVENS, writing for the majority, noted Wyeth's argument that it would be impossible for it to comply with both the state-law duties underlying those claims and its federal labeling duties. Stevens rejected this argument, holding that the FDA's "changes being effected" (CBE) regulation permitted certain preapproval labeling changes that add or strengthen a warning to improve drug safety. Pursuant to the CBE regulation, Wyeth could have unilaterally added a stronger warning about the administration of the drug. In addition, there was no evidence that the FDA would ultimately have rejected such a labeling change. A central premise of the (FDCA) and the FDA's regulations is that the manufacturer bears responsibility for the content of its label at all times.

Wyeth also argued that requiring it to comply with a state-law duty to provide a stronger warning would interfere with Congress' purpose of entrusting an expert agency with drug labeling decisions. Justice Stevens found no merit in this claim, for Wyeth relied on an untenable interpretation of congressional intent and an overbroad view of an agency's power to preempt state law. The history of the FDCA showed that Congress did not intend to preempt state-law failure-to-warn actions. Wyeth relied not on any statement by Congress but on the preamble to a 2006 FDA regulation declaring that state-law failure-to-warn claims threaten the FDA's statutorily prescribed role. Although an agency regulation with the force of law can preempt conflicting state requirements, this case involved no such regulation. It was

Diana Levine celebrates U.S. Supreme Court verdict at her home in Vermont, March 2009.

AP IMAGES

merely an agency's assertion that state law is an obstacle to achieving its **statutory** objectives.

Stevens concluded that when Congress has not authorized a federal agency to preempt state law directly, the weight the Court accords the agency's explanation of state law's impact on the federal scheme depends on its thoroughness, consistency, and persuasiveness. Under this standard, the FDA's 2006 preamble did not merit deference. It was inherently suspect in light of the FDA's failure to offer interested parties notice or opportunity for comment on the **preemption** question, it was at odds with the available evidence of Congress' purposes, and it reversed the FDA's own longstanding position that state law is a complementary form of drug regulation without providing a reasoned explanation.

PRODUCT LIABILITY

The responsibility of a manufacturer or vendor of goods to compensate for injury caused by a defective good that it has provided for sale.

Texas and New Jersey Courts Reverse Vioxx Decisions

In two completely separate cases decided on May 29, 2008, **appellate** courts in Texas and New Jersey reversed trial court decisions in litigation focused on the painkiller drug, Vioxx. The case that arose in Texas was especially eye-opening, as the plaintiff who was originally awarded more than $253 million took nothing as a result of the appellate court's decision.

Prostaglandins are hormone-like substances that are produced by the body and which affect pain and inflammation. The enzymes that produce prostaglandins are different forms of cyclooxygenase (COX). Certain drugs known as non-steroidal anti-inflammatory drugs (NSAIDs) help to ease pain and inflammation by decreasing production of prostaglandins in the body. The drugs work by inhibiting COX. Examples of NSAIDs are ibuprofen (used to make Advil and Motrin), naproxen (used to make Aleve), and aspirin. NSAIDs are commonly used to treat inflammation and acute and chronic pain caused by rheumatoid arthritis and osteoarthritis. These NSAIDs, though, are known to cause such problems as ulcers, perforations, and bleeding on the gastrointestinal tract.

During the early 1990s, scientists discovered that cyclooxygenase appears in two forms. The first form is known as cyclooxygenase-1 (COX-1), which protects the gastrointestinal tract. The second form is known as cyclooxygenase-2 (COX-2), which promotes inflammation and pain. Scientists began to work on a drug that could inhibit COX-2 while not affecting COX-1. Such a drug could be superior to NSAIDs because the drug would not cause the gastrointestinal problems associated with NSAIDs. Scientists also believed that such a drug could benefit treatment of other conditions, such as cancer and Alzheimer's disease.

Merck & Co., Inc. during the 1990s faced the loss of the patents for several of the company's major drugs, and so the company began to look for replacement products. Merck researchers worked on a product known generically as rofecoxib, which would serve as a COX-2 inhibitor. Rofecoxib was later marketed as Vioxx. Merck submitted a new drug application for Vioxx to the FOOD AND DRUG ADMINISTRATION (FDA) in November 1998. The FDA concluded that Vioxx was a safe and an effective treatment for certain types of pain, and in May 1999, the FDA initially approved Vioxx. Merck launched Vioxx in June 1999 with a massive marketing campaign.

The FDA subjected Vioxx to a series of studies and tests. In one study conducted in March 2000, researchers administered the drug to 8,000 patients to determine what effects Vioxx had on gastrointestinal functions. This study compared Vioxx with naproxen. The results of the tests showed that Vioxx caused fewer gastrointestinal problems, but the study also showed that Vioxx patients showed a greater risk of developing blood clots due to

the drug's effect on hormones that relate to clotting. At the time of these trials, the Vioxx label did not warn users of potential cardiovascular problems.

Merck submitted Vioxx to further testing, and the company submitted several revised labels between 2000 and 2002. In 2001, Merck estimated that Vioxx would generate sales of between $1.6 and $2.1 billion. The company did not express significant concern about the study results suggesting that the drug may cause clotting problems. However, the company expected a substantial decrease in sales if cardiovascular effects were stated in the "warnings" section of the drug label. During 2001, the *New York Times* published an article noting that a patient who took Vioxx ran a higher risk of having a heart attack.

Merck continued to dispute study results suggesting that Vioxx may cause cardiovascular problems. The company in 2000 began a study of Vioxx's possible effects on colon polyps. The study was known as Adenomatous Polyp Prevention on Vioxx (APPROVe) and continued for three years. In September 2004, an external safety board that was monitoring the APPROVe study informed Merck that that study had revealed that the drug caused cardiovascular problems. On September 30, 2004, Merck withdrew Vioxx from the market.

By 2005, Merck faced more than 4,200 lawsuits related to Vioxx. One of those cases arose in Texas when a doctor in September 2000 prescribed Vioxx to Bob Ernst to alleviate tendinitis in Ernst's hands. On May 6, 2001, Ernst suffered a heart attack and died. Merck's wife alleged that her husband's ingestion of Vioxx is what caused his heart attack, and she sued Merck on a variety of grounds. A jury in Brazoria County determined that Merck was liable. The jury originally awarded Ernst's wife more than $24 million in **compensatory damages** and $229 million in **punitive damages**. However, Texas law capped the punitive damages award, and the court reduced the final award to $26.1 million.

In New Jersey, two Vioxx users named John McDarby and Thomas Cona also suffered heart problems as a result of their use of Vioxx. Both men had taken Vioxx prior to 2002, which is when Merck changed its label to provide additional warnings about potential cardiovascular problems. In 2007, a New Jersey superior court in Atlantic County awarded $15.7 million to McDarby and $2.27 million to Cona.

Merck appealed the judgments from the cases in Texas and New Jersey. In Ernst's case, the 14th **District Court** of Appeals in Houston heard the appeal. Much of the opinion focused on whether Ernst had proven that Vioxx actually caused the blood clotting that caused her husband's heart attack. Ernst acknowledged that she had not provided **direct evidence** that Vioxx had caused the clotting, but she argued that circumstantial evidence supported the jury's decision. However, the court discredited expert testimony from two doctors because their opinions were not supported by scientifically reliable facts. The court therefore concluded that the evidence did not support the jury's award, and the court ordered that Ernst should take nothing. *Merck & Co., Inc. v. Ernst*, No. 14-06-00835-CV, 2008 WL 2201769 (Tex. App. May 29, 2008).

In the New Jersey case, the Appellate Division of the Superior Court of New Jersey reviewed the trial court's decision on a number of grounds. The court concluded that parts of the New Jersey **product liability** law at issue in the case was preempted by federal law. Based on this reasoning, the court reversed the trial court's punitive damages award. The court also reversed the award of attorney's fees. However, the court affirmed the compensatory damage awards given to both McDarby and Cona. *McDarby v. Merck & Co., Inc.*, 949 A.2d 223 (N.J. Super. A.D. 2008).

Mark Lanier, the attorney involved in both the Texas and New Jersey cases, expressed disappointment with both decisions. He was especially critical of the Texas court, saying that the court had taken a "simpleton approach" and accusing "activist judges" of protecting corporate executives. Lanier said his clients would appeal both decisions.

PUNITIVE DAMAGES

Monetary compensation awarded to an injured party that goes beyond that which is necessary to compensate the individual for losses and that is intended to punish the wrongdoer.

Philip Morris USA Inc. v. Williams

Since the 1990s the Supreme Court has reviewed a number of cases involving large awards of **punitive damages**. The Court has sought ways to limit the amount of punitive damages a jury may award and has developed standards for deciding whether an award is excessive. The U.S. tobacco industry has been the target of punitive damages. Not surprisingly, the industry has challenged these awards. Such was the case in *Philip Morris USA Inc. v. Williams*, __U.S.__, 129 S.Ct. 436, __L.Ed.2d__ (2009), which involved an Oregon jury's award of punitive damages that has grown over the time of the lengthy litigation to almost $150 million. The Supreme Court issued decisions in 2003 and 2007 that sent the case back to the Oregon state courts for reconsideration of the punitive damages award but the state courts upheld the awards both thimes. In a highly unusual move, the U.S. SUPREME COURT, after hearing arguments in 2008, dismissed the tobacco company's appeal.

Mayola Williams sued Philip Morris, the maker of Marlboro cigarettes, claiming that the company caused the death of her husband, Jesse Williams, a heavy smoker of Marlboros. Williams alleged negligence and deceit by Philip Morris. A jury found that his death was caused by smoking, that Williams smoked because he thought it was safe to do so, and that Philip Morris knowingly and falsely led him to believe that smoking was safe. The jury found that the company was negligent and had used deceit. On the deceit claim the jury awarded Williams in **compensatory damages** of about $821,000 and $79.5 million in punitive damages. The trial judge ruled that the punitive damages award was excessive and reduced the award to $32 million. Both sides appealed to the Oregon Court of Appeals, which sided with Williams and restored the $79.5 million jury award. Philip Morris appealed to the U.S. Supreme Court, which remanded the case to the Oregon Court of Appeals to reconsider based on the factors detailed in *State Farm Mutual Automobile Insurance Company v. Campbell*,538 U.S. 408, 123 S.Ct. 1513, 155 L.Ed.2d 585(2003). In that case the Court used three "guideposts" to determine whether a punitive damages award is excessive. A court must consider: (1) the degree of reprehensibility of the defendant's misconduct; (2) the disparity between the actual harm suffered by the plaintiff and the punitive damages award; and (3) the difference between the punitive damages award and the civil penalties authorized or imposed in comparable bases. The state appeals court upheld the award again and the Oregon Supreme Court did the same, finding that the trial judge properly refused a proposed jury instruction by the company that sought to limit punitive damages to the Williams family and not to others. The instruction would have gone against the purposes of punitive damages: to punish misconduct and deter misconduct against society as a whole.

The U.S. Supreme Court, in *Philip Morris USA Inc. v. Williams*, 549 U.S. 346, 127 S.Ct. 1057, 166 L.Ed.2d 940 (2007), ruled that the Due Process Clause forbids a state from using a punitive damages award to punish a defendant for injuries inflicted on "strangers to the litigation." To permit such an award would magnify the due process risks of arbitrariness, uncertainty, and lack of notice. The Court could find no authority for using punitive damages for the purpose of punishing a defendant for harming others. It was acceptable that a jury consider a punitive damages award "in light of the *potential* harm the defendant's conduct could have caused." However, the "potential harm at issue was harm potentially caused *the plaintiff*." The Oregon Supreme Court was correct that the U.S. Supreme Court had never explicitly held that a jury "may not punish for

the harm caused others. But we do so now." Therefore, the Court remanded the case to the Oregon Supreme Court so it could apply the correct constitutional standard. The Court acknowledged that the application of the standard might require a new trial or a change in the amount of punitive damages award. In light of this possibility the Court declined to analyze whether the $79.5 million was excessive.

The Oregon Supreme Court upheld the punitive damages award in a 2008 decision. 344 Or.45, 176 P.3d 1255. The court found that the jury instruction offered by Philip Morris at trial was flawed but this time looked to "independent state standards" rather than the standard articulated by the U.S. Supreme Court. The decision by the trial judge to refuse the proposed jury instruction could be upheld without reaching the federal Due Process Clause question if there is "an independent and adequate state grounds for doing so." The court found such grounds and Morris took its third appeal to the U.S. Supreme Court. With the dismissal of the appeal by the Court, the $143 million will be split between Mayola Williams and the state of Oregon, as required by state law.

RELIGION

Raid of Polygamist Sect Leads to Numerous Legal Problems

Acting on a tip phone call allegedly made by a 16-year-old girl, authorities in Texas in April 2008 raided a compound of the Fundamentalist Church of Jesus Christ of the Latter Day Saints (FLDS). State authorities removed hundreds of children from the ranch, leading to what looked to be a massive and drawn out child custody dispute in the Texas courts. However, the Texas Supreme Court in May 2008 ruled that the trial judge in the case had overstepped her bounds by removing the children from their parents. Several adult members of the sect were later indicted for crimes related to the sexual abuse of underage girls at the compound.

Members of the FLDS believe in practices that have long been rejected by the mainstream MORMON CHURCH. The leader of the FLDS has been Warren Jeffs, who established ranches in Utah and Arizona. The FLDS believed in **polygamy** based on practices of early Mormons. Girls as young as 12 were often required to marry much older men and to **consummate** the marriage immediately. These practices led to Jeffs' arrest in 2005 and 2006 for forcing these underage girls into the marriages. In September 2007, a Utah court convicted Jeffs of being an accomplice to rape. He may serve the rest of his life in prison.

The FLDS sect bought property near San Angelo, Texas and constructed a compound. The sect engaged in the same practices as was the case in Utah and Arizona, and Texas officials knew it. However, authorities were not able to act on credible evidence, even with visits by police officers, and so the sect carried on its marriage practices for several years. According to a local sheriff, had authorities heard an outcry from anyone inside the sect prior to 2008, his office would have taken action "in a heartbeat."

On March 29, the Texas Department of Family and Protective Services received a call from a girl who called herself "Sarah." The girl said she was 16 years old and was married to a 50-year-old man named Dale Barlow. According to the girl's call, Barlow had beaten and raped her. Two days later, state police officers entered the compound, known as the Yearning for Zion Ranch. Investigators interviewed both adults and children at the compound and searched for relevant documents. Convinced that the children at the compound were in danger, the Department of Family and Protective Services took all 468 children into possession. Authorities never found a 16-year-old named Sarah, though.

The department immediately filed an action known in Texas as a suit affecting the parent-child relationship (SAPCR). The department asked for emergency orders that would allow state officials to separate children from their parents and to limit access by the parents to the

Members of the Fundamentalist Church of Latter Day Saints sect being interviewed on the Today show, May 12, 2008.

AP IMAGES

children. Numerous attorneys, participants, and observers packed a courthouse in San Angelo for two weeks of hearings, after which Judge Barbara Walther issued temporary orders allowing the department to retain custody of the children.

Authorities began to suspect that the alleged 16-year-old girl who originally contacted authorities may have been a 33-year-old named Rozita Swinton of Colorado. On April 28, police in Colorado Springs arrested Swinton on a charge of making a false report to police, which is a **misdemeanor**. Swinton was reportedly very convincing while acting like a young girl, but authorities later discovered holes in her story. At least one of the calls came from a telephone number that authorities traced back to Swinton.

By the time of Swinton's arrest, all of the children had been separated from their families and placed in state foster care. On May 1, Texas RioGrande **Legal Aid** filed petition for a **writ** of **mandamus** with the Third District Texas Court of Appeals in Austin. A total of 38 mothers filed the petition, which asked the court to return 126 of the children. The vast majority of these children were under the age of 13. The mothers argued that the state had failed to meet its burden necessary under Texas law to separate the children from their parents. In a *per curiam* opinion (meaning no singled judge signed it), the court directed the **district court** to vacate its decision. According to the court:

> Removing children from their homes and parents on an emergency basis before fully litigating the issue of whether the parents should continue to have custody of the children is an extreme measure. It is,

unfortunately, sometimes necessary for the protection of the children involved. However, it is a step that the legislature has provided may be taken only when the circumstances indicate a danger to the physical health and welfare of the children and the need for protection of the children is so urgent that immediate removal of the children from the home is necessary.

In re Steed, No. 03-08-00235-CV, 2008 WL 2132014 (Tex. App. 2008).

The state appealed the decision to the Texas Supreme Court. In another *per curiam* decision, the court refused to disturb the court of appeals order. The court noted that the SAPCR proceedings would continue notwithstanding the rulings by the **appellate** courts. Nevertheless, the Texas Supreme Court agreed with the lower appeals court that the state had not met its burden to allow the state to separate the children from their parents. *In re Texas Dep't of Family Protective Servs.*, 255 S.W.3d 613 (Tex. 2008).

Most of the children were returned to their parents after the court's ruling. The investigation did not end, however. A **grand jury** convened in June and July to investigate the activities of the FLDS, and on July 22, the grand jury indicted Warren Jeffs and five others on charges of sexual assault and bigamy. Three more men were indicted in September on similar charges. Other than these indictments, the investigation into the FLDS compounded ended by December 2008.

RICO

A set of federal laws (18 U.S.C.A. § 1961 et seq. [1970]) specifically designed to punish criminal activity by business enterprises.

Boyle v. United States

The Racketeer Influenced and Corrupt Organizations Act (RICO), 18 USC §1961 *et seq.* was enacted, in part, to help officials break up, then prosecute activities associated with organized crime; this was because the most pervasive instances of racketeering were at one time associated with "mob activity". ("Racketeering" more generally means the extortive demand, **solicitation**, or receipt of anything of value, by means of a threat or promise, in order to cause persons with an interest in something of value to compromise that interest.) Since then, RICO has been invoked in all sorts of cases alleging some form of conspiratorial activity to extort, bribe, or otherwise illegally pressure persons against their own interests.

Section 18 USC §1962(c) of RICO forbids "any person.associated with any enterprise engaged in, or the activities of which affect, interstate or foreign commerce, to conduct or participate, directly or indirectly, in the conduct of such enterprise's affairs through a pattern of racketeering activity." More simply put, RICO makes it a federal crime for individuals to participate in, or profit from, any association with a criminal racketeering organization. At issue in *Boyle v. United States,* No. 07-1309, 556 U.S. ___ (2009) was a clarification of what constituted an "association-in-fact" enterprise under RICO in order to invoke violation thereof. A split among circuit courts of appeal on the matter had prompted the U.S. SUPREME COURT to grant review when this case came before it. The precise issue in *Boyle* focused on a jury instruction provided by the trial court on the meaning of a RICO "enterprise."

A jury in the United States **District Court** for the Eastern District of New York had convicted Edmund Boyle and eight other men of bank **robbery**, racketeering, and conspiracy charges under RICO. At trial, evidence was sufficient to prove, among other things, that Boyle and several others committed a series of bank thefts in several different states, that the participants in the robberies included a core group of individuals, along with others recruited as needed, and that the core group was loosely and informally organized, but not to the point of having a leader or internal hierarchy; neither was there any long-term master plan among them.

Most of Boyle's co-defendants had pleaded guilty by the start of trial, and the United States proceeded against Boyle alone. What it needed to prove to charge him under RICO was to show an existence of an association-in-fact enterprise, and that the enterprise was engaged in racketeering activity.

The original charges brought against Boyle and the others claimed that they all participated in a series of bank robberies as members of an organization (enterprise) referred to as the "Night Drop Crew." Boyle attempted to dismiss the charges with a pre-trial motion that cited some of the other eight men's convictions claiming groups named the "New Springville Boys" and the "Bank Crew" were responsible for the robberies. The United States responded that the different names were just labels applied to the same associated group, which had similar and overlapping members over the years. The pre-trial motion was dismissed and the case proceeded to trial.

During the trial against Boyle alone, the U.S. district attorneys (prosecutors) referred to the individuals in question as the "Boyle Crew" instead of the "Night Drop Crew." For his part, Boyle denied any association with any group and claimed that he and the other men were individuals acting on an impromptu basis with no formal organizational structure.

In instructing the jury on the meaning of a RICO "enterprise," the district court told them that, in order to establish the existence of such an enterprise, the Government needed to prove that,

"(1)There [was] an ongoing organization with some sort of framework, formal or informal, for carrying out its objective; and (2) the various members and associates of the association function[ed] as a continuing unit to achieve a common purpose."

Over objections by defense counsel, the jury convicted Boyle of racketeering and racketeering conspiracy under RICO, as well as bank burglary, conspiracy to commit bank burglary, and attempted bank burglary. He was sentenced to 151 months in prison.

Boyle's appeal followed. In it, he claimed that the Government's case was factually contradictory, because at its convenience (depending on who was up for trial) it arbitrarily changed the name(s) of the "enterprise" responsible, e.g., "Night Drop Crew," "New Springville Boys," "Bank Crew," "Boyle's Crew." This, according to Boyle, violated his right to due process under the FIFTH AMENDMENT.

The U.S. Court of Appeals for the Second Circuit rejected that argument, holding that the Government's case was not factually contradictory. "Nothing dictates that a single crime cannot be committed by two enterprises working together, each in furtherance of its own interests," said the opinion.

The U.S. Supreme Court agreed and affirmed. Writing for the majority 7-2 opinion, Justice Alito wrote that, while an association-in-fact enterprise under RICO must have a "structure," a jury instruction need not be framed in the precise language that Boyle had proposed, i.e., that there be an "ascertainable structure beyond that inherent in the pattern of racketeering activity in which it engages." By explicitly instructing the jury that they could not convict under RICO unless they found that the Government had proved the existence of an enterprise, the district court made clear that this was a separate element (to be proved) from the pattern of racketeering activity. The district court's instruction was therefore adequate and correct, the majority concluded, affirming the judgment of the Court of Appeals. Justice Alito was joined in the majority opinion by Chief Justice Roberts and Justices Scalia, Keneedy, Souter, Thomas, and Ginsburg.

Justice Stevens filed a dissenting opinion, primarily for the reason articulated in his first sentence: "In my view, Congress intended the term `enterprise' as it is used in [RICO] to refer only to business-like entities that have an existence apart from the predicate acts committed by their employees or associates." He was joined in dissent by Justice Breyer.

RIPARIAN RIGHTS

The rights, which belong to landowners through whose property a natural watercourse runs, to the benefit of such stream for all purposes to which it can be applied.

Kansas v. Colorado

States that are separated from each other by rivers sometimes become embroiled in legal disputes as to who controls these waters. In come cases the lawsuits are protracted. The U.S. Constitution grants the Supreme Court general or **original jurisdiction** over federal lawsuits between the states. The Court serves as a trial court and must be the finder of fact. However, the Court always appoints a Special Master, who acts as the finder of fact and files a report with the Court as to these findings and to conclusions of law. Once the report is filed the Supreme Court reviews the report and the "exceptions" the states make to the report. Since 1985 the states of Kansas and Colorado have been locked in a dispute over the Arkansas River. Kansas claimed that Colorado had violated an agreement by drilling irrigation wells that depleted water that should have gone to Kansas residents. The Special Master in the lawsuit filed five reports over 24 years, with the

states filing exceptions each time. The case finally appeared to draw to a close when the Court resolved how much Colorado would have to pay Kansas for the cost of that state's expert witnesses. *Kansas v. Colorado*, __U.S.__, 129 S.Ct. 1294, 173 L.Ed.2d 245 (2009)

Kansas filed suit in the Supreme Court in 1985, claiming Colorado had violated the federal Arkansas River Compact that the states had negotiated and signed in 1948. The agreement allowed development in Colorado provided that it did not cause material depletions of usable stateline Arkansas River flows. Kansas alleged that the drilling of irrigation wells depleted water that should have been available to Kansas users. The Supreme Court appointed a Special Master and ten years later the master filed a report with the recommendation that Colorado had violated the Compact. The Court accepted the recommendation and sent the case back to the Special Master to determine the appropriate remedies. In 2001 the Special Master recommended awarding monetary damages to Kansas. The Supreme Court accepted all but one of the recommendations, modifying the starting date for an award of prejudgment interest. In 2004 the case returned to the Court, which accepted additional recommendations by the Special Master. The Court approved calculating river depletions on a 10-year basis, so as to even out possible inaccuracies in computer modeling and that a Colorado Water Court be granted authority to make certain decisions involving the implementation of the agreement.

The Court again remanded the case. This time the Special Master used experts hired by the states to discuss and resolve the remaining issues. Through the use of expert witnesses and the use of a computer model to determine compliance with the Compact, the parties resolved most of the contested issues. The Special Master determined that Kansas was the **prevailing party** for the purposes of award litigation costs. Kansas proposed two ways for calculating the amount it was entitled to recover for retaining expert witnesses. The first proposal, which Kansas advocated, was based on the actual amount of **money paid** to the witnesses. Using that standard, Colorado would pay $9.2 million. The second proposal was calculated on the assumption that a federal **statute** governed, which limited the amount paid for a witness attendance fee to $40 per day. Using this calculation, Colorado would pay just $162,000. The Special Master concluded that the statute applied and awarded Kansas the smaller amount for costs. Kansas filed an exception with the Supreme Court, challenging the applicability of the law to the Court's original jurisdiction cases.

The Court, in a unanimous decision, agreed that Kansas should be awarded the smaller amount. Justice Samuel Alito, writing for the Court, noted Kansas's argument that the statute only applied to federal district courts and appeals courts. Colorado countered that the statute's language clearly stated that it applied to a proceeding in "any court of the United States." Justice Alito found it was unnecessary to decide whether Congress intended to have the law apply to the Court's original jurisdiction. Instead, assuming that the Court had the discretion to determine the fees recoverable in original actions, Alito concluded that it was "appropriate" to follow the statute. Cases brought in **district court** were "no less complex" than original actions brought in the Supreme Court. The "best approach is to have a uniform rule that applies in all federal cases." Chief Justice JOHN ROBERTS, in a concurring opinion, emphasized that the decision "in no way infringes this Court's authority to decide on its own, in original cases, whether there should be witness fees and what they should be."

SAFE HAVEN

Nebraska's Safe Haven Law Backfires

In July 2008, Nebraska became the 50th and last of the states to pass legislation under what is collectively referred to as "safe haven laws." Such state laws decriminalize the relinquishment of unharmed infants, primarily newborns, to state authorities for proper care and protection. Safe haven laws were generally enacted as incentives to assist new mothers/parents in crisis by allowing them to surrender their babies to designated "safe havens" (generally hospitals, fire departments, police departments, etc.) where the babies would be protected and provided with medical and custodial care until permanent foster or adoptive homes could be found. In return, many state safe haven laws provided the parent(s) with anonymity and shielded them from prosecution for **abandonment** of their unwanted infant, negligent care, or other legal repercussions. Texas became the first state to pass such a law in 1999.

Although last to enact a safe haven law, Nebraska became the first of all fifty states to not specify an age limit for relinquishing a "child" within the language of its **statute**. The other 49 states expressly specified that their laws pertained only to infants, ranging in age (depending on the state) from a few hours to no more than one year old.

Nebraska's Legislative Bill 157 was introduced in the 2008 legislative session. Forty-eight state senators voted for its final version. Because they could not agree on an age limit, the legislators did not include such provision in the bill. The full text of LB 157 stated:

> No person shall be prosecuted for any crime based solely upon the act of leaving a child in the custody of an employee on duty at a hospital licensed by the State of Nebraska. The hospital shall promptly contact appropriate authorities to take custody of the child.

Though LB 157's **original intent** was to protect unwanted newborns from abandonment and insufficient care, it soon became evident that Nebraska's law had created a quagmire of unintended results. What began as a generous and humane legislative initiative soon became a legal excuse for abandoning parental responsibilities, not unwanted newborns. Within the first six weeks following enactment, 14 children had been abandoned at Nebraska hospitals, all in September 2008. None of the children was an infant; none was in any immediate danger. This prompted **state action**, in the form of public communication.

On September 26, 2008, a press release from Kathie Osterman of Nebraska's Office of Communications and Legislative Services attempted to caution the state's citizens about the parameters of the new law. "The Department of Health and Human Services (DHHS) is letting Nebraskans know that leaving a child at a hospital does not terminate parental rights," the press release began. "While they cannot be charged for abandoning a child, parents and guardians using Nebraska's 'safe haven' law can be charged for other offenses." The press release continued by noting, "There seems to be a misconception that when a child is dropped off at a hospital, the parents are absolved of responsibility. That couldn't be further from the truth." It then provided information about local resources, including United Way organizations and faith-based community services, that could offer assistance ranging from parent support groups to crisis hotlines.

In truth, the floodgates had just begun to open. On October 7, 2008, Nebraska's Governor Dave Heineman released a press statement discussing the state's safe haven law.

> "Today, under Nebraska statutes, any child up to the age of 18 meets the criteria. Unfortunately Nebraska has seen several instances of exactly what no one hoped would ever happen. Parents and guardians have abandoned older children at hospitals."

He then went on to advise those who would abandon their children at local hospitals that they could be charged with several offenses. "Safe haven laws were not designed to allow families having difficulty with older youths and teenagers to abandon their children or responsibilities as parents," warned the governor. "Courts are also likely to require parents and guardians to participate in parenting classes, family therapy, conflict resolution or other services in an effort to reunite youth with their families. Child support payments may be ordered while children are in state custody."

The warning apparently failed in its intent. By November 2008, 34 children had been abandoned at area hospitals; most were teenagers, not one was newborn. In an incident reported by the Associated Press, one man left nine siblings, aged 1-17, at an Omaha hospital, stating that his wife had died and he "no longer knew how to care for them." Moreover, because of the law's vague wording, children from California, Georgia, Indiana, Iowa, and Michigan were anonymously dropped off at Nebraska hospitals.

On behalf of Governor Heineman, a special session of the state legislature was called. Legislative Bill 1 was introduced and approved by a 43-5 vote among state senators. Governor Heineman signed LB1 into law on November 21, 2008. The new law limited the age of a "child" dropped off at a hospital to "30 days or younger."

SEARCH AND SEIZURE

A hunt by law enforcement officials for property or communications believed to be evidence of crime, and the act of taking possession of this property.

Arizona v. Johnson

Though police usually must obtain a search warrant before searching an individual, there are circumstances where the Supreme Court has altered this requirement. In *Terry v. Ohio*, 392 U.S. 1, 88 S.Ct. 1868, 20 L.Ed.2d 889 (1968), the Court authorized police officers to "stop and frisk" individuals whose conduct has attracted their attention. Such investigatory stops may be used when officers have reasonable suspicions that criminal activity is taking place. Officers may conduct a limited search of outer clothing for weapons. The *Terry* precedent was extended to drivers and passengers of motor vehicles during traffic stops. In *Arizona v. Johnson*, __U.S.__, 129 S.Ct. 781, __L.Ed.2d__ (2009), the Court addressed legality of search of a passenger in a car stopped for a minor infraction. It held that the officer acted properly in conducting the patdown of the passenger, which led to the discovery of a handgun.

Three members of the Arizona gang force were on patrol in Tucson in the early evening near a neighborhood associated with the Crips gang. The officers pulled over a car for lacking valid registration, a violation of which is a civil infraction. The driver and a passenger were in the front seat, and Lemon Johnson was in the back seat. The three officers began to interview the three men separately. The driver was asked to step out of the car. The officer dealing with Johnson observed that he was wearing clothing associated with membership in the Crips gang and that he had a scanner in his jacket pocket. She thought the scanner's presence was unusual and that possession of the scanner suggested he might want to use it as a way to avoid police after committing criminal activity. Johnson talked with the officer and volunteered that he was from a town in Arizona that was home to a Crips gang and that he had been served time in prison for **burglary**. The officer wanted to continue the questioning away from the front seat passenger, so she asked Johnson to get out of the car. After he did she patted him down and felt the butt of a gun near his waist. Johnson began struggle but was subdued and placed in handcuffs. A jury convicted Johnson of illegally possessing a firearm.

Johnson appealed his conviction, arguing that the search was illegal under the FOURTH AMENDMENT. The Arizona Court of Appeals agreed. The appeals court acknowledged that Johnson was lawfully seized when the officers stopped the car but concluded that prior to the frisk the detention had "evolved into a separate, consensual encounter stemming from an unrelated investigation" by the officer into Johnson's possible gang affiliations. The officer failed to show a reasonable belief that Johnson was involved in criminal activity, making the the patdown for weapons illegal, "even if she had reason to suspect he was armed and dangerous." The Arizona Supreme Court denied review and the state appealed to the U.S. SUPREME COURT.

The Court, in a unanimous decision, reversed the state court decision, ruling that the patdown of Johnson was lawful. Justice RUTH BADER GINSBURG, writing for the Court, restated the importance of *Terry* in analyzing the stop, and the patdown and noted that the Court had applied it to traffic stops. Most traffic stops are similar to those authorized in *Terry*, as they are short in duration and seek to minimize harm to the police. In a prior case the Court found that police officers may order the driver out of the car that had been lawfully stopped without violating the Fourth Amendment. Once outside the vehicle, the driver could be patted down for weapons. Justice Ginsburg also cited a Court decision that permitted police officers to order passengers to get out of a vehicle that has been lawfully stopped. Based on this holding, the Court applied the rule to allow police to pat down passengers for weapons.

The Court had little problem applying this rule to Johnson, rejecting the appeals court conclusion that the interaction between the officer and Johnson became a consensual encounter. In fact, the encounter took place within minutes of the stop and the patdown took place within moments of Johnson exiting the car. There was no point where Johnson would have felt free to leave. The stop of the car by police communicated to a "reasonable passenger that he or she is not free to terminate the encounter with the police and move about at will." The officer in this case was not constitutionally required to give Johnson a chance to leave the scene after he stepped out of the vehicle "without first ensuring that, in so doing, she was not permitting a dangerous person to get behind her."

SECURITIES

Evidence of a corporation's debts or property.

Payouts in the Tyco Securities Settlement

In March 2009, class-action claimants in one of the largest securities fraud settlements ever recorded began receiving checks from the Claims Administrator handling *In re Tyco International Ltd. Securities Litigation,* No. 02-266-PB, pending in the U.S. District Court for the District of New Hampshire. Initial distribution was authorized by a February 3, 2009 Order of the court, representing a payout of approximately 90 percent of the Net Settlement Fund. (The total settlement fund was $3.2 billion. The March 2009 distribution was about $2.8 billion paid to class action plaintiffs, plus a 14.5 percent payment made to plaintiffs' attorneys and reimbursement of expenses in the amount of $28.9 million. A reserve amount was being withheld pending certain contingencies, the resolution of which would result in a second distribution of the remaining funds approximately 12 to 18 months later. Pursuant to the Plan of Allocation approved by the court, claimants whose distribution amount would be less than $10.00 did not receive a payment.

The settlement was the culmination of consolidated litigation that began in January

Dennis Kozlowski, June 16, 2005.

AP IMAGES

2003 with a 330-page Consolidated Securities Class Action Complaint. The lawsuit was filed against Tyco International Limited (Tyco), several of its former officers and directors, and PricewaterhouseCoopers. The alleged wrongful acts were in violation of Section 14, 20A, and 20(a) of the Securities Exchange Act of 1934. In the Complaint, representative plaintiffs alleged that the defendants, individually and collectively, made false and misleading public statements and omitted material information about Tyco's finances. Plaintiffs claimed that the false and misleading statements about Tyco's finances causeed Plaintiffs to invest their money in Tyco securities at artificially-inflated prices during the Class Action period from December 12, 1999 to June 7, 2002. Persons who purchased or otherwise acquired Tyco Securities common stock, notes, or options on common stock between those dates were potential claimants. The claim-filing deadline was December 28, 2007.

Chronologically, the action began in February 2002 when 40 class action suits were filed, naming the defendants above as wrongdoers in alleged acts of securities fraud. Most (32) were transferred to the U.S. District Court for the District of New Hampshire in 2003 for coordinated or consolidated pretrial proceedings.

In June 2006, the court entered an order certifying a class

> "consisting of all persons and entities who purchased or otherwise acquired Tyco securities between December 13, 1999 and June 7, 2002, and were damaged thereby, excluding defendants, all of the officers, directors and partners thereof, members of their immediate families and their legal representatives, heirs, successors or assigns, and any entity in which any of the foregoing have or had a controlling interest."

Tyco settled the 32 consolidated class actions in May 2007. The settlement released all claims against Tyco and the other settling defendants (including individuals) in return for the payment of $2.975 billion. In the settlement, the class agreed to assign to Tyco all of their claims against non-settling defendants L. Dennis Kozlowski, Mark K. Schwartz, and Frank E. Walsh, Jr. In return, Tyco agreed to pay to the certified class 50 percent of any net recovery against those defendants.

The following securities cases/actions were not resolved by the settlement and remained outstanding: *Stumpf v. Tyco International Ltd, New Jersey v. Tyco International Ltd, Ballard v. Tyco International, Ltd, Sciallo v. Tyco International Ltd, et al., Jasin v. Tyco International Ltd, et al.,* and *Hall v. Kozlowski, et al.*

Also not covered in the settlement were claims arising under the Employee Retirement Income Securities Act of 1974 (ERISA), 29 USC 1001 *et seq.,* which were not common to all class members, including claims asserted in *Overby, et al. v. Tyco International Ltd,* Docket No. 02-MD-1357-PB, also before the federal district court in New Hampshire. In an important ruling in April 2009, the court granted plaintiff's motion for summary judgment based on defendants' attempted assertion of an affirmative defense available for certain fiduciaries against ERISA claims brought by plan participants or beneficiaries. Plaintiffs had argued that this defense was not available to fiduciaries who were sued because of a decision to designate the investment options available to participants. Plaintiffs sued for breach of those and other fiduciary duties. Tyco also failed in its motion to exclude certain 401(k) contributions that were inherited through Tyco's mergers with other companies from plaintiffs' calculation of damages.

In May 2009, Tyco reached a tentative settlement with the investment firms of Black-Rock Inc. and Nuveen Asset Management in separate, direct securities fraud actions also charging the theft of corporate assets and fraudulent accounting entries concealing Tyco's true financial condition from investors.

Of related interest, in June 2009, the U.S. Supreme Court declined certiorari review of the criminal convictions of former corporate executives (CEO) L. Dennis Kozlowski and (CFO) Mark H. Swartz. They were serving prison terms of 8 to 25 years. Kozlowski's lavish spending and parties were the subject of media attention during their criminal trials. They argued on appeal that the trial was flawed because they had been denied access to documents relating to the company's internal investigation. Kozlowski's attorney vowed he would continue the battle by filing a petition for writ of habeas corpus next.

SENTENCING

The postconviction stage of the criminal justice process, in which the defendant is brought before the court for the imposition of a penalty.

Chambers v. United States

The desire by the public to impose tougher criminal sanctions has led state legislatures and Congress to enact laws that increase the length of prison sentences for repeat violent offenders. The federal Armed Career Criminal Act of 1984 (ACCA) requires courts to impose a mandatory minimum 15-year sentence on anyone who has been convicted of three prior violent felonies or serious drug offenses. Due to its severity, the ACCA has spawned numerous lawsuits by prisoners seeking to have their prior convictions thrown out or downgraded from the list of crimes that are defined as a "violent felony." In *Chambers v. United States*, __U.S.__, 129 S.Ct. 687, __L.Ed.2d__ (2009), the Supreme Court reviewed whether a felon's conviction on a failure to report to a local prison for 11 weekends of incarceration qualified as a violent **felony** under ACCA. The Court ruled that it did not.

Deondery Chambers had numerous convictions before he pleaded guilty to a charge of being a felon unlawfully in possession of a firearm. At sentencing in an Illinois federal **district court** the prosecutor asked the judge to apply ACCA'a 15-year mandatory prison term. The prosecutor contended that three of Chambers' prior offenses qualified under ACCA as either violent felonies or serious drug offenses. Chambers admitted that his 1998 conviction for **robbery** and aggravated **battery** and his 1999 drug crime conviction met ACCA's definitions but denied that a third conviction did so. The third conviction arose out of his sentence on the 1998 robbery and battery conviction. The sentence required Chambers to report to a local prison for 11 weeks of incarceration. He failed to report on four of the weekends and was then convicted of the Illinois state crime of failing to report to a penal institution. The federal district court treated this crime as a form of what the Illinois **statute** called an escape from a penal institution and ruled that this conviction qualified as a violent felony for ACCA purposes. Chambers was sentenced to a mandatory minimum 15-year sentence. The Seventh **Circuit Court** of Appeals upheld the ruling, but other circuit courts of appeal had ruled otherwise. Therefore, the Supreme Court took Chambers' appeal to resolve the conflict.

In a unanimous ruling the Court reversed the Seventh Circuit decision. Justice STEPHEN BREYER, writing for the Court, noted that the Court looks to the classification of a crime in the most general sense. Whether a crime is a "violent felony" must be based not on a crime committed on a particular occasion but on the generic crime category. This means that the "categorical" approach requires a court to choose the correct category. Reviewing the Illinois statute in question, Justice Breyer identified seven different kinds of behavior that constitute crimes. They ranged from a prison escape to failing to abide by the terms of home confinement. In this case Chambers pleaded guilty to failing to report for periodic imprisonment.

Justice Breyer concluded that the Court had to decide whether the "failing to report" provisions of the state constituted a separate crime from the two provisions dealing with escape from a penal institution. He found that the behavior underlying a failure to report "would seem less likely to involve a risk of physical harm than the less passive, more aggressive behavior underlying an escape from custody." In addition, the statute placed the escape and failing to report provisions separately in its title and its body. It also placed the behaviors in two different felony classes of different degrees of seriousness. Therefore, Breyer grouped the failure to report provisions as a single category.

The failure to report crime satisfied ACCA's requirement that the crime be punishable by a term of imprisonment exceeding one year. However, the Court found that the crime did not satisfy the remaining requirements. There was no element of physical force used against another person, nor did it involve **burglary**, arson, extortion, or the use of explosives. Most importantly, it did not involve conduct that presented "a serious risk of physical injury to another." In Breyer's view the crime amounted to a "form of inaction," which was a "far cry" from violent and aggressive conduct covered by ACCA. He pointed to a study by the U.S. Sentencing Guidelines Commission that showed that not one felon who failed to report for incarceration was involved with a crime of violence in the period between nonappearance and later apprehension. This study strongly supported the Court's "intuitive belief" that failure to report did not involve a "serious potential risk of physical injury." Therefore, Chambers should not have been sentenced under ACCA.

Justice Samuel Alito, in a concurring opinion joined by Justice Clarence Thomas, argued that Congress needed to rewrite ACCA so as to provide the courts with a "specific list of expressly defined crimes that are deemed worthy of ACCA's sentencing enhancement." Only this approach could rescue the **federal courts** from the "mire" into which ACCA's draftsmanship and the Court categorical approach had "pushed us."

Dean v. United States

In *Dean v. United States,* No. 08-5274, 556 U.S. ___ (2008), the U.S. SUPREME COURT addressed the classic challenge of **statutory** language vs. factual exception. The quintessential question before the Court was whether a statutorily- enhanced sentence (for a firearm being discharged during the course of another crime) should apply, if the firearm was accidentally discharged? The Supreme Court said yes, affirming the decision of the U.S. Court of Appeals for the Eleventh Circuit.

Title 18 USC §924(c)(1)(A) makes criminal the carrying or use of a firearm during or related to the commission of a violent or drug-trafficking crime. Any individual convicted under this provision receives an enhanced five-year mandatory minimum sentence in addition to the sentence for the underlying crime. Moreover, the mandatory minimum sentence increases to seven years if "the firearm is brandished," and to ten years "if the firearm is discharged."

On November 4, 2004, a masked man, later identified as Christopher Dean, entered a bank in Rome, Georgia, waving a gun and yelling for everyone to get down. Dean then walked behind the teller counter and began removing money from the teller stations. The teller stations were manned with employees. While Dean was holding his gun in his right hand and grabbing bills with his left, his gun discharged, leaving a bullet hole in the partition between two stations. Witnesses later testified that he appeared surprised when the gun discharged, cursed to himself, then fled the bank. No one was injured in the **robbery**.

Dean and his brother-in-law were later arrested and charged with conspiracy to commit a robbery affecting interstate commerce under 18 USC §1951(a) and aiding and **abetting** each

other in using, carrying, possessing, and discharging a firearm during an armed robbery, under the subject federal law, 18 USC §924(c)(1)(A). At trial, Dean admitted that he had committed the robbery, and a jury found him guilty on both charges.

The U.S. **District Court** for the Northern District of Georgia sentenced Dean to a mandatory minimum term of ten years for the firearm conviction, because the firearm "discharged" during the course of the robbery. Dean appealed, arguing that the firearm discharge was unintentional and accidental. He further argued that, in order to impose the mandatory minimum sentence under 18 USC §924(c)(1)(A), prosecutors would have to prove that Dean intended to discharge the firearm. But the government argued that sentence enhancement statutes are not "stand alone" crimes. Therefore, no intent is required to establish them. The district court agreed and found that the **statute** could be applied without proof of intent.

A three-judge panel of the Eleventh **Circuit Court** of Appeals affirmed the district court's conclusion that no intent need be established in order to apply the mandatory minimum sentence under 18 USC §924(c)(1)(A). It expressly held that a sentence enhancement statute "merely reflects factors that will enhance sentencing, not elements of an offense." However, its decision created a conflict among circuit courts of appeal, for which reason the Supreme Court granted **certiorari** (review).

Chief Justice JOHN ROBERTS, Jr. delivered the opinion of the Court, joined by Justices Scalia, Kennedy, Souter, Thomas, Ginsburg, and Alito. The Court, noting that it "ordinarily resist[s] reading words or elements into a statute that do not appear on its face," affirmed the Eleventh Circuit's decision, refusing to add the element of "intent" into the statute. Specifically, it held that 18 USC §924(c)(1)(A) (iii) ("if the firearm is discharged, be sentenced to a term of imprisonment of not less than 10 years") required no separate proof of intent. The Court concluded that the plain text of the statute did not require the discharge of a firearm to be done knowingly or intentionally. The statute contained no **words of limitation**. "The 10-year mandatory minimum applies if a gun is discharged in the course of a violent or drug trafficking crime, whether on purpose or by accident," Justice Roberts wrote. He further observed that it was not unusual for a criminal to be punished for the unintended consequences of his crime.

Justice Breyers and Stevens each filed separate dissenting opinions. "Accidents happen," wrote Justice Stevens. "[B]ut they seldom give rise to criminal liability." His dissent opined that a mandatory enhanced sentence was "a species of criminal liability." He further opined that the structure of the statute suggested that Congress intended to provide escalating levels of imprisonment for increasingly culpable conduct, which accidental discharges were not. Second, at **common law**, provisions that impose criminal penalties require proof of intent, and that presumption should carry to an interpretation of 18 USC §924(c)(1)(A).

Justice Breyer agreed with Justice Stevens, adding that the accidental discharge did not constitute "use" of a firearm, as explained in an earlier Supreme Court decision, *Bailey v. United States*, 516 U.S. 137 (1995). Justice Breyer would have imposed the lesser of the enhanced minimum mandatory sentences, for "possession" only.

United States v. Hayes

The craft of writing legislation requires great attention to every detail of a law. The placement of a sentence, a clause, a comma, or a semicolon in a **statute** may affect how the law is interpreted and applied by a court. Over the years the courts have developed rules of **statutory** construction and U.S. Congress has enacted the Dictionary Act, which defines how words and grammar are to be construed. These concerns are heightened when a **criminal law** is at issue, for individuals should not have to guess whether there behavior may be governed by a statute. All of these elements converged in *United States v. Hayes*, __U.S.__, 129 S.Ct. 1079, __L.Ed.2d__ (2009), where the U.S. SUPREME COURT had to decide whether a federal criminal law barring persons convicted of domestic violence from possessing firearms required the person to have been convicted of a specific domestic violence law or whether it was sufficient to show that the person had assaulted someone with whom he had a domestic relationship. The Court held that the latter showing was sufficient, for the opposite

construction would contradict the intent of Congress. In making this decision the Court debated the use of various tools of statutory construction.

Randy Hayes was a resident of Marion County, West Virginia. In 2004 county law officers came to his house in response to a 911 call reporting domestic violence. Hayes consented to a search of his home and officers found a rifle. The officers also discovered that Hayes had recently possessed other firearms as well. Based on this evidence a federal **grand jury** indicted him, charging Hayes with a violation of the federal Gun Control Act of 1968. Hayes was indicted under a provision that makes it a **felony** for a person convicted of a crime of domestic violence from possessing a firearm. Hayes had been convicted in 1994 for **misdemeanor battery** in violation of West Virginia law. The victim of his battery was his then-wife who shared a child with Hayes who was cohabiting with him as a spouse.

Hayes contested the charge, arguing that under the Gun Control Act he would have had to been charged with a crime that contained that contained as an element a domestic relationship between aggressor and victim. In his case he charged under the generic crime of battery. After the federal **district court** rejected his argument, Hayes entered a conditional guilty plea and appealed. The Fourth **Circuit Court** of Appeals sided with Hayes, even though nine other courts of appeal had ruled that the Gun Control Act provision did not require that the the predicate (prior) offense had to contain as an element a domestic relationship between the offender and the victim. For that reason the Supreme Court agreed to hear the case and resolve the conflict.

The Court, in a 7-2 decision, reversed the Fourth Circuit Ruling. Justice RUTH BADER GINSBURG, writing for the majority, noted that both sides agreed that a Gun Control Act conviction required that a misdemeanor crime of domestic violence must have as an element the use or attempted use of physical force. Second, the crime must be committed by a person who has a specified domestic relationship with the victim. The only question was whether the law called for a further limitation: must the statute defining the prior offense include, as a discrete element, the existence of a domestic relationship between the offender and the victim? The Court concluded that the nine courts of appeal got it right when they concluded that the Gun Control Act does not require a prior offense law of that specificity. Instead, the government has to prove **beyond a reasonable doubt** that the prior conviction was, in fact, an offense committed by the defendant against a spouse or other domestic victim.

Justice Ginsburg examined the domestic violence provision of the Gun Control Act, which was added in 1996 in recognition of the problem of domestic violence. She reviewed the grammar and punctuation of the provision and concluded that the most sensible way of construing it was to require that a domestic relationship be established at trial rather than through a "denominated element" of the prior offense. Ginsburg admitted that the provision could have been drafted more clearly but restricting the application of the law to specific crimes of domestic violence would "frustrate Congress' manifest purpose." As of 1996, when the provision was added, only about one-third of the states had criminal statutes that specifically proscribed domestic violence. Given that fact, she concluded that it was "highly improbable" that Congress meant to extend the firearm possession ban "only to the relatively few domestic abusers prosecuted under laws rendering a domestic relationship an element of the offense." Lacking a legislative record on this provision, the Court found that the intent of Congress was best served by not requiring the more specific domestic violence offense.

Chief Justice JOHN ROBERTS, in a dissenting opinion joined by Justice ANTONIN SCALIA, rejected the construction of the provision supplied by the majority. In his view the rules of construction supported a more restrictive reading of the provision's application.

SEX DISCRIMINATION

AT&T Corporation v. Hulteen

Until the end of the 1970s, employers routinely discriminated against women who went on pregnancy leave. For those women who were part of an employer **pension** plan based on seniority, the time spent on pregnancy leave was treated differently than for other medical disability leaves. In the case of the telecommunications

company AT&T, those who took disability leave did not lose service credits, while women on pregnancy leave lost service credits. The U.S. SUPREME COURT found this practice legal, leading Congress in 1978 to enact legislation to end this discrimination. As women began to retire, they noted that the service credits they lost before the law was changed were not restored when calculating their pension benefits. Several circuit courts of appeals disagreed whether this calculation was legal, leading the Supreme Court, in *AT & T Corporation v. Hulteen*, __U.S.__, 129 S.Ct. 1962, __L.Ed.2d__ (2009), to consider the issue. The court concluded that AT&T did not violate the law when it gave the women less service credit for pregnancy leave than they would have accrued on the same leave for disability.

Noreen Hulteen and three other women employed by AT & T, lost between two and seven months of service credit while on pregnancy leaves before 1979. Leave for pregnancy was treated as personal rather than disability leave. AT & T, like other companies, relied on the Supreme Court 1976 decision in *General Elec. Co. v Gilbert*, 429 U.S.125, 97 S.Ct. 401, 50 L.Ed.2d 343. In this case the court concluded that a disability benefit plan excluding disabilities related to pregnancy was not sex-based discrimination within the meaning of Title VII of the Civil Rights Act of 1964. 42 U.S. C.A. §2000e *et seq.* In 1978 Congress amended Title VII when it passed the Pregnancy Discrimination Act (PDA). The law overturned the *Gilbert* decision and made it illegal to treat pregnancy-related conditions less favorably than other medical decisions. The law became effective in 1979, at which time AT&T adopted a new disability plan that provided service credit for pregnancy leave on the same basis as leave taken for other temporary disabilities. The company did not make any retroactive adjustments to the service credit calculations of women who had taken pregnancy leave prior to 1979. When Hulteen and the other three employees retired, they found that their pension benefits were less because of the loss of service credits.

The women filed a complaint with the EQUAL EMPLOYMENT OPPORTUNITY COMMISSION (EEOC), which agreed that AT&T had violated the PDA by not crediting the pre-PDA pregnancy leaves back to employees. Hulteen then filed a civil rights lawsuit in California federal **district court**. The district court ruled in favor of Hulteen, citing a Ninth **Circuit Court** decision which found a Title VII violation where post-PDA retirement eligibility calculations incorporated pre-PDA accrual rules that differentiated on the basis of pregnancy. The Ninth Circuit upheld the district court ruling as well as its prior decision. This decision conflicted with rulings by the Sixth and Seventh Circuits, which found no violation of Title VII in similar circumstances. The Supreme Court agreed to hear the company's appeal to resolve this conflict.

The Court, in a 7-2 decision, overturned the Ninth Circuit ruling. Justice DAVID SOUTER, writing for the majority, noted that the company's pensions were based on a seniority system; the longer an employee worked, the greater the amount of the pension upon retirement. Under a provision of Title VII, employers may legally apply different standards of compensation, terms and conditions of employment under a "bona fide" seniority system so long as "such differences are not the result of an intention to discriminate because of race, color, religion, sex, or national origin." In this case AT&T's system was **bona fide**. The pre-PDA rules were not discriminatory because of the *Gilbert* decision.

Justice Souter concluded that the only way Hulteen could prove discrimination would be to show that the PDA applied retroactively to "recharacterize the acts as having been illegal when done, contra *Gilbert*." However, there was "no such clear intent" by Congress to apply the law retroactively. Therefore, AT&T had a legitimate right to manage the pension plan without recalculating service time.

Justice RUTH BADER GINSBURG, in a dissenting opinion joined by Justice STEPHEN BREYER, contended that the loss of service credits was not protected by the pre-PDA state of the law. She argued that AT&T "committed a current violation of Title VII when, post-PDA, it did not totally discontinue reliance upon a pension calculation premised on the notion that pregnancy-based classifications display no gender bias."

Fitzgerald v. Barnstable School Committee

The federal civil rights law 42 U.S.C. § 1983 provides an avenue for plaintiffs to sue local governments and government officials for damages for deprivations of rights guaranteed by the Constitution and by federal laws. However, the Supreme Court has ruled that when a federal **statute** contains a comprehensive set of procedures for pursuing claims against governments and government officials, a plaintiff cannot sue under § 1983. For more than twenty years the Court has reviewed federal statutes to make a final determination as to whether a private **right of action** under these laws prevent plaintiffs from using § 1983. In *Fitzgerald v. Barnstable School Committee*, U.S.__, 129 S.Ct. 788, L.Ed.2d __, (2009), the Court held that the private right of action provided under Title IX of the Education Amendments of 1972 does not bar plaintiffs from also using § 1983. Title IX prohibits education systems that received federal funds from discriminating on the basis of sex.

The daughter of Lisa and Robert Fitzgerald was a kindergarten student in the Barnstable, Massachusetts, school system, and rode the bus to school each morning. One day she told her parents that, whenever she wore a dress, a third-grade boy on the school bus would bully her into lifting her skirt. Lisa Fitzgerald immediately called the school principal, who met that day with the Fitzgeralds, their daughter, and another school official. The principal and the other official then questioned the alleged bully, who denied the allegations. The other official also interviewed the bus driver and several students who rode the bus. She concluded that she could not corroborate the girl's version of the events. The Fitzgeralds' daughter then provided new details of the alleged abuse to her parents, who relayed them to the principal. Specifically, she told her parents that in addition to bullying her into raising her skirt, the boy coerced her into pulling down her underpants and spreading her legs.

The local police department conducted an independent investigation and concluded there was insufficient evidence to bring criminal charges against the boy. Based partly on the police investigation and partly on the school's own investigation, the principal similarly concluded there was insufficient evidence to warrant discipline. The principal proposed remedial measures to the Fitzgeralds. He suggested transferring their daughter to a different bus or leaving rows of empty seats between the kindergartners and older students on the original bus. The Fitzgeralds felt that these proposals punished their daughter instead of the boy and countered with alternative proposals. They suggested transferring the boy to a different bus or placing a monitor on the original bus, but the school superintended declined to act. The Fitzgeralds drove their daughter to school to avoid further bullying on the bus, but she continued to report unsettling incidents at school. The Fitzgeralds reported each incident to the principal. The Fitzgeralds' daughter had an unusual number of absences during the remainder of the school year.

The Fitzgeralds filed a lawsuit in federal **district court**, alleging that the school system's response to their allegations of sexual harassment had been inadequate, resulting in further harassment to their daughter. Their complaint included a claim for violation of Title IX against the Barnstable School Committee (the school system's governing body), and claims under § 1983 for violations of Title IX and the **Equal Protection** Clause of the FOURTEENTH AMENDMENT against the school committee and the superintendent. The district court dismissed both claims. The First **Circuit Court** of Appeals upheld the dismissal of the Title IX claim on the grounds that it lacked merit; the response of the school committee and the superintendent to the reported harassment had been objectively reasonable. As to the § 1983 claim, the court upheld the dismissal because Title IX's implied private remedy was "sufficiently comprehensive" to preclude the use of § 1983 to **advance statutory** claims based on Title IX itself. The court concluded that Congress intended the Title IX remedy to be the sole means of vindicating constitutional rights "to be free from gender discrimination perpetrated by educational institutions."

The Supreme Court, in a unanimous decision, disagreed. It held that that Title IX did not preclude a § 1983 claim. Justice Samuel Alito, writing for the court, reviewed the Court's prior **case law** on this issue and noted that unlike other statutes that provide detailed procedures for pursuing claims against governments and government officials, Title IX has no such procedures. In addition, unlike other statutes that preclude private rights of action under § 1983, Title IX does not require the exhaustion of administrative remedies before filing suit. Moreover, the grounds for establishing liability under both statutes are not "congruent." In light of the divergent coverage

of Title IX and the Equal Protection Clause, as well as the absence of a comprehensive remedial scheme comparable to those at issue in other federal statutes, the Court held that that Title IX was not meant to be an exclusive mechanism for addressing gender discrimination in schools, or a substitute for § 1983 suits as a means of enforcing constitutional rights. Therefore, § 1983 lawsuits based on the Equal Protection Clause are available to plaintiffs alleging unconstitutional gender discrimination in schools.

SEX OFFENSES

A class of sexual conduct prohibited by the law.

New Jersey Supreme Court Voids Residency Restrictions for Sex Offenders

In 1994, the New Jersey State Legislature enacted the landmark MEGAN'S LAW (N.J.S.A. 2C: 7-1 to 7-19) that required convicted sex offenders to register with local police authorities after being released from prison. The law was passed following the brutal kidnapping, rape, and murder of 7-year-old Megan Kanka by her neighbor, Jesse Timmendequas, a repeat sex offender who had just been released from prison.

Under Megan's Law, offenders were required to give police, among other things, their address, Social Security Number, offender classification, details of the crime(s) and ages of the victim(s), and a photograph of the offender. The law created three tiers of offenders, the most serious (Tier III) having the strictest reporting and residency requirements. Many states and communities quickly enacted their own versions of the law. Several included new requirements and restrictions not covered in Megan's Law.

On May 7, 2009, the New Jersey State Supreme Court, by an unanimous 6-0 vote, ruled that towns could not ban sex offenders from living near schools, parks, or other places where children gather. The court concluded that since Megan's Law already gave the state's Parole Board the authority and responsibility to decide where sex offenders could live, more restrictive local ordinances were in conflict with the state's uniform requirements. *G.H. v. Township of Galloway,* No. A-64/65-08 (N.J. 2009). The decision served to void at least 120 municipal laws across the state.

The case was filed on behalf of G.H., a minor whose name was protected, who in 2009 was a senior at Richard Stockton College in Galloway, New Jersey. When G.H. was 15, he was caught engaging in sex with a 13-year-old girl and was convicted as a minor for improper sexual contact. Years later, after enrolling in college, he was told by police that the college's predator **ordinance** banned him from the campus.

The AMERICAN CIVIL LIBERTIES UNION (ACLU) had been waiting for the right case to use as a flagship in its challenge to residency restrictions placed on sex offenders. This case represented the perfect, sympathetic scenario to prove ACLU's point that municipalities had overreached their authority by enacting such ordinances. The ACLU had argued that such ordinances were ineffective because they either forced sex offenders to "go underground" (not register with local authorities) or forced them out of living environments that could have been supportive and rehabilitative. This was particularly true in small municipalities, where community buildings or parks are located within closer proximity to one another. The only way that offenders could find residential quarters that were not near schools, parks, playgrounds, or daycare centers was to essentially move away from the community or town in its entirety. This raised civil rights issues to present squarely before a court.

Two of the challenged local ordinances, in the communities of Galloway and Cherry Hill, New Jersey, were consolidated in the case. Cherry Hill's ordinance prohibited sex offenders from living within 2,500 feet of schools, parks, and daycare centers. But under Megan's Law, an offender is barred from residing in any place only if not approved by his/her parole officer, and using a sex offender criminal record to deny housing is prohibited. The Cherry Hill law was challenged by two offenders who were found guilty in municipal court for residing in a hotel near a school, even though that location had been approved by their parole officer(s).

The New Jersey Supreme Court wrote no full opinion in the case. Rather, it affirmed the judgment of the lower **Appellate** Division, based substantially on the same reasons. It declined to offer guidance to local public and county attorneys about the limits to Megan's Law's **preemption** of municipal action, or how to draft ordinances that would withstand

legal challenge. "The judicial function operates best when there is a concrete dispute presented," noted the court. "The only matter before the court is the validity of the challenged ordinances."

Within days of the decision, state legislators and angry community leaders were working together to create a statewide, uniform law to supplement Megan's Law. The proposed bill, A-641, would limit local residency restrictions for Megan's Law registrants to no closer than 2,000 feet from places frequented by children. Supporters also wanted to ensure that each local ordinance would be consistent and could not be manipulated to create **zoning** schemes which could effectively block offenders from residing anywhere in the town.

On June 8, 2009, the state's Assembly Judiciary Committee unanimously approved legislation restricting sex offenders from living within 500 feet of schools, playgrounds, or daycare centers. However, at that time, the measure did not have the support of local communities or the public defender's office. The New Jersey State League of Municipalities also declined support. While agreeing that a statewide standard was needed to supplement Megan's Law, local officials believed the proposed bill would not withstand legal challenge (as overly-restrictive), which would result in significant legal fees and litigation costs imposed on taxpayers.

SIXTH AMENDMENT

Montejo v. Louisiana

In an important **criminal law** and procedure case involving police questioning outside the presence **of counsel**, the U.S. SUPREME COURT, in a complex and narrow 5-4 decision, overruled one of its own previous decisions [*Michigan v. Jackson*, 475 US 625 (1986)] and vacated the judgment of the Supreme Court of Louisiana. *Montejo v. Louisiana*, No. 07-1529, 556 U.S. ___ (2009). The case received less media coverage than expected because the high court did not render a dispositive opinion on the underlying merits of the present case, but instead remanded for further proceedings consistent with its overruling of *Michigan v. Jackson*.

The SIXTH AMENDMENT to the U.S. Constitution provides that "[i]n all criminal prosecutions, the accused shall enjoy the right. to have the Assistance of Counsel for his defence." The earlier *Jackson* decision, argued on Sixth Amendment grounds, held that "if police initiate interrogation after a defendant's assertion, at an arraignment or similar proceeding, of his right to counsel, any waiver of the defendant's right to counsel for that police-initiated interrogation is invalid." On the other end of the spectrum, the Supreme Court has at a minimum *noted* that once the right to counsel attaches, the police may nonetheless initiate interrogation without the presence of defense counsel if the accused has not yet requested, retained, or "accepted by appointment" counsel. *Patterson v. Illinois,* 487 US 285 at 290 n.3 (1988).

Jesse Jay Montejo, an indigent, seemed to fall in the cracks between these cases, although only the *Jackson* case was at issue. On September 6 and 7, 2002, after waiving his *Miranda* rights, he was taken into custody and questioned by police in connection with a **robbery** and murder. During this time he admitted that he had shot and killed the victim, and the police interrogation was videotaped. Under Louisiana's "72-hour hearing" law, he was brought before a judge on the morning of September 10, 2002 for Louisiana's version of a **preliminary hearing**. At the hearing, where he was charged with first-degree murder, he stood mute. The court then appointed a public defender to represent him.

Later that same afternoon, two police detectives visited him in his prison cell and asked that he accompany them on an excursion to locate the murder weapon (which he had previously told police he had thrown into a lake). He was again read his *Miranda* rights and agreed to go along. During this excursion, he wrote a letter of apology to the victim's widow. When he was later returned to his cell, he met for the first time his court-appointed counsel.

At trial, Montejo's letter of apology was admitted into evidence over the objection of defense counsel. He was ultimately convicted of first-degree murder and sentenced to death. The admission of the letter into evidence at trial became the substantive issue on appeal.

Montejo's argument on appeal was that the letter should have been suppressed under *Michigan v. Jackson.* The Louisiana Supreme Court upheld his conviction and sentence and rejected his argument under *Michigan v. Jackson.* The state high court found that the *Jackson* provisions were not triggered unless and until the defendant actually requested counsel or otherwise affirmatively asserted his Sixth Amendment right to counsel. Since Montejo had stood mute at his preliminary hearing, he had made no such request or assertion. So, according to the Louisiana Supreme Court, the only question was whether he had knowingly and voluntarily waived his right, to which the court concluded he had. The U.S. Supreme Court then granted review.

Justice Scalia, writing the majority opinion for a very divided Court, wrote, "The *only* question raised by this case, and the only one addressed by the *Jackson* rule, is whether courts must *presume* that such a waiver is invalid under certain circumstances." (emphasis in the original). While he then endorsed (as "correct") the Louisiana Supreme Court's rejection of Montejo's *Jackson* claim, he went on to show why Louisiana's interpretation of *Jackson* would not work in other states. It might work in states where there exists a requirement for an indigent defendant to formally request counsel before an appointment is made. But in at least half the states, counsel is appointed at the discretion of the court, without request from the defendant.

However, eliminating the "invocation requirement" (requirement that a defendant must affirmatively request his Sixth Amendment right to counsel) would totally defeat the rationale of *Jackson,* which created a presumption. Accordingly, concluded the majority opinion, *Michigan v. Jackson* did not "pay its way" and should be, and was now, overruled. "Because of the protections created by this Court in *Miranda* and related cases, there is little if any chance that a defendant will be badgered into waiving his right to have counsel present during interrogation," Justice Scalia wrote. He also took time to explain why *stare decisis* (to adhere to decided cases) would not require the retention of the *Jackson* holdings, since other decisions provided ample protections for defendants.

One of those "other" decisions was *Edwards v. Arizona,* 451 US 477 (1981), which was designed to prevent police from coercing suspects into waiving previously-asserted *Miranda* FIFTH AMENDMENT rights against self-incrimination. Justice Scalia remanded the case to provide

Montejo with "an opportunity to contend that his letter of apology should still have been suppressed under the rule of *Edwards*."

Justice Scalia was joined by Chief Justice Roberts and Justices Kennedy, Thomas, and Alito. Justice Alito also wrote a concurring opinion, joined by Justice Kennedy. Justice Stevens filed a dissenting opinion, in which Justices Ginsburg and Souter joined. Justice Stevens, who authored the *Jackson* decision, found insufficient rationale for it being overruled. Justice Breyer also wrote a separate dissent in which he agreed with Justice Stevens and further asserted that *stare decisis* should have applied.

Oregon v. Ice

Since 2000, the U.S. SUPREME COURT has addressed the constitutionality under the SIXTH AMENDMENT of various schemes that authorized judges to increase criminal sentences. The Court has prohibited the use of any sentencing scheme that allows a judge to impose a sentence above the **statutory** maximum based on a fact, other than a prior conviction, not found by a jury. The Court established the standard in *Apprendi v. New Jersey*, 530 U.S. 466, 120 Ct. 2348, 147 L.Ed.2d 435 (2000). In *Blakely v. Washington*, 542 U.S. 296, 124 S.Ct. 2531, 159 L.Ed.2d 403 (2005) the Court struck down the state of Washington's sentencing guidelines system as violating the Sixth Amendment. One year later the Court did the same with the Federal Sentencing Guidelines in *United States v. Booker*, 543 U.S. 220, 125 S.Ct. 738, 160 L.Ed.2d 621(2005). In 2007 the Court, in *Cunningham v. California*, __U.S.__, 127 S.Ct. 856, 166 L.Ed.2d 856 (2007), invalidated a California determinate sentencing law that gave judges the ability to raise the maximum sentence based on additional facts. However, the application of the *Apprendi* precedent was rejected in *Oregon v. Ice*, __U.S.__, 129 S.Ct. 711, __L.Ed.2d__ (2009), where the Court held that states were free to assign judges the task of finding facts necessary to impose consecutive rather than concurrent sentences for multiple sentences.

An Oregon jury convicted Thomas Ice on two counts of first-degree **burglary** and four counts of first-degree sexual assault. Ice twice entered an 11-year-old girl's apartment in the complex he managed and sexually assaulted her. Ice was sentenced under a state law that generally provided for concurrent sentences. However, the trial judge was given the authority to impose consecutive sentences in certain circumstances. The judge in this case first found that the two burglaries constituted separate incidents and imposed consecutive sentences for these crimes. He also found that two of the sexual assaults qualified as well under the sentencing law for consecutive sentences. By imposing four consecutive sentences, Ice was given 340 months of imprisonment instead of the 90 months if served concurrently. Ice appealed his sentences, arguing that under the Sixth Amendment it was the jury and not the sentencing judge that had to find the facts that permitted the imposition of consecutive sentences. The Oregon Court of Appeals upheld the sentencing, but the Oregon Supreme Court reversed that decision. It concluded that *Apprendi* required a jury to to find the facts required under the **statute** for consecutive sentences. Because other state supreme courts had ruled differently, the U.S. Supreme Court agreed to hear Oregon's appeal.

The Court, in a 5-4 decision, reversed the Oregon Supreme Court. Justice RUTH BADER GINSBURG, writing for the majority, concluded that there was a significant difference between *Apprendi* and the current case: juries traditionally played no part in this part of the sentencing function. Most states have continued the common-law tradition of entrusting to judges the "unfettered discretion" to decide whether sentences for discrete offenses should be served consecutively or concurrently. Some states presume that sentences for multiple offenses are to be served consecutively but give the trial judges the ability to order concurrent sentences upon finding specific causes. Other states, including Oregon, presume that multiple offenses are to be served concurrently; a judge can order consecutive sentences only by finding certain facts.

Justice Ginsburg distinguished *Apprendi* and the other Court rulings from the Oregon case, as they had all involved sentencing for a discrete crime, not for multiple offenses different in character or committed at different times. The Court found that historical practice and respect for state sovereignty required the rejection of jury-based findings of fact for determinations of consecutive and concurrent sentencing. Juries had never played a role in this part of the sentencing process. At the time the Sixth

Amendment was ratified the Framers would not have contemplated juries having such a responsibility. In addition, **federal courts** should defer to the states as to how they make consecutive and concurrent sentences. If the Court applied *Apprendi*, it would soon expand into sentencing determinations that went beyond the length of incarceration. Trial judges "often find facts about the nature of the offense or the character of the defendant in determining, for example, the length of supervised release following service of a prison sentence."

Justice ANTONIN SCALIA, in a dissenting opinion joined by three justices, attacked the majority's reasoning. As the architect of *Apprendi*, Scalia contended that it should apply to the Oregon sentencing scheme. He noted that for many defendants, "the difference between consecutive and concurrent sentences is more important than a jury verdict of innocence on any single count." In his view only a jury could find the facts to support a consecutive sentence.

Kansas v. Ventris

It has long been well-established that a jailhouse informant cannot deliberately elicit an incriminating statement from an inmate about a crime for which the inmate has been charged, without violating the inmate's SIXTH AMENDMENT right to counsel. (This would make the statement inadmissible at trial for purposes of proving or tending to prove guilt.) *Massiah v. United States,* 377 U.S. 201 (1964). Later, in *Kuhlman v. Wilson,* 477 U.S. 436, 459 (1986), the U.S. SUPREME COURT pointed out that a Sixth Amendment violation does not occur if the informant merely acts as an "ear" or "listening post" and simply reports what the suspect had said. Such incriminating statements, if not deemed violations of the suspect's Sixth Amendment rights, can often be admitted into evidence as non-hearsay statements or exceptions because they are "admissions" or statements made against the speaker's own interest.

In the present case, *Kansas v. Ventris,* No. 07-1356, 556 U.S. ___ (2009), the U.S. Supreme Court was faced with the novel question of whether a concededly-elicited statement from a suspect to an informant, in violation of his Sixth Amendment rights, could still be used at trial for purposes of impeachment (but not to prove guilt). By a 5-2 majority, the Court said yes.

In *Ventris,* Donnie Ray Ventris and his girlfriend, Rhonda Theel, after two days of alleged drug use and lack of sleep, decided to confront a third person, Ernest Hicks, at his house. One or both of them ultimately shot and killed Hicks, took money and his cell phone, and drove off in his truck. Officers received a tip from persons who had helped transport the couple to Hick's house, and arrested the pair. Among other things, they were both charged with murder and aggravated **robbery**. The murder charge was ultimately dropped against Theel in return for her guilty plea to robbery and her testimony identifying Ventris as the shooter.

Prior to trial, officers had planted an informant in Ventris's holding cell, telling him to keep his ears open and to listen for incriminating statements. However, the over-zealous informant attempted to elicit statements from Ventris by suggesting that Ventris appeared to have something serious weighing on his mind. In response, Ventris divulged to the informant that "he'd shot [Hicks] in his head and in his chest" and taken "his keys, his wallet, about $350, and.a vehicle." The informant reported this to the government officers.

At trial, defendant Ventris took the stand in his own defense and identified his girlfriend Theel as the perpetrator of both the murder and the robbery. Prosecutors then sought to call the informant as an impeachment witness to testify to Ventris's prior contradictory statement. While the State conceded there was "probably a violation" of Ventris's Sixth Amendment right to counsel, it argued that the informant's testimony of Ventris's earlier conflicting statement should be admitted for purposes of impeachment. Prosecutors argued that just because there may have been a violation of his right to counsel, this did not give Ventris "a license to just get on the stand and lie."

The trial court agreed and allowed the testimony, but instructed the jury to "consider with caution" any testimony given in exchange for benefits from the State. Ventris was acquitted on the **felony** murder charge, but found guilty of aggravated **burglary** and aggravated robbery.

Ultimately, the Kansas Supreme Court reversed the conviction, holding that "[o]nce a criminal prosecution has commenced, the defendant's statements made to an undercover informant surreptitiously acting as an agent for the State are not admissible at trial for any reason, including the impeachment of the defendant's testimony."

In reversing the Kansas Supreme Court, the U.S. Supreme Court articulated two key reasons for its conclusion. First, the resulting exclusion of incriminating statements as inadmissible, if obtained in violation of Sixth Amendment rights, is intended to serve as a deterrent against such illegal actions by interrogators or police officials. But admitting such statements for impeachment purposes hardly provides an incentive to violate the law. Rather, said the Court, "Officers have significant incentive to ensure that they and their informants comply with the Constitution's demands, since statements lawfully obtained can be used for all purposes rather than simply for impeachment."

Second, suppressing such statements would encourage perjury and undermine the integrity of the whole legal process, said the Court. If a defendant testifies in a way that contradicts prior statements, prosecution would be denied the use of traditional truth-testing trial tactics normally part of the adversarial process. This would be a very high price for prosecutors to pay for infringement of the right to counsel at a prior stage. Therefore, introduction of prior inconsistent statements made to an informant, for impeachment purposes, are admissible.

Justice ANTONIN SCALIA delivered the opinion of the Court, joined by Chief Justice Roberts and Justices Kennedy, Souter, Thomas, Breyer, and Alito. Justice Stevens filed a dissenting opinion, in which he was joined by Justice Ginsburg. The dissent objected to the Court's characterization of a violation as occurring solely at the time the State subjects a counseled defendant to an un-counseled interrogation, "not when the fruits of the encounter are used against the defendant at trial." The dissent further opined that "permitting the State to cut corners in criminal proceedings taxes the legitimacy of the entire criminal process."

Vermont v. Brillon

In *Vermont v. Brillon*, No. 08-88, 556 U.S. ___ (2009), defendant Brillon lost his appeal to have his conviction overturned on the basis of being deprived of a speedy trial under the Sixth Amendment to the U.S. Constitution. In rejecting

A mug shot of Michael Brillon, 2001.

AP IMAGES

his argument, the high court reversed a decision of the Vermont Supreme Court.

Brillon had alleged that his trial delays were caused by the public defender (defense counsel) assigned to him. The Vermont Supreme Court agreed, holding that the delay in bringing him to trial was a violation of his constitutional right. But the U.S. Supreme Court said that the constitutional right to a speedy trial was intended to protect against the *government's* unjustified delay in bringing about a trial. Conversely, a public defender stands in the shoes of the defendant, and represents *him* before the court. A public defender is not a state actor. It was not the government that caused the delay, but rather the defendant and defense counsel. Therefore, no Sixth Amendment violation occurred.

In July 2001, Brillon had been arrested and charged with domestic violence. Although domestic violence was a misdemeanor crime in Vermont, Brillon had three prior felony convictions and was charged with an enhanced felony domestic assault as an habitual offender. Being indigent, he was assigned a public defender to represent him in this matter. Three years after being charged, in June 2004, Brillon was convicted and sentenced to 12 to 20 years. He had spent the entire period between being charged in 2001 and his trial in 2004 in jail, without bail.

Prosecution argued that Brillon delayed his own case by filing incessant and repetitive motions seeking to dismiss six different lawyers assigned to him. They also argued that Brillon created other conflicts that he hoped might lead to dismissal of his case.

Sonia Sotomayor.
AP IMAGES

On the other hand, Brillon argued that his first counsel told him that he was unprepared for trial because of a heavy caseload, so he fired him. Brillon then argued that other counsel assigned to him "subsequently did little or nothing to bring the case to trial."

In determining whether a Sixth Amendment right to a speedy trial has been violated, courts generally look to the U.S. Supreme Court's four-prong balancing test established in *Barker v. Wingo*, 407 U.S. 514 (1972). The *Wingo*, test considers (1) the length of the delay; (2) the reason for the delay, (3) the extent to which the defendant asserted the right to a speedy trial; and (4) the prejudice to the defendant caused by the delay.

The Supreme Court of Vermont did in fact rely on *Wingo* for guidance in reviewing Brillon's case. For the first factor, the Vermont court found that a nearly three-year delay was far more than what would be necessary to trigger review. As to the second prong (the reason for delay), the Vermont high court acknowledged Brillon's role in causing much of the delay (about eleven months' worth). Notwithstanding, the Vermont court found that most of the remaining period of delay was attributed to the state, more specifically, by the "inability or unwillingness of assigned [defense] counsel to move the case forward." Delays caused by the Vermont Defender General's office were attributable to the state, said the Vermont court, because that office "is part of the criminal justice system." As to the fourth prong (prejudice), the Vermont court held that the three years in waiting for trial were sufficient in length to potentially erode evidence such as witnesses' memories, and unfairly prejudice Brillon. Accordingly, the Vermont Supreme Court dismissed the charges against Brillon, vacated his conviction, and prohibited prosecutors from again trying him on those charges. The majority opinion found that "the failure of the system to provide the defendant a constitutionally guaranteed speedy trial is attributable to the prosecution, and not defendant."

On appeal to the U.S. Supreme Court, state prosecutors referred to the ruling as "what appears to be a first in the history of American jurisprudence" wherein the Vermont Supreme Court "vacated a felony conviction and barred a retrial due to speedy trial right violations that were caused solely by the defendant and his public defender(s)."

Writing for the 7-2 majority U.S. Supreme Court, Justice Ruth Ginsburg stated at the outset, "The Vermont Supreme Court erred in ranking assigned counsel essentially as state actors in the criminal justice system…Assigned counsel, just as retained counsel, act on behalf of their clients, and delays sought by counsel are ordinarily attributable to the defendants they represent."

(The Court did note that it was possible to charge the state for delay caused from a systemic breakdown in the public defender system (*Polk County v. Dodson,* 454 U.S. 312). However, in this case, the Vermont Supreme Court made no determination (and nothing in the record suggested) that institutional problems caused any part in Brillon's delay.

Justices Breyer and Stevens dissented, opining that the case did not squarely present the question reviewed. They would have dismissed the writ of certiorari as improvidently granted.

❖ SOTOMAYOR, SONIA

Sonia Sotomayor became the first Hispanic-American woman to be confirmed to a seat on the U.S. Supreme Court, on August 6, 2009. Nominated by President Barack Obama to replace retiring Associate Justice David Souter, Sotomayor declared that her heart was "bursting with gratitude" to her family and friends, and called the nomination "the most humbling honor of my life." President Obama called Sotomayor "an inspiring woman who I believe will make a great justice."

Sotomayor was born in New York City in 1954, the elder of two children, to parents of Puerto Rican birth. The Sotomayor family lived in a housing project called Bronxdale Houses in the Bronx. As a child, Sonia was diagnosed with juvenile diabetes at age 8. One year later her father died, leaving Sotomayor's mother, a registered nurse, to raise her daughter and son alone, putting both children through Catholic school. Upon graduating from high school, she was accepted into Princeton University, graduating summa cum laude from that institution in 1976, with a bachelor's degree in history. Three years later she earned a law degree from Yale University, where she had edited the Yale Law Journal.

After graduating from Yale, Sotomayor worked for several years as an assistant district

1954	Born, New York City
1976	Graduated from Princeton University
1991	Named to judgeship for U.S District Court
1997	Named to Second Circuit Court of Appeals
2009	Nominated to U.S. Supreme Court

attorney in New York. She married for a short time, but her marriage ended with no children. Sotomayor then became a private-practice attorney specializing in intellectual property at the New York-based firm of Pavia & Harcourt. In 1991 she was nominated by President George H. W. Bush to fill a seat on the U.S. District Court for the Southern District of New York. (Interestingly, a year earlier, Bush had nominated David Souter—the justice Sotomayor is slated to replace—to the U.S. Supreme Court.) Bush's successor, President Bill Clinton, nominated Sotomayor to the 2nd Circuit Court of Appeals, and she was confirmed by the Republican-majority Senate in 1997.

On May 1, 2009 David Souter announced his retirement, and within a short time President Obama's short list of nominees was released to and discussed among the national press. Most of the candidates listed were women and two were Hispanic—Sotomayor being among the two. Hispanic and women's groups encouraged Obama to nominate a Hispanic or a woman, in part to fill a gap left by Associate Justice Sandra Day O'Connor, who retired in 2006. In speaking of the task of finding a replacement for Souter, Obama stated that he would search for a justice who embraces both the rule of law and "the quality of empathy, of understanding and identifying with people's hopes and struggles."

Upon confirmation by the Senate Judiciary Committee and then by the Senate, Sotomayor is expected to be a firm anchor on the activist liberal wing of the Supreme Court. In light of this, much debate among American political commentators will center upon the perennial question of whether jurists should interpret established law or (in effect) create new laws, a debate between the ends and means of law.

SOVEREIGN IMMUNITY

The legal protection that prevents a sovereign state or person from being sued without consent.

Ministry of Defense of Iran v. Elahi

In a case touching upon international terrorism, retribution, **sovereign immunity**, and the reaches of American courts, the U.S. SUPREME COURT ruled in April 2009 that the brother of a murdered Iranian dissident could not collect $2.8 million in damages awarded to him by a U.S. federal **district court** by attaching money damages awarded to Iran in another unrelated contract case. *Ministry of Defense and Support for the Armed Forces of the Islamic Republic of Iran v. Elahi,* No. 07-615, 556 U.S. ___ (2009). (The case was commonly referred to in media sources as the "Iran Compensation Case.") It also represented the second time this matter was before the high court.

Two separate and unrelated cases led up to this controversy. In 1977, Iran's then-Ministry of Defense ("Iran") had entered into a contract with an American defense contractor, Cubic Defense Systems (Cubic), for the purchase of military equipment to be used for an Iranian air combat training system. However, after the Iranian Revolution in 1979, during which the Shah of Iran was deposed and fled the country, Cubic breached its contract and sold the equipment elsewhere (Canada). In 1997, Iran was successful against Cubic before the International Court of Arbitration, which awarded the Iranian Ministry of Defense $2.8 million in damages. Cubic refused to pay the award, and Iran filed suit in U.S. District Court for the Southern District of California in San Diego. Again, Iran prevailed, and the district court ordered Cubic to pay the award plus accrued interest (the Cubic Judgment).

Meanwhile, on the opposite U.S. coast a few years later (2000), and while the Cubic judgment was pending, plaintiff Dariush Elahi filed a **wrongful death** suit against Iran in the U.S. District Court for the DISTRICT OF COLUMBIA. He alleged that Iranian agents had assassinated his brother in Paris in 1990. He obtained a **default judgment** against Iran of approximately $312 million in damages. Since it was a default judgment, Elahi sought to collect some of the money immediately by attaching the $2.8 million that had been awarded to Iran in the Cubic Judgment.

Iran then asserted a defense of sovereign immunity under the Foreign Sovereign Immunities Act of 1976, 28 USC §1610. The federal district court in California (where the Cubic Judgment was pending) held that Iran had waived its immunity from attachment when it submitted to the jurisdiction of the International Court of Arbitration and International Chamber of Commerce, as well as the district court. The U.S. Court of Appeals for the Ninth Circuit affirmed, but the U.S. Supreme Court vacated that decision and remanded in *Ministry of Defense and Support for the Armed Forces of the Islamic Republic of Iran v. Elahi,* 546 U.S. 450 (the first time the matter came before the Court).

On remand, the Ninth Circuit still affirmed the district court's ruling, but on different grounds. It relied instead on an exception to immunity found in the Terrorism Risk Insurance Act of 2002 (TRIA), which allows private creditors of terrorism-related judgments to attach "the blocked assets of [a] terrorist party." The **appellate court** characterized Iran as a "terrorist party" and further held that the Cubic Judgment was a "blocked asset" subject to attachment. (The United States had blocked Iranian assets following the Iranian hostage crisis in 1979. The crisis was resolved by the Algiers Accords in 1981, resulting in the issuance of unblocking orders. Notwithstanding, the Ninth Circuit held that the Cubic Judgment was still a blocked asset because the previously-issued unblocking orders had omitted military goods such as those involved in the Cubic Judgment.)

Complicating matters still further, while appeals were pending, Elahi had accepted $2.3 million from the U.S. government from a 2000 fund established to compensate victims of Iranian terrorism in cases where Iran would not pay damages awarded by courts. Section 2002 of the Victims of Trafficking and Violence Protection Act of 2000 (VPA) offered compensation to persons holding terrorism-related judgments against Iran. However, the Act required that any person accepting payment must relinquish "all rights to attach property that is at issue in claims against the United

States before an international tribunal." Elahi had signed a waiver mirroring the **statutory** language.

The U.S. Supreme Court dissected and addressed the issues, one by one. Justice Breyer delivered the opinion of the Court, joined by all justices as to Parts I and II, which essentially resolved the controversy. First, the Court held that the Cubic judgment was not a "blocked asset" at the time of the Ninth Circuit's decision (2007). It disagreed with the Ninth Circuit's characterization of Iran's asset as an interest in the air combat training system. Instead, the Court ruled that the true nature of Iran's asset was simply a judgment enforcing an arbitration award, based upon Cubic's breach of accounting to Iran for its share of the proceeds of the systems' eventual sale to Canada. Neither the Cubic judgment itself nor the sale proceeds represented in the judgment were blocked assets in 2007.

Second, Elahi could not attach the judgment because he waived his right to do so, said the majority. Since Iran is a sovereign nation, Elahi needed to find an exception to sovereign immunity in order to attach the Cubic judgment against Iran. The Court noted that the Cubic judgment was "at issue" in a claim against the United States pending before the Iran-United States **Tribunal**. This, according to the majority, fell within the **purview** of Elahi's signed waiver. (Iran had filed a case against the United States in 1982, claiming that between 1979 and 1981, the United States had wrongfully barred the transfer of the Cubic training system and other military equipment to Iran. Iran had requested that the Tribunal order the United States to pay damages. In response, the United States argued that the Tribunal should use the $2.8 million represented by the Cubic judgment as a setoff against any award.) Accordingly, the majority opinion said this made the Cubic judgment property "at issue" and non-attachable under the terms of Elahi's waiver.

Justices Kennedy, Souter, and Ginsburg joined in all but the part about the waiver. The dissent opined that Elahi had not relinquished his right to attach the Cubic judgment under the waiver. This position, said the dissent, "departs from the plain meaning and the purpose of the statutes Congress enacted to compensate Elahi and other victims of terrorism."

SOVEREIGNTY

The supreme, absolute, and uncontrollable power by which an independent state is governed and from which all specific political powers are derived; the intentional independence of a state, combined with the right and power of regulating its internal affairs without foreign interference.

Hawaii v. Office of Hawaiian Affairs

The U.S. SUPREME COURT on March 31, 2009 rendered a decision in a dispute regarding the sale of Hawaiian public land that had been reserved for the native people of Hawaii. The dispute focused on the effect of a congressional resolution, which purportedly reserved this land for Hawaiians after Congress acknowledged that the overthrow of the Hawaiian monarchy in 1893 had been wrongful. The Supreme Court of Hawaii ruled that the sale of the land in question should be enjoined, but the Supreme Court reversed.

Native Hawaiians lived on the island for many hundreds of years prior to the arrival of Europeans in 1778. The people of Hawaii established a unified monarchy in 1810, with Kamehameha I serving as the first king of Hawaii. The United States recognized the Kingdom of Hawaii as an independent sovereignty from 1826 to 1893. During this time, the U.S. had engaged in diplomatic relations with the Kingdom, negotiating treaties and conventions with the monarchy. During the 19th century, the Congregational Church, which was the predecessor to the United Church of Christ, sent missionaries to the island.

On January 14, 1893, a minister named John L. Stevens conspired with a group of non-native Hawaiian residents, including U.S. citizens, to overthrow the existing Hawaiian government. Just days after Stevens and his group put the action into effect, U.S. naval forces invaded Hawaii. Those responsible for the overthrow established a provisional government on January 17, 1893. The queen of the island chose instead to cede control of Hawaii to the U.S. government. President Grover Cleveland in December 1893 acknowledged that the actions in Hawaii were wrongful. Nevertheless, as the U.S. engaged in the SPANISH-AMERICAN WAR in 1898, President William McKinley signed a resolution that called for the **annexation** of Hawaii. Through this resolution, those who had purportedly established the Republic of Hawaii ceded sovereignty of Hawaii to the

Students rally for Hawaii public lands, February 25, 2009.

AP IMAGES

United States, including 1.8 million acres that had once belonged to the Kingdom of Hawaii. The United States added Hawaii as the 50th state on August 21, 1959.

In 1993, Congress officially apologized to the people of Hawaii by issuing what became known as the Apology Resolution, Pub. L. No. 103-150, 107 Stat. 1510. This **joint resolution** acknowledged that the overthrow of the Kingdom of Hawaii was wrongful and that the native Hawaiian people had never relinquished their claims to the lands of the Kingdom of Hawaii. The resolution noted, though, that nothing in its provisions was intended to serve as a settlement of claims against the United States.

During the 1980s, the State of Hawaii suffered from a "critical shortage of safe and sanitary housing units which are affordable to lower income residents of the State." In response to this concern, the state's legislature in 1987 established the Housing and Finance Development Corporation (HFDC). This **entity** was authorized to develop land for the purpose of providing low-cost housing. During the same year HFDC was established, the organization identified two areas that could serve as potential sites for this housing. The two areas included Leiali'i in West Maui and La'i'opua in North Kona. To develop this land, the HFDC had to obtain approval from the state's Office of Hawaiin Affairs (OHA). In 1990, the OHA approved the proposal. In 1992, the Hawaiian Legislature approved the **conveyance** of the property to HFDC, with the law authorizing the transaction specifying that the OHA would receive a certain percentage of the sale of the land.

When Congress approved the Apology Resolution in November 1993, the issues surrounding the conveyance of the land to the HFDC became more difficult. Legal counsel for OHA concluded that the congressional resolution had a legal effect on the ownership of the lands in question. OHA requested that HFDC agree to a disclaimer regarding the lands, with the disclaimer effectively preserving the native Hawaiian claims to the land. The HFDC refused OHA's request, arguing that this disclaimer would cloud the title for any future buyers and would prevent these buyers from obtaining **title insurance** on the property. In November 1994, the HFDC received about 500 acres of the ceded land and subsequently sought to transfer more than $5.5 million to OHA but did not include the disclaimer. OHA refused the check and then subsequently filed suit seeking to enjoin any future sale of the ceded land.

The litigation that ensued dragged on for the rest of the decade and beyond. On December 5, 2002, a Hawaiian trial court concluded that OHA's claims were barred on several grounds, including sovereign immunity, waiver and estoppel, and justiciability. The Supreme Court reviewed the case, and in January 2008, vacated the trial court's decision. With regard to the Apology Resolution, the court concluded the following: "[W]e believe Congress has clearly recognized that the native Hawaiian people have unrelinquished claims over the ceded lands, which were taken without consent or compensation and which the native Hawaiian people are determined to preserve, develop, and transmit to future generations." Accordingly, the court held that the HFDC should be permanently enjoined from selling the ceded lands. *Office of Hawaiian Affairs v. Housing & Community Development Corp. of Hawaii*, 177 P.3d 884 (Haw. 2008).

The HDFC, now known as the Housing and Community Development Corporation of Hawaii (HCDCH), appealed the decision to the U.S. Supreme Court. A unamimous Supreme Court reversed the Hawaii Supreme Court. In an opinion written by Justice Samuel Alito, the Court first determined that it had jurisdiction in the case. The Court then turned to the substantive questions, which focused principally on the Apology Resolution. The Court noted that while it must give effect to the words used by Congress, the Court should not "turn an irrelevant **statutory** provision into a relevant one." The Court concluded that the Hawaiian state court placed too much emphasis on words on the so-called "whereas" clauses of the resolution, which stated the factual basis for the apology. The Court noted that the resolution could not have the legal effect of clouding the title of the Hawaiian lands. Accordingly, the Court reversed and remanded the case to the Hawaiian courts. *Hawaii v. Office of Hawaiian Affairs*, ___ U.S. ___, 129 S. Ct. 1436, ___ L. Ed. ___ (2009). On remand, the Hawaiian courts must resolve the state law claims in light of the Supreme Court's ruling regarding the effect of the Apology Resolution.

SPORTS LAW

Seattle Supersonics Settle on Oklahoma

In *City of Seattle v. Professional Basketball Club, LLC*, No. 2:2007 cv01620 (settled), as in a real game, there was plenty of huffing and puffing and bluffing before differences were settled and both sides claimed victory. What should have been a simple breach of contract case between the City of Seattle and the famous Seattle Supersonics (Sonics) NBA basketball team ended up a four-way free-for-all that neither a six day trial nor several intervening parties could bring closure to. Tempers flared, acrimonious arguments hit the press, dirty little secrets came out. Finally, just hours before U.S. **District Court** Judge Marsha Pechman issued her decision, the parties agreed to shake hands on it and move on.

At issue was a lease agreement for Seattle's KeyArena. Plaintiff City of Seattle sued Defendant Professional Basketball Club, LLC (a sports franchise that owned the Supersonics) for a **declaratory judgment** seeking "specific performance," i.e., forcing the Sonics to play out their final two seasons under the contract at KeyArena in Seattle (2010). But previous Supersonics owner Howard Schultz had sold the team to Clay Bennett's franchise group in

2006; Bennett's group was from Oklahoma City. Bennett wanted to buy out the remaining two years under the lease contract and move to Oklahoma City immediately. The lawsuit was filed in 2007.

Much more was at stake. The Sonics had begun playing in Seattle in 1967. If the team left, the National Basketball Association (NBA) was unlikely to return in the near future, leaving the city, its fans and businesses, and a huge arena without a team. Yet, the NBA had approved the Sonics' move to Oklahoma. One of the Sonics' core reasons for wanting to buy out the remainder of time under the lease was that KeyArena was unsuitable for basketball, due to (among other things) a lack of luxury suites. This would cost the Sonics $60 million to honor the final two years under the lease. Conversely, Oklahoma City's Ford Center had new court-side suites, and trendy new exclusive lounge areas being installed just off the court, and the Sonics could make $17 million over the next two years. But the City of Seattle rejected Bennett's $26.5 million offer to buy out the final two years and move the team to Oklahoma City for the next season. And funding for renovations to KeyArena would be dependent upon the Sonics staying two more years.

Enter Howard Schultz, the previous Sonics owner, who decided to file his own lawsuit against Bennett for breach of contract. He sought to **rescind** his 2006 sale of the team to Bennett, claiming that Bennett made a good-faith promise to keep the Sonics in Seattle. Then Oklahoma notified Schultz that it would sue Schultz if he prevailed in his lawsuit and the Sonics did not move to Oklahoma. Schultz's case was also assigned to Judge Pechman. U.S. District Court Judge Ricardo Martinez was originally assigned to the City's case, and in October 2007 denied the Sonics' request for arbitration to avoid trial. He was later moved off the case with no public explanation.

Judge Pechman, undaunted by the publicity surrounding the high-profile case, put the **bench trial** on a strict timetable. Each side was to get exactly 15 hours for arguments, witnesses and objections.

Trial began as scheduled in mid-June 2008. City of Seattle lawyers argued, "a deal is a deal," and in this case, one which should compel **specific performance** under the contract. The City further argued that the Sonics had intangible

A Seattle Supersonics fan holds sign protesting team move, February 11, 2009.
AP IMAGES

value such as civic pride and goodwill to Seattle that could not be quantified or compensated by a lease buyout. Finally, the City tried to show that Bennett and his partners had planned all along to move the team to Oklahoma soon after they bought it in 2006. This was evidenced by some damaging e-mails between Bennett and his partners.

Not to be outdone with courtroom drama, The Sonics' lawyers brought forth their own damning evidence against the City of Seattle, in the form of a document entitled, "The Sonics Challenge, Why a Poisoned Well Affords a Unique Opportunity." The Sonics alleged that former U.S. Senator Slade Gorton, who had been retained by the City to lead their fight to retain the Sonics, had carried this document to a meeting at the home of one of the City's key players in the controversy. The "Poisoned Well" document outlined a plan to drain the finances of Bennett's franchise group and force him to sell the Sonics to local Seattle investors. By producing evidence of an alleged Machiavellian plan to defraud Bennett's business, Sonics' legal team argued that Seattle officials had "unclean hands" and were in no position to ask for specific performance. City officials took the stand and testified that Gorton had acted alone and they had no knowledge of his plan. The Sonics rested their case after Sonics' lawyer Brad Keller injected humor into the closing arguments by producing an electronic drawing of a human silhouette with a bifurcated brain inside the skull, depicted by two different colors. "Are we to assume the left side wasn't talking to the right side?" Keller asked, arguing that it defied logic and common sense that the City and its retained expert, Gorton, were not acting as one.

Meanwhile, the NBA had filed a motion to intervene in Schultz's case against Bennett. It reminded Schultz that the "release and indemnification" document executed at the time Schultz sold the team to Bennett's group required Schultz to be responsible for all expenses and reasonable legal fees incurred in connection with any lawsuits, even if Schultz prevailed. The motion further noted that legal counsel for the NBA was billing at $900 per hour and that NBA would pursue any and all legal remedies against Schultz for pursuing his suit against Bennett and obstructing the Sonics' attempted settlement with the City.

Schultz's attorney then filed a motion to bifurcate the trial into two separate trials: the first to determine whether Bennett's group was guilty of breaching its contract with Schultz or of negligent misrepresentation, the second phase to determine an appropriate legal remedy for Schultz.

On July 3, 2008, the City of Seattle and the Sonics reached a settlement. It was literally hours before Judge Pechman was to announce her verdict in the bench trial. The settlement allowed the Sonics to proceed with an immediate move to Oklahoma City, in exchange for a $45 million contract buyout to Seattle. Importantly, the settlement also provided for an additional $30 million payout to Seattle in five years should the City fail to attract a new NBA franchise. Under the terms of the settlement, Seattle retained the name Supersonics, as well as the history and records of the franchise.

The former Sonics NBA team physically moved to Oklahoma City in August 2008 and is now known as the Oklahoma City Thunder.

SUICIDE

The deliberate taking of one's own life.

Montana Judge Supports Doctor-Assisted Suicide for Terminally Ill

In October 2008, two patients and four physicians sued the State of Montana, claiming that Montana's state constitution afforded them the right to assisted suicide. More than one year later, in December 2008, First **District Court** Judge Dorothy McCarter ruled that mentally competent patients with terminal illnesses did indeed have the right to physician-assisted suicides under Montana's constitution. *Baxter v. State of Montana,* No. DA-09-0051 (2008). Montana State Attorney General Steve Bullock appealed the decision. In January 2009, Judge McCarter rejected Bullock's request to stay her order during the pendency of the appeal. In a one-page order, the judge noted that any stay would "deny the fundamental right of Montanans to die with dignity for a lengthy period of time while the case is being appealed." The Montana Supreme Court was not expected to rule on the matter for close to a year.

Meanwhile, a divided Montana state legislature failed to act on the matter with either a supportive **statute** or a ban, deciding instead to await the state high court's ruling and guidance. A spokesman for State Attorney General Bullock did not indicate whether the state JUSTICE DEPARTMENT would prosecute physicians for assisting in suicides while the matter was still pending before the state's high court. As of June 2009, only two other states, Oregon and Washington, allowed physician-assisted suicides, and both states had passed restrictive legislation that expressly outlined end-of-life care and procedure (see below).

Judge McCarter's December 5, 2008 ruling was premised on her opinion that Montana's constitutional rights of privacy and human dignity included the "right" of terminally-ill patients to request an end to their suffering and to die with dignity. While proponents lauded the decision and believed that it would put sympathetic physicians on more secure legal ground in the interim, others were cautious. Oregon and Washington had clearly-defined terms for what constituted "terminal illness" and "mentally-competent" patients capable of understanding options and making choices. Judge McCarter's ruling, on the other hand, gave no guidelines. It specified only three prerequisites: that the patient be mentally competent, be terminally ill, and that the physician's involvement be limited to prescribing the lethal medication.

As in most public-interest cases, a barrage of intervening and/or interested parties filed *amicus curiae* briefs with the Montana Supreme Court (briefs filed by non-parties who nonetheless have strong interest and/or expertise in the subject matter and/or who would be affected by the outcome of the court's ruling).

Arguments in support of the judge's ruling tended to express a recurring theme: death with dignity. Proponents also compared the fundamental right to create life (procreation) to a [proffered] fundamental right to end life. Moreover, an advocacy group called Compassion for Choices argued that supportive legislation was not a requirement, because Judge McCarter's ruling had mirrored the "most significant" aspects of Oregon's and Washington's statutes already.

Opposition to assisted suicide had historically been couched in moral/religious grounds. Additionally, the AMERICAN MEDICAL ASSOCIATION opposed such measures on the principle of conflict with physicians' Hippocratic oaths to treat with compassion, heal, and to preserve life. But over the years, arguments in opposition had broadened in scope and appeal.

In Montana's case, an *amicus* brief filed by the Americans United for Life (AUL) argued on behalf of 28 Montana legislators (bi-partisan) that the district court's ruling failed to give proper weight to the unanimous decisions in other courts that found no right to assisted suicide. Rather, the state had a compelling interest in protecting those citizens who were vulnerable because of illness.

An organization known as Not Dead Yet also coalesced with the Disability Rights Education and Defense Fund, the National Council on Independent Living, and the National Spinal Cord Injury Association, all of which jointly filed an *amicus* brief. They argued that there was no compelling **state interest**, let alone a legitimate one, to find a constitutional right to assisted suicide for only some (the "terminally ill") but not other state citizens. This, in effect, discriminated against persons with disabilities by degrading the value of their lives and their worth as human beings, making them and only them expendable in the eyes of the law. The brief further argued that such a move would be in violation of the Americans with Disabilities Act, 42 USC 12101, *et seq.*

The International Task Force on Euthanasia & Assisted Suicide, joined by Dr. Herbert Hendin and renowned law Professor Yale Kamisar, filed an *amicus* brief cautioning the high court of probable future scenarios. The brief argued that the lack of transparency in nearby Oregon made it an unreliable laboratory for assessing the practice of assisted suicide. Once assisted suicide was transformed from a crime to a medical treatment, the brief argued, the forces of economic gravity would make it a "preferred" treatment more readily endorsed

Judge Dorothy McCarter in court, Montana, October 10, 2008, during assisted suicide trial.

AP IMAGES

and authorized by health insurance companies and programs. More costly treatments that patients might want or need would be resisted for the more cost-effective "treatment of choice," i.e., the cessation of life.

Other briefs in opposition to assisted suicide cited the potential for masking domestic and elder abuse. Still others pointed to the assisted suicide program in the Netherlands, where rampant abuse had been found, including the tendency for doctors to decide which lives were worth saving based on economic gain for proposed treatments and the encouraged elimination of patients with no economic value.

Many more briefs were filed with the Montana Supreme Court both in support of and opposition to the district court's ruling. Meanwhile, many Montana citizens and lawmakers felt immobilized by the pending case. Montana Family Foundation president Jeff Laszloffy told the *Bozeman Daily Chronicle* that the district court's ruling could be a "wide-open decision" subject to abuse without legislative containment. On the other hand, he noted, any legislative action to outline or limit procedures in physician-assisted suicides only served to further legalize the practice. In the end, he said, waiting for the Montana Supreme Court's decision was the best, albeit imperfect, strategy.

SUPREMACY CLAUSE

The clause of Article VI of the U.S. Constitution that declares that all laws and treaties made by the federal government shall be the "supreme law of the land."

Haywood v. Drown

State and federal governments have sought to reduce the number of civil lawsuits filed by prisoners. Congress passed the Prison Litigation Reform Act of 1995 (PLRA), 28 U.S.C.A. § 1932, to deal with which placed a number of restrictions on prisoners who used the federal civil rights **statute** 42 U.S.C.A. § 1983 to pursue actions challenging prison conditions. Under the PLRA, prisoners must exhaust all administrative remedies before they are allowed to file a § 1983 lawsuit or any other **civil action** based on a federal law in federal court. Once filed, a federal **magistrate** will determine whether the prisoner has met the PLRA conditions. If not, the court will dismiss the lawsuit. The State of New York took a different approach, enacting a provision in its Correction Law that prohibits state trial courts from hearing any § 1983 lawsuit for damages against correction officers. A prisoner challenged the law, contending it violated the Constitution's **Supremacy Clause**. The Supreme Court agreed with the prisoner, ruling in *Haywood*, __U.S.__, 129 S.Ct. 2108, __L.Ed.2d__ (2009) that the state could not selectively remove certain § 1983 actions from its courts of **general jurisdiction**.

Keith Haywood, an inmate at New York's Attica Correctional Facility, started two § 1983 actions against several correction employees, alleging that they had deprived him of his civil rights at three disciplinary hearings and one altercation. He filed the suits in State Supreme Court, the state's trial court of general jurisdiction, seeking compensatory and **punitive damages**, as well as attorney's fees. The court dismissed the actions, citing the provision of the Correction Law for its lack of jurisdiction to hear the case. The intermediate court of appeals upheld this ruling as did the state's highest court, the New York Court of Appeals. The court believed there was no Supremacy Clause violation because the law treated state and federal damages actions against correction officers equally-neither action could be brought in state court.

The Supreme Court, in a 5-4 decision, overruled the New York court. Justice JOHN PAUL STEVENS, writing for the majority, acknowledged that the purpose of the Correction Law provision was to stop prisoner lawsuits that were largely frivolous and vexatious. New York did provide an alternate procedure for the prisoner, allowing the inmate to file the claim for damages in the state's **court of claims**.

Stevens pointed out, however, that in this court the inmate is not provided the same relief and same options as in a state trial court. An inmate must file a claim within 90 days of the alleged injury, he is not entitled to a jury trial, punitive damages, or attorney's fees. In addition, the inmate cannot seek an injunction.

Justice Stevens stated that the Court had long held that federal law "is as much the law of the several States as are the laws passed by their own legislature." Although § 1983 was enacted during RECONSTRUCTION to help newly freed slaves protect their rights in federal court, the Court has ruled that such actions can be heard in state court as well. The only way New York could justify its law was by demonstrating it was a "neutral rule of judicial administration." Otherwise, the states lack the authority "to nullify a federal right or **cause of action** they believe is inconsistent with their local policies."

The Court concluded that the state's policy of prohibiting prisoner lawsuits for damages was not a neutral rule of **judicial administration**. The law was contrary to the intent of Congress that all persons who violate federal rights while acting under color of state law should be held liable for damages. Justice Stevens admitted that prior Court decisions had not been clear as to what was an acceptable neutral rule. He stated that "equality of treatment" does not equal neutrality. Just because there was the absence of discrimination in the law did not mean the law was neutral: "A jurisdictional rule cannot be used as a device to undermine federal law, no matter how evenhanded it may appear." Ensuring the equality of treatment is just the beginning and not the end of the Supremacy Clause. Therefore, the state could not bar inmates from filing § 1983 lawsuits in state court.

Justice Clarence Thomas, in a dissenting opinion joined by Chief Justice Roberts and Justices ANTONIN SCALIA and Samuel Alito, contended that the state had the absolute right to refuse to hear a § 1983 action or any other federal action that it chose. Justice Thomas reviewed the history of the Constitutional Convention and the drafting of the Supremacy Clause, concluding that "the States have the unfettered authority to determine whether their local courts may entertain a federal cause of action." Once the state chooses to do so, "it is the end of the matter as far as the Constitution is concerned."

TERRORISM

The unlawful use of force or violence against persons or property in order to coerce or intimate a government or the civilian population in furtherance of political or social objectives.

President Obama Orders Closure of Guantanamo Bay Detention Camp

Closing the Guantanamo Bay (Cuba) Detention Camp, where more than 240 "enemy combatants" were still being held indefinitely for further **disposition**, was one of presidential candidate Barack Obama's most important campaign promises in the November 2008 election. Newly-elected President Obama made good on his promise, signing Executive Order 13492 on January 22, 2009, within 48 hours of taking office, which directed the closure of Guantanamo within one year. He also ordered the temporary suspension (for 120 days) of all proceedings conducted by the Guantanamo Military Commission, and an immediate assessment of the prison itself to ensure that conditions for the remaining detainees would meet the humanitarian requirements of the Geneva Conventions. But the Obama administration was about to face a plethora of legal, diplomatic, logistic and political hurdles that would make that closure more troublesome and complicated than many officials were willing to admit.

The indefinite detention of persons at Guantanamo had been a volatile political issue for years, as human rights activists, politicians,

and even foreign governments expressed their concern for the status of the detainees. The prior Bush administration had asserted that detainees were not entitled to the protections of the Geneva Convention. But the U.S. SUPREME COURT, in *Hamdan v. Rumsfeld,* 126 S.Ct. 2749 (2005)held that neither the U.S. Constitution (including the inherent powers of the Executive) nor any act of Congress expressly authorized the type of "military commissions" created by the Bush Administration to try detained enemy combatants for war crimes. Absent that express authorization, the commissions had to comply with the ordinary laws of the United States and the laws of war, including parts of the Geneva Conventions and the **statutory** UNIFORM CODE OF MILITARY JUSTICE (UCMJ).

In response to the Court's ruling, Congress enacted the U.S. Military Commissions Act, Pub. L. 109-366, 120 Stat. 2600, on September 29, 2006. Its stated purpose was to "facilitate bringing to justice terrorists and other unlawful enemy combatants [defined therein] through full and fair trials by military commissions, and for other purposes." But four years later, in 2009, only one combatant had been tried by the military commission's **tribunal**, and the rest were still waiting in custody at Guantanamo.

Section 2 of Obama's Executive Order ("Findings") noted that

(a) Over the past 7 years, approximately 800 individuals who the Department of Defense

A prisoner sleeping in his cell at Guantanamo Bay.
AP IMAGES

has ever determined to be, or treated as, enemy combatants have been detained at Guantanamo. The Federal Government has moved more than 500 such detainees from Guantanamo, either by returning them to their home country or by releasing or transferring them to a third country. The Department of Defense has determined that a number of the individuals currently detained at Guantanamo are eligible for such transfer or release. (b) Some individuals currently detained at Guantanamo have been there for more than 6 years, and most have been detained for at least 4 years. In view of the significant concerns raised by these detentions, both within the United States and internationally, prompt and appropriate disposition of the individuals currently detained at Guantanamo and closure of the facilities in which they are detained would further the national security and foreign policy interests of the United States and the interests of justice. Merely closing the facilities without promptly determining the appropriate disposition of the individuals detained would not adequately serve those interests. To the extent practicable, the prompt and appropriate disposition of the individuals detained at Guantanamo should precede the closure of the detention facilities at Guantanamo. (c) The individuals currently detained at Guantanamo have the constitutional privilege of the **writ** of **habeas corpus**. Most of those individuals have filed petitions for a writ of habeas corpus in

Federal court challenging the lawfulness of their detention.

The very language of the executive order attested to the complexity of the situation. The Bush administration's secret and protracted detention of persons at Guantanamo had attracted international scorn and condemnation, even from friendly European countries and allies. It was clear that all eyes, expectant and hopeful, would be on Obama and his eventual resolution of these pending concerns.

First, for the remaining 241 detainees (as of April 2009), the government needed to produce sufficient evidence to justify their detention in pending habeas corpus proceedings, as well as their eventual trials. Among one of the most sensitive challenges was to build effective cases against the detainees without using evidence obtained by coercion or torture, an issue expected to be exploited by attorneys representing the detainees. In light of the April 2009 release by the JUSTICE DEPARTMENT of internal documents and memoranda of the Bush administration (the "torture memos") indicating that indeed, torture tactics had been employed in many circumstances, many cases may have been compromised. Moreover, for those detainees who really constituted little threat when they were first detained, they were expected to have been "hardened" in their animosity toward the United States, because of the lengthy and tortuous detention.

Second, if Guantanamo and all other "secret" detention camps were to be closed by Obama's order, where and how would the United States detain and interrogate suspects it would later pick up in the continuing battle against al-Qaeda and global terrorism? According to *The Washington Post*, Obama advisers denied reports that the administration was contemplating some form of **preventive detention** backed by a new civilian national security court. More likely, suspects would be incrementally referred to federal court for prosecution.

Further, where would released detainees go? It was undeniable that global sentiment supported Obama's decision to close Guantanamo. Therefore, European countries and the Persian Gulf states, previously resistant to accepting Guantanamo prisoners under the Bush administration, might hopefully be more receptive and accommodating with the new administration. Moreover, some 100 of the 241 remaining detainees were Yemenis. The Bush administration had been unable to secure assurances that Yemenis returned to Yemen would be closely monitored, as Yemen had a history of allowing al-Qaeda suspects to escape from prison. What countries and allies would be willing to take some of them? According to Eric Holder Jr., the newly appointed Attorney General under Obama, some 60 other detainees were expected to be placed in Portugal, Ireland, Switzerland, Spain, and Lithuania, which agreed to help (but as of April 2009 had not made firm commitments). The United Kingdom would also help; France agreed to take one. Holder reported that after a three-day European tour, he was "pleasantly surprised" at the number of countries willing to help.

Finally there was the question of whether any U.S. officials would face prosecution for alleged torture. Several European officials and civil liberties groups were pressing Obama to hold Bush administration officials legally accountable for their harsh treatment of the detainees. Obama had previously indicated that he would not, because officials at the time believed they were acting under "approved" guidelines. However, with the revelation of some of the tactics actually employed, pressure was mounting for high-level officials to be held accountable.

Holy Land Foundation former executive Shukri Abu Baker, October 22, 2007.

AP IMAGES

Holy Land Foundation Convicted of Supporting Terrorism

In November 2008, a federal jury convicted the Holy Land Foundation of Relief and Development (HLF), a non-profit domestic corporation organized in Texas, along with five of its key leaders, of funding the terrorist Palestinian militant organization Hamas under the ruse of collecting and distributing charitable donations. The government's successful convictions followed an earlier mistrial in October 2007. The defendants argued that they had been engaged in legitimate humanitarian aid for community welfare programs and Palestinian orphans. The matter was considered the largest terrorism financing case in U.S. history.

Specifically, the U.S. **District Court** for the Northern District of Texas in Dallas returned guilty verdicts on all 108 criminal counts filed under what is commonly referred to as the "material support statute," a component of the Antiterrorism and Effective Death Penalty Act of 1996 (AEDPA), 110 Stat. 1214, 28 USC §2254. Convictions included counts for providing material support and resources to a foreign terrorist organization; providing funds, goods, and services to a specially-designated terrorist; and **money laundering**. The defendants were also convicted of conspiracy to commit all of the above substantive crimes. Two of the individual defendants were additionally convicted of filing false tax returns and conspiring to impede and impair the INTERNAL REVENUE SERVICE (IRS).

According to prosecutors, the defendants funneled approximately $12.4 million to Hamas in support of its goal of creating an Islamic Palestinian state by eliminating the State of Israel through violent jihad. The prior Clinton administration had declared Hamas a terrorist group in 1995 for its role in sponsoring suicide bombings targeting Israelis.

The HLF organization, considered the largest Muslim charity in the United States, had been shut down by the U.S. Government in 2001 and its assets frozen. It was based in Richardson, Texas, a Dallas suburb. It was originally incorporated by Defendants Shukri Abu Baker, Mohammad El-Mezain, and Ghassan Elashi. The HLF functioned as the chief fundraising arm of its parent organization, the Muslim Brotherhood.

In its case-in-chief, the U.S. government presented evidence that as early as the 1990s, the Muslim Brotherhood intended to establish a network of organizations within the United States to raise money for Hamas and spread militant Islamic messages. According to a wiretap of a 1993 Palestine Committee meeting in Philadelphia, former HLF President Shukri Abu Baker spoke to the attendees about downplaying connections to Hamas in order to keep fundraising activities viable in the United States.

Evidence further showed that the defendants sent HLF-raised funds to Hamas-controlled "zakat" committees (an Arabic word referring to the religious obligation to give alms) and charitable societies in the West Bank and Gaza. The money was then used to support, among other things, the families of Hamas martyrs, detainees, and activists. According to evidence presented, the HLF was so concerned about its activities being discovered that its leaders kept a private "policies and procedures" manual. It addressed such things as hiring a security company to search the HLF for listening devices, training one person on advanced methods in detecting wiretaps, shredding board meeting documents, and keeping incriminating documents at off-site locations.

On May 27, 2009, the defendants were sentenced, and were described in various media articles as "defiant." The *Dallas Morning News* quoted defendant HLF board chairman Elassi as complaining that "We gave the essentials of life-oil, rice, flour." before receiving his 65-year sentence. He argued that the HLF intended to

assist Palestinians in their steadfastness against the brutal apartheid regime. Other defendants received sentences ranging from 15-20 years in prison. Defendant El-Mezain, former HLF endowments director and Muslim **prayer** leader who delivered fiery speeches on confiscated tapes in the case, declared, "We did it all in the name of America. The Holy Land Foundation was no different than any other Jewish or Baptist charity."

The federal jury deliberated for eight days (compared to 19 days in the 2007 trial). Prosecutors spent more time in the second trial to paint a more clear picture of the money trail and explain the complexities of the organization. The government also dropped some of its previous charges.

Within 24 hours of the sentencing, three defendants had filed notices of appeal with the U.S. Fifth **Circuit Court** of Appeals, with the remaining defendants vowing to do the same. Counsel for at least one defendant stated that appeals would be based on a number of issues, including testimony evidence from an anonymous "expert" witness. Counsel also complained that the government was permitted to use wiretapped statements of defendants that were made over a number of years, without defendants being allowed to review them (because they were classified).

TOBACCO

Altria Group, Inc. v. Good

Civil lawsuits against tobacco companies by cigarette smokers have become a part of the contemporary legal landscape. A contentious and important issue has been whether smokers could use state laws to pursue their claims. The tobacco companies have argued that federal laws regulating tobacco, tobacco labeling, and advertising preempt conflicting state laws. A dispute over state jurisdiction in claims that a tobacco company fraudulently misrepresented the safety of "light" and "lowered tar and nicotine" cigarettes reached the U.S. SUPREME COURT in *Altria Group, Inc. v. Good*, __U.S.__, 129 S.Ct. 538, __L.Ed.2d__ (2009). In an important ruling, the Court held that federal laws did not preempt the state lawsuit.

Stephanie Good and a group of cigarette smokers filed suit against Altria Group and its subsidiary Philip Morris USA, Inc., claiming that the companies had violated the Maine Unfair Trade Practices Act (MUTPA) by fraudulently advertising that their "light" cigarettes delivered less tar and nicotine than regular cigarettes. The plaintiffs had smoked Marlboro Lights and Cambridge Lights cigarettes for over 15 years. Though the plaintiffs acknowledged that both brands did have lower tar and nicotine levels than those of regular cigarettes, they claimed the companies had known all along that smokers unconsciously engage in compensatory behaviors not addressed by the method of testing cigarette filters. By covering ventilation holes with their lips or fingers, smokers take larger or more frequent puffs, and they hold the smoke in their lungs longer. Because of this, plaintiffs contended that smokers of light cigarettes unknowingly inhale as much tar and nicotine as do smokers of regular cigarettes. Moreover, they claimed that light cigarettes are more harmful than regular cigarettes because the light filter design produces smoke with more tar content. The plaintiffs alleged that the companies had fraudulently concealed this troubling information and had affirmatively represented that such light cigarettes posed fewer health risks.

The federal **district court** dismissed the case on the grounds that the the MUTPA claim was preempted by the Federal Cigarette Labeling and Advertising Act (Labeling Act). The Fifth **Circuit Court** of Appeals reversed the district court decision. The appeals court held that the case was not about a failure-to-warn claim, which is preempted from state law, but rather a **fraud** claim that alleged the companies falsely represented their cigarettes as light or having lowered tar and nicotine levels. The federal Labeling Act did not expressly preempt this type of claim. Because the Fifth Circuit Court of Appeals had ruled that this type of claim was preempted, the Supreme Court accepted the case for review so as to resolve the conflict.

The Supreme Court, in a 6-3 decision, upheld the First Circuit ruling and concluded that the Maine **statute** could be used against the companies. Justice JOHN PAUL STEVENS, writing for the majority, noted that the police powers of the states are not to be superseded by a federal law unless "that was the clear and manifest purpose of Congress." The Labeling Act, which was enacted in 1965, came in response to the Surgeon General's finding that cigarette smoking was harmful to health. The

act requires a warning to that effect on each package of cigarettes sold in the United States. The act has been amended several times, with more explicit warning language added each time. A provision also preempted the states from imposing labeling warnings or advertising regulations on tobacco companies. This section of the act formed the basis of the Altria's legal argument. To allow the plaintiffs to sue under state fraud law would defeat the purpose of preventing nonuniform state warning requirements

Justice Stevens acknowledged the purposes of the law but pointed out that under its prior case precedents fraud claims "rely on a single, uniform standard: falsity." These prior rulings had set out a standard for determining whether a common-law claim is preempted: "whether the legal duty that is the predicate of the common-law damages action constitutes" a requirement based on smoking and health with respect to advertising or promotion. If so, the claim was preempted. In this case, however, the claim was not preempted because the manufacturer's duty was not to deceive. This duty, which was codified in MUTPA, was not based on smoking or health. MUPTA only dealt with the general rule that creates a duty not to deceive and it had no connection with tobacco regulations. The Court rejected Altria's argument that **preemption** turned on the distinction between misleading and false statements. Altria had contended that the law was preempted because the company's statements on light cigarettes "might create a false impression" rather than those statements being "inherently false."

Altria argued in the alternative that the law must be preempted because it would contradict a FEDERAL TRADE COMMISSION (FTC) policy that has for over 40 years encouraged the promotion of low tar cigarettes and has encouraged consumers to rely on the tar and nicotine content information in choosing among cigarette brands. Justice Stevens found no merit in this claim, as the FTC has never authorized the use of "light" and "low tar" descriptors. None of the FTC's decisions over the years on statements of tar and nicotine content impliedly preempted MUTPA.

Florida Restarts Tobacco Lawsuits

Litigation by tobacco smokers seeking damages from tobacco companies for injuries caused by smoking has been a constant in U.S. law since the 1980s. State and **federal courts** have had to wrestle with numerous issues. One critical issue has been whether smokers could be joined in a **class action** suit or whether each individual had to sue individually. Class actions are a more efficient means of settling civil disputes, but some types of litigation are not appropriate for this method. The Florida Supreme Court, in a 2006 decision, overturned a tobacco class-action verdict, ruling that each smoker's claims had to be heard individually on their own merits. At the time of the verdict in 2000, the class of smokers was estimated up to 700,000. With the 2006 decision, the Florida state court system had to prepare for up to 8,000 individual tobacco lawsuits. The first lawsuit was tried in February 2009 and the widow of the smoker was awarded $3 million in **compensatory damages** and $5 million in **punitive damages**. The case could set a standard for the thousands of other lawsuits awaiting trial.

The saga of Florida tobacco litigation began in 1996 with the class action lawsuit of *Engle v. Reynolds*. The class action suit was certified to include approximately 700,000 smokers in the state of Florida. The plaintiffs, who sought damages from five major tobacco companies, alleged that they had been entrapped by a defective product that caused addiction and illness. Moreover, they alleged that the tobacco companies were guilty of **fraud** for using deceptive advertising and for years of covering up the true health effects of smoking. In July 2000, the jury awarded the plaintiffs $145 billion in damages, by far the largest class action award in U.S. history. On appeal the Florida Court of Appeals and later the Florida Supreme Court overturned the verdict. The appeals courts first attacked the idea of class certification for smokers' lawsuits. The class should not have been certified because the individual health complaints of each plaintiff were unique. Therefore, no single person could fairly represent an "average member" of the group. This was the type of case where proof of damages was essential to proving liability. Damages could not be determined on a class-wide basis because the issue of damages required individualized proof for each plaintiff. In 2006, the Supreme Court ultimately tossed out the $145 million award as excessive. Individual smokers were free to pursue their claims, but some observers expressed skepticism that many would do so. Their skepticism seemed

to be merited, as the hundreds of thousands of potential plaintiffs had been reduced to 8,000 cases filed by January 2009. Despite the reduction of the plaintiff pool, 8,000 civil trials would place great burdens on the state court system.

The first case to go to trial took place in Fort Lauderdale in February 2009. Elaine Hess, whose husband Stuart Hess died of lung cancer in 1997 at the age of 55, alleged that her husband had chain smoked for decades. She sued the tobacco manufacturer Philip Morris, claiming that it and other companies had used deceptive advertising, criticized health studies about smoking risks, and spread doubts about links to cancer. Though the companies knew they sold dangerous products, they hid the true risks from the public for decades. Hess's lawyer made these arguments to a six-person jury that heard the tobacco company lawyer contend that Mr. Hess had it within his power to stop smoking at any time. He made a personal choice to continue smoking, even in the face of long-term health concerns. Hess bore personal responsibility for his choices.

The trial included video of 1994 testimony by the heads of the tobacco companies before Congress, where they denied that smoking was addictive. This long-discredited message likely had an impact on the jury, which found Philip Morris liable for Hess's health problems and death. The jury then deliberated on damages. Mrs. Hess asked the jury for $130 million dollars, but the jury awarded her $3 million in compensatory damages and $5 million in punitive damages.

The Hess trial could serve as a template for the thousands of cases yet to be tried. If similar verdicts are rendered in the coming years the tobacco industry will be facing large payouts. There is also the strong likelihood that the companies will ask trial judges to reduce damages and, if unsuccessful, appeal the verdict and the damages decision.

TORT LAW

A body of rights, obligations, and remedies that is applied by courts in civil proceedings to provide relief for persons who have suffered harm from the wrongful acts of others. The person who sustains injury or suffers pecuniary damage as the result of tortious conduct is known as the plaintiff, and the person who is responsible for inflicting the injury and incurs liability for the damage is known as the defendant or tortfeasor.

Burlington Northern & Santa Fe R.R. Co. v. United States

The U.S. SUPREME COURT in 2009 reviewed a case involving efforts of state and federal agencies to recoup cleanup costs caused by spilling of hazardous waste at a facility in California. In *Burlington Northern & Santa Fe Railway Co. v. United States*, ___ U.S. ___, 129 S. Ct. 1870, ___ L. Ed. 2d ___ (2009), the Court ruled that a chemical supplier that did not intend for disposal of hazardous waste could not be held liable under the Comprehensive Environmental Response, Compensation, and Liability Act.

Brown & Bryant, Inc. (now a defunct company) began operation of an agricultural chemical storage and distribution facility in 1960. The facility was located on a 3.8-acre piece of land in Arvin, California. By 1975, Brown & Bryant had outgrown the parcel of land it used and began to lease a 0.9-acre parcel that was adjacent to the Brown and Bryant land. The 0.9-acre parcel was then owned by the Atchison, Topeka & Santa Fe Railroad Co. and the Southern Pacific Transportation Co. These companies were the predecessors in interest to the Burlington Northern & Santa Fe Railway Co. and the Union Pacific Transportation Co.

The parcel leased from the railroad companies was west of the main Brown & Bryant site. Brown & Bryant used the railroad parcel to park rigs used to haul fertilizer. The land on which the Brown and Bryant operation sat, including the railroad parcel, graded towards a drainage pond on the Brown and Bryant parcel. Brown and Bryant used the land to receive delivery of chemicals. The company also stored the chemicals on the land and distributed the chemicals from the land. Brown & Bryant bought two types of agricultural chemicals from Shell Oil Co., including D-D and Nemagon. These chemicals were designed to kill microscopic worms that attack the roots of crops. Brown & Bryant also purchased and stored on its land a weed killer manufactured by Dow Chemical Company.

Shell requested that its customers purchase chemicals in bulk, which requires the customers to maintain large storage tanks. Shell delivered the chemicals to Brown & Bryant in **common carrier** trucks. These trucks transferred the chemicals to storage tanks at the Arvin facility by pumping the chemicals through hoses. This process resulted in numerous spills. To apply chemicals to agricultural fields, Brown & Bryant used rigs that were stored on the railroad parcel and loaded with the chemical.

In 1978, a windstorm destroyed a storage tank used to store Shell's D-D. Brown & Bryant then started using stainless steel milk trailers to store the D-D chemical. This chemical is highly corrosive and ate through some of the steel cans. Nevertheless, Brown & Bryant kept these tanks all over the Arvin facility. Chemicals such as those stored at the Arvin facility evaporates quickly in air but are soluble in water. These chemicals tend to move through soil and can contaminate drinking water.

The leakage of chemicals at the Arvin occurred for more than 20 years. In 1983, the California Department of Toxic Substances Control (DTSC) investigated the facility and found Brown & Bryant to be in violation of several hazardous waste laws. In a separate investigation, the ENVIRONMENTAL PROTECTION AGENCY (EPA) discovered evidence of soil and ground-water contamination at the facility. Pursuant to authority under the Comprehensive Environmental Response, Compensation, and Liability Act (CERCLA), 42 U.S.C. §§ 9601-9675, the EPA and DTSC exercised cleanup authority, incurring substantial costs during the remediation. In 1989, Brown & Bryant went out of business, requiring the EPA and the DTSC to take over the remediation efforts.

The EPA in 1991 ordered the railroads to take specific preventative steps at the railroad parcel, including the installation of groundwater monitoring wells. The railroad parcel, though, did not have any contamination that required immediate remediation. In 1992, the railroads filed an action against Brown & Bryant and its principals, seeking contribution of costs that were incurred during the cleanup process. In 1996, the EPA and DTSC filed actions under CERCLA against Brown & Bryant, the railroads, and Shell for reimbursement of the investigation and for cleanup costs.

Congress enacted CERCLA in 1980 to provide for effective responses to health and environmental threats posted by hazardous waste. The **statute** allows state and federal agencies to being the cleanup of toxic areas and then sue potentially responsible parties for costs incurred in the cleanup process. The statute shifts the cost of cleaning up environmental harm from the government to the parties who benefited from disposal of the harmful wastes. Under the statute, a party can be held liable for cleanup of toxic chemicals at a facility if the party fits into one of four categories, including:

> (1) the owner and operator of … a facility; (2) any person who at the time of disposal of any hazardous substance owned or operated any facility at which such hazardous substances were disposed of;(3) any person who by contract, agreement, or otherwise arranged for disposal or treatment, or arranged with a transporter for transport for disposal or treatment, of hazardous substances owned or possessed by such person …; and (4) any person who accepts or accepted any hazardous substances for transport to disposal or treatment facilities….

The U.S. **District Court** for the Central District of California ruled in favor of the government on July 15, 2003. According to the district court, the railroads were liable because they owned portions of the facility, and Shell was liable because the company had "arranged for" the hazardous waste disposal by selling and delivering the chemicals. The district court also determined that harm caused could be divided among the parties. The parties appealed the decision to the Ninth **Circuit Court** of Appeals. The Ninth Circuit agreed with the district court that Shell could be liable as an "arranger." However, the court ruled that the district court had erred by apportioning the costs. The **appellate court** concluded that no reasonable basis existed to apportion these costs, and so the Ninth Circuit held that the railroads and Shell should be jointly and severally liable for the cleanup costs. *United States v. Burlington Northern & Santa Fe Railway Co.*, 479 F.3d 1113 (9th Cir. 2007).

The Supreme Court agreed to review the case and reversed the Ninth Circuit's decision. Justice JOHN PAUL STEVENS wrote for an 8-1 majority, which disagreed with both lower courts regarding the extent to which arranger liability extends. Stevens concluded that so-called "arranger liability" under CERCLA is "fact intensive and case specific." The Court concluded that for a party to arrange for disposal of a hazardous substance, the party needs to have some intent to dispose of the substance. In the case, Shell did not intend to dispose of the

hazardous substance, and its knowledge that the substance may be illegally disposed was not enough to establish liability. The Court also concluded that the Ninth Circuit was wrong that liability could not be apportioned. Therefore, the Court reversed the Ninth Circuit regarding the lower court's conclusion that the parties should be held jointly and severally liable.

RUTH BADER GINSBURG dissented, arguing that the majority's decision was inconsistent with the purpose behind CERCLA. Commentators noted that the result of the majority's decision will limit the range of parties that may be responsible for cleanup. Unless the party that arranged for disposal of hazardous waste actually intended for the waste to be dispose, the party will not be liable under the statute.

TORTURE

Obama Administration Releases "Torture Memos"

Only days before Barack Obama was sworn in as the 45th President of the United States on January 20, 2009, Deputy Assistant Attorney General Steven Bradbury authored a new "Memorandum for the Files." In it, he noted that the legal opinions expressed in nine national security legal opinion memos, written during the Bush administration, were no longer being relied upon and were "not consistent with the current views" of the Office of Legal Counsel (OLC) (operated under the Attorney General within the U.S. Department of Justice). The later release (to the public) of those memos by the Obama administration on March 2, 2009 signaled the beginning of an unraveling of policies and ostensible legal guidance during the Bush years that would cast shadows upon, and create havoc for, future administrations as well.

At the heart of the controversy were the so-called "torture memos," legal opinions coming from OLC that offered guidance and legal authority for, among other things, the treatment and interrogation of persons following the terror attacks of September 11, 2001. The memoranda dealt with such topics as warrantless wire tapping, an expanded scope of executive power, and the seizure of terrorism suspects. In one example, the "Memorandum Regarding Authority for Use of Military Force to Combat Terrorist Activities within the United States," dated October 23, 2001, the lawyers opined that FOURTH AMENDMENT protections would not apply for domestic military operations "designed to deter and prevent further terrorist attacks." The memorandum reasoned that "In our view, however well suited the warrant and **probable cause** requirements may be as applied to criminal investigation or to other law enforcement activities, they are unsuited to the demands of wartime and the military necessity to successfully prosecute a war against an enemy."

Moreover, the memo expressed, the First Amendment's protections for speech and press might also be "subordinated to the overriding need to wage war successfully." (In his 11-page memo distancing those memos from current thinking, Bradbury offered that many of them had been written "in the wake of the atrocities of 9/11.")

Obama released several memos after accepting a recommendation from newly-appointed Attorney General Eric Holder to declassify and release three other 2005 memos that described interrogation techniques approved for CIA use against Al Qaeda suspects (suspected of orchestrating the 9/11 attacks). The collective memoranda would become even more provocative, as U.S. Intelligence officials, led by senior national security aide John Brennan, mounted an intense campaign to reverse the decision for their release. Brennan (along with former Vice President Dick Cheney and others) strongly argued that release of the memos could embarrass foreign intelligence services who had cooperated with the CIA, either by direct participation in overseas renditions, or by housing detainees in overseas "black site" prisons. But Obama, who had campaigned on a platform of "government transparency," decided in favor of release.

Several memos were the subject of a FREE-DOM OF INFORMATION ACT (FOIA) lawsuit filed by the AMERICAN CIVIL LIBERTIES UNION (ACLU). The Obama administration, in return for requesting from the **district court** a two-week extension for release, proffered release of another controversial and long-sought-after memo, written in 2002 by former OLC lawyers Jay Bybee and John Yoo (which had been publicly withdrawn in 2004 after its contents were first revealed to the public).

It was the 2002 Bybee/Yoo memo that became the watershed for all that followed, creating the most controversy and commanding

the most media attention. In the now infamous memo, Yoo and Bybee concluded that "waterboarding" and other harsh interrogation techniques could be used against al-Qaeda suspects without violating federal law prohibiting "torture." Yoo further advised that the military could employ "any means necessary" to hold terror suspects. Importantly, Yoo declared that treatment of detainees would constitute "torture" only if they rose to the level of, e.g., "organ failure, impairment of bodily function, or even death."

Those same legal opinions were again repeated by a new set **of counsel** in 2005, including Bradbury (see above), who also approved techniques such as head-slapping, frigid temperatures, and taunting one suspect frightened of insects with a crawling one in the suspect's narrow cubicle. The memos further concluded that such techniques, if used by the CIA, would not violate Geneva Conventions or other international restrictions against "cruel, inhuman and degrading" treatment of prisoners. Such physical and psychological "techniques" could be used, said the memos, because there was "no specific intent to inflict severe mental pain or suffering."

On April 16, 2009 (the district court's extended deadline), the Obama administration released four memos, dating from 2002 to 2005, which outlined, in graphic detail, a series of practices intended to garner information from prisoners and detainees. The techniques were designed to inspire "dread," said one footnote. They included slapping prisoners in the face or abdomen, dousing them with water, confining them in cramped quarters (up to two hours in small boxes), exposing them to frigid temperatures, removing their privacy, depriving them of sleep (for up to 11 days), waterboarding, and nude shackling.

President Obama and Attorney General Holder had both indicated their desire to move forward rather than conduct investigations that could **alienate** the intelligence community and/or incite partisan bickering. "This is a time for reflection, not retribution," said Obama, although he referred to the memos and their origin as a "dark and painful chapter in our history." Both he and Holder also assured that "dedicated men and women" would not be prosecuted for good-faith conduct that was "sanctioned in **advance** by the Justice Department." But they left open the

DILEMMA OVER PROSECUTIONS FOR THE 'TORTURE MEMOS'

In the early months and years following the September 11, 2001 terrorist attacks on the United States, former Department of Justice attorneys John Yoo and Jay Bybee of the DOJ's Office of Legal Counsel (OLC) wrote memoranda offering legal opinions ostensibly justifying the use of questionable interrogation techniques of detainees in government custody. The legal memos, authored during the early years of the Bush administration, further opined that the president had a constitutional right (executive power) to authorize such techniques without involvement from Congress. The later release (to the public) of those memos by the subsequent Obama administration on March 2, 2009 signaled a watershed of revealed policies and controversial legal guidance during the Bush years that would cast shadows upon, and create havoc for, future administrations as well.

In one of the now-infamous 2002 memos (which had been publicly withdrawn in 2004 after its contents were first revealed to the public), Yoo and Bybee concluded that "waterboarding" and other harsh interrogation techniques could be used against al-Qaeda suspects without violating federal and international law prohibiting "torture." Yoo further advised that the military could employ "any means necessary" to hold terror suspects. Importantly, Yoo declared that treatment of detainees would constitute "torture" only if it rose to the level of, e.g., "organ failure, impairment of bodily function, or even death."

On June 13, 2009, Judge Jeffrey White, presiding in the U.S. **District Court** for the Southern District of California in San Francisco, ruled that convicted Islamic terrorist Jose Padilla could maintain his civil lawsuit against John Yoo for authoring the so-called "torture memos" authorizing harsh treatments for "enemy combatant" detainees. *Padilla v. Yoo*, No. CV-08-0035, D.C.N.D.Cal, pending. The court's ruling represented the first judicial opinion holding that government lawyers could be potentially responsible for detainee abuse. The decision rejected defendant Yoo's motion to dismiss, based on a defense of qualified immunity.

The DOJ, representing Yoo in the case, further argued for judicial abstention in favor of deferring review to the coordinate branches of government with **purview** of the substantive areas of law raised in the memoranda. DOJ lawyers also argued that courts were barred from examining top-level administrative decisions in wartime. Moreover, making public "allegations of unconstitutional treatment of an American citizen on American soil" would damage national security or foreign relations (those arguments repeated by former Vice President Dick Cheney to the media). The district court rejected all.

Padilla, a Brooklyn-born American citizen who converted to Islam, is serving a 17-year sentence on terror charges relating to a dirty bomb plot. He claimed that he was tortured while being held in a Navy brig in Charleston, South Carolina

as a suspected terrorist for nearly four years. The Complaint alleged, among other counts, denial of access to counsel and the court; unconstitutional conditions of confinement and interrogation; denial of freedom of religion, speech, and association; denial of the right to information; denial of due process; and unconstitutional military detention.

The decision was, of course, controversial. Legal critics questioned how liability for constitutional violations could attach to the forming of legal opinions as part of policy development. But the district court held that Yoo went beyond the boundaries of legal counsel when he crafted legal opinions designed to facilitate the plans (for harsh interrogations) that the Bush administration had already decided upon, and/or helped to legally formulate those very policies. "Like any other government official, government lawyers are responsible for the foreseeable consequences of their conduct," said the district court.

That was the question for Obama. To find, perchance, that Americans might wake up angry, having elected a president who promised transparency and palpable change, but who looked the other way when confronted with prior officials' wrongdoing. Worse yet, if the new administration decided to criminally prosecute those former government officials responsible for espousing what amounted to dark mistreatment of post-September 11, 2001 prisoners and detainees, would future cooperation from domestic and international intelligence

possibility that higher-level officials could face charges if they ventured beyond the parameters outlined in the memos.

No Trial for Alleged Terrorist Because of "Approved Torture"

The Bush administration (during the presidency of GEORGE W. BUSH, 2000-2008) had

long maintained that "torture" was not a tactic employed by government investigators when questioning "enemy combatants" in the WAR ON TERRORISM. But in May 2008, the top official responsible for overseeing military trials of suspected terrorists held at the U.S. detention prison at Guantanamo Bay, Cuba, dismissed the pending case against Mohammed al-Qahtani communities, at a time when national security interests and global relations were so tenuous, be threatened? The stakes were high.

Obama and Attorney General Holder had both indicated their desire to move forward rather than conduct investigations that could **alienate** the intelligence community and/or incite partisan bickering. "This is a time for reflection, not retribution," said Obama, although he referred to the memos and their origin as a "dark and painful chapter in our history." Both he and Holder also assured that "dedicated men and women" would not be prosecuted for good-faith conduct that was "sanctioned in **advance** by the Justice Department." But they left open the possibility that higher-level officials could face charges if they ventured beyond the parameters outlined in the memos.

In the end, President Obama deferred to the recommendations of the DOJ as to whether the lawyers who prepared the legal memos and made recommendations should be criminally prosecuted. He also continued with his pledge that interrogators would not be investigated or prosecuted for using techniques the lawyers approved.

The Senate Select Committee on Intelligence was conducting its own investigation into the treatment and interrogation of detainees, which was not expected to be completed till the latter part of 2009. Leading senators wanted to delay potential prosecution until this report was finalized.

Meanwhile, in May 2009, an internal DOJ investigation concluded that Bush administration officials [including Loo and others] suffered some serious lapses of judgment but probably should not be

prosecuted. The 220-page draft report, by the office of Professional Responsibility (an internal ethics unit of the DOJ) reviewed, among other things, whether the legal memos were the products of independent judgment on the limits of the federal anti-torture **statute**, or were deliberately skewed to accommodate justification of proposed techniques. (Several legal scholars had noted that in approving waterboarding, the technique described by the Obama administration as "torture," Yoo and others failed to cite known cases in which the United States had previously prosecuted both American law enforcement officials and Japanese WORLD WAR II interrogators for using the same procedure.)

Although the report did not recommend criminal prosecutions for the lawyers, it did, however, imply that referrals to state bar associations were likely, which could result in formal reprimands, suspensions, or even disbarment for some of the lawyers involved in writing the legal opinions.

The 110th Congress attempted to amend the federal "anti-torture act," (The Detainee Treatment Act of 2005, P.L. 109-148, 42 USC 21D), but the bill (H.R. 5460) expired before action. It would have, among other things, amended the definition of "torture" and the definition of cruel, inhumane or degrading treatment or punishment to include waterboarding. In January 2009, House Judiciary Chairman John Conyers (D-MI) reintroduced a bill, the American Torture Act of 2009 (H.R. 893), which had similar objectives and provisions. It also proposed to extend the **statute of limitations** from eight to ten years. (It is noteworthy that the most controversial of memoranda was the 2002 Yoo/Bybee one, which meant that the

time remaining to prosecute could expire in 2010.) With the ticking time and the lack of definitional language in the existing law [could amended language even be used retroactively?], there was reasonable cause for deliberation.

The 1984 International Convention Against Torture, approved by 145 nations and adopted by the United States in 1994, compels member nations to prosecute any and all who are responsible for torture. The Convention declares, "No exceptional circumstances whatsoever, whether a state of war or a threat of war, internal political instability or any other public emergency, may be invoked as a justification for torture." It was this limitation that the Bush administration lawyers sought to circumvent in their legal memoranda.

But the World was not waiting for President Obama to decide. Global opinion was sharp and often critical. Spanish **magistrate** Baltasar Garzon launched his own investigation into the Bush administration in May 2009 over the alleged torture of four Spanish nationals at Guantanamo. He also ordered an independent inquiry into whether Bush administration lawyers created the legal framework that authorized the mistreatment. Other countries hinted at similar independent investigations.

In June 2009, President Obama released a statement marking the 25th anniversary of the Convention Against Torture. He called on the international community "to join with the United States and the community of law-abiding nations in prohibiting, investigating, and prosecuting all acts of torture and in undertaking to prevent other cruel and unusual punishment."

for precisely that concern. According to Susan J. Crawford, convening authority of military commissions, interrogation techniques used against Qahtani were authorized at the time (2002), but "his treatment met the legal definition of torture," causing her to order war-crime charges against him dropped. Crawford's

remarks were made during an interview for *The Washington Post* published in January 2009. She previously had not made public her reasons for the May 2008 dismissal of charges.

Qahtani, a Saudi Arabian national, was believed by FBI officials to be "the 20th hijacker" associated with the September 11, 2001 terrorist attacks on the United States. Investigators later established that the leader who plotted those attacks (Mohammed Atta), who died after steering American Airlines Flight 11 into the World Trade Center in New York, had gone to Orlando Airport in Florida on August 4, 2001, to meet Qahtani. However, Qahtani was denied entry by a suspicious immigration inspector. He was later captured in Afghanistan and transported to Guantanamo in 2002.

While Crawford agreed that Qahtani was a "muscle hijacker" and "very dangerous man," she told interviewers she was shocked, upset, and embarrassed by what she learned of interrogation techniques used against him. Crawford told interviewers that the techniques did not involve "some horrendous physical act" of torture, but rather consisted of authorized techniques that were applied in an "overly aggressive and too persistent" manner. "It was the medical impact [on him] that pushed me over the edge" to call it torture, Crawford said.

Crawford, a retired judge who had previously served as general counsel for the Army during the Reagan administration as well as Pentagon Inspector General, personally reviewed Qahtani's interrogation records and other military documents before rendering her decision. She found that Qahtani had undergone 18-to-20-hour interrogations during 48 of 54 consecutive days from November 2002 to January 2003. His only contact for 160 straight days was with interrogators. "Standing naked in front of a female agent. Subject to strip searches. And insults to his mother and sister," Crawford noted. A military report had indicated that Qahtani was threatened with a military working dog, forced to wear a woman's bra, had a thong placed on his head during interrogation, and was told that his mother and sister were "whores." At one point, a leash had been tied to his chains as he was led around a room, forced to perform dog tricks. Additionally, interrogation techniques included sustained isolation, sleep deprivation, and prolonged exposure to cold temperatures.

But it was the fact that Qahtani was hospitalized twice following interrogations that pushed Crawford to her conclusion. His diagnosis was bradycardia, a condition in which the heart rates slows to dangerously low levels, leading to heart failure and death. Bradycardia can be directly linked to cold body temperature and fatigue. In October 2006, Qahtani recanted a confession he said he had made after enduring such interrogation methods.

In considering the impact her decision to drop charges against Qahtani would have upon the new Obama administration and the United States, Crawford expressed concern. "I sympathize with the intelligence gatherers in those days after 9/11, not knowing what was coming next and trying to gain information to keep us safe," she told The Post. "But there still has to be a line that we should not cross.If we tolerate this and allow it, then how can we object when our servicemen and women.[are] subjected to the same techniques? .Where is our moral authority to complain?"

In fact, the alleged techniques had been the subject of several Pentagon investigations, and were found to be authorized and legal when briefly used for a small number of detainees following the September 11, 2001 attacks. But following the Supreme Court's decision in *Hamdan v. Rumsfeld*, 126 S.Ct. 2749 (2005), Congress rewrote the Army field manual rules and passed the Military Commissions Act, which created a new structure for trials and the military commission. It also created Crawford's position as a neutral official with ultimate decision-making power over all cases coming before the military commissions, including prosecutorial charges, trials, and sentencing.

In early April 2009, the U.S. Department of Justice released internal papers showing the extent of interrogative techniques used during the Bush years. President Obama referred to this as a "dark period" in American history and vowed to end it and "move on." Notwithstanding, the release of information triggered massive controversy, not only among government officials but also the American public. As of July 2009, no new charges had been filed against Qatani, despite a government in November 2008 stating new charges were forthcoming. He remains imprisoned at Guantanamo Bay.

TRADE

United States v. Eurodif S.A

The United States has in place a law that seeks to prevent foreign companies from selling their merchandise in the U.S. at less than its fair value. This law, which was enacted as part of the **Tariff** Act of 1930, calls for placing "anti-dumping" tariffs on such goods in an amount equal to the amount by which the normal value exceeds the export price for the merchandise. The purpose of anti-dumping **statute** is to protect U.S. industries from unfair competition. However, this law only applies to the export of foreign goods at an unfair price; it does not apply to international sale of services. Foreign companies may seek to characterize their work as a service rather than the production of merchandise to avoid paying the tariffs. The Supreme Court, in *United States v. Eurodif S.A*, __U.S.__, 129 S.Ct. 878, __L.Ed.2d__ (2009), upheld the U.S. Commerce Department's conclusion that a French exporter of enriched uranium was not providing a service to U.S. energy utilities by enriching the material but instead was selling a product subject to the anti-dumping laws.

There are a small number of companies in the U.S. and the rest of the world that enrich uranium. Enriched uranium comes in weapons-grade concentrations and in lower concentrations for use as fuel in nuclear power plants. Power utilities typically obtain low enriched uranium (LEU) by paying cash and providing unenriched uranium to the enricher. There are only five major uranium enrichers in the world. Eurodif, a French company, and other European enrichers have provided U.S. utilities with LEU, to the detriment of the sole U.S. domestic enricher, which claimed that the foreign enrichers were selling LEU at less than fair value. The U.S. company asked the COMMERCE DEPARTMENT to investigate its charges. Eurodif agreed that its contracts were for the sale of LEU but argued that the contracts involved only the sale of uranium enrichment services and were outside the scope of the anti-dumping provision. It contended that the U.S. utilities provided it with unenriched uranium and, as a service, it enriched and returned the uranium.

The Commerce Department rejected Eurodif's interpretation. It found that the enrichment process accounted for about 60 percent of the value of the LEU and worked a "substantial transformation" on uranium feedstock. Eurodif also had complete control over the level of usage of the natural uranium provided and the utilities took no part in the manufacture of the product. The department also ruled that the parties could not control the characterization of

their contract so as to allow them to "convert trade in goods into trade in so-called manufacturing services." This would expose U.S. industries to injury from unfair trade practices without the anti-dumping remedy. Finding that Eurodif was selling LEU below fair value, the department levied a tariff on the LEU. Eurodif challenged the decision before the Court of International Trade, which sided with Eurodif. The Court of Appeals for the Federal Circuit upheld this ruling, finding that nothing in the contract displayed "any intention by the parties to vest the enrichers with ownership rights in the delivered unenriched uranium of the finished LEU."

The Supreme Court, in a unanimous decision, overturned the Federal Circuit ruling. Justice DAVID SOUTER, writing for the Court, noted that the issue before the Court was not whether the challenged contract was for the sale of services or good; the statute gave that decision-making authority to the Commerce Department. The Court will find that the department's interpretation "governs in the absence of unambiguous **statutory** language to the contrary or unreasonable resolution of language that is ambiguous." Justice Souter agreed with the department that the anti-dumping law was not limited to cash-only sales and that the department was not bound by the "legal fiction" in the contract that the same uranium delivered to Eurodif for enrichment was returned as LEU to the utility.

Justice Souter concluded that the contract in question occupied a middle ground in the debate over goods and services. On one extreme is the sale of a service, such as contracting with a dry cleaner to clean as shirt. The customers pays the cleaner for the service and receives back the same shirt. On the other extreme a customer provides cash and sand to a manufacturer of silicon processors and receives back computer chips that are more than "sand enhancement services." In the case of LEU, the transaction occupied a middle ground not clearly defined in the anti-dumping statute. However, the Court concluded that the department made a reasonable interpretation in deciding the contract was for the sale of LEU. The utility did not receive back the same uranium it delivered to Eurodif and the enrichment process resulted in a "substantial transformation of the unenriched uranium."

VETERANS' RIGHTS

Shinseki v. Sanders

Veterans of the U.S. military services who have served on active duty are entitled to receive benefits for disabilities caused or aggravated by their military service. Veterans must file disability claims with the Department of Veterans Affairs (VA), which determines whether a disability is linked to military service. Under federal law the VA must give claimants information on what kinds of evidence the veterans must supply and what evidence the VA will provide. If a claim is denied, the veteran has the right to appeal the denial. The failure of the VA to meet the notice requirements has been a common basis for appeal. The Federal **Circuit Court** of Appeals, which hears all VA benefits appeals, developed a **harmless error** rule that made it difficult for the VA to prevail, as the burden of proving harmlessness fell on the agency. The Supreme Court, in *Shinseki v. Sanders*, __U.S.__, 129 S.Ct. 1696, __L.Ed.2d__ (2009), overturned the harmless error rule, finding it too complex and rigid.

The case involved appeals by Woodrow Sanders, a WORLD WAR II veteran, and Patricia Simmons, who served between 1978 and 1980. Sanders claimed that a bazooka exploded near his face in 1944, causing later blindness in his right eye. However, his wartime records did not disclose this injury, and the VA denied him benefits in 1948 and 1949. The VA agreed to reopen his claim in 1992, but after examining his military medical records and arranging for a medical examination, the VA again denied his claim. Sanders then appealed to the VA's Board of Veterans' Appeals, an **administrative board** with the power to consider certain types of new evidence. The board concluded that Sanders had failed to show that his eye injury was service connected. He then appealed to the Court of Appeals for Veterans Claims, an executive branch court. In this appeal he argued for the first time that the VA had made a notice error. The VA had sent him a notice telling him what further information was needed to substantiate his claim, but he said the VA had failed to tell him which parts of the information the VA would provide or which parts he would have to provide. The Veterans Court ruled that these notice errors were harmless, as Sanders had failed to explain how he would have acted differently if provided with the notices.

Patricia Simmons claimed she had lost hearing in her left ear while working in a noisy environment. She applied for disability benefits in 1980, but the VA denied her claim. The VA agreed to reopen her claim in 1998, which now included hearing loss in her right ear. The VA denied her claim, the board upheld the ruling, and she filed an appeal with the Veteran's **Court of Appeal**. She claimed that she had not received a notice about a right-ear examination that the VA arranged and therefore did not attend. She also argued that she had not received the required notice from the VA telling her what was needed to prove her claim. The Veterans Court agreed with her on both points and found the error prejudicial in respect to her left-ear hearing loss. It remanded her case to the board.

Sanders appealed to the Federal Circuit Court of Appeals, as did the VA in Simmons' case. The Federal Circuit ruled that the Veterans Court was wrong to find the notice error harmless regarding Sanders. It held that when the VA provides a claimant with a notice letter deficient in any respect, the VA should presume that the notice error is "prejudicial, requiring reversal unless the VA can show that error did not affect the essential fairness of the adjudication." The court applied this holding to the Simmons appeal and again found that the error was not harmless, upholding the Veterans Court.

The Supreme Court, in a 6-3 ruling, overruled the Federal Circuit. Justice STEPHEN BREYER, writing for the majority, concluded that the Veterans Court must apply the same kind of harmless error rule that courts ordinarily use in civil cases. The Federal Circuit's harmless error rule was complex, rigid and mandatory. It imposed "an unreasonable evidentiary burden upon the VA, as the rule required the VA to prove that Sanders knew that he, not the VA, would have to provide more convincing evidence that the accident caused his eye injury. Proving a claimant's state of mind about such a matter would be difficult, if not impossible. Finally, the Federal Circuit rule required the VA, not the claimant, to explain why the error was harmless. This was wrong, for the harmless error rule in administrative cases places the burden of showing harmful error on the party attacking the agency's determination.

Based on the application of the normal harmless rule, the Court found that the VA's notice error in Sanders' case was harmless. In the Simmons case the Court concluded that the Veterans Court should decide whether reconsideration was necessary.

Justice DAVID SOUTER, in a dissenting opinion joined by Justices JOHN PAUL STEVENS and RUTH BADER GINSBURG, argued that placing the **burden of persuasion** on the veteran to show harmful error disregarded the special place veterans occupy in federal law. Federal statutes direct the VA to give veterans the

benefit of the doubt in close cases; veterans should have a "comparable benefit" in the Veterans Court.

VOTING

Bartlett v. Strickland

The VOTING RIGHTS ACT OF 1965, 42 USC 1973 *et seq.* endeavored to eliminate discriminatory treatment of minorities exercising their fundamental right to vote. Section 2 of the Act, at issue in *Bartlett v. Strickland,* No. 07-689, 556 U.S. ___ (2009), parallels the protections of the 15th Amendment to the U.S. Constitution. ("The right of citizens of the United States to vote shall not be denied or abridged by the United States or by any State on account of race, color, or previous condition of servitude.") The 1982 amendments to §2 established a violation of the Act "if, based on the totality of circumstances, it is shown that the [election] processes leading to nomination or election in the State or political subdivision are not equally open to participation by members of a [protected] class [who] have less opportunity than other members of the electorate to participate in the political process and to elect representatives of their choice."

A racial minority is identified as such because it comprises a lesser percentage of a given population than the majority. The larger question is whether any racial minority could ever elect its candidate of choice, if its votes were to be continually outnumbered (or "diluted") by the votes of the majority? More narrowly then, if the Act is intended to protect minority populations from being hindered in exercising their voting rights, can the Act be construed to actually require proactive measures that would facilitate minority populations in electing their candidate(s) of choice?

The precise question before the U.S. SUPREME COURT in *Bartlett v. Strickland* was whether §2 of the Act could be invoked to require state officials to draw up/create voting districts in a way that would help racial minority populations (who comprised less than 50 percent of the voting-age population within the district) elect their candidates of choice? By a 5-4 **plurality** opinion (which also included three separate dissenting opinions), the Supreme Court said no. Its decision affirmed a decision of the North Carolina Supreme Court. The decision is expected to have a significant impact on state redistricting plans following the 2010 census.

As background, North Carolina's state constitution contained a provision that prohibited the state's legislative branch (the General Assembly) from dividing state counties when drawing legislative districts (the "Whole County Provision"). As early as 1991, the General Assembly had tried to create District 18 by including portions of four different counties. The ostensible reason was to create a district that would have a majority African-American voting-age population.

Following the 2000 census, the North Carolina Supreme Court rejected two separate (and legally-challenged) district plans on the grounds that they violated the state constitution's Whole County Provision. The General Assembly's third attempt at creating District 18 resulted in the present controversy. Unable to draw up a geographically-compact "majority-minority" district (one in which the majority of the population was comprised of members of a minority class, in this case African-American), the General Assembly drew new district lines that split portions of Pender and New Hanover Counties. Without splitting the counties, District 18 would have had an African-American voting population of 35 percent. By splitting portions of Pender and New Hanover Counties, that percentage was increased to 39 percent. The General Assembly's stated rationale was to enhance the potential for minority voters to join with "crossover" majority voters to elect the minority group's candidate of choice.

Pender County and its Board of Commissioners (Strickland, et al.) sued, alleging that the plan violated the Whole County Provision by splitting the county into two House districts. The state-official defendants (Bartlett, et al.) answered that dividing the county was required to satisfy §2 of the Act.

The state trial court noted that this case immediately differed from other §2 cases, in that §2 was raised as a defense rather than raised by plaintiffs as an alleged violation. Therefore, procedurally, defendant state officials carried the burden of proving that §2 required their action of splitting Pender County.

In making its decision, the trial court relied on a previous U.S. Supreme Court case, *Thornburg v, Gingles,* 478 U.S. 30 (1986).

In that case, the Supreme Court identified three threshold requirements needed to establish a §2 violation, (1) that the minority group is "sufficiently large and geographically compact to constitute a majority in a single-member district," (2) that the minority group is "politically cohesive," and (3) "that the white majority votes sufficiently as a bloc to enable it.usually to defeat the minority's preferred candidate." The trial court then concluded that the above requirements had been met, and it sustained the boundary lines of District 18, even though splitting the counties violated the state's Whole County Provision. (It is well-established that such state election-law requirements can be superseded by federal law.)

On appeal, the Supreme Court of North Carolina reversed. It held that a "minority group must constitute a numerical majority of the voting population in the area under consideration" before §2 could be invoked to authorize or justify a legislative district specifically created or drawn up "to prevent dilution of the votes of that minority group." Accordingly, because African-Americans still did not constitute a geographic numerical majority, the defendants failed to establish that creation of District 18 was mandated by §2 of the Act.

The U.S. Supreme Court accepted **certiorari** (review) to resolve a split among five circuit courts of appeal and at least two state supreme courts over what §2 required or did not require. Four other states, the NAACP, and the League of Women Voters also filed amicus briefs with the Court.

Justice ANTHONY M. KENNEDY, writing as well for Chief Justice JOHN ROBERTS, Jr. and Justice Samuel Alito, articulated the narrow majority opinion. Justice Clarence Thomas, joined by Justice ANTONIN SCALIA, filed an opinion concurring in the judgment. The high court upheld the decision of the North Carolina Supreme Court. Justice Kennedy noted that the Court has previously held that §2 could require the creation of a "majority-minority" district, in which a minority group composes a numerical, working majority of the voting age population, e.g., *Voinovich v. Quilter,* 507 U.S. 146, 154-155. But §2 did not require the creation of an "influence" district, in which a minority group could try to influence the outcome of an election even if its preferred candidate was not elected.

THE INTERNET IS THE NEW FACE OF POLITICAL CAMPAIGNING

In 1996, only four percent of adults in the United States used the Internet as a source of news or politics. Twelve years later, that number had increased to 44 percent, according to a survey conducted by the Pew Internet and American Life Project for the People and the Press. Statistics such as this are not surprising, given that they are consistent with overall numbers related to Internet usage. Evaluations of the use of the Internet for campaigning shows that modern national campaigns cannot survive without a strong Internet presence.

By the time that races had begun for the 2008 election, major national candidates had developed their strategies for persuading voters through the Internet. As the Democratic and Republican presidential primaries raged on in December and January, a survey showed that 24 percent of all adults regularly used the Internet to learn about the presidential race. This number was merely 9 percent in 2000 and 13 percent in 2004. In the same survey,

respondents said that they used more traditional sources less frequently. For instance, use of a daily newspaper as a main source of information for campaign news fell from 40 percent in 2000 to 31 percent in 2008. Likewise, only 40 percent of those responding said they relied on local television news for campaign news. In 2000, the number was 48 percent.

Age of voters also heavily affected how much they relied on the Internet. In 2004, 20 percent of those ages 18 to 29 used the Internet as a source for campaign news, compared with 16 percent of those ages 30 to 49 and 7 percent of those over the age of 50. In 2008, the numbers increased significantly. Of those between the ages of 18 and 29, 42 percent said they used the Internet regularly for campaign news. The same survey showed that these younger voters relied much less than older voters on the more traditional sources, such as local news, newspapers, and radio.

Throughout the decades of the 1990s and 2000s, most expected the use of the Internet as a major campaign tool to grow. However, the change was not as dramatic as the change caused by the use of television in 1960. The 2000 election marked the first time that candidates first made significant use of the Internet for fundraising, as well as e-mail and websites for campaigning. The amount spent on online campaigning was relatively minimal, as only about $50 million of the $3 billion spent on the 2000 election was raised online. After the election, many thought that e-mail would be one of the major tools used for future elections.

The Internet played a much more significant role in the 2004 election. Democratic candidate John Kerry reportedly raised $82 million from online sources, which was more than the entire total that AL GORE had raised in the 2000 campaign. Special interest groups established websites and raised significant donations for political candidates. For

---

In the present case, even the re-drawn District 18 contained only 39 percent African-Americans in the voting population. While that minority might rely on "crossover" voters from the majority to elect a preferred candidate, "Nothing in §2 grants special protection to a minority group's right to form political coalitions," Justice Kennedy summarized. Justice Thomas, in his concurring opinion, noted that nothing in the text of §2 even authorized a vote dilution claim.

The three dissenting justices disagreed with the plurality's stricter interpretation of §2. Justice Ginsberg called on Congress to overturn the decision by "clarify[ing] beyond debate the appropriate reading of §2."

Common Cause/Georgia v. Billups

Concerns about potential voter **fraud** has led some states to impose voter identification

requirements on their citizens. In Georgia the state legislature enacted laws in 2005 and 2006 that required voters to present a government-issued photo identification to election officials to be admitted to the polls and to vote in person. Civil rights organizations challenged these laws, arguing that they violated constitutional and **statutory** provisions and would make it harder for thousands of people to vote. A federal **district court** upheld the Georgia Voter ID law and the Eleventh **Circuit Court** of Appeals, in *Common Cause/Georgia v. Billups*, 554 F.3d 1340 (11th Cir.2009), agreed. The appeals court found that the law was supported by a strong **state interest** in protecting the integrity of elections and that the way it was implemented did not substantially burden citizens seeking to vote.

Until 1997, the state of Georgia did not require voters to present identification when example, the liberal website MoveOn.org raised an estimated $750,000 for Democratic candidates in 2004. The DEMO-CRATIC PARTY saw first hand how the Internet could be used effectively based on the popularity of candidate (and former Vermont governor) Howard Dean, who used the Internet as his principal staging ground.

Between 2004 and 2008, the Internet evolved considerably. Static web pages used to provide information developed into more fully interactive sites that allowed users to comment back and forth more easily. Blogs became more standard as source of news and opinions. Moreover, social networking sites such as MySpace and Facebook became hugely popular. Technological developments allowed candidates to use the web in ways that were far more effective than use of e-mail alone. According to Phil Tajitsu Nash of Campaign Advantage, which helps organizations develop and implement online fundraising strategies:

> Good online fundraising requires not just the technology, and not just the candidate, but also a message that resonates with online audiences. And what that means is that the insurgent candidates, generally speaking,

have a better chance of raising money.

Candidates in 2008 were fully aware of the power of the Internet. Barack Obama had used the Internet in 2004 during his U.S. Senate race in Illinois, but he made more complete use of the Internet by hiring staff members who worked on the campaigns of Dean and Kerry. Obama used social networking as a major part of his campaign, and he even hired Facebook co-founder Chris Hughes to join the Obama campaign. Obama eventually had more than a million supporters on Facebook and had developed a presence on other sites, such as MySpace, Twitter, MyBatanga, MiGente and AsianAve.

Republicans also used the new online tools as part of their campaigns. Candidate Ron Paul found support from his online campaign, even as the mainstream media paid little attention to him. On one day during November 2007, Paul raised more than $4 million online. As McCain's campaign progressed, he also relied more heavily on social networking. His daugther, Megan, maintained a blog designed to attract younger voters, and the McCain campaign established McCainSpace, his own social network. However, these efforts could not match those of Obama. For instance, at one

point during the election McCain had fewer than one-fifth the number of supporters on Facebook as Obama.

Obama was also innovative in use of other web tools, such as online video. His campaign created video that was uploaded to the video-sharing site You-Tube. Viewers watched Obama campaign videos for a combined total of 14.5 million hours. If the Obama campaign were to run 14.5 million hours of advertisements on television, the ads would cost more than $47 million. On YouTube, the campaign clips ran for free.

Many credit the Internet for Obama's victory in 2008. Arianna Huffington, who runs the popular site The Huffington Post, said that Obama would not have won the Democratic nomination, let alone the presidential race, were it not for the Internet. Use of the Internet of fundraising and campaigning will likely to continue to grow in importance. Data from the Pew Internet & American Life Project shows that 55 percent of the entire adult population used the Internet for information about the election in 2008, representing the first time that more than half of the American public used the Internet in this manner during an election.

---

they went to the polls. In that year the legislature enacted a law that required voter identification. A person could present, among other documents, a driver's license, birth certificate, a copy of a current utility bill, or a payroll to satisfy the the law. In 2005 the legislature amended the law to require voters to present a government-issued photo ID. For voters who did not already possess an acceptable form of identification, the law provided that voter ID cards could be obtained for a free of $20 to $35. The NAACP of Georgia, Common Cause of Georgia, and other groups challenged the law in federal district court, claiming that the voter ID card fee constituted an unconstitutional **poll tax**. The district court agreed and issued a **preliminary injunction** that prevented the law from going into effect.

In 2006 the state legislature repealed the **statute** and enacted a new one that listed six specific kinds of photo identification that would allow a person to vote. They included a driver's license, a voter identification card, a U.S. passport, a government employee ID card, a U.S. military ID card, or a tribal ID card. The new law also required each county to issue free of charge a Georgia voter ID card with a photograph of the voter to anyone who did not possess an acceptable form of identification. The same organizations challenged the new law in federal court by amending their complaint. The judge preliminarily enjoined the enforcement of the new law in 2006 because the court believed the state needed to educate its citizens about the new requirement. In August 2007 a **bench trial** was held, in which the plaintiffs solely argued that the new law unduly burdened the right to vote in violation of the FOURTEENTH AMENDMENT. The district court denied the plaintiffs a permanent injunction, ruling that the interest of Georgia in preventing voter fraud outweighed the burden of the voters' rights.

In a unanimous decision, a three-judge panel of the Eleventh Circuit Court of Appeals agreed with the district court. Judge William Pryor, writing for the court, relied on the Supreme Court's 2008 decision upholding an Indiana voter photo identification law similar to Georgia's. In *Crawford v. Marion County Election Board*, __U.S.__,128 S.Ct. 1610, 170 L.Ed.2d 174 (2008), the Court stated that for an election law to be constitutional, the state must convince the Court that the interests put forward to justify voting qualifications outweigh the burden imposed on citizens by the law. Each law must be evaluated on a case-by-case basis, with the Court balancing the interests on both sides. Judge Pryor noted that the district court's ruling, though decided before *Crawford*, used the same means of evaluating the law. The NAACP claimed that the state had failed to put forth sufficiently weighty state interests to justify the limitation imposed by the photo identification requirement. Pryor found that concerns about curbing voter fraud were sufficient to justify the state's interests in passing the law. The state did not have to prove that in-person voter fraud existed and that photo IDs were an effective remedy. He noted that the Supreme Court did not require Indiana to prove specific instances of voter fraud.

The appeals court found that the only burdens imposed by the law were those that affected persons who were eligible to vote but did not possess a current photo identification that complied with law. Those most affected were person who might have difficulty obtaining a photo ID. The district court had ruled that the burden was not undue or significant. Pryor agreed, rejecting the claim by the NAACP that between five and ten percent of all registered voters would be burdened. The statistical data presented by the NAACP was, in the court's view, "incomplete and unreliable." Because the plaintiffs "failed to prove that any individual would bear a significant burden," the court found in favor of the state, clearing the way for the implementation of the law for the next elections.

Thousands of Voters Blocked from Voting

On October 9, 2008, just weeks before the November 2008 presidential and national elections, *The New York Times* published a lengthy and provocative article entitled, "States' Actions to Block Voters Appear Illegal." The attention-grabbing first paragraph read as follows:

> "Tens of thousands of eligible voters in at least six swing states have been removed from the rolls or have been blocked from registering in ways that appear to violate federal law, according to a review of state records and Social Security data by The New York Times."

The second paragraph was more conciliatory:

> "The actions do not seem to be coordinated by one party or the other, nor do they appear to be the result of election officials intentionally breaking rules, but are apparently the result of mistakes in the handling of the registrations and voter files as the states tried to comply with a 2002 federal law, intended to overhaul the way elections are run."

Nonetheless, the article continued, because Democrats had more aggressively pursued and registered new voters, any enhanced screening of new applications may have the potential to affect Democratic Party supporters disproportionately.

The "federal law" referred to in the article included the Help America Vote Act of 2002 (HAVA), 42 U.S. 15301 *et seq.*, designed to "strengthen" the election process. Under the Act, states were required to establish statewide electronic voter registration lists and clear the electronic lists of duplicates or otherwise ineligible names (deaths, etc.). This was intended to prevent "voter fraud," i.e., ineligible voters casting ballots.

But according to *The Times*, many states were purging their lists for the first time in 2008 and appeared to be unfamiliar with the requirements of the 2002 law. Media attention had been focused on millions of new voters being added to the voter rolls by the candidacy of Senator Barack Obama. Yet, for every voter added to the rolls in some states, election officials had removed two, leaving a net result of less voters on the rolls.

The Times identified the six swing states with the highest screening or purging of voter registration lists as Colorado, Indiana, Ohio, Michigan, Nevada, and North Carolina.

Its inquiry found that Michigan and Colorado were removing voters from registration rolls within 90 days of a federal election. This was prohibited under federal law, excepting for the death of a voter, notification to the state that the voter had moved, or a finding that the voter was otherwise declared unfit to vote. Other data suggested that states may have removed voters who had relocated within the state.

In Colorado, Louisiana, and Michigan, the number of people removed from election registration rolls since August 2008 greatly exceeded the number who had died or relocated during that period by a ratio of approximately 3:1. For example, in Louisiana, 18,000 voters were removed from the rolls in a five-week period during July and August 2008. But over the same period, only 1,600 moved out of the state and there were approximately 3,300 deaths, according to data from the U.S. Postal Service and death records. Colorado recorded a net loss of 100,000 voters since 2004, despite a significant population increase and major voter registration drives held in 2008.

Four other states, Indiana, Nevada, North Carolina, and Ohio, appeared to be improperly using Social Security data to verify registration applications for new voters. Alabama and Georgia also appeared to be improperly using Social Security information to screen new voter applications.

For example, Nevada election officials used the Social Security database 740,000 times to check voter files or registration applications and found more than 715,000 discrepancies. Georgia's election officials ran more than 1.9 million checks and found more than 260,000 discrepancies.

The U.S. Social Security Administration found these numbers far too high to represent cases where names were not in state databases. This implied improper use of the Social Security database, a violation of federal law contained in the contract that states signed with the Social Security Administration, setting limitations on use of the database only as a last resort. The requirement for limited use/access existed because the federal database was less reliable than state lists, and was more likely to flag otherwise valid voter applications.

Following inquiry by *The Times*, Michael J. Astrue, commissioner of the Social Security Administration, advised the U.S. Department of Justice of the problem and also sent letters to election officials in Alabama, Georgia, Indiana, Nevada, and North Carolina, and Ohio, asking that they ensure their states were complying with federal law.

Rosemary E. Rodriguez, chairperson of the federal Election Assistance Commission which oversees elections, said these statistics could represent "extremely serious problems ... the law is pretty clear about how states can use Social Security information."

According to *The Times*, purge estimates were calculated by using data from state election officials compared with U.S. Postal Service data and state/county death records. *The Times'* methodology for calculating the purge data was reviewed by national voting experts.

Several state officials did not immediately respond to *The Times'* report. Later, Nevada officials reported that the large number of Social Security checks were the result of county clerks entering Social Security numbers and drivers' license numbers in the wrong data fields before records were sent to the state. Nevada Secretary of State Ross Miller issued a formal statement calling *The Times'* report misleading.

Indiana officials also defended their procedures, saying that the use of all available technologies was the best way to fight voter fraud. A spokesman for the Louisiana Secretary of State acknowledged that it was unclear why approximately 11,000 additional persons (more than deaths and relocations) were removed from its registration rolls.

Chris Thomas, Michigan Elections Director, ultimately denied that there were 33,000 voter names removed since August, stating that it was more like 11,000, and those represented deaths, relocations, or instances of otherwise ineligible voters. But *The Times* stood by its figures. After explaining its methodology to Mr. Thomas, Catherine Mathis remarked that Thomas could not explain the discrepancy between the state's numbers and those reported by *The Times*.. No response was listed for Colorado's Secretary of State.

WAR CRIMES

Those acts that violate the international laws, treaties, customs, and practices governing military conflict between belligerent states or parties.

Former Nazi Guard Deported to Germany

After years of litigation, the United States deported a former Nazi prison guard to Germany. John Demjanjuk has faced allegations for his role at several Nazi camps during WORLD WAR II, and the 89-year-old former auto worker will face more charges before a court in Germany. Demjanjuk was stripped of his U.S. citizenship twice.

Demjanjuk (then known as Ivan) was born in Ukraine in 1920. He served in the Soviet Red Army during World War II and was captured by German forces in 1942. He allegedly trained at the Treblinka death camp in Poland to became a guard. For the next two years, authorities claim he spent two years at two camps in Poland (Sobibor and Majdanek) and one in Bavaria (Flossenburg). Historians have noted that after the war, many war crimes suspects posed as Nazi victims to avoid prosecution. In 1948, Demjanjuk registered as a displaced person, which typically meant that that person was a former concentration camp prisoner or forced laborer. He asked to be transferred to Argentina, but he eventually entered the United States on an immigrant visa. He became a U.S. citizen in 1958.

Demjanjuk lived quietly as an autoworker for the next several years. However, some Holocaust victims identified Demjanjuk as the cruel death camp guard known as "Ivan the Terrible." The Immigration and Naturalization Service began an investigation, and in 1977, the JUSTICE DEPARTMENT submitted a request to the U.S. **District Court** for the Northern District of Ohio to revoke Demjanjuk's citizenship. A federal judge in 1981 concluded that Demjanjuk had lied on his application for citizenship and that he had served as a guard at the Nazi camps. Thus, the judge granted the request to revoke Demjanjuk's citizenship.

The State of Israel requested extradition so that Demjanjuk could stand trail for his alleged role in running the gas chamber at Treblinka. An estimated 870,000 Jews were murdered at the Treblinka camp, and Holocaust victims believed that Demjanjuk was the man ("Ivan the Terrible") who operated the machines that sent gas into the gas chambers. In 1988, an Israeli court found Demjanjunk guilty of war crimes and crimes against humanity, and he was sentenced to death. However, evidence found in the KGB archives in 1992 revealed that other guards at Treblinka identified Ivan the Terrible as someone named Ivan Marchenko rather than Ivan Demjanjuk. One year after this discovery, the Israel Supreme Court reversed Demjanjuk's conviction.

Demjanjuk regained his U.S. citizenship in 1998, but in 1999, the Justice Department filed another complaint in federal court in Ohio to

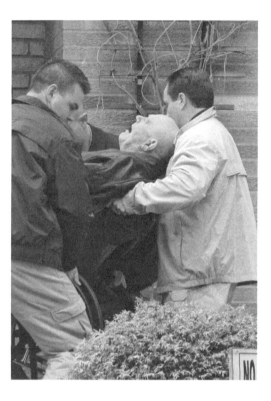

John Demjanjuk, being taken from his home April 14, 2009.

AP IMAGES

revoke Demjanjuk's citizenship once again. According to the three-count complaint, Demjanjuk was never lawfully admitted into the United States in 1952 because of his role at the death camps in Poland and Bavaria. Since he was not eligible for the visa, the government argued, he was not eligible for citizenship. After a trial, the court ruled in the government's favor. The court in 2002 revoked Demjanjuk's citizenship. *United States v. Demjanjuk*, No. 1:99CV1193, 2002 WL 544622 (N.D. Ohio Feb. 21, 2002). Demjanjuk appealed the decision twice to the Sixth **Circuit Court** of Appeals, but the **appellate court** twice affirmed the lower court's decision.

In 2004, the Department of Homeland Security served Demjanjuk with notice that he was subject to removal from the United States. The Executive Office for Immigration Review (EOIR) then initiated removal proceedings. Chief Immigration Judge Michael J. Creppy presided over the proceedings, and on December 28, 2005, Creppy ordered Demjanjuk's removal from the United States. As part of the order, Creppy determined that Demjanjuk could be deported to Germany, Poland, or Ukraine. Demjanjuk continued the litigation by arguing that Creppy was not authorized to preside over the removal proceedings. The Sixth

Circuit reviewed the case and held that Creppy was authorized under **statute** to serve as a presiding judge in the case. *Demjanjuk v. Mukasey*, 514 F.3d 616 (6th Cir. 2008).

On March 11, 2009, German prosecutors decided to seek to have Demjanjuk extradited to Germany to face 29,000 counts of being an accessory to murder. Less than two weeks later, U.S. officials confirmed that they had requested travel documents from Germany so that the United States could begin the deportation. Demjanjuk asked an immigration judge to stay the deportation, arguing that sending him to Germany would amount to torture. In a statement, Demjanjuk said that deporting him would expose him "to severe physical and mental pain that clearly amount to torture under any reasonable definition of the term." On April 6, U.S. Immigration Judge Wayne Iskra denied Demjanjak's request to stay the deportation. Four days later, the Board of Immigration Appeals also denied Demjanjak's request.

U.S. immigration agents arrived at Demjanjuk's home on April 14 to take him into federal custody. On the same day, though, the Sixth Circuit granted Demjanjak's motion to stay his removal. Federal authorities released Demjanjuk for several weeks, but on May 1, the Sixth Circuit revoked the emergency stay. Demjanjuk asked the U.S. SUPREME COURT to review the case, but the Court on May 7 denied **certiorari**. On day later, the immigration agents served Demjanjuk with a notice to surrender. He was deported on May 11.

WHISTLEBLOWING

The disclosure by a person, usually an employee, in a government agency or private enterprise; to the public or to those in authority, of mismanagement, corruption, illegality, or some other wrongdoing.

Source of Story on Warrantless Surveillance Reveals Himself

One of the principal sources of information for a story that ran in the *New York Times* in 2005 regarding the National Security Agency's warrantless wiretapping of U.S. citizens revealed his identity in 2008. The writers of the *Times* article eventually received the Pulitzer Prize for the story, which cited several unnamed sources. Agents with the FEDERAL BUREAU OF

INVESTIGATION opened a criminal probe to identify the sources for the story. The main source turned out to be Thomas Tamm, a former prosecutor with the JUSTICE DEPARTMENT.

Following the SEPTEMBER 11TH ATTACKS in 2001, the administration of President GEORGE W. BUSH implemented several programs and investigation methods designed to prevent terrorist attacks. Several of these programs and methods became the source of great controversy later in Bush's presidency and even after his presidency ended. For example, lawyers in the Attorney General's office wrote a series of memos providing legal justification for certain interrogation methods that many claim amounted to torture. These memos and their authors became the subject of scrutiny in 2008 and 2009 when the contents of these memos were released to the public.

One of the memos focused on a warrantless surveillance program run by the National Security Agency (NSA). The opinion was written by John Yoo, then an attorney with the Office of Legal Counsel of the Justice Department. Yoo was also the author of a 2003 memo concluding that the interrogation technique known as "waterboarding" was justifiable. In another memo, dated September 25, 2001, Yoo concluded that the United States government could conduct warrantless searches due to "national security reasons." These reasons included the investigation of potential terrorists and terrorist activity.

The specific context of Yoo's September 25, 2001 memo focused on possible amendments to the Foreign Intelligence Surveillance Act, 50 U.S.C. §§ 1801 *et seq.* (FISA). The FISA was enacted in 1978 out of concern of abuses within the U.S. intelligence community. The FISA established the Foreign Intelligence Surveillance Court (FISC), which now consists of 11 U.S. **district court** judges appointed by the chief justice of the U.S. SUPREME COURT. The FISC reviews applications for warrants related to national security investigations. The focus of proposed surveillance may be a U.S. citizen, but only if the U.S. citizen is acting as an agent of a foreign power and is involved in the commission of a crime.

In 2002, Bush signed a secret order authorizing the NSA to conduct surveillance on U.S. citizens without going through the FISC process that is prescribed by **statute**. The NSA identified targets for this surveillance based on information found on computers and cell phones seized from al-Qaeda agents. If authorities found a number or email address of a U.S. citizen, Bush's order authorized the authorities to eavesdrop on calls made or emails sent from the number or email address to a foreign country. This eavesdropping required no warrant under the order. The code name for the NSA's collection activities was "Stellar Wind."

On December 16, 2005, *New York Times* writers James Risen and Eric Lichtblau wrote a story entitled "Bush Lets U.S. Spy on Callers Without Warrants." The story described the program as follows:

> The previously undisclosed decision to permit some eavesdropping inside the country without court approval was a major shift in American intelligence-gathering practices, particularly for the National Security Agency, whose mission is to spy on communications abroad. As a result, some officials familiar with the continuing operation have questioned whether the surveillance has stretched, if not crossed, constitutional limits on legal searches.

Risen and Lichtblau won the Pulitzer Prize in 2006 for national reporting. Both authors later wrote books related to their investigation.

Risen and Lichtblau referred to "nearly a dozen current and former officials" as sources for the story. The story also quoted a specific official, identified as a "former senior official who specializes in national security law." Bush later referred to the leak as a "shameful act." In late December 2005, the Justice Department announced that it would run an investigation to determine who leaked the information. The leak was largely responsible for increasing the public consciousness about the investigation tactics used in the WAR ON TERRORISM.

The identities of the officials who blew the whistle on the program remained secret until 2008, when *Newsweek* featured a cover story on Thomas Tamm, who was the principal source for the *New York Times* story. Tamm's uncle and father were both high-ranking officials within the bureau, and it was only natural that Tamm would work for the federal government. He was originally a state prosecutor in Maryland, but by the late 1990s, he had joined the prosecution team within the Justice Department's Capital Case Unit.

In early 2003, Tamm accepted a transfer to the Office of Intelligence Policy and Review

(OIPR). OIPR lawyers are responsible for applying to the FISC so that investigating agencies could install wiretaps for purposes of national security. According to Tamm, members of the Bush administration had become frustrated with the OIPR process because it was cumbersome and time-consuming. While working for OIPR, Tamm became aware of the secret eavesdropping program and began to ask questions. Few familiar with the program were willing to discuss the program with him, and those that did suggested that he drop the matter. The lawyer who reviewed Tamm's work for OIPR told him that she assumed the program was illegal.

Tamm's position required a security clearance above top secret. Any information to which he was **privy** was considered highly sensitive. After being rebuked by those within his department, Tamm said he became frustrated. He said his conscience would not allow him to remain silent, and he believed his only choice was to go to the press. He contacted Lichtblau, who had written several stories focusing on the Justice Department. The two met several times, and Lichtblau later said that Tamm was rather vague in his accounts. More than a year passed between Tamm's meetings with Lichtblau (and later Risen), and President Bush personally tried to stop the *Times* from publishing the story. However, the story finally ran in the December 16, 2005 edition.

Tamm was the subject of an FBI investigation, and he could still face possible criminal charges. He gave several interviews after the *Newsweek* article ran and explained his motivation for blowing the whistle on the program. He told NBC's Rachel Maddow, "My entire life really was based on trying to enforce the law— my entire career. I believed that the law was being broken in the place where I was working." Some commentators (mostly liberal) applauded Tamm for bringing the program to light. Other commentators, however, noted that Tamm had been entrusted to maintain classified information and that he had breached his duty by taking the story to the press.

WIRETAPPING

A form of electronic eavesdropping accomplished by seizing or overhearing communications by means of a concealed recording or listening device connected to the transmission line.

In re Directives Pursuant to Section 105B of the Foreign Intelligence Surveillance Act

The United States Foreign Intelligence Surveillance Court (FISC) is a U.S. federal court that reviews requests for surveillance warrants against suspected foreign intelligence agents inside the United States by federal police agencies. It was created by the Foreign Intelligence Surveillance Act of 1978 (FISA). As part of the Bush Administration's "war on terror," the government secretly sought the cooperation of telecommunication providers without seeking warrants from the FISC. After a newspaper reported on the program and allegations were raised about domestic wiretapping, Congress enacted in 2007 an amendment to FISA that was known as the Protect America Act (PAA). This amendment authorized the U.S. government to direct communications service providers to assist in the warrantless gathering foreign intelligence when it involved targeted third persons, such as the provider's customers, reasonably believed to be located outside the United States. The act expired in February 2008 and the provisions were repealed in July 2008. However, a legal controversy over the constitutionality of the act did not come to a conclusion until August 2008, when the FISC ruled on the matter. However, the heavily redacted decision was not released to the public until January 2009. The decision, which upheld the constitutionality of the act, placed national security over FOURTH AMENDMENT privacy rights. *In re Directives Pursuant to Section 105B of the Foreign Intelligence Surveillance Act*, 551 F.3d 1004 (2008).

Under the 2007 law the Director of National Intelligence (DNI) and the Attorney General (AG) were permitted to authorize, for periods of up to one year, the acquisition of information on foreign agents reasonably believed to be outside the United States if the acquisition met certain criteria. These criteria included reasonable procedures for ensuring the targeted person was outside the United States, the assistance of communications service providers to acquire information from their customers, and that a significant purpose of the surveillance was to obtain foreign intelligence information. Pursuant to this authorization, the DNI and AG were permitted to issue directives to the providers, detailing the assistance needed to acquire the information.

One communication provider whose identity has been concealed, refused to cooperate, challenging the legality of the directives. The government then asked the FISC to compel compliance. Federal **District Court** Judge Reggie Walton, who also served as a member of the FISC, heard the matter. Walton found the directives lawful and ordered the company to comply. The company then appealed to a three-judge panel of the FISC but asked that Judge Walton stay his compliance order while the case was under review. Walton refused, and the company complied under the threat of civil contempt.

The appeals court ruled unanimously in favor of the government. Judge Bruce Selya from the First **Circuit Court** of Appeals, serving as chief judge, issued the ruling. The central issue was whether the Fourth Amendment barred warrantless surveillance. The company made two claims that were limited to the harm that may be inflicted upon U.S. persons: (1) the government, in issuing its directives, must comply with the warrant clause of the Fourth Amendment; and (2) Even if a foreign intelligence exception exists that makes a warrant unnecessary, the surveillance mandated by the directives is unreasonable. Judge Selya characterized the argument an as-applied challenge, which meant that the company had to prove more than a theoretical risk that the PAA could on certain facts produce unconstitutional applications. The company had to show that the PAA was unconstitutional as implemented.

The court found no merit in the argument that there is no foreign intelligence exception to the Fourth Amendment's requirement that searches and seizures must be authorized by a warrant signed by a judge. Though the Supreme Court has never explicitly recognized such an exception, it has made exceptions outside the foreign intelligence area. In so-called "special needs" cases the Court has deemed a warrant unnecessary when the purpose behind the governmental action goes beyond routine law enforcement and requiring a warrant would materially interfere with the accomplishment of the government action. Judge Selya applied the reasoning in these cases to the surveillance carried out through the PAA. Requiring a warrant would, with a "high degree of probability …hinder the government's ability to collect time-sensitive information" and would impede vital national security interests.

The Court rejected the claim that such warrantless surveillance is unreasonable under the Fourth Amendment. Judge Selya stated that the government did not have "carte blanche." The court was required to look at the totality of the circumstances and balance the interests at stake. The government's interest in national security was "of the highest order of magnitude." As to the "parade of horrible" presented by the company , the court concluded that it had failed to present any evidence of "actual harm, any egregious risk of error, or any broad potential for abuse." Fears that placing discretion entirely in the hands of the Executive Branch would invite abuse were off the mark as well. There was no evidence that the government's procedures to prevent abuse were implemented in **bad faith**. Therefore, the balancing of interests fell decidedly on the side of the government and the PAA.

Discrimination

LILLY LEDBETTER FAIR PAY ACT OF 2009

SEC. 202. FINDINGS.

Congress finds the following:

(1) Women have entered the workforce in record numbers over the past 50 years.

(2) Despite the enactment of the Equal Pay Act in 1963, many women continue to earn significantly lower pay than men for equal work. These pay disparities exist in both the private and governmental sectors. In many instances, the pay disparities can only be due to continued intentional discrimination or the lingering effects of past discrimination.

(3) The existence of such pay disparities—

(A) depresses the wages of working families who rely on the wages of all members of the family to make ends meet;

(B) undermines women's retirement security, which is often based on earnings while in the workforce;

(C) prevents the optimum utilization of available labor resources;

(D) has been spread and perpetuated, through commerce and the channels and instrumentalities of commerce, among the workers of the several States;

(E) burdens commerce and the free flow of goods in commerce;

(F) constitutes an unfair method of competition in commerce;

(G) leads to labor disputes burdening and obstructing commerce and the free flow of goods in commerce;

(H) interferes with the orderly and fair marketing of goods in commerce; and

(I) in many instances, may deprive workers of equal protection on the basis of sex in violation of the 5th and 14th amendments.

(4)(A) Artificial barriers to the elimination of discrimination in the payment of wages on the basis of sex continue to exist decades after the enactment of the Fair Labor Standards Act of 1938 (29 U.S.C. 201 et seq.) and the Civil Rights Act of 1964 (42 U.S.C. 2000a et seq.).

(B) These barriers have resulted, in significant part, because the Equal Pay Act has not worked as Congress originally intended. Improvements and modifications to the law are necessary to ensure that the Act provides effective protection to those subject to pay discrimination on the basis of their sex.

(C) Elimination of such barriers would have positive effects, including—

(i) providing a solution to problems in the economy created by unfair pay disparities;

(ii) substantially reducing the number of working women earning unfairly low wages, thereby reducing the dependence on public assistance;

(iii) promoting stable families by enabling all family members to earn a fair rate of pay;

(iv) remedying the effects of past discrimination on the basis of sex and ensuring that in the future workers are afforded equal protection on the basis of sex; and

(v) ensuring equal protection pursuant to Congress' power to enforce the 5th and 14th amendments.

(5) The Department of Labor and the Equal Employment Opportunity Commission have important and unique responsibilities to help ensure that women receive equal pay for equal work.

(6) The Department of Labor is responsible for–

(A) collecting and making publicly available information about women's pay;

(B) ensuring that companies receiving Federal contracts comply with anti-discrimination affirmative action requirements of Executive Order No. 11246 (relating to equal employment opportunity);

(C) disseminating information about women's rights in the workplace;

(D) helping women who have been victims of pay discrimination obtain a remedy; and

(E) being proactive in investigating and prosecuting equal pay violations, especially systemic violations, and in enforcing all of its mandates.

(7) The Equal Employment Opportunity Commission is the primary enforcement agency for claims made under the Equal Pay Act, and issues regulations and guidance on appropriate interpretations of the law.

(8) With a stronger commitment by the Department of Labor and the Equal Employment Opportunity Commission to their responsibilities, increased information as a result of the amendments made by this Act to the Equal Pay Act of 1963, wage data, and more effective remedies, women will be better able to recognize and enforce their rights.

(9) Certain employers have already made great strides in eradicating unfair pay disparities in the workplace and their achievements should be recognized.

Drugs and Narcotics

MICHIGAN MEDICAL MARIJUANA ACT

2. Findings.

Sec. 2. The people of the State of Michigan find and declare that:

(a) Modern medical research, including as found by the National Academy of Sciences' Institute of Medicine in a March 1999 report, has discovered beneficial uses for marihuana in treating or alleviating the pain, nausea, and other symptoms associated with a variety of debilitating medical conditions.

(b) Data from the Federal Bureau of Investigation Uniform Crime Reports and the Compendium of Federal Justice Statistics show that approximately 99 out of every 100 marihuana arrests in the United States are made under state law, rather than under federal law. Consequently, changing state law will have the practical effect of protecting from arrest the vast majority of seriously ill people who have a medical need to use marihuana.

(c) Although federal law currently prohibits any use of marihuana except under very limited circumstances, states are not required to enforce federal law or prosecute people for engaging in activities prohibited by federal law. The laws of Alaska, California, Colorado, Hawaii, Maine, Montana, Nevada, New Mexico, Oregon, Vermont, Rhode Island, and Washington do not penalize the medical use and cultivation of marihuana. Michigan joins in this effort for the health and welfare of its citizens.

3. Definitions.

Sec. 3. As used in this act:

(a) "Debilitating medical condition" means 1 or more of the following:

(1) Cancer, glaucoma, positive status for human immunodeficiency virus, acquired immune deficiency syndrome, hepatitis C, amyotrophic lateral sclerosis, Crohn's disease, agitation of Alzheimer's disease, nail patella, or the treatment of these conditions.

(2) A chronic or debilitating disease or medical condition or its treatment that produces 1 or more of the following: cachexia or wasting syndrome; severe and chronic pain; severe nausea; seizures, including but not limited to those characteristic of epilepsy; or severe and persistent muscle spasms, including but not limited to those characteristic of multiple sclerosis.

(3) Any other medical condition or its treatment approved by the department, as provided for in section 5(a).

(b) "Department" means the state department of community health.

(c) "Enclosed, locked facility" means a closet, room, or other enclosed area equipped with locks or other security devices that permit access only by a registered primary caregiver or registered qualifying patient.

(d) "Marihuana" means that term as defined in section 7106 of the public health code, 1978 PA 368, MCL 333.7106.

(e) "Medical use" means the acquisition, possession, cultivation, manufacture, use, internal possession, delivery, transfer, or transportation of marihuana or paraphernalia relating to the administration of marihuana to treat or alleviate a registered qualifying patient's debilitating medical condition or symptoms associated with the debilitating medical condition.

(f) "Physician" means an individual licensed as a physician under Part 170 of the public health code, 1978 PA 368, MCL 333.17001 to 333.17084, or an osteopathic physician under Part 175 of the public health code, 1978 PA 368, MCL 333.17501 to 333.17556.

(g) "Primary caregiver" means a person who is at least 21 years old and who has agreed to assist with a patient's medical use of marihuana and who has never been convicted of a felony involving illegal drugs.

(h) "Qualifying patient" means a person who has been diagnosed by a physician as having a debilitating medical condition.

(i) "Registry identification card" means a document issued by the department that identifies a person as a registered qualifying patient or registered primary caregiver.

(j) "Usable marihuana" means the dried leaves and flowers of the marihuana plant, and any mixture or preparation thereof, but does not include the seeds, stalks, and roots of the plant.

(k) "Visiting qualifying patient" means a patient who is not a resident of this state or who has been a resident of this state for less than 30 days.

(l) "Written certification" means a document signed by a physician, stating the patient's debilitating medical condition and stating that, in the physician's professional opinion, the patient is likely to receive therapeutic or palliative benefit from the medical use of marihuana to treat or alleviate the patient's debilitating medical condition or symptoms associated with the debilitating medical condition.

Terrorism

PRESIDENT OBAMA ORDERS CLOSURE OF GUANTÁNAMO BAY DETENTION CAMP

By the authority vested in me as President by the Constitution and the laws of the United States of America, in order to effect the appropriate disposition of individuals currently detained by the Department of Defense at the Guantánamo Bay Naval Base (Guantánamo) and promptly to close detention facilities at Guantánamo, consistent with the national security and foreign policy interests of the United States and the interests of justice, I hereby order as follows:

Sec. 2. Findings.

(a) Over the past 7 years, approximately 800 individuals whom the Department of Defense has ever determined to be, or treated as, enemy combatants have been detained at Guantánamo. The Federal Government has moved more than 500 such detainees from Guantánamo, either by returning them to their home country or by releasing or transferring them to a third country. The Department of Defense has determined that a number of the individuals currently detained at Guantánamo are eligible for such transfer or release.

(b) Some individuals currently detained at Guantánamo have been there for more than 6 years, and most have been detained for at least 4 years. In view of the significant concerns raised by these detentions, both within the United States and internationally, prompt and appropriate disposition of the individuals currently detained at Guantánamo and closure of the facilities in which they are detained would further the national security and foreign policy interests of the United States and the interests of justice. Merely closing the facilities without promptly determining the appropriate disposition of the individuals detained would not adequately serve those interests. To the extent practicable, the prompt and appropriate disposition of the individuals detained at Guantánamo should precede the closure of the detention facilities at Guantánamo.

(c) The individuals currently detained at Guantánamo have the constitutional privilege of the writ of habeas corpus. Most of those individuals have filed petitions for a writ of habeas corpus in Federal court challenging the lawfulness of their detention.

(d) It is in the interests of the United States that the executive branch undertake a prompt and thorough review of the factual and legal bases for the continued detention of all individuals currently held at Guantánamo, and of whether their continued detention is in the national security and foreign policy interests of the United States and in the interests of justice. The unusual circumstances associated with detentions at Guantánamo require a comprehensive interagency review.

(e) New diplomatic efforts may result in an appropriate disposition of a substantial number of individuals currently detained at Guantánamo.

(f) Some individuals currently detained at Guantánamo may have committed offenses for which they should be prosecuted. It is in the interests of the United States to review whether and how any such individuals can and should be prosecuted.

(g) It is in the interests of the United States that the executive branch conduct a prompt and thorough review of the circumstances of the individuals currently detained at Guantánamo who have been charged with offenses before military commissions pursuant to the Military Commissions Act of 2006, Public Law 109-366, as well as of the military commission process more generally.

Sec. 3. Closure of Detention Facilities at Guantánamo. The detention facilities at Guantánamo for individuals covered by this order shall be closed as soon as practicable, and no later than 1 year from the date of this order. If any individuals covered by this order remain in detention at Guantánamo at the time of closure of those detention facilities, they shall be returned to their home country, released, transferred to a third country, or transferred to another United States detention facility in a manner consistent with law and the national security and foreign policy interests of the United States.

Sec. 4. Immediate Review of All Guantánamo Detentions.

(a) Scope and Timing of Review. A review of the status of each individual currently detained at Guantánamo (Review) shall commence immediately.

(b) Review Participants. The Review shall be conducted with the full cooperation and participation of the following officials:

(1) the Attorney General, who shall coordinate the Review;

(2) the Secretary of Defense;

(3) the Secretary of State;

(4) the Secretary of Homeland Security;

(5) the Director of National Intelligence;

(6) the Chairman of the Joint Chiefs of Staff; and

(7) other officers or full-time or permanent part-time employees of the United States, including employees with intelligence, counterterrorism, military, and legal expertise, as determined by the Attorney General, with the concurrence of the head of the department or agency concerned.

(c) Operation of Review. The duties of the Review participants shall include the following:

(1) Consolidation of Detainee Information. The Attorney General shall, to the extent reasonably practicable, and in coordination with the other Review participants, assemble all information in the possession of the Federal Government that pertains to any individual currently detained at Guantánamo and that is relevant to determining the proper disposition of any such individual. All executive branch departments and agencies shall promptly comply with any request of the Attorney General to provide information in their possession or control pertaining to any such individual. The Attorney General may seek further information relevant to the Review from any source.

(2) Determination of Transfer. The Review shall determine, on a rolling basis and as promptly as possible with respect to the individuals currently detained at Guantánamo, whether it is possible to transfer or release the individuals consistent with the national security and foreign policy interests of the United States and, if so, whether and how the Secretary of Defense may effect their transfer or release. The Secretary of Defense, the Secretary of State, and, as appropriate, other Review participants shall work to effect promptly the release or transfer of all individuals for whom release or transfer is possible.

(3) Determination of Prosecution. In accordance with United States law, the cases of individuals detained at Guantánamo not approved for release or transfer shall be evaluated to determine whether the Federal Government should seek to prosecute the detained individuals

for any offenses they may have committed, including whether it is feasible to prosecute such individuals before a court established pursuant to Article III of the United States Constitution, and the Review participants shall in turn take the necessary and appropriate steps based on such determinations.

(4) Determination of Other Disposition. With respect to any individuals currently detained at Guantánamo whose disposition is not achieved under paragraphs (2) or (3) of this subsection, the Review shall select lawful means, consistent with the national security and foreign policy interests of the United States and the interests of justice, for the disposition of such individuals. The appropriate authorities shall promptly implement such dispositions.

(5) Consideration of Issues Relating to Transfer to the United States. The Review shall identify and consider legal, logistical, and security issues relating to the potential transfer of individuals currently detained at Guantánamo to facilities within the United States, and the Review participants shall work with the Congress on any legislation that may be appropriate.

Sec. 5. Diplomatic Efforts. The Secretary of State shall expeditiously pursue and direct such negotiations and diplomatic efforts with foreign governments as are necessary and appropriate to implement this order.

Sec. 6. Humane Standards of Confinement. No individual currently detained at Guantánamo shall be held in the custody or under the effective control of any officer, employee, or other agent of the United States Government, or at a facility owned, operated, or controlled by a department or agency of the United States, except in conformity with all applicable laws governing the conditions of such confinement,

including Common Article 3 of the Geneva Conventions. The Secretary of Defense shall immediately undertake a review of the conditions of detention at Guantánamo to ensure full compliance with this directive. Such review shall be completed within 30 days and any necessary corrections shall be implemented immediately thereafter.

Sec. 7. Military Commissions. The Secretary of Defense shall immediately take steps sufficient to ensure that during the pendency of the Review described in section 4 of this order, no charges are sworn, or referred to a military commission under the Military Commissions Act of 2006 and the Rules for Military Commissions, and that all proceedings of such military commissions to which charges have been referred but in which no judgment has been rendered, and all proceedings pending in the United States Court of Military Commission Review, are halted.

Sec. 8. General Provisions.

(a) Nothing in this order shall prejudice the authority of the Secretary of Defense to determine the disposition of any detainees not covered by this order.

(b) This order shall be implemented consistent with applicable law and subject to the availability of appropriations.

(c) This order is not intended to, and does not, create any right or benefit, substantive or procedural, enforceable at law or in equity by any party against the United States, its departments, agencies, or entities, its officers, employees, or agents, or any other person.

BARACK OBAMA

The White House,

January 22, 2009.

ABORTION

FOURTH CIRCUIT STRIKES DOWN BAN ON PARTIAL BIRTH ABORTIONS

Associated Press, "Court Strikes Down Late-Term Abortion Ban," *Washington Times*, May 21, 2008.

Mauro, Tony, "Abortion Ban Back at 4th Circuit," Law.com, October 29, 2007.

ANTI-CHOICE MEASURES FAIL IN THREE STATES

O'Sullivan, Mike. "U.S. Voters Weigh in on Gay Marriage, Abortion." Voice of America News, 08 November 2008. Available at http://voanews. com/english/archive/2008-11/2008-11-08-voal.cfa

Riccardi, Nicholas. "Ballot Initiatives to Curtail Abortions Defeated." *Los Angeles Times*, 05 November 2008.

Text of Proposed Measure 11 available at http://www. sdsos.gov/electionsvoteregistration/electvoterpdfs/ 2008/2008regulateperformanceofabortions

"Voters Reject Amendment 48 'Personhood' Issue. *Rocky Mountain News*, 05 November 2008.

ADMIRALTY AND MARITIME LAW

ATLANTIC SOUNDING CO. V. TOWNSEND

Force, Robert. 2004. *Admiralty and Maritime Law*. Washington, D.C.: Federal Judicial Center.

Maraist, Frank L. and Thomas C. Galligan, Jr. 2005. *Admiralty in a Nutshell*. St. Paul, Minn.: Thomson/West.

AGE DISCRIMINATION

GROSS V. FBL FINANCIAL SERVICES

Lewis, Harold S., Jr. and Elizabeth J. Norman. 2004. *Employment Discrimination Law*. 2d ed. St. Paul, Minn.: Thomson/West.

Lindemann, Barbara T. and Paul Grossman, eds. 2007. *Employment Discrimination Law*. 4th ed. Washington, D.C.: BNA Books.

ALIEN

REPORT FINDS U.S. HOMELAND SECURITY FAILED TO PROTECT UNDOCUMENTED MINORS

"A Child Alone and Without Papers." Center for Public Policy Priorities, 13 November 2008. Available at http://www.cppp.org/ repatriation/

"Recent Reviews of U.S. Policy on Unaccompanied Children." Center for Public Policy Priorities, November 2008. Available at http://www.cppp. org/repatriation/backgrounder1.pdf

"Unaccompanied Immigrant and Refugee Minors." National Conference of State Legislatures, August 2005. Available at http://www.ncsl.org/issue research/immigratioin/ unaccompaniedimmigrantandrefugeeminors/

AMERICANS WITH DISABILITIES ACT

CONGRESS OVERTURNS SUPREME COURT ADA RULINGS

Goren, William. *Understanding the Americans with Disabilities Act, 2nd Edition*. 2007, American Bar Association.

Mezey, Susan. *Disabling Interpretations: The Americans With Disabilities Act In Federal Court*. 2005, University of Pittsburgh Press.

Tucker, Bonnie, and Milani, Adam. *Federal Disability Law in a Nutshell, 3rd Edition*. 2004, West Publishing.

ANTITRUST LAW

PACIFIC BELL TELEPHONE COMPANY, DBA AT&T CALIFORNIA, V. LINKLINE COMMUNICATIONS, INC.

American Bar Association. *Market Power Handbook : Competition Law and Economic Foundation.* Chicago, Ill.: 2006.

Gellhorn, Ernset. *Antitrust Law And Economics In A Nutshell.* Saint Paul, MN.: West Group. Fifth Edition, 2004.

Kwoka, John and White, Lawrence. *The Antitrust Revolution. 4th Edition.* Oxford University Press, 2003.

APPELLATE ADVOCACY

BELL V. KELLY

Eisenberg, Brian. "Bell v. Kelly." *The Federalist Society* publication, 13 January 2009. Available at http://fed-soc.org/publications/pubID.1241/pub_detail.asp.

Bell v. Kelly, No. 07-1223, 555 US. ____ (2008). Available at www.supremecourtus.gov/opinions/08pdf/07-1223.pdf

Bell v. Kelly, No. 06-22(2008) Unpublished opinion available through http://pacer.ca4.uscourts.gov/opinion.pdf/0622.U.pdf

ARBITRATION

ARTHUR ANDERSEN LLP V. CARLISLE

Nolan-Haley, Jaqueline. *Alternative Dispute Resolution In A Nutshell.* Saint Paul, MN: West Group. Second Edition. 2001.

Barett, Jerome. *A History of Alternative Dispute Resolution: The Story of a Political, Social, and Cultural Movement.* Hoboken, N.J.: Jossey-Bass. 2004.

Ware, Stephen. *Alternative Dispute Resolution.* Saint Paul, MN: Westgroup. 2001.

VADEN V. DISCOVER BANK

Goldberg, Stephen B., *Dispute Resolution: Negotiation, Mediation, and Other Processes.* Austin, Tex.: Wolters Kluwer Law & Business/Aspen Publishers, 2007.

Carbonneau, Thomas E., *The Law and Practice of Arbitration.* Huntington, N.Y.: Juris Pub., 2007.

14 PENN PLAZA LLC V. PYETT

Barett, Jerome. *A History of Alternative Dispute Resolution: The Story of a Political, Social, and Cultural Movement.* Hoboken, N.J.: Jossey-Bass. 2004.

Nolan-Haley, Jaqueline. *Alternative Dispute Resolution In A Nutshell.* Saint Paul, MN: West Group. Second Edition. 2001.

Ware, Stephen. *Alternative Dispute Resolution.* Saint Paul, MN: Westgroup. 2001.

ARMED ROBBERY

O.J. SIMPSON SENTENCED TO 33 YEARS IN HOTEL HOLDUP CASE

Arsenuik, Melissa, "Simpson Guilty on All Counts," *Las Vegas Sun*, October 3, 2008.

Associated Press, "O.J. Simpson Sentence to Long Prison Term," MSNBC.com, Dec. 5, 2008.

ATTORNEY

ATTORNEYS CONVICTED IN FEN-PHEN SETTLEMENT PROCEEDS CASE

"Disbarred Fen-Phen Lawyers Convicted, Ordered to Return Money." *Legal News*, 22 May 2009. available at http://www.legalinfo.com//legal-news/05-22-09.html

"Fen-Phen Lawyers Convicted of Wire Fraud and Wire Fraud Conspiracy." Dept. of Justice, FBI Press Release, 3 April 2009. Available at www.louisville.fbi.gov/dojpressrel/pressrel09/lo040309.htm

"Kentucky Fen-Phen Lawyers Ordered to Return $30M." *Insurance Journal*, 9 April 2009. Available at www.insurancejournal.com/news/southeast/2009/04/09/99485.htm

"Newsroom." Fordham University School of Law, 16 February 2009. Available at www.law.fordham.edu/ihtml/news-2ihtml?id=638&nid=967

Wolfson, Andrew. "Fen-Phen Lawyers Convicted." *The Courier-Journal*, 03 April 2009.

DEMOCRATIC FUND RAISER CONVICTED FOR UNAUTHORIZED PRACTICE OF LAW

Malan, Denise. "Celis Indicted on Two Charges." *Corpus Christi Caller-Times.* April 26, 2008.

Malan, Denise. "Celis Sentenced to 1 Year, Headed to Appeal." *Corpus Christi Caller-Times.* March 26, 2009.

ATTORNEY GENERAL

REPORT FINDS ALBERTO GONZALES MISHANDLED CLASSIFIED DOCUMENTS

Johnson, Carrie. "Report Describes Careless Handling of U.S. Secrets." *The Washington Post*, 3 September 2008.

"Report of Investigation Regarding Allegations of Mishandling of Classified Documents by Attorney General Alberto Gonzales." U.S. Department of Justice, Office of the Inspector General. 2 September 2008. Available at http://www.usdoj.gov/oig/special/50809/final.pdf

"Report Says Alberto Gonzales Mishandled Classified Information." American Bvar Association *ABA Journal*, 2 September 2008.

AUTOMOBILES

AUTOMAKER BAILOUT TALKS LEADS TO GREATER OVERSIGHT OF THE AUTOMOTIVE INDUSTRY

Feulner, Ed, "CEObama, the Car Czar," *Washington Times*, April 9, 2009, A17

BANKRUPTCY

TRAVELERS INDEMNITY V. BAILEY

"Justices Agree to Review Insurer's Asbestos-Related Lawsuits." *On the Docket*, 12 December 2008. Available at www.onthedocket.org/cses/2008/travelers-indemnity-v-bailey.

Travelers Indemnity v. Bailey and *Common Law Settlement Counsel v. Bailey*, Nos. 08-295 and 08-307, 556 U.S. ___ (2009). Available at www.supremecourtus.gov/opinions/08pdf/08-295.pdf

Travelers Indemnity v. Bailey, Legal Information Institute (LII) of Cornell University School of Law. Available at http://www.law.cornell.edu/supct/cert/08-295.html

BANKS AND BANKING

CUOMO V. CLEARING HOUSE ASSOCIATION

Aman, Alfred C. and William Mayton. 2001. *Administrative Law*. 2d ed. St. Paul, Minn.: West Group

Beerman, Jack M. 2006. *Administrative Law*. New York: Aspen Publishers.

Vinici, James. "Top Court Allows NY State's Home Lending Probe." Reuters.com, June 29, 2009.

THE DEBATE OVER NATIONALIZATION OF BANKS

Newman, Rick. "Why Bank Nationalization is So Scary." *U.S. News and World Report*. February 22, 2009.

Richardson, Matthew and Nouriel Roubin. "Nationalize the Banks! We're All Swedes Now." *Washington Post*. February 15, 2009.

BIRTH CONTROL

ILLINOIS COURTS WRESTLE WITH EMERGENCY CONTRACEPTION LAWS

Associated Press, "Illinois Can't Force Dispensing 'Morning-After' Pill," Chicago Tribune, April 6, 2009.

Johnson, Carla K., "Druggists Can Object to 'Morning-After' Pill Rule," Chicago Tribune, December 18, 2008.

CAPITAL PUNISHMENT

KENTUCKY CONDUCTS ITS FIRST CRIMINAL EXECUTION IN NINE YEARS

Barrouquere, Betty. "Kentucky Executes First Inmate in Nine Years." Louisville *Courier-Journal*, 22 November 2008.

Chapman v. Commonwealth, No. 2005-SC-000070-MR, 19 November 2008. Available at http://www.findlaw.com

"Child Killer Marco Chapman Executed." Lexington WLEX-TV News, 21 November 2008. Available at http://www.wlextv.com/global/story.asp?=9396152

Hamrich, Brian. "Police Suspect Made Mom Watch Murders." Cincinnati WLWT Eyewitness News 5. 23 August 2008. Available at http://www.wlwt.com/news/1629037/detail.html

"Marco Chapman Closer to Execution." *Kentucky Post*, 7 November 2008.

"Young Hero Saves Self, Mother." ABC Primetime News, 21 July 2005. Available at http://abcnews.go.com/Primetime/Story?id-965806

LETHAL INJECTIONS RESUME IN STATES AFTER BAZE

Chase, Randall. "Delaware Hears Arguments Challenging Lethal Injections." *Delco Times*, 29 January 2009.

Dolan, Maura. "Schwarzenegger Changes Strategy in Execution Debate." *Los Angeles Times*, 24 February 2009.

Green, Jeff. "Lawsuit: Moore Upholds Constitutionality of Ohio's Lethal Injection Protocol." *Morning Sentinel*, 14 May 2009.

La Corte, Rachel. "Supreme Court Stays Execution Set for Today." The *Spokesman Review*, 13 March 2009.

Moritz, Rob. "Court Postpones Arguments in Lawsuit Challenging Lethal Injection." The *Arkansas News*, 14 May 2009.

"Order Granting Stay." *Stenson v. Vail*, Available at http://www.law.berkeley.edu/clinics/dpclinic/lethalinjection/LI/documetns/courtorders/washington/stenson/2008

Ovaska, Sarah. "North Carolina Court: Doctors Can Participate in Executions." *The Charlotte Observer*, 01 May 2009.

Stohr, Greg and Deborah Denno. "Executions to Resume After High Court Upholds Lethal Injections." *Bloomberg News*, 17 April 2008.

"U.S. Supreme Court Lifts Execution Stay." The *Spokesman Review*, 3 December 2008.

"Washington State's Execution Team Resigns." The *Spokesman Review*, 2 April 2009.

Williams, Carol. "New Death Penalty Rules Rejected by California Court." *Los Angeles Times*, 22 November 2008.

Williams, Carol. "State Opens Comment Period on Lethal Injection Regs." *Los Angeles Times*, 1 May 2009.

SUPREME COURT DENIES REVIEW OF VICTIM IMPACT EVIDENCE CASES

Kelly v. California, No. 07-11073, 555 US. ____ (2009). Available at www.supremecourtus.gov/opinions/08pdf/07-11073Stevens.pdf

Savage, David. "Supreme Court Upholds 'Victim Impact Evidence' Rule." *Los Angeles Times*, 11 November 2008.

CLEAN WATER ACT

ENTERGY CORPORATION V. RIVERKEEPER, INC.

Findley, Roger. *Environmental Law in Nutshell*. St. Paul, MN: West Group. 2004. Sixth Edition.

Getches. David. *Water Law in a Nutshell*. St. Paul, MN: West Group. 1997. Third Edition.

Shiva, Vandana. *Water Wars: Privatization, Pollution, and Profit*. Cambridge, MA: South End Press. 2002.

COMMERCE CLAUSE

SIXTH CIRCUIT STRIKES DOWN KENTUCKY WINE LAW

Barron, Jerome A. and C. Thomas Dienes, *Constitutional Law*. St. Paul, Minn.: Thomson/West, 2003.

Nowak, John E. and Ronald T. Rotunda, *Constitutional Law*. St. Paul, Minn.: Thomson/West, 2004.

COMPUTER CRIME

VA AGREES TO $20 MILLION SETTLEMENT OVER STOLEN LAPTOP

Files, John. "VA Laptop is Recovered, Its Data Intact." *New York Times*, June 29, 2006.

Yen, Hope. "$20 Million Settlement Reached for Veterans in ID Theft Suit." *New York Times*, January 28, 2009.

CONFRONTATION

MELENDEZ-DIAZ V. MASSACHUSETTS

Liptak, Adam. "Justices Rule Lab Analysts Must Testify on Results." *New York Times*, June 26, 2009.

Barnes, Robert. "Defendants Have Right to Confront Analysts of Forenscs, Court Rules." *Washington Post*, June 26, 2009.

Savage, David. "Defendant Can Cross-Examine Forensic Experts, Supreme Court Rules." *Los Angeles Times*, June 26, 2009.

COPYRIGHT

CONGRESS ENACTS LAW THAT AUTHORIZES APPOINTMENT OF COPYRIGHT CZAR

Miller, Arthur R., and Davis, Michael H. *Intellectual Property: Patents, Trademarks, and Copyright, 3rd Edition*. West Group, 2000.

Poltorak, Alexander, and Lerner, Paul. *Essentials of Intellectual Property*. Wiley, 2002.

Shaw, Russell, and Mercer, David. *Caution! Music & Video Downloading: Your Guide to Legal, Safe, and Trouble-Free Downloads*. Wiley, 2004.

ORPHAN WORKS ACT OF 2008

Albanese, Andrew. "As 109th Congress Nears Close is Orphan Works Bill Unlikely? *Library Journal*, 25 September 2008.

Kravets, David. "'Orphan Works' Copyright Law Dies Quiet Death." *Wired*, 30 September 2008.

"Leahy, Hatch, Berman, Smith Introduce IP Legislation." Freedom for Intellectual Property. 30 April 2008. Available at http://freedomforip. org/2008/04/24/shawn-bentley-orphan-works-act-of-2008/

"Legislative Agenda 2009: Executive Summary." Association of College and Research Libraries (ACRL). Available at www.crl.org/ala/mgrps/divs/ acrl/issues/washingtonwatch/ALA

"Senator Hatch Speaks at World Copyright Summit." *IP Watchdog*, June 2009. Available at http://www. ipwatchdog.com/

"Shawn Bentley Orphan Works Act of 2008." Text available at http://thomas.loc.gov/cgi-bin/query/z? c110:S.2913:

"Statement of Marybeth Peters, Register of Copyrights, before the Subcommittee on Courts, the Internet, and Intellectual Property, Committee on the Judiciary. 13 March 2008. Available at www.copyright.gov/docs/ regstat031308.html

RIAA CHANGES POSITION ON SUING INDIVIDUALS WHO ILLEGALLY DOWNLOAD MUSIC

Miller, Arthur R., and Davis, Michael H. *Intellectual Property: Patents, Trademarks, and Copyright, 3rd Edition*. West Group, 2000.

Poltorak, Alexander, and Lerner, Paul. *Essentials of Intellectual Property*. Wiley, 2002.

Shaw, Russell, and Mercer, David. *Caution! Music & Video Downloading: Your Guide to Legal, Safe, and Trouble-Free Downloads*. Wiley, 2004.

STUDIOS CLASH OVER RIGHTS TO "WATCHMAN" MOVIE

Cieply, Michael. "Judge Says Fox Owns Rights to a Warner Movie." *New York Times*. December 24, 2008.

Horn, John. "A Super Battle over 'Watchman'." *Los Angeles Times*. November 16, 2008.

CORRUPTION

ILLINOIS GOVERNOR ROD BLAGOJEVICH IMPEACHED

Long, Ray and Rick Pearson. "Impeached Illinois Gov. Rod Blagojevich Has Been Removed from Office." *Chicago Tribune*. Jan. 30, 2009.

Saulny, Susan. "Portrait of a Politician: Vengeful and Profane." *New York Times*. Dec. 9, 2008.

SENATE TED STEVENS LOSES SENATE ELECTION FOLLOWING CONVICTION

"Sen. Ted Stevens' Conviction Set Aside." CNN.com. April 7, 2009.

Bolstad, Erika. "Stevens Bids Farewell in Speech to Senate." *Anchorage Daily News*. November 20, 2008.

COVENANT

RIGHT TO DRY LAWS

Rosenthal, Elizabeth. "A Line in the Yard: The Battle Over the Right to Dry Outside." *New York Times*, April 17, 2008.

Russell, Jenna. "Clothesline Rule Creates Flap." *Boston Globe*, March 13, 2008.

CRIME

FBI REPORTS TWO-YEAR DECLINE IN VIOLENT CRIME

"FBI Releases Preliminary Annual Crime Statistics for 2007." FBI Press Release, 9 June 2008. Available at http://www.fbi.gov/pressrel/prressrel08/prelim_ucr060908.htm

"FBI Reports Drop in Crime Including Arson." *Insurance Journal*, 12 January 2009.

"Some Good News: Crime is Declining." 2008 Crime in the United Sates Preliminary Semiannual Uniform Crime Report: January through June. FBI Press Release, 12 June 2009. Available at http://www.fbi.gov/page2/jan09/ucr_statistics011209.html

CRIMINAL LAW

CRAIG V. STATE

Cammack, Mark and Garland, Norman. *Advanced Criminal Procedure in a Nutshell*. St. Paul, MN: West Publishing Co. 2001.

Dripps, Donald. *About Guilt and Innocence: The Origins, Development, and Future of Constitutional Criminal Procedure*. Praeger, 2002.

Sprack, John. *A Practical Approach to Criminal Procedure, 11th Edition*. Oxford University Press, 2006.

CRIMINAL PROCEDURE

CONE V. BELL

Federman, Cary. *The Body And the State: Habeas Corpus And American Jurisprudence*. New York, NY: State University of New York Press. 2006.

Frank, Jerome. *Courts on Trial*. Princeton, NJ: Princeton University Press. 1973.

Freedman, Eric. *Habeas Corpus: Rethinking the Great Writ of Liberty*. New York: New York Univ. Press. 2003.

HEDGPETH V. PULIDO

LaFave, Wayne R. and Jerold H. Israel, *Criminal Procedure*. St. Paul, Minn: Thomson/West 2007.

Emanuel, Steven, *Criminal Procedure*. New York: Aspen Publishers, 2004.

PUCKETT V. UNITED STATES

Puckett v. United States, No. 07-9712, 556 U.S. ___ (2009), Available at www.supremecourtus.gov/opinions/08pdf/07-9712.pdf

Puckett v. United States, Legal Information Institute (LII) of Cornell University School of Law. Available at http://www.law.cornell.edu/supct/cert/07-9712.html

Puckett v. United States, Supreme Court Media, The Oyez Project, available at http://www.oyez.org/cases/2000-2009/2007/2007_07_9712

"Puckett v. United States." Legal Information Institute (LII), Cornell University School of Law, available at http://topics.law.cornell.edu/supct/cert/07-9712

DEPARTMENT OF JUSTICE

JUSTICE DEPARTMENT PROBE FINDS MISCONDUCT IN POLITICALLY-MOTIVATED HIRINGS

Cassens Weiss, Debra. "Lawyers Ask Va. Bar to Investigate Monica Goodling." *ABA Law Journal*, 16 September 2008.

Palazzolo, Joe. "Report: Ex-DOJ Officials Improperly Politicized Hiring, Broke Law." *Legal Times*, 29 July 2008.

U.S. Department of Justice. "An Investigation of Allegations of Politicized Hiring by Monica Goodling and Other Staff in the Office of the Attorney General," 28 July 2008. Available at www.usdoj.gov/oig/special/s0807/final.pdf

DISCRIMINATION

ASHCROFT V. IQBAL

Hardy, Colleen E. *The Detention of Unlawful Enemy Combatants During the War on Terror*. El Paso: LFB Scholarly Pub., 2009.

Miller, Mark C. *Exploring Judicial Politics*. New York: Oxford University Press, 2009.

CONGRESS ENACTS GENETIC INFORMATION NONDISCRIMINATION ACT

"Genetic testing and employment litigation." *Journal of Law and Health*. 2001. Vol. 16:1, 61.

Jones, Nancy et al. *Genetic Discrimination*. 2008, Nova Science Publishers.

Stewart, Alison et al. *Genetics, Health Care and Public Policy*. 2007, Cambridge University Press.

CONGRESS ENACTS THE LILLY LEDBETTER FAIR PAY ACT

Covington, Robert and Decker, Kurt. *Employment Law in a Nutshell.* Saint Paul, MN: West Group. 2002. Second Edition.

Lewis, Jr., Harold and Norman, Elizabeth. *Civil Rights Law and Practice.* Saint Paul, MN: West Group. 2004.

Vieira, Norman. *Constitutional Civil Rights in a Nutshell.* Saint Paul, MN.: West Group. 1998.

DNA EVIDENCE

OSBORNE V. DISTRICT ATTORNEY'S OFFICE FOR THE THIRD JUDICIAL DISTRICT

Federal Judicial Center. 2000. *Reference Manual on Scientific Evidence.* New York: LEXIS Publishing.

Moore, Solomon. 2009. "F.B.I. and States Vastly Expand DNA Databases," *New York Times.*

DOUBLE JEOPARDY

YEAGER V. UNITED STATES

Yeager v. United States, No. 08-67, 557 U.S. ___ (2009), Available at www.supremecourtus.gov/opinions/08pdf/08-67.pdf

Yeager v. United States, Legal Information Institute (LII) of Cornell University School of Law. Available at http://www.law.cornell.edu/supct/cert/08-67.html

Yeager v. United States. Supreme Court Media, The Oyez Project, available at http://www.oyez.org/cases/2000-2009/2008/2008_08_67/

Yeager v. United States, Legal Information Institute (LII) of Cornell University School of Law. Available at http://www.law.cornell.edu/supct/cert/08-67.html

DRUGS AND NARCOTICS

VOTERS APPROVE MARIJUANA INITIATIVES

Abel, David, "Voters Approve Marijuan Law Change," *Boston Globe,* Nov. 5, 2008.

Chambers, Jennifer, "Medical Marijuna Law Mired in Confusion," *Detroit News,* April 22, 2009.

DUTY OF TONNAGE

POLAR TANKERS, INC. V. CITY OF VALDEZ

Chemerinsky, Erwin. 2005. *Constitutional Law.* 2d ed. New York, NY: Aspen Publishers.

Nowak, John E. and Ronald D. Rotunda. 2004. *Constitutional Law.* 7th ed. St. Paul, Minn.: Thomson/West.

ECONOMY

CONGRESS ENACTS $789 BILLION STIMULUS PACKAGE

Labaton, Stephen and David M. Herszenhorn, "Treasury to Unveil Bailout Plan Tuesday," New York Times, February 9, 2009.

Rich, Frank, "They Sure Showed That Obama," New York Times, February 15, 2009.

EDUCATION LAW

THE LOUISIANA SCIENCE EDUCATION ACT OF 2008

"Act No. 473 (Senate Bill No. 733)." Text available at http://www.legis.state.la.us/billdata/streamdocument.asp?did=503483

"Final Louisiana Survey Report." The Public Policy Research Lab. 2009. Available at http://www.survey.lsu.edu/downloads/2009/lasurveyreport_final.pdf

Gefter, Amanda. "New Legal Threat to Teaching Evolution in the US." *New Scientist,* Issue 2664, 9 July 2008.

Forrest, Barbara. "Louisiana is Reaping What it Sowed." Louisiana Coalition for Science article, 16 February 2009.

Hvitved, Angela. "Academic Freedom Is a Good Thing, Right?" *ASBMB Today,* August 2008.

"Polling Education in Louisiana." The National Center for Science Education News article, 14 April 2009. Available at http://ncseweb.org/news/2009/04/polling-evolution-louisiana-004730

NO PRIVATE CAUSE OF ACTION UNDER NO CHILD LEFT BEHIND ACT

Duffy, Shannon P., "3rd Circuit: Parents Can't Sue Under No Child Left Behind Act," Law.com, November 21, 2008.

Rapp, James A., *Education Law.* New York: Matthew Bender & Co., 2007.

ELECTIONS

CONTEST OF GENERAL ELECTION HELD ON NOVEMBER 4, 2008, FOR THE PURPOSE OF ELECTING A UNITED STATES SENATOR FROM THE STATE OF MINNESOTA

Doyle, Pat. "At Last, a Second Senator for Minnesota." *Minneapolis Star Tribune.* July 1, 2009.

Horwith, Justin. "Coleman and Franken: Fighting Over the Minnesota Recount." *Time.* November, 17, 2008.

Phillips, Kate. "Court Rules Franken has won the Senate Race; Coleman Concedes." *New York Times.* June 30, 2009.

EMPLOYMENT LAW

A TIGHTENING JOB MARKET AND ITS LEGAL IMPLICATIONS

"2008 Job Market Report." March 2008. Published by Lee Hecht Harrison. Available as retrieved on 23 June 2009 at http://marketing.adeccoma.com/jobmarket_mod_0308/pdf/jobmkt08_lhh.pdf

"Fewer Grads Have Jobs, More Headed to Graduate School." National Association of Colleges and Employers. 13 May 2009. Available at www.naceweb.org/spotlight/2009/c51309a.htm

Johns, Gregg. "Legal Issues: H-1B Visa Quota Still Not Exhausted." National Association of Colleges and Employers. 24 June 2009. Available at www.naceweb.org/spotlight/2009/e052809.htm

Robison, Jennifer. "Teens Squeezed Out: Summer Job Market Especially Tough for Poor Kids." *The Las Vegas Review-Journal,* 18 June 2008.

CRAWFORD V. METROPOLITAN GOVERNMENT OF NASHVILLE AND DAVIDSON COUNTY, TENNESSEE

Covington, Robert and Decker, Kurt. *Employment Law in a Nutshell.* Saint Paul, MN: West Group. 2002. Second Edition.

Lewis, Jr., Harold and Norman, Elizabeth. *Civil Rights Law and Practice.* Saint Paul, MN: West Group. 2004.

Vieira, Norman. *Constitutional Civil Rights in a Nutshell.* Saint Paul, MN.: West Group. 1998.

ENVIRONMENTAL LAW

COEUR ALASKA, INC. V. SOUTHEAST ALASKA CONSERVATION COUNCIL

Craig, Robin Kundis. 2009. *The Clean Water Act and the Constitution.* 2d ed. Environmental Law Institute.

Gaba, Jeffrey M. *Environmental Law.* 4th ed. St. Paul, Minn.: Thomson/West.

OBAMA ADMINISTRATION SHIFTS POLICY ON AUTO EMISSIONS REGULATION

Findley, Roger and Farber, Daniel. *Environmental Law in a Nutshell. 6th Ed.* West Publishing, 2006.

Coile, Zachary. State Renews Push for Tougher Emission Rules. San Francisco Chronicle. March 6, 2009.

SUMMERS V. EARTH ISLAND INSTITUTE

Breen, Rioabart. *Approaching Ecosystem Management: Change and Challenge in Forest Planning in the US Forest Service.* 2008, VDM Verlage.

Findley, Roger and Farber, Daniel. *Environmental Law in a Nutshell.* 2004, 6th edition. West Publishing.

U.S. Forest Service. *The National Forest Manual.* 2008. Bibliolife.

ESPIONAGE

U.S. NATURALIZED CITIZEN SENTENCED AS CHINESE SPY

"China Denied Spying Claims Made in U.S. Case." MSNBC News, 14 May 2009. Available at http://www.msnbcnews.com

"China Denies Spying Claims Made in U.S. Court Case." ABC News, 14 May 2009. Available at http://www.abcnews.go.com/International/wirestory?id=7583418

"Chinese High-Tech Spy Case Inches Closer to Trial." *Network World,* 19 March 2009.

"Chinese Spy Sentenced to Nearly 16 Years." *The New York Times,* 9 August 2008.

"Former Pentagon Official Pleads Guilty in China Spy Case." *Christian Science Monitor,* 2 April 2008.

"U.S. Man Who Spied for China Gets Nearly 16 Years." FOX News, 8 August 2008. Available at http://www.foxnews.com/wires/2008Aug08/0,4675,ChineseSpies,00.html

EVIDENCE

CORLEY V. UNITED STATES

Corley v. United States, No. 07-10441, 556 US. ____ (2008). Available at www.supremecourtus.gov/opinions/09pdf/07-10441.pdf

"Corley v. United States." Legal Information Institute (LII) Cornell University School of Law. Available at http://www.law.cornell.edu/supct/html/07-10441.ZS.html

"Corley v. United States." Supreme Court Media, The Oyez Project, available at http://www.oyez.org/cases/2000-2009/2009/07_10441

FEDERAL COMMUNICATIONS COMMISSION

FEDERAL COMMUNICATIONS COMMISSION V. FOX TELEVISION STATIONS, INC.

Carter, T. Barton. *Mass Communications Law in a Nutshell. 6th ed.* West Group, 2006.

Tomlinson, Richard. *Tele-Revolution.* Penobscot Press, 2000.

Zarkin, Kimberly and Zarkin, Michael. *The Federal Communications Commission.* Greenwood Press, 2006.

FEDERAL DEPOSIT INSURANCE CORPORATION

FDIC STEPS IN TO TRY TO CURB FORECLOSURE CRISIS

Mullins, Luke, "FDIC Chief Calls for a Housing Rescue," U.S. News and World Report, April 9, 2008.

Zibel, Alan, "FDIC Proposes to Modify 2.2M Mortgages to Fight Foreclosure," USA Today, Nov. 14, 2008.

FIRST AMENDMENT

ELEVENTH CIRCUIT PARTIALLY REJECTS CHALLENGE TO FLORIDA PLEDGE OF ALLEGIANCE LAW

Palmer, Alyson M. and Jonathan Ringel, "11th Circuit Rejects Most of Florida Pledge Challenge," Law.com, July 24, 2008.

Ringel, Jonathan, "11th Circuit Rejects Flag Pledge Case," Law.com, Jan. 27, 2009.

"The Pledge of Allegiance and the Law," *Wall Street Journal*, Jan. 27, 2009.

THIRD CIRCUIT AGAIN STRIKES DOWN CHILD ONLINE PROTECTION ACT

Duffy, Shannon P., "3d Circuit Strikes Down COPA – Again," Law.com, July 23, 2008.

"Supreme Court Will Not Consider Internet Children's Safety Law," Congress Daily, Jan. 21, 2009

PLEASANT GROVE CITY, UTAH V. SUMMUM

Barnes, Robert. "City Can Reject Religious Display." *Washington Post*, February 26, 2009.

Liptak, Adam. "Court Denies a Religion Its Monument in a Park." *New York Times*, February 26, 2009.

Savage, David. "Supreme Court rejects free-speech argument for 'Seven Aphorisms' display." *Los Angeles Times*, February 26, 2009.

YSURSA V. POCATELLO EDUCATION ASSOCIATION

Barron, Jerome, Dienes, Thomas. *First Amendment Law in a Nutshell, 3rd ed.* West Group, 2004.

Farber, Daniel. *The First Amendment: Concepts and Insights.* Foundation Press, 2002.

Sunstein, Cass. *Democracy and the Problem of Free Speech.* Free Press, 1995.

JUSTICE DEPARTMENT REPORTS INCREASE IN SURVEILLANCE WARRANTS

Ryan, Jason. "Secret Wiretap Warrants Double Since 9/11." ABC News, 30 April 2008. Available at http://abcnews.go.com/id=4761476

Singel, Ryan. "Secret Spying Court Stays Secret, Rejects ACLU Plea Again." *Wired*, 29 August 2008. Available at http://www.wired.com/threatlevel/2008/08/secret-spying-c/

"The Foreign Intelligence Surveillance Act of 1978." U.S. Department of Justice Publication, last date revised: 27 February 2009. Available at http://www.it.ojp.gov/default.aspx?area=privacy&page=1286.

FOOD AND DRUG ADMINISTRATION

SALMONELLA OUTBREAK LEADS TO HUNDREDS OF ILLNESSES

Doering, Christopher. "Peanut Recall Having Big Impact on Small Firms." Reuters.com. March 11, 2009.

Stark, Lisa, Brian Hartman, and Kate Barrett. "Major Expansion Announced in Peanut Recall." ABC News. Jan. 28, 2009.

FDA COMES UNDER FIRE

Kling, Jim. "FDA's Biggest Blunders." MSN.com. March 18, 2008.

Moss, Michael. "Food Companies Are Placing the Onus for Safety on Consumers." *New York Times.* May 14, 2009.

Mundy, Alicia and Jared A. Favole. "FDA Scientists Ask Obama to Restructure Drug Agency." *Wall Street Journal.* January 8, 2009.

FOURTH AMENDMENT

ARIZONA V. GANT

Cammack, Mark and Garland, Norman. *Advanced Criminal Procedure in a Nutshell.* West Publishing Co. 2001.

Dash, Samuel. *The Intruders: Unreasonable Searches and Seizures from King John to John Ashcroft.* Rutgers University Press. 2004.

Long, Carolyn. *Mapp V. Ohio: Guarding Against Unreasonable Searches And Seizures.* University Press of Kansas. 2006.

HERRING V. UNITED STATES

Cammack, Mark and Garland, Norman. *Advanced Criminal Procedure in a Nutshell.* St. Paul, MN: West Publishing Co. 2001.

Dash, Samuel. *The Intruders: Unreasonable Searches and Seizures from King John to John Ashcroft.* Rutgers, NJ: Rutgers University Press. 2004.

Long, Carolyn. *Mapp V. Ohio: Guarding Against Unreasonable Searches And Seizures.* Lawrence, KS: University Press of Kansas. 2006.

NINTH CIRCUIT RULES THAT EMPLOYEE TEXT MESSAGES ARE PROTECTED BY THE FOURTH AMENDMENT

Associated Press, "Court Limits Employer Access to Worker Messages," FoxNews.com, June 19, 2008.

Boehning, H. Christopher and Daniel J. Toal, "Reasonable Expectations of Privacy Expand," New York Law Journal, August 26, 2008.

FRAUD

INVESTORS LOSE BILLIONS IN BERNARD MADOFF'S PONZI SCHEME

Gandel, Stephen, "Wall Street's Latest Downfall: Madoff Charged with Fraud," Time, Dec. 12, 2008.

Henriques, Diana B., "Madoff Scheme Kept Rippling Outward, Across Borders," New York Times, Dec. 19, 2008.

FREEDOM OF INFORMATION

PRESIDENT OBAMA SIGNS EXECUTIVE ORDER AMENDING PRESIDENTIAL RECORDS ACT

"Executive Order 133489 of January 21, 2009." Presidential Documents, Federal Register, Vol. 74 No. 15, 26 January 2009. Also available at http://edocket.access.gpo.gov/2009/pdf/E-9-1712.pdf

"Obama Executive Order Limits Privilege for Presidential Records." Information Management Journal, March-April 2009.

"President Obama Revokes Bush Presidential Records Executive Order." National Coalition for History, 26 January 2009. Available at http://www.historycoalition.org/2009/01/21/president-obama-revokes-bush-presidential-records-executive-order/

"Presidential Records Act of 1978." As accessed on 23 June 2009 at www.archives.gov/presidential-libraries/laws/1978-act.html

FREEDOM OF SPEECH

THIRD CIRCUIT STRIKES DOWN TEMPLE UNIVERSITY SEXUAL HARASSMENT POLICY

Duffy, Shannon P. "Court Rejects Temple's Sexual Harassment Policy." Law.com. August 5, 2008.

Lederman, Doug. "Court Strikes Down 'Overbroad' Harassment Policy." Inside Higher Ed. August 5, 2008.

GAY AND LESBIAN RIGHTS

ARKANSAS VOTERS BAN ADOPTION AND FOSTER PARENTING BY UNMARRIED COUPLES

Pinello, Daniel. Gay Rights and American Law. Cambridge University Press, 2003.

Alsenas, Linda. Gay America: Struggle for Equality. Amulet Press, 2008.

CALIFORNIA SUPREME COURT UPHOLDS SAME-SEX MARRIAGE

"California Supreme Court Declares Prohibition of Same-Sex Marriages Unconstitutional." Harvard Law Review, March 2009. Available at http://www.hlr.org/issues/122/march09/recentcases/in_re_marriage_case.pdf

"California Supreme Court Rules in Marriage Cases." News Release No. 26, The Judicial Council of California, 15 May 2008. Available at http://www.courtinfo.ca.gov/presscenter/newsreleases/NR26-08.PDF

Crary, David. "Iowa Court Ruling Transforms the Gay-Marriage Map." The Boston Herald, 03 April 2009.

Dolan, Maura. "California Supreme Court Looks Unlikely to Kill Proposition 8." Los Angeles Times, 06 March 2009.

Dolan, Maura. "Prop. 8 Gay Marriage Ban Goes to Supreme Court." Los Angeles Times, 20 November 2008.

In re Marriage Cases, 15 May 2008. Available at http://www.courtinfo.ca.gov/opinions/archives/S147999.PDF

O'Sullivan, Mike. "U.S. Voters Weigh in on Gay Marriage, Abortion." Voice of America News, 08 November 2008. Available at http://voanews.com/english/archive/2008-11/2008-11-08-voal.cfa

CONNECTICUT AND IOWA SUPREME COURTS FIND SAME-SEX MARRIAGE BANS UNCONSTITUTIONAL UNDER STATE CONSTITUTIONS

Crary, David. "Iowa Court Ruling Transforms the Gay-Marriage Map." The Boston Herald, 03 April 2009.

Ewers, Justin "As Connecticut Allows Same-Sex Marriage, the Debate Continues in California." U.S. News & World Reports, 13 November 2008.

Kerrigan v. Commissioner of Public Health, 28 October 2008. Available at http://www.jud.ct.gov/external/supapp/Cases/AROcr/CR289/289CR152.pdf

Kerrigan v. Commissioner of Public Health, OLR Research Report, 7 November 2008. Available at http://www.cga.ct.gov/2008/rpt/2008-R-0585.htm

Lorentzen, Amy. "Iowa High Court Legalizes Gay Marriage in State. The Berkeley Independent, 3 April 2009.

CONSTITUTIONAL AMENDMENTS TO SAME-SEX MARRIAGES

"California High Court Upholds Same-Sex Marriage Ban." CNN.com. May 27, 2009.

Kornblum, Janet. "California Approves Gay Marriage Ban." USA Today. November 5, 2008.

McKinley, Jesse and Laurie Goodstein. "Bans in 3 States on Gay Marriage." N.Y. Times. November 5, 2008.

MICHIGAN SUPREME COURT PROHIBITS PUBLIC EMPLOYERS FROM PROVIDING HEALTHCARE BENEFITS TO SAME-SEX PARTNERS

National Pride at Work v. Granholm, available at http://www.courts.michigan.gov/supremecourt/Clerk/11-07/133554

"State Constitutional Law-Same-Sex Relations-Supreme Court of Michigan Holds that Public Employers May Not Provide Healthcare Benefits to Same-Sex Domestic Partners of Employees." *Harvard Law Review*, Issue 122, February 2009, p. 1263.

Thelen, Sara Lynne. "High Court Bars Same-Sex Benefits." *The Daily News*, 11 May 2008.

NORTH COAST WOMEN'S CARE MEDICAL GROUP, INC. v. SAN DIEGO COUNTY SUPERIOR COURT

Pinello, Daniel. *Gay Rights and American Law*. Cambridge University Press, 2003.

Alsenas, Linda. *Gay America: Struggle for Equality*. Amulet Press, 2008.

HABEAS CORPUS

HARBISON v. BELL

Harbison v. Bell, Cornell University School of Law Available at http://www.law.cornell.edu/supct/cert/07-8521.html

Harbison v. Bell, No. 07-8521, Available at www.supremecourtus.gov/docket/07-8521.htm

"Professor Dan Kobil's Amicus Curiae Brief Helps Influence U.S. Supreme Court Ruling in *Harbison v. Bell*." Capital University Law School News Release, 2 April 2009. Available at http://www.law.capital.edu/news/archive/2009/20090402kobil.asp

Rutledge, Sarah. "Harbison v. Bell." *Duke Journal of Constitutional Law & Public Policy*, p. 215 Sidebar, 2009.

JIMINEZ v. QUARTERMAN

Federman, Cary. *The Body And the State: Habeas Corpus And American Jurisprudence*. New York, NY: State University of New York Press. 2006.

Frank, Jerome. *Courts on Trial*. Princeton, NJ: Princeton University Press. 1973.

Freedman, Eric. *Habeas Corpus: Rethinking the Great Writ of Liberty*. New York: New York Univ. Press. 2003.

KNOWLES v. MIRZAYANCE

"Justices Overturn Another Ineffective Assistance of Counsel Ruling." 24 March 2009. *On the Docket*, Supreme Court Media, The Oyez Project, available at http://www.oyez.org/cases/2000-2009/2008/2008_07_1315

Knowles v. Mirzayance, No. 07-1315, 556 US. ____ (2009). Available at www.supremecourtus.gov/opinions/08pdf/07-1315.pdf

Knowles v. Mirzayance, Global Legal Information Network (GLIN). Retrieved on 30 May 2009 at www.glin.gov/view.action?glinid=217410

Knowles v. Mirzayance, Legal Information Institute (LII). Available at www.topics.law.cornell.edu/supct/cert/07-1315

IDENTITY THEFT

FLORES-FIGUEROA v. UNITED STATES

Cammack, Mark and Garland, Norman. *Advanced Criminal Procedure in a Nutshell*. St. Paul, MN: West Publishing Co. 2001.

Dripps, Donald. *About Guilt and Innocence: The Origins, Development, and Future of Constitutional Criminal Procedure*. Praeger, 2002.

Sprack, John. *A Practical Approach to Criminal Procedure, 11th Edition*. Oxford University Press, 2006.

IMMIGRATION

LOZANO v. CITY OF HAZELTON, PENNSYLVANIA

"Local Laws Barring 'Illegal Aliens' From Jobs, Housing Are Preempted, Violate Due Process." *U.S. Law Week*, Vol 76 No. 5, 7 August 2007.

"Case Detail: Lozano v. City of Hazelton." Washington Legal Foundation, 19 February 2008. Available at http://www.wlf.org/litigating/case_detail.asp?id=528

Lozano v. City of Hazelton, Pennsylvania, 496 F.Supp.2d 477.

NEGUSIE v. HOLDER

Phelan, Margaret and Gillespie, James. *Immigration Law Handbook*. Oxford University Press, 2007.

Scaros, Constantinos. *Learning About Immigration Law*. Thomson Delmaer Learning, 2006.

Weissbrodt, David and Danielson, Laura. *Immigration Law and Procedure in a Nutshell, 5th Edition*. West Group, 2005.

NKEN v. HOLDER

Nken v. Holder, No. 08-681, 556 U.S. ____ (2009). Available at www.supremecourtus.gov/opinions/08pdf/08-681.pdf

Nken v. Holder, Legal Information Institute (LII) of Cornell University School of Law. Available at http://www.law.cornell.edu/supct/cert/08-681.html

Nken v. Holder, Supreme Court Media, The Oyez Project, available at http://www.oyez.org/cases/2000-2009/2007/2007_06_11612/

"Justices Make it Easier to Fight Deportation." *On the Docket*, 22 April 2009. Available at www.onthedocket.org/cses/2008/nken-v-holder.

"Justices Will Review Stay Standard in Removal Case." *On the Docket*, 25 November 2008. Available at www.onthedocket.org/cses/2008/nken-v-holder.

IMMUNITY

PEARSON v. CALLAHAN

Currie, David. *Federal Jurisdiction in a Nutshell*. West Group, 1999.

Lewis, Jr., Harold, and Norman, Elizabeth. *Civil Rights Law and Practice.* West Group, 2004.

Vieira, Norman. *Constitutional Civil Rights in a Nutshell.* West Group, 1998.

VAN DE KAMP V. GOLDSTEIN

Currie, David. *Federal Jurisdiction in a Nutshell.* West Group, 1999.

Lewis, Jr., Harold and Norman, Elizabeth. *Civil Rights Law and Practice.* West Group, 2004.

Vieira, Norman. *Constitutional Civil Rights in a Nutshell.* West Group, 1998.

INTERNET

SEATTLE "SPAM KING" CONVICTED

Carter, Mike. "Spammer Sentenced to 47 Months in Prison." *The Seattle Times*, 22 July

Greenemeier, Larry. "A Tale of Two 'Spam Kings'." *Scientific American*, 24 July 2008.

"Seattle Spammer Pleads Guilty to Mail Fraud, Spam and Tax Charges." Press Release, U.S. Attorney's Office, Western District of Washington. 14 March 2008. Available at www.usdoj.gov/usao/waw/press/2008/mar/soloway.html

JUDGES

CAPERTON V. A.T. MASSEY COAL CO., INC.

Alfini, James J. *Judicial Conduct and Ethics.* Newark, N.J.: LexisNexis, 2007.

Flamm, Richard E. *Judicial Disqualification: Recusal and Disqualification of Judges.* Berkeley, Cal.: Banks & Jordan Law Publishers, 2007.

TWO PENNSYLVANIA JUDGES PLEAD GUILTY TO KICKBACK SCHEME

Urbana, Ian. "Despite Red Flags About Judges, a Kickback Scheme Flourished." *New York Times.* March 28, 2009.

Roche, Jr., Walter. "Juvenile Records Cleared in Luzerne Judge Bribery." *Pittsburgh Tribune-Review.* March 27, 2009.

JURISDICTION

CARLSBAD TECHNOLOGY, INC. V. HIF BIO, INC.

Freer, Richard D. and Martin H. Redish. *Federal Courts.* 3d ed. Eagan, Minn.: Thomson West, 2004.

Yackle, Larry W. *Federal Courts.* 3d ed. Durham, N.C.: Carolina Academic Press, 2009.

JURY

KANSAS SUPREME COURT RULES THAT JUVENILES ENTITLED TO JURY TRIAL

"Court Says Juveniles Have Right to Trial," Associated Press Wire Release, June 21, 2008.

Fry, Steve, "Jury Trial for Youths May Strain Local Courts," *Topeka Capital-Journal*, June 21, 2008.

WADDINGTON V. SARAUSAD

Federman, Cary. *The Body And the State: Habeas Corpus And American Jurisprudence.* New York, NY: State University of New York Press. 2006.

Frank, Jerome. *Courts on Trial.* Princeton, NJ: Princeton University Press. 1973.

Freedman, Eric. *Habeas Corpus: Rethinking the Great Writ of Liberty.* New York: New York Univ. Press. 2003.

LABOR LAW

LOCKE V. KARASS

Covington, Robert and Decker, Kurt. *Employment Law in a Nutshell.* Saint Paul, MN: West Group. 2002. Second Edition.

Gould, William. *A Primer on American Labor Law.* Cambridge, MA: MIT Press. 2004. Fourth Edition.

Leslie, Douglas. *Labor Law in a Nutshell.* Saint Paul, MN: West Group. 2000. Fourth Edition.

LIBEL

LIBEL SUIT AGAINST AUTHOR JOHN GRISHAM DISMISSED

Kehe, Marjorie. "John Grisham Libel Suit Results." *The Christian Science Monitor.* September 18, 2008.

Neil, Martha. "Federal Judge Axes Ex-DA's Libel Suit Over John Grisham's 'Innocent Man'" *ABA Journal.* September 18, 2008.

HATFILL V. THE NEW YORK TIMES

Hatfill v. The New York Times Company, No. 07-1124. Available at http://pacer.ca4.uscourt.gov/apinion.pdf/07-11124.P.pdf

"4th Circuit Uphold Dismissal of Anthrax Libel Suit." Associated Press article, 15 July 2008. Available at www.firstamendmentcenter.org/news/aspx?id=20299

Stout, David. "Justices Reject Appeal in Anthrax Libel Suit." *The New York Times*, 15 December 2008.

FORMER BASEBALL STAR ROGER CLEMENS SUES TRAINER FOR LIBEL

Associated Press, "FBI Opens Probe Into Clemens' Testimony on Mitchell Report," ESPN.com, February 28, 2008.

"Clemens Apologizes for 'Mistakes,' Continues to Deny Steroid Use," ESPN.com, May 4, 2008.

MANSLAUGHTER

BLACKWATER SECURITY INDICTED FOR KILLING IRAQI CIVILIANS

Londono, Ernesto and Qais Mizher. "Iraq to Deny New License to Blackwater Security Firm." *Washington Post*, 29 January 2009 p. A12.

"Five Blackwater Employees Indicted on Manslaughter and Weapons Charges for Fatal Nisur Square Shooting in Iraq." U.S. Department of Justice Press Release, 8 December 2008. Available at http://www.usdoj.gov/opa/pr/2008/December/08-nsd-1068.html

Schall, Jeremy. "Blackwater Operatives Indicted for Slaughter of Iraqi Citizens." *The Nation*, 9 December 2008.

The Federalist Society publication, 13 January 2009. Available at http://fed-soc.org/publications/pubID.1241/pub_detail.asp

MILITARY LAW

UNITED STATES V. DENEDO

Schlueter, David A. *Military Crimes and Defenses.* Newark, N.J.: LexisNexis, 2007.

Schlueter, David A. *Military Criminal Justice: Practice and Procedure.* Newark, N.J.: LexisNexis, 2008.

MILITARY TRIBUNAL

MILITARY TRIBUNAL CONVICTS BIN LADEN'S DRIVER

"Hamdan Gets 5 <<Years on Terror Charge-Guantanamo." 07 August 2008. Available at http://www.msnbc.com/id/26055301

Markon, Jerry. "Hamdan Guilty of Terror Support." *The Washington Post*, 07 August 2008 http://jurist.law.pitt.edu/paperchase/2007/05/appeals-court-hears-challenge-to.php

Schmickle, Sharon. "Historic Trial, Unlikely Historic Figure." *The Minnesota Post*, 06 August 2008.

"U.S. v. Salim Ahmed Hamdan." MC Form 458, 5 April 2007. Available at http://news.findlaw.com/hdocs/tribunals/ushamdan07chrgs3.html

Wilber, Del Quentin and Peter Finn. "U.S. Retires 'Enemy Combatant,' Keeps Broad Right to Detain." *The Washington Post*, 14 March 2009, p. A06.

Williams, Carol J. "Bin Laden Driver Convicted at Guantanamo of Aiding Terror." *Los Angeles Times*, 07 August 2008.

MORTGAGE

SUBPRIME LENDING CRISIS TURNS INTO A FINANCIAL MELTDOWN

Browning, Lynnley, "Ex-Executive Faults Mortgage Giants for 'Orgy' of Nonprime Loans," New York Times, December 9, 2008.

Ellis, David, "The Meltdown," CNNMoney.com, September 21, 2008.

MURDER

CASEY ANTHONY MURDER CASE DRAWS NATIONAL ATTENTION

Edwards, Amy L. and Sarah Lundy, "Casey Anthony Weeps, Chuckles in Evidence Photos, Videos," *Orlando Sentinel*, April 7, 2009.

Edwards, Amy L. and Sarah Lundy, "State to Seek Death Penalty in Casey Anthony Case," *Newsday*, April 13, 2009.

NATIONAL SECURITY

WINTER V. NATIONAL RESOURCES DEFENSE COUNCIL, INC.

Findley, Roger and Farber, Daniel. *Environmental Law in a Nutshell.* 2004, 6th edition. West Publishing.

Liptak, Adam. "Supreme Court Rules for Navy in Sonar Case." *New York Times.* November 13, 2008.

Savage, David. "U.S. Supreme Court OKs Navy use of Sonar." *Los Angeles Times.* November 13, 2008.

NATIVE AMERICAN RIGHTS

CARCIERI V. SALAZAR

Canby, William. *American Indian Law in a Nutshell.* St. Paul, MN: West. 2004 Fourth Edition.

NATIVE AMERICANS AWARDED $455 MILLION IN LAND TRUST CASE

Lumpkin, Beverley. "Judge Awards Native Americans $455 Million in Trust Case-Far Less Than Sought." The Indian Trust, 9 August 2008. Available at www.indiantrust.com/index.cfm?

Rave, Jodi. "Interior Secretary Disappoints Landowners." *The Bismarck Tribune*, 30 March 2009.

Rave, Jodi. "Native Trust Lawsuit Likely Headed Back to Court." *The Missoulian*, 26 March 2009.

"Welcome to the Special Trust for American Indians." As retrieved on 11 May 2009. Available at www.doi/gov/specialtrustee/

Wilber, Del Quentin. "Judge Rules Indians Owed Over $455 Million." *The Washington Post*, 08 August 2008.

UNITED STATES V. NAVAJO NATION

Canby Jr., William C., *American Indian Law in a Nutshell.* St. Paul, Minnesota: Thomson/West, 2004.

Long, Larry, *American Indian Law Deskbook.* Boulder, Colorado: University Press of Colorado, 2008.

OBSTRUCTION OF JUSTICE

DETROIT MAYOR PLEADS GUILTY TO OBSTRUCTION OF JUSTICE

Schaefer, Jim, and Elrick. M.L. "Detroit Mayor, Aide Lied Under Oath, Texts Show." *Detroit Free Press*, January 24, 2009.

McGraw, Bill. "The Rise and Fall of Kwame Kilpatrick ." *Detroit Free Press*, September 5, 2008.

PENSIONS

KENNEDY V. PLAN ADMINISTRATOR FOR DUPONT SAVINGS AND INVESTMENT PLAN

Conison, Jay. *Employee Benefits in a Nutshell, 3rd Ed.* West Group, 2003.

Rosenbloom, Jerry. *The Handbook of Employee Benefits, 6th Ed.* McGraw-Hill, 2005.

Ziesenheim, Ken. *Understanding ERISA: A Compact Guide to the Landmark Act.* Marketplace Books, 2002.

PEREMPTORY CHALLENGE

RIVERA V. ILLINOIS

Rivera v. Illinois, No. 07-9995, 556 US. ____ (2009). Available at www.supremecourtus.gov/opinions/08pdf/07-9995.pdf

Rivera v. Illinois, Supreme Court Media, The Oyez Project, available at http://www.oyez.org/cases/2000-2009/2008/2008_07_9995

Rivera v. Illinois, Legal Information Institute (LII) of Cornell University School of Law. Available at http://www.law.cornell.edu/supct/cert/07-9995.html

"Justices Uphold Conviction in Peremptory Challenge Case." *On the Docket*, 31 March 2009. Available at www.onthedocket.org/cases/2007/rivera-v-illinois.

PERJURY

DISGRACED TRACK STAR MARION JONES SPENDS SIX MONTHS IN PRISON FOR PERJURY

Littman, Jonathan, "Marion Jones Gives Truth the Runaround," Yahoo! Sports, January 22, 2009.

Wilson, Duff and Michael S. Schmidt, "Olympic Champion Acknowledges Use of Steroids," *New York Times*, October 5, 2007.

PREEMPTION

WYETH V. LEVINE

Epstein, Richard. *Federal Preemption.* AEI Press, 2007.

O' Reilly, James. *Federal Preemption of State and Local Law.* American Bar Association, 2006.

Zimmerman, Joseph. *Congressional Preemption.* State University of New York Press, 2006.

PRODUCT LIABILITY

TEXAS AND NEW JERSEY COURTS REVERSE VIOXX DECISIONS

Axtman, Kris. "Jury's Vioxx Award: Not So Texas-Sized After All." *Christian Science Monitor.* August 25, 2005.

Longstreth, Andrew. "Mark Lanier's Faith Tested: He Loses Two Vioxx Appeals in One Day." AmLaw Daily. May 29, 2008.

PUNITIVE DAMAGES

PHILIP MORRIS USA INC. V. WILLIAMS

Chemerinsky, Erwin. *Federal Jurisdiction, 4th Ed.* Aspen Publishers, 2003.

Currie, David. *Federal Jurisdiction in a Nutshell.* West Group, 1999.

Wright, Charles Alan. *Law of Federal Courts, 6th Ed.* West Group, 2002.

RELIGION

RAID OF POLYGAMIST SECT LEADS TO NUMEROUS LEGAL PROBLEMS

Michels, Scott, "Texas High Court: Sect Children Can Return to Families," ABCNews.com, May 29, 2008.

Von Drehle, David, "The Texas Polygamist Sect: Uncoupled and Unchartered," Time, April 24, 2008.

RICO

BOYLE V. UNITED STATES

Boyle v. United States, No. 07-1309, 556 U.S. ___ Available at www.supremecourtus.gov/opinions/08pdf/07-1309.pdf

Boyle v. United States, Legal Information Institute (LII) of Cornell University School of Law. Available at http://www.law.cornell.edu/supct/cert/07-1309.html

Gonzalez v. United States, Supreme Court Media, The Oyez Project, available at http://www.oyez.org/cases/2000-2009/2007/2007_07_1309/

RIPARIAN RIGHTS

KANSAS V. COLORADO

Wright, Kennth. Ed. *American Water Works Association, 1998.*

Sherk, George. *Dividing the Waters: The Resolution of Interstate Water Conflicts in the United States.* Springer, 2000.

Arnold, Craig, and Jewell, Leigh. Ed. *Beyond Litigation: Case Studies in Water Rights Disputes.* Environmental Law Institute, 2002.

SAFE HAVEN

Nebraska's Safe Haven Law Backfires

Flanigan, Katie. "Nebraska Clarifies Its 'Safe Haven' Law." *Health Care News*, January 2009. Published by the Heartland Institute.

"Governor Heineman Signs Safe Haven Update Into Law." 21 November 2008. Press Release from the Communications Office of the Governor. Available at http://www.hhs.state.ne.us/SafeHaven/GovRelease112108.pdf

Osterman, Kathie. "Safe Haven Law Does Not Absolve Parents of Responsibility." Press Release, Office of Communications and Legislative Services, 26 September 2008. Available at http://www.hhs.state.ne.us/newsroom/newsreleases/2008/Sep/safehaven2.htm

"Safe Haven Law." Nebraska DHHS, Children and Family Services. 22 November 2008. Available at http://www.hhs.state.ne.us/SafeHaven/

"Safe Haven Law Needs Changing." Press Release from the Communications Office of the Governor, 7 October 2008. Available at http://www.hhs.state.ne.us/children_family_services/SafeHaven/GovernorColumn.pdf

SEARCH AND SEIZURE

Arizona v. Johnson

Dash, Samuel. *The Intruders: Unreasonable Searches and Seizures from King John to John Ashcroft.* Rutgers University Press. 2004.

Cammack, Mark and Garland, Norman. *Advanced Criminal Procedure in a Nutshell.* West Publishing Co. 2001.

Long, Carolyn. *Mapp V. Ohio: Guarding Against Unreasonable Searches And Seizures.* University Press of Kansas. 2006.

SECURITIES

Payouts in the Tyco Securities Settlemen

"ERISA Doesn't Shield Tyco From Fraud Action: Judge…" 06 April 2009. *Law 360 Newswire for Business Lawyers*, Available at http://www.law360.com/company_articles/4158

"Ex-Tyco Bosses Take Convictions to Supreme Court." 14 April 2009. *Law 360 Newswire for Business Lawyers*, Available at http://www.law360.com/company_articles/4158

"Ex-Tyco CEO Perseveres in Conviction Fight." (8 June 2009. *Law 360 Newswire for Business Lawyers*, Available at http://www.law360.com/company_articles/4158

In re Tyco International Ltd. Securities Litigation, Various court documents accessed through www.bostonerisalaw.com/uploads/tyco and www.findlaw.com and www.erisafraud.com

"Supreme Court Rejects Appeal From 2 Ex-Tyco Executives." *The New York Times*, 9 June 2009.

"Tyco Can't Exclude Premerger Contributions: Judge…" 13 April 2009. *Law 360 Newswire for Business Lawyers*, Available at http://www.law360.com/company_articles/4158

"Tyco International Direct Litigation." Available from plaintiffs' counsel at www.lieffcabrasersecurities.com/cases/tyco.htm on 4 June 2009.

Tyco settlement documents and related memoranda accessed on 23 June 2009 from www.tycoclasssettlement.com and www.tycoclasssettlement.com/faq/php3

SENTENCING

Chambers v. United States

Branham, Lynm. *The Law of Sentencing and Corrections in a Nutshell.* West Group, 2005.

Stith, Kate. *Fear of Judging: Sentencing Guidelines in the Federal Courts.* University of Chicago Press, 1998.

Tonry, Michael. *Sentencing Matters.* Oxford University Press, 2004.

Dean v. United States

"Court Accepts New Statutory Mandatory Minimum Case." *On the Docket*, SCOTUS News, 14 November 2008. Available at http://www.otd.oyez.org/cases/2008/dean-v-us.

Dean v. United States, No. 08-5274, 556 US. ____ (2008). Available at www.supremecourtus.gov/opinions/08pdf/08-5274.pdf

"Dean v. United States," LLI (Legal Information Institute of Cornell University School of Law). Available at http://www.law.cornell.edu/supct/cert/06-11612.html

"Justices Back Enhanced Sentencing Requirements." *On the Docket*, SCOTUS News, 29 April 2009. Available at http://www.otd.oyez.org/cases/2008/dean-v-us.

United States v. Hayes

Branham, Lynm. *The Law of Sentencing and Corrections in a Nutshell.* West Group, 2005.

Stith, Kate. *Fear of Judging: Sentencing Guidelines in the Federal Courts.* University of Chicago Press, 1998.

Tonry, Michael. *Sentencing Matters.* Oxford University Press, 2004.

SEX DISCRIMINATION

AT & T CORPORATION V. HULTEEN

Covington, Robert and Decker, Kurt. *Employment Law in a Nutshell.* Saint Paul, MN: West Group. 2002. Second Edition.

Lewis, Jr., Harold and Norman, Elizabeth. *Civil Rights Law and Practice.* Saint Paul, MN: West Group. 2004.

Vieira, Norman. *Constitutional Civil Rights in a Nutshell.* Saint Paul, MN. : West Group. 1998.

FITZGERALD V. BARNSTABLE SCHOOL COMMITTEE

Currie, David. *Federal Jurisdiction in a Nutshell.* West Group, 1999.

Lewis, Jr., Harold and Norman, Elizabeth. *Civil Rights Law and Practice.* West Group, 2004.

Vieira, Norman. *Constitutional Civil Rights in a Nutshell.* West Group, 1998.

SEX OFFENSES

NEW JERSEY SUPREME COURT VOIDS RESIDENCY RESTRICTIONS FOR SEX OFFENDERS

Fuchs, Mary and Favid Giambusso. "N.J. Supreme Court Invalidates Restrictions on Where Sex Offenders Can Live." *The Star-Ledger*, 07 May 2009.

G.H. v. Township of Galloway, No. A-64/65-08 (N.J. 2009). Available at http://www.judiciary.state.nj.us/opinions/supreme/A-64-08

Hester, Tom. "Panel Approves New Jersey Sex Offender Residency and Legislation." NewJerseyNewsroom.com, 08 June 2009. Available at www.newjerseynewsroom.com/stateassembly/panel-approves-tougher-penalties-for-sex-offenders

McHugh, Margaret. "Supreme Court Bans Towns' Residency Laws on Sex Offenders." NewJerseyNewsroom.com, 07 May 2009. Available at www.newjerseynewsroom.com/state/supreme-court-bans-towns-residency-laws-on-sex-offenders.

Shipkowski, Bruce. "New Push to Impose Sex Offender Residency Limit. The Associated Press, 7 June 2009.

Wright, E. Assata. "Sex Offenders Live in Hoboken JC But Supreme Court Bans Local Towns..." *The Hudson Reporter*, May 2009.

SIXTH AMENDMENT

MONTEJO V. LOUISIANA

"Court Eases Limits on Questioning Suspects Without Counsel." *On the Docket*, 26 May 2009.

Available at www.onthedocket.org/cses/2008/nontejo-v-louisiana.

Montejo v. Louisiana, No. 07-1529, 556 U.S. ___ (2009). Available at www.supremecourtus.gov/opinions/08pdf/07-1529.pdf

Montejo v. Louisiana. Legal Information Institute (LII) of Cornell University School of Law. Available at http://www.law.cornell.edu/supct/cert/07-1529.html

"Montejo v. Louisiana." Legal Information Institute (LII), Cornell University School of Law, available at http://topics.law.cornell.edu/supct/cert/07-1529

OREGON V. ICE

Branham, Lynm. *The Law of Sentencing and Corrections in a Nutshell.* West Group, 2005.

Stith, Kate. *Fear of Judging: Sentencing Guidelines in the Federal Courts.* University of Chicago Press, 1998.

Tonry, Michael. *Sentencing Matters.* Oxford University Press, 2004.

KANSAS V. VENTRIS

Kansas v. Ventris, No. 07-1356. Available at www.supremecourtus.gov/opinions/08pdf/07-1356.pdf

"Kansas v. Ventris." The Oyez Project, available at http://oyez.org/cases/2000-2009/2008/2008_7_1356

"Kansas v. Ventris." Legal Information Institute (LII), Cornell University School of Law , available at http://topics.law.cornell.edu/supct/cert/07-1356

"U.S. Supreme Court Sides with AG in Kansas v. Ventris Case." Office of the Kansas Attorney General, 29 April 2009. Available at http://www.ksag.org/content/page/id/532

VERMONT V. BRILLON

"Justices Accept Case Involving the Right to a Speedy Trial." *On the Docket*, 01 October 2008. Available at www.onthedocket.org/cses/2008/vermont-v-brillon

"Justices Overturn Vermont Decision in Speedy Trial Case." *On the Docket*, 09 March 2009. Available at www.onthedocket.org/cses/2008/vermont-v-brillon

Vermont v. Brillon, No. 08-88, 556 US. ___ (2009). Available at www.supremecourtus.gov/opinions/08pdf/08-88.pdf

Vermont v. Brillon, Legal Information Institute (LII) of Cornell University School of Law. Available at http://www.law.cornell.edu/supct/cert/08-88.html

"Vermont v. Brillon." Legal Information Institute (LII), Cornell University School of Law, available at http://topics.law.cornell.edu/supct/cert/08-88

SOVEREIGN IMMUNITY

MINISTRY OF DEFENSE OF IRAN V. ELAHI

Ministry of Defense and Support for the Armed Forces of the Islamic Republic of Iran v. Elahi, No. 07-615, 556 US. ____ (2009). Available at www.supremecourtus.gov/opinions/08pdf/07-615.pdf

"Ministry of Defense and Support for the Armed Forces of the Islamic Republic of Iran v. Elahi," Legal Information Institute (LII) at Cornell University School of Law. Available at http://www.law.cornell.edu/supct/cert/07-615.html

Ministry of Defense and Support for the Armed Forces of the Islamic Republic of Iran v. Elahi, "On the Docket," Supreme Court Media, The Oyez Project, available at http://www.oyez.org/cases/2000-2009/2008/2008_07_615/

SOVEREIGNTY

HAWAII V. OFFICE OF HAWAIIAN AFFAIRS

Niesse, Mark, "Hawaiians Extend Their Influence," AP Alert, April 20, 2009.

Savage, David G., "Court Leaves Hawaii's Land Dispute to the State," *Los Angeles Times*, April 1, 2009.

SPORTS LAW

SEATTLE SUPERSONICS SETTLE ON OKLAHOMA

Allen, Percy. "Seattle v. Sonics: Trial Starts Next Week, if There's No Settlement." *The Seattle Times*, 11 June 2008.

Bell, Gregg. "Sonics Trial Ends, Judge May Issue Decision Wednesday." ABC News, 26 June 2008. Available at http://abcnews.go.com/sports/wirestory?id=5255194

Brunner, Jim. "This Judge Will Decide the Fate of the Sonics." *The Seattle Times*, 15 June 2008.

City of Seattle v. Professional Basketball Club LLC, No. 2:2007cv01620 (2008). Available at http://news.justia.com/cses/featured/washington/wawdce/2:2007cv01620/146857/

Fitzgerald, Dan. "Seattle Cashes In, Settles Lawsuit Against Supersonics." 3 July 2008. Available at http://www.ctsportslaw.com/category/national-basketball-association

Johns, Gregg. "Lawsuit Would Delay NBA's Role in Case." 11 July 2008. Available at http://www.ctsportslaw.com/category/national-basketball-association

SUICIDE

MONTANA JUDGE SUPPORTS DOCTOR-ASSISTED SUICIDE FOR TERMINALLY ILL

Baxter v. State, No. DA-09-0051, proceedings and court filings available at www.mt-govinfo.com/2009/06/baxter-v-state.html

O' Reilly, Kevin B. "Montana Judge Rejects Stay of Physician-Assisted Suicide Ruling." *AMA News*, American Medical Association. Available at www.ama-assn.org/amednews/2009/01/26/prsd0129.htm

Person, Daniel. "No Physician-Assisted Suicide Bills Heard in Legislature." *Bozeman Daily Chronicle*, 30 May 2009.

SUPREMACY CLAUSE

HAYWOOD V. DROWN

Lewis, Jr., Harold and Norman, Elizabeth. *Civil Rights Law and Practice*. Saint Paul, MN: West Group. 2004.

TERRORISM

PRESIDENT OBAMA ORDERS CLOSURE OF GUANTANAMO BAY DETENTION CAMP

"Executive Order-Review and Disposition of Individuals Detained at the Guantanamo Bay Naval Base and Closure of Detention Facilities." White House Press Release, 22 January 2009. Available at http://www.whitehouse.gov/the_press_office/closureofguantanamodetentionfacilities/

Finn, Peter. "Guantanamo Closure Called Obama Priority." *The Washington Post*, 12 November 2008.

"Obama Issues Directive to Shut Down Guantanamo." *New York Times*, 22 January 2009.

Whitlock, Craig. "Europe Seen Willing to Take Detainees." *The Washington Post*, 30 April 2009.

HOLY LAND FOUNDATION CONVICTED OF SUPPORTING TERRORISM

"Federal Jury in Dallas Convicts Holy Land Foundation and Its Leaders for Providing Material Support to Hamas Terrorist Organization." U.S. Department of Justice Press Release, 24 November 2008. Available at http://www.usdoj.gov/opa/pr/2008/November/08-nsd-1046.html

Kovach, Gretel C. "Five Convicted in Terrorism Financing Trial." *The New York Times*, 25 November 2008.

Rozen, Miriam. "Appeals Follow Sentencing of Defendants in Holy Land Foundation Case." *The Texas Lawyer*, 01 June 2009.

Trahan, Jason. "Five Decry Jail Terms in Holy Land Foundation Case." *The Dallas Morning News*, 27 May 2009.

TOBACCO

ALTRIA GROUP, INC. V. GOOD

Epstein, Richard. *Federal Preemption*. AEI Press, 2007.

O' Reilly, James. *Federal Preemption of State and Local Law*. American Bar Association, 2006.

Zimmerman, Joseph. *Congressional Preemption*. State University of New York Press, 2006.

FLORIDA RESTARTS TOBACCO LAWSUITS

Derthick, Martha. 2nd Edition. *Up In Smoke: From Legislation To Litigation In Tobacco Politics*, CQ Press, 2004.

Michaels, David. *Doubt is Their Product: How Industry's Assault on Science Threatens Your Health*, Oxford University Press, 2007.

TORT LAW

BURLINGTON NORTHERN & SANTA FE R.R. CO. V. UNITED STATES

Eggen, Jean Macchiaroli. *Toxic Torts in a Nutshell*. 5th ed. St. Paul, Minn. : Thomson/West.

Stohr, Greg. "Shell Gets U.S. High Court Hearing on Cleanup Suits." Bloomberg.com. Oct. 1, 2008.

TORTURE

OBAMA ADMINISTRATION RELEASES "TORTURE MEMOS"

"Author of Torture Memos Can Be Sued." CBS News, 13 June 2009. Available at www.cbsnews.com

deVogue, Ariane, Pierre Thomas, and Jason Ryan. "DOJ Memos Reveal Legal Thinking Behind Controversial Bush Terrorism Policy." ABC News, 2 March 2009. Available at www.abcnews.go.com/thelaw/doj/story?id=6989424&page=1

deVogue, Ariane. "DOJ Releases Controversial 'Torture Memos'." ABC News, 16 April 2009. Available at www.abcnews.go.com/thelaw/doj/

Johnson, Carrie and Julie Tate. "New Interrogation Details Emerge." *The Washington Post*, 17 April 2009.

"Obama Team Divided Over Release of Torture Memos." *Newsweek*, 3 April 2009.

Mazetti, Mark and Scott Shane. "Interrogation Memos Detail Harsh Tactics by the CIA." *The New York Times*, 17 April 2009.

DILEMMA OVER PROSECUTIONS FOR THE 'TORTURE MEMOS'

Complaint in *Padilla v. Yoo*, CV-08-0035, D.C.N.D. Cal, pending. Available at www.jurist.law.pitt.edu/pdf/yoocomplaint.pdf

"H.R. 893: American Anti-Torture Act of 2009." Available at http://www.govtrack.us/congress/bill.xpd?bill-111-893

Cox, Larry. "Obama Must Prosecute Bush-era Torture Enablers." Editorial article, *The Christian Science Monitor*, 15 June 2009.

Johnston, David and Scott Shane. "Interrogation Memos: Inquiry Suggests No Charges." *The New York Times*, 6 May 2009.

Leopold, Jason. "Obama Vows to Prosecute Torturers, But There's a Catch." *The Atlantic Reporter*, 29 June 2009. Available at http://pubrecord.org/torture/977-obama-vows-to-prosecute-torture-but-theres-a-catch.html

Schwartz, John. "Judge Allows Civil Lawsuit Over Claims of Torture." *The New York Times*, 13 June 2009.

NO TRIAL FOR ALLEGED TERRORIST BECAUSE OF "APPROVED TORTURE"

Geary, Ann. "White House Answers Judge's Finding of U.S. Torture." ABC News, 14 January 2009. Available at http://abcnews.go.com.print?id=6643535

"USA: Torture Acknowledged, Question of Accountability Remains." Amnesty International Report, 14 January 2009. Available at http://amnestyinternational.org/doc.php?lang=e&id=ENGAMR510032009.

Wilber, Del Quentin and Peter Finn. "U.S. Retires 'Enemy Combatant,' Keeps Broad Right to Detain." *The Washington Post,* 14 March 2009, p. A06.

Woodward, Bob. "Guantanamo Detainee Was Tortured, Says Official Overseeing Military Trials." *Washington Post*, 14 January 2009.

TRADE

UNITED STATES V. EURODIF S.A

Folsom, Ralph. *International Trade and Economic Relations in a Nutshell, 4th Ed.* West, 2008.

Folsom, Ralph. *International Business Transactions in a Nutshell, 7th Ed.* West, 2004.

VETERANS' RIGHTS

SHINSEKI V. SANDERS

Gaytan, Peter, and Borden, Marian. *For Service To Your Country: The Insider's Guide to Veterans' Benefits*. Citadel, 2008.

Shinseki v. Sanders, No. 07-1209, 556 U.S. ___ (2009). Available at www.supremecourtus.gov/opinions/08pdf/07-1209.pdf

Shinseki v. Sanders Legal Information Institute (LII) of Cornell University School of Law. Available at http://www.law.cornell.edu/supct/cert/07-1209.html

Shinseki v. Sanders, Supreme Court Media, The Oyez Project, available at http://www.oyez.org/cases/2000-2009/2008/2008_07_1209/

Roche, John. *Claim Denied!: How to Appeal a VA Denial of Benefits*. Potomac Books, 2008.

VOTING

BARTLETT V. STRICKLAND

Bartlett v, Strickland, No. 07-689, 556 U.S. ___ (2009), Available at www.supremecourtus.gov/opinions/08pdf/07-1223.pdf

Bartlett v, Strickland, On the Docket, available at http://otd.oyez.org/cases/2008/bartlett-v-strickland.

COMMON CAUSE/GEORGIA V. BILLUPS

Jewell, Malcom, and Morehouse, Sally. *Political Parties and Elections in American States. 4th ed.* CQ Press, 2000.

Hershey, Marjorie. *Party Politics in America. 13th ed.* Longman, 2008.

Cain, Bruce, and Gerber, Elizabeth, editors. *Voting at the Political Fault Line: California's Experiment with the Blanket Primary.* University of California Press, 2002.

THE INTERNET IS THE NEW FACE OF POLITICAL CAMPAIGNING

Miller, Claire Cain. "How Obama's Internet Campaign Changed Politics." *New York Times.* November 7, 2008.

Smith, Aaron. "The Internet's Role in Campaign 2008." Pew Research Center. April 15, 2009.

Terhune, Lea. "Internet Revolutionizes Campaign Fundraising." America.gov. July 10, 2008.

THOUSANDS OF VOTERS BLOCKED FROM VOTING

"Election Officials Deny Illegally Purging Voters." FOX News, 09 October 2008. Available at http://origin.foxnews.com/wires/2008Oct09/0,4670,VoterPurges,00.html

"Election Officials Dispute Illegal Removal of Voters From Rolls." *TopNews*, U.S. Edition, 10 October 2008. Available at http://www.topnews.in/usa/elections-officials-dispute-illegal-removal-voters-rolls-21682

Urbina, Ian. "States' Actions to Block Voters Appear Illegal." *The New York Times*, 9 October 2008.

WAR CRIMES

FORMER NAZI GUARD DEPORTED TO GERMANY

Associated Press. "Accused Nazi Guard Won't Be Deported to Germany Yet, After Wheelchair Removal from Home." FoxNews.com. April 14, 2009.

Associated Press. "Court OKs Deportation of Alleged Ex-Nazi Guard." MSNBC.com. April 6, 2009.

WHISTLEBLOWER

SOURCE OF STORY ON WARRANTLESS SURVEILLANCE REVEALS HIMSELF

Isikoff, Michael, "The Fed Who Blew the Whistle," *Newsweek*, December 22, 2008.

Risen, James and Eric Lichtblau, "Bush Lets U.S. Spy on Callers Without Courts," *New York Times*, December 16, 2005.

WIRETAPPING

IN RE DIRECTIVES PURSUANT TO SECTION 105B OF THE FOREIGN INTELLIGENCE SURVEILLANCE ACT

Bazan, Elizabeth, Ed. 2008 *The Foreign Intelligence Surveillance Act: Overview and Modifications.* Nova Science Publishers.

Volkman, Earnest. 2008. *The History of Espionage: The Clandestine World of Surveillance, Spying and Intelligence, from Ancient Times to the Post-9/11 World.* Carlton Publishing Group.

Abandonment: The surrender, relinquishment, disclaimer, or cession of property or of rights. Voluntary relinquishment of all right, title, claim, and possession, with the intent of not reclaiming it.

The giving up of a thing absolutely, without reference to any particular person or purpose, as vacating property with the intention of not returning, so that it may be appropriated by the next comer or finder. The voluntary relinquishment of possession of thing by owner with intention of terminating ownership, but without vesting it in any other person. The relinquishing of all title, possession, or claim, or a virtual, intentional throwing away of property.

Term includes both the intention to abandon and the external act by which the intention is carried into effect. In determining whether one has abandoned property or rights, the intention is the first and paramount object of inquiry, for there can be no abandonment without the intention to abandon.

Abandonment differs from surrender in that surrender requires an agreement, and also from forfeiture, in that forfeiture may be against the intention of the party alleged to have forfeited.

Abet: To encourage or incite another to commit a crime. This word is usually applied to aiding in the commission of a crime. To abet another to commit a murder is to command, procure, counsel, encourage, induce, or assist. To facilitate the commission of a crime, promote its accomplishment, or help in advancing or bringing it about.

In relation to charge of aiding and abetting, term includes knowledge of the perpetrator's wrongful purpose, and encouragement, promotion or counsel of another in the commission of the criminal offense.

A French word, *abeter* : to bait or excite an animal.

Abeyance: A lapse in succession during which there is no person in whom title is vested. In the law of estates, the condition of a freehold when there is no person in whom it is vested. In such cases the freehold has been said to be *in nubibus* (in the clouds), *in pendenti* (in suspension), and *in gremio legis* (in the bosom of the law). Where there is a tenant of the freehold, the remainder or reversion in fee may exist for a time without any particular owner, in which case it is said to be in abeyance. A condition of being undetermined or in a state of suspension or inactivity. In regard to sales to third parties of property acquired by county at tax sale, being held in *abeyance* means that certain rights or conditions are in expectancy.

Abuse of discretion: A failure to take into proper consideration the facts and law relating to a particular matter; an arbitrary or unreasonable departure from precedents and settled judicial custom.

Academic Freedom: The right to teach as one sees fit, but not necessarily the right to teach evil. The term encompasses much more than teaching-related speech rights of teachers.

Academic year: That period of time necessary to complete an actual course of study during a school year.

Ad valorem: According to value.

Adequate remedy at law: Sufficient compensation by way of monetary damages.

Adjudication: The legal process of resolving a dispute. The formal giving or pronouncing of a judgment or decree in a court proceeding; also the judgment or decision given. The entry of a decree by a court in respect to the parties in a case. It implies a hearing by a court, after notice, of legal evidence on the factual issue(s) involved. The equivalent of a determination. It indicates that the claims of all the parties thereto have been considered and set at rest.

Administrative board: A comprehensive phrase that can refer to any administrative agency but usually means a public agency that holds hearings.

Advance: To pay money or give something of value before the date designated to do so; to provide capital to help a planned enterprise, expecting a return from it; to give someone an item before payment has been made for it.

Affirmative defense: A new fact or set of facts that operates to defeat a claim even if the facts supporting that claim are true.

Aggravated assault: "A person is guilty of aggravated assault if he or she attempts to cause serious bodily injury to another or causes such injury purposely, knowingly, or recklessly under circumstances manifesting extreme indifference to the value of human life; or attempts to cause or purposely or knowingly causes bodily injury to another with a deadly weapon. In all jurisdictions, statutes punish such aggravated assaults as assault with intent to murder (or rob or kill or rape) and assault with a dangerous (or deadly) weapon more severely than "simple" assaults."

Aggravation: Any circumstances surrounding the commission of a crime that increase its seriousness or add to its injurious consequences.

Alienate: To voluntarily convey or transfer title to real property by gift, disposition by will or the laws of descent and distribution, or by sale.

Allocation: The apportionment or designation of an item for a specific purpose or to a particular place.

Annexation: The act of attaching, uniting, or joining together in a physical sense; consolidating.

Antitrust law: Legislation enacted by the federal and various state governments to regulate trade and commerce by preventing unlawful restraints, price-fixing, and monopolies, to promote competition, and to encourage the production of quality goods and services at the lowest prices, with the primary goal of safeguarding public welfare by ensuring that consumer demands will be met by the manufacture and sale of goods at reasonable prices.

Appellate: Relating to appeals; reviews by superior courts of decisions of inferior courts or administrative agencies and other proceedings.

Appellate court: A court having jurisdiction to review decisions of a trial-level or other lower court.

Apportionment: The process by which legislative seats are distributed among units entitled to representation. Determination of the number of representatives that a state, county, or other subdivision may send to a legislative body. The U.S. Constitution provides for a census every ten years, on the basis of which Congress apportions representatives according to population; but each state must have at least one representative. *Districting* is the establishment of the precise geographical boundaries of each such unit or constituency. Apportionment by state statute that denies the rule of one-person, one-vote is violative of equal protection of laws.

Also, the allocation of a charge or cost such as real estate taxes between two parties, often in the same ratio as the respective times that the parties are in possession or ownership of property during the fiscal period for which the charge is made or assessed.

Arrest warrant: A written order issued by authority of the state and commanding the seizure of the person named.

Bad faith: The fraudulent deception of another person; the intentional or malicious refusal to perform some duty or contractual obligation.

Bargaining agent: A union that possesses the sole authority to act on behalf of all the employees of a particular type in a company.

Battery: At common law, an intentional unpermitted act causing harmful or offensive contact with the person of another.

Bench trial: A trial conducted before a judge presiding without a jury.

Beyond a reasonable doubt: The standard that must be met by the prosecution's evidence in a criminal prosecution: that no other logical explanation can be derived from the facts except that the defendant committed the crime, thereby over-coming the presumption that a person is innocent until proven guilty.

Bona fide: [*Latin, In good faith.*] Honest; genuine; actual; authentic; acting without the intention of defrauding.

Burden of persuasion: The onus on the party with the burden of proof to convince the trier of fact of all elements of his or her case. In a criminal case the burden of the government to produce evidence of all the necessary elements of the crime beyond a reasonable doubt.

Burglary: The criminal offense of breaking and entering a building illegally for the purpose of committing a crime therein.

Case law: Legal principles enunciated and embodied in judicial decisions that are derived from the application of particular areas of law to the facts of individual cases.

Case or controversy: A term used in Article III, Section 2, of the Constitution to describe the structure by which actual, conflicting claims of individuals must be brought before a federal court for resolution if the court is to exercise its jurisdiction to consider the questions and provide relief.

Cause of action: The fact or combination of facts that gives a person the right to seek judicial redress or relief against another. Also, the legal theory forming the basis of a lawsuit.

Certiorari: [*Latin, To be informed of.*] At common law, an original writ or order issued by the Chancery of King's Bench, commanding officers of inferior courts to submit the record of a cause pending before them to give the party more certain and speedy justice.

A writ that a superior appellate court issues on its discretion to an inferior court, ordering it to produce a certified record of a particular case it has tried, in order to determine whether any irregularities or errors occurred that justify review of the case.

A device by which the Supreme Court of the United States exercises its discretion in selecting the cases it will review.

Circuit Court: A specific tribunal that possesses the legal authority to hear cases within its own geographical territory.

Civil action: A lawsuit brought to enforce, redress, or protect rights of private litigants (the plaintiffs and the defendants); not a criminal proceeding.

Civil Procedure: The methods, procedures, and practices used in civil cases.

Claim for relief: The section of a modern complaint that states the redress sought from a court by a person who initiates a lawsuit.

Class action: A lawsuit that allows a large number of people with a common interest in a matter to sue or be sued as a group.

Clemency: Leniency or mercy. A power given to a public official, such as a governor or the president, to in some way lower or moderate the harshness of punishment imposed upon a prisoner.

Closing argument: The final factual and legal argument made by each attorney on all sides of a case in a trial prior to a verdict or judgment.

Collateral: Related; indirect; not bearing immediately upon an issue. The property pledged or given as a security interest, or a guarantee for payment of a debt, that will be taken or kept by the creditor in case of a default on the original debt.

Collective bargaining agreement: The contractual agreement between an employer and a labor union that governs wages, hours, and working conditions for employees and which can be enforced against both the employer and the union for failure to comply with its terms.

Color of law: The appearance of a legal right.

Commerce Clause: The provision of the U.S. Constitution that gives Congress exclusive power over trade activities between the states and with foreign countries and Indian tribes.

Common carrier: An individual or business that advertises to the public that it is available for hire to transport people or property in exchange for a fee.

Common law: The ancient law of England based upon societal customs and recognized and enforced by the judgments and decrees of the courts. The general body of statutes and case law that governed England and the American colonies prior to the American Revolution.

The principles and rules of action, embodied in case law rather than legislative enactments, applicable to the government and protection of persons and property that derive their authority from the community customs and traditions that evolved over the centuries as interpreted by judicial tribunals.

A designation used to denote the opposite of statutory, equitable, or civil; for example, a common-law action.

Common Pleas: Trial-level courts of general jurisdiction. One of the royal common-law courts in England existing since the beginning of the thirteenth century and developing from the Curia Regis, or the King's Court.

Compensatory damages: A sum of money awarded in a civil action by a court to indemnify a person for the particular loss, detriment, or injury suffered as a result of the unlawful conduct of another.

Comptroller: An officer who conducts the fiscal affairs of a state or municipal corporation.

Consumer credit: Short-term loans made to enable people to purchase goods or services primarily for personal, family, or household purposes.

Consumer protection: Consumer protection laws are federal and state statutes governing sales and credit practices involving consumer goods. Such statues prohibit and regulate deceptive or unconscionable advertising and sales practices, product quality, credit financing and reporting, debt collection, leases and other aspects of consumer transactions.

Consummate: To carry into completion; to fulfill; to accomplish.

Conveyance: The transfer of ownership or interest in real property from one person to another by a document, such as a deed, lease, or mortgage.

Court of Appeal: An intermediate federal judicial tribunal of review that is found in thirteen judicial districts, called circuits, in the United States.

A state judicial tribunal that reviews a decision rendered by an inferior tribunal to determine whether it made errors that warrant the reversal of its judgment.

Court of claims: A state judicial tribunal established as the forum in which to bring certain types of lawsuits against the state or its political subdivisions, such as a county. The former designation given to a federal tribunal created in 1855 by Congress with original jurisdiction: initial authority: to decide an action brought against the United States that is based upon the Constitution, federal law, any regulation of the executive department, or any express or implied contracts with the federal government.

Criminal law: A body of rules and statutes that defines conduct prohibited by the government because it threatens and harms public safety and welfare and that establishes punishment to be imposed for the commission of such acts.

Criminal procedure: The framework of laws and rules that govern the administration of justice in cases involving an individual who has been accused of a crime, beginning with the initial investigation of the crime and concluding either with the unconditional release of the accused by virture of acquittal (a judgment of not guilty) or by the imposition of a term of punishment pursuant to a conviction for the crime.

Cruel and unusual punishment: Such punishment as would amount to torture or barbarity, and cruel and degrading punishment not known to the common law, or any fine, penalty, confinement, or treatment so disproportionate to the offense as to shock the moral sense of the community.

Declaratory judgment: Statutory remedy for the determination of a justiciable controversy where the plaintiff is in doubt as to his or her legal rights. A binding adjudication of the rights and status of litigants even though no consequential relief is awarded.

Deed of trust: A document that embodies the agreement between a lender and a borrower to transfer an interest in the borrower's land to a neutral third party, a trustee, to secure the payment of a debt by the borrower.

Defamation: Any intentional false communication, either written or spoken, that harms a person's reputation; decreases the respect, regard, or confidence in which a person is held; or induces disparaging, hostile, or disagreeable opinions or feelings against a person.

Default judgment: Judgment entered against a party who has failed to defend against a claim that has been brought by another party. Under rules of civil procedure, when a party against whom a judgment for affirmative relief is sought has failed to plead (i.e., answer) or otherwise defend, the party is in default and a judgment by default may be entered either by the clerk or the court.

Direct evidence: Evidence in the form of testimony from a witness who actually saw, heard, or touched the subject of questioning. Evidence that, if believed, proves existence of the fact in issue without inference or presumption. That means of proof which tends to show the existence of a fact in question, without the intervention of the proof of any other fact, and which is distinguished from circumstantial evidence, often called *indirect.*

   Evidence that directly proves a fact, without an inference or presumption, and which in itself, if true, conclusively establishes that fact.

Disorderly conduct: A broad term describing conduct that disturbs the peace or endangers the morals, health, or safety of a community.

Disposition: Act of disposing; transferring to the care or possession of another. The parting with, alienation of, or giving up of property. The final settlement of a matter and, with reference to decisions announced by a court, a judge's ruling is commonly referred to as disposition, regardless of level of resolution. In criminal procedure, the sentencing or other final settlement of a criminal case. With respect to a mental state, denotes an attitude, prevailing tendency, or inclination.

District Court: A designation of an inferior state court that exercises general jurisdiction that it has been granted by the constitution or statute which created it. A U.S. judicial tribunal with original jurisdiction to try cases or controversies that fall within its limited jurisdiction.

Docket: A written list of judicial proceedings set down for trial in a court.

   To enter the dates of judicial proceedings scheduled for trial in a book kept by a court.

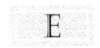

Embezzlement: The fraudulent conversion of another's property by a person who is in a position of trust, such as an agent or employee.

En banc: [*Latin, French. In the bench.*] Full bench. Refers to a session where the entire membership of the court will participate in the decision rather than the regular quorum. In other countries, it is common for a court to have more members than are usually necessary to hear an appeal. In the United States, the Circuit Courts of Appeal usually sit in panels of judges but for important cases may expand the bench to a larger number, when the judges are said to be sitting *en banc.* Similarly, only one of the judges of the U.S. Tax Court will typically hear and decide on a tax controversy. However, when the issues involved are unusually novel or of wide impact, the case will be heard and decided by the full court sitting *en banc.*

Entice: To wrongfully solicit, persuade, procure, allure, attract, draw by blandishment, coax, or seduce. To lure, induce, tempt, incite, or persuade a person to do a thing. Enticement of a child is inviting, persuading, or attempting to persuade a child to enter any vehicle, building, room, or secluded place with intent to commit an unlawful sexual act upon or with the person of said child.

Entity: A real being; existence. An organization or being that possesses separate existence for tax purposes. Examples would be corporations, partnerships, estates, and trusts. The accounting entity for which accounting statements are prepared may not be the same as the entity defined by law.

Entity includes corporation and foreign corporation; not-for-profit corporation; profit and not-for-profit unincorporated association; business trust, estate, partnership, trust, and two or more persons having a joint or common economic interest; and state, U.S., and foreign governments.

An existence apart, such as a corporation in relation to its stockholders.

Entity includes person, estate, trust, governmental unit.

Entrapment: The act of government agents or officials that induces a person to commit a crime he or she is not previously disposed to commit.

Equal protection: The constitutional guarantee that no person or class of persons shall be denied the same protection of the laws that is enjoyed by other persons or other classes in like circumstances in their lives, liberty, property, and pursuit of happiness.

Escrow: Something of value, such as a deed, stock, money, or written instrument, that is put into the custody of a third person by its owner, a grantor, an obligor, or a promisor, to be retained until the occurrence of a contingency or performance of a condition.

Et seq.: "An abbreviation for the Latin *et sequentes* or *et sequentia,* meaning "and the following."

Exclusionary rule: The principle based on federal constitutional law that evidence illegally seized by law enforcement officers in violation of a suspect's right to be free from unreasonable searches and seizures cannot be used against the suspect in a criminal prosecution.

Fair market value: The amount for which real property or personal property would be sold in a voluntary transaction between a buyer and seller, neither of whom is under any obligation to buy or sell.

Federal courts: The U.S. judicial tribunals created by Article III of the Constitution, or by Congress, to hear and determine justiciable controversies.

Felonious: Done with an intent to commit a serious crime or a felony; done with an evil heart or purpose; malicious; wicked; villainous.

Felony: A serious crime, characterized under federal law and many state statutes as any offense punishable by death or imprisonment in excess of one year.

Felony-murder rule: A rule of law that holds that if a killing occurs during the commission or attempted commission of a felony (a major crime), the person or persons responsible for the felony can be charged with murder.

Fiduciary: An individual in whom another has placed the utmost trust and confidence to manage and protect property or money. The relationship wherein one person has an obligation to act for another's benefit.

First impression: The initial presentation to, or examination by, a court of a particular question of law.

First instance: The initial trial court where an action is brought.

Fiscal: Relating to finance or financial matters, such as money, taxes, or public or private revenues.

Foreclosure: A procedure by which the holder of a mortgage:an interest in land providing security for the performance of a duty or the payment of a debt:sells the property upon the failure of the debtor to pay the mortgage debt and, thereby, terminates his or her rights in the property.

Forensic: Belonging to courts of justice.

Fraud: A false representation of a matter of fact:whether by words or by conduct, by false or misleading allegations, or by concealment of what should have been disclosed: that deceives and is intended to deceive another so that the individual will act upon it to her or his legal injury.

Fraudulent: The description of a willful act commenced with the specific intent to deceive or cheat, in order to cause some financial detriment to another and to engender personal financial gain.

Freedom of association: The right to associate with others for the purpose of engaging in constitutionally protected activities.

General jurisdiction: The legal authority of a court to entertain whatever type of case comes up within the geographical area over which its power extends.

Good faith: Honesty; a sincere intention to deal fairly with others.

Grand jury: A panel of citizens that is convened by a court to decide whether it is appropriate for the government to indict (proceed with a prosecution against) someone suspected of a crime.

Habeas corpus: "[*Latin, You have the body.*] A writ (court order) that commands an individual or a government official who has restrained another to produce the prisoner at a designated time and place so that the court can determine the legality of custody and decide whether to order the prisoner's release."

Harmless error: "A legal doctrine in criminal law that allows verdicts to stand without new trials being ordered despite errors of law at trial as long as all errors were insufficient to affect the final outcome. Rule 52(a) of the Federal Code of Criminal Procedure explains it as, "Any error, defect, irregularity or variance which does not affect substantial rights shall be disregarded.""

Interlocutory: Provisional; interim; temporary; not final; that which intervenes between the beginning and the end of a lawsuit or proceeding to either decide a particular point or matter that is not the final issue of the entire controversy or prevent irreparable harm during the pendency of the lawsuit.

Inure: To result; to take effect; to be of use, benefit, or advantage to an individual.

Irreparable injury: Any harm or loss that is not easily repaired, restored, or compensated by monetary damages. A serious wrong, generally of a repeated and continuing nature, that has an equitable remedy of injunctive relief.

Jeopardy: Danger; hazard; peril. In a criminal action, the danger of conviction and punishment confronting the defendant.

Joint resolution: A type of measure that Congress may consider and act upon, the other types being bills, concurrent resolutions, and simple resolutions, in addition to treaties in the Senate.

Judicial administration: The practices, procedures, and offices that deal with the management of the administrative systems of the courts.

Judicial review: A court's authority to examine an executive or legislative act and to invalidate that act if it is contrary to constitutional principles.

Junk bond: A security issued by a corporation that is considered to offer a high risk to bondholders.

Jurisprudence: "From the Latin term *juris prudentia,* which means "the study, knowledge, or science of law"; in the United States, more broadly associated with the philosophy of law."

Larceny: The unauthorized taking and removal of the personal property of another by a person who intends to permanently deprive the owner of it; a crime against the right of possession.

Legal Aid: A system of nonprofit organizations that provide legal services to people who cannot afford an attorney.

Lewdness: Behavior that is deemed morally impure or unacceptable in a sexual sense; open and public indecency tending to corrupt the morals of the community; gross or wanton indecency in sexual relations.

Magistrate: Any individual who has the power of a public civil officer or inferior judicial officer, such as a justice of the peace.

Mail fraud: A crime in which the perpetrator develops a scheme using the mails to defraud another of money or property. This crime specifically requires the intent to defraud, and is a federal offense governed by section 1341 of title 18 of the U.S. Code. The mail fraud statute was first enacted in 1872 to prohibit illicit mailings with the Postal Service (formerly the Post Office) for the purpose of executing a fraudulent scheme.

Malice: The intentional commission of a wrongful act, absent justification, with the intent to cause harm to others; conscious violation of the law that injures another individual; a mental state indicating a disposition in disregard of social duty and a tendency toward malfeasance.

Mandamus: [*Latin, We command.*] A writ or order that is issued from a court of superior jurisdiction that commands an inferior tribunal, corporation, municipal corporation, or individual to perform, or refrain from performing, a particular act, the performance or omission of which is required by law as an obligation.

Manslaughter: The unjustifiable, inexcusable, and intentional killing of a human being without deliberation, premeditation, and malice. The unlawful killing of a human being without any deliberation, which may be involuntary, in the commission of a lawful act without due caution and circumspection.

Market value: The highest price a willing buyer would pay and a willing seller would accept, both being fully informed, and the property being exposed for sale for a reasonable period of time. The market value may be different from the price a property can actually be sold for at a given time (market price). The market value of an article or piece of property is the price that it might be expected to bring if offered for sale in a fair market; not the price that might be obtained on a sale at public auction or a sale forced by the necessities of the owner, but such a price as would be fixed by negotiation and mutual agreement, after ample time to find a purchaser, as between a vendor who is willing (but not compelled) to sell and a purchaser who desires to buy but is not compelled to take the particular article or piece of property.

Misdemeanor: Offenses lower than felonies and generally those punishable by fine, penalty, forfeiture, or imprisonment other than in a penitentiary. Under federal law, and most state laws, any offense other than a felony is classified as a misdemeanor. Certain states also have various classes of misdemeanors (e.g., Class A, B, etc.).

Money laundering: The process of taking the proceeds of criminal activity and making them appear legal.

Money paid: The technical name given a declaration in assumpsit in which the plaintiff declares that the defendant had and received certain money. A common-law pleading, stating that the defendant received money that, in equity and good conscience, should be paid to the plaintiff.

Monopoly: An economic advantage held by one or more persons or companies deriving from the exclusive power to carry on a particular business or trade or to manufacture and sell a particular item, thereby suppressing competition and allowing such persons or companies to raise the price of a product or service substantially above the price that would be established by a free market.

Nominal damages: Minimal money damages awarded to an individual in an action where the person has not suffered any substantial injury or loss for which he or she must be compensated.

Notary public: A public official whose main powers include administering oaths and attesting to signatures, both important and effective ways to minimize fraud in legal documents.

Of counsel: A term commonly applied in the practice of law to an attorney who has been employed to aid in the preparation and management of a particular case but who is not the principal attorney in the action.

Omnibus: [*Latin, For all; containing two or more independent matters.*] A term frequently used in reference to a legislative bill comprised of two or more general subjects that is designed to compel the executive to approve provisions that he or she would otherwise reject but that he or she signs into law to prevent the defeat of the entire bill.

Open court: "Common law requires a trial in open court; "open court" means a court to which the public has a right to be admitted. This term may mean either a court that has been formally convened and declared open for the transaction of its proper judicial business or a court that is freely open to spectators."

Ordinance: A law, statute, or regulation enacted by a municipal corporation.

Original intent: The theory of interpretation by which judges attempt to ascertain the meaning of a particular provision of a state or federal constitution by determining how the provision was understood at the time it was drafted and ratified.

Original jurisdiction: The authority of a tribunal to entertain a lawsuit, try it, and set forth a judgment on the law and facts.

Parens patriae: [*Latin, Parent of the country.*] A doctrine that grants the inherent power and authority of the state to protect persons who are legally unable to act on their own behalf.

Pecuniary: Monetary; relating to money; financial; consisting of money or that which can be valued in money.

Pension: A benefit, usually money, paid regularly to retired employees or their survivors by private business and federal, state, and local governments. Employers are not required to establish pension benefits but do so to attract qualified employees.

Per curiam: [*Latin, By the court.*] A phrase used to distinguish an opinion of the whole court from an opinion written by any one judge.

Peremptory challenge: The right to challenge a juror without assigning, or being required to assign, a reason for the challenge.

Personal actions: Lawsuits initiated in order, among other things, to recover damages for some injury to a plaintiff's personal right or property, for breach of contract, for money owed on a debt, or for the recovery of a specific item of personal property.

Plurality: The opinion of an appellate court in which more justices join than in any concurring opinion.

The excess of votes cast for one candidate over those votes cast for any other candidate.

Poll tax: A specified sum of money levied upon each person who votes.

Polygamy: The offense of having more than one wife or husband at the same time.

Ponzi scheme: A fraudulent investment plan in which the investments of later investors are used to pay earlier investors, giving the appearance that the investments of the initial participants dramatically increase in value in a short amount of time.

Prayer: The request contained in a bill in equity that the court will grant the process, aid, or relief that the complainant desires.

Preemption: A doctrine based on the Supremacy Clause of the U.S. Constitution that holds that certain matters are of such a national, as opposed to local, character that federal laws preempt or take precedence over state laws. As such, a state may not pass a law inconsistent with the federal law.

A doctrine of state law that holds that a state law displaces a local law or regulation that is in the same field and is in conflict or inconsistent with the state law.

Preliminary hearing: A proceeding before a judicial officer in which the officer must decide whether a crime was committed, whether the crime occurred within the territorial jurisdiction of the court, and whether there is probable cause to believe that the defendant committed the crime.

Preliminary injunction: A temporary order made by a court at the request of one party that prevents the other party from pursuing a particular course of conduct until the conclusion of a trial on the merits.

Presidential powers: The executive authority given to the president of the United States by Article II of the Constitution to carry out the duties of the office.

Prevailing party: The litigant who successfully brings or defends an action and, as a result, receives a favorable judgment or verdict.

Preventive detention: The confinement in a secure facility of a person who has not been found guilty of a crime.

Privy: One who has a direct, successive relationship; to another individual; a coparticipant; one who has an interest in a matter; private.

Pro bono: Short for *pro bono publico* [*Latin, For the public good*]. The designation given to the free legal work done by an attorney for indigent clients and religious, charitable, and other nonprofit entities.

Probable cause: Apparent facts discovered through logical inquiry that would lead a reasonably intelligent and prudent person to believe that an accused person has committed a crime, thereby warranting his or her prosecution, or that a cause of action has accrued, justifying a civil lawsuit.

Probative: Having the effect of proof, tending to prove, or actually proving.

Product liability: The responsibility of a manufacturer or vendor of goods to compensate for injury caused by a defective good that it has provided for sale.

Profanity: Irreverence towards sacred things; particularly, irreverent or blasphemous use of the name of God. Vulgar, irreverent, or course language.

Public domain: Land that is owned by the United States. In copyright law, literary or creative works over which the creator no longer has an exclusive right to restrict, or receive a royalty for, their reproduction or use but which can be freely copied by the public.

Public figure: A description applied in libel and slander actions, as well as in those alleging invasion of privacy, to anyone who has gained prominence in the community as a result of his or her name or exploits, whether willingly or unwillingly.

Public Policy: A principle that no person or government official can legally perform an act that tends to injure the public.

Punitive damages: Monetary compensation awarded to an injured party that goes beyond that which is necessary to compensate the individual for losses and that is intended to punish the wrongdoer.

Purview: The part of a statute or a law that delineates its purpose and scope.

Putative: Alleged; supposed; reputed.

Rational basis test: A judicial standard of review that examines whether a legislature had a reasonable and not an arbitrary basis for enacting a articular statute.

Redress: Compensation for injuries sustained; recovery or restitution for harm or injury; damages or equitable relief. Access to the courts to gain reparation for a wrong.

Repeal: The annulment or abrogation of a previously existing statute by the enactment of a later law that revokes the former law.

Rescind: To declare a contract void:of no legal force or binding effect: from its inception and thereby restore the parties to the positions they would have occupied had no contract ever been made.

Restitution: In the context of criminal law, state programs under which an offender is required, as a condition of his or her sentence, to repay money or donate services to the victim or society; with respect to maritime law, the restoration of articles lost by jettison, done when the remainder of the cargo has been saved, at the general charge of the owners of the cargo; in the law of torts, or civil wrongs, a measure of damages; in regard to contract law, the restoration of a party injured by a breach of contract to the position that party occupied before she or he entered the contract.

Revised Statutes: A body of statutes that have been revised, collected, arranged in order, and reenacted as a whole. The legal title of the collection of compiled laws of the United States, as well as some of the individual states.

Right of action: The privilege of instituting a lawsuit arising from a particular transaction or state of facts, such as a suit that is based on a contract or a tort, a civil wrong.

Robbery: The taking of money or goods in the possession of another, from his or her person or immediate presence, by force or intimidation.

Search and seizure: In international law, the right of ships of war, as regulated by treaties, to examine a merchant vessel during war in order to determine whether the ship or its cargo is liable to seizure.

A hunt by law enforcement officials for property or communications believed to be evidence of crime, and the act of taking possession of this property.

Self-determination: The political right of the majority to the exercise of power within the boundaries of a generally accepted political unit, area, or territory.

Solicitation: Urgent request, plea, or entreaty; enticing, asking. The criminal offense of urging someone to commit an unlawful act.

Sovereign immunity: The legal protection that prevents a sovereign state or person from being sued without consent.

Specific performance: An extraordinary equitable remedy that compels a party to execute a contract according to the precise terms agreed upon or to execute it substantially so that, under the circumstances, justice will be done between the parties.

State action: A requirement for claims that arise under the Due Process Clause of the Fourteenth Amendment and civil rights legislation, for which a private citizen seeks relief in the form of damages or redress based on an improper intrusion by the government into his or her private life.

State interest: A broad term for any matter of public concern that is addressed by a government in law or policy.

Statute: An act of a legislature that declares, proscribes, or commands something; a specific law, expressed in writing.

Statute of limitations: A type of federal or state law that restricts the time within which legal proceedings may be brought.

Statutory: Created, defined, or relating to a statute; required by statute; conforming to a statute.

Strict liability: Absolute legal responsibility for an injury that can be imposed on the wrongdoer without proof of carelessness or fault.

Strict scrutiny: A standard of judicial review for a challenged policy in which the court presumes the policy to be invalid unless the government can demonstrate a compelling interest to justify the policy.

Subject matter jurisdiction: The power of a court to hear and determine cases of the general class to which the proceedings in question belong.

Substantive due process: The substantive limitations placed on the content or subject matter of state and federal laws by the Due Process Clauses of the Fifth and Fourteenth Amendments to the U.S. Constitution.

Summary judgment: A procedural device used during civil litigation to promptly and expeditiously dispose of a case without a trial. It is used when there is no dispute as to the material facts of the case and a party is entitled to judgment as a matter of law.

Supremacy Clause: "The clause of Article VI of the U.S. Constitution that declares that all laws and treaties made by the federal government shall be the "supreme law of the land.""

Tariff: The list of items upon which a duty is imposed when they are imported into the United States, together with the rates at which such articles are taxed.

Taxable situs: The location where charges may be levied upon personal property by a government, pursuant to provisions of its tax laws.

Third party: A generic legal term for any individual who does not have a direct connection with a legal transaction but who might be affected by it.

Time, place, and manner restrictions: Limits that government can impose on the occasion, location, and type of individual expression in some circumstances.

Title insurance: A contractual arrangement entered into to indemnify loss or damage resulting from defects or problems relating to the ownership of real property, or from the enforcement of liens that exist against it.

Tort law: A body of rights, obligations, and remedies that is applied by courts in civil proceedings to provide relief for persons who have suffered harm from the wrongful acts of others. The person who sustains injury or suffers pecuniary damage as the result of tortious conduct is known as the plaintiff, and the person who is responsible for inflicting the injury and incurs liability for the damage is known as the defendant or tortfeasor.

Tortious: Wrongful; conduct of such character as to subject the actor to civil liability under tort law.

Tribunal: A general term for a court, or the seat of a judge.

Trustee: An individual or corporation named by an individual, who sets aside property to be used for the benefit of another person, to manage the property as provided by the terms of the document that created the arrangement.

Usury: The crime of charging higher interest on a loan than the law permits.

Venue: A place, such as the territory from which residents are selected to serve as jurors.

A proper place, such as the correct court to hear a case because it has authority over events that have occurred within a certain geographical area.

Vicarious liability: The tort doctrine that imposes responsibility upon one person for the failure of another, with whom the person has a special relationship (such as parent and child, employer and employee, or owner of vehicle and driver), to exercise such care as a reasonably prudent person would use under similar circumstances.

Words of limitation: The words in a deed or will that indicate what type of estate or rights the person being given the land receives.

Writ: An order issued by a court requiring that something be done or giving authority to do a specified act.

Wrongful death: The taking of the life of an individual resulting from the willful or negligent act of another person or persons.

Zoning: The separation or division of a municipality into districts, the regulation of buildings and structures in such districts in accordance with their construction and the nature and extent of their use, and the dedication of such districts to particular uses designed to serve the general welfare.

A.	Atlantic Reporter	ACS	Agricultural Cooperative Service
A. 2d	Atlantic Reporter, Second Series	ACT	American College Test
AA	Alcoholics Anonymous	Act'g Legal Adv.	Acting Legal Advisor
AAA	American Arbitration Association; Agricultural Adjustment Act of 1933	ACUS	Administrative Conference of the United States
		ACYF	Administration on Children, Youth, and Families
AALS	Association of American Law Schools	A.D. 2d	Appellate Division, Second Series, N.Y.
AAPRP	All African People's Revolutionary Party	ADA	Americans with Disabilities Act of 1990
AARP	American Association of Retired Persons	ADAMHA	Alcohol, Drug Abuse, and Mental Health Administration
AAS	American Anti-Slavery Society	ADC	Aid to Dependent Children
ABA	American Bar Association; Architectural Barriers Act of 1968; American Bankers Association	ADD	Administration on Developmental Disabilities
		ADEA	Age Discrimination in Employment Act of 1967
ABC	American Broadcasting Companies, Inc. (formerly American Broadcasting Corporation)	ADL	Anti-Defamation League
		ADR	Alternative dispute resolution
		AEC	Atomic Energy Commission
ABM	Antiballistic missile	AECB	Arms Export Control Board
ABM Treaty	Anti-Ballistic Missile Treaty of 1972	AEDPA	Antiterrorism and Effective Death Penalty Act
ABVP	Anti-Biased Violence Project	A.E.R.	All England Law Reports
A/C	Account	AFA	American Family Association; Alabama Freethought Association
A.C.	Appeal cases		
ACAA	Air Carrier Access Act		
ACCA	Armed Career Criminal Act of 1984	AFB	American Farm Bureau
		AFBF	American Farm Bureau Federation
ACF	Administration for Children and Families	AFDC	Aid to Families with Dependent Children
ACLU	American Civil Liberties Union	aff'd per cur.	Affirmed by the court
ACRS	Accelerated Cost Recovery System	AFIS	Automated fingerprint identification system

AFL	American Federation of Labor	Ann. Dig.	Annual Digest of Public International Law Cases
AFL-CIO	American Federation of Labor and Congress of Industrial Organizations	ANRA	American Newspaper Publishers Association
AFRes	Air Force Reserve	ANSCA	Alaska Native Claims Act
AFSC	American Friends Service Committee	ANZUS	Australia-New Zealand-United States Security Treaty Organization
AFSCME	American Federation of State, County, and Municipal Employees	AOA	Administration on Aging
		AOE	Arizonans for Official English
AGRICOLA	Agricultural Online Access	AOL	America Online
AIA	Association of Insurance Attorneys	AP	Associated Press
AIB	American Institute for Banking	APA	Administrative Procedure Act of 1946
AID	Artificial insemination using a third-party donor's sperm; Agency for International Development	APHIS	Animal and Plant Health Inspection Service
		App. Div.	Appellate Division Reports, N.Y. Supreme Court
AIDS	Acquired immune deficiency syndrome	Arb. Trib., U.S.-British	Arbitration Tribunal, Claim Convention of 1853, United States and Great Britain Convention of 1853
AIH	Artificial insemination using the husband's sperm		
AIM	American Indian Movement	Ardcor	American Roller Die Corporation
AIPAC	American Israel Public Affairs Committee	ARPA	Advanced Research Projects Agency
AIUSA	Amnesty International, U.S.A. Affiliate	ARPANET	Advanced Research Projects Agency Network
AJS	American Judicature Society		
ALA	American Library Association	ARS	Advanced Record System
Alcoa	Aluminum Company of America	Art.	Article
		ARU	American Railway Union
ALEC	American Legislative Exchange Council	ASCME	American Federation of State, County, and Municipal Employees
ALF	Animal Liberation Front		
ALI	American Law Institute	ASCS	Agriculture Stabilization and Conservation Service
ALJ	Administrative law judge		
All E.R.	All England Law Reports	ASM	Available Seatmile
ALO	Agency Liaison	ASPCA	American Society for the Prevention of Cruelty to Animals
A.L.R.	American Law Reports		
ALY	American Law Yearbook		
AMA	American Medical Association	Asst. Att. Gen.	Assistant Attorney General
AMAA	Agricultural Marketing Agreement Act	AT&T	American Telephone and Telegraph
Am. Dec.	American Decisions	ATFD	Alcohol, Tobacco and Firearms Division
amdt.	Amendment		
Amer. St. Papers, For. Rels.	American State Papers, Legislative and Executive Documents of the Congress of the U.S., Class I, Foreign Relations, 1832–1859	ATLA	Association of Trial Lawyers of America
		ATO	Alpha Tau Omega
		ATTD	Alcohol and Tobacco Tax Division
		ATU	Alcohol Tax Unit
AMS	Agricultural Marketing Service	AUAM	American Union against Militarism
AMVETS	American Veterans (of World War II)	AUM	Animal Unit Month
		AZT	Azidothymidine
ANA	Administration for Native Americans	BAC	Blood alcohol concentration

BALSA	Black-American Law Student Association	CAFE	Corporate average fuel economy
BATF	Bureau of Alcohol, Tobacco and Firearms	Cal. 2d	California Reports, Second Series
BBS	Bulletin Board System	Cal. 3d	California Reports, Third Series
BCCI	Bank of Credit and Commerce International	CALR	Computer-assisted legal research
BEA	Bureau of Economic Analysis	Cal. Rptr.	California Reporter
Bell's Cr. C.	Bell's English Crown Cases	CAP	Common Agricultural Policy
Bevans	United States Treaties, etc. *Treaties and Other International Agreements of the United States of America, 1776–1949* (compiled under the direction of Charles I. Bevans, 1968–76)	CARA	Classification and Ratings Administration
		CATV	Community antenna television
		CBO	Congressional Budget Office
		CBS	Columbia Broadcasting System
BFOQ	Bona fide occupational qualification	CBOEC	Chicago Board of Election Commissioners
BI	Bureau of Investigation	CCC	Commodity Credit Corporation
BIA	Bureau of Indian Affairs; Board of Immigration Appeals	CCDBG	Child Care and Development Block Grant of 1990
BID	Business improvement district	C.C.D. Pa.	Circuit Court Decisions, Pennsylvania
BJS	Bureau of Justice Statistics	C.C.D. Va.	Circuit Court Decisions, Virginia
Black.	Black's United States Supreme Court Reports	CCEA	Cabinet Council on Economic Affairs
Blatchf.	Blatchford's United States Circuit Court Reports	CCP	Chinese Communist Party
BLM	Bureau of Land Management	CCR	Center for Constitutional Rights
BLS	Bureau of Labor Statistics		
BMD	Ballistic missile defense	C.C.R.I.	Circuit Court, Rhode Island
BNA	Bureau of National Affairs	CD	Certificate of deposit; compact disc
BOCA	Building Officials and Code Administrators International	CDA	Communications Decency Act
BOP	Bureau of Prisons	CDBG	Community Development Block Grant Program
BPP	Black Panther Party for Self-defense	CDC	Centers for Disease Control and Prevention; Community Development Corporation
Brit. and For.	British and Foreign State Papers		
BSA	Boy Scouts of America		
BTP	Beta Theta Pi	CDF	Children's Defense Fund
Burr.	James Burrows, *Report of Cases Argued and Determined in the Court of King's Bench during the Time of Lord Mansfield* (1766–1780)	CDL	Citizens for Decency through Law
		CD-ROM	Compact disc read-only memory
		CDS	Community Dispute Services
BVA	Board of Veterans Appeals	CDW	Collision damage waiver
c.	Chapter	CENTO	Central Treaty Organization
C³I	Command, Control, Communications, and Intelligence	CEO	Chief executive officer
		CEQ	Council on Environmental Quality
C.A.	Court of Appeals	CERCLA	Comprehensive Environmental Response, Compensation, and Liability Act of 1980
CAA	Clean Air Act		
CAB	Civil Aeronautics Board; Corporation for American Banking		
		cert.	*Certiorari*

CETA	Comprehensive Employment and Training Act	CLP	Communist Labor Party of America
C & F	Cost and freight	CLS	Christian Legal Society; critical legal studies (movement); Critical Legal Studies (membership organization)
CFC	Chlorofluorocarbon		
CFE Treaty	Conventional Forces in Europe Treaty of 1990		
C.F. & I.	Cost, freight, and insurance	C.M.A.	Court of Military Appeals
C.F.R	Code of Federal Regulations	CMEA	Council for Mutual Economic Assistance
CFNP	Community Food and Nutrition Program	CMHS	Center for Mental Health Services
CFTA	Canadian Free Trade Agreement	C.M.R.	Court of Military Review
CFTC	Commodity Futures Trading Commission	CNN	Cable News Network
		CNO	Chief of Naval Operations
Ch.	Chancery Division, English Law Reports	CNOL	Consolidated net operating loss
CHAMPVA	Civilian Health and Medical Program at the Veterans Administration	CNR	Chicago and Northwestern Railway
		CO	Conscientious Objector
CHEP	Cuban/Haitian Entrant Program	C.O.D.	Cash on delivery
		COGP	Commission on Government Procurement
CHINS	Children in need of supervision		
CHIPS	Child in need of protective services	COINTELPRO	Counterintelligence Program
		Coke Rep.	Coke's English King's Bench Reports
Ch.N.Y.	Chancery Reports, New York		
Chr. Rob.	Christopher Robinson, *Reports of Cases Argued and Determined in the High Court of Admiralty* (1801– 1808)	COLA	Cost-of-living adjustment
		COMCEN	Federal Communications Center
		Comp.	Compilation
		Conn.	Connecticut Reports
CIA	Central Intelligence Agency	CONTU	National Commission on New Technological Uses of Copyrighted Works
CID	Commercial Item Descriptions		
C.I.F.	Cost, insurance, and freight		
CINCNORAD	Commander in Chief, North American Air Defense Command	Conv.	Convention
		COPA	Child Online Protection Act (1998)
C.I.O.	Congress of Industrial Organizations	COPS	Community Oriented Policing Services
CIPE	Center for International Private Enterprise	Corbin	Arthur L. Corbin, *Corbin on Contracts: A Comprehensive Treatise on the Rules of Contract Law* (1950)
C.J.	Chief justice		
CJIS	Criminal Justice Information Services		
		CORE	Congress on Racial Equality
C.J.S.	Corpus Juris Secundum	Cox's Crim. Cases	Cox's Criminal Cases (England)
Claims Arb. under Spec. Conv., Nielsen's Rept.	Frederick Kenelm Nielsen, *American and British Claims Arbitration under the Special Agreement Concluded between the United States and Great Britain, August 18, 1910* (1926)		
		COYOTE	Call Off Your Old Tired Ethics
		CPA	Certified public accountant
		CPB	Corporation for Public Broadcasting, the
		CPI	Consumer Price Index
CLASP	Center for Law and Social Policy	CPPA	Child Pornography Prevention Act
CLE	Center for Law and Education; Continuing Legal Education	CPSC	Consumer Product Safety Commission
		Cranch	Cranch's United States Supreme Court Reports
CLEO	Council on Legal Education Opportunity; Chief Law Enforcement Officer	CRF	Constitutional Rights Foundation

CRR	Center for Constitutional Rights	D.C. Md.	United States District Court, Maryland
CRS	Congressional Research Service; Community Relations Service	D.C.N.D.Cal.	United States District Court, Northern District, California
CRT	Critical race theory	D.C.N.Y.	United States District Court, New York
CSA	Community Services Administration	D.C.Pa.	United States District Court, Pennsylvania
CSAP	Center for Substance Abuse Prevention	DCS	Deputy Chiefs of Staff
CSAT	Center for Substance Abuse Treatment	DCZ	District of the Canal Zone
CSC	Civil Service Commission	DDT	Dichlorodiphenyl-tricloroethane
CSCE	Conference on Security and Cooperation in Europe	DEA	Drug Enforcement Administration
CSG	Council of State Governments	Decl. Lond.	Declaration of London, February 26, 1909
CSO	Community Service Organization	Dev. & B.	Devereux & Battle's North Carolina Reports
CSP	Center for the Study of the Presidency	DFL	Minnesota Democratic-Farmer-Labor
C-SPAN	Cable-Satellite Public Affairs Network	DFTA	Department for the Aging
CSRS	Cooperative State Research Service	Dig. U.S. Practice in Intl. Law	Digest of U.S. Practice in International Law
CSWPL	Center on Social Welfare Policy and Law	Dist. Ct.	D.C. United States District Court, District of Columbia
CTA	*Cum testamento annexo* (with the will attached)	D.L.R.	Dominion Law Reports (Canada)
Ct. Ap. D.C.	Court of Appeals, District of Columbia	DMCA	Digital Millennium Copyright Act
Ct. App. No. Ireland	Court of Appeals, Northern Ireland	DNA	Deoxyribonucleic acid
Ct. Cl.	Court of Claims, United States	Dnase	Deoxyribonuclease
Ct. Crim. Apps.	Court of Criminal Appeals (England)	DNC	Democratic National Committee
Ct. of Sess., Scot.	Court of Sessions, Scotland	DOC	Department of Commerce
CTI	Consolidated taxable income	DOD	Department of Defense
CU	Credit union	DODEA	Department of Defense Education Activity
CUNY	City University of New York		
Cush.	Cushing's Massachusetts Reports	Dodson	Dodson's Reports, English Admiralty Courts
CWA	Civil Works Administration; Clean Water Act	DOE	Department of Energy
		DOER	Department of Employee Relations
DACORB	Department of the Army Conscientious Objector Review Board	DOJ	Department of Justice
		DOL	Department of Labor
Dall.	Dallas's Pennsylvania and United States Reports	DOMA	Defense of Marriage Act of 1996
DAR	Daughters of the American Revolution	DOS	Disk operating system
		DOT	Department of Transportation
DARPA	Defense Advanced Research Projects Agency	DPT	Diphtheria, pertussis, and tetanus
DAVA	Defense Audiovisual Agency	DRI	Defense Research Institute
D.C.	United States District Court; District of Columbia	DSAA	Defense Security Assistance Agency
D.C. Del.	United States District Court, Delaware	DUI	Driving under the influence; driving under intoxication
D.C. Mass.	United States District Court, Massachusetts	DVD	Digital versatile disc

DWI	Driving while intoxicated	et seq.	*Et sequentes* or *et sequentia* ("and the following")
EAHCA	Education for All Handicapped Children Act of 1975	EU	European Union
		Euratom	European Atomic Energy Community
EBT	Examination before trial		
E.coli	Escherichia coli	Eur. Ct. H.R.	European Court of Human Rights
ECPA	Electronic Communications Privacy Act of 1986	Ex.	English Exchequer Reports, Welsby, Hurlstone & Gordon
ECSC	Treaty of the European Coal and Steel Community		
EDA	Economic Development Administration	Exch.	Exchequer Reports (Welsby, Hurlstone & Gordon)
EDF	Environmental Defense Fund	Ex Com	Executive Committee of the National Security Council
E.D.N.Y.	Eastern District, New York		
EDP	Electronic data processing		
E.D. Pa.	Eastern-District, Pennsylvania	Eximbank	Export-Import Bank of the United States
EDSC	Eastern District, South Carolina	F.	Federal Reporter
EDT	Eastern daylight time	F. 2d	Federal Reporter, Second Series
E.D. Va.	Eastern District, Virginia	FAA	Federal Aviation Administration; Federal Arbitration Act
EEC	European Economic Community; European Economic Community Treaty	FAAA	Federal Alcohol Administration Act
EEOC	Equal Employment Opportunity Commission	FACE	Freedom of Access to Clinic Entrances Act of 1994
EFF	Electronic Frontier Foundation	FACT	Feminist Anti-Censorship Task Force
EFT	Electronic funds transfer	FAIRA	Federal Agriculture Improvement and Reform Act of 1996
Eliz.	Queen Elizabeth (Great Britain)		
Em. App.	Temporary Emergency Court of Appeals	FAMLA	Family and Medical Leave Act of 1993
ENE	Early neutral evaluation	Fannie Mae	Federal National Mortgage Association
Eng. Rep.	English Reports		
EOP	Executive Office of the President	FAO	Food and Agriculture Organization of the United Nations
EPA	Environmental Protection Agency; Equal Pay Act of 1963	FAR	Federal Acquisition Regulations
ERA	Equal Rights Amendment	FAS	Foreign Agricultural Service
ERDC	Energy Research and Development Commission	FBA	Federal Bar Association
		FBI	Federal Bureau of Investigation
ERISA	Employee Retirement Income Security Act of 1974	FCA	Farm Credit Administration
ERS	Economic Research Service	F. Cas.	Federal Cases
ERTA	Economic Recovery Tax Act of 1981	FCC	Federal Communications Commission
ESA	Endangered Species Act of 1973	FCIA	Foreign Credit Insurance Association
ESF	Emergency support function; Economic Support Fund	FCIC	Federal Crop Insurance Corporation
ESRD	End-Stage Renal Disease Program	FCLAA	Federal Cigarette Labeling and Advertising Act
ETA	Employment and Training Administration	FCRA	Fair Credit Reporting Act
		FCU	Federal credit unions
ETS	Environmental tobacco smoke	FCUA	Federal Credit Union Act
		FCZ	Fishery Conservation Zone

FDA	Food and Drug Administration	F.O.B.	Free on board
FDIC	Federal Deposit Insurance Corporation	FOIA	Freedom of Information Act
		FOMC	Federal Open Market Committee
FDPC	Federal Data Processing Center	FPA	Federal Power Act of 1935
FEC	Federal Election Commission	FPC	Federal Power Commission
FECA	Federal Election Campaign Act of 1971	FPMR	Federal Property Management Regulations
Fed. Cas.	Federal Cases	FPRS	Federal Property Resources Service
FEHA	Fair Employment and Housing Act	FR	Federal Register
		FRA	Federal Railroad Administration
FEHBA	Federal Employees Health Benefit Act	FRB	Federal Reserve Board
FEMA	Federal Emergency Management Agency	FRC	Federal Radio Commission
		F.R.D.	Federal Rules Decisions
FERC	Federal Energy Regulatory Commission	FSA	Family Support Act
		FSB	Federal'naya Sluzhba Bezopasnosti (the Federal Security Service of Russia)
FFB	Federal Financing Bank		
FFDC	Federal Food, Drug, and Cosmetics Act	FSLIC	Federal Savings and Loan Insurance Corporation
FGIS	Federal Grain Inspection Service	FSQS	Food Safety and Quality Service
FHA	Federal Housing Administration	FSS	Federal Supply Service
FHAA	Fair Housing Amendments Act of 1998	F. Supp.	Federal Supplement
		FTA	U.S.-Canada Free Trade Agreement of 1988
FHWA	Federal Highway Administration	FTC	Federal Trade Commission
FIA	Federal Insurance Administration	FTCA	Federal Tort Claims Act
FIC	Federal Information Centers; Federation of Insurance Counsel	FTS	Federal Telecommunications System
		FTS2000	Federal Telecommunications System 2000
FICA	Federal Insurance Contributions Act	FUCA	Federal Unemployment Compensation Act of 1988
FIFRA	Federal Insecticide, Fungicide, and Rodenticide Act	FUTA	Federal Unemployment Tax Act
FIP	Forestry Incentives Program	FWPCA	Federal Water Pollution Control Act of 1948
FIRREA	Financial Institutions Reform, Recovery, and Enforcement Act of 1989	FWS	Fish and Wildlife Service
		GAL	Guardian ad litem
FISA	Foreign Intelligence Surveillance Act of 1978	GAO	General Accounting Office; Governmental Affairs Office
FISC	Foreign Intelligence Surveillance Court of Review	GAOR	General Assembly Official Records, United Nations
FJC	Federal Judicial Center	GAAP	Generally accepted accounting principles
FLSA	Fair Labor Standards Act		
FMC	Federal Maritime Commission	GA Res.	General Assembly Resolution (United Nations)
FMCS	Federal Mediation and Conciliation Service	GATT	General Agreement on Tariffs and Trade
FmHA	Farmers Home Administration	GCA	Gun Control Act
		Gen. Cls. Comm.	General Claims Commission, United States and Panama; General Claims United States and Mexico
FMLA	Family and Medical Leave Act of 1993		
FNMA	Federal National Mortgage Association, "Fannie Mae"	Geo. II	King George II (Great Britain)

Geo. III	King George III (Great Britain)	HNIS	Human Nutrition Information Service
GHB	Gamma-hydroxybutrate	Hong Kong L.R.	Hong Kong Law Reports
GI	Government Issue	How.	Howard's United States
GID	General Intelligence Division		Supreme Court Reports
GM	General Motors	How. St. Trials	Howell's English State Trials
GNMA	Government National Mortgage Association, "Ginnie Mae"	HUAC	House Un-American Activities Committee
GNP	Gross national product	HUD	Department of Housing and Urban Development
GOP	Grand Old Party (Republican Party)	Hudson, Internatl. Legis.	Manley Ottmer Hudson, ed., *International Legislation: A Collection of the Texts of Multipartite International Instruments of General Interest Beginning with the Covenant of the League of Nations* (1931)
GOPAC	Grand Old Party Action Committee		
GPA	Office of Governmental and Public Affairs		
GPO	Government Printing Office		
GRAS	Generally recognized as safe		
Gr. Br., Crim. Ct. App.	Great Britain, Court of Criminal Appeals	Hudson, World Court Reps.	Manley Ottmer Hudson, ea., *World Court Reports* (1934–)
GRNL	Gay Rights-National Lobby		
GSA	General Services Administration	Hun	Hun's New York Supreme Court Reports
Hackworth	Green Haywood Hackworth, *Digest of International Law* (1940–1944)	Hunt's Rept.	Bert L. Hunt, *Report of the American and Panamanian General Claims Arbitration* (1934)
Hay and Marriott	Great Britain. High Court of Admiralty, *Decisions in the High Court of Admiralty during the Time of Sir George Hay and of Sir James Marriott, Late Judges of That Court* (1801)	IAEA	International Atomic Energy Agency
		IALL	International Association of Law Libraries
		IBA	International Bar Association
HBO	Home Box Office	IBM	International Business Machines
HCFA	Health Care Financing Administration	ICA	Interstate Commerce Act
H.Ct.	High Court	ICBM	Intercontinental ballistic missile
HDS	Office of Human Development Services	ICC	Interstate Commerce Commission; International Criminal Court
Hen. & M.	Hening & Munford's Virginia Reports		
HEW	Department of Health, Education, and Welfare	ICJ	International Court of Justice
HFCA	Health Care Financing Administration	ICM	Institute for Court Management
HGI	Handgun Control, Incorporated	IDEA	Individuals with Disabilities Education Act of 1975
HHS	Department of Health and Human Services	IDOP	International Dolphin Conservation Program
Hill	Hill's New York Reports	IEP	Individualized educational program
HIRE	Help through Industry Retraining and Employment	IFC	International Finance Corporation
		IGRA	Indian Gaming Regulatory Act of 1988
HIV	Human immunodeficiency virus	IJA	Institute of Judicial Administration
H.L.	House of Lords Cases (England)	IJC	International Joint Commission
H. Lords	House of Lords (England)		
HMO	Health Maintenance Organization	ILC	International Law Commission
		ILD	International Labor Defense

Ill. Dec.	Illinois Decisions
ILO	International Labor Organization
IMF	International Monetary Fund
INA	Immigration and Nationality Act
IND	Investigational new drug
INF Treaty	Intermediate-Range Nuclear Forces Treaty of 1987
INS	Immigration and Naturalization Service
INTELSAT	International Telecommunications Satellite Organization
Interpol	International Criminal Police Organization
Int'l. Law Reps.	International Law Reports
Intl. Legal Mats.	International Legal Materials
IOC	International Olympic Committee
IPDC	International Program for the Development of Communication
IPO	Intellectual Property Owners
IPP	Independent power producer
IQ	Intelligence quotient
I.R.	Irish Reports
IRA	Individual retirement account; Irish Republican Army
IRC	Internal Revenue Code
IRCA	Immigration Reform and Control Act of 1986
IRS	Internal Revenue Service
ISO	Independent service organization
ISP	Internet service provider
ISSN	International Standard Serial Numbers
ITA	International Trade Administration
ITI	Information Technology Integration
ITO	International Trade Organization
ITS	Information Technology Service
ITT	International Telephone and Telegraph Corporation
ITU	International Telecommunication Union
IUD	Intrauterine device
IWC	International Whaling Commission
IWW	Industrial Workers of the World
JAGC	Judge Advocate General's Corps
JCS	Joint Chiefs of Staff
JDL	Jewish Defense League

JNOV	Judgment *non obstante vere-dicto* ("judgment nothing to recommend it" or "judgment notwithstanding the verdict")
JOBS	Jobs Opportunity and Basic Skills
John. Ch.	Johnson's New York Chancery Reports
Johns.	Johnson's Reports (New York)
JP	Justice of the peace
K.B.	King's Bench Reports (England)
KFC	Kentucky Fried Chicken
KGB	Komitet Gosudarstvennoi Bezopasnosti (the State Security Committee for countries in the former Soviet Union)
KKK	Ku Klux Klan
KMT	Kuomintang (Chinese, "national people's party")
LAD	Law Against Discrimination
LAPD	Los Angeles Police Department
LC	Library of Congress
LCHA	Longshoremen's and Harbor Workers Compensation Act of 1927
LD50	Lethal dose 50
LDEF	Legal Defense and Education Fund (NOW)
LDF	Legal Defense Fund, Legal Defense and Educational Fund of the NAACP
LEAA	Law Enforcement Assistance Administration
L.Ed.	Lawyers' Edition Supreme Court Reports
LI	Letter of interpretation
LLC	Limited Liability Company
LLP	Limited Liability Partnership
LMSA	Labor-Management Services Administration
LNTS	League of Nations Treaty Series
Lofft's Rep.	Lofft's English King's Bench Reports
L.R.	Law Reports (English)
LSAC	Law School Admission Council
LSAS	Law School Admission Service
LSAT	Law School Aptitude Test
LSC	Legal Services Corporation; Legal Services for Children
LSD	Lysergic acid diethylamide

LSDAS	Law School Data Assembly Service	MIRVed ICBM	Multiple independently targetable reentry vehicled intercontinental ballistic missile
LTBT	Limited Test Ban Treaty		
LTC	Long Term Care		
MAD	Mutual assured destruction	Misc.	Miscellaneous Reports, New York
MADD	Mothers against Drunk Driving		
MALDEF	Mexican American Legal Defense and Educational Fund	Mixed Claims Comm., Report of Decs	Mixed Claims Commission, United States and Germany, Report of Decisions
Malloy	William M. Malloy, ed., *Treaties, Conventions International Acts, Protocols, and Agreements between the United States of America and Other Powers* (1910–1938)	M.J.	Military Justice Reporter
		MLAP	Migrant Legal Action Program
		MLB	Major League Baseball
		MLDP	Mississippi Loyalist Democratic Party
		MMI	Moslem Mosque, Incorporated
Martens	Georg Friedrich von Martens, ea., *Noveau recueil général de traités et autres actes relatifs aux rapports de droit international* (Series I, 20 vols. [1843–1875]; Series II, 35 vols. [1876–1908]; Series III [1909–])	MMPA	Marine Mammal Protection Act of 1972
		Mo.	Missouri Reports
		MOD	Masters of Deception
		Mod.	Modern Reports, English King's Bench, etc.
		Moore, Dig. Intl. Law	John Bassett Moore, *A Digest of International Law*, 8 vols. (1906)
Mass.	Massachusetts Reports		
MCC	Metropolitan Correctional Center	Moore, Intl. Arbs.	John Bassett Moore, *History and Digest of the International Arbitrations to Which United States Has Been a Party*, 6 vols. (1898)
MCCA	Medicare Catastrophic Coverage Act of 1988		
MCH	Maternal and Child Health Bureau		
MCRA	Medical Care Recovery Act of 1962	Morison	William Maxwell Morison, *The Scots Revised Report: Morison's Dictionary of Decisions* (1908–09)
MDA	Medical Devices Amendments of 1976		
Md. App.	Maryland, Appeal Cases	M.P.	Member of Parliament
M.D. Ga.	Middle District, Georgia	MP3	MPEG Audio Layer 3
Mercy	Movement Ensuring the Right to Choose for Yourself	MPAA	Motion Picture Association of America
		MPAS	Michigan Protection and Advocacy Service
Metc.	Metcalf's Massachusetts Reports	MPEG	Motion Picture Experts Group
MFDP	Mississippi Freedom Democratic party	mpg	Miles per gallon
MGT	Management	MPPDA	Motion Picture Producers and Distributors of America
MHSS	Military Health Services System		
Miller	David Hunter Miller, ea., *Treaties and Other International Acts of the United States of America* (1931–1948)	MPRSA	Marine Protection, Research, and Sanctuaries Act of 1972
		M.R.	Master of the Rolls
		MS-DOS	Microsoft Disk Operating System
Minn.	Minnesota Reports	MSHA	Mine Safety and Health Administration
MINS	Minors in need of supervision	MSPB	Merit Systems Protection Board
MIRV	Multiple independently targetable reentry vehicle	MSSA	Military Selective Service Act
		N/A	Not Available

NAACP	National Association for the Advancement of Colored People	NCJA	National Criminal Justice Association
NAAQS	National Ambient Air Quality Standards	NCLB	National Civil Liberties Bureau
NAB	National Association of Broadcasters	NCP	National contingency plan
NABSW	National Association of Black Social Workers	NCSC	National Center for State Courts
NACDL	National Association of Criminal Defense Lawyers	NCUA	National Credit Union Administration
NAFTA	North American Free Trade Agreement of 1993	NDA	New drug application
		N.D. Ill.	Northern District, Illinois
NAGHSR	National Association of Governors' Highway Safety Representatives	NDU	National Defense University
		N.D. Wash.	Northern District, Washington
NALA	National Association of Legal Assistants	N.E.	North Eastern Reporter
NAM	National Association of Manufacturers	N.E. 2d	North Eastern Reporter, Second Series
NAR	National Association of Realtors	NEA	National Endowment for the Arts; National Education Association
NARAL	National Abortion and Reproductive Rights Action League	NEH	National Endowment for the Humanities
NARF	Native American Rights Fund	NEPA	National Environmental Protection Act; National Endowment Policy Act
NARS	National Archives and Record Service	NET Act	No Electronic Theft Act
NASA	National Aeronautics and Space Administration	NFIB	National Federation of Independent Businesses
NASD	National Association of Securities Dealers	NFIP	National Flood Insurance Program
NATO	North Atlantic Treaty Organization	NFL	National Football League
		NFPA	National Federation of Paralegal Associations
NAVINFO	Navy Information Offices	NGLTF	National Gay and Lesbian Task Force
NAWSA	National American Woman's Suffrage Association	NHL	National Hockey League
NBA	National Bar Association; National Basketball Association	NHRA	Nursing Home Reform Act of 1987
		NHTSA	National Highway Traffic Safety Administration
NBC	National Broadcasting Company	Nielsen's Rept.	Frederick Kenelm Nielsen, *American and British Claims Arbitration under the Special Agreement Concluded between the United States and Great Britain, August 18, 1910* (1926)
NBLSA	National Black Law Student Association		
NBS	National Bureau of Standards		
NCA	Noise Control Act; National Command Authorities		
NCAA	National Collegiate Athletic Association	NIEO	New International Economic Order
NCAC	National Coalition against Censorship	NIGC	National Indian Gaming Commission
NCCB	National Consumer Cooperative Bank	NIH	National Institutes of Health
NCE	Northwest Community Exchange	NIJ	National Institute of Justice
NCF	National Chamber Foundation	NIRA	National Industrial Recovery Act of 1933; National Industrial Recovery Administration
NCIP	National Crime Insurance Program		

NIST	National Institute of Standards and Technology
NITA	National Telecommunications and Information Administration
N.J.	New Jersey Reports
N.J. Super.	New Jersey Superior Court Reports
NLEA	Nutrition Labeling and Education Act of 1990
NLRA	National Labor Relations Act
NLRB	National Labor Relations Board
NMFS	National Marine Fisheries Service
No.	Number
NOAA	National Oceanic and Atmospheric Administration
NOC	National Olympic Committee
NOI	Nation of Islam
NOL	Net operating loss
NORML	National Organization for the Reform of Marijuana Laws
NOW	National Organization for Women
NOW LDEF	National Organization for Women Legal Defense and Education Fund
NOW/PAC	National Organization for Women Political Action Committee
NPDES	National Pollutant Discharge Elimination System
NPL	National priorities list
NPR	National Public Radio
NPT	Nuclear Non-Proliferation Treaty of 1970
NRA	National Rifle Association; National Recovery Act
NRC	Nuclear Regulatory Commission
NRLC	National Right to Life Committee
NRTA	National Retired Teachers Association
NSA	National Security Agency
NSC	National Security Council
NSCLC	National Senior Citizens Law Center
NSF	National Science Foundation
NSFNET	National Science Foundation Network
NSI	Network Solutions, Inc.
NTIA	National Telecommunications and Information Administration

NTID	National Technical Institute for the Deaf
NTIS	National Technical Information Service
NTS	Naval Telecommunications System
NTSB	National Transportation Safety Board
NVRA	National Voter Registration Act
N.W.	North Western Reporter
N.W. 2d	North Western Reporter, Second Series
NWSA	National Woman Suffrage Association
N.Y.	New York Court of Appeals Reports
N.Y. 2d	New York Court of Appeals Reports, Second Series
N.Y.S.	New York Supplement Reporter
N.Y.S. 2d	New York Supplement Reporter, Second Series
NYSE	New York Stock Exchange
NYSLA	New York State Liquor Authority
N.Y. Sup.	New York Supreme Court Reports
NYU	New York University
OAAU	Organization of Afro American Unity
OAP	Office of Administrative Procedure
OAS	Organization of American States
OASDI	Old-age, Survivors, and Disability Insurance Benefits
OASHDS	Office of the Assistant Secretary for Human Development Services
OCC	Office of Comptroller of the Currency
OCED	Office of Comprehensive Employment Development
OCHAMPUS	Office of Civilian Health and Medical Program of the Uniformed Services
OCSE	Office of Child Support Enforcement
OEA	Organización de los Estados Americanos
OEM	Original Equipment Manufacturer
OFCCP	Office of Federal Contract Compliance Programs
OFPP	Office of Federal Procurement Policy

OIC	Office of the Independent Counsel	PBGC	Pension Benefit Guaranty Corporation
OICD	Office of International Cooperation and Development	PBS	Public Broadcasting Service; Public Buildings Service
OIG	Office of the Inspector General	P.C.	Privy Council (English Law Reports)
OJARS	Office of Justice Assistance, Research, and Statistics	PC	Personal computer; politically correct
OMB	Office of Management and Budget	PCBs	Polychlorinated biphenyls
OMPC	Office of Management, Planning, and Communications	PCIJ	Permanent Court of International Justice Series A-Judgments and Orders (1922–30) Series B-Advisory Opinions (1922–30) Series A/B-Judgments, Orders, and Advisory Opinions (1931–40) Series C-Pleadings, Oral Statements, and Documents relating to Judgments and Advisory Opinions (1923–42) Series D-Acts and Documents concerning the Organization of the World Court (1922–47) Series E-Annual Reports (1925–45)
ONP	Office of National Programs		
OPD	Office of Policy Development		
OPEC	Organization of Petroleum Exporting Countries		
OPIC	Overseas Private Investment Corporation		
Ops. Atts. Gen.	Opinions of the Attorneys-General of the United States		
Ops. Comms.	Opinions of the Commissioners		
OPSP	Office of Product Standards Policy		
O.R.	Ontario Reports		
OR	Official Records	PCP	Phencyclidine
OSHA	Occupational Safety and Health Act	P.D.	Probate Division, English Law Reports (1876–1890)
OSHRC	Occupational Safety and Health Review Commission	PDA	Pregnancy Discrimination Act of 1978
OSM	Office of Surface Mining	PD & R	Policy Development and Research
OSS	Office of Strategic Services	Pepco	Potomac Electric Power Company
OST	Office of the Secretary		
OT	Office of Transportation	Perm. Ct. of Arb.	Permanent Court of Arbitration
OTA	Office of Technology Assessment	PES	Post-Enumeration Survey
OTC	Over-the-counter	Pet.	Peters' United States Supreme Court Reports
OTS	Office of Thrift Supervisors		
OUI	Operating under the influence	PETA	People for the Ethical Treatment of Animals
OVCI	Offshore Voluntary Compliance Initiative	PGA	Professional Golfers Association
OWBPA	Older Workers Benefit Protection Act	PGM	Program
		PHA	Public Housing Agency
OWRT	Office of Water Research and Technology	Phila. Ct. of Oyer and Terminer	Philadelphia Court of Oyer and Terminer
P.	Pacific Reporter	PhRMA	Pharmaceutical Research and Manufacturers of America
P. 2d	Pacific Reporter, Second Series		
		PHS	Public Health Service
PAC	Political action committee	PIC	Private Industry Council
Pa. Oyer and Terminer	Pennsylvania Oyer and Terminer Reports	PICJ	Permanent International Court of Justice
PATCO	Professional Air Traffic Controllers Organization	Pick.	Pickering's Massachusetts Reports

PIK	Payment in Kind	Rec. des Decs.	G. Gidel, ed., *Recueil des*
PINS	Persons in need of	des Trib.	*décisions des tribunaux ar-*
	supervision	Arb. Mixtes	*bitraux mixtes, institués par*
PIRG	Public Interest Research		*les traités de paix* (1922–30)
	Group	Redmond	Vol. 3 of Charles I. Bevans,
P.L.	Public Laws		*Treaties and Other Interna-*
PLAN	Pro-Life Action Network		*tional Agreements of the*
PLC	Plaintiffs' Legal Committee		*United States of America,*
PLE	Product liability expenses		*1776–1949* (compiled by
PLI	Practicing Law Institute		C. F. Redmond) (1969)
PLL	Product liability loss	RESPA	Real Estate Settlement
PLLP	Professional Limited Liability		Procedure Act of 1974
	Partnership	RFC	Reconstruction Finance
PLO	Palestine Liberation		Corporation
	Organization	RFRA	Religious Freedom
PLRA	Prison Litigation Reform Act		Restoration Act of 1993
	of 1995	RIAA	Recording Industry
PNET	Peaceful Nuclear Explosions		Association of America
	Treaty	RICO	Racketeer Influenced and
PONY	Prostitutes of New York		Corrupt Organizations
POW-MIA	Prisoner of war-missing in	RLUIPA	Religious Land Use and
	action		Institutionalized Persons
Pratt	Frederic Thomas Pratt, *Law of*		Act
	Contraband of War, with a	RNC	Republican National
	Selection of Cases from		Committee
	Papers of the Right Hon-	Roscoe	Edward Stanley Roscoe, ed.,
	ourable Sir George Lee		*Reports of Prize Cases*
	(1856)		*Determined in the High*
PRIDE	Prostitution to Independence,		*Court Admiralty before the*
	Dignity, and Equality		*Lords Commissioners of*
Proc.	Proceedings		*Appeals in Prize Causes and*
PRP	Potentially responsible party		*before the judicial Commit-*
PSRO	Professional Standards		*tee of the Privy Council from*
	Review Organization		*1745 to 1859* (1905)
PTO	Patents and Trademark	ROTC	Reserve Officers' Training
	Office		Corps
PURPA	Public Utilities Regulatory	RPP	Representative Payee Program
	Policies Act	R.S.	Revised Statutes
PUSH	People United to Serve	RTC	Resolution Trust Corp.
	Humanity	RUDs	Reservations, understandings,
PUSH-Excel	PUSH for Excellence		and declarations
PWA	Public Works	Ryan White	Ryan White Comprehensive
	Administration	CARE Act	AIDS Research Emergency
PWSA	Ports and Waterways Safety		Act of 1990
	Act of 1972	SAC	Strategic Air Command
Q.B.	Queen's Bench (England)	SACB	Subversive Activities Control
QTIP	Qualified Terminable Interest		Board
	Property	SADD	Students against Drunk
Ralston's Rept.	Jackson Harvey Ralston, ed.,		Driving
	Venezuelan Arbitrations of	SAF	Student Activities Fund
	1903 (1904)	SAIF	Savings Association Insurance
RC	Regional Commissioner		Fund
RCRA	Resource Conservation and	SALT	Strategic Arms Limitation
	Recovery Act		Talks
RCWP	Rural Clean Water Program	SALT I	Strategic Arms Limitation
RDA	Rural Development		Talks of 1969–72
	Administration	SAMHSA	Substance Abuse and Mental
REA	Rural Electrification		Health Services
	Administration		Administration

Sandf.	Sandford's New York Superior Court Reports	SNCC	Student Nonviolent Coordinating Committee
S and L	Savings and loan	So.	Southern Reporter
SARA	Superfund Amendment and Reauthorization Act	So. 2d	Southern Reporter, Second Series
SAT	Scholastic Aptitude Test	SPA	Software Publisher's
Sawy.	Sawyer's United States Circuit Court Reports		Association
		Spec. Sess.	Special Session
SBA	Small Business Administration	SPLC	Southern Poverty Law Center
SBI	Small Business Institute	SRA	Sentencing Reform Act of
SCCC	South Central Correctional Center		1984
		SS	Schutzstaffel (German,
SCLC	Southern Christian Leadership Conference		"Protection Echelon")
		SSA	Social Security
Scott's Repts.	James Brown Scott, ed., The Hague Court Reports, 2 vols. (1916–32)		Administration
		SSI	Supplemental Security Income
SCS	Soil Conservation Service; Social Conservative Service	START I	Strategic Arms Reduction Treaty of 1991
		START II	Strategic Arms Reduction Treaty of 1993
SCSEP	Senior Community Service Employment Program	Stat.	United States Statutes at Large
S.Ct.	Supreme Court Reporter	STS	Space Transportation Systems
S.D. Cal.	Southern District, California	St. Tr.	State Trials, English
S.D. Fla.	Southern District, Florida	STURAA	Surface Transportation and
S.D. Ga.	Southern District, Georgia		Uniform Relocation
SDI	Strategic Defense Initiative		Assistance Act of 1987
S.D. Me.	Southern District, Maine	Sup. Ct. of	Supreme Court of Justice,
S.D.N.Y.	Southern District, New York	Justice, Mexico	Mexico
SDS	Students for a Democratic Society	Supp.	Supplement
		S.W.	South Western Reporter
S.E.	South Eastern Reporter	S.W. 2d	South Western Reporter,
S.E. 2d	South Eastern Reporter, Second Series		Second Series
		SWAPO	South-West Africa People's
SEA	Science and Education Administration		Organization
		SWAT	Special Weapons
SEATO	Southeast Asia Treaty Organization		and Tactics
		SWP	Socialist Workers Party
SEC	Securities and Exchange Commission	TDP	Trade and Development Program
Sec.	Section	Tex. Sup.	Texas Supreme Court
SEEK	Search for Elevation, Education and Knowledge		Reports
		THAAD	Theater High-Altitude Area Defense System
SEOO	State Economic Opportunity Office	THC	Tetrahydrocannabinol
SEP	Simplified employee pension plan	TI	Tobacco Institute
		TIA	Trust Indenture Act
Ser.	Series		of 1939
Sess.	Session	TIAS	Treaties and Other
SGLI	Servicemen's Group Life Insurance		International Acts Series (United States)
SIP	State implementation plan	TNT	Trinitrotoluene
SLA	Symbionese Liberation Army	TOP	Targeted Outreach
SLAPPs	Strategic Lawsuits Against Public Participation		Program
		TPUS	Transportation and Public Utilities Service
SLBM	Submarine-launched ballistic missile	TQM	Total Quality Management

Tripartite Claims Comm., Decs. and Ops.	Tripartite Claims Commission (United States, Austria, and Hungary), Decisions and Opinions	UNICEF	United Nations Children's Fund (formerly United Nations International Children's Emergency Fund)
TRI-TAC	Joint Tactical Communications	UNIDO	United Nations Industrial and Development Organization
TRO	Temporary restraining order		
TS	Treaty Series, United States	Unif. L. Ann.	Uniform Laws Annotated
TSCA	Toxic Substance Control Act	UN Repts. Intl. Arb. Awards	United Nations Reports of International Arbitral Awards
TSDs	Transporters, storers, and disposers		
TSU	Texas Southern University	UNTS	United Nations Treaty Series
TTBT	Threshold Test Ban Treaty	UPI	United Press International
TV	Television	URESA	Uniform Reciprocal Enforcement of Support Act
TVA	Tennessee Valley Authority		
TWA	Trans World Airlines		
UAW	United Auto Workers; United Automobile, Aerospace, and Agricultural Implements Workers of America	U.S.	United States Reports
		U.S.A.	United States of America
		USAF	United States Air Force
		USA PATRIOT Act	Uniting and Strengthening America by Providing Appropriate Tools Required to Intercept and Obstruct Terrorism Act
U.C.C.	Uniform Commercial Code; Universal Copyright Convention		
U.C.C.C.	Uniform Consumer Credit Code	USF	U.S. Forestry Service
		U.S. App. D.C.	United States Court of Appeals for the District of Columbia
UCCJA	Uniform Child Custody Jurisdiction Act		
UCMJ	Uniform Code of Military Justice	U.S.C.	United States Code; University of Southern California
UCPP	Urban Crime Prevention Program		
		U.S.C.A.	United States Code Annotated
UCS	United Counseling Service		
UDC	United Daughters of the Confederacy	U.S.C.C.A.N.	United States Code Congressional and Administrative News
UFW	United Farm Workers		
UHF	Ultrahigh frequency	USCMA	United States Court of Military Appeals
UIFSA	Uniform Interstate Family Support Act		
		USDA	U.S. Department of Agriculture
UIS	Unemployment Insurance Service	USES	United States Employment Service
UMDA	Uniform Marriage and Divorce Act		
		USFA	United States Fire Administration
UMTA	Urban Mass Transportation Administration		
		USGA	United States Golf Association
U.N.	United Nations		
UNCITRAL	United Nations Commission on International Trade Law	USICA	International Communication Agency, United States
UNCTAD	United Nations Conference on Trade and Development	USMS	U.S. Marshals Service
		USOC	U.S. Olympic Committee
UN Doc.	United Nations Documents	USSC	U.S. Sentencing Commission
UNDP	United Nations Development Program	USSG	United States Sentencing Guidelines
UNEF	United Nations Emergency Force	U.S.S.R.	Union of Soviet Socialist Republics
UNESCO	United Nations Educational, Scientific, and Cultural Organization	UST	United States Treaties
		USTS	United States Travel Service
		v.	*Versus*

VA	Veterans Administration	WFSE	Washington Federation of State Employees
VAR	Veterans Affairs and Rehabilitation Commission	Wheat.	Wheaton's United States Supreme Court Reports
VAWA	Violence against Women Act	Wheel. Cr. Cases	Wheeler's New York Criminal Cases
VFW	Veterans of Foreign Wars		
VGLI	Veterans Group Life Insurance	WHISPER	Women Hurt in Systems of Prostitution Engaged in Revolt
Vict.	Queen Victoria (Great Britain)		
VIN	Vehicle identification number	Whiteman	Marjorie Millace Whiteman, *Digest of International Law,* 15 vols. (1963–73)
VISTA	Volunteers in Service to America		
VJRA	Veterans Judicial Review Act of 1988	WHO	World Health Organization
		WIC	Women, Infants, and Children program
V.L.A.	Volunteer Lawyers for the Arts	Will. and Mar.	King William and Queen Mary (Great Britain)
VMI	Virginia Military Institute		
VMLI	Veterans Mortgage Life Insurance	WIN	WESTLAW Is Natural; Whip Inflation Now; Work Incentive Program
VOCAL	Victims of Child Abuse Laws		
VRA	Voting Rights Act	WIPO	World Intellectual Property Organization
WAC	Women's Army Corps		
Wall.	Wallace's United States Supreme Court Reports	WIU	Workers' Industrial Union
		W.L.R.	Weekly Law Reports, England
Wash. 2d	Washington Reports, Second Series	WPA	Works Progress Administration
WAVES	Women Accepted for Volunteer Service	WPPDA	Welfare and Pension Plans Disclosure Act
WCTU	Women's Christian Temperance Union	WTO	World Trade Organization
		WWI	World War I
W.D. Wash.	Western District, Washington	WWII	World War II
W.D. Wis.	Western District, Wisconsin	Yates Sel. Cas.	Yates's New York Select Cases
WEAL	*West's Encyclopedia of American Law;* Women's Equity Action League	YMCA	Young Men's Christian Association
Wend.	Wendell's New York Reports	YWCA	Young Women's Christian Association

A

14 Penn Plaza LLC v. Pyett, 14–15
ACLU v. Ashcroft, 102
ACLU v. Gonzales, 102
ACLU v. Mukasey, 103
ACLU v. Reno, 102
AT & T Corporation v. Hulteen, 202–203
Abuelhawa v. United States, 73–74
Altria Group, Inc. v. Good, 222–223
Amnesty International v. McConnell, 110
Apprendi v. New Jersey, 207
Arizona v. Gant, 110–111
Arizona v. Johnson, 196–197
Arthur Andersen LLP v. Carlisle, 12–13
Ashcroft v. Iqbal, 65–66
Ashe v. Swenson, 73
Atlantic Sounding Co. v. Townsend, 4–5

B

Bailey v. United States, 201
Ballard v. Tyco International, Ltd, 198
Barker v. Wingo, 210
Bartlett v. Strickland, 234–236
Baxter v. State of Montana, 216
Baze v. Rees, 33, 34
Bell Atlantic Corp. v. Twombly, 66
Bell v. Kelly, 11–12
Beneficial Nat'l Bank v. Anderson, 14
Bivens v. Six Unknown Federal Narcotics Agents, 65
Blakely v. Washington, 207
Booth v. Maryland, 36
Boyle v. United States, 190–192
Brady v. Maryland, 57, 71
Brooke Group Ltd. v. Brown and Williamson Tobacco Corp., 10
Burlington Northern & Santa Fe Railway Co. v. United States, 225–226
Bush v. Gore, 85

C

Caperton v. A.T. Massey Coal Co., Inc., 145–146
Capitol Records Inc. v. Thomas, 47–48

Carcieri v. Salazar, 171–172
Carlsbad Technology, Inc. v. HIF Bio, Inc., 148–149
Caterpillar Inc. v. Williams, 14
Chambers v. United States, 199–200
Chapman v. Commonwealth, 34
Cherry Hill Vineyards, L.L.C. v. Hudgins, 41
Cherry Hill Vineyards, L.L.C. v. Lilly, 42
Chevron U.S.A., Inc. v. Natural Res. Def. Council, 28
Chimel v. California, 111
City of Seattle v. Professional Basketball Club, LLC, 214–215
City of Valdez v. Polar Tankers, Inc., 77
Clearing House Ass'n v. Cuomo, 28
Clemens v. McNamee, 157–158
Clyde Mallory Lines v. Alabama ex rel. State Docks Commission, 76
Cobell v. Babbitt, 172
Cobell v. Kempthorne, 172
Cobell v. Salazar, 172
Coeur Alaska, Inc. v. Southeast Alaska Conservation Council, 89–91
Common Cause/Georgia v. Billups, 236–238
Common Law Settlement Counsel v. Bailey, 25–26
Complete Auto Transit, Inc. v. Brady, 76
Cone v. Bell, 57–58
Contest of General Election Held on November 4, 2008, for the Purpose of Electing a United States Senator from the State of Minnesota, 84–86
Corley v. United States, 94–96
Craig v. State, 56–57
Crawford v. Marion County Election Board, 238
Crawford v. Metropolitan Government of Nashville and Davidson County, Tennessee, 88–89
Crawford v. Washington, 43
Cunningham v. California, 207

D

DeJohn v. Temple University, 117–118
Dean v. United States, 200–201
Demjanjuk v. Mukasey, 242
Denedo v. United States, 161–162
Discover Bank v. Vaden, 14

District Attorney's Office for the Third Judicial
    District v. Osborne, 71
Dolan v. Postal Service, 74

E

Edwards v. Arizona, 206
Engle v. Reynolds, 224
Entergy Corporation v. Riverkeeper, Inc., 37–38

F

Federal Communications Commission v.
    Fox Television Station, 97–98
Fedorenko v. United States, 138
Findlay v. State, 150
Fitzgerald v. Barnstable School Committee, 203–204
Flores-Figueroa v. United States, 135–136
Frazier ex rel. Frazier v. Winn, 100–101

G

G.H. v. Township of Galloway, 204–205
General Elec. Co. v. Gilbert, 202
Goetz v. Ansell, 100
Gonzaga University v. Doe, 84
Gonzales v. Carhart, 2
Granholm v. Heald, 41
Gross v. FBL Financial Services, Inc. 5–6
Guthrie v. Harkness, 27

H

HIF Bio, Inc. v. Yung Shin Pharmaceuticals
    Industrial Co., 149
Hall v. Kozlowski, et al., 198
Hamdan v. Rumsfeld, 163, 219, 230
Harbison v. Bell, 129–130
Hatfill v. The New York Times, 155–157
Hawaii v. Office of Hawaiian Affairs, 213–214
Hedgpeth v. Pulido, 58–60
Herring v. United States, 111–112
Hines v. J.A. LaPorte, Inc., 4
Holloman ex rel. Holloman v. Harland, 101

I

In re Directives Pursuant to Section 105B of the Foreign
    Intelligence Surveillance Act, 244–245
In re L.M., 150
In re Marriage Cases, 120–121
In re Steed, 190
In re Texas Dep't of Family Protective Servs., 190
In re Tyco International Ltd. Securities Litigation, 197–198
Iqbal v. Hasty, 66

J

Jasin v. Tyco International Ltd, et al., 198
Jiminez v. Quarterman, 130–131

K

Kansas v. Colorado, 192–193
Kansas v. Ventris, 208–209
Kelly v. California, 36–37

Kennedy v. Plan Administrator for DuPont Savings
    and Investment Plan, 180–181
Kerrigan v. Commissioner of Public Health, 121
Knowles v. Mirzayance, 131–132
Kuhlman v. Wilson, 208

L

Ledbetter v. Goodyear Tire & Rubber
    Company, Inc., 68–70
Locke v. Karass, 153–154
Lockyer v. City and County of San Francisco, 120
Los Angeles County v. Davis, 118
Lozano v. City of Hazelton, Pennsylvania, 136–137

M

Mallory v. United States, 95
Massiah v. United States, 208
McDarby v. Merck & Co., Inc., 186–187
McKeiver v. Pennsylvania, 149
McNabb v. United States, 95
Melendez-Diaz v. Massachusetts, 43–44
Merck & Co., Inc. v. Ernst, 187
Michigan v. Jackson, 205–206
Miles v. Apex Marine Corp., 4
Miller v. California, 102
Ministry of Defense and Support for the Armed Forces
    of the Islamic Republic of Iran v. Elahi, 211–212
Miranda v. Arizona, 95, 206
Montejo v. Louisiana, 205–206
Morr-Fitz, Inc. v. Blagojevich, 31

N

National Pride at Work v. Granholm, 123
Navajo Nation v. United States, 174
Negusie v. Holder, 137–138
New Jersey v. Tyco International Ltd, 198
New York Times Co. v. Sullivan, 155
New York v. Belton, 110
Newark Parents Association v. Newark Public
    Schools, 83–84
Nken v. Holder, 138–139
North Carolina Department of Corrections v.
    North Carolina Medical Board, 35
North Coast Women's Care Medical Group, Inc. v.
    San Diego County Superior Court, 125–126

O

Office of Hawaiian Affairs v. Housing & Community
    Development Corp. of Hawaii, 214
Office of the Comptroller of the Currency v. Spitzer, 28
Ohio v. Ruben Rivera, 35
Oregon v. Ice, 207–208
Osborne v. District Attorney's Office for the Third
    Judicial District, 71
Ott v. Miss. Valley Barge Line Co., 76
Overby, et al. v. Tyco International Ltd, 198

P

Pacific Bell Telephone Company, dba AT&T
    California, v. Linkline Communications, Inc., 9–10

Padilla v. Yoo, 228
Patterson v. Illinois, 206
Payne v. Tennessee, 36
Pearson v. Callahan, 140–141
People v. Pulido, 59
Perez v. Sharp, 121
Peterson v. Grisham, 154–155
Philip Morris USA Inc. v. Williams, 187–188
Pleasant Grove City, Utah v. Summum, 103–104
Plyler v. Doe, 137
Polar Tankers, Inc. v. City of Valdez, Alaska, 77
Polk County v. Dodson, 210
Powerex Corp. v. Reliant Energy Services, Inc., 149
Price Waterhouse v. Hopkins, 6
Puckett v. United States, 60–61
Pulido v. Chrones, 60
Pulido v. Lamarque, 59

Q

Quon v. Arch Wireless Operating Co., 113

R

Reno v. ACLU, 101
Richmond Medical Center for Women v. Herring, 2
Richmond Medical Center v. Hicks, 2
Rivera v. Illinois, 181–182
Roe v. Wade, 2

S

Sable Communications of Cal., Inc. v. FCC, 102
Saucier v. Katz, 140
Sciallo v. Tyco International Ltd, et al., 198
Shinseki v. Sanders, 233–234
Southeast Alaska Conservation Council v. United States
    Army Corps of Engineers, 90
State Farm Mutual Automobile Insurance Company v.
    Campbell, 187
Stenson v. Vail, 35
Stormans inc. v. Selecky, 32
Straights and Gays for Equality v. Osseo Area
    Schools-District, 279
Strickland v. Washington, 132
Stumpf v. Tyco International Ltd, 198
Summers v. Earth Island Institute, 92–93
Sutton v. United Airlines, 8

T

Terry v. Ohio, 196
The Osceola, 5
Thermtron Products, Inc. v. Hermansdorfer, 149
Thornburg v. Gingles, 235
Toyota Motor Manufacturing, Kentucky, Inc. v.
    Williams, 8
Travelers Indemnity v. Bailey, 25–26
Twentieth Century Fox Film Corp. v. Warner Brothers
    Entertainment Corp., 48–49

U

United States v. Booker, 207
United States v. Burlington Northern & Santa Fe
    Railway Co., 226
United States v. Demjanjuk, 242
United States v. Denedo, 161–162
United States v. Eurodif S.A, 231–233
United States v. Hayes, 201–202
United States v. Morgan, 161
United States v. Navajo Nation, 173–174
United States v. Oakland Cannibis Buyers' Co-op., 74
United States v. Ramos, 40

V

Vaden v. Discover Bank, 13–14
Van de Kamp v. Goldstein, 141–142
Varnum v. Brien, 123
Vermont v. Brillon, 209–210
Voinovich v. Quilter, 235

W

Wachovia Bank, N.A. v. Burke, 27
Waddington v. Sarausad, 150–152
West Virginia State Board of Education v.
    Barnette, 100
Winter v. National Resources Defense
    Council, Inc., 170–171
Wyeth v. Levine, 184–185

Y

Yeager v. United States, 72–73
Ysursa v. Pocatello Education Association, 104–105

Z

Zamudio v. California, 36–37

NOTE: *Page numbers appearing in bold face indicate major treatment of entries. Italicized page numbers refer to photos.*

A

Abortion, **1–3**
Abuelhawa, Salman Khade, 73–74
ADA *See* Americans With Disabilities Act (ADA)
ACLU *See* American Civil Liberties Union (ACLU)
ADEA *See* Age Discrimination in Employment Act (ADEA)
AEDPA *See* Antiterrorism and Effective Death Penalty Act of 1996 (AEDPA)
Age Discrimination in Employment Act (ADEA), 5, 15
   anti-choice measures, 2–3
   partial birth abortion bans, 1–2
Administrative Maximum Special Housing Unit, 65–66
Admiralty and Maritime Law, **3–5**
Age Discrimination, **5–6**
al-Qaeda, 162–163, 221, 227, 243
Alabama
   exclusionary rule and evidence, 111–112
Alaska
   Kensington Gold Mine, 89–91
   Ted Stevens, 51–52
   City of Valdez, 76–77
Aldrete-Davila, Osvaldo, 38–39
Alexandre, Cynthia, 100–101
Alien, **6–8**
Alito, Samuel
   discrimination, 66
   duty of tonnage, 77
   First Amendment, 104
   immunity, 140
   labor law, 154

maritime law, 5
riparian rights, 193
sentencing, 200
sex discrimination, 204
sovereignty, 214
Supremacy Clause, 218
voting discrimination, 235
Altria Group, 222–223
American Civil Liberties Union (ACLU), 57, 110, 136, 205, 227
American Indian Trust Fund Management Reform Act, 173
American Library Association, 45
American Telephone and Telegraph (AT&T), 9–10
Americans With Disabilities Act (ADA), **8–9**, 217
Anthony, Casey, 165–167
Anthony, Caylee, 165–167, *166*
Antiterrorism and Effective Death Penalty Act of 1996 (AEDPA), 11, 151–152, 221
Antitrust Law, **9–11**
Appeals Reform Act, 92
Appellate Advocacy, **11–12**
Arbitration, **12–16**
Arizona
   search and seizure, 110–111
Arkansas
   execution protocols, 35
Armed Robbery, **16–17**
Arthur Andersen LLP, 12–13
Asbestos, 25
Ashcroft, John, 63, 65–66
AT&T *See* American Telephone and Telegraph (AT&T)
A.T. Massey Coal Co., 145–146
Attorney, **17–20**
Attorney General, **20–21**
   politically motivated staff hirings in office of, 63–64
Automobiles, **21–23**

B

Baby Bells, 10
Bair, Sheila, 99
Baker, Shukri Abu, *222*
Bamberger, Joseph, 18–19
Bañales, J. Manuel, 20
Bank of America, 99
Bankruptcy, **25–26**
Banks and Banking, **26–29**
   nationalization of banks, 28–29
Barofsky, Neil, 29
Beardsley, Alfred, 17
Beatty, Christine, 175
Bell, Edward, 10–11
Benitez, Guadalupe, 125–126
Benjamin, Brent, 145
Bennett, Clay, 214–215
Bergersen, Gregg W., 93–94
Bernanke, Ben, 29, 99
BIA *See* Bureau of Indian Affairs
Biden, Joseph, *29*, **29–30**
"Big Three" automakers, 21–22
bin Laden, Osama, 162
Birth Control, **30–32**
BizBioTech, 148
Blackwater Worldwide, 159–160
Blagojevich, Rod, 31, *50*
   impeachment, 49–50
Blankenship, Don, 145
Board of Immigrant Appeals (BIA), 137–138
Boggs, J. Caleb, 30
Boyle, Edmund, 191–192
Boynton Beach Community High School, 100
Breyer, Stephen
   discrimination, 66
   duty of tonnage, 77
   environmental law, 93
   Federal Communications Commission, 98

Breyer, Stephen (*continued*)
  identity theft, 136
  immunity, 141
  jurisdiction, 149
  labor law, unions, 154
  sex discrimination, Title VII, 203
  veterans' rights, 234
Bricolage Capital, LLC, 12
Brillon, Nathan, 209–210
Brody, Dr. Christine, 125–126
Buffalo Bills, 16
Bureau of Customs and Border
  Protection, 7
Bureau of Immigration and
  Customs Enforcement (ICE), 7
Bureau of Indian Affairs, 173
Burlington Northern & Santa Fe
  Railway Co., 225–226
Bush administration
  credit monitoring for veterans,
    military personnel, 42
  torture under, 228
  wiretapping under, 243
Bush, George W.
  and "car czar,", 22
  clemency grants, 38–39
  copyright law, 45
  economic crisis, 79, 165
  Food and Drug Administration,
    108
  military tribunals under, 163
  and Gonzales, Alberto, 20
  No Child Left Behind Act, 83
  and Presidential Records Act, 116
Bybee, Jay, 227

C

CAAF *See* United States Court of
  Appeals for the Armed Forces
  (CAAF)
California
  anti-choice abortion measures, 2
  medical marijuana, 74
  same-sex fertility services, denial
    of, 125–126
Callahan, Afton, 140–141
CAN-SPAM Act, 142–143
Caperton, Hugh, 145–146
Capital Punishment, **33–37**
  and execution protocols, 34–36
Carter, Debra Sue, 154–155
  Chapman execution, 33–34
  and victim impact evidence,
    36–37
Carlisle, Wayne, 12–13
CDC *See* Centers for the Disease
  Control and Prevention (CDC)
Celis, Mauricio, 19–20
Centers for the Disease Control
  and Prevention (CDC), 107
Center for Public Policy Priorities
  (CPPP), 6–7

Center for Reproductive Rights, 2
CGT Law Group, 19
Chambers, Deondery, 199
Chapman, Marco Allen, 33–34, *34*
Chesley, Stanley, 19
*Child Alone and Without
  Papers, A*, 6–7
Child Online Protection Act,
  101–102
Chun, Yang-Sook, 148
Ciavarella, Mark, 147–148
CIS *See* U.S. Citizenship and
  Immigration Services (CIS)
Citizens Protecting Michigan's
  Kids, 75
Civil Rights Act
  Title VII, 5–6, 67, 68, 88, 202
Clark, Joanne, 125–126
Clean Water Act, **37–38**, 90
Clemency, **38–40**
Clemens, Roger, 157–158
Clinton, Bill, 2
  clemency grants, 40, 116
  and Craig, Gregory, 54–55
  and Holder, Eric, 133
  and Sotomayor, Sonia, 211
Coastal Zone Management Act, 170
Cobell, Elouise, 173
Colorado
  Arkansas River dispute, 192–193
  Measure 48 anti-abortion
    measure, 2
Commerce Clause, **40–42**, 76–77
  wine sales, 40–42
Communications Decency Act, 101
Compean, Jose Alonso, 38–39
Comprehensive Drug Abuse Pre-
  vention and Control Act of
  1970, 73
Comprehensive Environmental
  Response, Compensation, and
  Liability Act (CERCLA), 225
Computer Crime, **42–43**
Conahan, Michael, 147
Cone, Gary, 57–58
Congress
  Americans with Disabilities Act,
    overturning rulings, 8
  automakers loan, 22
Confrontation Clause, **43–44**
Conte, Victor, 183
Controlled Substances Act
  (CSA), 73
Copyright, **44–49**
  copyright czar, 44–45
  Orphan Works Act of 2008,
    46–47
  RIAA lawsuits, 47–48
  Watchmen case, 48–49
Copyright Office, 46
Corruption, **49–53**
  Blagojevich impeachment, 49–51
  Stevens conviction, 51–52

Coeur Alaska, Inc., 89–90
Court of Federal Claims, 174
Covenant, **53–54**
CPPP *See* Center for Public Policy
  Priorities (CPPP)
Craig, Gregory, **54–55**, *54*
Craig, Larry, 56–57
Crawford, Susan J., 229–230
Creationism, 81–83
Crime, **55–56**
Criminal Law, **56–57**
Criminal Procedure, **57–61**
  due process, 57–58
  jury instructions, 58–60
  plea arrangement, 60–61
CSA *See* Controlled Substances
  Act (CSA)
Cubic Defense Systems, 212–212
Cunningham, Shirley, Jr., 17–19
Cuomo, Andrew, 48

D

Dawes Act, 172
Dean, Christopher, 200
DeJohn, Christian, 117–118
Delaware
  stay on executions, 35
Demjanjuk, John, 241–242, *242*
Denedo, Jacob, 161–162
Department of Justice, U.S., **63–64**
Department of Veterans Affairs
  (VA), 42
Detroit, Michigan, 175–177
DFS *See* Discover Financial
  Services (DFS)
Dictionary Act, 201
Discover Financial Services, Inc.
  (DFS), 13
Discrimination, **64–70**
  fair pay, 68–70
  genetic discrimination, 66–68
  prisoner treatment, 65–66
DNA, **70–72**
Dodd, Christopher, 22
Double Jeopardy, **72–73**
Drugs and Narcotics, **73–75**
Duke, Stephen, 112–113
Duty of Tonnage, **76–77**

E

E-Verify, 87
Earth Island Institute, 92–93
Economy, **79–80**
  stimulus package, 79–80
Economic Stimulus Act, 165
Education Law, **80–84**
creationism, 81–83
  Equal Access Act violations,
    80–81
  No Child Left Behind Act,
    83–84
Ehrlich, Charles, 17

Eighth Amendment, 35
E.I. DuPont de Nemours &
    Company, 180–181
Elahi, Dariush, 211–212
Elections, **84–86**
    Coleman, Norm, 84–86,
    Franken, Al, 84–86
Electronic Frontiers Foundation, 45
Emergency Economic
    Stabilization Act of 2008, 79
Employee Retirement Income
    Security Act (ERISA), 180–181
Employment Law, **86–89**
    tightening job market, 86–87
Endangered Species Act, 170
Energy Independence and
    Security Act of 2007, 91
Enron Corporation, 72
Environmental Protection Agency
    (EPA), 37–38, 89–90, 91–92
Environmental Law, **89–93**
Enzi, Michael, 22
EPA *See* Environmental
    Protection Agency (EPA)
Equal Access Act (EAA), 80–81
Equal Employment Opportunity
    Commission, 69–70, 88
Equal Pay Act, 69
ERISA *See* Employee Retirement
    Income Security Act (ERISA)
Ernst, Bob, 186–187
Espionage, **93–94**
    and China, 93–94
Establishment Clause, 103–104
Eurodif, 231
Evidence, **94–96**
    confessions, 95–96

F

FAA *See* Federal Arbitration Act
    (CDC)
Family Educational Rights and
    Privacy Act (FERPA), 84
Family Foundation of Virginia, 2
FBI *See* Federal Bureau of
    Investigation (FBI)
FBL Financial Services, 5–6
FCC *See* Federal Communications
    Commission (FCC)
FDCA *See* Federal Food, Drug,
    and Cosmetic Act (FDCA)
FDIA *See* Federal Deposit
    Insurance Act (FDIA)
FDIC *See* Federal Deposit
    Insurance Corporation (FDIC)
Federal Arbitration Act (FAA),
    12–13
Federal Bureau of Investigation
    (FBI)
    anthrax attacks, 156
    Blackwater killings, 159
    copyright, 46
    and Corley, Johnny, 95

drug trafficking, 74
Foreign Intelligence Surveillance
    Court, 109
and Qahtani, Mohammed al, 229
report on crime, 55–56
salmonella scare, 108–109
September 11th attacks, 65
spam investigation, 143
stolen documents, 94
and Tamm, Thomas, 244
and Ted Stevens, 52
Federal Cigarette Labeling and
    Advertising Act (Labeling Act),
    223
Federal Communications
    Commission (FCC), 10, **97–98**
    indecent language, 97–98
Federal Deposit Insurance Act
    (FDIA), 14
Federal Deposit Insurance Cor-
    poration (FDIC), 29, **98–100**
    foreclosure crisis, 98–100
Federal Food, Drug, and
    Cosmetic Act (FDCA), 184
Fen-Phen
    mishandling of settlement
    money, 17–19
Federal Rules of Criminal
    Procedure, 95
Federal Trade Commission
    (FTC), 223
FERPA *See* Family Educational
    Rights and Privacy Act
    (FERPA)
First Amendment, **100–106**
    Child Online Protection Act,
    101–103
    payroll deductions for political
    activities, 104–106
    Pledge of Allegiance laws,
    100–101
    religious monuments, 103–104
FISA *See* Foreign Intelligence
    Surveillance Act (FISA)
FISC *See* Foreign Intelligence
    Surveillance Court (FISC)
Fitzgerald, Lisa, 203
Fitzgerald, Robert, 203
Fitzhugh, William G., 1
FLDS *See* Fundamental Church of
    Latter-Day Saints (FLDS)
Flores-Figueroa, Ignacio,
    135–136
Florida
    Anthony, Caylee, murder case,
    165–167
    tobacco lawsuits, 224–225
Food and Drug Administration
    (FDA), **106–109**
    birth control pills, 31
    Vioxx, 186
Foreclosure, 98–100

Foreign Intelligence Surveillance
    Act (FISA), 109, 244
Foreign Intelligence Surveillance
    Court (FISC), **109–110**,
    244–245
Foreign Sovereign Immunities
    Act, 212
14 Penn Plaza LLC, 15
Fourteenth Amendment
    Due Process Clause, 57, 76–77
Fourth Amendment, **110–114**
    automobile searches, 110–111
    exclusionary rule and evidence,
    111–112
    text messages, 112–113
Fox Television Network, 97–98
Franken, Al, 84–86, *85*
Frazier, Cameron, 100–101
Fraud, **114–116**
    Madoff, Bernard, 114–115
Freedom of Information, **116–117**
    Presidential Records Act,
    116–117
Freedom of Speech, **117–118**
    Temple University harassment
    policy, 117–118
Fritz, Dennis, 154–155
Fromong, Bruce, 17
FTC *See* Federal Trade Commis-
    sion (FTC)
Fundamentalist Church of Jesus
    Christ of the Latter Day Saints
    (FLDS) sect, 189–190, *190*

G

Gallion, William, 17–19
Gant, Rodney, 110–111
Gay and Lesbian Rights, **119–126**
    Arkansas adoption ban, 119–120
    fertility procedures, denial of,
    125–126
    same-sex marriage, California,
    120–121
    same-sex marriage, Connecticut,
    121–122
    same-sex marriage, constitu-
    tional amendments, 124–125
    same-sex marriage, Iowa,
    121–122
    same-sex partner benefits,
    Michigan, 123–124
Geithner, Timothy, **126–127**
    automakers crisis, 23
Genetic Information Nondiscrim-
    ination Act of 2008 (GINA),
    66–67
Gilbert, Mike, 16
    How I Helped O.J. Get Away
    With Murder: The Shocking
    Inside Story of Violence,
    Loyalty, Regret and
    Remorse, 17

Ginsburg, Ruth Bader
  arbitration, 14
  bankruptcy, 26
  Clean Water Act, 38
  criminal procedure, 60
  discrimination, 66, 69
  double jeopardy, 73
  environmental law, Clean Air
    Act, 91
  Fourth Amendment, 112
  habeas corpus, 130, 132
  peremptory challenge, 182
  RICO, 192
  search and seizure, 197
  sentencing, 200, 201
  sex discrimination, 203
  Sixth Amendment, 207,
    209, 210
  sovereign immunity, 212
  tort law, 226
  veterans' rights, 233
Glass, Jackie, 17
Goldman, Fred, 16
Goldman, Ron, 16
Goldstein, Thomas, 141–142
Gonzales, Alberto, 63
  document mishandling, 20–21
  hiring practices in office of
    attorney general, 63–64
Good, Stephanie, 222–223
Goodling, Monica, 63–64
Goodyear Tire and Rubber,
    68–70
Gordon, Lawrence, 48–49
Gribbon-Motz, Diane, 2
Grisham, John, 154–155
Gross, Jack, 5–6
Guantanamo Bay prison camp,
    219–221, *220*, 228
Gun Control Act, 201–202

H

Habeas Corpus, **129–132**
  clemency, death row inmates,
    129–130
  ineffective counsel, 131–132
  procedural rules, 130–131
Hamas, 222
Hamdan, Salid Ahmed, 162–163
Harbison, Edward, 129–130
Hatch, Orrin, 46
Hatfill, Stephen J., 155–156
Hawaii
  Apology Resolution, 213
  public land sale, 213–214
Hayes, Dean, 201–202
Haywood, Keith, 218
Heisman Trophy, 16
Help America Vote Act, 238
Henry, Thomas J., 19–20
Herring, Bernie, 111–112

Hess, Elaine, 224
Hett, Melvin, 155
HFDC *See* Housing and Finance
    Development Corporation
    (HFDC)
Hicks, Ernest, 208
HIF Bio, Inc., 148
Hill, Anita, 169
HMDA *See* Home Mortgage Dis-
    closure Act (HFDC)
Holder, Eric, **132–133**
Holy Land Foundation, 221–222,
    221
Homeland Security Act of 2002, 7
Home Mortgage Disclosure Act
    (HMDA), 27
Housing and Finance Develop-
    ment Corporation (HFDC),
    213–214
*How I Helped O.J. Get Away With
    Murder: The Shocking Inside
    Story of Violence, Loyalty, Regret
    and Remorse, 17*
Hughes, Gene, 88
Hulteen, Noreen, 202–203
Hunter, C.J., 182–183
Hunter, Neilia, 29

I

ICE *See* Bureau of Immigration
    and Customs Enforcement
Ice, Thomas, 207
Idaho
  Right to Work Act, 105
Identity Theft, **135–136**
*If I Did It: Confessions of the
    Killer,* 16–17
IIRIRA *See* Illegal Immigration
    Reform and Immigrant
    Responsibility Act (IIRIRA)
Illegal Immigration Reform and
    Immigrant Responsibility Act
    (IIRIRA), 138–139
Illinois Health Care Right of
    Conscience Act, 32
Illinois Religious Freedom
    Restoration Act, 32
Immigration, **136–140**
  aliens, removal of, 138–139
  city ordinances, 136–137
  refugees, rules allowing, 137–138
Immigration and Nationality Act
    (INA), 137–138
Immigration and Naturalization
    Service (INS), 7
Immigration Reform and Control
    Act (IRCA), 137
Immunity, **140–142**
  criminal prosecutors, 141–142
  right to sue police officers,
    140–141
INA *See* Immigration and
    Nationality Act (INA)

Indian Reorganization Act, 171
The Innocent Man, 154–155
INS *See* Immigration and
    Naturalization Services (INS)
Insanity plea, 131–132
Insider Trading, 72–73
Intellectual Property Enforcement
    Representative (IPEC), 45
Interlocutory appeals, 12–13
Internal Revenue Service (IRS),
    12–13, 143, 221
International Court of
    Arbitration, 211
Internet, **142–143**
  Seattle "spam king," 142–143
IPEC *See* Intellectual Property
    Enforcement Representative
    (IPEC)
Iqbal, Javaid, 65–66
Iran, 211–212
IRCA *See* Immigration Reform
    and Control Act (IRCA)
IRS *See* Internal Revenue Service
    (IRS)

J

Jackson, Dexter, 70–71
Jeffs, Warren, 189–190
Jin, Hanjuan, 94
Jindal, Bobby, 81
Johns-Manville Corporation, 25
Johnson, Lemon, 196–197
Jones Act, 4–5
Jones, Marion, 182–184, *183*
Judges, **145–148**
  kickback scheme of, 146–147
  recusal of, 145–146
Jurisdiction, **148–149**
  authority to remand, 148–149
Jury, **149–152**
  jury instructions, criminal
    trials, 150–151
  juveniles, entitled to jury,
    149–150

K

Kang, Yu Xin, 93–94
Kansas
  Arkansas River dispute,
    192–193
  juvenile offenders, jury trials,
    150
Kansas Juvenile Offenders Code
    (KJOC), 150
Karsnia, David, 56–57
Kashkari, Neel T., 99
Kazaa, 47
Kennedy, Anthony M.
  confrontation clause, 44
  discrimination, 66
  environmental law, Clean Air
    Act, 90

judges, recusal, 146
military tribunals, 162
partial birth abortion, 2
Kennedy, William, 1801–81
Kensington Gold Mine, 89–91, 89
Kentucky
Chapman execution, 33–34
Fen-Phen settlement money, 17–19
wine statute, 40–41
Kentucky Trust for Healthy Living, 18
Kerrigan, Beth, 122
Kilpatrick, Kwame, 175–176, 176
KJCC See Kansas Juvenile Justic Code (KJCC)
KJOC See Kansas Juvenile Offenders Code (KJOC)
Kozlowski, Dennis, 197–198, 197
Kristof, Nicholas, 156–157
Kuo, Tai Shen, 93–94

L

Labor Law, 153–154
union fees, 153–154
Lanier, Mark, 187
Leahy, Patrick, 45, 47
Levine, Diane, 184–185, 185
Ledbetter, Lilly, 68–70, 68
Libel, 154–158
Clemens, Roger, 157–158
Grisham, John, 154–155
New York Times, 156–157
Lilly Ledbetter Fair Pay Act of 2009, 68–70
Linkline Communications, 10
Louisiana
science education, 81–82
Louisiana Science Education Act, 81–82
Lozano, Pedro, 137

M

Madoff, Bernard, 114–115, 114
Madoff, Ruth, 114–115
Maine
union fees, 153–154
Maine Unfair Trade Practices Act (MUTPA)
Maintenance and Cure (maritime law), 4
Manslaughter, 159–160
Blackwater deaths, 159–160
Marijuana
medical usage, 74–75
Massachusetts
confrontation clause, 43–44
medical marijuana, 74–75
McCain, John, 179–180
McCarter, Dorothy, 216–217
McNamee, Brian, 157–158

Megan's Law, 204
Melendez-Diaz, Luis, 43–44
Merck, 186–187
Merkin, J. Ezra, 115
Michael, M. Blane, 2
Michigan
medical marijuana, 43–44
same-sex partner benefits, 123–124
Michigan Coalition for Compassionate Care, 75
Military Law, 160–162
coram nobis writs, 161–162
Military Tribunal, 162–164
Hamdan trial, 162–163
Minnesota
Equal Access Act violations, 80–81
Franken-Coleman election, 84–86
Mirzayance, Alexandre, 131–132
Mock, Judy, 122
Montgomery, Tim, 183
Mormon Church, 189–190
Montejo, Jesse Jay, 206–207
Mortgage, 164–165
sub prime lending meltdown, 164–165
Motor Tug Thomas, 4
Mueller, Robert, 66
Mukasey, Michael, 64
Murder, 165–167
Anthony, Caylee, 165–167
MUTPA See Maine Unfair Trade Practices Act (MUTPA)

N

NAACP See National Association for the Advancement of Colored People (NAACP)
Napolitano, Janet, 169–170
NARA See National Archives and Records Administration (NARA)
Narragansett Indian Tribe, 171–172
National Association for the Advancement of Colored People (NAACP), 237–238
National Bank Act (NBA), 14, 26–27
National Basketball Association (NBA), 214–215
National Football League (NFL), 16
National Records and Archive Administration (NARA), 116
National Security, 170–171
military testing and sea mammals, 170–171
National Security Agency (NSA), 20, 242–243
Native American Rights, 171–174
fiduciary duty, 173–174
Indian Reorganization Act, 171–172

land trust withholdings, 172–173
Navajo-Hopi Rehabilitation Act, 174
Navajo Nation, 173–174
Navy-Marine Corps Court of Criminal Appeals (NMCCA), 161
NBA See National Bank Act or National Basketball Association (NBA)
Nebraska
safe haven law, 195–196
Negusie, Daniel, 137–138
The New York Times, 155–157, 186, 238, 243
Newport International Marketing Corporation (NIM), 142–143
NFL See National Football League (NFL)
Niemeyer, Paul V., 2
NIM See Newport International Marketing Corporation (NIM)
Nken, Jean Marc, 139–140
NMCCA See Navy-Marine Corps Court of Criminal Appeals (NMCCA)
No Child Left Behind Act, 83–84
North Carolina
execution protocols, 35
NSA See National Security Agency (NSA)

O

Obama administration
automobile emissions, 91–92
automobile industry, 22
bank nationalization, 28
Cobell land trust case, 172
Food and Drug Administration, 108
foreclosure crisis, 98–99
and recession, 79–80
and terrorist suspects, 164
"torture memo" release, 226–229
Obama, Barack, 68. See also Obama administration
and Craig, Gregory, 54
and economy, 79–80
foreclosure crisis, 80
and Geithner, Timothy, 126
Guantanamo Bay closure, 219–220
and Holder, Eric, 132–33
Intellectual Property Enforcement Representative, appointment of, 46
Internet campaigning, 237
and Ledbetter, Lilly
and Napolitano, Janet, 169

Obama, Barack (*continued*)
Presidential Records Act,
116–117
and Sotomayor, Sonia, 210
U.S. Senate seat, 50
Obstruction of Justice, **175–177**
Kilpatrick, Kwame, 175–176,
176
OCC *See* Office of Comptroller of
Currency (OCC)
O'Connor, Sandra Day, 6
Office of Hawaiian Affairs (OHA),
214
Office of Historical Trust
Accounting, 173
Office of the Comptroller of
Currency (OCC), 26–27
Office of the Inspector General
(OIG), 20
Office of Refugee Resettlement
(ORR), 7
Ohio
execution protocols, 35
OHA *See* Office of Hawaiian
Affairs (OHA)
OIG *See* Office of the Inspector
General (OIG)
Oklahoma
supersonics basketball move,
215–216
Orphan Works Act of 2008, 46–47
ORR *See* Office of Refugee
Resettlement (ORR)
Osborne, William, 70–72, *70*

P

PAA *See* Protect America Act
(PAA)
Palin, Sarah, **179–180**
Park, Jong-Wan, 148
PDA *See* Pregnancy Discrimina-
tion Act (PDA)
Peabody Coal Company, 173–174
Peanut Corporation of America,
106–107
Pennsylvania
ordinances, immigration,
136–137
Pensions, **180–181**
ERISA standards, 180–181
Peremptory Challenge, **181–182**
and due process, 181–182
Perjury, **182–184**
Jones, Marion, 182–184, *183*
Peterson, William, 155
Phenergan, 184–185
Philip Morris, 187–188, 222–223,
224
Pleasant Grove City, Utah, 103–104
PLRA *See* Prison Litigation
Reform Act of 1995 (PLRA)
Polar Tankers, Inc., 76–77
Ponzi schemes, 114–115

Powell, Robert, 147
Preemption, **184–185**
drug labelling, 184–185
Pregnancy Discrimination Act
(PDA), 202
Preliminary Semiannual Uniform
Crime Report, 55–56
Presidential Records Act of 1978,
116–117
Prince, Erik, 159–160
Prioritizing Resources and
Organization for Intellectual
Property ACT (Pro-IP), 45
Prison Litigation Reform Act of
1995 (PLRA), 218
Product Liability, **185–187**
Vioxx decisions, 185–187
Proposition 8, 121
Protect America Act (PAA),
244–245
Puckett, James, Benjamin, 60–61
Pulido, Michael, 58–60
Punitive Damages, 4, **187–188**
and tobacco industry, 187–188
Pyett, Steven, 15

Q

Qahtani, Mohammed al-, 228–230
Quon, Jeff, 112–113

R

RAB *See* Realty Advisory Board on
Labor Relations (RAB)
Ramos, Ignacio, 38–39, *39*
Rattner, Steven, 23
Reagan, Ronald, 30, 40, 54, 116
and Holder, Eric, 133
Realty Advisory Board on Labor
Relations (RAB), 15
Recording Industry Association of
America (RIAA), 47–48
Recovery Rebates and Stimulus
for the American People Act of
2008, 79
Reeves, Danny, 18
Rehabilitation Act of 1973, 9
Religion, **189–190**
FLDS sect, 189–190, *190*
Revised Kansas Juvenile Justice
Code (KJJC), 150
Rezko, Antoin, 50
RIAA *See* Recording Industry
Association of America (RIAA)
Riccio, Thomas, 17
Racketeer Influenced and Corrupt
Organizations Act(RICO), 148,
190–192
enterprise under statute,
190–192
RICO *See* Racketeer Influenced
and Corrupt Organizations Act
(RICO)
Ridgeway, Jeremy, 160

Right to dry laws, 53–54
Riparian Rights, **192–193**
Arkansas River dispute,
192–193
Rivera, Michael, 181–182
Riverkeeper, Inc., 37–38
Roberts, John
antitrust law, 10
arbitration, 13, 14
discrimination, 66
DNA, 71
duty of tonnage, 77
evidence, 95
First Amendment, state
and local government
employees, 105
Fourth Amendment, arrest
warrants, 112
judges, 146
labor law, 154
military law, 162
national security, 172
riparian rights, 193
sentencing, 200, 202
voting discrimination, 235
Rogers, Gary, 155
Rohrabacher, Dana, 40
Ronquillo, Brian, 151–152
Ryan, George, 50

S

Safe Haven, **195–196**
Nebraska law, 195–196
SAGE *See* Straights and Gays for
Equality (SAGE)
Said, Mohammed, 73–74
Salmonella, 106–107
Sampson, D. Kyle, 63–64
Sanders, Woodrow, 233–234
Sarausad, Cesar, 151–152
Scalia, Antonin
arbitration, 13
banking, 28
Clean Water Act, 38
confrontation clause, 43
criminal procedure, 58
discrimination, 66
environmental law, 92
Federal Communications
Commission, 98
Fourth Amendment, arrest
warrants, 111
jurisdiction, 149
Native American rights, 174
sentencing, 202
Sixth Amendment, 208, 209
Supremacy Clause, 218
voting discrimination, 235
Schultz, Howard, 215–216
Schumer, Chuck, 29

Search and Seizure, **196–197**
  automobile searches, 196–197
Seattle Supersonics, 214–215
Securities, **197–198**
  Tyco settlement, 197–198
Sentencing, **198–202**
  Armed Career Criminal Act
    (ACCA), 198–199
  statutorily-enhanced sentences,
    199–201
  statutory language, 201–202
Sentry Royalty Company, 173
September 11th Attacks, 65–66, 156
Service Employees International
  Union, 15
Sex Discrimination, **202–204**
  pregnancy leave, 202–203
  Title IX violations, 203–204
Sex Offenses, **204–205**
  sex offenders residency
    restrictions, 204–205
Sexual Assault Survivors
  Emergency Treatment Act, 31
Shell Oil, 225
Sherman Antitrust Act, 10
Simmons, Patricia, 233–234
Simpson, Nicole Brown, 16
Simpson, O.J., *16*
  armed robbery trial, 16–17
  *If I Did It: Confessions of
    the Killer*, 16–17
Sixth Amendment, **205–210**
  informant-elicited statements,
    208–209
  judge-increased sentences,
    207–208
  questioning without counsel,
    205–207
  speedy trials, rights to, 209–210
Sky-Tel, 176–177
Smith, Lamar, 47
Soloway, Robert Alan, 142–143
Sotomayor, Sonia, **210–211**
Souter, David
  arbitration, 13
  Clean Water Act, 38
  criminal procedure, 60
  discrimination, 66
  employment law, 88
  First Amendment, 102
  jury, 152
  pensions, 181
  retirement of, 210–211
  sex discrimination, 203
  trade, 231
  veterans' rights, 234
South Dakota
  "Measure 11" anti-choice
    measure, 2
Southeast Alaska Conservation
  Council, 89–90

Sovereign Immunity, 211–212
  Iran, 211–212
Sovereignty, **213–214**
  Hawaiian public land sale,
    213–214
Spector, Arlen, 45
Spitzer, Eliot, 27
Sports Law, **214–216**
  Seattle Supersonics move,
    214–216
Stevens, John Paul
  age discrimination, 6
  arbitration, 13, 15
  Clean Water Act, 38
  criminal procedure, suppressed
    evidence, 58
  criminal procedure, jury
    instructions, 60
  discrimination, 66
  DNA, 71
  duty of tonnage, 77
  First Amendment, 105
  Fourth Amendment, 111
  jurisdiction, 149
  Native American rights, 172
  preemption, 185,
  Supremacy Clause, 218
  tobacco, 223
  tort law, 226
  veterans' rights, 234
Stevens, Ted, 51–53, *51*
Stewart, Clarence "C.J.", 17
Stored Communications Act, 113
Straights and Gays for Equality
  (SAGE) 81
Suicide, **216–217**
  Montana assisted suicide law,
    216–217
Summers, Lawrence, 23
Summum, 103–104
Supremacy Clause, **217–218**
  prisoner civil suits, 218
Supreme Court, U.S.
  anti-dumping tariffs, 230–231
  arbitration of civil rights claims,
    15–16
  Armed Career Criminal Act,
    interpretation of, 199–200
  asylum seekers and "persecu-
    tion bar," 137–138
  authority of bankruptcy courts,
    25–26
  automobile searches, 110–11
  and Clean Water Act, 37–39
  Congress overturning ADA
    rulings, 8–9
  Controlled Substances Act, 73–74
  criminal evidence conflicts, 94–96
  and death row inmates'
    clemency claims, 129–130

DNA testing, 70–71
  discrimination, 65–66
  district courts compelling
    arbitration, 13–14
  district courts remanding cases,
    148–149
  double jeopardy, 72–73
  and due process, 57–58
  duty of tonnage, 76–77
  employee service credit for
    pregnancy, 202–203
  employment discrimination,
    88–89
  environmental cleanup costs,
    recouping of, 225–226
  exclusionary rule, 111–112
  and FAA stays, 12–13
  and FCC indecent language
    policy, 97–98
  forensic analysts and
    confrontation clause, 43–44
  free speech protections,
    103–104
  government burden of proof,
    135–136
  housing regulations for illegal
    immigrants, 136–137
  immunity qualifications,
    140–141
  Indian Reorganization Act,
    application of, 171–172
  informants, statements elicited
    by, 208–209
  judge recusal, 145–146
  jury instructions, 151–152
  jury instructions in ADEA
    cases, 5–6
  jury instructions in criminal
    cases, 58–60
  military courts and coram nobis
    writs, 161–162
  and National Bank Act,
    26–29
  national security interests,
    170–171
  and partial birth abortion, 1–2
  pensions and ERISA standards,
    180–181
  and peremptory challenges,
    181–182
  and permit-issuing agencies,
    89–91
  and plea arrangement, 60–61
  police questioning without
    counsel, 205–207
  preemption, 184–185
  price squeeze claims, 10–11
  procedural rules for habeas
    writs, 130–131

Supreme Court, U.S. (*continued*)
prosecutorial immunity, 141–142
punitive damages, 187–188
punitive damages for injured seamen, 4–5
removal of aliens, 138–140
RICO, interpretation of, 191–192
right to a speedy trial, 209–210
riparian rights, 192–193
sale of public lands, 213–214
search and seizure, 196–197
sentencing guidelines, 207–208
sex discrimination suits under Title IX, 203–204
sovereign immunity, 211–212
statutorily-enhanced sentences, 200–201
statutory construction, 201–202
strict scrutiny, application of, 105–106
supremacy clause, 218–219
tobacco lawsuits, 222–223
union fees, 153–154
veterans, disability claims, 233–234
victim evidence cases, 36–37
voting rights, 234–236

T

Taiwan, 93–94
Tamm, Thomas, 243–244
TARP *See* Troubled Asset Relief Program (TARP)
Telecommunications Act of 1996, 9, 101
Temple University, 117–118
Ten Commandments, 103–104
Tennessee
employment discrimination, 88
Terrorism, **219–222**
Guantanamo Bay closing, 219–221, *220*
Holy Land Foundation, 221–22
Texas
FDLS sect, 189–190
Theel, Rhonda, 208
Thomas, Clarence
age discrimination, 6
arbitration, 15
confirmation hearing, 169
discrimination, 66
First Amendment, 98
habeas corpus, 131, 132
jury instructions, 152
maritime law, 5
Native American rights, 172
sentencing, 200
Supremacy Clause, 218
voting discrimination, 235

Thomas, Jammie, 47
Thomson, Linda Chatman, 115
Tobacco, **222–224**
Florida lawsuits, 223–224
state laws to pursue claims, 222–223
Tonnage Clause, 76–77
Tort Law, **224–226**
hazardous waste cleanup, 224–226
Torture, **226–230**
al-Qahtani, Mohammed, 228–230
prosecution for memos, 228–229
"torture memos" release, 226–228
Townsend, Edgar, 4
Toyota plant, Georgetown, Kentucky, 8
Trade, **230–231**
foreign trade tariffs, 230–231
Travelers Indemnity, 25
Treblinka, 241–242
Troubled Asset Relief Program (TARP), 28–29
Twentieth Century Fox, 48–49
Tyco International Ltd., 197–198

U

UAW *See* United Auto Workers (UAW)
UCMJ *See* Uniform Code of Military Justice (UCMJ)
UCR *See* Uniform Crime Recording Program (UCR)
Uniform Code of Military Justice (UCMJ), 162, 219
Uniform Crime Reporting Program (UCR), 55
United Auto Workers (UAW), 22
U.S. Army Corps of Engineers, 89–90
U.S. Chamber of Commerce, 44–45
U.S. Citizenship and Immigration Services (CIS), 86–87
U.S. Court of Appeals for the Armed Forces (CAAF), 161
U.S. Department of Defense, 170
U.S. Department of Education, 84
U.S. Department of Homeland Security, 6–7, 161
Office of Inspector General (OIG), 38
U.S. Department of the Interior, 172
U.S. Department of Justice, 20, 45, **63–64**, 109, 157, 241–242, 243
politically motivated hirings, 63–64
U.S. Department of the Treasury, 79, 99

U.S. Navy, 170–171
U.S. Forest Service, 89–91, 92
U.S. Postal Service, 60

V

Vaden, Betty, 13–14
Valdez, AL, 76–77
Van de Kamp, John, 141–142
VECO Corporation, 52
Ventris, Donnie Ray, 208–209
Veterans Rights, **233–234**
disability claims, 233–234
Victims of Trafficking and Violence Protection Act, 212
Virginia
drug trafficking, 73–74
stolen laptop, 42–43
Virginia Supreme Court
ineffective counsel, 11
partial birth abortion ban, 1–2
Vitale, Adam, 143
Vioxx, 185–186
Voting, **234–239**
blocked voters, 2008 election, 238–239
identification cards, 236–238
Internet campaigning, 236–237
minority rights, 234–236
Voting Rights Act of 1965, 234–235

W

Wagoner, Rick, 23
Wainstein, Kenneth, 20–21
Walsh, David, 29
War Crimes, **241–242**
Demjanjuk, John, 241–242, *242*
Warner Brothers, 49
Washington
execution protocols, 35–36
jury instructions, 150–152
Watchmen, 48–49
Whistleblowing, **242–244**
warrantless surveillance, 242–243
Wilkinson, James H., III, 14
Williams, Ella, 8
Williams, Jan, 64
Williams, Mayola, 187
Williamson, Ron, 154–155
Wiretapping, **244–245**
Foreign Intelligence Surveillance Act, 244–245
Wyden, Ron, 45
Wyeth (drug company), 184–185

Y

Yeager, F. Scott, 72–73
Yoo, John, 227, 228–229, 243